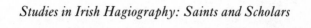

Studies in Irish Hagiography: Saints and Scholars

Studies in Irish Hagiography
Saints and Scholars

*John Carey, Máire Herbert
& Pádraig Ó Riain*

EDITORS

FOUR COURTS PRESS

This book was set in 10.5 on 12.5 point Ehrhardt by
Carrigboy Typesetting Services for
FOUR COURTS PRESS LTD
Fumbally Court, Fumbally Lane, Dublin 8, Ireland
email: info@four-courts-press.ie
web: http://www.four-courts-press.ie
and in North America for
FOUR COURTS PRESS
c/o ISBS, 5824 N.E. Hassalo Street, Portland, OR 97213.

A catalogue record for this title
is available from the British Library.

ISBN 1-85182-486-3

Printed in Great Britain by
MPG Books Ltd, Bodmin, Cornwall.

Contents

Abbreviations

AASS	Bollandists, *Acta sanctorum*
AU	Mac Airt and Mac Niocaill, *Annals of Ulster*
B.Br.	*Bethu Brigte*
BHL	Bollandists, *Bibliographia hagiographica latina*
BL	Stokes, *Lives of the Saints from the Book of Lismore*
BLSM	Stokes, *The Birth and Life of Saint Moling*
BNE	Plummer, *Bethada Náem nÉrenn*
CCSL	Corpus Christianorum Series Latina
CGH	O'Brien, *Corpus genealogiarum Hiberniae*
CGSH	Ó Riain, *Corpus genealogiarum sanctorum Hiberniae*
DLS	Adomnán, *De locis sanctis*
Fin.	Macalister, 'The Life of Saint Finan'
PL	Migne, *Patrologia latina*
VAed.	*Vita Aedi*
VC	Adomnán, *Vita Columbae*
VCainn.	*Vita Cainnechi*
VSH	Plummer, *Vitae sanctorum Hiberniae*
Wortk.	Meyer, 'Zur keltische Wortkunde I–IX'

BIBLICAL CITATIONS

Gn	Genesis	Mt	Matthew
Ex	Exodus	Mc	Mark
Nm	Numbers	Lc	Luke
Dt	Deuteronomy	Io	John
Ios	Joshua	Act	Acts of the Apostles
I–II Sm	1–2 Samuel	Rm	Romans
III–IV Rg	1–2 Kings	I–II Cor	1–2 Corinthians
I–II Par	1–2 Chronicles	Gal	Galatians
Iob	Job	Phil	Philippians
Ps	Psalms	I–II Th	1–2 Thessalonians
Sap	Wisdom	Hbr	Hebrews
Is	Isaiah	I–II Pt	1–2 Peter
Ier	Jeremiah	I–III Io	1–3 John
Ez	Ezekiel	Apc	Apocalypse/
Dn	Daniel		Revelation

Contributors

WALTER BERSCHIN, Ruprecht-Karls-Universität Heidelberg

EDEL BHREATHNACH, The Discovery Programme, Dublin

ANDRÉ-YVES BOURGÈS, Centre International de Recherche et de Documentation sur le Monachisme Celtique (CIRDoMoC), Landévennec

DOROTHY ANN BRAY, McGill University

JOHN CAREY, University College Cork

FRANÇOIS DE VRIENDT, Université de Namur

DAVID N. DUMVILLE, Girton College, Cambridge

ROBERT GODDING, Société des Bollandistes

MÁIRE HERBERT, University College Cork

KAREN JANKULAK, University of Wales Lampeter

GWENAËL LE DUC, Université de Haute Bretagne, Rennes 2

AIDAN MACDONALD, University College Cork

ELIZABETH MCLUHAN, Centre for Medieval Studies, University of Toronto

BERNARD MERDRIGNAC, Université de Haute Bretagne, Rennes 2

JOSEPH FALAKY NAGY, University of California, Los Angeles

THOMAS O'LOUGHLIN, University of Wales Lampeter

GUY PHILIPPART, Université de Namur

JEAN-MICHEL PICARD, University College Dublin

PAUL RUSSELL, Radley College, Oxon

NATHALIE STALMANS, Fonds National de la Recherche Scientifique, Université Libre de Bruxelles

CLARE STANCLIFFE, Durham

D.J. THORNTON, University College Cork

MICHEL TRIGALET, Université de Namur

JONATHAN M. WOODING, University of Wales Lampeter

Preface

The present collection records proceedings of an international conference on hagiography, organised by the Department of Early and Medieval Irish, University College Cork, as part of the commemoration of the 1400th anniversary of the death of St Colum Cille. Participants from at least thirteen countries came to Cork in April 1997 to discuss a broad range of topics relating to the Lives of Irish saints. Along with a focus on Columban hagiography in acknowledgement of the saint's anniversary year, attention was given to a variety of other hagiographical writings, and to their transmission both in Ireland and in Continental Europe. In addition, hagiographical scholarship itself was treated, both the discipline's seventeenth-century beginnings and a modern international project.

We had a most enjoyable and fruitful gathering in delightful spring weather, and we hope that these proceedings recall pleasant memories of the conference for the participants, as well as providing a more permanent record for the wider scholarly community. We would like to thank all who agreed so readily to contribute papers, and the many others who attended the conference and participated enthusiastically in all its activities.

We should like to acknowledge also the many people and organizations who supported the conference, and made its success possible. The editors (who were the organizing committee) received invaluable assistance from Caoimhín Ó Muirigh, Meidhbhín Ní Úrdail, Aideen O'Leary, Pádraigín Riggs, Shane Lehane, Regina Sexton, Elmarie Uí Cheallacháin and Siobhán Ní Dhonghaile. We are grateful to Helen Davis, Boole Library, UCC; Stella Cherry, Cork Public Museum; Fr Ignatius Fennessy, Franciscan Library, Killiney; and Michael Graham and René de Ruest, St Fin Barre's Cathedral, Cork, for their co-operation in the preparation of exhibitions coinciding with the conference, and we thank also Jerome O'Leary of Waterstones Bookshop.

The conference and its proceedings were aided by financial assistance from Toyota Ireland, a generous benefactor of the Department; from the Arts Faculty Fund, UCC; and from Bord na Gaeilge, UCC. We thank them sincerely, as we thank also the sponsors of overseas speakers: Deutscher Akademiker Austauschdienst, The Embassy of Austria, The Embassy of France, The British Council, and the Irish Office of the European Commission.

We are grateful to Four Courts Press, and, in particular, to Martin Fanning, for cordial assistance and co-operation through all the stages of the book's production. We hope that this record of the first international conference on Irish hagiography will stimulate further research into the rich resources of the subject.

JOHN CAREY
MÁIRE HERBERT
PÁDRAIG Ó RIAIN

The Tombs of the Saints: Their Significance for Adomnán

Thomas O'Loughlin

Reconstructing the mental world of an early medieval author is a fraught task. If it is possible at all, then it is at best a tentative affair: we only gain glimpses. Often it is only by noting where their views and our own are so at variance that they consciously jar that we can have any degree of certainty about our understanding of how they constructed their view of reality. This is a particular problem in hagiographical writing, for the very reason for the genre was that 'holiness', whatever that may be, was manifested in an individual by means of 'the miraculous'. The miraculous is a category *sui generis* in the hagiographer's world,[1] and one which is alien to our own.[2] Hence there is a special complexity in reading these texts. To the author, the world of the saint is perceived as a special world and so he writes of it as one foreign to his everyday world; yet the world he so constructs – and shares with his ideal reader – is one that is, therefore, doubly alien to us. So if we wish to enter that world (and unless we read saints' Lives simply as accidental witnesses to our historical

---

1 We can see this in the New Testament: the miracle is that which produced 'amazement' (ἔκστασις/*stupor*), e.g. at Lc 5.26 in the Synoptics; while in John, e.g. Io 2.18, the miracle is a 'sign' (σημεῖον/*signum*): in both cases it is the recognition of the event that reveals the person who instigates it. The miraculous is testimony to the power that is present; this can be seen from the number of occasions when there is a connection between seeing 'signs and wonders' (σημεῖα καὶ τέρατα/*signa et prodigia*) and belief/faith in some way or other (Mt 24.24; Mc 13.22; Io 4.48; Act 4.30, 5.12, 14.3, 15.12; Rm 15.19; II Cor 12.12; II Th 2.9; and Hbr 2.4). That the miraculous is noteworthy within the tradition of Christianity can be seen in the practice in Hippo, in Augustine's time, of keeping a *libellus* of miraculous cures (cf. Delehaye, 'Libelli miraculorum' and 'Recueils antiques'). Such divine interventions were not only noteworthy in the sense of being out of the ordinary, but were to be recorded as in some way significant in that they pointed to God making his power manifest (thus Brown, *Augustine of Hippo*, pp. 414–15). As such, they do not belong to the ordinary mechanisms of the universe, but are contingent on Providence, and thus constitute the stuff of history which should be narrated: cf. Augustine, *De doctrina christiana* II.xxviii.42–4, especially 44.   2 It is alien to our world in that we do not accept the notion of divine interventions as a satisfactory explanation of events. But we should note that the miraculous was also alien within the world of early medieval writers in that it was not produced from within that world, but was extrinsic to the world within the divine freedom. Hence the intrinsic worth of miracles: these are the judgements of God quite apart from all that we ordinarily know.

I

concerns, we must enter that world),[3] then we need pathways which allow us to estimate the intellectual distance between our world and the hagiographer's, and which are meaningful within the world of the hagiographer while being capable of translation into our world.

The world brought before us in the writings of Adomnán is just such a foreign world. In looking at the *Vita Columbae*,[4] while we may do so out of interest in the historical Columba, or in the life of an early Irish monastery, we enter this world of the miraculous. The story is not that of a sixth-century 'significant person' as we define it, but of one who is defined in terms of prophetic revelations (*profeticae reuelationes*), divine wonders (*diuinae ... uirtutes*), and epiphanies of one sort or another (*angelicae apparitiones ... et ... caelestis claritudinis manifestationes*), which are the divisions consciously employed in the work.[5] This is a portrait of a man who inhabits a parallel world for Adomnán and to that extent one that was alien to him. To us, even the notion of such a parallel world, let alone the details of how Adomnán understood its relation to his own world, is foreign. Likewise his *De locis sanctis* (DLS),[6] for all the use that is made of the text by historians of architecture, travel, and the late seventh-century middle and near east, is not a guide to places, but to *holy* places.[7] It is not the details of the seventh-century places that are the primary focus of the text, but places in the past (*martyria*) that witness to things beyond history.[8] It is an account not of ordinary cities, but of cities that are miraculously cleansed,[9] illuminated,[10] or located by the direct manifestation of the will of God.[11] These are not everyday places but places where there is literally the

---

3 This use of *vitae* as sources of historical information *per accidens* is legitimately pursued by many historians: an example is Doherty, 'Some Aspects'. 4 Citations will be from Anderson and Anderson, *Life of Columba*. 5 *Praefatio secunda*. The fact that VC seems to bring a 'real person' before us has had the effect that it has been treated as wholly different from such contemporary works as the *Vita Brigidae* of Cogitosus or the *Vita Patricii* of Muirchú. Yet however we may consider Adomnán to be a more competent author, his work is still hagiography, and its authorial rationale is at one with that of Cogitosus and Muirchú. 6 Citations will be from Meehan and Bieler, *Adamnan's De locis sanctis*. 7 I have tried to bring out this 'other' aspect of the text in my article 'Exegetical Purpose'. More recently I have tried to show that the physical world of Adomnán and the geography of the text are at variance ('Adomnán's Mental Maps'). The physical world of the text is a sacred landscape. 8 The places of events in Scripture are described in the same terms as in Scripture, the intervening years being of no account: see DLS II.vii on the burial place of Rachel; and cf. DLS I.vi.1 and I.vii.1 where the word *martyrium* is used by Adomnán. While in both these cases he thinks of it as the name of a specific place rather than as a common noun for a place that witnesses to an important belief (... *quae et martirium appellatur* ... ; *Inter ... basilicam et martirium* ...; and cf. Meehan's introduction, *Adamnan's De locis sanctis*, p. 22), he was also familiar with the notion of witness-places (cf. Davies, *Pilgrimage*, p. 9; and Murphy, 'Martyrium'). This is evident at many points in DLS, his description of Mount Olivet (I.xxiii) being a very fine example. 9 DLS I.i.7–13. 10 DLS I.xxiii.11–3. 11 Jerusalem is located by a special manifestation of the divine will (DLS I.i.11) at the centre of the lands,

imprint of the divine,[12] and where wondrous water springs forth from rocks.[13] In these places the miraculous is the norm. As places they may be ultimately contiguous with Adomnán's island in that one could travel to them, but as worlds they are apart, qualitatively different as places,[14] as the saint is qualitatively different as a man.

Both DLS and VC describe what is 'other', but not 'wholly other', for the description of this other world is made to encourage and facilitate the transition from the everyday to the sacred.[15] The world of the holy appears as a state manifested in the ordinary world in special places and persons, and one which is entered by imitation and liturgy.[16] Here I wish to consider just one point of contact between the two worlds of the ordinary and the holy in Adomnán's work: his reports of tombs and burials. One of the striking features of both VC and DLS is just how many references there are to burials, graves, and tombs. When these are examined we notice that apart from obvious concerns such as relics, other themes are also evident in his descriptions, in particular the view that in the tombs are the bodies of those who are waiting for the resurrection. The tombs are of two sorts: ordinary 'full' tombs containing a body, and empty tombs like the sepulchre of Christ.[17] When all tombs are looked at together, the evidence appears to reflect Adomnán's theology of the resurrection, and to be an extension of the preaching of Peter (Act 2.25–36) that God would not leave the Holy One in the place of death as David was left in his tomb with them there: Christ was raised from the tomb and `his body did not see corruption', and thus there is resurrection for his followers. In examining this theme I wish

and so is the *omphalos* of the earth (DLS I.xi, especially sentence 4); the site of Constantinople was selected directly by God (DLS III.ii). 12 DLS I.xii.4 and I.xxiii.6–7. 13 DLS II.iii. Adomnán brings out its miraculous nature quite explicitly: just as it is *contra naturam* for the Christ to come as saviour, so it is miraculous for water to flow from this source (DLS II.iii.3). 14 Anthropologists note that 'sacred space' is not just a special piece of space ('space apart', in the language of Rudolf Otto), but is space with a different quality to the places of living and farming. See further Brereton, 'Sacred Space'. 15 I have argued that one purpose of DLS is to describe the future Jerusalem, 'our mother' (Gal 4.26), which Adomnán would have considered to be the city at the end of the Christian's life. See O'Loughlin, 'Adomnán's Mental Maps', pp. 118–20. 16 Throughout DLS, and in works concerned with the Holy Places such as the *Peregrinatio Egeriae*, there is a concern with liturgical details. This is not simply an interest in how things are done in faraway parts, but rather a concern over the ideal liturgy. The liturgy compressed time and space, so that the original event in Palestine, the event there and then in a particular place such as Iona in the seventh century, and the perfect liturgy of heaven were brought together. Location metaphors, most notably that of Jerusalem, were the key to this compression of time and space. Thus the monks on Iona going through the liturgy of the Ascension saw themselves as on the summit of Olivet being told by the angels that they were the *uiri Galilaei* (Act 1.11–12) and were waiting for Christ to return. DLS I.xxiii has to be understood as providing information which enables them to enter more fully into this celebration. On this liturgical theme the classic study is Casel, 'Mysteriengedächtnis der Messliturgie'. 17 Throughout this study, 'tombs' will be used as a generic term to cover any type of burial.

first to look at the burials mentioned in VC, where there are over a dozen references to death and burial, along with interesting comments by Adomnán about their significance.[18] The theme can then be followed in a more articulated way in DLS, where we have not only descriptions of tombs, but explicit theological reflections on their religious role. As with VC, while we should expect to find in DLS some record of the burial places of the saints who died in Palestine (e.g. Jerome),[19] or of tombs mentioned in Scripture (e.g. Machpelah),[20] the scale of Adomnán's interest is surprising. No less than eleven of its fifty-nine[21] chapters are devoted to tombs directly,[22] while five more refer to tombs incidentally.[23]

In the opening chapter of VC (I.1) we are presented with Columba as someone who can know the final destinies of human beings. He can see the souls of the just being carried upwards to paradise, while the damned are brought down to the depths (*ad inferna*) by the demons. This is a theme which recurs on two other occasions in VC: at I.35 and II.25. In all three cases Columba is being made to conform to a model of holiness drawn from the *Dialogi* of Gregory the Great.[24] Gregory, in a discussion on the nature of the punishment of souls by fire, introduces the story of a holy man on one of the Lipari Islands who saw the soul of Theodoric being carried into Mount Vulcanus.[25] This passage from Gregory was clearly of great importance to Adomnán in forming his views of the destiny of the wicked, for it also formed the basis of the last chapter of DLS.[26] While this process appears to be a two-fold one (the just go upwards, the reprobate go downwards), the situation is not that simple. For Gregory and Adomnán, the demons drag the wicked souls away to hell, while the saints are watching. Once in hell they have arrived at their final destination and at once begin their punishments. No further change in their state lies in the future. Gregory builds his argument on the parable of the rich man and Lazarus (Lc 16.19–31). Once the rich man is in hell, nothing further can happen to change or alleviate his state. 'Between us and you a great chasm has been fixed,

---

18 In VC we expect a reference to Columba's tomb (III.23), for knowing the location of the tomb of a saint is a crucial element in the development of the cult. But we should note that there is considerable interest in burials apart from that of Columba. We also observe a concern with relics: these create the focus of the cult for they provide a legacy to be guarded, and a source of power. We see this link most clearly in the importance attached to the tombs of the apostles in Rome (see Ortenberg, 'Sigeric's Journey to Rome') or, in an Irish context, the warfare over the relics of Patrick (Muirchú II.13 [Bieler, *Patrician Texts*, p. 120]). Yet, significantly, there is no mention of relics in VC. This is a question that deserves exploration. 19 DLS II.v; see Lanzoni, 'Sepolcro do S. Girolamo'. 20 DLS II.x; and O'Loughlin, 'Adam's Burial'. 21 Counting DLS II.ix and II.x as one chapter. 22 DLS I.ii; I.iii; I.xii; I.xiii; I.xiv; I.xxv; II.iv; II.v; II.vi; II.vii; and II.x. 23 DLS I.iv; I.ix; I.xvii; I.xix and II.xxx. 24 *Dialogi* IV.31 (de Vogüé, iii.104–5). 25 For an emendation of the text of Gregory and a discussion of this passage's underlying theology, see O'Loughlin, 'Gates of Hell'. See also Hillgarth, 'Julian of Toledo', p. 18. 26 Cf. O'Loughlin, 'Library of Iona', p. 45; and 'Gates of Hell', pp. 105–10.

in order that those who would pass from here to you may not be able, and none may cross from there to us' (Lc 16.26). On the other hand, the righteous, although they are in heaven, are not yet in their final state. They must await the final resurrection when their souls are re-united with their bodies. This reunion of soul and body constitutes their final 'situation'.[27] It is the third of these three uses of Gregory that supplies an insight for this paper. The brute (*homo ... crudilis*) in VC II.25 is punished for his crime immediately by the word of the saint. Adomnán reminds us that Ananias and Sapphira were struck down in similar fashion by the apostle Peter (Act 5.1–11).[28] However, there is an interesting difference between the scene in VC and that in Acts. In Acts we are told of the burial first of Ananias (vv. 6 and 9) and then of Sapphira (v. 10), but Adomnán does not mention a burial or even hint at it. That this is a deliberate omission, rather than a detail not recorded, becomes clear when we compare other deaths mentioned in VC. Aid the Black (I.36) is an evil and bloody man who returns to his old wicked ways after an unworthy ordination. Eventually he is killed in pursuit of evil, and perishes (*disperiit*) by drowning. He has no grave. A similar fate befalls Ioan, another wicked man (II.22). Like Aid, he does not repent nor reform himself, but is an obstinate evil-doer (*malefactor*). After a miraculously induced storm at sea, Ioan is brought into the depths (*ad inferna*) of the sea (and thus of hell), and has no grave.[29] Something similar happens to Feradach in the next chapter (II.23). Feradach is responsible for the death of a guest whom he had promised to protect, and so must suffer the punishment of sudden death himself. A strange detail in this story is that the punishment is not for murdering his guest, but for lying to God, through his saint, by promising protection to the exiled noble Pict, Tarain. The key to this scene lies in the phrase: *cuius nomen de libro uitae delebitur*. The notion that God keeps a record book in heaven is found in many places in Scripture (e.g. Ex 32.32), but the precise phrase 'Book of Life' (*librum uitae*)[30] is confined to Paul and the

---

27 This final situation is presented in the final line of many early credal formulae: *Credo in ... carnis resurrectionem* (cf. Denzinger and Schönmetzer, *Enchiridion symbolorum*, nrs 10–36 and expecially n. 29).   28 This comparison of miracles is most interesting. It would seem that Adomnán's point is simply that in both cases the punishments meted out are similar, or that Columba is similar in power to Peter. However, the two miracles also share a more profound similarity for the punishment is an expression of the role of the saint as the instrument of the divine law. In both cases the miracle expresses the author's conviction that the justice of God is made manifest in the actions of the saints. On the structure of such miracles ('Rule Miracles of Punishment') in the early Christian period, see Theissen, *Miracle Stories*, pp. 106–12.   29 The Andersons translate *inferna* simply as 'hell' (corrected to 'depths of hell' by Sharpe, *Life of St Columba*, p. 172; see the parallel case in VC II.23). But it should be noted that there is a connection in Adomnán's mind between the depths of the ocean which swallowed Ioan, and the depths of hell which is his eschatological destination. The depths of the sea is the location of the Biblical demonic beasts; see Borsje, *From Chaos to Enemy*, chapter 2; and O'Loughlin, 'Living in the Ocean', pp. 11–23.   30 Cf. McKenzie's article 'Book of Life' in his *Dictionary of the Bible*, p. 103, for a survey of the theme in general.

Apocalypse.[31] Adomnán has at least three, and possibly four, of these texts in mind here. First, Apc 3.5 says that the one who is going to be saved will not have his name blotted out from that book (*non delebo nomen eius de libro uitae*), but in VC Feradach's name is going to be removed, so he will not be with the saints. Second, Apc 21.27 states there is no overlap between those who tell lies (*mendacium*) and those whose names are in the Book of Life: Feradach has lied (*mentitus est*) so his name cannot remain in that book. Thirdly, those who are not listed in the Book of Life will be slaughtered (Apc 13.8) and cast into the lake of fire (Apc 20.15). Hence Feradach will die suddenly (*subita ... morte*) and will be brought down to hell (*ad infernalia rapietur loca*).[32] For Adomnán, Feradach is now dead, and so among the damned in hell. There is no mention of either burial or a grave. In stark contrast to these tomb-less evildoers, on every other occasion when a death is mentioned in VC, there is also mention of a burial and/or a tomb.

The clearest contrast to the way that the evildoers are described is the case of the old pagan of natural goodness (*bonum naturale*) who comes to the saint, is baptised, and then immediately dies (VC I.33). Adomnán is at pains to point out that he was then buried and his grave marked with a heap of stones, still visible, in a way reminiscent of the marker stone on Rachel's tomb (Gn 35.20; and DLS II.vii). The righteous man may be dead, but he has not perished, and we can even know where his body lies. When Columba prophesies that the good monk Baitán will not settle 'in a desert in the ocean' (*in oceano desertum*, i.e. an island hermitage) he does so with reference to where he will be buried (VC I.20). We are then told of the fulfilment of the prophecy concerning his burial place. Another burial mentioned incidentally is that of the Pict who was killed by an evil beast (*bilua*)[33] in the river Ness (VC II.27).[34] Since he was attacked by an evil one, we can infer that this was a good man who was being buried as the saint passed by. Indeed, his goodness may have made it possible for his friends to rescue his corpse for burial. A less clear case of a good man's burial is that of the thief Erc (I.41), as it is unclear whether he had stopped thieving. Probably Adomnán wishes us to assume that he had repented: hence Columba's concern with providing for his funeral.

The other burials mentioned in VC give us a more precise picture of the religious worth which Adomnán attached to tombs. The prophecies concerning the two sons (I.16) show that already burial on monastery ground was of importance. Others apart from its community can be given a share in its special

---

31 Phil 4.3; Apc 3.5, 13.8, 17.8, 20.12, 20.15, and 21.27.   32 On the identification of the *stagnum ignis* and hell for Adomnán, see O'Loughlin, 'Gates of Hell', p. 108.   33 See VC I.19. The use of *bilua* [*belua*] implies one of the monsters of the deep who, while being under God's power, are evil; see O'Loughlin, 'Living in the Ocean', p. 22.   34 This incident has been studied in detail in Borsje, 'Monster in the River Ness'.

status as holy ground. This is developed upon in the story of Librán (in II.39). The incident regarding the son of Meldán has curious liturgical echoes: the father is told on a Sabbath that his son will die after a seven-day period (*in fine ... septimanae*).[35] This puts the death on the sixth day (*sexta feria*) of the next week, and exactly an octave (*octaua*)[36] after the prophecy, he will be buried on the Sabbath. This language, with its joining of Sabbath to Sabbath, is intended to link the death of this youth to the time-scale of the passion of Christ. Both deaths take place on the sixth day of the week,[37] both enter the world of tombs on the day of rest after life's exertions, and in both cases this involves an 'octave' – Christ rises on 'the eighth day'. A similar liturgical sense of time is found in DLS III.vi for *Mons Vulcanus*.[38] This interpretation of Adomnán's intentions in the story of Meldán's son is highly speculative, but regarding his understanding of burial in the case of Librán (II.39) we are on much firmer ground. Librán, having served his father and carried out his filial duty in burying him, returns to Iona as a monk. Having made his vows he is told that he will not die nor be buried on Iona, but in another monastery belonging to Columba in Ireland. What is important in this context is how this is described: to die in a Columban monastery in Ireland (*in uno meorum morieris monasteriorum*) is exactly equivalent to saying 'you will arise' (*resurges*) there. The place of death and burial is the place of final resurrection, for it is there that the deceased will be when the Kingdom comes (*cum electis ... in regno*). This reference to the final resurrection by means of the Biblical image of the Kingdom is based on Mt 25.31–4. Buried with the brethren of that monastery, it is with them that Librán 'will awake from the sleep of death into the resurrection of life' (*in resurrectionem uitae de somno mortis euigelabis*).[39] This phrase, *in resurrectionem uitae*, is taken from Io 5.29, and recalls the whole passage in John about those to whom the Son will give life on the Last Day. Those who hear his voice will rise to life, those who do not will arise to judgement. But the key statement is this: *quia uenit hora in qua omnes qui in monumentis sunt audient uocem eius et procedent qui bona fecerunt in resurrectionem uitae qui uero mala egerunt in resurrectionem iudicii* (Io 5.28–9). Those who have lived good lives will be in their tombs when they hear the voice of Christ, and having listened from there (note now Adomnán's choice of *euigilare*) they will arise from there to perfect life. This notion, while most often cited with reference to these verses of John, is also found elsewhere, and is made particularly pointed with reference to burials in Dn 12.2: *et multi de his qui dormiunt in terrae puluere euigilabunt alii in uitam aeternam et alii in*

---

35 This should not be translated 'week' as the Andersons have done.   36 The Andersons have 'the eighth day from now', and Sharpe 'one week today'; both fail to bring out the liturgical significance of *octaua*. On the liturgical significance of octaves, cf. Cabrol, 'Octave'. 37 On the time-scale of the death of Christ for Adomnán, see O'Loughlin, '*Res, Tempus, Locus, Persona*'. 38 See O'Loughlin, 'Gates of Hell', p. 106. 39 There is an allusion here to Ps 12.4 (LXX numeration).

obprobrium. What we have in Adomnán's story is another reflection of a theological vision of death and burial that is built up, like a mosaic, of these different Biblical images. The burial place is the place of the sleep and waiting between earthly death and the final call from Christ to rise.[40] The story in VC ends with the fulfilment of Columba's prophecy – Librán goes to the Lord in peace, and is buried in Durrow whence he will rise again (*resurrecturus*)[41] into eternal life.[42] A similar view of burial is found in the story of the holy monk Ernéne (VC III.23) stated to be buried with the saints waiting for the resurrection (*resurrectionem exspectat*). This waiting for, looking out for, longing for, is something that he is doing now while his body is in the grave in the ridge of Tóimm. Adomnán's words echo the phrase of the 'Nicene' creed: *et exspecto resurrectionem mortuorum.*[43] From the way that these burials are described, we can infer that Adomnán believes in a sequence something like this: death, burial, a waiting for the resurrection of the body, and then the life of the world to come.[44]

Having displayed the theological motif of awaiting the resurrection in these stories, it is surprising that in the episode of Columba's burial (VC III.23) Adomnán does not use it. Rather the image is that of the Sabbath rest after life's labours, and the entry to the Lord's day of resurrection. Thus Columba goes the way of his fathers (cf. Ios 23.14), which is that of burial.[45] His death comes at the happy 'last hour'[46] when Columba, in a Christ-like fashion, breathes out his spirit,[47] and so leaves 'the tabernacle of the body'.[48] Of his burial, all that we are told is that it is marked with the stone that was once his pillow.[49]

---

40 This call, which is presented as 'a word' or 'a voice' in John, is often conflated in exegesis of this verse with the 'trumpet' that announces the gathering of the saints at the eschaton. Cf. Mt 24.31; I Cor 15.52; Apc 11.15; and especially I Th 4.16.   41 The use of the future participle *resurrecturus* is an echo of the Vulgate of Iob 19.25: *scio enim quod redemptor meus uiuat et in nouissimo de terra surrecturus sim.*   42 The concept of 'eternal life' is a commonplace in the Scriptures, and the phrase *in uitam aeternam* occurs on many occasions (e.g. Mt 25.45): here it is perhaps most interesting to draw attention to its use in Dn 12.2 and Io 5.24.   43 Cf. Denzinger and Schönmetzer, *Enchiridion symbolorum*, nr 150. This phrase in turn can be seen to echo Act 24.15: *spem habens in Deum quam et hii ipsi ex[s]pectant resurrectionem futuram iustorum et iniquorum.*   44 This final state could be described with several of the New Testament metaphors already noted, such as that of 'the Kingdom'; or in the Creed's phrase: *et uitam uenturi saeculi*, where this is understood to come after the *resurrectio mortuorum.*   45 This Scriptural quotation in VC is non-Vulgate, being used here by way of the Latin translation of Athanasius's *Vita Antonii*, cap. 91. See Brüning, 'Adamnans Vita Columbae', p. 246, where it is said to fall in cap. 58 of the *Vita Antonii* following the divisions in the PL printing of Evagrius's translation.   46 An allusion to I Io 2.18, but without invoking that text's purpose or theology.   47 This phrase *spiritum exalauit* echoes a conflation of how Mc 15.37 (with Lc 23.46) describes the death of Christ with the word *exspirauit*, and the phrase used in Mt 27.50 (and cf. Io 19.30), *emisit spiritum*, for the same event.   48 This is an allusion to I Cor 6.19.   49 As with the good man who was baptised and died (VC I.33), there is a reminiscence in the description of the burial place of Columba (*hodie ... iuxta sepulchrum ... titulus ... monumenti*) of the marker stone on Rachel's tomb (Gn 35.20: *super sepulchrum ... titulus monumenti ... in presentem diem*; and DLS II.vii).

The tombs mentioned in DLS, holy places with an established importance within Christian belief, present us with a far more developed theology of tombs. Many of Adomnán's references to tombs are quite simply descriptive of location and appearance, along with occasional details of associated cult. Thus we have basic information on the tombs of Iosaphat,[50] Simeon and Joseph,[51] Jerome,[52] the Shepherds of Bethlehem,[53] Rachel,[54] and Mark the Evangelist.[55] While in several of these cases Adomnán may have had specific reasons for mentioning these tombs, his descriptions do not add to our understanding of what importance he attached to burials, except to show that tombs were of particular interest to him.

Adomnán's theological interests are more apparent in other cases. I begin with an argument from a silence which, viewed alongside similar silences in VC, can hardly be accidental. In DLS I.xviii the place where Judas Iscariot hanged himself is described, and a theological reflection on his fate is offered from Juvencus. Judas is almost the archetype of the evil man being condemned by Christ himself.[56] Adomnán's account follows Mt 27.3–5 closely,[57] but he uses the term 'he perished' – the word used of the end of the wicked in VC. As with the evil ones of VC, while the place of his death is known, there is no mention of a burial or a tomb.

The tombs of David, Lazarus, and the burial place for 'pilgrims' in Jerusalem present us with more complex evidence as they are linked in various ways with Christ. David's tomb is stated to be in Bethlehem where he is buried in the earth.[58] Here Adomnán is following his source, Eusebius/Jerome's *Liber de situ et locorum*,[59] which states: *Bethleem ... ubi et sepulchrum Iesse et David ostenditur ... ut in Paralipomenon uolumine plenius dicitur.* Jerome wrily adds in his own voice: *Lege diligenter historiam.*[60] However, no amount of careful reading will furnish the text that inspired Eusebius to make this statement. The Biblical tradition is unanimous that David was buried in 'his city' – Jerusalem (III Rg 2.10, followed by Act 2.29).[61] For our purpose here what is significant is that

---

50 Iosaphat is the Vulgate form of Jehoshaphat. That he was buried in Jerusalem is based on III Rg 22.50 (Vulgate: 22.51) and II Par 21.1. In both these texts the death and burial are described with the formula 'buried in the city of David'; in these historical books this is identified as Jerusalem (cf. II Sm 5.7 and III Rg 8.1), which Adomnán follows despite Lc 2.4 and 11. The question of the valley and the tower are beyond the scope of this paper, but see Warren, 'Jehoshaphat'; and Morgenstern, 'Gates of Righteousness', p. 15. 51 DLS I.xiv. 52 DLS II.v. 53 DLS II.vi. 54 DLS II.vii. 55 DLS II.xxx.25. 56 E.g. Mt 26.24. 57 Mt reads: *paenitentia ductus ... laqueo se suspendit*; DLS reads: (title) *De loco ... se suspendit. ... locus ubi Iudas Scariothis disperatione coactus* [an exegesis of his motive, given that he was repentant] *laqueo se suspendens disperierat.* 58 See O'Loughlin, 'Exegetical Purpose', p. 48. 59 See O'Loughlin, 'Library of Iona', p. 38. 60 Eusebius (in Jerome's translation), *Onomastikon* (Klostermann, pp. 43 and 45). 61 A possible explanation is that III Rg 2.10 says that he was buried with his fathers, and since his father, Jesse, was from Bethlehem it may not have seemed unlikely to Eusebius that there were generations of ancestors there, and so there too David was buried. This interpretation of 'the city of David' would agree with Lc 2.4.

Adomnán states David is there buried in the earth (*Sepulchrum Dauid regis in terra humati*). This is necessary for the Christian reading of Davidic prophecy in Ps 15.8 (LXX numeration) that the Lord would not abandon the soul of his anointed nor let him see corruption. This is used on two occasions in the New Testament (Act 2.29 and 13.36) as proof that Christ has risen from the grave and has not seen corruption. The argument runs like this: David spoke of not seeing corruption or being abandoned in the grave; but he is in his grave (Act 2.29: *sepulchrum eius est apud nos*) and he did see corruption. His grave is still there to be seen (Act 13.36). Therefore he must have prophesied, not about himself, but another: this other is the Christ. The interred, and therefore corrupt,[62] body of David is thus a direct pointer to Christ, who is the one who has risen from the tomb, and whom God will not let any tomb contain nor will he let him see corruption (Act 13.36: *quem* [i.e. Christ] *uero Deus suscitauit non uidit corruptionem*). The second case is the tomb of Lazarus at Bethany.[63] This tomb was famous as the site of the miracle in Io 11. Lazarus, dead for four days and stinking, 'was raised from sleep' by Christ.[64] The *spelunca*, with a church over it, was significant as the *martyrium* to this event.[65] For Adomnán the tomb is exactly as it was on the day before Christ's triumphal entry into Jerusalem (i.e., without Lazarus's body), since the topic is raised in DLS just before that of the Holy Week chronology. Among the Latin Fathers the raising of Lazarus was a type of Christ's own resurrection, and an antetype of the resurrection of all those who are in their tombs waiting. Christ at the End will call everyone from their tombs (see the comments on Io 5.28 above), just as he has called forth Lazarus and forgiven him his sins.[66] Its significance is that this is an empty tomb which points out the power of God (cf. Io 11.4, 15, and 40) and points to the other empty tomb, Christ's. If both David's tomb and what had been Lazarus's tomb are significant for the theme of viewing tombs as waiting places for the final resurrection, the description of the burial place known as the Acheldemach presents a further nuance on the situation of the dead.[67] Adomnán closely follows the Vulgate form of Matthew's account of this field as

---

62 That burial in the earth should amount to corruption is a point we shall examine in connection with the burial at Hebron, and is based on Gn 3.19.   63 DLS I.xxiv. 64 Adomnán's language echoes John. DLS reads: *illam ... speluncam ... quadriduanum mortuum suscitauit Lazarum*; John reads: *erat autem speluncam* (11.38) *... dicit ei* [i.e. Jesus] *Martha soror eius qui mortuus fuerat*: '*Domine iam fetet quadriduanus enim est*' (11.39), and *Iesus ... uenit Bethaniam ubi fuerat Lazarus mortuus quem suscitauit Iesus* (12.1; and cf. 12.9, 12.17 and 11.17).   65 On the notion of a *martyrium* see n. 8 above.   66 To attempt to survey this material for the period before Adomnán in Latin would be impossible here. Suffice it to note that the theme can be followed in medieval or renaissance catena-style commentaries which note their Patristic authorities, e.g. Cornelius a Lapide's commentary on John (first published in 1639, and continuing in print until the end of the 19th century).   67 DLS I.xix. Since the English spelling in modern versions varies (e.g. *Akeldama* in the R.S.V., *Hakeldama* in the N.R.S.V.), I shall retain the Latin form.

the place for the burial of 'pilgrims' (*peregrini*) (Mt 27.7–8),[68] and then adds some details. Many pilgrims receive a proper and careful burial in the earth there (*humantur*), as we should expect, but there are others left there rotting without being interred (*inhumati*), covered only with rags and skins. This seems a strange oversight. If some are properly buried, why not all? We might presume the cause to be poverty or lack of associates to undertake the task, but there is no such hint in the text. A clue may be provided by Adomnán's use of a curious phrase to describe these bodies: they are thrown upon the face of the earth and are rotten (*super terrae faciem putrefacti iacentes*). Part of this phrase, *super faciem terrae*, is used four times in connection with death in the Old Testament. In IV Rg 9.37 the body of Jezebel is left like dung to rot upon the face of the earth; while Ier 8.2 says that sinners shall be left like dung on the face of the earth, their bodies not to be gathered up nor buried. Ier 16.4 and 25.23 repeat this, adding that these bodies are not to be lamented, but to become food for birds and wild animals. The combined message of these texts is that sinners are to be thrown like dung on the face of the earth. There appear to be two distinct ways to mark the end of human life in Adomnán's mind. The first is proper burial. This belongs to the saints in their tombs, his brethren and those pilgrims in their decent graves. The other is the lot of sinners. Judas, and wicked people closer home, either have no burial place or are just thrown on the surface of the earth in squalor. This is the reward and lot of the sinners, as predicted by the prophets.[69]

The more elaborately described tomb of the Virgin Mary[70] provides us with a clearer indication of how Adomnán thought of burial.[71] Adomnán states that

---

68 In the Greek text, Acheldemach is mentioned only in Act 1.19, where we find the tradition that Judas himself bought the field and then simply exploded, without mention of suicide. The more usual story, followed by Adomnán, is given in Mt 25.5–8: 'And throwing down the pieces of silver in the temple, he [i.e. Judas] departed; and he went and hanged himself. But the chief priests, taking the pieces of silver, said, "It is not lawful to put them into the treasury, since they are blood money." So they took counsel, and bought with them the potter's field, to bury strangers (ξένοις) in. Therefore that field has been called the Field of Blood to this day'. The Latin gospel text assimilated the Aramaic name from Acts and the key verses read: *consilio autem inito emerunt ex illis agrum figuli in sepulturam peregrinorum propter hoc uocatus est ager ille Acheldemach ager sanguinis usque in hodiernum diem.*
69 Adomnán was surely familiar with Ez 39.14 which directs that men be 'set apart to pass through the land continually and bury those remaining upon the face of the land, so as to cleanse it'. These unburied corpses of Acheldemach would be a defilement of the holy city, but no doubt this was part of the pollution miraculously cleansed annually from the city (DLS I.i.7–13). 70 DLS I.xii. 71 This is the most studied chapter of DLS. In the period before the Catholic Church proclaimed as one of its dogmas that Mary was assumed into heaven two key debates concerned (1) whether or not Mary died and (2) whether there was agreement in the tradition as to a belief in her assumption. Adomnán's text clearly assumed her death, and implied that there was no notion of an assumption: hence the theologians arguing in the case needed to be able either to ignore this chapter (always taking it as factual eye-witness evidence), or else read it as in some way anticipating the later Roman Catholic

this tomb is now empty because her body has been removed. The result is that no one knows with certainty where 'she awaits the resurrection' (*in quo loco resurrectionem exspectat*).[72] The implication is clear: wherever a saint lies buried, there is where he/she awaits the resurrection. Mary too is awaiting the resurrection, wherever her body is now, only that place is unknown.

Adomnán's underlying theology of burial/resurrection can be viewed through his sources in the case of his description of the tombs of the patriarchs at Machpelah: one of the most detailed accounts surviving in Christian sources of the tomb of Adam and Eve, Abraham, Isaac, Jacob, and their wives.[73] Moreover, his presentation of the material, and his analysis of the Scriptural references to this tomb, is among his most accomplished interweavings of the sources at his disposal into a single consistent picture. However, his main interest in this place is because it is Adam's tomb. For his facts, he uses the key western source, Jerome.[74] For his analysis of its importance, he uses the greatest Latin authority on this burial, Augustine.[75] Augustine in the passage employed by Adomnán was concerned with Paul's teaching about the resurrection in I Th 4.13–7.[76] There, death is described as a falling asleep until the Lord comes, with a word of power and the trumpet call to arise. Then the Christian dead will arise from the earth and meet Christ in the air as he comes down to them. This future event Augustine understands to be the resurrection of the dead, as that is professed in the creeds. Then people will have immortal bodies (cf. I Cor 15.53–4) and will be brought back to life (cf. I Cor 15.22), but this requires that the present body first die.[77] This is equivalent to the seed being sown in the earth, and dying in order to rise to its new life (cf. I Cor 15.36–9).[78] For Augustine, this corresponds allegorically to the human body dying and being sown in the earth in burial. This burial is the sentence on sin in Gn 3.19, and the saints are not exempt from it, for death, burial and putrefaction are no more than the lot of Adam's children. Because of Christ, however, they await a new flesh and new life after being called from their graves. This is 'the celestial body' (I Cor 15.40) which is 'caught up ... in the clouds to meet the Lord in the air' (I Th 4.17). Augustine then notes that this is to be believed, though how it actually happens humans are unable fully to understand. Adomnán takes over Augustine's argument and expresses it with simplicity. Adam, in whom is all humanity, was prevented from reaching his eternal destination by sin. This sin

---

position. This debate does not concern us here, but it is perhaps useful to note the following discussions: Agius, 'On Pseudo-Jerome Epistle IX'; Lambot, 'L'homélie du Pseudo-Jérôme'; Jugie, *La mort et l'assomption de la Sainte Vierge*; Faller, *De priorum saeculorum silentio*; H. Barré, 'La lettre du Pseudo-Jérôme'; and O'Carroll, *Theotokos*, s.v. 'Adamnan, St', p. 5. See also Meehan's extended footnote, *Adamnan's De locis sanctis*, p. 59. 72 DLS I.xii.3. 73 DLS II.ix–x. 74 See O'Loughlin, 'Adam's Burial'. 75 See O'Loughlin, 'Latin Version', pp. 20–1. 76 Augustine, *De ciuitate Dei* XX.20. 77 Augustine makes this point as an exegesis of I Cor 15.36. 78 Cf. also Io 12.24.

diverted him to another destiny. Earth goes back to earth, so now he waits in the earth for resurrection. Christ will call him back from the earth to heaven, but this has not happened yet. Thus 'Adam the protoplast' (*protoplaustus*) in his tomb is the cause of all human burials, but as the oldest awaiting resurrection (*exspectans resurrectionem*) he is the archetype of all who are in their tombs now.[79]

The tomb described in greater detail than any other in DLS is the sepulchre of Christ.[80] But this tomb is empty: it is a tomb whose body has gone from it. The location of Christ's tomb is none other than the place of his resurrection (... *in loco Dominicae resurrectionis fabricata est*).[81] In this fascination with the empty tomb of Christ Adomnán is doing no more than following the lead of the gospels, where the news of the empty tomb is the first announcement of the resurrection.[82] But he is also adding a significant element of interpretation: this tomb stands as a sign of what will happen to all the other tombs where there are still bodies. Adomnán's frequent use of the Scriptural/credal echo, *expectans resurrectionem*, stands in contrast to the tomb whose occupant has risen (*surrexit a mortuis*).[83]

This paper has sought to examine why tombs figure so prominently in Adomnán's writings, in VC and DLS. Tombs are the places of waiting for the resurrection – a part of the great divine plan that began with Adam's sin and his condemnation to return to the earth, and which shall end at the last trumpet when the bodies of the saints come forth from their tombs. In this divine plan, the central moment is the risen Christ who has left his tomb, and will one day call the other saintly tomb-dwellers to join him. As such Adomnán's interest is not just a curiosity about the saints or relics or places of intercession, but a key part of a systematic theology of the resurrection.

This study has attempted to be as minimalist as possible: it has only looked at Scriptural texts that seemed warranted by Adomnán's use of or allusion to them, and has only sought to use Patristic authorities, namely Augustine and Gregory, where there is clear evidence not only for their presence on Iona, but that they were used by Adomnán in what he wrote about the present state of the dead. A fuller study would have to situate this in terms of a more synthetic presentation of notions of bodily resurrection in the Patristic period and the early medieval west, and, especially, combine it with a study of the theme of Christ's *descensio ad inferos* in writing,[84] liturgy,[85] and iconography.[86] Such an

---

79 DLS II.x.5. The connection between 'the first Adam' and Christ as 'the last Adam' in I Cor 15 (see verses 22 and 45 especially) is in the immediate background to this treatment as the Christ-Adam contrast is there discussed as part of Paul's teaching on the resurrection of the dead. See Barrett, *From First Adam to Last*, pp. 92–120.   80 DLS I.ii; I.iii; I.iv; and I.ix.   81 DLS I.iv.   82 Mt 28.8; Mc 16.2–8; Lc 24.1–24; and Io 20.1–11.   83 This phrase is found in many forms in the New Testament, e.g. Mt 27.64.   84 See MacCulloch, *Harrowing of Hell*.   85 See Kennedy, 'Dead, Cult of the', pp. 107–8, on the place of tombs in early Christian worship.   86 See McDonnell, 'Descent of Jesus', a study which supplies a context in which several other elements in DLS could be seen as reflecting this aspect of

approach would be out of place here, but my hope is that this paper shows that in such a broader study Adomnán should be seen as having had a well thought out position on these questions, and to have made a definite contribution to western theology.[87]

Adomnán's theology.   **87** This paper has steered clear of Insular evidence from archaeology, and other texts in Latin and the vernacular, as this would have taken it too far from its purpose. But clearly this is the most important context in which this should be seen: see, for example, Doherty, 'Monastic Town', pp. 53–4; and O'Brien, 'Archaeological Study', pp. 160–2. The topic is far from closed.

Aspects of the Monastic Landscape in Adomnán's *Life of Columba*

Aidan MacDonald

I believe a case can be made that Adomnán provides evidence for a triple boundary system delimiting and defining the monastic settlement and its adjacent farmland, and for the view that the entire area thus enclosed was regarded as, in some sense at least, sacred space. The broad validity of this contention will be argued, and some of its possible implications briefly explored. The bulk of the material I shall examine concerns, as one might expect, Iona.

I THE OUTERMOST BOUNDARY

The foreshore of the island seems to me to function as more than a merely natural outer boundary. In *Vita Columbae* (hereafter VC) I.22, Columba orders to be put ashore on Mull a man of lurid sins, 'so that he may not set foot upon the sod of this island' (*ne huius insulae cispitem calcet*): the man must not be allowed to profane holy ground. Then he and Baithéne go to the harbour to confront the man. Columba knows in his heart that he is fundamentally impenitent and, in effect, persists in refusing to receive him on Iona. I interpret this direct exchange as a formal, almost ceremonial, refusal of admittance: the reverse of a ceremonial, or at least formal, reception. The harbour (singular) can be seen as the outer gateway. In VC I.4 Cainnech of Aghaboe, whose imminent arrival, despite bad weather, Columba has foretold, is formally received by the saint and the community of Iona – at the harbour, by clear implication. In VC I.30 the saint meets at the harbour a true penitent, Féchna, whose arrival he has foreseen. Féchna publicly confesses his sins there and then, and Columba pronounces him forgiven. 'And Féchna rising was joyfully received by the saint' (*Qui surgens gaudenter a sancto susceptus...*). He remains with Columba on Iona for a few days, before being sent to Baithéne at the monastery of *Campus Lunge* on Tiree. There is clearly a formal, perhaps almost ceremonial, aspect to this exchange: Féchna kneels and confesses, Columba bids him rise and so receives him. The formality of the occasion is, I suggest, enhanced by its setting at the harbour, though otherwise there is apparent an element of spontaneity that might seem to border on informality. Féchna, moreover, is forgiven, not absolved: he is presumably sent to *Campus Lunge* for a more or less protracted period of penance, during which, like Librán in VC II.39, he was not permitted to receive communion.[1] In VC I.45 Columba goes to meet his dying uncle Ernán, arriving from *Hinba*, at the harbour. The case here is rather different, since Ernán has clearly left the harbour when he collapses and dies, and Columba has not yet reached it. In order that 'the saint's word should not be rendered vain in any way' (he has predicted, on sending Ernán as prior to Hinba, that he will not see him again alive in this world), it is necessary that Ernán die before they meet; and the two men are some twenty-four paces (*pas(s)us*) apart and, the Andersons suggest, apparently out of sight of each other, when death overtakes Ernán.[2] Clearly, no formal reception was contemplated here, and the outer boundary and its gateway are in the event ignored. Perhaps Adomnán wishes to emphasise, in this seeming breach of proper procedure, the vanity of Ernán's attempt in his extremity to evade the divine dispensation that Columba has already announced. The contrast with the order and dignity of Ernán's commission and departure for *Hinba* is marked. For Adomnán, the two crosses surviving in his own day are commemorative: one marks the spot where Ernán died, the other the spot where Columba stood at that moment. It is equally clear, however, that they do not stand at the harbour itself and fulfil, perhaps *inter alia*, an apotropaic function. Rather, they are probably on the way from the harbour to the monastery – perhaps beside the path linking the harbour with the (main?) entrance through the *uallum monasterii* (discussed below). In VC III.23 Adomnán mentions a cross, likewise commemorative and surviving, that is also situated beside a path, that linking the monastery with farm buildings, half way between the monastery and the nearest barn.[3] In VC II.14 Columba has bidden farewell to Cainnech at the harbour. He is not alone, since Cainnech's forgotten staff is given to him there when found. It seems quite likely that a formal communal valediction here balances the formal reception of VC I.4 – in terms of literary composition, if not of actual fact.

In Adomnán's text, those who come to Iona by sea under their own sail, who steer themselves into the harbour, are generally more favoured than those who

---

1 There does not seem to be much detailed circumstantial information on confession, as distinct from penance, in the early Irish church: see the *Canones Hibernenses* II.3 (P and B) and II.4 (P and B) (Bieler, *Irish Penitentials*, pp. 164–5); *Paenitentiale S. Columbani* B 23 and B 30 (ibid., pp. 104–7); and the 'Old Irish Penitential' III.19 (ibid., p. 268). Both monastic and non-monastic situations seem to be envisaged here. Discussion of the dating of these texts in Bieler's introduction, ibid., pp. 8–9, 47–51. In a strictly monastic context, Columbanus ordains that confession be made 'before meat or before entering our beds or whenever it is opportune' (Walker, *Sancti Columbani opera*, pp. 144–5). Cf. Warren, *Liturgy and Ritual*, pp. 147–52; Ryan, *Irish Monasticism*, pp. 353–7. Penitents were apparently not housed on Iona, but were sent to *Campus Lunge* or *Hinba*: MacDonald, 'Adomnán's Monastery', p. 44. 2 Anderson and Anderson, *Life of Columba*, p. 82 n. 106. 3 For discussion of the functions of crosses, as evidenced by literary sources, see A. Hamlin, 'Crosses in Early Ireland'. In VC II.16, a demon has been inadvertently carried within the monastic enclosure at the bottom of a milk-pail: it is expelled by the *sign* of the cross.

have to ask for passage across the Sound of Iona from the Mull shore. In addition to Cainnech (VC I.4) and Féchna (VC I.30), there is Colmán (VC I.5); and also, though their circumstances are special in either case, there are Finten moccu Moie (VC I.2) and Librán (VC II.39). This group has a decidedly clerical hue. In comparison, those who have to be ferried across the Sound form a more mixed group, with a strong lay element. These people are represented as shouting across the strait to announce their arrival and to request a passage. There is no question in any of these cases of a formal reception at the harbour. A clumsy guest arrives thus in VC I.25. The arrival of a religious guest in VC I.26 – Aidán, Fergno's son, the attendant for twelve years of Brendan – causes the relaxation of the customary Wednesday fast and thus his presence may be regarded as in some sense intrusive. Also notable are a wretched man in VC I.27, more concerned with his material needs than with his spiritual welfare, whose death is imminent; two brothers – laymen – on pilgrimage in VC I.32, who enter the community at Columba's bidding and die shortly afterwards; and a traveller from Ireland in VC I.43, who confirms a prophecy of the saint.

The Sound of Iona, the strait, certainly seems to function here as a means of protecting the community by regulating access to the island, symbolically as well as physically. In VC III.22, Columba sees angels, who have come to conduct his soul to heaven, held back and 'standing on a rock beyond the strait of our island; they wish to approach, in order to summon me from the body, but they are not allowed to come nearer, and will presently return to the highest heavens'. During the three days and nights of the saint's funeral (VC III.23), 'a great storm of wind blew without rain, and forbade anyone in a small ship to cross the strait in either direction. And after the burial of the blessed man had been completed, straightway the storm was stilled, the wind ceased, and the whole sea was calmed'. The community was thus effectively immured and the world – *promiscuum populi uulgus* – excluded for the crucial period, fulfilling Columba's prophecy that only his monastic family – *mei soli familiares monaci* – would solemnise the rites of his funeral.

For Adomnán the Sound is, I suggest, a reinforcement of the outer boundary system facing the only nearby coast. The choice of the practice of shouting across it, however, to obtain a passage, frankly puzzles me. I should have thought the channel generally too wide for so uncertain a means of communication. Dr Richard Sharpe, on the other hand, who knows the locality far better than I do, accepts it as possible under the right conditions: 'The distance is nearly a mile; on still days, especially in the early morning or the evening, the voice would carry easily, but there must have been many days when the noise of wind and waves would have defeated the ears of the most attentive boatman'.[4] The practical

---

4 Sharpe, *Life of St Columba*, p. 285 n. 126. In a letter to me dated 2 September 1992, Patrick Cashman, Area Officer for Scottish Natural Heritage in Mull, Coll and Tiree, writes: 'The

effectiveness of the method, it seems to me, is likely to have been so haphazard under most circumstances that I wonder if Adomnán chose 'shouting' (*clamor*) to denote symbolically any petition, by whatever means, for access to the monastery, for whatever purpose.[5] It probably did not escape his notice, furthermore, as it certainly did not escape that of Isidore of Seville, that the root of Latin *fretum* (n.), *-us* (m.), 'strait, sound, channel', was said to be that also seen in the verb *ferueo*, 'boil, ferment, glow, foam, rage, etc.': hence it can also mean by extension, 'a raging, swelling, heat, violence'.[6] The appositeness, in that case, of the symbolism of a cry across the fretful waters of worldly concerns and dangers to be brought into the safe shelter of a monastic haven would surely not have been lost on a learned but also religious author.[7]

II THE MIDDLE BOUNDARY

The middle boundary is, I propose, the monastic enclosure itself, the *ual(l)um monasterii*: perhaps a single rather than a multiple line of enceinte in Adomnán's scheme of things, but its detailed physical character (which may, after all, have varied from one settlement to another) does not really affect my argument. It is mentioned explicitly only in relation to Clonmacnoise (VC I.3) and Iona (VC II.29). In the case of Clonmacnoise, Adomnán may or may not have known the place personally. If he did not, then one must assume either that he knew of the existence of a *uallum* there by reliable report, or that he assumed its existence from his own knowledge of Iona and of other Columban houses. In the case of Iona, the fact that a monk goes outside the *uallum* to kill a cow (VC II.29) may reflect a religiously motivated prohibition against the taking of life even for purposes of food within the enclosure, an area of presumably greater sanctity in the eyes of the community. (It is perhaps unlikely, on the other hand, that cows or other livestock were kept within the *uallum* anyway). Since lay people are apparently allowed, at least under supervision, onto the *platea monasterii* (VC I.50) – the courtyard of the monastery which, as I would argue, was centrally situated within the enclosure among the main public buildings[8] – then

Sound of Iona is unlikely to have been much different in the fifth and sixth centuries than it is today. If anything, the channel may have been a little deeper and thus the Sound a little wider with the raised sea level.' 5 Cf. perhaps the opening verses of the *De profundis* (Ps 129.1–2 in the Vulgate): *De profundis clamaui, ad te Domine; Domine, exaudi vocem meam.* 6 Isidore, *Etymologiae* XIII.xviii.2; cf. Varro, *De lingua latina* VII.22 (Kent, i.290–1). I am most grateful to Dr P.A.J. Cronin, Department of Ancient Classics, U.C.C., for discussion and help with regard to the passages here quoted. On Adomnán's knowledge and use of the works of Isidore see O'Loughlin, 'Living in the Ocean', p. 15, and reference there cited. 7 Cf. Meister Eckhart, beginning of Sermon 54 and note 1 thereto, in Walshe, *Meister Eckhart*, ii.69–74. 8 MacDonald, 'Adomnán's Monastery', p. 40.

this area was probably integral to the space specifically delimited by the middle boundary (see further below).

As with the outer boundary, Adomnán does not seem to envisage here an enclosure defended by standing crosses, whether of wood or stone, having an apotropaic function. In VC II.16, a demon that has been lurking in the bottom of a milk-vessel is inadvertently carried by a young brother within the enclosure. There Columba expels it with the sign of the cross; and rebukes the brother for not taking this precaution himself at the outset.[9]

III THE INNERMOST BOUNDARY

This, I believe, is an enclosure around the church, probably also containing the monastic cemetery. Lay people are not said to enter the church save as prospective monks (VC I.32), or as penitents like Librán, who subsequently takes monastic vows (VC II.39).[10] The attempted assassination of Columba (VC II.24) may have involved violation of the church on *Hinba*; but in any case the would-be assassin subsequently meets an exemplary end. Towards the end of his work, Adomnán mentions that certain privileged individuals witnessed Columba's grave surrounded by heavenly light and frequented by angels (VC III.23). Sharpe notes that 'the continuance of such manifestations at the grave of the saint is something not mentioned of other Irish saints'.[11] I have argued elsewhere that, in view of Adomnán's clearcut attitude to monastic burial, he would certainly not have tolerated, in fact or in theory, a mixed cemetery for monks and laity.[12]

IV THE BOUNDARY SYSTEM IN PRACTICE

This tripartite arrangement can be seen in action. At Clonmacnoise (VC I.3), Columba's reception, described as 'a ceremonial *adventus* recalling Christ's entry into Jerusalem',[13] moves with 'hymns and praises' from the fields (*agelluli*) adjacent to the monastery, through the *uallum*, to the church (*ec(c)lesia*). The saint is protected, moreover, from the enthusiastic throng as he walks. When

---

9 In VC III.8 Columba, praying alone in a remote part of Iona, has a vision of a host of demons making war on him with iron spits; they wish to attack his monastery 'and with these same spikes to slaughter many of the brothers' – by the infliction of diseases as it transpires. After a contest lasting nearly all day between the saint and his adversaries, the demons are driven off by the arrival of angelic help. The demons are attempting to invade Columba's island – *sua insula*: they are repulsed by his prayer and heavenly aid – at the shore? (But cf. Anderson and Anderson, *Life of Columba*, p. 193 n. 219). 10 Cf. n. 1 above. 11 *Life of St Columba*, pp. 377–8 n. 421. 12 MacDonald, 'Adomnán's Monastery', pp. 32–3. 13 O'Reilly, 'Reading the Scriptures', p. 103.

Adomnán and his companions, who have been delayed by contrary winds on their return from Ireland, eventually reach the harbour of Iona after the third hour on 9 June, having finished their voyage in the early morning and in miraculous time with Columba's help, they wash their hands and feet, presumably within the monastery, and at the sixth hour mass is celebrated in the church – for the festival of Columba and Baithéne (VC II.45). The aged Columba, sitting in a wagon on or near the western coast of Iona, turns east to bless the island and its inhabitants (VC III.23). As in the earlier version of the same episode in VC II.28, where the blessing is performed 'on higher ground', the saint's blessing renders men and beasts there safe from snakebite (see further below). Then, from a small hill overlooking his monastery,[14] he blesses it and prophesies its future greatness; finally, the saint blesses his community as he lies dying before the altar in the church. Cumulatively, this is the solemn blessing of a patriarch about to die, just as Jacob blessed his twelve sons (Gn 49) and Moses the twelve tribes of Israel (Dt 33).

Right of sanctuary for the local lay population seems to be involved in the episode (VC I.20) in which Columba prophesies of a certain Baitán, who has sought his blessing before setting out to seek 'a desert place in the sea' (*in mari herimum*) that he will not be buried in any such hermitage, but 'in that place (*illo in loco*) in which a woman will drive sheep across his grave'. Baitán's quest ends in failure and, returning to his own district, he is for many years head of a small church there. Then he dies and is buried at Derry. Shortly thereafter, the neighbouring lay people take refuge there during a raid and Columba's prophecy is duly fulfilled. Baitán has not been a member of the community of Derry, but he may have been a Columban monk.[15] If so, he may have been buried in the monastic cemetery, as Librán, from *Campus Lunge*, was buried at Durrow (VC II.39). Has a lay person – and a woman at that – breached the innermost boundary, sheep and all, during the dislocation caused by the crisis? Does Adomnán, then, wish to emphasise the contrast between Baitán's earthly expectation and the actual treatment of his grave by drawing attention to a serious violation of due order? Even if he was buried elsewhere, within or outside the main enclosure, such a contrast seems implicit: concentration is on his burial-place alone, to the exclusion of all others. I think, however, that

---

14 Both the Andersons (*Life of Columba*, pp. xlvi and 222 n. 243) and Sharpe (*Life of St Columba*, p. 374 n. 409) think that this *monticellus* was Cnoc nan Carnan, the rocky hillock immediately overlooking the main monastic area from the west. Both point out that Cnoc nan Carnan (or at least part of it) lay within the *uallum*; and this was certainly true at some stage. If, however, its steep eastern face originally bounded the west side of the monastic enclosure, then Columba stands on my middle boundary. If so, was one of the reasons for its eventual inclusion within the *uallum* the fact that it was the traditional site of this penultimate general blessing of the saint? 15 Sharpe, *Life of St Columba*, p. 281 n. 111. For the church of Derry at this time, see ibid., pp. 28–9 and 255–6 n. 54.

solitary burial, especially in an ecclesiastical context, is unlikely. Adomnán seems distinctly reserved about Baitán. Perhaps he was regarded, because of spiritual pride or some other fault, as unsuited for the eremitical life. We are not actually told that Columba did bless him, and the saint's farewell prophecy seems to distance Columba somewhat from the seeker and his enterprise. The background details are opaque. An innermost enclosure may be implied, as far as Baitán's place of burial is concerned, and the use of the term *ecclesia* for the place of refuge may convey the existence of a *uallum* at least, possibly an outermost boundary also.[16] Further than that, however, it does not seem possible to go.

To be respected, all three boundaries would have to be visible, though not necessarily formidable or defensible in any military sense (a practical impossibility in any case). In the Second Preface to VC, the farmlands – *agelluli* – of a monastery of Mochta of Louth and a monastery of Columba (*monasteriola*) share a 'small hedge' (*sepiscula*) as a common boundary. The use of these diminutives here may have no material significance. Adomnán's boundary system, however, is apparent only in the context of somewhat formal movement inward, from the outside world to the church at the centre. When the direction is reversed, these boundaries make no appearance. Twice, indeed, an outward movement is depicted by Adomnán as threefold. Firstly, as the moment of Columba's death approaches, his attendant Diormit and a few other brothers, as they draw near, see the whole church filled with angelic light about the dying saint. In the hour of Columba's death, a monk in a monastery in Ireland has a vision of the whole island of Iona illuminated by the light of the angels descending from heaven to receive Columba's soul. At the same time, Columban monks and others fishing in the River Finn in Donegal see the whole sky lit up by a great column of light rising in the direction of sunrise and seeming to light the whole world 'like the summer sun at midday' (VC III.23). These three manifestations of heavenly light are, moreover, explicitly linked by Adomnán. The limits are, however, different: first the church, then Iona, finally the world. I am inclined to see in this a scheme in some sense complementary to that outlined by O'Loughlin, wherein the preaching of the gospel is also envisaged as a threefold movement: first in Jerusalem, then to all Israel, finally to the ends of the earth.[17] Iona, at those ends, has received the gospel message and now she makes in return her own contribution: 'You received without charge, give without charge' (Mt 10.8). Secondly and similarly, at the end of the work, Adomnán describes how Columba's fame has reached out from Iona to embrace not only Ireland and Britain; but also Spain, Gaul and Italy; and finally Rome itself, 'which is the chief of all cities' – and, of course, the centre of Latin Christendom (VC III.23).

---

16 Sharpe, *Life of St Columba*, p. 281 n. 112; MacDonald, 'Adomnán's Monastery', p. 32.
17 O'Loughlin, 'Living in the Ocean', p. 19, writing in the context of Adomnán's *De locis sanctis*.

V ADOMNÁN AND THE LAITY

Adomnán's scheme of things, whether it reflects the reality of his own or Columba's day, or both, or an ideal only, pretty clearly envisages no resident lay population on Iona. The significance of the timely windstorm, which effectively closes the island to outsiders for the duration of the saint's funeral ceremonies and allows his family of monks only to be present at them (VC III.23), would apparently be nullified if there had in fact been laity living on the island at the time. If this impression is right, then though the *plebeus* Findchán is implicitly a tenant of the monastery (VC II.3), his home place, *Delcros*, must have been elsewhere, probably on Mull. This conclusion is supported to some extent by the fact that the wattles for building, taken from his land, are brought to the monastery by ship. It appears that only monks work on the land (VC I.18, 37; II.28 ,39; III.23), in the steading (VC II.16, 29), in the workshop (VC II.29), on building (VC I.29; II.3, 45; III.15), or at general tasks (VC III.12).[18]

The attitude of VC to the laity generally seems ambivalent. Adomnán shows, on the one hand, a lively interest in secular, especially royal and aristocratic affairs. His attitude to women in particular, mostly laywomen, is not unsympathetic as a rule (VC I.17; II.3, 5, 7, 39, 40, 41; III.10; but contrast I.47; II.37; cf. II, 7); and can be actively compassionate (VC II.25 and 33). Laymen are received in Columban monasteries in various circumstances and capacities: as guests (VC I.13, 25, 27; cf. I.2); as penitents (VC I.21, 30; II.39; cf. I.22); as pilgrims (VC I.32); as students (VC III.21); to be buried (VC I.16). On the other hand, Adomnán seems to show concern over unrestricted access to Iona on the part of the laity – a concern reflected, not only by the reference to the funeral windstorm (VC III.23), but also, I suggest, by the end of VC III.7. And, as I have already observed, most of those requiring passage across the Sound seem to be lay people.

It is in the context of a public cult of relics, however, that this concern appears most noticeable. Recourse to or veneration of relics (in particular relics of Columba himself) are not conspicuous features of the Life as a whole.[19] Such instances as are noted, moreover, are clearly not intended to attract or encourage the devotion of the laity at large. Most conspicuous, however, by its absence is any reference to pious recourse to Columba's grave,especially reference to posthumous miracles effected there. The reports of heavenly light about his grave and angelic visits to it (VC III.23) do not appear to be intended to stimulate lay interest generally in any way. Posthumous cures effected at the saint's grave, or more widely by means of his relics, simply do not occur. And the protective patronage afforded by St Columba (VC II.46) is, in the first instance, too vague (the Picts and Scots) and, in the second, too restricted (the Columban

---

18 Sharpe too concludes that Iona did not support a resident lay population in Columba's time (*Life of St Columba*, pp. 19–20).   19 See VC II.44–5; and cf. II.8–9.

community in Scotland and Adomnán and his companions on the two
Northumbrian journeys) to be considered in this context. It does not, in any
case, direct attention to Iona itself (or to a named dependent church for that
matter), a surprising omission if the intention had been to foster pilgrimage. I
have, in fact, the definite impression that Adomnán was concerned positively to
discourage such developments. I think that he would have found much with
which to agree in the words attributed by Bede to the dying St Cuthbert: '...
I ... think that it will be more expedient for you (i.e. the community of
Lindisfarne) that I should remain here (i.e. at his hermitage on Farne), on
account of the influx of fugitives and guilty men of every sort, who will perhaps
flee to my body because, unworthy as I am, reports about me as a servant of
God have nevertheless gone forth; and you will be compelled very frequently to
intercede with the powers of this world on behalf of such men, and so will be
put to much trouble on account of the presence of my body'. And even when
he has finally consented to be buried on Lindisfarne, Cuthbert recommends
that he be buried in the church there, so that, while having ready access to his
tomb themselves, the brothers may also control access to it by visitors.[20] If I
have interpreted Adomnán's system of boundaries correctly in broad outline,
Columba's mortal remains lay within the innermost enclosure, where lay people
may have been excluded, or only allowed entry under strict supervision. The
accommodation, then, of public access to them could have involved more or less
fundamental changes for the community, and would probably have presented
the monastery of Iona with problems – indeed dangers – that, I believe,
Adomnán wished at all costs to avoid.

VI IONA AS A SACRED LANDSCAPE

Adomnán affords evidence which may reasonably be interpreted as indicating
that the island was regarded as substantially more than just the home farm.

It frequently happens that the island and monastery of Iona are so closely
identified as to be, at least by implication, one and the same. This practical
identification probably occurs most frequently in formulaic phrases employed
to establish Columba's situation at a given time. Thus: *cum esset uir sanctus in
Ioua insula* (VC I.8); *cum uir sanctus in Ioua conuersaretur insula* (VC II.39); *cum
(uir) sanctus in Ioua commoraretur insula* (VC II.42; III.6); *sanctus (Columba) in
Ioua commanens insula* (VC II.40; III.9); *dum uir beatus in Ioua commaneret insula*
(VC III.22; cf. III.7: an Irish pilgrim *in Ioua commanebat insula* with Columba
for some months); *uir sanctus/beatus in Ioua conuersans insula* (VC III.10, 16);
dum uir uenerandus in Ioua conuersaretur insula (VC III.11; in the closely similar

20 Bede, *Vita S. Cudbercti*, cap. 37 (Colgrave, *Two Lives*, pp. 279–81).

episode of VC III.12, Columba and his monks are in the *monasterium*: presumably Iona is meant); *uir uenerandus cum in Ioua conuersaretur insula* (VC III.13). In all these instances and in VC I.31 (*ad eum* [i.e. Columba] *in Ioua insula commorantem*), though the island is named, the setting is actually the monastery: in fact the monastery is meant. This also appears to be the case when Librán crosses from Ireland to Columba's island monastery, *insulanum monasterium* (VC II.39); and when a British monk 'first among us has died in this island' (*primus apud nos in hac insula mortuus est*, VC III.6). Demons wishing to inflict diseases on Columba's community of monks, *super eius cenubialem coetum*, are repelled 'from this our principal island' (*hac nostra de insula... primaria*, VC I.1). In the full version of the same episode Columba is described as living in the island of Io (*uir sanctus in Ioua conuersans insula*), and the demons as wishing to attack his monastery (*monasterium*), and to kill many of the brothers (*fratres*): he defends 'his island' (*sua insula*) against them (VC III.8).[21] Finten moccu Moie sails to the island of Io, *transnauigans Iouam deuenit insulam*; and is received there as a guest (VC I.2). Monastic hospitality is extended to an exhausted bird on the western shore of Io (*cum sanctus in Ioua inhabitaret insula / in occidentali huius insulae parte*): the crane is described as being 'in pilgrimage with us' (*apud nos perigrinari*), and as a 'pilgrim guest' (*perigrina hospita*, VC I.48). In VC II.45, the monastery is the destination, but is described usually as the island of Io (*Ioua insula*), or 'our island' (*nostra insula*).

As might be expected, however, the identification is not total: in VC I.30, 37, 48; and III.8, 16 and 23 (six times [thrice in 128a alone]), the monastery is quite clearly also *within* the island. The *uallum monasterii* is, after all, a significant boundary.

There are other considerations, however, that, I think, reflect much more explicitly the sacred character of the island as a whole for Adomnán and the Columban community. In the first place, there is Columba's pillow-stone. The saint is said to have used the bare rock for his bed, 'and for pillow, a stone which even today stands beside his burial-place as a kind of grave-pillar' (*et pro puluillo lapidem qui hodieque quasi quidam iuxta sepulchrum eius titulus stat monumenti*, VC III.23). The Andersons briefly discuss the use of *titulus* in Gn 28.18, where Jacob sets up his stone pillow *in titulum*; and in Gn 35.20, where a *titulus* is set up by Jacob over Rachel's tomb (*sepulchrum*): *est titulus monumenti Rachel usque in praesentem diem*.[22] I am not concerned here so much with the stone as grave-marker, as with the stone as pillow; and with its implications for Iona in the context of Gn 28.

---

21 There is, of course, only one monastery on Iona. Compare the situation on Tiree, which supported several *fratrum monasteria*, and where Baithéne successfully defends the *eclesiae ... collectio* or *congregatio* of *Campus Lunge* against the same demons (VC III.8).   22 Anderson and Anderson, *Life of Columba*, pp. 224–5 n. 247. Sharpe too draws attention to Gn 35.20 in this connection: *Life of St Columba*, pp. 374–5 n. 411.

In Gn 28.10–19, Jacob stopped for the night at a certain place and, 'taking one of the stones of that place, he made it his pillow and lay down where he was'. In the ensuing dream, he saw a ladder stretching from earth to heaven, with angels ascending and descending; and God appeared to him and promised him that '"The ground on which you are lying I shall give to you and your descendants ... Be sure, I am with you; I shall keep you safe wherever you go, and bring you back to this country, for I shall never desert you until I have done what I have promised you." Then Jacob awoke from his sleep and said, "Truly, Yahweh is in this place and I did not know!" He was afraid and said, "How awe-inspiring this place is! This is nothing less than the abode of God, and this is the gate of heaven!" Early next morning, Jacob took the stone he had used for his pillow, and set it up as a pillar, pouring oil over the top of it. He named the place Bethel ...'.[23] The common use of *titulus* in the two Genesis passages and in Adomnán makes it a reasonable inference that Columba's pillow-stone symbolised for his spiritual descendants Jacob's pillow before it served finally as a grave-marker. Iona is then, like Bethel, nothing less than the abode of God and the gate of heaven. The island is, in other words, an especially holy place, where the divine may choose to reveal itself more clearly to 'elect persons'.[24]

In the second place, the monastery and its locality can be sensed as being or representing, for Adomnán, the earthly paradise restored, or at least returning. Here a passage from the Life of St Gall by Walahfrid Strabo (died 849) may serve as a link, since it both quotes Gn 28.16 and introduces snakes in the context of a sacred place. So it is both retrospective and prospective for purposes of the present discussion:

> ... these two faithful lovers of the wilderness continued their way through the valley and espied at last between two streams a spot [i.e. the future site of St Gall] which they judged well fitted for a settlement, for it offered much that they desired, a fine wood and mountains around enclosing a small plain. Then the Saint, recalling the words of Jacob after he had beheld the vision of the ladder and the angels ascending and descending thereon, said, 'Truly the Lord is in this place!' (Gn 28.16). Up to that time there had been a great many serpents in that valley, but from that day forth they vanished so completely that not one was ever after seen there.[25]

---

23 The translation is cited from the *New Jerusalem Bible*. Cf. the Vulgate of Gn 28.18: *Surgens ergo Iacob mane, tulit lapidem quem supposuerat capiti suo, et erexit in titulum, fundens oleum desuper* ('Rising then in the morning, Jacob took the stone which he had put under his head, and set it up as a pillar, pouring oil from above'); and references in n. 22 above. 24 'And even after the departure of his most gentle soul from the tabernacle of the body, this same heavenly brightness, as well as the frequent visits of holy angels, does not cease, down to the present day, to appear at the place in which his holy bones repose; as is established through being revealed to certain elect persons (*quibusdam electis*)' (VC III.23). 25 *Vita Galli* I.13 (Joynt, *Life of St Gall*, p. 82).

In VC II.28, Columba, shortly before his death, visited the brothers working in the western plain of Iona. Standing on higher ground and prophesying that they will not see him again in that vicinity, 'raising both his holy hands he blessed all this island of ours, and said: "From this moment of this hour, all poisons of snakes shall be powerless to harm men or cattle in the lands of this island, so long as the inhabitants of that dwelling-place shall observe the commandments of Christ".' The chapter-heading makes it clear that this is the focal point of the chapter. The episode must have been important to Adomnán, since he repeats it at the beginning of VC III.23 as a kind of first prelude to his account of Columba's death. In this second version the saint, 'still sitting in the wagon … turned his face to the east, and blessed the island, with the islanders its inhabitants. And from then to the present day, as has been written in the above-mentioned book, the poison of three-forked tongues of vipers has not been able to do any injury to either man or beast.' Here the prophecy of his impending death is more explicit. The primary version is clearly that of VC II.28; but in VC III.23, too, the formality of the moment is marked when Columba turns his face to the east, over the island to his monastery, to give his blessing (see above). There are actually no adders on Iona and there probably never have been any.[26] It is unlikely, however, that Adomnán wrote the story just to explain why there were no snakes on the island: that is not his purpose and he does not, in any case, say that Columba *expelled* an insular population of snakes.[27] His message must, therefore, be sought elsewhere than in the material or natural order. O'Reilly has discussed more generally the Biblical, Patristic and early monastic exegetical tradition in which the snake represents the devil and all his works (including schism and heresy); and in particular the passages under review as depicting, *inter alia*, the earthly (here monastic) paradise as a foreshadowing of the heavenly paradise and realisable now as long as the community perseveres in the monastic life and in the quest for Christian perfection.[28] I am concerned here only with the implications of this metaphor for a sacred landscape. So I would observe that, while there is no question that the snake symbolises the diabolic at important levels of early and medieval Christian thinking, it is also and equally incontrovertibly a creature in the natural realm. It has to be dealt with, therefore, under both aspects. At one and

---

26 In his letter to me of 2 September 1992 (see n. 4 above), Patrick Cashman writes: 'I have found no biological record of the adder on Iona, and I have confirmed this with local islanders.' Cf. Reeves, *Life of St Columba*, pp. 142–3 n. d.   27 Lérins was 'uninhabited because of its utter desolation and unvisited for fear of its venomous snakes'. But St Honoratus is not said to expel the snakes: 'The terrors of the solitude were put to flight; the army of serpents fell back … not once was he ever in danger or even startled by an encounter with a snake, although encounters are so frequent in those arid wastes (as I can bear witness), especially when provoked by heavy seas.' So says Hilary of Arles, quoting just beforehand Ps 90(91).13 and Lc 10.19 (*De uita S. Honorati Arelatensis episcopi*, cap. 15, in Hoare, *Western Fathers*, pp. 259–60).   28 'Reading the Scriptures', pp. 94–7.

the same time, the devil must be overcome if even an earthly paradise is to be restored, let alone heaven attained; but the snake is also an integral part of that fallen creation whose redemption as a direct consequence of the final salvation of humanity St Paul confidently expects (Rm 8.18–25). If the state of paradise before the fall was to be realised, as far as possible, in the monastic settlement – or, to put it another way, if the monastic community and its place of habitation were to be an incarnation (therefore physical as well as spiritual) of that paradise – then it might have been thought desirable or appropriate at one level that the site and its surroundings be free of snakes. It was not necessary, however, that, if naturally present, they should actually be expelled. Snakes, like other wild animals, could indeed be a danger or a nuisance. Like other wild animals, though, they could be assumed into the renewed order of a cosmos becoming whole again (as in Is 11.6–9). The reintegration of the cosmic order does not, of course, raise brute creation to the destiny of rational humanity: the animal kingdom serves and will continue to serve mankind. Columba's blessing, nevertheless, protects beasts as well as men: beasts, too, participate in the reconciliation of heaven and earth. God, moreover, gave the created order to humanity for its right use in integrity and holiness (Gn 1.26–8; compare, e.g., Ps 8, Sap 9.1–4): the true relationship of *all* creatures is one of mutual dependence (and respect on the part of human beings) under the eye of divine providence.

Adomnán's attitude to animals in general is not sentimental: they were, often enough in practice, for work or food only. So the compassionate hospitality bestowed upon the exhausted crane in VC I.48, where the bird is tended in the way that a sick or weary human visitor to a monastic guest-house might reasonably anticipate; and the sorrow of the white workhorse at the impending death of its master, which has been in some way divinely revealed to it (VC III.23), should also be seen in all probability as reflecting the ideal reintegration of the animal kingdom, wild and domestic, into a redeemed order of creation.

Angels, too, frequent the earthly paradise and, in the new dispensation, the sword is withdrawn (Gn 3.24), save, of course, to keep evil at bay. Columba reveals that certain places within the enclosure at Clonmacnoise were frequented by angels at the time of his visit there (VC I.3). The saint is eventually given help by angels in his fight against the disease-bearing demons in VC III.8. His conversation with angels on *Cnoc Angel* – the *colliculus angelorum* – on the western plain is observed (VC III.16).[29] The frequent visits of angels to Columba's grave are mentioned (VC III.23). Indeed, angels often visited the saint, according to Adomnán (VC III.16; cf. III.23).[30]

29 In VC II.44, Adomnán, some seventeen years before the time of writing, has to take action to try to end a severe spring drought on Iona. Part of his plan involves elders of the community in opening and reading from books in Columba's handwriting on the hill of the angels, 'where at one time the citizens of the heavenly country were seen descending to confer with the holy man'. This is immediately successful: heavy rain falls and, eventually, a very good harvest ensues.   30 The idea that the monastic life was the angelic life, that the

VII COLUMBA ON THE MOUNTAIN

Iona and its community are also the Promised Land and the Children of Israel,in which and for whom Columba moves and acts as a patriarchal and prophetic figure.[31] In this context it is surely significant that on a number of occasions the saint receives prophetic knowledge on, or gives his patriarchal blessing from, a hill or at least higher ground. In VC I.30 Columba, sitting 'on the top of the hill that at a little distance overlooks this monastery of ours',[32] foresees the imminent arrival by sea of the penitent Féchna; but it is his attendant Diormit who actually sees the ship's sail a short while later. In VC II.4 the saint sits 'on the little hill (*in monticulo*) that is in Latin called "great fortress" (*munitio magna*),'[33] from which he sees 'a heavy rain-cloud that had risen from the sea in the north, on a clear day'. Foretelling that the cloud will bring disease to both men and beasts in a certain part of Ireland, he sends one of his monks thither with bread that he has blessed as a cure. In VC III.16 he has the conference with angels, standing 'on a certain knoll of that [i.e. the western] plain' (*in quodam illius campuli colliculo*) – the *Cnoc angel* referred to earlier. In VC III.23 he blesses his monastery and prophesies its future renown from the summit of the small hill (*monticell(ul)us*) overlooking the monastery that both the Andersons and Sharpe have suggested was Cnoc nan Carnan.[34]

Adomnán's exemplars were doubtless Scriptural and drawn mainly from the Old Testament accounts of patriarchs and prophets. I see nothing to indicate that we need look further afield than the Biblical tradition. Abraham encounters God in the supreme test of his faith – the sacrifice of Isaac – on the mountain of Moriah (Gn 22.1–18), traditionally identified with the hill on which the

monks lived the life of paradise restored, in a reintegrated relationship with the created order, especially the animal world, is already found in the desert: see Benedicta Ward's introduction to Russell, *Lives of the Desert Fathers*, pp. 36–7, 43–4. A hermit of the Thebaid called Amoun, much troubled by thieves, employs two large serpents to guard the door of his cell – to good effect. But the same hermit destroys a monstrous serpent that has been ravaging the countryside around: ibid., pp. 80–1 (IX) and notes, p. 132. **31** O'Reilly draws attention to the identification of the monastery of Iona with Jerusalem: 'Reading the Scriptures', p. 97. **32** Cnoc Mór? See Anderson and Anderson, *Life of Columba*, pp. 56–7 n. 62; Sharpe, *Life of St Columba*, p. 292 n. 140. **33** Anderson and Anderson (*Life of Columba*, p. 98 n. 126) and Sharpe (*Life of St Columba*, p. 319 n. 215) identify this hill with Dún Í. **34** Cf. note 14 above. In VC II.22 Columba predicts the impending doom of Ioan and his associates from 'higher ground' (*eminentiore loco*) in Ardnamurchan. The setting seems entirely secular. It might be argued that the saint and his companions needed to be elevated in order to witness the destruction of the thieves and their ship out at sea between Mull and Coll. The circumstances of the patriarchal blessing of VC II.28 and III.23 differ from one another in some details: in the former the saint stands 'on higher ground' (*in eminentiore loco*) for the prophecy and presumably for the blessing also; but in the latter he refers to his own impending death and then, 'still sitting in the wagon' (*ut erat in uechiculo sedens*), he gives his blessing.

temple of Jerusalem was later built.[35] Moses meets God in the burning bush at Sinai; there also he is given his mission; and the divine name is revealed to him (Ex 3.1–4.17). On the mountain also he sees what is allowed him of the glory of Yahweh (Ex 33.18–23). At Sinai Moses receives the Law from God (Ex 19–40, especially 19.3–25, 24.12–18, 31.18, 34.1–9, 28; Nm 1–10). In III Rg 19.1–18, Elijah, recalling Moses, journeys to Horeb-Sinai to find God and be confirmed in his own mission. On the mountain of the Transfiguration (traditionally Tabor), it is Moses and Elijah who appear to Peter, James and John, talking with Jesus (Mt 17.1–8; Mc 9.2–8; Lc 9.28–36).

CONCLUSION

Adomnán's triple boundary scheme, if acceptable, frames this sacred landscape. The outer boundary, the foreshore, delimited the island at large: an area access to which may have been closely supervised rather than actively restricted, and one where mundane agricultural and no doubt other domestic activities were carried on. The island was, nevertheless, I have argued here, formally a *locus sanctus*. The intermediate boundary, then, the *uallum monasterii*, defined the immediate area of the monastic settlement, access to which may have been restricted (certain categories of persons perhaps being excluded), or at least more tightly controlled – a *locus sanctior* in fact. Finally, I have postulated an innermost zone, the church and any enclosure around it, access to which may have been highly privileged – the *locus sanctissimus*. More work in detail is certainly necessary, but it is pertinent to notice here that the scheme I have adumbrated is at least reminiscent of that advocated in the *Collectio canonum Hibernensis*. This work is of early eighth-century date and one of its editors, Cú Chuimne, was himself a monk of Iona.[36] In it is found legislation for a system of ecclesiastical *termini*, varying in number between two and four, but in which three actually seems to be the implied norm, enclosing zones that are progressively *sanctus*, *sanctior* and *sanctissimus*.[37] One of the two main recensions of this collection actually names Adomnán as its latest authority. I would not argue, however, that he was necessarily the author of the scheme; or that it originated within the Columban federation – though the latter is a possibility. On the other hand, the fact that Adomnán envisages the same or something very similar as operating at Clonmacnoise leads me to suppose that he took it for granted that a system of progressively more sacred enclosures was usual around seventh-

---

35 'Solomon then began to build the house of Yahweh in Jerusalem on Mount Moriah where David his father had a vision' (II Par 3.1).   36 Kenney, *Sources*, p. 249.   37 I have discussed this matter briefly, in the context of a discussion of Adomnán's *plate(ol)a monasterii*, in 'Aspects', pp. 293–7, esp. 295–6, with reference to Wasserschleben, *Irische Kanonensammlung*, pp. 174–5. See also Kenney, *Sources*, pp. 247–50 (nr 82).

century monastic – perhaps more broadly ecclesiastical – sites. The concept of sacred space, enclosed or unenclosed, is probably universal. The ultimate exemplar behind the particular scheme or schemes outlined here, however, is, I suggest, Ezekiel's ideal temple in his restored Jerusalem of the (post-exilic) future (Ez 40–8). Here the sanctuary area as a whole has three divisions: an outer court (40.5–27), to which the people are confined (42.14, 44.17–19, 46.19–24 – save on solemn festivals, 46.9?); an inner court (40.28–47, 44.17–19);[38] and the Temple (40.48–41.26), itself having three parts – the *Ulam* (the Vestibule, 40.48–9), the *Hekal* (the Hall, the 'Holy', 41.1–2) and the *Debir* (the Sanctuary, the 'Holy of Holies', 41.3–4). Admittance to the Temple and Sanctuary is strictly circumscribed (44.4–9).[39] For the present, however, these final observations must be regarded as very tentative.[40]

---

38 Possibly also Ez 42.15–20, unless these are the outer dimensions of the whole sanctuary area, including the outer court: cf. 45.2.   39 Cf. the account of Solomon's temple in III Reg. Other threefold divisions *possibly* discernible in Ezekiel's scheme are:– (i) the Holy Land (Ez 45.1), Jerusalem (48.15–16, 30–5), the Sanctuary (45.2); (ii) Jerusalem – the Sanctuary – the Temple proper.   40 The text of the *Collectio* in particular requires examination in detail, so that the complex evidence of VC can be more fully illuminated.

The *Vita Columbae* and Irish Hagiography: A Study of *Vita Cainnechi*

Máire Herbert

The surviving manuscript witnesses to the *Vita Columbae* (VC) by Adomnán indicate how the text circulated in Continental Europe and in Britain in the aftermath of its compilation around the year 700 AD[1] There is no comparable Irish evidence to establish that the text was being read and copied contemporaneously in the saint's homeland. Up to recently it could only be asserted that the unabbreviated version of VC was used as a source by the author of the vernacular Life of Colum Cille around the mid-twelfth century, while a copy of the shortened recension was included in the collection of Hiberno-Latin hagiography in the fifteenth-century MS Z 3.1.5 in Primate Marsh's Library, Dublin.[2] Though it was suggested that Hiberno-Latin *vitae* of saints like Colmán Elo, Munnu, and Cainnech, saints who are mentioned in VC, drew in their turn on Adomnán's work,[3] none of these *vitae* had been securely dated, and the manuscript collections of Hiberno-Latin hagiography in which they survived were no earlier than the fourteenth century.[4] Thus, their evidence could not securely establish when VC became known in Ireland.

Recently, however, Richard Sharpe's examination of the medieval manuscript collections of Hiberno-Latin hagiography has noted within them groups of Lives sharing a common textual source. In particular, Sharpe has identified a group of nine or ten Lives, common to all three collections, which he assigns to an exemplar datable within the period 750–850 AD. He claims that the texts of the Lives in one of these collections, the *Codex Salmanticensis*, best represent this exemplar. Thus, a group of *vitae* in the *Codex Salmanticensis* may be seen as providing access to hagiographical works composed around the eighth century.[5] Moreover, the group includes the *vitae* which I have noted as deriving

<hr/>

1 Anderson and Anderson, *Life of Columba*, pp. liv–lxv; Picard, 'Adomnán's *Vita Columbae*'.
2 Herbert, *Iona*, pp. 182–4; Brüning, 'Adamnan's Vita Columbae', pp. 272–6; Sharpe, 'Maghnus Ó Domhnaill's Source'. 3 Brüning, 'Adamnan's Vita Columbae', pp. 290–1; Plummer, VSH i.lxxxvi, 263–4 n. 14. 4 For a listing of the collections see Lapidge and Sharpe, *Bibliography*, pp. 110–29. 5 Sharpe, *Medieval Irish Saints' Lives*, in particular pp.

material from VC. Therefore, does their witness help to provide a new date for the use of Adomnán's work in Ireland?

As Sharpe did not provide analysis of the content of each particular Life to cross-check its dating indications against those provided by the larger scrutiny of the collections, I have opted to do a test-case here. I have chosen to analyze the *Codex Salmanticensis* version of *Vita Cainnechi* (hereafter *VCainn.*)[6] since it is a composition in which the use of VC extends beyond the simple borrowing of particular episodes to be a constitutive element of the text. Therefore, what is at stake is not simply the dating of *VCainn.* but also its evidence regarding the formative influence of VC on Irish hagiographical composition.

Initial examination for dating purposes reveals no glaring late feature in the text of *VCainn.* Several of the forms of its personal and place-names have been cited in Sharpe's listing of items diagnostic of a date in the Old Irish period.[7] The fourteenth-century date of the manuscript in which the forms occur, however, means that purely orthographical evidence must be used with caution. More telling are instances of correct grammatical usage in vernacular forms in the text such as *haut longe o Birraib* (§35), and *i nAchuth Bo* (§54). Moreover, it is possible to compare other onomastic features in the text with external records. For example, the usage *apud dexterales Laginenses* (§41) for the realm of king *Cormaccus filius Dyarmici* correctly designates the realm of the Uí Bairrche king. Moreover, the locution in *VCainn.* finds a parallel in the annal phrase *apud Laginenses Dexteriores*, unattested after the eighth century.[8] The form of the place-name *Cella Achith Drummoto* (§39) seems to be a rendering of *Cell Achaid Drommo Foto* of the eighth-century annals, abbreviated to *Cell Achaid* from the following century.[9] The monastic site *Letube Kainnich* (§19) is otherwise unknown apart from two eighth-century annal notices, and it is probable that the foundation was among the many which ceased to function in the Viking era.[10]

While *VCainn.* sets out to depict a sixth-century reality, it is to be expected that the content of the text will be influenced by the contemporary circumstances of its composition. As a ground-clearing exercise, we may cite at the outset a lack of evidence of postViking date. Literary derivation might serve as an explanation for the fact that the circumstances of Iona appear very similar to those depicted in VC. It does not suffice, however, to explain how the independent material from the author of *VCainn.* also reflects the conditions of preViking times. Sea-travel is unhindered. Menaces to Irish society which require saintly intervention in the Life are those involving the misdeeds of local kings and of *laici*.[11] There is

---

297–339. **6** Text ed. Heist, *Vitae*, pp. 182–98. **7** Sharpe, *Medieval Irish Saints' Lives*, pp. 318–34. **8** AU s.a. 712.9. For the substitution by subsequent redactors of the anachronistic *Uí Cheinnselaig*, see VSH i.164. See also Sharpe, *Medieval Irish Saints' Lives*, pp. 308–9; and Byrne, *Irish Kings and High-Kings*, pp. 136–7. **9** AU s.aa. 746.6, 796.4. Pádraig Ó Riain suggests that the *VCainn.* form may, indeed, be the older. **10** AU s.aa. 773.2, 779.2. I take the instance in CGSH §707.463 to be derivative: the form there is *Lethdubi*. **11** See Sharpe,

no sense of external threat. All in all we may hypothesize that as far as the composition of *VCainn.* is concerned the use of VC provides a *terminus a quo* of *c.*700 AD, while the content of the work may suggest a *terminus ante quem* of the early ninth century, before the beginning of Viking impact on ecclesiastical life.

VCainn. has a biographical structure. It recounts the circumstances of the saint's birth and early upbringing, his departure to Britain to study with the holy man Docc, his ordination and onward travel to Rome, and his performance of various miracles in Italy. Then, divine intervention reminds him that his destiny lies in Ireland, whereupon he returns home. He is depicted as performing miracles in various places throughout Ireland, and subsequently appears in Britain, where he has various encounters, particularly with Colum Cille on Iona. Another round of travelling and miracle-working throughout Ireland follows. Finally, and rather abruptly, his approaching death is announced, and the Life recounts how he received the final eucharist, not from one of his own *familia*, but from *Fintan Meldub*, 'sent by God'.

The Life appears to be a carefully-wrought hagiographical construction by an author well-acquainted with the conventions of his genre. Throughout the text there is emphasis on Cainnech's role as *electus Dei,* and on the manner in which heavenly agency marks all stages of his life. Indeed, there is conscious stylization to underline this. The Life reveals how the Lord parted flood-waters for him, saved him from fire and drowning and was willing to move a mountain for him.[12] Cainnech himself had parents who were 'poor like those of Christ', he fasted for forty days and forty nights, *excemplo Domini*, and he raised the dead to life.[13]

Yet the individuality of the saint emerges also, with a good deal of plausible information about persons and places in his career, even the detail that in appearance Cainnech was small and bald.[14] While annal evidence indicates that ecclesiastical and secular figures brought in contact with the saint are, indeed, his contemporaries,[15] there is no other means of ascertaining whether the hagiographer drew on genuine historical records of Cainnech's career. In any case, *VCainn.* is a work of literature, and we need to look further at its compositional aspect in order to discover more about its outlook and purposes.

VCainn. reflects conventional practice in its reliance on miracle-working as the chief affirmation of sanctity. Its connection with VC is evident immediately in its direct borrowing of two miracle stories involving sea-travel through

---

'Hiberno-Latin *Laicus*'. I do not agree with Plummer's assumption (VSH i.xii n. 4) that *gial[l]cherd* (*VCainn.* §41) is necessarily inferior to *gallcherd* in the other manuscripts; nor do I accept his inference that *gallcherd* necessarily refers to Viking practice. 12 *VCainn.* §§5, 8, 21. 13 Ibid. §§1, 48, 59. 14 Ibid. §§46, 57. 15 Plummer, VSH i.xlv. Clearly, my focus is on the literary representation of Cainnech, and I do not propose to enter into speculation about the saint's putative origins or identity. In this regard, see Ó Riain, 'Cainnech *alias* Colum Cille'; on the onomastic aspects of the name, see Paul Russell's contribution elsewhere in this volume.

storms.[16] Certainly these are borrowed from VC because they show Cainnech being viewed in a positive light by the Columban community. When re-set in *VCainn.*, however, the Columban aspect of the stories is diminished. For example, Adomnán's work (VC II.13) asserted that the prayers of both saints had worked together to ensure the safety of the Columban crew. Cainnech's hagiographer, however, gives his subject sole credit.

On further examination we see a continuation of this pattern. The hagiographer depicts instances in which Cainnech's career is made to track that of Colum Cille in places associated with the Iona saint, across the Spine of Britain, in Tiree, and in Iona itself. Thus Cainnech's sanctity is affirmed in Colum Cille's own bailiwick, but without Columban accompaniment.[17] Elsewhere, Cainnech's saintly attributes implicitly parallel those of Colum Cille. For example, books, learning, and preaching the word of God are given prominence in the *vitae* of both saints, and Cainnech's books, like those of the Iona saint, are undamaged by exposure to the elements.[18]

Probably the most evident aspect of saintly portrayal which *VCainn.* shares with VC is that of supernatural visitations and otherworldly contacts. Book III of VC, which is devoted to this topic, seems to provide the unacknowledged model for episodes which have been termed 'vertical' in import, illustrating the saint's relationship with the divine sphere.[19] Like Colum Cille, Cainnech was rebuked by an angel when he took an unapproved initiative.[20] He not only saw angels,[21] but also had the facility of seeing distant events through the Spirit.[22] Heavenly light surrounded him.[23] He retreated from human company, and spent three days and three nights in uninterrupted contemplation.[24] *VCainn.* not only highlights angelic visitations to the saint, it also shares with VC a parallel focus on encounters with demons. Both *vitae* recount aerial contests against demons for the possession of souls,[25] and tell of saints being enveloped in diabolically induced mist.[26]

Clearly, the author of *VCainn.* did not slavishly follow his exemplar, but used it shrewdly to complete a portrait of his subject which would reveal him as having been affirmed in his sanctity by the same range of supernatural signs which marked the Columban Life.[27] Yet it emerges that this definition of Cainnech is not framed as homage for he appears not as a second Columba, but rather as a superior alternative.

---

16 VC I.4, reflected in *VCainn.* §28; VC II.13, reflected in *VCainn.* §54.   17 *VCainn.* §§24, 25, 26.   18 See, for instance, VC I.25, II.8, 9, III. 23; *VCainn.* §§18, 22, 23, 33, 43.   19 On this topic see Stancliffe, 'Miracle Stories', especially pp. 94–110.   20 VC III.5, *VCainn.* §9. 21 VC I.1, III.1, III.5, III.15, III.16, III.23; *VCainn.* §§9, 18, 21.   22 VC I.1, I.29, I.41, II.39, II.42; *VCainn.* §§17, 38.   23 VC III.19, 20, 21; *VCainn.* §§42, 46.   24 VC III.18, *VCainn.* §37.   25 VC III.6, 10, 13; *VCainn.* §§13, 27.   26 VC II.34, *VCainn.* §46. We may note further that the phrase *instinctu diabuli* is used with similar effect in VC II.24 and *VCainn.* §5.   27 Other episodes which may be characterized as VC-type *uirtutes* include *VCainn.* §§17, 47, 50.

Of course, the aggrandizement of his subject is the hagiographer's task and there is nothing particularly remarkable in the revelation of a saint's status through comparison with others. Indeed, in one instance *VCainn.* follows the example of VC itself in representing a gathering of eminent churchmen in which the superiority of one is demonstrated. In VC, a ball of fire is seen to shine over the head of Colum Cille as he celebrates Mass with Brendan, Comgall and Cainnech. In *VCainn.* the narrative depicts how inclement weather soaked the clothing of Colum Cille and of Comgall, while their companion, Cainnech, remained entirely dry.[28] What is significant about *VCainn.*, however, is that the author goes beyond conventional hagiographical competitiveness to draw a pointed contrast between Columban moral misguidedness and Cainnech's unimpeachable judgement.

The particular narrative demonstration gains added literary force from the fact that it is a calculated reworking of a narrative of VC.[29] Adomnán's work (I.2) relates how Finten, son of Tailchán, arriving to join the monastic community of Iona in the aftermath of Colum Cille's death, learns from the new abbot, Baithéne, that the saint had prophetically advised that Finten should not remain in Iona, but should found his own monastery in Ireland. The episode as it appears in *VCainn.*, however, recounts how Finten (here called Munnu, the hypocoristic form of his name) is brought to Iona by his pilgrim father. *Bithinus* (Baithéne) alleges that the father loves his son more than he does God, and demands that the boy be cast into the sea. Grieving, but obedient, the father does so, a fact which the Holy Spirit revealed to Cainnech as he was sailing from Tiree. He snatches the boy from the waves and proceeds to Iona to vent his anger on Colum Cille. The latter in turn orders Bithinus to present himself to Cainnech for judgement. After a three-year search throughout Ireland, Bithinus reaches Cainnech. He is told that the years of his quest suffice as punishment, and he is enabled to return to Iona. Cainnech clearly holds the high moral ground, and his humane decisions contrast with the doctrinaire attitude on Iona. The narrative concludes by indicating that despite closure of the matter the legacy of Columban culpability remained.

There is no doubt that the hagiographer designed this material as polemic. What was the context in which he did so? Just as the influence of VC signals a particular emphasis in *VCainn.*, we now find that affinities with another hagiographical work provide further illumination. An episode relating how Cainnech came to the aid of Bishop Áed mac Bricc clearly proclaims a positive association between the two saints,[30] while at the literary level, the narrative of *VCainn.* has echoes of the *vita* of the bishop (hereafter *VAed.*).[31] Indeed, there

---

28 VC III.17; *VCainn.* §20. Note also *VCainn.* §§18, 52, which duplicate an episode of Cainnech's superiority. 29 *VCainn.* §§26, 27. 30 Ibid. §32. 31 Text in Heist, *Vitae*, pp. 167–81.

are several other narratives in *VCainn.* which recall miracle-stories in *VAed.*, though they do not mention the bishop. Like Bishop Áed, Cainnech had unbroken horses become tame for him, he revealed the deceptive power of a *magus*, he removed an unwanted pregnancy through his blessing, and restored an eaten animal.[32] Stories of bishop Áed's extraordinary powers of travel have their cognate in *VCainn.*,[33] as have accounts of the immobilization of the saint's attackers,[34] and the story of miraculous provision of his Lenten fare.[35]

It is possible that *VCainn.* and *VAed.* were both simply drawing on the same stock of hagiographical lore, but the episode in *VCainn.* which makes explicit mention of the bishop seems to be based directly on two narratives in *VAed.*[36] What are the implications of this? *VAed.*, like *VCainn.*, belongs to the group of *vitae* in the *Codex Salmanticensis* for which Sharpe proposes a preViking date.[37] My own examination suggests that *VAed.* was compiled in the first half of the eighth century.[38] If the text, as we have it, was directly used by the compiler of *VCainn.*, therefore, the latter's work must be placed no earlier than the mid-eighth century.

Before proceeding further with the matter of date, however, we should note that the association portrayed between Cainnech and Bishop Áed highlights another important feature of *VCainn.*, that it locates several episodes of the saint's career in Southern Uí Néill territory, and in the borderlands between Uí Néill and Munster.[39] Certainly the author of *VCainn.* sought to demonstrate that his subject had widespread associations both within and without Ireland. We have already noted the Columban resonance of episodes set in Britain. In Ireland, the saint's family origins explain links with the north of Ireland in the *vita*[40] while Cainnech's association with the church of Achad Bó and thereby with Ossory and South Leinster is already attested in VC.[41] The text goes further afield, moreover, depicting Cainnech even in Munster, beside Loch Léin.[42] While this episode is probably intended to enhance the idea of a country-wide cult of Cainnech, the unlikelihood of the location may have chronological implications. In the second half of the eighth century, up to the year 786, it was the Éoganacht of Loch Léin who held Munster kingship.[43] It is possible, therefore, that the hagiographer simply drew on such contemporary information to represent Munster interest in *VCainn.* through a Loch Léin setting.

---

32 *VCainn.* §11, *VAed.* §14; *VCainn.* §14, *VAed.* §39; *VCainn.* §56, *VAed.* §15; *VCainn.* §58, *VAed.* §20. 33 *VCainn.* §57, *VAed.* §§36, 42. 34 *VCainn.* §7, *VAed.* §42. 35 *VCainn.* §15, *VAed.* §47. 36 *VCainn.* §32, drawing on *VAed.* §24 and §31. 37 Sharpe, *Medieval Irish Saints' Lives*, pp. 297–339. 38 I hope to publish my views in the forthcoming volume of the *Ireland and Europe* series, edited by Próinséas Ní Chatháin and Michael Richter. 39 *VCainn.* §§32–5, 38, 59. 40 *VCainn.* §§10–2, 14, 17–8. 41 VC II.13, *VCainn.* §§41, 46–7, 50, 54. 42 *VCainn.* §45. 43 Byrne, *Irish Kings and High-Kings*, pp. 216–9; *Annals of Inisfallen*, s.a. 786.

What of the episodes associated with Southern Uí Néill territory? Dedication evidence links Cainnech with the church of Kilkenny West in Westmeath, which, in turn, was not far distant from Bishop Áed's church of Killare.[44] Both saints also are associated with churches close to the Uí Néill-Munster boundary.[45] Cainnech's activities in Uí Néill territory, however, involve secular as well as ecclesiastical associations. The hagiographer depicts his subject assisting Bishop Áed in a confrontation with the Uí Néill king, Colmán Bec (*Colmanus Modicus*). Struck down by divine intervention, the king was miraculously resurrected by Cainnech who received thereafter not only royal submission but also the gift of a church-site.[46] Subsequently, *VCainn.* recounts how the saint, on his travels *in regionibus Neill*, came upon a wayside cross, and was told that it marked the spot where the king, Colmán Bec, had been slain. Cainnech prayed so fervently and tearfully at the cross that surrounding snow melted, until finally he received a revelation through the Holy Spirit that the soul of Colmán had been brought out of hell.[47]

Cainnech's role in Southern Uí Néill territory, therefore, is associated with the secular power of Colmán Bec's branch of the Uí Néill. In the historical record it was the families of the brothers of Colmán Bec, Colmán Mór and Áed Sláne, who dominated Southern Uí Néill politics from the end of the sixth century up to the 760s. Then there was a brief interlude of prominence for Colmán Bec's family, after which they were again eclipsed.[48] Is it the case, therefore, that Cainnech's hagiographical association with Colmán Bec had contemporary resonance for an author whose work we have tentatively placed around the second half of the eighth century?

Examination of the historical record of Southern Uí Néill over-kingship indicates that after a period of Síl nÁedo Sláne dominance the long reign of Domnall mac Murchada (*c.* 728–763) initiated an era of power for his Clann Cholmáin Móir dynasty. Annal evidence suggests, moreover, that Domnall was allied from the early years of his reign with Follomon, head of the dynasty of Colmán Bec.[49] Another significant alliance, attested from the latter part of Domnall's reign, was with the *familia* of Colum Cille. While there were immediate connections with the Columban monastery of Durrow within Domnall's own realm, the Columban connection extended beyond the local to the headship of the *familia* in Iona. As over-king of all the Uí Néill kingdoms, a position which he attained after 743,[50] Domnall appears to have been the main secular ally of

44 O'Donovan, 'Ordnance Survey Letters', pp. 10–1, 20–3.   45 *VCainn.* §§35–7, *VAed.* §§1, 7, 42, 44. Bishop Áed's church of *Enach Midbren* has not been identified, but it is evidently in Muscraige Tíre.   46 *VCainn.* §32.   47 *VCainn.* §38.   48 Byrne, *Irish Kings and High-Kings*, pp. 93–4, 116, 281–2.   49 AU s.a. 733.7 indicates that both rulers were targets of attack by the Munster ruler, Cathal mac Finguine; see also Byrne, *Irish Kings and High-Kings*, pp. 207–10. Another view is expressed by Ó Riain, *Cath Almaine*, p. xii n. 3.   50 His succession follows the defeat and killing of Áed Allán of Northern Uí Néill in that year (AU s.a.743.4).

the Iona successors of Colum Cille, kin-saint and patron of all the Uí Néill. The alliance is reflected in the annal record of Domnall's proclamation of a church-state legal measure called 'The Law of Colum Cille' in the year 753. Sléibéne, newly-elected abbot of Iona, came to Ireland in the following year, and himself proclaimed *Lex Columbe Cille* in the year 757.[51]

The death of Domnall in the year 763 was followed by conflict amongst his sons, and it appears that at this juncture Follomon of the family of Colmán Bec, the long-time associate of the dead king, took the kingship of Mide. Yet he remained engaged with the fortunes of Domnall's family also, since he is reported as having been on the side of Donnchad, son of Domnall in his victory over another of the king's sons in the year 765. Follomon apparently got no reward for his loyalty, however, but rather he was slain *dolose* in the following year.[52] As Donnchad son of Domnall succeeded to the kingship thereafter, there is at least a strong suspicion of his involvement in the killing. The murder of Follomon, a senior political figure, must have been widely deplored. Yet the author of *VCainn.*, who declares his interest through representation of Follomon's ancestor Colmán Bec, nevertheless directs the hostile focus of his composition not against treacherous political colleagues of the king but against the Columban community. Why should this be?

If we examine church-state interaction in Southern Uí Néill lands in the aftermath of Follomon's killing, we see that the Columban community, and its Iona leaders, continued to ally themselves with the leading political power in Southern Uí Néill, and thereby with the king Donnchad. Indeed, the annals record an Irish visitation by the abbot of Iona in the same year that Follomon was murdered. Though Donnchad seems to have gained power through this violent deed, and though his reign was marked by aggression, the Columban *familia* of Durrow were involved on his side in a conflict against the Munstermen in 776. Moreover, the annals reveal that *Lex Coluim Chille* was jointly proclaimed by Donnchad and by Bresal, abbot of Iona in the year 778.[53]

This state of affairs, therefore, appears as a likely catalyst for the critical attitude of *VCainn.* toward the Columban community. The Life acknowledges the former friendship between Cainnech and Colum Cille, which is reflected in VC. In Southern Uí Néill lands, the two communities were on the same side politically for as long as the dynasties of Colmán Mór and Colmán Bec were allies. For the followers of Cainnech, however, the aftermath of Follomon's killing and Donnchad's accession must have estranged them from a Columban community which appeared to put politics before principle. The author of *VCainn.* represents the Iona leadership of the Columban community as having lost its moral compass. The rigidity shown in its ecclesiastical life seems to stand

---

51 See Herbert, *Iona*, pp. 60–7; and AU s.aa. 753.4, 754.3, 757.9. 52 See AU s.aa. 763.1, 765.5, 766.2. 53 AU s.aa. 766.6, 770.8, 775.5, 776.11, 778.4.

for a more general inflexibility which failed to take account of specific circumstance. Moreover, there is an episode in *VCainn.* where even demons are
represented as mouth-pieces of the watch-word *Relinque mundum.*[54] Is this also
a veiled criticism of monastic concern with worldly support at the expense of
humane values?

While the main counter-Columban episodes of *VCainn.* are played out in
Britain, the Life makes it clear that Ireland is at the centre of its concerns. The
hagiographer sets out to depict Cainnech, not only as a saint who embodied and
surpassed Columban virtues, but also as a saint whose presence was asserted in
many Irish regions, and in several religious communities. He is credited with
miracles of assistance to fellow ecclesiastics[55] and favoured rulers,[56] as well as
with punishment-miracles wrought against erring kings[57] and churchmen.[58]
What is significant in an Irish context is that the Columban presence is edited
out. In Southern Uí Néill lands, the saint favoured by Cainnech is Bishop Áed
mac Bricc. Moreover, hints of Patrician partisanship may be a direct rebuff to
Columban interests.[59] Cainnech is depicted as working a miracle for Brendan,
and as choosing to receive the last rites from Fintan Maeldub, successor of
Fintan of Clonenagh.[60] The hagiographer is depicting a network of alliances
which implicitly repudiate the Columban community in nearby Durrow.

Given the historical context which I have outlined, the hagiographer is most
likely to have compiled his work during the period 766–780. He presents a strongly
individualized picture of Cainnech, while also projecting the shadow-image of
Colum Cille through literary parallelism. Episodes in *VCainn.* derived from VC
reflect the close bonds that had existed between Cainnech and Colum Cille, as
well as the rupture of those bonds in the second half of the eighth century. The
testimony in VC to friendship between the saints surely implies continuation of
this friendship by their communities down to Adomnán's day. This in turn
suggests that the community of Cainnech was a likely destination for a copy of
VC. We still have not discovered how soon the work reached Ireland after its
completion around the year 700. It seems to me that if VC had not immediately
been circulated in Ireland, it must surely have become available from the year
727 when Adomnán's *reliquie* were brought from Iona to Ireland.[61]

Early Hiberno-Latin saints' Lives seem to have been addressed primarily to
an ecclesiastical public, aware of the local and of the literary contexts of
hagiographical composition. For the Columban community, the use of VC by
the author of *VCainn.* must have considerably intensified the impact of the *vita*.

---

54 *VCainn.* §57. Note also that *VCainn.* §20 opposes spiritual and worldly concerns.
55 Ibid. §§35–7, 39, 40, 53, 58, 59.   56 Ibid. §§46–7.   57 Ibid. §§10, 32.   58 Ibid. §47.
59 Note the testimony to the power of 'Patrick's hymn', *VCainn.* §48. There are echoes of
Patrician hagiography in *VCainn.* §§12, 19, 46. Compare Tírechán, *Collectanea* § 40; *Muirchú*
I.23 (22) and II.3 (Bieler, *Patrician Texts*, pp. 154–5; 102–7, 114–17).   60 *VCainn.* §§53, 60.
61 AU s.a. 727.5. The *reuersio reliquiarum Adomnani* is recorded at AU s.a. 730.3.

VCainn. could be viewed as having impugned the iconic status both of Columban sanctity, and of its hagiographical memorial. In literary terms, moreover, *VCainn.* not only testifies to the presence of VC in Ireland in the second half of the eighth century, it also testifies to the development of the genre of hagiography in Ireland about a century after the earliest works were compiled. It shows Irish hagiography drawing on exemplars from within its own tradition, and developing its own rhetorical strategies, while also retaining generic conventions adopted from external models during the seventh century.

Le jugement de l'âme dans la Vie de Columba

Nathalie Stalmans

Dans la Vie de Columba rédigée à la fin du VIIème siècle[1], Adomnán relate treize récits mettant en scène des visions de damnation ou d'élection[2]. Ceux-ci nous permettent de comprendre la conception de l'auteur du destin de l'homme après la mort et du jugement de l'âme. Nous étudierons la nature de la sentence et les modalités selon lesquelles elle se décide.

Le sort de l'individu se règle immédiatement après la mort. Adomnán le montre par les termes qu'il utilise: *eodem horae momento* (VC I.35)[3], *eadem hora* (II.25, III.9)[4], *hac in hora ... hoc momento* (III.13)[5], *continuo* (III.14)[6]. Il le suggère par le sens du récit: Columba voit une âme s'envoler alors même que la mort n'a pas encore été annoncée (III.7, III.11, III.12)[7], un moine meurt et

---

1 *Vita Sancti Columbae*, ed. trad. Reeves, *The Life of St. Columba*; Anderson and Anderson, *Adomnán's Life of Columba*. Le texte sera abrégé VC; les citations renverront à l'édition des Anderson et donneront les numéros de livre et de chapitre. 2 VC I.35, I.39, II.22, II.23, II.25, III.6, III.7, III.9, III.10, III.11, III.12, III.13, III.14. 3 *eodem horae momento obiisse ab acculis eiusdem regionis percunctatus inuenit, quo uir beatus eidem a demonibus raptum enarrauit* (I.35). 4 *'eadem hora qua interfectae ab eo filiae anima ascendit ad caelos, anima ipsius interfectoris discendat ad inferos'. Et dicto citius, cum uerbo; sicut Annanias coram Petro, sic et ille innocentium iugulator coram oculis sancti iuuenis in eadem mortuus cicidit terrula* (II.25). *eadem hora qua de corpore eductus est sanctus Columba in Ioua commanens insula paucis quibusdam se circumstantibus sic profatus senioribus: (...) qui de propria manuum laboratione suarum praemia emax felix conparauit aeterna. Ecce enim nunc anima eius a sanctis uehitur angelis ad caelestis patriae gaudia* (III.9). 5 *uir uenerandus cum in Ioua conuersaretur insula quadam subitatione incitatus signo personante collectis fratribus: 'Nunc', ait, 'oratione monacis abbatis Comgilli auxiliemur, hac in hora in stagno dimersis uituli. Ecce enim hoc momento in aere contra aduersarias belligerant potestates'* (III.13). 6 *Ibidemque quidam repertus senex Emchatus nomine audiens a sancto uerbum dei praedicatum et credens babtizatus est; et continuo laetus et securus cum angelis obuiantibus ei ad dominum commigrauit* (III.14). 7 *'Nunc', ait, 'quidam de conprouincialibus tuis clericus ad caelum ab angelis portatur, cuius adhuc ignoro nomen'. (...) 'Alium Christi scio militonem qui sibi in eodem territorio in quo et ego commanebam monasteriolum construxit, nomine Diormitium'. Cui sanctus ait : 'Ipse est de quo dicis qui nunc ab angelis dei in paradisum deductus est'* (III.7). *'Nullus enim ad nos de Scotia sancti illius uiri obitus peruenit nuntius'. 'Vade tum', ait sanctus, 'meae obsecundare iusioni debes. Hac enim nocte praeterita uidi subito apertum caelum, angelorumque choros sancti Brendini animae obuios discendere ... '* (III.11). *'ob uenerationem illius animae quae hac in nocte inter sanctos angelorum choros uecta ultra siderea caelorum spatia ad paradisum ascendit' (...) aliqui de lagenica commeantes prouincia ea nocte eundem obisse nuntiant episcopum qua sancto ita reuelatum est* (III.12).

Columba a une vision (III.6)[8], les hommes maudits sont condamnés à être tués et ravis par les démons (I.39, II.22, II.23)[9]. Enfin, dans un récit, Adomnán ne stipule pas le moment de la mort de l'individu mais précise pour le moment de la vision *subito oculos ad caelum diregens* (III.10), suggérant que le décès vient de se produire[10]. L'idée que le sort individuel soit directement décidé après la mort est commune au VIIème siècle[11]. D'ailleurs, les visions de la damnation d'un roi ou de l'élection d'un saint au moment de leur mort sont des emprunts d'Adomnán à Grégoire le Grand[12].

Cependant, contrairement à son époque, Adomnán considère que le destin de l'individu est alors définitivement scellé. L'idée communément admise dans l'Irlande du VIIème siècle tient à une quadripartition de la société tenue de Grégoire le Grand, en non jugés et élus, non jugés et damnés, jugés et élus, jugés et damnés, ou selon l'appellation d'Augustin *boni ualde, mali ualde, boni non ualde, mali non ualde*[13]. Cette conception implique généralement l'existence d'un état purgatoire pour les deux groupes pas assez bons pour être élus de suite, pas assez mauvais pour être damnés de suite, et qui doivent donc attendre le jugement en tentant de se purifier.

Pendant ce temps purgatoire, une aide des vivants peut être octroyée au mort[14]. Parallèlement, comme le sort du mort n'est pas scellé, la localisation de

---

8 *qui eodem momento post sancti de domu secessum uiri praesentem finiit uitam. Tum uir praedicabilis in plateola sui deambulans monasterii porrectis ad caelum oculis diutius ualde obstupescens ammirabatur* (III.6). 9 *'Inimici tui repperient te in eodem cum meritrice cubantem cubiculo, ibidemque trucidaberis; daemones quoque ad loca penarum tuam rapient animam'* (I.39). *' ... quas appetit terras subita praeuentus morte cum suis perueniet malis cooperatoribus'* (...) *Mirumque in modum toto circumquaque manente tranquillo equore, talis una rapaces ad inferna submersos prostrauit procella, misere quidem sed digne* (II.22). *'subita praeuentus morte ad infernalia rapietur loca'* (II.23). 10 *uir sanctus ... subito oculos ad caelum diregens haec profatus est ...* (III.10). 11 A partir d'Origène, le jugement particulier directement après la mort se formule clairement. Voir à ce sujet van Uytfanghe, *Stylisation biblique*, pp. 229–35; idem, 'Essor du culte', pp. 93–8. 12 Chez Adomnán comme chez Grégoire le Grand, la damnation d'un grand d'une province est annoncée par un solitaire (Columba est dans une petite cabane) à un ou plusieurs sujets qui, ayant noté le moment de la vision, découvrent une fois rentrés chez eux qu'un chef/un roi est bien mort à cet instant (VC I.35; Grégoire, *Dialogi* IV.31 [de Vogüé, iii.104–6]; rééd. du passage de Grégoire, O'Loughlin, 'Gates of Hell', pp. 110–1 avec *Vulcani* pour *vulcani*). Le prototype peut être la Vie d'Antoine dans sa traduction par Evagre où il y a également mise par écrit du moment de la vision, puis vérification (*Vita Antonii* c.32, PL lxxiii.153–4). On trouve dans VC III.11 et III.12 l'influence de la mort de saint Germain dans les *Dialogues* de Grégoire le Grand: mort nocturne, grande lumière qui envahit le monde, existence de messagers, âme menée au ciel par des anges directement après la mort (II.35 et IV.8 [de Vogüé, ii.238, iii.42–4]). 13 Grégoire, *Moralia in Iob* XXVI. xxvii. 49–51 (PL lxxvi.378–80); Augustin, *Enchiridion* §110 (PL xl.283). Voir Rivière, art. 'jugement' dans le *Dictionnaire de théologie catholique* viii, 2, col. 1801. Sur l'usage de ces appellations dans les sources irlandaises à partir du VIIème siècle, voir Seymour, 'Eschatology', pp. 191–7; McNamara, 'Some Aspects', pp. 57–9. 14 De façon générale sur le sujet, voir Le Goff, *Naissance du purgatoire*, pp. 64–173; Carozzi, 'Géographie de l'au-delà'; Gurevich, 'Au Moyen Age', pp. 261–6; idem, *Voyage de l'âme*, pp. 14–98; Atwell, 'From Augustine to Gregory the Great'; McNamara, 'Some Aspects', pp. 49–52. Pour la croyance

la sépulture et son aspect peuvent avoir des conséquences sur le destin de l'âme[15].

La Vie de Columba présente par contre une bipartition de l'au-delà, traite de la pénitence terrestre comme du seul rachat possible et ne confère aucun rôle aux vivants ou au corps mort vis-à-vis du destin de l'âme. Nous allons étudier les trois points successivement ci-dessous.

Les morts sont divisés en deux catégories: ceux dont l'âme prend le chemin des enfers et ceux dont l'âme monte vers le ciel, ou les cieux. La nomenclature utilisée pour les enfers regroupe les termes *inferni* (I.35[16], II.22), *loca penarum* (I.39), *infernalia loca* (II.23), *inferi* (II.25). Les *loca penarum* ne sont certainement pas des lieux de peines provisoires vu le contexte de malédiction de l'âme qui y est emmenée[17]. Pour définir le ciel, nous trouvons les termes *paradisus* (III.12) ou *caelum* (III.7, III.11) synonymes l'un de l'autre (III.7), ou encore *caeli* (II.25). *Paradisus* pour sa part est également donné comme synonyme de *aeternae refrigerationis locus* (III.10). Sont encore mentionnés les *caelestis patriae gaudia* (III.6, III.9) et les *summi caeli regiones* synonyme de *ad dominum* (III.14). Nous apprenons que les *siderea caelorum spatia* sont la région qui mène au *paradisus* (III.12)[18].

On pourrait imaginer que chacun des treize récits traite de non jugés et élus, non jugés et damnés, soit les saints et les maudits pour lesquels aucun autre recours n'existe. Tel n'est pas le cas. Certaines âmes élues sont celles de personnages dont l'état moral est à peine – ou pas du tout – décrit[19], et l'un des

en un temps et un feu purgatoire et l'aide que peuvent recevoir les morts des vivants en Irlande, voir notamment *Collectio canonum* XV.1–6, XV.9, XVIII.8 (Wasserschleben. pp. 42–5, 58); Tírechán, *Collectanea* §§16 et 39 (Bieler, *Patrician Texts*, pp. 136 et 152); la Règle de Tallaght §§18 et 86 (Gwynn and Purton, 'Monastery of Tallaght', pp. 133, 163–4). Voir sur le sujet, Warren, *Liturgy and Ritual*, pp. 102–5; Seymour, 'Eschatology', pp. 191–7, 200–3; Grogan, 'Eschatological Teaching', pp. 48–50; Charles-Edwards, 'Pastoral Role', pp. 75–6; Carey, 'Posthumous Quatrain'; McNamara, 'Some Aspects', pp. 53–60. La *Collectio canonum Hibernensis* citée ci-dessus stipule aussi qu'il n'y a pas de risque pour l'âme lorsque le corps est enterré dans un lieu sauvage L.1–2 (Wasserschleben p. 208); voir Charles-Edwards, *Early Irish and Welsh Kinship*, pp. 263–5). Il ne se dégage donc pas de ce traité un discours uniforme et cohérent. Le traité irlandais *Liber de ordine creaturarum* (fin VIIème siècle) traite de la quadripartition de la société et du feu purgatoire (c.XIII 'De la diversité des péchés et du lieu des peines' [Díaz y Díaz, pp. 178–84]). C. Carozzi a montré les profondes particularités qui animent ce texte, notamment l'absence de temps purgatoire (le feu appelé 'purgatoire' n'agit effectivement qu'après le Jugement final) (*Voyage de l'âme*, pp. 189–92). **15** Pour cette croyance sur le continent, voir Brown, *Cult of the Saints*, pp. 4–12 et 36–8; idem, *Society and the Holy*, pp. 222–50; Pietri, 'Sépultures privilégiées', p. 135 et nn. 32–4; idem, 'Évolution du culte', p. 28; Duval, *Auprès des saints*. Pour cette croyance en Irlande, voir notamment *Collectio Canonum* XV.3, XVIII.8, L1.2 (Wasserschleben, pp. 43, 58–9, 209). Voir à ce sujet Stalmans, 'Inhumation laïque'. **16** Le passage des *Dialogues* de Grégoire qui inspire ce récit (voir n. 12) est également la source d'inspiration d'Adomnán pour sa description de l'entrée de l'enfer dans le *De locis sanctis* III.6 (voir O'Loughlin, 'Gates of Hell', pp. 105–6). **17** voir citation n. 9. **18** *ultra siderea caelorum spatia ad paradisum.* **19** Nous ne savons rien par exemple de la femme (III.10) ou de l'hôte des moines (III.13). De

exemples de vision de damnation concerne un homme dont aucun forfait n'est mentionné (I.35). Après la mort, l'humanité se divise en deux groupes. La préface de la Vie nous le disait d'ailleurs déjà[20].

Sans nier à proprement parler l'existence d'un état intermédiaire permettant une purification entre mort et sentence définitive, Adomnán ne lui laisse aucune place. En atteste sa conception de la pénitence.

Le tableau ci-dessous reprend tous les cas de mort subite de la Vie, soit attestés explicitement (en italique), soit implicitement.

§	Identité	Type de miracle	Type de mort
I.17	Colcu, ecclésiastique	prophétie	âgé, lors d'un souper avec amis
I.21	Nemán, mauvais pénitent	malédiction	avec voleurs, mangeant chair jument volée
I.22	pécheur, incestueux, fratricide	malédiction	tué par ses ennemis
I.36	Aid, prêtre	malédiction	triple mort subite
I.38	Luguid, riche	prophétie d'un cas de damnation[21]	pauvre, avec prostituée, ayant mangé
I.39	Nemán	malédiction/ prophétie	par ennemis, avec prostituée
I.42	poète Crónán	prophétie	*ocius*, tué par ses ennemis
I.45	prêtre Ernán, oncle de Columba	prophétie	âgé, après un temps de maladie, *subita*
II.20	Vigenus, riche pas hospitalier	malédiction	frappé d'un pieu par ennemis
II.22	malfaiteur	malédiction	*subita morte*
II.23	criminel	malédiction	*subita morte*
II.24	criminel	malédiction	transpercé par javelot
II.25	jeune fille innocente	vision élection	tuée par criminel
II.25	criminel	malédiction	tombe mort, *subita uindicta*
III.13	moines	vision élection	noyés
III.13	hôte	vision combat puis élection	noyé
III.22	Columba	vision, prophétie	*subita emigratione*

Diormit nous ne connaissons que sa qualité de moine (III.7), du païen baptisé à la dernière minute que sa 'bonté naturelle' (III.14). **20** *Quorundam iustorum animas crebro ab angelis ad summa caelorum uehi sancto revelante spiritu uidebat. Sed et reproborum alias ad inferna a daemonibus ferri sepe numero aspiciebat. Plurimorum in carne mortali adhuc conuersantium futura plerumque praenuntiabat merita, aliorum laeta, aliorum tristia* (I.1). **21** I.38 est un doublet du I.39 et peut donc être également considéré comme un cas de malédiction. **22** VC I.15, I.17,

Si nous considérons ces cas de mort subite, nous constatons qu'ils atteignent tous des damnés, à l'exception de Columba, un personnage dont l'élection ne fait aucun doute. Le meurtre de la 'jeune fille innocente', et la noyade des moines de Comgell (nous reviendrons plus loin sur le cas de leur hôte) ne sont mentionnés qu'incidemment pour expliquer la malédiction de l'assassin et le combat pour l'âme de l'hôte. Les morts de Colcu, Crónán et Ernán sont présentées comme 'subites' pourtant elles surviennent après un temps de maladie et, pour Colcu, à un âge avancé.

La mort subite est crainte. Des personnages très différents (roi, moine, laïc) viennent interroger Columba sur la façon dont ils mourront[22]. La mauvaise mort équivaut à une damnation car elle empêche de faire pénitence. Columba espère que le poète Crónán se repentira avant la mort subite qui le guette (I.42)[23]; ailleurs, le saint regrette qu'un malade ne profite pas de l'opportunité qui lui est donnée de faire pénitence[24]; on lit la crainte de Librán de mourir avant la fin de sa pénitence[25]; ou encore que la miséricorde divine ne peut être obtenue que s'il y a pénitence avant la mort[26]. Inversement, empêcher quelqu'un de faire pénitence signifie sa damnation : ce refus est donné par Columba à un 'fils de perdition' (I.36)[27] et à tous ceux qui, maudits par le saint, tombent morts. En dehors des certainement élus (Columba) et des certainement damnés (le 'fils de perdition' et les individus maudits par le saint), il y a tous ceux qui ne sont ni justes ni mauvais, et pour lesquels un temps avant la mort est nécessaire pour faire pénitence. Nous constatons que la quadripartition *boni ualde* (non jugé et élu), *mali ualde* (non jugé et damné), *boni* et *mali non ualde* telle qu'elle s'applique dans d'autres sources à l'au-delà, est ici liée à la pénitence terrestre, non à la purgation *post mortem*.

I.47. L'invocation du nom de Columba empêche de tomber sur un champ de bataille (VC I.1). Dans l'hagiographie de Patrice, le saint demande à un cadavre enterré le type de mort qu'il a eue (Muirchú II.2 [Bieler, *Patrician Texts*, p. 114]); Tírechán omet cette question dans la narration du même récit (§41 [ibid., pp. 154–6]). 23 C'est le fait d'exercer une activité quelle qu'elle soit au lieu de se repentir qui est signe de damnation, non pas l'activité elle-même comme l'a cru Stevenson, 'Literacy and Orality', pp. 21–2. 24 *Cui oportunius erat ueram de peccatis hodie penitudinem gerere, nam in huius fine ebdomadis morietur* (I.27). 25 *'ego et tu usque quo numerum expleas septinalium annorum deo donante uicturi sumus'* (II.39). 26 *'... ut quia noster sis alumnus lacrimosam ante exitum agas penitudinem, et a deo misericordiam consequaris'* (III.21). 27 L'idée d'être damné d'office est contraire aux pénitentiels selon lesquels toute faute est pardonnable tant qu'on est en vie (*Pénitentiel de Vinnian* §29 [Bieler, *Irish Penitentials*, p. 84]). Le refus de Columba suscitera l'indignation de Baithéne. Sur ce récit et l'interdiction de Columba de laisser un pécheur mettre pied à terre pour préserver la terre de pollution, voir Charles-Edwards, 'Social Background', pp. 50–1. Les compilateurs de la *Collectio*, citant I Io 5.16, définiront le péché mortel en tant que 'péché commis jusqu'au moment de la mort' et dont le coupable est puni n'ayant pas eu le temps de se repentir (*Collectio canonum* XV.8 [Wasserschleben, p. 45]). Dans l'oeuvre de Jonas de Bobbio, se confesser trois fois par jour est souhaité, un refus de faire pénitence amenant la damnation (II.19 [Krusch, pp. 138–40; trad. de Vogüé, pp. 220–3 (et voir pp. 56–7)]). En outre, Columban annonce régulièrement à ses moines le moment de leur mort de sorte qu'ils puissent s'y préparer. Nous remercions C. Stancliffe et B. Merdrignac de nous avoir suggéré ce rapprochement.

Le silence d'Adomnán vis-à-vis d'actions des vivants en relation avec le destin d'une âme est en accord avec l'idée du sort fixé dès la mort. Adomnán mentionne la célébration de messes pour les âmes de Colmán et de Brendan mais ceci après sa vision de l'ascension des âmes au ciel. Ce sont de simples messes de commémoration.

De même, l'auteur tait toute possibilité d'influence du corps mort: la tombe n'a pas d'incidence sur le destin eschatologique de l'âme. Un élu peut n'avoir pas de lieu d'inhumation (comme les moines noyés de Comgell dont l'élection est immédiatement assurée). L'enterrement *ad sanctos* n'est pas considéré comme une garantie d'élection mais comme un moyen de ressusciter plus heureux[28]. Le surplus de joie qui attend l'élu au jour du jugement, en particulier par le fait de ressusciter entouré d'amis est d'ailleurs signalé chez les Pères[29]. La tombe est importante dans la pensée d'Adomnán et correspond à un signe d'élection ou de damnation[30], mais le fait d'être ou n'être pas inhumé n'a pas d'influence sur le sort de l'âme.

La conception d'une sentence immédiate définitive répond peut-être à une volonté d'Adomnán de contrer certaines pratiques de son époque : l'existence d'un temps purgatoire, la croyance en l'efficacité de la prière, des offrandes pour les morts, pouvaient amener un certain laxisme face à la pénitence terrestre[31]. Si le sort est définitif, deux problèmes se posent cependant pour l'auteur: quelle place laisser à l'intercession du saint, comment faire en sorte que le jugement final ne soit pas une simple modalité? Nous allons voir que la pensée d'Adomnán relative au processus du jugement individuel permet de repenser le rôle d'intercesseur du saint et laisse au jugement final sa force théocentrique.

Dans le cas de dix visions sur les treize, on voit soit les démons soit les anges venir chercher l'âme au moment de la mort et la conduire vers l'endroit qui lui est fixé. Anges et démons n'ont pour rôle que d'assurer l'exécution d'une décision dont l'origine, lorsqu'elle est indiquée, est divine[32]. Les anges sont décrits comme 'descendant' à la rencontre de l'âme[33]. Les démons par contre

---

28 C'est le cas de Librán, convaincu d'être élu mais désespéré de la prédiction de Columba comme quoi il ne sera pas inhumé à Iona mais en Irlande. Il se console en apprenant que ce sera parmi des fidèles de Columba (II.39). 29 van Uytfanghe, 'Essor du culte', p. 103; McNamara, 'Some Aspects', p. 52. 30 Voir à ce sujet le texte de la conférence de O'Loughlin, 'Tombs of the Saints' (dessus). 31 Pour une réflexion similaire, voir Fros, 'Eschatologie médiévale', p. 218. 32 *'Quanto', ait, 'sancte puer Columba, hoc scelus cum nostra dehonoratione temporis spatio inultum fieri iudex iustus patietur deus?'* (II.25). Grégoire le Grand attribue lui aussi d'ordinaire aux démons le rôle d'exécuteurs des décrets divins, leur conférant cependant parfois un rôle d'accusateurs. A ce sujet voir Rivière, 'Rôle du démon', pp. 60–2. 33 *angelorum choros sancti Brendini animae obuios discendere* (III.11); *sancti angeli sanctis obuiantes animabus* (III.13); *'properemus' ait, 'sanctis obuiam angelis qui de summis caeli regionibus ad praeferendam alicuius gentilici animam emisi' … cum angelis obuiantibus ei ad dominum commigrauit* (III.14); *'angelos enim sanctos de excelso uidi misos throno ad meam de carne animam obuios educendam …'* (III.22).

semblent se trouver sur place au moment voulu. Ainsi, en cas de damnation, les anges sont totalement absents, alors que, lorsqu'il y a élection, les démons sont parfois là. Nous retrouvons la conception de l'omniprésence des démons dans les airs[34] et de leur éventuelle attaque de l'âme montant vers le ciel, présente dans la Vie d'Antoine et chez Sulpice Sévère[35].

Les trois visions restantes sont des récits d'attaque. Ces combats sont décrits dans le troisième livre de la Vie de Columba. Adomnán essaie d'y montrer les rapports privilégiés du saint avec l'au-delà, les apparitions angéliques qui ne sont visibles que de lui. Dans le premier récit, les anges remportent la victoire sur les démons pour l'âme d'un moine; Columba rend grâce au Christ, arbitre du combat (III.6). Dans le deuxième récit, l'âme d'une femme accompagnée d'anges combat les démons et remporte l'âme de son mari, aidée par les vertus de celui-ci (III.10). Dans le troisième récit, les âmes de moines noyés combattent des démons voulant ravir l'âme d'un hôte laïc qui s'est noyé avec eux; par les prières du saint et celles de ses moines, des anges interviennent et sont victorieux (III.13).

Dans le premier récit c'est le Christ 'agonothète' au sens que lui donne Cassien d'"arbitre', de 'président du combat'[36] qui permet la victoire des anges; dans le deuxième, l'âme de l'épouse est aidée par les anges et par la vertu de son mari; dans le troisième récit, les âmes des noyés sont secourues par des anges suite à la prière de Columba et de ses moines.

Contrairement à la Vie d'Antoine où l'âme tente par elle-même de monter aux cieux, l'âme dans les treize récits d'Adomnán a un caractère passif. Après la mort, elle ne peut plus rien et attend passivement son destin, exécuté par les démons si l'individu a été mauvais, par les anges sinon. En cas de combat, ce n'est pas l'âme qui est attaquée par les démons et secourue par les anges; ce sont les démons emportant l'âme qui sont attaqués par des anges appelés à la rescousse. Cette passivité de l'âme rejoint ce que nous avons déjà dit: c'est sur terre que se joue le destin de l'âme, c'est durant son existence terrestre que l'homme se donne les moyens de recevoir après la mort l'aide adéquate. On comprend alors qu'Adomnán n'ait pas emprunté, à Sulpice Sévère par exemple[37], le thème du tribunal de l'au-delà.

Les démons étant sur les lieux de la sortie aérienne de l'âme du corps, il arrive qu'ils ravissent une âme qui ne leur appartient pas, ce qui explique les combats. Vu l'omniprésence démoniaque, il s'agit non seulement d'avoir été

---

34 Déjà chez S. Paul (Eph 6.12).   35 Vie d'Antoine par Athanase dans sa traduction par Evagre (cap. 37–8 [PL lxxiii.155–6]); Vie de Martin par Sulpice Sévère (II.4 et III.15–6 [Fontaine, i.326 et 342]).   36 Christ arbitre et agonothète président le combat pour sauver l'âme de l'homme de la tentation et de la mort (*arbiter atque agonotheta residens pugnam cursus et certaminis, De coenobiorum institutis* VI.9 [Guy, p. 272]); *Conlationes* VII.20 [Pichery, p. 262]), contrairement aux emplois de l'hagiographie mérovingienne cités par Du Cange où ne paraît que l'idée de 'président le monde'.

vertueux mais également d'avoir vénéré le Christ qui peut jouer le rôle d'arbitre, ainsi que les défunts qui ont le pouvoir d'appeler les anges. Incidemment, l'auteur affirme donc ici que si les prières _pour_ les morts sont sans efficacité, celles _aux_ morts sont utiles. En outre, il y a le risque d'une mort subite, sans avoir eu le temps de se repentir. C'est le cas de l'hôte des moines de Comgell: les âmes d'autres morts ne suffisent pas à repousser les démons, il faut les prières de Columba. Le saint demeure le seul recours en cas de mauvaise mort[38]. Le jugement final demeure important dans la pensée d'Adomnán[39]. Il se fera par Dieu seul, verra la résurrection des corps et concernera l'humanité entière[40]. Il se situe à un autre niveau, et démons, anges, intercesseurs ne s'y impliqueront pas[41]. C'est le sort de l'individu qui occupe ceux-ci, et ce destin est alors scellé.

Dans la Vie de Columba, Adomnán garantit l'élection de son âme à l'individu croyant, méritant, confessé régulièrement et qui a adressé ses dévotions aux défunts et au bon saint. Cette certitude apaise la terreur de l'au-delà. Adomnán adresse un message de réconfort qui illustre, à un autre niveau, toute l'importance qu'il attache à l'homme.

---

37 Vie de Martin III.3 (Fontaine, i.266–70). **38** Pour peu qu'il agisse rapidement après la mort. La hâte de Columba dans III.13 rappelle celle de Martin dans la Vie par Sulpice: Martin se dépêche de prier pour le catéchumène dont le procès céleste est déjà en cours (III.3 [Fontaine, i.266–70]). Pour une typologie des formes d'interventions d'un saint, voir Philippart, 'Patrons de la bonne mort', p. 88. **39** VC II.39 par exemple. L'importance du thème est particulièrement évidente dans le _De locis sanctis_. Voir les études de O'Loughlin, 'Exegetical Purpose', pp. 48–50; idem, 'Library of Iona', p. 41; idem, 'Tombs of the Saints'. **40** 'Celui qui croit en lui n'est pas jugé; celui qui ne croit pas est déjà jugé' (Io 3.18). Comme Jean, Adomnán croit que le sort de l'âme dépend de l'existence terrestre, de la foi de l'individu, de ses mérites, de sa dévotion à Columba. Et comme chez Jean (12.48), cela ne signifie pas pour Adomnán que le jugement final soit oublié. Ainsi que l'explique Grégoire de Tours à l'hérétique' qui ne comprend pas la pensée de Jean, 'Il (celui qui n'a pas cru) a déjà été jugé pour le supplice éternel, mais son corps ressuscitera pour endurer ce supplice' (Grégoire de Tours, _Historiae_ X.13 [Krusch, pp. 497–8; trad. Latouche, pp. 278–9]). **41** Sur ce point encore, Adomnán a une conception très différente de celle des hagiographes de Patrice. Pour ceux-ci, le saint est juge non seulement au moment de la mort mais également à la fin des temps (_Liber angeli_ §23 [Bieler, _Patrician Texts_, p. 188]; Muirchú II.6 [ibid., p. 116]). Pour les implications politiques et sociales de ces différences, voir Stalmans, 'Fonction du travail'.

Varieties of Supernatural Contact in the Life of Adamnán

John Carey

The Middle Irish Life of Adamnán, as its editors Pádraig Ó Riain and Máire Herbert have both observed, touches only glancingly upon the career of the historical saint. Instead, to quote Professor Herbert,

> the able leader of the Columban *familia* is depicted either in stock saintly attitudes, performing miracles and routing the devil in debate, or in the role of influential and irascible churchman, whose curse heralded the downfall of the secular leaders who opposed him.[1]

While they have by no means ignored the first of these two aspects of the Life, Herbert and Ó Riain have accorded most attention to its political dimension, and to those episodes in which Adamnán is portrayed confronting royal authority. In the present paper, I hope to show that the Life's account of its hero's meetings with a series of unearthly beings may have an interest comparable to that of the fascinating web of dynastic allegories which my colleagues have already elucidated. In essence, I shall be advancing two contentions: first, that a comparison of these episodes with one another reveals them to be a tightly interrelated group, conveying a specific message; second, that they reflect a distinct body of traditions about Colum Cille, which seem to have bulked problematically large in the latter's legendary profile.

At the outset, let me quickly summarise the material under consideration. One of the relevant chapters (§2) occurs at the beginning of the Life, while the others (§§14–7) are grouped in a block at its end:

> §2. The men of Munster send a demon in the shape of a youth (*óclach*) to question Adamnán. This being asks the saint about the sins of Lucifer and Adam, boasts that he witnessed the Fall, and disappears when Adamnán makes the sign of the cross against him.

---

1 *Iona*, p. 151. Cf. Herbert and Ó Riain, *Betha Adamnáin*, p. 1; in line with the statement of the editors, ibid. pp. vii–viii, I take the introduction to the edition to represent Professor Ó Riain's views specifically.

§14. When the corpse of the Pictish king Bruide mac Bili is brought to Iona, Adamnán spends a night watching over it and it begins to revive. A member of the community objects that if Adamnán raises the dead, all of his successors will also be obliged to do so: acknowledging the truth of this, the saint sends the king's soul to heaven with his blessing.

§15. Adamnán fasts alone in a closed house for three days and nights. When his monks peep through the keyhole they see a beautiful little boy in his lap; they conclude that this is an apparition of Jesus.

§16. A corpse which has been brought to Iona demands an interview with a 'man of learning'. It poses many abstruse questions, all of which Adamnán answers. Recognising from the last of these that a devil is speaking out of the body, the saint banishes it.

§17. An 'unknown youth' (*óccláech anaithnidh*) is in the habit of relating wonders to a hermit named Colmán at Croaghpatrick. He explains to Colmán that Adamnán's prophecies of a disaster on the feast of John the Baptist refer to the saint's own death: this proves to be the case.

Before looking at these episodes in more detail, let us consider them in the aggregate. Of the five, three involve Adamnán's meetings with supernatural entities: a devil in the form of a youth (§2), a devil possessing a corpse (§16), and Jesus appearing in the guise of a child (§15). Each of the remaining two episodes is suggestively analogous to one of these three: the *ócláech* who reveals wonders to Colmán in §17 recalls the *óclach* who boasts of his preternatural knowledge to Adamnán in §2; and the partially resuscitated king in §14 may be compared with the diabolically animated corpse in §16. These pairings, furthermore, seem like positive and negative counterparts of one another: the hermit's informant appears benevolent while the being sent to Adamnán by the Munstermen is a demon; of the two corpses, one is evidence of the power of sanctity, the other of the wiles of hell. Already this looks like more than a haphazard gathering of marvels; I hope that the deliberate sophistication of the material's arrangement will become still more apparent in what follows.

We may now consider the anecdotes one by one. Herbert and Ó Riain translate §2 as follows:

> It is related hereafter how the demon came in human form to accost and address Adamnán, because he had been compelled by the Munstermen to come to Adamnán. He arrived, then, with many questions. One of the questions was: 'Did the devil sin in his beauty or in his disfigurement, and did Adam sin wittingly or unwittingly?' 'It is audacious [to enquire]' said Adamnán. 'Do not make a wonder of it', said the [Otherworld] youth,

'one who knows is addressing you, for I was present at the Fall'. Adamnán looked at him angrily and immediately made the sign of the cross in his direction. Thereupon the trouble-maker disappeared, leaving his stench in the assembly. Thus all the crowd knew that he was a demon in human guise who had come to deceive the multitudes. And through his expulsion by Adamnán God's name was magnified.[2]

The most obvious comparandum here is the brief tale *Immacallam Choluim Chille 7 ind Óclaig*, possibly dating from the seventh century.[3] While standing beside Lough Foyle, Colum Cille is approached by a mysterious youth or *óclach* who asks him a riddling question. Instead of answering, the saint interrogates the youth first concerning the remote past of the lough, then about the regions beneath the sea. In conclusion,

> Colum Cille arose as his followers watched, and went aside to speak with him and to ask him about the heavenly and earthly mysteries. While they were together thus for half the day, or from one hour to the next, Colum Cille's followers watched them from a distance. When they separated, they saw that the youth was suddenly hidden from them. They did not know where he went nor from where he came. When Colum Cille's followers were asking him to reveal something of what had passed between them, Colum Cille told them that he could not tell them even a single word of anything that he had been told; and he said that it was better for mortals not to know it.[4]

The author, or a later redactor, tentatively identifies the youth as Mongán mac Fíachnai; this identification is taken for granted in later versions of the tale.[5]

Here a saint – none other than Adamnán's own famous predecessor – is approached and questioned by a mysterious *óclach* in the presence of a group of witnesses; but he does not answer the latter's questions. The youth's supernatural origin, already apparent from the range of his knowledge, is confirmed when he vanishes suddenly at the close of the interview. The resemblances to §2 are obvious, and surely significant: but so are the differences. For in *Immacallam Choluim Chille* there is nothing to indicate that the stranger is sinister, let alone

---

2 Herbert and Ó Riain, *Betha Adamnáin*, p. 49.   3 On linguistic indications of the text's early date see Carney, 'Earliest Bran material', p. 181 n. 19; cf. Mac Cana, '"Prehistory" of *Immram Brain*', pp. 37–8. In 'Interrelationships', pp. 77–83, 91, I have proposed that the *Immacallam* may belong to one of the earliest strata in *Cín Dromma Snechtai*.   4 Translation from Koch and Carey, *Celtic Heroic Age*, pp. 208–9; text edited by Grosjean, 'S. Columbae ... colloquium'.   5 On the background of this identification, see my remarks in 'Interrelationships', pp. 82–3. References to the later versions are provided by Mac Cana, '"Prehistory" of *Immram Brain*', pp. 34–5.

diabolical. Nor is there anything hostile in Colum Cille's attitude toward him: on the contrary, he is eager to learn all that the youth has to tell. Finally, the older text does not situate the youth within a Christian category such as angel or devil; and indeed his talk of a lake engulfing an ancient kingdom, of his own existence through the ages in the shapes of various creatures, and of populous regions beneath the sea points to a background in native tradition.[6]

Further parallels to §2 are suggested by the fact that this debate about events at the beginning of the world takes place at an 'assembly' (*airecht*), in the presence of a 'crowd' (*slúag*). Here we may recall a passage at the conclusion of *Scél Tuáin meic Cairill*:

> Whatever history and genealogy there is in Ireland, its origin is from Tuán son of Cairell. Patrick had spoken with him before that, and he related it to him; and Colum Cille had spoken with him; and Finnia related it to him [sic] in the presence of the folk of the land.[7]

Again, a preternatural informant hands knowledge of the remote past on to various saints (including Colum Cille) in the presence of a multitude; and again, as it happens, the account of the past involves a series of metamorphoses.

There are similar accounts relating to the undying Fintan mac Bóchra. The tale *Suidigiud Tellaig Temro*, perhaps composed in the tenth century, describes how Fintan gave an account of Ireland's geography and early history to Díarmait mac Cerbaill at a great assembly, held at Tara; this seems to be based on an earlier, shorter text in which Fintan is questioned by the seventh-century scholar Cenn Fáelad mac Ailello.[8] Writing at the tenth century's end, the historical poet Eochaid úa Flainn telescoped the incidents, stating that Fintan as well as Tuán passed his knowledge on to Patrick, Colum Cille, and Finnia. Speaking of the lore transmitted by the long-lived informants, Eochaid says that

---

6 Herbert and Ó Riain note verbal parallels between §2 in the Life and the story of Moling's conversation with Satan in the commentary to *Féilire Óengusso* in Laud Misc. 610 – itself based on Sulpicius Severus's account of a similar conversation involving Martin of Tours (*Betha Adamnáin*, p. 67). One of these parallels is the use of the word *óclach* to designate the masquerading devil; this is also, of course, the term applied to the youth in the *Immacallam*. Given the great popularity of the *Vita Martini*, it may well have influenced the author of the Life (perhaps also the author of the *Immacallam*); it may be worth while to consider the possibility that the Life in turn exercised some influence on the Moling anecdote. 7 Carey, 'Scél Tuáin', p. 107. 8 Best, 'Manor of Tara'; the text of the *Interrogatio Cinn Fhaelad do Fhintan* appears on pp. 162–4. Perhaps derived from the *Suidigiud*, and certainly closely resembling it, is the introductory anecdote which attributes the *Dindshenchas* to Fintan: again, an assembly at Tara provides the setting (Stokes, 'Rennes Dindsenchas', pp. 277–9).

The ancients reckoned it for the saints
in the presence of the lords of the enduring world.
As it was composed and verified
it was written upon their knees.[9]

A significant body of evidence, accordingly, points to a tale-type in which the eyewitness of primeval events communicates his knowledge to a saint in the presence of a large gathering. By contrast with the Adamnán anecdote, there is nothing evil about the protagonists of such tales, or about the information which they provide. Not only *Immacallam Choluim Chille*, but also *Scél Tuáin* and Eochaid úa Flainn, associate Colum Cille with such encounters.

Next, we may look at §14:

> Once upon a time, the body of Bruide son of Bile, king of the Cruithin, was brought to Iona. Adamnán was distressed and grieved at the death. He asked that Bruide's corpse should be brought to him in his house that night. Adamnán watched over the corpse in that house until morning. On the following morning, the corpse began to move and to open its eyes. Thereupon an unsympathetic member of the faithful arrived at the door of the house, and said: 'If, as seems likely, the dead are being raised by Adamnán, I declare that no cleric will be appointed abbot to succeed him unless he too raises the dead.' 'Some implications may indeed be involved here,' said Adamnán. 'If it be more appropriate, let us, therefore, utter a blessing over this body in the interests of Bruide's soul.' Then Bruide died once more and went to Heaven, with the blessing of Adamnán and of the community of Iona.[10]

I believe that this episode was inspired by *Vita Columbae*, specifically by chapters 32 and 33 of the second book. The first of these describes the only occasion on which Colum Cille was believed to have restored a dead person to life: while in Pictland he prays in a house apart beside the recently deceased son of two of his converts, 'and the boy that was dead opened his eyes and lived again'.[11] In the next chapter the saint imbues a white stone with healing powers,

9 Macalister, *Lebor Gabála*, iv.280. The translation is my own: *cáem* is to be rendered as 'noble, lord', rather than (following Macalister) as 'scholar'. Cf. the derivative passage in the prose text, ibid. v.22.   10 Herbert and Ó Riain, *Betha Adamnáin*, pp. 56–9.   11 Herbert and Ó Riain point out §14's similarity to the account of a miracle in Sulpicius's *Vita Martini* (*Betha Adamnáin*, p. 81; cf. Herbert, *Iona*, p. 174 n. 85). Again, the influence of this very popular text is certainly a possibility. The resemblances in question may, however, rather reflect Elijah's revival of the son of the Shunnamite in IV Rg 4:18–37: this was clearly the source of the miracle in Sulpicius, and is explicitly alluded to in *Vita Columbae*.

and by the Lord's mercy it brought about the healing of many ailments among the people. But if the sick person seeking help from the stone was one whose appointed term of life was finished, then – strange to say – no way could the stone be found. So it happened on the day King Bridei [= Bruide] died. The stone was sought but it could not be found in the place where till then it had been kept.[12]

Here, in adjacent episodes of the *Vita*, we have both a scenario recalling that of Adamnán's interrupted miracle, and an occasion when a saint's healing powers are denied to another Pictish king named Bruide. The double parallel is unlikely to be coincidental, especially as this is the only resuscitation with which Colum Cille is credited.

Of all of the incidents in the Life to be considered in this paper, that related in §15 seems to accord least problematically with the conventions of hagiography:

At another time when Adamnán was in Iona, he fasted in his closed house for three days and nights and did not come into the monastery. A few of the faithful went to the house to see how the cleric was. They looked through the keyhole and saw a very beautiful little boy in Adamnán's lap. Adamnán was showing affection to the infant in a manner which convinced them that it was Jesus who had come in the form of a child in order to bring solace to Adamnán.[13]

Professor Ó Riain has suggested that this scene too was inspired by an incident in *Vita Columbae*: in this case one from the *Vita*'s third book, devoted to apparitions of angels and heavenly light:

On another occasion when St Columba was living in *Hinba*, the grace of the Holy Spirit was poured upon him in incomparable abundance and miraculously remained over him for three days. During that time he remained day and night locked in his house, which was filled with heavenly light. No one was allowed to go near him, and he neither ate nor drank. But from the house rays of brilliant light could be seen at night, escaping through the chinks of the doors and through the keyholes. He was also heard singing spiritual chants of a kind never heard before. And, as he afterwards admitted to a few people, he was able to see openly revealed many secrets that had been hidden since the world began (*occulta ab exordio mundi arcana*), while all that was most dark and difficult in the sacred Scriptures lay open, plain, and clearer than light in the sight of his most pure heart.

St Columba regretted that his foster-son Baithéne was not there. If he had been present for those three days, he could have recorded from the

---

12 VC II.32–3 (Anderson and Anderson, pp. 138–45). I cite the translation in Sharpe, *Life of St Columba*, pp. 179–82.   13 Herbert and Ó Riain, *Betha Adamnáin*, pp. 58–9.

saint's lips a great number of mysteries, both of ages past and future, unknown to other men, together with some interpretations of the sacred books.[14]

Some parallels are certainly striking here: the saint's strict seclusion in a separate house for three days and nights, and the mention of keyholes. Also striking, I think, is the fact that the passage is specifically concerned with Colum Cille's acquisition, through supernatural agency, of knowledge of 'a great number of mysteries, both of ages past and future'. In the Irish Life, the divine child's visit to Adamnán is portrayed simply as a mark of heavenly favour; but its background seems, as with much of the other material considered in this paper, to lie in traditions concerning Colum Cille's access to unearthly sources of information.

In this connection it is also worth while to look at the *Breviary of Aberdeen*, compiled *c.*1500 by William Elphinstone. Here the lections for Adamnán's feast include brief versions of the incidents related in §§2, 15, and 16 of the Irish Life. The third lection, which has no clear counterpart in the Life, is the most interesting:

> While pigs, according to their wont, were rooting up the earth, a living infant was found beneath a turned-up sod. When Saint Adamnán found him, he brought him up like a son, and exerted himself to have him trained in the liberal arts. When at length brought before the man of God, he set him many questions (*multa ei probleumata proposuit*). Then with the sign of the cross the saint banished the Enemy, who had sought to tempt the blessed man in the form of an infant.[15]

Here a supernatural child (recalling §15) turns out to be a diabolical questioner (as in §§2 and 16): the Aberdeen lection fits remarkably well into the group of anecdotes which we are considering. We can be more specific. If as I have suggested the devilish *óclach* of §2 is a negative version of the benevolent *óclaech* of §17, and the possessed corpse of §16 a negative version of the blessed corpse of §14, it seems natural to see the demon child of the present story as a negative version of the child Jesus of §15. If the five episodes of the Irish Life are supplemented with this one, peculiar to the *Breviary*, a clear symmetry appears in the group as a whole.

Alarmingly precocious children are also found in the secular tradition, where however they are presented in a positive light: the obvious examples are Aí mac Ollaman, Morann, and Noídiu Noíbrethach, described for instance in the text

---

14 VC III.18 (Anderson and Anderson, p. 208; Sharpe, pp. 219–20). Ó Riain's discussion in *Betha Adamnáin*, pp. 33–4.   15 From the Latin text as given in Herbert and Ó Riain, *Betha Adamnáin*, p. 37.

edited by Rudolf Thurneysen under the title 'Die drei Kinder, die gleich nach ihrer Geburt sprachen'.[16] A further parallel is provided by the Welsh poet Taliesin, as he appears in legend.[17] The child's discovery by pigs also suggests his native antecedents: the supernatural associations of swine in Celtic tradition, while they should not be emphasised at the expense of their everyday economic importance, were nevertheless pervasive and significant.[18] A pagan analogue for the child can be cited from another European (though not Indo-European) culture: an Etruscan myth held that Tages, 'a boy in appearance but an old man in wisdom', sprang from a furrow as a field was being ploughed, revealing all of the mysteries of divination to the throng which quickly gathered around him.[19] Although the account in the *Breviary* identifies the wonder-child with the devil, therefore, it is not too adventurous to posit an earlier tale in which he, like the youth beside Lough Foyle, came from the indigenous Otherworld.

In §16, a corpse is again brought to Iona. Before it can be taken from the boat, it rises up and speaks: 'It would have been more fitting to have found a learned man (*fer léiginn*) to converse with me than to have come in order to bury me.' It then poses 'many extraordinary questions' (*cestu imda incchantu*), all of which Adamnán answers. The text continues:

> 'Since Adamnán responds well to questions', said he, 'enquire of him the meaning of the phrase in the baptismal rite *Urget te Melthiel*'. They related that to Adamnán who said: 'From hell was that question brought to put to Colum Cille and it should cause no wonderment that Amelthiel should be the name of the [angelic] grade from which the demon transgressed'. 'Open up the reliquary (*erdamh*) of Colum Cille', said Adamnán. This was done, and Adamnán made the sign of the cross in the direction of the corpse. The shrieking and screaming of the satanic presence were to be heard as it departed the body for hell.[20]

No baptismal formula *Urget te Melthiel* has yet to come to light, nor has any other evidence been found of *Melthiel* or *Amelthiel* as the name of an angel or angelic order.[21] But this tantalising conundrum is not the episode's only interesting feature. Again, there is a tight thematic connection with the other stories in the group: as in §2, a devil tests Adamnán with questions relating to the beginning of the world; as in §14, a body brought to Iona for burial seems to be restored to life.

Another intriguing detail, noted by Herbert, is Adamnán's statement that the question about Melthiel had already been put by a demon to Colum Cille.[22]

---

16 Thurneysen, 'Drei Kinder'.　17 Ford, *Ystoria Taliesin*, p. 69.　18 References in Ross, *Pagan Celtic Britain*, pp. 308–21; Ní Chatháin, 'Swineherds'. For a Welsh tale in which a sow leads a man to the place where his preternatural fosterson is concealed, cf. Williams, *Pedeir Keinc*, p. 89.　19 Cicero, *De divinatione* II.xxiii.50 (Falconer, pp. 49–52).　20 Herbert and Ó Riain, *Betha Adamnáin*, pp. 60–1.　21 Ibid., pp. 35–6.　22 Herbert, *Iona*, p. 153.

Once more, the Life appears to furnish us with evidence of traditions that Colum Cille engaged in debate with supernatural beings.

§17 is devoted to Adamnán's death. Its most relevant section for our present purposes runs as follows:

> ... In the last years of his life, [Adamnán] proclaimed that an affliction would come upon the men of Ireland and of Britain around the feast of John. A young stranger (*óccláech anaithnidh*) used to visit Colmán of Cruachan Aigle [=Croaghpatrick], an anchorite of Connacht, and he would relate many remarkable things (*mór do ingantaibh*) to Colmán. He asked him if Adamnán had foretold tribulation for the men of Ireland and Britain around the feast of John. 'Yes', said Colmán. 'It will prove true for him', said the young man, 'for the tribulation consists of Adamnán's departure for heaven around this feast of John'.[23]

Who is the 'young stranger'? Herbert and Ó Riain, alluding once more to *Immacallam Choluim Chille*, have observed that 'the scenario is that of the well-established encounter between the saint and an Otherworld visitor, whose function is to provide knowledge of (future) wondrous events';[24] furthermore, as I have mentioned, use of the term *óclaech* for this mysterious figure recalls the *óclach* whose role in §2 we have already considered. I believe that additional evidence can be cited which points in the same direction.

First of all, there is a curious passage in the *Tripartite Life of Patrick*:

> There are guardians (*cométaidi*) of Patrick's household still alive in Ireland. A man of his is on Crúachan Aigle: the sound of his bell is heard, and he is not found. And there is a man of his on Gulban Guirt. The third of his men is to the east of Clonard, together with his wife. There is a man of his in Drommann Breg. There is another man on Slíab Slánga: Domangart mac Echach. It is he who will raise up Patrick's relics a little before the Judgement. His church is Ráith Murbuilc on the side of Slíab Slánga; and a haunch of meat together with its trimmings, and a pitcher of ale, are set before him every Easter, and it is always given to those who celebrate the mass on Easter Monday.[25]

Proinsias Mac Cana has observed that 'as it stands, the story of the ... survivors is wholly Christian, but its origins may of course be older.'[26] Support for this plausible supposition is provided by two secular tales: *Mesca Ulad* and *Airne Fíngein*.

---

23 Herbert and Ó Riain, *Betha Adamnáin*, pp. 60–1.   24 Ibid., p. 85; cf. p. 33.
25 Mulchrone, *Bethu Phátraic*, p. 75.   26 'Placenames and Mythology', p. 324. For a

In the Book of Leinster text of *Mesca Ulad*, the introductory account of the Túatha Dé Donann concludes as follows:

> They left five men for each of the fifths of Ireland, to magnify battle and conflict and struggle and strife between the sons of Míl. They left five men for the fifth of Ulster in particular. These are the names of those five: Brea mac Belgain in Drommann Breg, Redg Rotbél in Slemna Maige Ítha, Tinnell mac Boclachtnai on Slíab Edlicon, Grice on Crúachan Aigle, Gulban Glass mac Gráice on Benn Gulbain Guirt meic Ungairb.[27]

And here is the version of the doctrine which appears in *Airne Fíngein*:

> There are four who fled before the Túatha Dé Donann at the battle of Mag Tuired, so that they have been under concealment, blighting grain and milk and mast and sea-produce: one of them in Slemna Maige Ítha, named Redg; one of them in Drommann Breg, named Brea; one of them in Slíab Smóil, named Grenn; one of them in the territories of Crúachu, named Tinell.[28]

In the *Tripartite Life*, Patrick leaves certain of his followers in specific places, to live on through the ages until the end of the world. In *Mesca Ulad* and *Airne Fíngein*, supernatural beings (whether Túatha Dé Donann or Fomoiri) exist for centuries in certain locations – survivors of the conquest of Ireland by the Gaels, or of the still earlier battle of Mag Tuired. *Mesca Ulad's* account is the closest to that in the *Tripartite Life*: in both five spots are involved, and three of these – Benn Gulbain, Drommann Breg, and Crúachan Aigle – are common to both sources.[29]

What is the relationship to one another of the hagiographic and saga versions of this doctrine; and what was the nature of the earlier tradition from which both presumably derive? Here of course we can only guess. The most natural hypothesis seems to me to be that the texts reflect two distinct Christianising strategies: in one case the 'guardians' were rendered innocuous, by having their immortality attributed to Patrick; in the other they were not admitted to the Christian fold, but demonised as agents of war or famine. At all events, the sources seem to concur in attesting to a belief that a deathless being dwelt on Croaghpatrick: I submit that this entity is to be identified with the 'unknown youth' who related wonders to the hermit Colmán.

discussion of the very suggestive body of traditions relating to Domangart and Slíab Slánga (now Slieve Donard), see Mac Neill, *Festival of Lughnasa*, pp. 84–96; further references in Grosjean, 'Hagiographica celtica IV'.   **27** Watson, *Mesca Ulad*, p. 1.   **28** Vendryes, *Airne Fíngein*, pp. 14–5.   **29** Drommann Breg also appears in the *Airne Fíngein* list; and *i críchaib Crúachna* (v.ll. *Cruachan, Cruach-*) could reflect an earlier reference to Crúachán Aigli here as well.

Of Colmán himself, O Riain plausibly suggests that 'this otherwise unknown saint may in fact have originated as Colum Cille, the patron of the parish containing Croaghpatrick'.[30] The episode, then, may well reflect yet another tradition that Colum Cille received preternatural knowledge from an immortal visitor; and this figure's provenance seems again likelier to have been secular than ecclesiastical.[31]

Let us now look at the episodes again as a group. As I have already mentioned, they occur at the beginning and end of the Life: §2 is the first anecdote following the exordium; while §§14–17 come at the conclusion, leading up to Adamnán's death. All save §2 are set on Iona, and a brief poem in §14 was almost certainly composed there.[32] If we accept the persuasive arguments which the text's editors have advanced for seeing Kells as the place where the Life as we know it was composed, it seems not unreasonable to imagine that the Kells author took a preexisting text from Iona and inserted into it his §§3–13.

Such a hypothesis is supported by the web of thematic links interconnecting §§2, 14–17 which have been discussed above. It is also supported, I think, by their sequence. If the five chapters are taken as a block, they exhibit a 'ring structure': to the youth in the first there corresponds a youth in the last, the corpse in the second is matched by a corpse in the fourth, and the unique child comes in the middle.

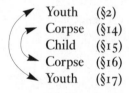

This line of reflection can be carried further if we take another look at the *Breviary of Aberdeen*. Its office for the feast of Adamnán includes six lections concerning the saint: as it happens, these too come at the beginning and end of the office, three lections concerning Saint Thecla having been interpolated in the middle. The material relating to Adamnán may be summarised as follows:

---

30 Herbert and Ó Riain, *Betha Adamnáin*, p. 33; cf. p. 85.   31 It is interesting to find in another text a collocation of a supernatural bell rung on Crúachan Aigle (as in the *Tripartite Life*), eschatological prophecy (the usual subject of Adamnán's warnings concerning the feast of John; cf. Herbert and Ó Riain's observations, *Betha Adamnáin*, p. 85), and the granting of knowledge of the future to Colum Cille. In an anecdote preserved in *Liber Flavus Fergusiorum*, Colum Cille prophesies that on the last day 'the bell will be rung on Crúachan Aigle, to awaken the men of Ireland, both living and dead, by the sound of the bell; that is, the Bernán Pátraic, which was broken upon the demons on Crúachan Aigle' (my trans.; text in Grosjean, 'Tale of Doomsday', p. 75; cf. idem, 'Addenda'). The statement recurs in O'Kelleher and Schoepperle, *Betha Colaim Chille*, pp. 114–15.   32 Herbert and Ó Riain, *Betha Adamnáin*, p. 32; Herbert, *Iona*, p. 173.

§i. Birth and early career; abbot of Lismore.

§ii. Becomes abbot of Iona; banishes a demon in the shape of a fox when it distracts a crowd from his preaching.

§iii. The demon child found by pigs (discussed above).

§uii. Apparition of Jesus as a child.

§uiii. A corpse brought to Iona for burial suddenly rises; Adamnán banishes the demon responsible.

§ix. Death.

Here §§ii, uii, and uiii obviously parallel §§2, 15, and 16 in the Life; there can be no doubt of a close relationship between the two works. Ó Riain has argued that the Life was itself taken to Iona some time after 1160, and the material in the *Breviary* excerpted from it once it was in Scotland;[33] Herbert prefers to see the *Breviary* and the Life as independent reflections of an earlier Iona document.[34] I incline at present toward the latter view: if, as I have suggested, the chapters which we have been considering from the Middle Irish Life were originally themselves part of a work concerning Adamnán composed on Iona, it would be a curious coincidence if only these chapters should have been drawn upon when the Life found its way to Iona some centuries later.

Here too, consideration of the arrangement of the material may be fruitful. We can note immediately that the anecdotes in the *Breviary* which have direct analogues in the Life appear in the same sequence as the latter: again, I think, an indication that both groups derive from a single integral document. But there is more. If, in line with my arguments for its thematic connectedness with the episodes in the Life, we suppose that the *Breviary*'s story of the demon child also figured in this earlier document, its position in the sequence of lections allows it to be inserted into the ring structure discernible in the Life without disrupting the latter's symmetry. In fact, the symmetry is enhanced: there are now three pairs, each with one evil and one good member; moreover, evil and good alternate regularly throughout the sequence as a whole.

---

33 Herbert and Ó Riain, *Betha Adamnáin*, pp. 38–41. Ó Riain points out that §15 in the Life shares details with its ultimate source in *Vita Columbae* (cf. discussion of §15 above), details which have no counterpart in the *Breviary*. While I agree that this militates against the Life's dependence on the *Breviary*, I see no difficulty in supposing that both Life and Breviary drew upon an earlier work, from which each has diverged in various ways.   34 Herbert, *Iona*, pp. 171–3.

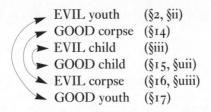

I contend, then, that the chapters of the Life of Adamnán considered above reflect a document composed with careful, not to say obsessive, attention to thematic coherence and internal symmetry. But what was its point? Here I can speak only tentatively; but I think that the Life offers us some very suggestive clues.

Throughout the relevant sections of the Life, as we have seen, Adamnán is explicitly or implicitly compared with his great predecessor. §2 recalls traditions of Colum Cille's conversations with Mongán and Tuán, while §§14 and 15 are based on Adamnán's own accounts of his hero's healing powers and celestial illumination. In §16, Adamnán is made to allude to an earlier conversation between Colum Cille and a demon. §17 seems to reflect a tradition that Colum Cille learned secrets from an immortal being resident on Croaghpatrick. Between the lines, then, these stories about Adamnán bear witness to an intriguing body of lore regarding Colum Cille: the latter appears as a visionary open to contact with the angelic and diabolical realms, and with the more equivocal representatives of the native supernatural.

But while it highlights this aspect of Colum Cille, the Life denies any comparable exploits to Adamnán. He may be able to hold his own when interrogated by devils;[35] but he seeks to learn nothing from them, and dismisses as 'audacious' (*esamain*) any curiosity regarding the subjects of which they claim to have special knowledge. Although able to raise the dead, he chooses not to do so. Colum Cille learns 'secrets that had been hidden since the world began' during his three days of solitude; Adamnán seeks not knowledge, but delight in the presence of the child Jesus. The youth on Croaghpatrick relates wonders not to Adamnán, but to the hermit Colmán.

Why should this be the case? In part, the idea may simply be that Adamnán does not try to compete with Colum Cille: this is almost certainly an element in §14, when he refrains from performing a miracle appropriate only to the founder saint. But I think that more may be involved as well.

The traditions regarding Colum Cille's relations with the supernatural appear to have involved several beings who were neither angels nor devils; and the saint's attitude to them is one of interest, not antagonism. Stories portraying him in this light seem on the basis of surviving evidence to have been fairly widespread, and are attested from an early date: it has been suggested that

---

35 Another of the features linking the six episodes on which I have focussed is that each of the three evil figures – the child, the youth, and the corpse – appears specifically as a questioner.

Immacallam Choluim Chille 7 *ind Oclaig* may well be as old as *Vita Columbae*, or indeed even older.[36]

I suggest that these traditions may have become something of an embarrassment to the Columban *familia*, and may even have been perceived as casting a shadow on the orthodoxy of the saint and his successors. This would be one way of interpreting the innuendo of Wilfrid at Whitby: Bede has him rebuff Colmán's assertion of the sanctity of the abbots of Iona with the words

> … So far as your father Columba and his followers are concerned, whose holiness you claim to imitate and whose rules and precepts (confirmed by heavenly signs) you claim to follow, I might perhaps point out that at the judgement, many will say to the Lord that they prophesied in His name and cast out devils and did many wonderful works, but the Lord will answer that He never knew them. Far be it from me to say this about your fathers, for it is much fairer to believe good rather than evil about unknown people.[37]

Do these roundabout insinuations imply that Colum Cille's powers might not have derived from Christ? If such suspicions were indeed in the air in the second half of the seventh century, this would have provided an additional motivation for Adamnán's desire that his *Vita Columbae* should, in Herbert's words, 'link Columban monastic tradition with the mainstream of Western hagiography, so that it should affirm that Colum Cille, venerated as a saint by his own community, merited acknowledgement also as a member of the communion of saints of Christendom'.[38] In remodelling his protagonist along Continental lines, Adamnán may have been seeking to extricate him from more awkward native associations.[39]

Whatever about Adamnán's portrayal of Colum Cille, the anecdotes which we have considered concerning Adamnán himself serve to distance him – and, by implication, the other heads of the Columban *familia* – from this *risqué* side of the patron saint. Such things belonged exclusively to the past, and were the preserve of the unimpeachable founder: Adamnán, when not dealing with God Himself, faces the beyond with the uncomplicated hostility of an exorcist. Even in the Gaelic world – in certain times and places, at all events – there were limits to the acceptability of the supernatural.

36 Cf. n. 3 above.   **37** *Historia ecclesiastica* III.25 (Colgrave and Mynors, pp. 304–7). **38** Herbert, *Iona*, p. 138.   **39** Cf. ibid., p. 144. In this context, it is tempting to see the most spectacular of Colum Cille's encounters with angels as a sort of Christian counterpart to the conversation in *Immacallam Choluim Chille*. The saint is suddenly joined by supernatural interlocutors, who just as suddenly depart; the dialogue is observed from a distance, and Colum Cille strictly enjoins secrecy upon the witness (VC III.16 [Anderson and Anderson, pp. 204–7; Sharpe, pp. 217–8]). Note that *Cnoc nan Aingeal* 'Hill of the Angels', where this apparition is said to have taken place, is now known locally as the *Sìthean* (i.e., *Síd*); I am grateful to Mairi McArthur for the information that it figures prominently in contemporary tradition as a dwelling of the fairies.

'*Ministerium seruitutis meae*': The Metaphor and Reality of Slavery in Saint Patrick's *Epistola* and *Confessio*

Elizabeth McLuhan

The Patrician texts comprise one of the earliest preserved examples of Insular Latin writing. Little about their author – the historical Patrick – is known or agreed upon by scholars. According to his own account, however, Patrick came from a British slave-owning family. While still a youth, he was kidnapped and taken as a slave to Ireland. He escaped and, as a runaway slave, lived like a fugitive under the law. But it was while he was enslaved that Patrick experienced a profound spiritual awakening to the religion to which he had belonged only nominally before. Eventually, Patrick returned to the land of his captivity as 'seruus in Christo'. For Patrick, like Saint Paul, the social reality of slavery provided a powerful paradigm for the imitation of Christ.

This paper will first examine Patrick's references to slavery in the *Confessio* and *Epistola*. Following this, I will consider Patrick's affinity with Saint Paul, especially Paul's theology of sin and slavery. Finally, I will step back to review Patrick's life within the broader socio-historical context of slavery and the Christian church of the fifth/sixth century.

I

In the *Confessio*, Patrick opens with an account of his capture as a youth, with many others, by slave traders. At the time, Patrick was staying on his father's estate.

> … ubi ego capturam dedi. Annorum eram tunc fere sedecim. Deum enim uerum ignorabam et Hiberione in captiuitate adductus sum cum tot milia hominum, secundum merita nostra, quia a Deo recessimus et praecepta eius non custodiuimus et sacerdotibus non oboedientes fuimus, qui nostram salutem admonebant … [1]

1 *Confessio* §1 (Hood, p. 23).

63

Patrick goes on to describe his increased spiritualization while in captivity:

> Sed postquam Hiberione deueneram, cotidie itaque pecora pascebam et
> frequens in die orabam; magis ac magis accedebat amor Dei et timor
> ipsius et fides augebatur et spiritus agebatur, ut in die una usque ad
> centum orationes et in nocte prope similiter, ut etiam in silua et monte
> manebam, et ante lucem excitabar ad orationem per niuem, per gelu, per
> pluuiam, et nihil mali sentiebam neque ulla pigritia erat in me – sicut
> modo uideo, quia tunc Spiritus in me feruebat.[2]

God later led, or directed, Patrick out of Ireland, ' ... terra captiuitatis
meae'.[3] In the second section, he asserts that God provided a vision whereby he
might escape and ' ... deinde postmodum conuersus sum in fugam et intermisi
hominem cum quo fueram sex annis ... '.[4] He returned to Britain, only to have
another vision telling him that he must go back to Ireland.[5] In the third section,
which deals with Patrick's rejection by the *seniores* or elders, he once again
extols the spiritual value of his enslavement. He commends those newly
converted slaves who bear witness to Christ at great personal risk. In the fourth
section Patrick recapitulates the nature of his mission, speaking 'fratribus et
conseruis meis'.[6] He ends by defending his conduct and 'ministerium seruitutis
meae'.[7] In the final words of the last section of the *Confessio*, Patrick reaffirms
his purpose in returning 'ad gentem illam unde prius uix euaseram'.[8]

In the *Epistola*, slavery is an overt issue. Patrick opens with a diatribe against a
certain Coroticus and the condemnation that ' ... qui facit peccatum seruus est et
filius zabuli nuncupatur'.[9] He demands that Coroticus and his men make amends
to God and 'liberent seruos Dei et ancillas Christi baptizatas'.[10] In a rhetorically
powerful section, Patrick presents slavery as the central motif in his life:

> Numquid a me, piam misericordiam quod ago erga gentem illam qui me
> aliquando ceperunt et deuastauerunt seruos et ancillas domus patris mei?
> Ingenuus fui secundum carnem; decorione patre nascor. Vendidi enim
> nobilitatem meam (non erubesco neque me paenitet) pro utilitate aliorum.
> Denique seruus sum in Christo genti exterae ob gloriam ineffabilem
> perennis uitae quae est in Christo Jesu Domino nostro.[11]

Patrick's early enslavement was the catalyst for his spiritual rebirth. This
same experience foreshadowed and defined his sense of personal mission among
the Britons in fifth-century Ireland. Profoundly influenced by the *exemplum* and

---

2 Ibid. §16 (Hood, p. 25).   3 Ibid. §3 (Hood, p. 23).   4 Ibid. §17 (Hood, p. 26).   5 Ibid.
§23 (Hood, p. 27).   6 Ibid. §47 (Hood, p. 32).   7 Ibid. §49 (Hood, p. 32).   8 Ibid. §61 (Hood,
p. 34).   9 *Epistola* §4 (Hood, p. 35).   10 Ibid. §7 (Hood, p. 36).   11 Ibid. §10 (Hood, p. 36).

epistles of Saint Paul, Patrick's evangelizing efforts are all the more distinctive given that he was working in what has been termed 'the first recognised Christian community beyond the western Imperial frontiers'.[12]

Scholars have speculated on Patrick's Biblical references and it is generally thought that he used pre-Jerome sources. Today, it is conceded that Patrick was a 'homo unius libri'[13] with very limited literary roots. At the same time, a more subtle reading of his works is emerging acknowledging the depth of Patrick's Biblical understanding and the quality of his writing as it was meant to be *heard*.[14]

Patrick would have been British-speaking, with the limited Latin and Biblical training available to him as a youth in sub-Roman Britain. He could have acquired Irish while a slave, and would have certainly needed it later for preaching. But Latin would of necessity have been the language in which Patrick read the Bible and in which it was read to his flock – of enslaved, nominally Christian, Britons and, possibly, new Irish converts. Almost certainly, Patrick wrote both the open letter or *Epistola* and the *Confessio* in Latin to be read aloud to his congregation.

D.R. Howlett has reconstituted Patrick's Latin phrase by phrase and clause by clause, in order to illustrate his use of the antiphonal structure of the Bible. Only then, Howlett believes, 'can one begin to hear the tenor of his explicit statements and the undertones and overtones of his implicit resonances'.[15] Patrick is no bumbling rube apologizing for his lack of learning. Rather, he wears his lack of human teaching as a badge of honour with the knowledge that his mission and his understanding come directly from God.

II

Indeed, Patrick's assumption of the mantle of 'seruus' can be seen as additionally validating his mission. Both Patrick and Paul, in their construction of a slave persona, can be placed within an early Christian literary tradition. Dale Martin in his recent study of the Classical literary sources of such slavery motifs observes that

> Paul's slavery to Christ did not connote humility but rather established his authority as Christ's agent and spokesperson. Even Paul's slavery to all was not unambiguously humbling, for it evoked in the minds of Paul's contemporary audience a model of leadership in which the leader exercised power by stepping down to the social level of those whom he was to lead.[16]

Paul announced his special calling in the first line of the first epistle: 'Paulus seruus Christi Iesu uocatus apostolus segregatus in euangelium Dei'.[17] He

---

12 Dumville, 'Some Aspects', p. 17.   13 Dronke, 'St Patrick's Reading', p. 21.   14 Howlett, *Book of Letters*, p. 11.   15 Ibid., p. 17.   16 Martin, *Slavery as Salvation*, p. 147.   17 Rm 1.1.

staked out his territory with Christ's authorization, 'per quem accepimus gratiam et apostolatum ad oboediendum fidei in omnibus gentibus pro nomine eius'.[18] Patrick, too, declares himself 'seruus'.[19] In both the *Confessio* and *Epistola*, he describes himself as set apart by God for a mission made special by virtue of the constituency to which he had been assigned.

> ... quis ego sum, Domine, uel quae est uocatio mea, qui mihi tanta diuinitate comparuisti, ita ut hodie in gentibus constanter exaltarem et magnificarem nomen tuum ubicumque loco fuero ... ut ego inscius et in nouissimis diebus hoc opus tam pium et tam mirificum auderem adgredere, ita ut imitarem quippiam illos quos ante Dominus iam olim praedixerat praenuntiaturos euangelium suum in testimonium omnibus gentibus ante finem mundi.[20]

It is interesting to compare Patrick's assertion 'Ecce testes sumus quia euangelium praedictum est usque ubi nemo ultra est'[21] with Paul's comment 'Sic autem hoc praedicaui evangelium non ubi nominatus est Christus ne super alienum fundamentum aedificarem'.[22] It is impossible to know for certain to which of Paul's epistles Patrick was indebted. While it has been established that not all of the Pauline epistles were actually written by Paul, the letters do share many contemporary cultural assumptions with regard to slavery.[23]

The letters of Saint Paul must have resonated on several levels with Patrick's own experience. Patrick's concerns over the acceptance and recognition of his text may have exacerbated the 'constant anxiety about authority which pervades both *Confessio* and *Epistola* ... due ... to Patrick's doubtful ecclesiastical status'.[24] It has been suggested that Patrick's possible lack of official episcopal status may account for his frequent references to a personal mission from God. Patrick's whole defensive posture against the *seniores* in the *Confessio* has been shown to derive in large part from Saint Paul's defense of his own mission in his letters to the Corinthians.[25]

Patrick certainly embraced Saint Paul's notion of sin as spiritual slavery: 'qui facit peccatum seruus est et filius zabuli nuncupatur'.[26] Paul wrote: 'Quod fuistis serui peccati, oboedistis autem ex corde in eam formam doctrinae in qua traditi estis; liberati autem a peccato, serui facti estis iustitiae'.[27] Patrick's notion of spiritual duality afforded Christians a choice of servitude: to God or Satan. The only freedom available to every Christian was the freedom of submission to God's will. Patrick's sixth vision in the *Confessio* could derive from Paul's

18 Rm 1.5.　19 *Epistola* §10 (Hood, p. 36).　20 *Confessio* §34 (Hood, p. 29).　21 Loc. cit. 22 Rm 15.20.　23 Garnsey, *Ideas of Slavery*, p. 173 n. 1.　24 Conybeare, 'Re-Reading St. Patrick', p. 43.　25 Nerney, 'St Patrick's Sources', p. 507.　26 *Epistola* §4 (Hood, p. 35). 27 Rm 6.17–18.

teaching on human will and the inner person who seeks God but needs God's help to realize his quest.[28] Certainly Patrick always acknowledged God's grace. Conybeare writes that 'the *Confessio*, indeed, can be read as a succession of surrenders to God, through faith, of Patrick's autonomy'.[29]

III

In their attitudes to slavery, Patrick and Paul were products of their respective time periods. In late Roman antiquity,

> the 'standard unit' of the Roman law was the freeborn Roman citizen, male, of age and sound mind and head of his family. Everyone else was legally inferior and by comparison subject to some sort of restriction, ranging from minor to total, upon his legal powers, rights or personality. There thus developed a stratified society in which every man had his legally appointed and legally defined place.[30]

The *Corpus iuris ciuilis* of Justinian, a codification completed in 534 of older laws and practices still in use from the past four centuries, defined slavery as 'an institution of the law of nations whereby one man is made the property of another, contrary to natural right'.[31] While masters did possess the power of life and death over their slaves, the law continued that

> at the present time, neither Roman citizens nor any other persons subject to the rule of the Roman people are allowed to treat their slaves with excessive harshness. ... Masters who show intolerable savagery are to be forced to sell their slaves to other owners.... This is the same principle by which prodigals are restrained from misuse of their own property.[32]

Coming from a family of slave owners in late fourth- and early fifth-century Britain, Patrick would have been aware of these general principles of governance within the Roman Empire. Paul's audience comprised Greek and Roman communities in the first century:

> When Paul wrote 1 Corinthians, about one-third of the population in Corinth was in slavery and another third had been in slavery and had been manumitted. It is clear that Paul was familiar with this social-legal

---

28 Shanzer, '"Iuvenes vestri"', p. 177.   29 Conybeare, 'Re-Reading St Patrick', p. 49.
30 Kolbert, *Justinian*, p. 49.   31 *Institutes* I.iii.2.   32 Ibid. XLVIII.l–liii (trans. Kolbert, *Justinian*, p. 52).

institution and the Greek and Roman laws which regulated its practice in Corinth. Indeed, some of the first people whom he baptized into Christ at Corinth were in slavery at the time.[33]

Slaves in the Roman Empire were frequently better off economically than freemen. Frequently, freemen are known to have opted for slavery as an escape from economic hardship and want. The possibility of manumission for first-century slaves is thought to have allowed the ancient system to enjoy long duration.[34]

The purpose of Christianity was not to emend society in any case. Paul's message was that salvation transcended social status and that human efforts should be directed to making ready one's soul for Christ and the end of the world as they knew it: 'praeterit enim figura huius mundi'.[35] Whether you were slave or master, your soul had to be entrusted – or enslaved – to God to realise salvation through Christ, the only true freedom. Paul's teaching (I Cor 7.21) might be interpreted thus:

> Let each one live his life in accord with the fact that the Lord has distributed [faith] to him and that God has called him ... Keeping the commands of God is what really counts. Each person should continue in that calling into which he was called.
>
> Were you a slave when you were called? Don't worry about it. But if, indeed, you become manumitted, by all means [as a freedman] live according to [God's calling]. For a slave who has been called in the Lord is the Lord's freedman. Likewise, a freedman who has been called [in the Lord] is Christ's slave. You were bought with a price: do not become slaves of men. Each one should continue to live in accord with his calling [in Christ] – in the sight of God.[36]

Patrick, like Paul, suggests no discontent with the slave system *per se*. Patrick's outrage against Coroticus in the *Epistola* is less a railing against the enslavement of freeborn Christians than an objection that those so enslaved would be sold to non-Christians and in this way exposed to sinful influences: most explicitly, the sexual dangers encountered by women. His anger was reserved for a fellow (perhaps nominally Christian) Briton who would capture for purposes of sale, and transport far away, other Britons and by implication fellow Christians.[37] Patrick urges local Christians to shun Coroticus until he has publicly repented with the requisite compunction, gruelling penance and release of the Christians who belong properly to God. God has purchased or redeemed their souls

---

33 Bartchy, *First-Century Slavery*, p. 173.   34 Ibid., p. 175.   35 I Cor 7.31.   36 Bartchy, *First-Century Slavery*, p. 183.   37 Thompson, *Who Was Saint Patrick?*, p. 18.

through the act of his Son's crucifixion: 'seruos Dei et ancillas Christi baptizatas, pro quibus mortuus est et crucifixus'.[38]

In the *Confessio* Patrick describes men and women from all classes converting to Christianity and adopting a celibate life. Within this context of promoting Christian celibacy, Patrick notes the persecution suffered by converts of royal families but singles out those converts from among the female slaves who suffer most, even to the point of death, in imitation of Christ.[39] Michael Herren comments that 'There is no sense of shock or outrage expressed in this passage, although there certainly is compassion ... . Patrick's virgins chose their fate with their eyes open'.[40]

In the *Epistola*, Patrick expresses admiration for Christians in Gaul who ransom Christian captives from the Franks and other presumably non-Christian peoples.[41] This practice is in sharp contrast to that of Coroticus, who is prepared to put the virginity of Christians at risk as surely as he might assign them to a whorehouse. Patrick was concerned that Christian slaves should have Christian masters, or at the least masters who tolerated their Christian beliefs and practices.

While Gallo-Roman Christians may have led the way in the reclamation of Christian captives, it was not with a view to dispensing with slavery as a social institution that they did so. Caesarius of Arles is a case in point. His tireless efforts to raise monies to ransom Christian captives in late fifth- and early sixth-century Gaul are well documented. Caesarius was considered an ascetic in comparison with the opulent living standards of other bishops at the time. Yet he himself owned slaves, and on his death left two slaves *as bequests* among his few personal possessions.[42] Even in life, Caesarius took a hard line to enforce the laws governing and delimiting the legal rights of the offspring of slaves and their masters.[43] He preached against the mixing of the classes.[44]

Even closer to Patrick's own time, the Council of Chalcedon in 451 stated that monasteries could not accept slaves without their owners' consent – upon threat of excommunication.[45]

Patrick goes to great pains to establish that he himself was under God's direction as a runaway slave.[46] It has been suggested that Patrick was deliberately vague as to where he went and what he did during that period to protect those who helped him who would also be judged criminal under Roman law for aiding and abetting a fugitive.[47] Slavery was probably a long-standing institution in pre-Christian Ireland, although much less is known about it there. Although Christianity may have provided some relief to the harsh lot of the slave,

---

38 *Epistola* §7 (Hood, p. 36). 39 *Confessio* §42 (Hood, p. 31). 40 Herren, 'Mission and Monasticism', pp. 79–80. 41 *Epistola* §14 (Hood, p. 37). 42 Klingshirn, *Caesarius of Arles*, p. 89. 43 Ibid., pp. 192–3. 44 Caesarius of Arles, *Sermons*, p. 213. 45 Westermann, *Slave Systems*, p. 158. 46 *Confessio* §17 (Hood, p. 26). 47 Thompson, *Who Was Saint Patrick?*, p. 21.

it is clear that slavery continued to be of considerable economic importance ... One indication is the number of references to slaves in the law texts, sagas, saints' lives, etc. and another is the use of the word *cumal* 'slave woman' as a unit of value.[48]

Another indication that traditional Irish laws on slaves persisted can be found in the accounts of Patrick by Muirchú and Tírechán, which took Patrick's own writings as their point of departure. In both texts the first order of business, upon Patrick's return to Ireland, is the payment of restitution for his slave price to his former owner.

Ubi uissum est ei nihil perfectius esse quam ut semet ipsum primitus redemeret; et inde appetens sinistrales fines ad illum hominem gentilem Milcoin, apud quem quondam in captiuitate fuerat, portansque ei geminum seruitutis praetium, terrenum utique et caeleste, ut de captiuitate liberaret illum cui ante captiuus seruierat.[49]

In both accounts by Muirchú and Tírechán, the former owner is portrayed as a powerful pagan who resists conversion to Christianity. In Muirchú's version, king Miliucc is deceived by the devil into destroying himself and all he possesses rather than to fall under Patrick's sway.[50] In Tírechán's tale, Patrick's owner is Miliucc moccu Boin, the druid, whose children are converted in his stead and who reject their pagan beliefs which are supplanted by the Christian Word of God. In a dream, Miliucc sees Patrick and the children transformed into birds.[51] In both accounts, Patrick's efforts to buy back his freedom are thwarted. The reasons for his failure to pay up, however, are nothing less than heroic and are victories for the church.

In looking back on his life in the *Confessio*, Patrick believes that he and his young friends deserved to be enslaved and that his own presence among foreign peoples is a direct result of God's intervention.[52] Patrick asserts that his abduction and captivity were the means by which he was 'emendatus ... a Domino'.[53] He was literally a new man. He also states that his life without God was but a living death, a prelude to the transformative experience that was in store for him.

... et Deum uiuum non credebam, neque ex infantia mea sed in morte et in incredulitate mansi donec ualde castigatus sum et in ueritate humiliatus sum a fame et nuditate, et cotidie.[54]

48 Kelly, *Early Irish Law*, p. 96.   49 Bieler, *Patrician Texts*, pp. 76–8.   50 Ibid., p. 80. 51 Ibid., p. 162.   52 *Confessio* §1 (Hood, p. 23).   53 Ibid. §28 (Hood, p. 28).   54 Ibid. §27 (Hood, p. 28).

Patrick vividly conveys the trauma of this experience even as he echoes the words of Paul.[55] Patrick's enslavement – and his voluntary exile back to Ireland – recall the theme of Christ's 'humiliation/exaltation' so embraced by Paul to characterize his own mission.[56] I would argue that Patrick, like Saint Paul,

> ... in viewing the condition of Christian slaves saw in it a unique and important opportunity for the imitation of Christ in union with him in his work of salvation ... The title 'slave' ... always described a fundamental condition of complete dedication to the divine will.[57]

Kenneth C. Russell, in the discussion just cited, goes on to assert that the metaphor of the slave in Paul's writing is 'never far from the secular root', although Paul adapted the term to describe the condition of all Christians.[58] Human society was only a prelude to the spiritual reward of salvation awaiting those who were reborn in Christ. Within this paradigm, the onus was upon both human slave and master to live together in as Christian a manner as possible while waiting for the end.

Nevertheless, the ransoming of Christian captives/slaves from masters or situations which threatened their virtue, or impeded the exercise of their religion, was deemed by Patrick to be a suitable practice for both Christians and the Church. It was the earthly counterpart to God's redemption of human souls. No human agent had ransomed Patrick. Patrick believed that his enslavement and escape were both providentially guided. Patrick's mission among the peoples of Ireland – his 'ministerium seruitutis' – was thus a reenactment of his earlier captivity and a celebration of his personal redemption by God.

---

55 II Cor 11.27.   56 Martin, *Slavery as Salvation*, p. 130.   57 Bartchy, *First-Century Slavery*, pp. 15–6; from Russell, 'Slavery as Reality', p. 17.   58 Ibid., p. 16.

Radegundis and Brigit

Walter Berschin

We have lost so much of the Latin biography of Antiquity that it seems almost impossible to say anything about it in general. Were there biographies of women during the Golden and Silver Ages of Latin literature? We don't know. The first surviving Latin biography of women is the *Passio Sanctarum Perpetuae et Felicitatis*, which dates from the first years of the third century of the Christian era.

About the year 400 Jerome wrote a dozen letters which can be viewed as biographies; most of them describe the lives of women. An increasing number of female heroines is characteristic of Merovingian biography or hagiography; I included a list of nine titles in my *Biographie und Epochenstil*.[1] The most prominent of these nine biographies is the *Vita S. Radegundis* written by Venantius Fortunatus soon after the year 587, when Radegundis died in Poitiers.

A hundred years later, a group of four, possibly even five, Latin biographies, composed in Ireland,[2] emerged out of the darkness of the seventh century – the *saeculum tenebricosum*, as it was called by Matthias Flacius Illyricus and the Centuriatiors of Magdeburg.[3] Some scholars consider the so-called *Vita secunda S. Brigidae* by Cogitosus to be the first of this group.[4] Muirchú, another of the four, tells us that Cogitosus did much for the introduction of sacred biography into Ireland: 'I have taken my ... boat ... out on this ... sea of sacred narrative ... , on which so far no boat has ventured except the one of my [spiritual] father Cogitosus.'[5]

The use of 'and' in the title of my article signifies affinity. It is my intention to compare the best Merovingian biography of a woman with one of the most important early Hiberno-Latin *vitae*. The differences are great; but in the end there is a coincidence which leads one to the question whether Cogitosus knew the *Vita S. Radegundis* by Venantius Fortunatus.

1 Berschin, *Biographie*, ii.307.   2 Namely, Cogitosus's Life of Brigit, the Lives of Patrick by Muirchú and Tírechán, and Adomnán's Life of Columba. Some scholars would also place the *Vita prima* of St Brigit in the seventh century (see n. 4).   3 Flacius Illyricus, *Historia ecclesiastica*, p. 22.   4 For the most recent discussions of the subject see McCone, 'Brigit in the Seventh Century' and Sharpe, '*Vitae S. Brigidae*'.   5 ' ... in hoc ... narrationis sanctae pylagus ... tantum uno patris mei Coguitosi expertum ... cymbam deduxi' (Bieler, *Patrician Texts*, p. 62).

Let us begin with a brief sketch of the two Lives. Venantius Fortunatus is the first mediaeval biographer to write a whole series of biographies; he is the first 'professional hagiographer' of Latin literature. All of his works were Lives of bishops, with the exception of the *vita* of St Radegundis which concerned a Thuringian princess, Frankish queen, and foundress of a convent at Poitiers, whom Venantius adored and loved.[6]

Radegundis's career was full of incredible events. For example, the princess, as a prisoner of war, brought together a group of children near St.Quentin, washed their heads and hands, fashioned a wooden cross and proceeded to a church. She also endured her arranged marriage for as long as she was able. Finally she forced a bishop to give her the veil and built herself in Poitiers a 'mighty fortress' in the form of a convent whose fire curtain of penitence and prayer no vile Merovingian could penetrate, not even her husband.

Perhaps it would be appropriate to mention also some details which are difficult to understand in a modern context. Radegundis began a process of mortification which, during the forty days of Lent, involved winding chains around her body and disfiguring herself with a glowing piece of iron. *In se ipsa tortrix*, 'tormenter unto herself', she was called by Venantius Fortunatus (cap. 26). Up to this point only the word *tortor* existed in Latin; Venantius Fortunatus seems to have invented the feminine counterpart *tortrix*, describing a new phenomenon with a new word. Subsequently, female forms of words spread widely in the Latinity of late Antiquity and the Middle Ages.[7]

Through her exercises of penitence Radegundis wanted to become a 'martyr by herself' (*a se ut fieret martyra*, cap. 26), experiencing the pain of crucifixion in her own flesh. Her monastery was dedicated to the Holy Cross, which she venerated not only spiritually, but also physically, in body and in mind. There was an enormous contrast between the glory of her former life, as the daughter of a king and as a queen, and the *passio* which she had chosen voluntarily. Turning points in the biography are like turning points in the human condition. Radegundis was a woman forging a new path. Departing from the glory of kingship, she willingly took upon herself the existence of a servant and penitent, which was tantamount to living *sub forma crucis* 'under the form of the cross'.

Reading the *Vita S. Brigidae* by Cogitosus, one quickly gains the impression that it is little more than a series of miracles.[8] At the beginning one finds some remarks on the birth and youth of Brigit (cap. 3) but, at the end, the death of the saint is unrecorded. In its place we read a description of the monastery of

---

6 Venantius Fortunatus, *Vita S.Radegundis* (Krusch, pp. 364–77). 7 It is for this reason that the Catholic Church still prays *pro famulis et famulabus* despite the fact that, according to Donatus (Keil, *Grammatici latini*, iv.378) and Priscian (ibid., ii.293), both *famulus* and *famula* yield *famulis* in the ablative plural. 8 AASS Februarii I, pp. 135–41; PL lxxii.775–90.

Kildare, where Brigit proves her saintly existence *post mortem* by the miracles she continues to work. Despite this emphasis, her life story is not only the chronicle of a centre of pilgrimage, a *Wallfahrts-Chronik*, but a *vita* as well. The author, who names himself in both preface and epilogue (cap. 40), had, I surmise, intended to give the Life of Brigit the form of a rapid sequence of miracles, a narrative technique developed by Venantius Fortunatus, who was *the* Merovingian master of biography.

Cogitosus presents some fascinating scenes, of which two are of interest here. An Irish king had a tame little fox, which amused him greatly. A stupid man killed it and was due to be punished severely, together with his wife and children. Hearing of this St Brigit went into her carriage and said a prayer and, lo and behold, a fox came, jumped into her carriage and 'neatly sat beside her' (cap. 23). Brigit went to the king, and the fox she brought with her turned out to be as well-trained as the one that had been killed. With its help Brigit freed the condemned wrong-doer and, as soon as everybody was safe and sound, the little fox escaped to freedom again.

This story is representative of many relating to animals, including dogs (cap. 6, 16), cattle (cap. 4, 8), goats (cap. 11), pigs (cap. 11), fish (cap. 28) and even ducks (cap. 24). I dare say that there is no other Latin *vita* of the early Middle Ages, where a biographer has so continuously told stories about his saint's involvement with animals. Even Adomnán's Life of Columba, with its stories of the crane arriving from Ireland 'tossed by winds through long circuits of the air' (VC I.48), and the white horse mourning and weeping 'on the lap of the saint' (VC III.23), is not so consistently determined by the involvement of animals as Cogitosus's *Vita S. Brigidae*. Brigit's miracles prove, as Cogitosus says, 'that the entire nature of the beasts and cattle and birds was subject to her command'.[9]

It is possible that oriental influences were partly responsible for this idea of absolute power over animals. The Egyptian Menas preferred to live with the beasts in the wilderness 'for they know God and honour Him'.[10] The martyr Mammas prayed in the wilderness in the company of many animals:[11] he is portrayed as a kind of Christian Orpheus. But there is also a western mythological tradition in which animals play an important role. The story of Orpheus was known in the Middle Ages through Ovid and other mythographical authors.

Another story in the *Vita S. Brigidae* recalls Ovid's tale of Philemon and Baucis.[12] Brigit, travelling on one of her journeys to different parts of Ireland,

---

9 '... quod omnis natura bestiarum et pecorum et volucrum subiecta eius fuit imperio' (ibid., cap. 24).   10 ' ... ferae enim deum cognoverunt et honoraverunt', *Passio S. Mennae* (Mombritius, ii.287).   11 *Passio S.Mammetis* §8 (Delehaye, p. 131). There is a new edition of Walahfrid's poem on Mammas by Pörnbacher, *Walahfrid Strabo: Zwei Legenden*. 12 Ovid, *Metamorphoses* VIII.611–724 (Miller, i.448–56).

spends the night with a poor woman who, in honour of her guest, slaughters the only calf she has beside her cow and, as there is no wood to roast the meat, uses parts of her loom to make a fire. The next morning she finds not only the calf alive beside her cow, but also the loom restored to its original condition (cap. 29). Like Jupiter drinking the wine of Philemon and Baucis, Brigit accepts the generosity of the poor without taking anything from them.

In comparing Radegundis and Brigit, it is not difficult to put one's finger on the differences between the two portraits of leading women of the early Middle Ages. Let us try to identify the main focus of each Life. Radegundis is a saint living under the spell of the Cross. Indeed, the veneration of the Holy Cross has evoked Radegundis's story throughout fifteen centuries and, for as long as *Pange, lingua, gloriosi proelium certaminis* and *Vexilla regis prodeunt, fulget crucis mysterium* are sung, it will continue to do so. These two poems were composed by Venantius Fortunatus for Radegundis and her nuns in honour of the relic of the Holy Cross venerated by them. In the last stanza of *Vexilla regis*, in the lines *Salue ara, salue uictima de passionis gloria*,[13] we find the most succinct summary of Radegundis's career, her 'glory of passion'.

The Holy Cross is almost absent from Brigit's Life, as are mortification and asceticism. How are we to form an impression of Brigit's monastery? Was she an abbess? Was she, who is so often sitting in her carriage (*in curru sedebat*), not subject to *stabilitas in congregatione*? Do we encounter something Celtic in the fascination with her carriage? Celtic princes on the Continent even took their carriages with them to their graves. Cogitosus's Brigit seems to live in an archaic world, surrounded by animals, 'praising the invisible Creator of everything through his visible creation, the Creator to whom the animals are subject and for whom they live'.[14]

I have already suggested that the form of Cogitosus's Life of Brigit may have been influenced by an element of biography characteristic of Venantius Fortunatus, for whom the Life of a saint should consist of a series of astonishing events. *Formulae praeteritionis* like *Nec praetereundum est* of the Life of Brigit (cap. 6, 23, 32), for example, are typical of chapter openings in the *vitae* of Venantius. Additionally, there is an important detail in Venantius's Life of Radegundis, which might have been a model for Cogitosus's Brigit.

Ludwig Bieler stated in 1962 that 'in one respect Cogitosus disappoints us: he has not succeeded in welding his material into a continuous narrative. After some brief chapters on Brigit's birth, childhood and vocation, he merely relates a number of miracles. He does not even describe the saint's death; instead he tells as an eye-witness some *miracula post mortem*'.[15] But this *praeteritio* of an

---

13 Bulst, *Hymni latini*, p. 129.   14 ' … collaudans creatorem omnium rerum invisibilem per creaturas visibiles, cui omnia subiecta sunt animantia et cui omnia vivunt' (cap. 24).
15 Bieler, 'Celtic Hagiographer', esp. p. 247.

existential event could be an imitation of Venantius Fortunatus's *Vita S. Radegundis*: for here too there is no chapter describing the death of the saint. Instead, Fortunatus details one of Radegundis's many miracles, one of which, we are told, happened the day she left this world.[16] Even in death, Radegundis helps others as a worker of miracles, a thaumaturge.[17] The saint is as much present beyond death as during her life. Venantius's contemporary, Gregory of Tours, filled the gaps the biographer had left,[18] as did Baudonivia, who added a second book to the *Vita S. Radegundis* about 600 AD.[19]

What both Venantius Fortunatus and Cogitosus achieved, by omitting the description of the deaths of their respective heroines, is by no means unique. Let me show this by a rather modern example. In his biography of Winckelmann, Goethe omitted any direct reference to the harsh reality of death. His penultimate chapter bears the title 'Restlessness' (*Unruhe*) and ends with the sentence 'and so, returning to his native country, he felt uneasy and burdened with the impossibility of continuing on his way'. The final chapter which follows, entitled 'Passing On' (*Hingang*), goes on immediately: 'thus he left the world, after having reached the highest degree of good fortune that he could have wished for'. In Goethe's presentation, Winckelmann, the saint of the Weimar classicists, imperceptibly ascended from the summit of human existence to the higher plain of the departed.[20] Birth and death may be the cornerstones of a person's life; but in some biographies, mediaeval and modern, these earthly realities are often presented as miraculous metamorphoses.

16 ' ... die, qua sanctissima migravit de saeculo' (*Vita S. Radegundis*, cap. 38).   17 Palermo, the most recent translator of the biography, writes: 'è come ... pur essendo ... già in paradiso ... fosse rimasta ancora vicina agli amici cari' (*Venanzio Fortunato*, p. 133 n. 54).   18 Gregory of Tours, *In gloria confessorum*, cap. 104 (Krusch, pp. 364–6).   19 Baudonivia, *Liber II vitae S. Radegundis* (Krusch, pp. 377–95). Radegundis's death is reported in cap. 21. 20 *Winckelmann und sein Jahrhundert*, pp. 287–9.

St Brendan's Boat: Dead Hides and the Living Sea in Columban and Related Hagiography

Jonathan M. Wooding

Hagiography has been widely used as a historical source for material life.[1] Such use proceeds from the assumption that data pertaining to technology, trade and consumption are preserved inadvertently in narratives of religious events. This assumption has been especially prevalent in early medieval studies, owing to the decision by the editors of the Monumenta Germaniae Historica to edit a selection of saint's *vitae* to supplement the limited picture of early medieval economic and social history available from diplomatic sources.[2] This use of hagiography as evidence for processes of travel, transport and *Gesellschaft* has been carried over into Insular studies through the work of Zimmer, Levison and their successors,[3] and in many areas of historical study fundamentally colours historians' perceptions of hagiography. Such use of saints' biographies, however, may have proved an obstacle to our understanding of the religious and literary function of such texts. If data on material life are to be recovered from the descriptive element in hagiography it must be with due regard to the functions of such data in the context of the entire narrative and not on an uncritical assumption that these are simply incidental details. This need is well illustrated by the treatment of details in the Lives of St Brendan and other

1 I would like especially to thank Jacqueline Borsje, Glyn Burgess, Michael Cahill, John Carey, David Dumville, Karen Jankulak, Séamus Mac Mathúna, Kevin Murray, Donnchadh Ó Corráin, Dáibhí Ó Cróinín, Tom O'Loughlin and Jennifer O'Reilly for encouragement and assistance with various aspects of this paper. 2 On the Monumenta and its use of sources see Knowles, *Great Historical Enterprises*, pp. 3–32. The historicist preoccupation of the MGH is well reflected in its treatment of a text such as the *Vita Fursei*, in which large sections of principally theological interest are excluded: with the edition of Krusch ('Vita uirtutesque Fursei') may be contrasted that of Heist (*Vitae*, pp. 37–40). 3 See, especially, Zimmer, 'Handelsverbindungen', esp. pp. 430–76 and 1098–1119; Levison, *England and the Continent*. On Zimmer's conception of history see Meyer, 'Nachlass Heinrich Zimmers', but now also Ó Lúing, 'Celtic Scholars of Germany', which contradicts Meyer's picture on some points and provides evidence for Mommsen's role in the development of Zimmer as a historian. For later studies which have brought the Monumenta's approach into insular historical studies see Mayr-Harting, *Coming of Christianity*; James, 'Ireland and Western Gaul'.

closely related *vitae,* as well as vernacular *immrama.* These 'voyage' tales have, of course, been subject to historicist interpretation of their broad narratives by exploration historians and hyper-diffusionists as representing pre-Columbian Atlantic crossings – without such claims finding much acceptance by more critical historians.[4] The argument that these texts are reliable sources for individual material details has found more widespread acceptance: especially with respect to their depiction of the hide-covered boat, or 'curragh', as a very common craft for voyaging around Irish waters in the first millennium A.D., and for monastic voyaging in particular. Study of a range of Hiberno-Latin and Irish texts indicates, however, that the hide-covering of such vessels has a significant, possibly central, narrative function in literary representation of penitential voyaging, and in exegesis of certain pertinent Biblical passages. While not necessarily disproving the actual use of hide-covered craft in early medieval Ireland, this identification of the hide-covering as an essential genre element in a penitential discourse has implications both for the attention which must be paid to all potential religious detail in hagiography and for the assumption by historians that any details in such texts can safely be regarded as *inadvertently* included from the broader material paradigm, and hence a reliable representation of everyday material life.

Most works of maritime history have accepted the assumption that the hide-covered craft was the most commonly built vessel in pre-Viking Ireland.[5] It has been accepted that references to ships in early Irish and Hiberno-Latin texts refer to curraghs, even where the lexical items used may be non-specific as to the method of construction of the craft.[6] The assumption has been made that the hide-covered craft was the 'indigenous' vessel of Celtic Britain and Ireland, and support is seen to lie in literary indications of the predominance of hide-covered over wooden craft, of which explicit descriptions are very rare. Adomnán's use on at least one occasion in the *Vita Columbae* of the generic item *nauis* to describe a hide-covered craft is also taken to suggest that all such *naues* were hide-covered.[7]

Debate has been frequently preoccupied with the question as to whether hide-covered craft are sturdy enough for extended ocean voyaging.[8] But there

---

4 See Wooding, 'Monastic Voyaging', in idem, *Otherworld Voyages*; O'Meara, Review. For a survey of hyper-diffusionist uses of Irish materials, see also Fingerhut, *Who First Discovered America?*, pp. 11–29. 5 See e.g. Johnstone, *Seacraft of Prehistory*, pp. 26–7; Evans, 'Saints and Skinboats'. Among general histories of prehistoric seafaring, only Seán McGrail's seems to present a balanced view on this point (*Ancient Boats*, pp. 185–7). 6 E.g. Marcus, *Conquest of the North Atlantic*, esp. pp. 3–32; MacCullagh, *Irish Currach Folk*. 7 See below. 8 The effect of this has been to draw most investigation down the path of hyper-diffusionist attempts to prove the capacity or incapacity of hide-covered craft to cross the Atlantic (a redundant question in view of the everyday use of curraghs in Atlantic coastal voyaging); and, following the successful prosecution of such a voyage by Tim Severin, into heated debate concerning the authenticity of his reconstruction. This challenge was set up by

has been little appreciation of the socio-economic reasons why either skin or wooden craft may have been chosen for use by the early Christian Irish, let alone any consideration of the literary contexts in which sea-going craft are described.

Two interpretive problems may be identified here. The first concerns the extent to which hagiographical texts, which are central to all of the models of early Irish seafaring so far presented, can be taken as representative of any real scenario. The Andersons, in their 1961 edition of the *Vita Columbae*, drew attention to Adomnán's inconsistent use of maritime terms,[9] which should give pause to any attempt to argue a meaning for his use of *nauis* on the basis of one episode. Other works of hagiography raise further questions. St Petroc is said to have travelled in a glass boat.[10] Other saints are said to have travelled in boats of stone.[11] Do we have any reason to believe that descriptions of saints travelling in hide-covered craft are more concerned with the reality of clerical voyaging than such obviously more miraculous representations? Presumably representations of stone and glass craft are made by their authors for narrative or iconographic associations. In other words, if glass and stone can have purely symbolic functions in a hagiographical narrative, why assume that hide is simply a representation of reality?

Certainly, there can be no serious doubt that a hide-covered craft did exist, and that its lineal descendant – generally termed a *naomhóg* in Munster Irish[12] – is still used in Ireland in the present day, though covered by tarred cloth rather than hide.[13] It is, however, one thing to prove that the hide-covered craft was a real vessel in use in medieval Ireland; it is another to argue that its common representation in hagiography is due to it being the ubiquitous 'native' craft in use.[14] In non-hagiographic early Irish sources, the hide-covered craft

comments by George Little (in the 1940s) and by Geoffrey Ashe (in the 1960s), and was explored by Tim Severin in his 1976–7 voyage from Ireland to Canada in a reconstruction of a medieval curragh. See Little, *Brendan*; Ashe, *Land to the West*, p. 119; Severin, *Brendan Voyage*. For comment on this issue see O'Meara, Review; also Wooding, 'Paradise'. 9 For example: *ratis* as a metonym for *nauis*. Adomnán, VC I.36 (Anderson and Anderson, pp. 66–7 and n. 79). 10 *Vita prima Sancti Petroci*, cap. 9, in Grosjean, 'S. Petroc', p. 493. Also in the *Vita secunda*. 11 Henken, *Welsh Saints*, pp. 98–9; Alonso, 'Galician Legends'. 12 For the most comprehensive ethnographic study, see Hornell, *British Coracles*. 13 The direct relationship of this craft to its medieval ancestor has been questioned by some critics (De Courcy Ireland, *Ireland and the Irish*, p. 38). Where the author of the *Nauigatio Sancti Brendani* describes such a craft as a type built in early medieval Munster, however (cap. 4; Selmer, p. 10), the similarity of the design of the modern *naomhóg* to that described in the *Nauigatio* – as well as to the depiction of a medieval curragh on the Kilnaruane Pillar in West Cork (Hourihane and Hourihane, 'Kilnaruane Pillar Stone'; Johnstone, 'Bantry Boat'; Wooding, 'Biblical Narrative') – leaves little doubt that the *naomhóg* descends, directly or indirectly, from a medieval ancestor which is essentially the same as that described in hagiography. 14 The widespread use of the *naomhóg* in areas of Kerry and Connemara in the nineteenth century cannot be taken to reflect any medieval ubiquity of such craft, as it is

appears as simply one type of vessel amongst several which were in use.[15]
Sufficient evidence exists to show that wooden craft were used alongside hide-
covered craft in early medieval Ireland.[16]

However, this evidence that wooden craft *were* used carries no implication
that wooden craft would have been regarded as superior for ocean voyaging or
that wooden craft would necessarily have been the commonest type of craft in
use, replacing the hide-covered vessel entirely as the 'Celtic' ship type. One of
the singular failings of maritime history as a genre has been its adherence to
evolutionary models which start from the assumption that individual ethnic
groups built only single types of craft as a matter of tradition.[17] The argument
that 'Celts' exclusively used hide-covered vessels, Germanic peoples clinker-
built craft, and Mediterraneans mortice-and-tenon built craft, reflects outdated
isolationist models which deny the probably various use of technology for
different functions, regardless of which ethnic group may have initially
designed any one type of craft.[18] This assumption that the early medieval Irish
were locked by tradition into one choice of maritime technology has not served
to advance our understanding of the specific roles played by the hide-covered
vessel as one of a number of types of craft available in early Ireland – let alone
the specific functions of its representation in hagiography.

When Adomnán in VC II.42 describes a voyage by monks in search of an
ocean *desertum*, in a *nauis* ('ship') with a *pellicium tectum* ('hide covering') and, three
chapters later (II.45), describes *curucae* in use for towing logs, should we accept
either of these descriptions as simply representing real events? The *curuca*[19]

most probably due to reintroduction from Clare in the mid-1800s: Synge, *In Wicklow*, p. 151;
Ó Criomhthain, *An tOileánach*, p. 170; Hornell, 'Curraghs of Ireland', p. 20. Also see De
Brún, 'Windele's Visit', pp. 100–1. Synge and Ó Criomhthain state that smaller, cheaper craft
were required as declining markets for fish made bulk fishing with larger crews, from 'Seine
Boats', less profitable.   **15** See e.g. the early Irish law tract *Uraicecht Becc's* discussion of the
status of boat-builders, who might be builders of: '*lerlonga* [sea ships], and *bárca* [merchant
ships], and *curaig*' (Binchy, *Corpus iuris*, pp. 1615, 2280 and 2332). *Long*, from the Latin
compound *longa nauis*, is undoubtedly a word for a wooden craft: see Wooding,
Communication and Commerce, p. 9.   **16** This evidence includes such archaeological finds as
the Lough Lene boat from County Westmeath (Raftery, *Pagan Celtic Ireland*, pp. 208–9;
Brindley and Lanting, 'Roman Boat', pp. 10–1; Ó hEailidhe, 'Monk's Boat') and the
controversial boat model from Broighter in County Derry, (Farrell and Penny, 'Broighter
Boat', pp. 15–28; Warner, 'Broighter Hoard'; Neill, 'How Carson Caught the Boat'); as well
as references in Adomnán and in the early Irish laws (Flanagan, 'Ships and Shipping', pp.
3–8; Wooding, *Communication and Commerce*, cap. 2).   **17** As Maarleveld has argued ('Type
or Technique?'), marine technology was by definition mobile and transferred easily from
community to community.   **18** For recent discussion of the movement of ships between
peoples in the late Roman period see e.g. Haywood, *Dark Age Naval Power*, p. 31. For
argument along the lines of ethnic singularity see Jones, 'Mast and Sail', p. 47; idem, *End of
Roman Britain*, p. 92 n.48; Brindley and Lanting, 'Roman Boat', p. 11.   **19** In Harvey et al.,
Archive, this item is cited only from Gildas and Adomnán, in both instances in ablative plural.
The nominative forms used here are those given in Latham and Howlett, *Dictionary*, q.v.

reference, which occurs in a phrase along with *scapha*,[20] may be an example of Adomnán's tendency, noted above, to employ a variety of different terms for boats as a form of elegant variation.[21] Nonetheless, such use of curraghs in inshore waters would harness notable advantages of the hide-covered craft, namely its ability to navigate shoal and estuarial waters,[22] so there appears no reason why in this case we should not accept his words at face value. The reference to the ocean voyage, however, may be seen to sit within a Classical and Patristic literary discourse in which hide-covered craft were used for ocean-voyaging, not always by British and Irish peoples. Here the question of whether a hide-covered craft was actually used becomes subject to issues of literary genre, as well as practical reality.

References by Classical authors of the first century B.C. and later to hide-covered craft frequently occur in the context of descriptions of the Ocean which themselves derive in whole or in part from Greek *periploi* of the fifth through second centuries B.C.[23] Such descriptions are found in the works of Diodorus,[24] Pliny,[25] and Strabo,[26] among others. A common denominator to several descriptions is the image of hide-covered craft in use by the Celtic barbarians to conduct commerce in and around coastal islands. This image later occurs as a poetic conceit in the works of Lucan,[27] Avienus[28] and Sidonius[29] – whether derived directly from the Greek *periploi* or not is unclear – in which the barbarians navigate the 'British' sea 'in a hide'. The most detailed of these occurs in Avienus's *Ora maritima* of the fourth century AD, which supposedly quotes a lost Massiliote Periplus describing a voyage along the Ocean shores:

> Under the head of this promontory, the Oestrymnic bay lies open for the natives. In it the islands called Oestrymnides stretch themselves out. They lie widely apart and are rich in tin and lead. There is much hardiness in the people here, a proud spirit, an efficient industriousness. They are all constantly concerned with commerce. They ply the widely troubled sea and swell of monster-filled Ocean with skiffs of skin. For these men do not know how to fashion keels with pine or maple. They do not hollow out yachts, as the custom is, from fir trees. Rather they always marvellously fit out boats with joined skins and often run through the vast salt water on leather. But from here, there is a two-day journey for a ship

---

20 VC II.45 (Anderson and Anderson, pp. 174–5). For discussion see below. 21 *Scapha* is indeed a term used to describe hide-covered craft by Isidore, *Etymologiae* XIX.i.21. 22 Cf. Strabo, *Geographica* (Jones, ii.76–7). 23 For the most recent comprehensive discussion of these sources see Roseman, *Pytheas*. 24 Diodorus Siculus, *Historical Library* V.22 (Oldfather and Walton, iii.154–7). 25 Pliny, *Naturalis historia* IV.16 (Rackham et al., ii.198). 26 See below, note 32. 27 Lucan, *Pharsalia* IV.134–5 (Duff, pp. 184–5). 28 See below, note 30. 29 *Panegyric on Avitus* lines 369–71; *Epistola* VIII.vi.13–14 (Anderson, i.150–1, ii.428–31).

to the Holy Island – thus the ancients called it. This island, large in extent
of land, lies between the waves. The race of Hierni inhabits it far and
wide. Again the island of the Albiones lies near.[30]

The canonical interpretation of this passage is that of O'Neill Hencken, who
argued that the Oestrymnides are Britain and Ireland, and that Avienus refers to
traders coming to Brittany with tin and lead from Cornwall.[31] It may be debated,
however, whether the (what I suspect to be) common underlying source for these
references to voyages in hide-covered craft was originally concerned with Britain
at all. There can be no doubt that by the late-Roman period the hide-covered craft
was most often understood as a purely British phenomenon. Strabo, however,
writing in the first century, states that hide-covered craft were previously built
in Atlantic Spain.[32] Christopher Hawkes has argued on the basis of the
distances and details in this account that Avienus's source described a voyage to
Spain rather than Britain,[33] with the Albiones and the Hierni being Iberian
peoples, in which case the hide-covered craft described may also be Iberian –
though by Avienus's time now confused with British craft and even perhaps one of
the bases of the conflation.[34] It is also worthy of note that Sidonius's reference
concerns Saxons, not Celts, as do references in Hegesippus and Isidore.[35] The
tendency has been to 'correct' the former to 'Irish'.[36] While again this is a matter
for another discussion, we may note that the identification of the hide-covered
craft as an exclusively British and Irish vessel for ocean voyaging is by no means as
clear cut as has been claimed. Rather, it is part of a much more general discourse
for the depiction of barbarians on the Ocean shore – who, in the case of the
Iberians and Saxons, may well have been actually using such craft in estuarial
contexts where their special qualities would have been entirely apposite.[37] On

---

30 Avienus, *Ora maritima* lines 94–112 (Murphy, pp. 8–9): 'Sub huius autem prominentis
vertice sinus dehiscit incolis Oestrymnicus, in quo insulae sese exerunt Oestrymnides laxe
iacentes et metallo divites stanni atquae plumbi. multa vis hic gentis est, superbus animus,
efficax solertia, negotiandi cura iugis omnibus, netisque cumbis turbidum late fretum et
beluosi gurgitem Oceani secant. non hi carinas quippe pinu texere et acere norunt, non
abiete, ut usus est, curvant faselo(s), sed rei ad miraculum navigia iunctis semper aptant
pellibus corioque vastum saepe percurrunt salum. ast hinc duobus in sacram, sic insulam
dixere prisci solibus cursus rati est. Haec inter undas multa[m] caespitum iacet, eamque late
gens Hiernorum colit. propinqua rursus insula Albionum patet'.   31 O'Neill Hencken,
Archaeology of Cornwall and Sicily, pp. 168, 181–3.   32 διφθερίνοις τε πλοίοις ἐχρῶντο
ἕως ἐπὶ Βρούτου διὰ τὰς πλημυρίδας καὶ τὰ τενάγη, νυνὶ δὲ καὶ τὰ μονόξυλα ἤδη
σπάνια: 'Up to the time of Brutus [136 BC] they [the Iberians] used boats of tanned leather,
on account of the flood tides and shoal waters, but now, already, even the dugout canoes are
rare', Strabo, *Geographica* III.3 (Jones, pp. 76–7).   33 Hawkes, *Pytheas*.   34 Another factor
may be the Classical error which saw Britain and Ireland lying adjacent to Spain: see
Baumgarten, 'Geographical Orientation'.   35 Isidore, *Etymologiae* XIX.i.21; Hegesippus,
Historiae V.150 (Ussher, p. 320). Hegesippus is quoted in Isidore's account.   36 E.g.
Marcus, 'Factors', p. 313; Jones, 'Mast and Sail', p. 47 and n. 40.   37 The Saxons in
question are evidently those whom Gregory of Tours describes as living on islands in the

the last point we may only note the surprisingly categorical and exclusive character of judgements which are made concerning sub-Roman seafaring on the basis of a handful of archaeological finds.[38]

These questions are of some relevance for our appreciation of how limited are the sources upon which the curragh thesis has been based. More pertinent, however, are the implications of this common motif of barbarians sailing the perilous Ocean in a hide for the literary representation of the curragh in early Irish hagiography. Both the lines of transmission of details from the Greek *periploi* into Roman texts and the Irish debt to Patristic authors are sufficiently poorly understood to make it difficult to trace the path of transmission of this image of the hide-covered craft into early Irish writing. Nonetheless, when we consider the common features of the contexts in which this craft is represented the likelihood that the Irish representation of voyaging in hide-covered craft derives from the Patristic and Classical images becomes increasingly clear. In literary contexts – separate from probably everyday use for fishing and other coastal navigation – hide-covered craft in Irish texts occur predominantly in a penitential context. They represent vehicles for travel in the 'monster-filled Ocean': a potentially permeable, perilous vehicle in which the voyagers are separated from the living sea only by a prophylactic layer, or layers, of dead hide. Such voyages took the form both of a legal penalty and, in a monastic context, a statement of *peregrinatio*, which is itself reasonably described as a penitential act.[39]

Voyages as a legal penalty are found in secular as well as ecclesiastical law codes, though Mary Byrne has argued that the secular punishment derived from ecclesiastical practice.[40] Examples of this punishment are found across a range of legal texts, from the early Irish laws through the *Collectio canonum Hibernensis*[41] and *Cáin Adomnáin*.[42]

Most often the penalty specifies the number of hides from which the craft is made. *Cormac's Glossary*, making a typically misleading learned etymology, derives the word *cimbith* ('a criminal') from Greek κύμβη, which is glossed as a 'boat of one hide'.[43] The penalty of a voyage in a vessel of one hide is explicitly described in the *vitae* of St Patrick, in which St Patrick sends Macc Cuill to sea after he has repented his impious deeds in front of his own people:

Loire in the fifth century and whom Sidonius describes as performing dangerous landings on the beach as a normal practice: Gregory of Tours, *Historia Francorum* II.19 (Krusch, p. 65); cf. Sidonius, *Epistola* VIII.vi.13–4 (Anderson, ii.430).   **38** Cf. John Haywood's sensible words on this point: *Dark Age Naval Power*, pp. 2–5.   **39** The *immrama* have also recently been frequently characterised as 'penitential': see Mac Mathúna, *Immram Brain*, p. 278; Hillers, 'Voyages', p. 69.   **40** Byrne, 'Punishment'. This is disputed by Jacqueline Borsje, 'Tragedie van Fergus'.   **41** *Collectio canonum* XLIV.8 (Wasserschleben, pp. 176–7). **42** Meyer, *Cáin Adamnáin*, pp. 24–5, 30–1. Meyer interestingly discussed examples in which the craft is not described as having a single hide, but a single oar (pp. 43–4).   **43** 'CIMBITH quasi cimba .i. on noi oensheiched' (Meyer, *Sanas Cormaic*, p. 21). Cf. Sidonius's use in a similar context of *myoparone*, also a Greek-derived word.

They all forthwith believed, and Macc Cuill believed, and at Patrick's behest he went on the sea in a coracle of [only] one hide.[44]

As we will see, the choice of a craft of one hide accentuates the peril of being on the ocean. The voyage is also most frequently made without oars or sail, so that where the victim may drift is truly in the hands of God.

The concept of penitential voyaging is not limited to this model of the placing of someone into the hands of God as a form of trial by ordeal. The idea of placing oneself in God's hands through an ocean voyage was an expression of *peregrinatio pro amore Dei* – the eremitical self-exile which constituted one of the fundamental expressions of the Irish monastic vocation.[45] The number of hides permitted in this case appears to have been greater, from which we may presume the degree of penance implied by an act of *peregrinatio* was less extreme than that required in a legal punishment.

In a famous episode in the *Anglo-Saxon Chronicle*, sub anno 891,

> Three Irishmen came to King Alfred in a boat without oars, having stolen away from Ireland for the love of God to go on pilgrimage, they cared not where. The boat was made of two-and-a-half-hides and they took with them sufficient that they might have food for seven nights; and they came to land in Cornwall after seven nights.[46]

These pilgrims are named for us by the chronicler and there can be no doubt that this is a historical episode.[47] In this case the figure given for the number of hides is 'two-and-a-half', which is the same in all recensions including the Latin.[48]

References in Irish 'voyage' narratives indicate that the number of hides from which a craft is made is a measure of the degree of peril in which the penitents place themselves. An episode in Adomnán's *Vita Columbae* presents a

---

44 'Rocreitset fóchetoir huli ocus rocreiti macc Cuill, ocus luid for muir hicurach oenseiched laforcongra Patraic', (Stokes, *Tripartite Life*, i.222–3). Cf. the 'nauim unius pellis' in Muirchú, *Vita* (Bieler, *Patrician Texts*, p. 104).   45 Charles-Edwards, 'Social Background'.
46 'Þrie Scottas comon to Ælfrede cyninge, on anum bate butan ælcum gereþrum of Hibernia, þonon hi hi bestælon forþon þe hi woldon for Godes lufan on elþiodignesse beon, hi ne rohton hwær. Se bat wæs geworht of þriddan hælfre hyde þe hi on foron, 7 hi namon mid him þæt hi hæfdun to seofon nihtum mete; 7 þa comon hie ymb vii niht to londe on Corn walum', *Anglo-Saxon Chronicle* s.a. 891 (Plummer and Earle, *Saxon Chronicles*, i.82).
47 See most recently Dumville, Review; Ireland, 'Some Analogues'. One feature which might give the reader pause, however, is the statement that the three exiles left in secret: this is strongly reminiscent of the formula, in Irish *immrama* and related texts, of the three supernumerary voyagers who travel without permission of their abbot. Nonetheless, the likelihood is that this is a real episode, whatever literary formulae might possibly have influenced its recording.   48 'In nauicula facta duobus coriis et dimidio' (Plummer and Earle, *Saxon Chronicles*, p. 83 n. 6).

good example of the nature of this peril. The *peregrinus* Cormac, while searching for a *desertum* in the ocean, was carried due north into an arctic region where he encountered *bestiolae* in the form of stinging beasts:

> While Cormac was labouring for the third time in the sea of Ocean, he came into dangers that nearly caused his death. When his ship, blown by the south wind, had driven with full sails in a straight course from land towards the region of the northern sky, for fourteen summer days and as many nights, such a voyage appeared to be beyond the range of human exploration, and one from which there could be no return. And so it happened, after the tenth hour of the fourteenth day, that there arose all around them almost overwhelming and very dreadful objects of terror; for they were met by loathsome and exceedingly dangerous small creatures covering the sea, such as had never been seen before that time; and these struck with terrible impact the bottom and sides, the stern and prow, with so strong a thrust that they were thought able to pierce and penetrate the skin-covering of the ship.[49]

The monks were rescued from their peril by their prayers and the *bestiolae* stopped short of fully penetrating the hide. Attempts have been made to associate these creatures with actual sea creatures – Tom Lethbridge's choice was Arctic mosquitoes![50] Jacqueline Borsje's explanation seems more sensible, however: they are one of the many varieties of mythical beasts of the sea, presenting differing forms of threat to the traveller, but in essence representing non-moral evil.[51] They extend a Classical and Patristic discourse in which Ocean is a perilous zone – as well as resonating with the experiences of Columba's namesake Jonah.

As Carney observed, the voyages of Cormac present the earliest example of a text which falls within the 'voyage' genre: the third being a voyage into a perilous, infernal zone, while the first is troubled by the presence of a traveller

---

49 'Cum idem Cormacus tertia in ociano mari fatigaretur uice, prope usque ad mortem periclitari coepit. Nam cum eius nauis a terrís per xiiii. aestei temporis dies totidemque noctes plenís uelís, austro flante uento, ad septemtrionalis plagam caeli directo excurreret cursu, eiusmodi nauigatio ultra humani excursus modum, et inremeabilis uidebatur. Vnde contigit, ut post decimam eiusdem quarti et decimi horam diei, quidam pene insustentabiles undique et ualde formidabiles consurgerent terrores. Quaedam quippe usque in id temporis inuisae mare obtegentes occurrerant tetrae et infestae nimis bestiolae, quae horribili impetu carinam et latera pupimque et proram ita forti feriebant percusura, ut pellicium tectum nauis penetrales putarentur penetrare posse' (Adomnán, VC II.42 [Anderson and Anderson, pp. 168–9]). 50 Lethbridge, *Herdsmen and Hermits*, p. 73. If they have any counterpart in actual geographical knowledge, it is more likely that they are some animation of Pytheas's *Mare Concretum*, in which e.g. Dicuil took considerable interest (*De mensura* VII.11–3 [Tierney, pp. 74–5]). 51 Borsje, *From Chaos to Enemy*, pp. 16off; see also Bray, 'Allegory'.

who has come without permission. The travellers in the third voyage are redeemed by their faith in face of peril – these are all genre features found in the *immrama* and the St Brendan dossier.[52] Cormac's voyages, however, are also most probably hagiographical representations of genuine voyages which were made from Iona – or which included Iona[53] – and which also provide data which occur in episodes in the *Nauigatio*, various *immrama*, and the *Liber de mensura orbis terrae* of the ninth-century geographer Dicuil. Whether the purpose of these voyages was principally for purposes of *peregrinatio* or experimental science – or, more probably, a combination of both – remains a matter for debate;[54] as indeed does the veracity of the different episodes which have been claimed to depict actual Atlantic or Arctic locations.[55] Without rehearsing these debates here, the fact that genuine voyages at least partially inspired Adomnán and the authors of the other voyage narratives requires us to consider whether these voyages were indeed conducted in hide-covered craft – whatever literary symbolism may also have become attached to the hide of such vessels.

Dicuil, who might be regarded as the soberest of the reporters of these voyages, describes a journey to islands north of Britain in a 'two-benched boat'.[56] The use of a taxonomy of benches to describe boats is found elsewhere in an Irish *milieu* where, for example, the *Senchus Fer nAlban* describes a warship as a 'seven-bencher'.[57] The latter is clearly a wooden craft, but there seems no reason to assume that the bench taxonomy is exclusive to wooden ships. A 'two-bencher' is probably a smaller vessel – though perhaps not proportionately, as a warship such as is described in the *Senchus* necessarily requires oarsmen for manoeuvrability as opposed to a sailing boat used for non-military purposes, which may only use oars when close inshore. A 'two-bencher' might very well be a hide-covered craft. Considering the evidence of the *Anglo-Saxon Chronicle*

---

52 Carney, Review.   53 Both St Brendan (of the Alltraige) and Cormac (of the Uí Líatháin) are most probably from south-west Ireland, and we should be careful not to assume that the voyages to such locations as the Orkneys, Faroes and Iceland were necessarily by monks of Iona, even if they are reported from there. The voyages of which Dicuil writes, for example, might be voyages from the south-west which simply visited Iona. Cormac's first voyage, for example, commenced from County Mayo (VC I.6 [Anderson and Anderson, pp. 30–1]). 54 See Ó Fiaich, 'Vergil's Irish Background'. For recent discussion of Dicuil's data see Bermann, 'Dicuils *De Mensura*'.   55 See Wooding, 'Monastic Voyaging'.   56 'Duorum nauicula transitorum' (Dicuil, *De mensura* VII.14 [Tierney, p. 74]).   57 For the term 'uii sese' see Bannerman, *Studies*, pp. 42, 59–60. Cf. 'sechtsesach', O'Davoren's Glossary §478 (Stokes, 'O'Davoren's Glossary', p. 272). John Carey, who has kindly advised me on a number of points with regard to this topic, has drawn my attention to a reference in *In Tenga Bithnúa* to the ability of an *óenses* ('single-bench boat') to penetrate a black poisonous sea in the north full of monsters (Stokes, 'Evernew Tongue', pp. 112–3). I would suggest that this is a reference to the same story as in the third voyage of Cormac and *Immram Curaig Úa Corra*. This seems to support an impression which I have had that the enumeration of either hides or benches in the order of one to three is in some cases synonymous in indicating a small craft used for penance. It is also possible, however, that *óenses* is a mishearing of *óenseiched* – they are certainly easily conflated by the ear.

for actual monastic voyages in hide-covered craft, we should admit the strong possibility that Dicuil is describing such a craft also, but without considering the material from which it is made a matter of interest to his audience.

Cormac's *nauis* has a *pellicium tectum*, but is not a *curuca*. Can we be sure then that it has a hide-covered hull, and not simply a leather cover – which is a possible alternative meaning of *tectum*?[58] The implication is that the *bestiolae* will sink the ship with their stings if they penetrate the hide, however, and the inescapable conclusion is that what is described here is a curragh.

Why then does Adomnán not use the term *curuca*, considering that he does so only three chapters further on? It is possible that he is incorporating into his narrative a 'voyage' tale which does not use this term. It is also possible that he understands a *curuca* as only a small craft. We should note here again, however, Adomnán's inconsistent use of marine terms. Adomnán's terminology may be varied here perhaps to highlight the hide from which the boat was made, which for narrative reasons was of central interest.

An incident which must be derived from Adomnán, or a common source, in the Irish *Immram Curaig Úa Corra* further articulates the conception of the peril presented to hide by the beasts of the sea. In this episode the travellers set out in a boat of three hides.[59] On a fiery sea they encounter beasts (*píasta*):

> 'That which we see is an abode of death', says one his brothers to the elder. The beasts (that lived in the sea) pierced through one of the two lower hides of the boat. 'Let that not trouble you', said the elder, 'God is able to save us though we be in (only) the one hide; and even though yon desire to destroy us, they cannot go against His will'.[60]

The boat is of a thickness of three hides, and the *píasta* reduce this thickness to two. To be on the sea in one hide is clearly the most extreme peril which confronts a penitent. Even in this case, however, the true penitent has nothing to fear, as the creatures of the sea must obey the Lord and the Lord is eternally vigilant.

This point is made most clearly in an image from the *Pseudo-Jerome Commentary on Mark*, to which Bischoff, in his 'Wendepunkte', ascribed an Irish authorship. On the basis of a manuscript list which names the author as *Cummeanus*, he suggested an Irishman by that name, perhaps Cummianus Albus of Iona, or Cummianus Longus (Cumméne Fota) of Clonfert – though this has been a controversial matter.[61] Michael Cahill, the *Commentary*'s most

---

58 Indeed, *tectum* is cognate with English 'deck'. 59 *Immram Curaig Úa Corra*, cap. 33 (Stokes, 'Húi Corra', pp. 38–9). 60 '"Is adba ega an ni atciam" ar an brathair frisin sruith. Ro-treaghdsat na piasta indara choduil inichtaracha don churach. "Na tabrad a snímh sibsi sin", ar in sruith. "As tualuing Dia ar n-anacul gidh isin aen choduil bem", ar se, "ocus masedh as áil do ar n-oided léo sút ní fettar toidhecht anagaid a thoili"' (*Immram Curaig Úa Corra*, cap. 66 [Stokes, 'Húi Corra', pp. 54–5]). 61 Gorman, 'Critique', esp. pp. 180–1.

recent editor, has cast doubt on its Irish authorship, though Maura Walsh and
Dáibhí Ó Cróinín, and most recently David Howlett, have argued strongly for
its authorship by Cumméne Fota[62] – the latter, however, basing his opinion on
a controversial method of textual criticism upon which the jury is still out. It
will be argued here, however, on the strength of Pseudo-Jerome's description of
hide-covered craft, which Bischoff regarded as one of its stronger claims to
authorship in an Irish *milieu*,[63] that authorship in a strongly Irish *milieu* is
unquestionable.

Mark 4.38 shows Christ, while crossing the Sea of Galilee, asleep in his boat:

> AND HE WAS IN THE STERN, ASLEEP ON THE CUSHION– The ship made of
> dead skins, contains living beings. It holds off the waves and is strength-
> ened with wood, that is to say, the church is saved by the cross and death
> of the Lord. The cushion represents the body of the Lord, on which
> divinity was bowed down like the head. The ship is the church at its
> beginning when Jesus sleeps in a bodily sense, because 'he never sleeps
> who guards Israel'. He rebukes the wind and the sea that it may be quiet.
> Concerning this, it is said, 'You control the might of the sea etc.'. The
> wind and the sea are the demons and the persecutors.[64]

As in the episodes in *Vita Columbae* and *Immram Curaig Úa Corra*, the sea is
the theatre for the manifestation of evil which will endanger the traveller –
though, on account of the demons, here moral rather than non-moral evil.
Unlike the travellers in the 'voyage' narratives, however, Christ has no need to
pray to God or an intercessory figure, and so the sea simply becomes calm at his
command.[65] This motif is more than simply that of Christ calming the waves –
which is found frequently in early medieval texts.[66] The wind and sea are not

---

62 Walsh and Ó Cróinín, *Cummian's Letter*, pp. 217–21; Howlett, 'Seven Studies', pp. 36–40.
63 Bischoff, 'Wendepunkte', pp. 199–200; his discussion of the boat motif is best consulted
in the revised translation 'Turning-Points', pp. 81–2. The importance of the boat motif to
Bischoff's ascription appears to have been mostly passed over by his critics (with the
exception of Coccia: see below). Michael Cahill has only now taken this matter up in the
introduction to his edition of the commentary. His discussion only appeared after this paper
was written, but I hope shortly in another paper to return to this question in the context of
the 'Wendepunkte'.   64 'ET ERAT IPSE IN PUPPI SUPER CERUICAL DORMIENS. Puppis mortuis
pellibus uiuos continet et fluctus arcet et ligno solidatur. Id est cruce et morte Domini
ecclesia saluatur. Ceruical corpus Domini est; cui diuinitas sicut caput inclinata est. Puppis
initium ecclesiae est, cum quo Dominus corporaliter dormit. Quia numquam "dormitet" qui
"custodit Israhel". Comminatur uento et mari ut taceat. De quo dicitur, "Tu dominaris
potestati maris", et reliqua. Uentus et mare daemones et persecutores sunt' (Cahill, *Expositio
Evangelii*, pp. 27–8; idem, *First Commentary*, pp. 52–3). I would like to thank Michael Cahill
for kindly allowing me to use his edition and translation in advance of publication.   65 This
episode has also been proposed by Peter Harbison as the subject of the boat motif on the
Kilnaruane Pillar (Harbison, *High Crosses*, i.254–5).   66 E.g. Adomnán, VC II.12–3
(Anderson and Anderson, pp. 110–3).

literally animate in this case. This is parallelled elsewhere in Adomnán, where the *magus* Broichan conjures the winds and waves to attack the saint:

> It is not strange that, with God's permission, these things can at times be done by the art of demons, so that even winds and waves can be roused to violence. Thus did hosts of evil spirits once attack the holy bishop Germanus in the midst of the sea, when he was sailing from the bay of Gaul to Britain, in the cause of man's salvation. They put perils in his way, and stirred up storms; they covered sky and daylight with a mist of darkness. But more quickly than speech, at the prayer of St Germanus all these things were calmed, and ceased.[67]

The forces and the beasts of the sea are all dangers which may be stirred up either by the mere presence of the travellers or by moral agency. The spiritual cargo of the ship is thinly separated from them by a prophylactic hide. Some of these dangers threaten the hide itself. As we will see below, however, the hide is only a metaphor for our mortality. The real protection is faith.

In Bischoff's thinking, an Irish author would regard a boat as being normally made of hide; therefore the hide boat is a circumstantial clue to the nationality of its author. In the face of the foregoing analysis this argument is unsustainable.[68] In fact the context is far more specific: this is a commentary by an author who is utilising the specific discourse concerning the voyage of a hide boat upon the living sea. The idea that voyaging in such a craft might be a perilous act could just possibly be derived from ancient sources by a non-Irish author. Here, however, the context is a more developed discourse in which the hide craft travels in a living sea, blown by winds, both of which must obey the will of God. The only parallels for this motif are those passages from Adomnán and the *Immram Curaig Úa Corra* cited above. It would appear safe to assume that it is uniquely Irish.

The number of the hides being a measure of the prophylactic qualities of the craft may not, however, be necessarily the basis of any real practice of penitential voyaging. The idea that the beasts of the sea pose a threat to the hide itself is only found in the *Vita Columbae* episode and the related passage in *Immram Curaig Úa Corra* – though it undoubtedly has a resonance with Avienus's motif of the 'monster-filled Ocean' being navigated in a hide. Hornell

---

67 'Nec mirum haec interdum arte daemonum posse fieri, deo permittente, ut etiam uenti et equora in asperius concitentur. Síc enim aliquando daemoniorum legiones sancto Germano episcopo de sinu gallico causa humanae salutis ad Brittanniam nauiganti medio in equore occurrerant, et oponentes pericula procellas concitabant; caelum diemque tenebrarum caligine obducebant. Quae tamen omnia sancto orante Germano dicto citius sedata detersa cessarunt caligine' (VC II.34 [Anderson and Anderson, pp. 144–5]). I would like to thank Jacqueline Borsje for drawing this passage to my attention.   68 This too was the view of Edmondo Coccia, who argued that the hide boat was not exclusively Irish ('Cultura irlandese', pp. 343–5).

estimated the dimensions of a 'hide' to be in the vicinity of around six feet by four feet – sufficient to make a coracle.[69] The voyage in such a vessel of only one hide *in size* might be sufficiently perilous to account for the original conception of the legal punishment. Two-and-a-half or three hides, the size used in the monastic voyages and *immrama*, would be a craft capable of carrying 3–4 persons. Two-and-a-half does not make sense as a measure of thickness, nor is any hide craft still made elsewhere in the world ever more than one hide thick – excluding doubled strips of hide as strengtheners or skids.[70] We should note here that *Immram Curaig Úa Corra* is the latest in date of the *immrama*,[71] and we may suspect that it has made a unique interpretation of a taxonomy usually used to distinguish hide-craft by size to develop further the image which it borrows from an earlier source.[72]

This leads us to contemplate the complex development of literary, legal and monastic imagery which interacts with actual traditions of boat-building. The Classical and Patristic discourse of sailing the sea in a hide may have influenced the formulation of an actual legal penalty using native craft of one hide; a complementary penitential monastic expression also evolved using larger versions of the same craft, 2–3 hides or more in size. This mixture of literary representation and actual penitential activity, along with the potentially wide range of iconographic motifs which could be derived from a vessel made of once-living hide, saw this type of vessel adopted into increasingly complex literary discourses. It became central to the interaction between pilgrims and the living sea in the *immram* tradition and the related texts of the St Brendan dossier.

The image of the human traveller perilously navigating the ocean in a hide obviously lent itself to imagery of more than simply oceanic peril. Dead hide is seen as a metaphor for mortality in literary and visual iconography from Patristic through to late medieval times, where Adam is depicted as clothed in dead flesh as a symbol of man's mortality.[73] The Pseudo-Jerome commentary makes a connection between the hide of a boat and mortal flesh in Book I.17:

> We are to loathe the boat of our former way of life. Indeed, Adam, our father according to the flesh, is clothed with dead skins. We now lay aside the old man with his actions, and seek to be a new man. We are clothed in the skins of Solomon, of which the bride boasts of having become as beautiful.[74]

69 Hornell, 'Curraghs of Ireland', p. 78.   70 Ibid.   71 See Mac Mathúna, 'Structure and Transmission'; specific discussion of the sea beasts on p. 335.   72 Probably from *Immram Curaig Maíle Dúin*, of which it is highly derivative: cf. Stokes, 'Mael Duin', pp. 458–9, where the vessel is also of three hides.   73 Jennifer O'Reilly, personal communication.   74 'Nauem pristinae conuersationis abominantes. Pellibus enim mortuis tegitur Adam qui est genitor noster secundum carnem. Et nunc deposito uetere homine "cum actibus suis", nouum sequentes hominem, "pellibus" tegimur "Salomonis", quibus sponsa gloriatur se factam esse "formosam" (*Expositio Evangelii* I.17 [Cahill, p. 15]; cf. idem, *First Commentary*, p. 37).

In the *Vita Brendani* St Brendan, after fruitlessly seeking to enter the Paradise of the Saints, is told by St Ita,

> 'As a passenger in the hides of dead animals you will not attain the land promised to you. You will attain it, however, in a boat made of planks'.[75]

He then finds himself required to build a boat of wood, which successfully takes him to his destination. It is possible that the wooden craft symbolises the cross, which is our redemption, though it is also possible that the absence of mortal flesh was sufficient.[76]

It is evident that from an early date the hide-covered craft – whether initially for reasons of simple availability, or as a penitential formula – was seen as a natural vehicle for voyages of *peregrinatio*. In this episode, however, while the hide boat will carry Brendan safely through the living sea on his *peregrinatio*, it is anathema to the environment of the Promised Land which he wishes to enter. The disentangling of this question may have implications for our understanding of the development of the *immram*/saints' voyage genre. In amongst various episodes, the monastic literary voyages for the most part ultimately take their participants into an infernal zone[77] – in the words of the brother in the *Immram Curaig Úa Corra*, 'an abode of death'.[78] This is the ultimate episode in the voyage of Cormac, and comes close to the conclusion of the *Nauigatio*. In this zone the pilgrim is subjected to the ultimate test of faith. The experience is still one of a transient encounter with an ever-present evil. The journey to a Christian otherworld, however, adds an eschatological dimension to this formula. The entry into this land becomes more than simply a matter of attainment through progressive development of the pilgrim's faith, but is a matter of the inherent otherworldliness of the saint. The sailing in a boat of hide carries with it the constant image of mortality, which St Brendan must shake off.[79]

The role of the rich image of the hide-covered craft is thus not constant, but evolves as part of a developing literature of monastic voyaging. In the context of these various literary representations which put hide-covered craft at the centre of complex penitential, allegorical and eschatological narrative discourses, these craft cannot be regarded as an incidental feature of representation in hagiography. The hide-covered craft was evidently used for ocean voyaging, but

---

75 'Mortuorum pellibus animalium uectus, promissam non adipisceris terram. Inuenies autem, facta de tabulis naue', *Vita altera S. Brendani* (*Salmanticensis*) cap. 10 (Heist, *Vitae*, p. 328). Cf. *Vita prima Sancti Brendani* (*Oxoniensis*), cap. 71 (Plummer, *Vitae*, i.136), also *Betha Brennain Clúana Ferta*, cap. 92 (Plummer, *Bethada*, i.64). 76 This, for example, may explain the case of St Ailbe who, in the *Salmanticensis* version of his *vita*, is depicted as travelling in a hideless coracle. *Vita Albei*, cap. 4 (Heist, p. 119). 77 See Borsje, *Chaos to Enemy*, p. 164. 78 See especially Esposito, 'Apocryphal Book', and Dumville, 'Two Approaches'.

this reality became integrated with literary models in which it was the ubiquitous vessel for penance and exile. The increasing centrality of the curragh to narratives of the travels of the *peregrini* is for this reason of vital importance to our understanding of the evolution of the 'voyage' tales. In these, as in the case of Pseudo-Jerome's commentary, the craft themselves are details which are integral, not incidental, to the formulae presented.

79 The particular episode of the transition to a wooden craft is not found in the *Nauigatio*. The *Nauigatio*'s account of Brendan's refusal of meat may, however, be an exploration of the same motif along slightly different lines: *Nauigatio*, cap. 16 (Selmer, p. 48).

Irish Saints in Brittany: Myth or Reality?

Gwenaël Le Duc

As everybody knows, Ireland has exported saints and scholars to Continental Europe for centuries, even if saints seem less numerous nowadays. To many people it has evidently seemed that Brittany was a favourite destination, not only because it is close, but also because it supposedly shared with Ireland a 'Common Celtic culture'. In fact, it seems to me that most of the Irish saints who came to the Continent had little interest in Brittany.

Nevertheless, the belief exists; the reasons for this are numerous, and can best be analysed by psychologists and sociologists. The fact is that the number of Irish saints in Brittany has been grossly exaggerated, without regard for history, documentation, philology, or even common sense. Dishonesty has at times played a role in these claims, but often mere fancy has been responsible.

When I tackled this subject, I wished first to list all the saints who were said to be Irish and to arrange them severally, scientifically, and reasonably. But the task soon got out of hand: I think that I could list nearly 8,000 Irish saints, if I had the courage. How's that?

Toward 400 AD there was stationed near Brest a Roman legion (that is, 6666 men: *sex milia sex centum sexaginta sex uiri*), who became 7777 martyrs (more precisely 7847: *seizh mil, seizh kant, seizh ugent ha seizh*). It seems that it is only in the course of this century – in the past ten years, in fact – that they became Irish.[1] Perhaps they did not even exist: in any case they were not Christians, they were not martyrs, and they were not Irish.

This is only one of the most glaring examples of the problem with which we are confronted. Just because it 'looks nicer' on pamphlets for tourists, or for other reasons, many saints in Brittany are, or were, or will be said to be Irish. It is a recurrent fashion, and does not belong only to the past. Such claims were made in the eleventh and twelfth, in the seventeenth, in the nineteenth, and in the twentieth centuries. They will certainly be made again.[2]

---

1 Pain, 'Actualisation des sources', p. 23 n. 93. 2 To refute such ideas is the same as saying that Galician is not a Celtic language, or that Saint Patrick was not a druid: it has, and will have, to be done again and again. Some time after I gave this lecture, a student showed me a

At the outset, it will perhaps be useful to define what I mean by an Irish saint in Brittany. Very simply, I mean someone born in Ireland, the child of people also born on the island, who came to Brittany.

I have excluded travellers who went to Ireland and then came or went back to Brittany. I also exclude Irish saints who are merely honoured in Brittany, like St Fiacre[3] or St Osmanne,[4] because they never set foot in Brittany. I have retained three Irish saints who supposedly came to Brittany, even if they did not die there.

I have excluded students, as they rather concern the history of relationships between Ireland and Brittany, and have already been studied elsewhere.[5]

I have limited my study to saints: that is, to those who were or are called 'saint', whatever the reason. No questions asked.

Finally, I have neglected saints who have nothing going for them: someone said that they were Irish,[6] but all that we have is a dedication to a saint with a Breton name. Indeed, if we ask why such and such a saint is said to be Irish, at times the only available answer is: Why not? This is no answer, and such cases are best left alone.

I have limited myself, therefore, to those saints who are said to be Irish by some authoritative source: a medieval text when we have one; Albert Le Grand in the seventeenth century, who is sometimes the first to state that a certain saint was Irish;[7] then Colgan;[8] then Loth;[9] and eventually Kenney.[10] I have also deliberately omitted St Briac and St Fingar (and therefore also St Piala and St Ia), who are discussed by my colleagues André-Yves Bourgès and Karen Jankulak elsewhere in this volume.

If these Irish saints are so numerous, they must be categorised scientifically. In some cases this can be done readily enough, but others will require closer scrutiny.

We must of course check the basis for any claim of Irish origin. Very often, it proves to be a late assertion, secondary in the text which contains it, and going back to that text's source solves the problem. Quite often, it is a case of confusion or assimilation. Nowadays, we distinguish between Wales, Cornwall, England, and Ireland; but these distinctions have not always been observed. In Breton saints' Lives of the nineteenth century, saints in Brittany are usually made to come from England, even St Andrew – and this even at the time when England was considered to be a pagan country.[11]

'typical' Breton saint's life which she had forged herself. S. Macrulus may not have existed last year, but he was Irish.   3 Kenney, *Sources*, p. 493 (nr 283).   4 Pain, 'Actualisation des sources', pp. 221–7; Duine, *Mémento*, nr 86; BHL pp. 918–9, *Supplementum*, p. 240; Lobineau, *Vies des saints*, p. 40; Duine, *Bréviaires et missels*, pp. 9, 174; Kenney, *Sources*, pp. 181–2 (nr 38); Lapidge and Sharpe, *Bibliography*, nr 947.   5 'Bretons et Irlandais'; see also Laurent and Davis, *Irlande et Bretagne*.   6 I refer in particular to de Garaby, *Vies*, and to the rightly anonymous *Dictionnaire des saints bretons*, *passim*.   7 Le Grand, *Vies des saints*. 8 Colgan, *Acta sanctorum*.   9 J. Loth, *Noms de saints*.   10 Kenney, *Sources*.   11 Even when I was young, Huguenots and English were looked upon as pagans – since they were not

At any rate, we seldom have ancient sources, even untrustworthy ones. Often, the oldest document that we have is the French text redacted by Albert Le Grand, published in 1637. Usually, such texts are in fact hardly better than nothing.

Therefore, the first test possible, and the most necessary one, is the saint's name. Is it Irish or not? In several cases we have good Brittonic names, or Latin ones. When we have what look like Irish names we are luckier, but also likelier to go astray. It must be admitted that some Irish names could in theory have been adapted to Brittonic, but in practice this seems never to be the case: even in cases of assimilation or confusion, the various forms are kept together, as if it were more glorious for a saint to have several names. In the Life of St Malo, after all, St Brendan is said to be Welsh, even though the stories told about him seem to have originated in Kerry.[12] The name was not modified. St Columban's name is not modified either.

Once the tree has been shaken, there are not many apples still hanging from the branch, and it is not easy to devise a single simple method for dealing with them: each case is peculiar, but there are not that many of them.

Finally, I have restricted the scope of this inquiry in order to keep it within reasonable limits. To my regret, this has kept me from getting to the heart of the matter. Some confusions must be of Cornish origin, while others perhaps derive from Glastonbury; but this is another subject.

IRISH SAINTS WHO CAME TO BRITTANY AS TRAVELLERS AND DID NOT STAY

St Patrick

It may well be that St Patrick landed in Brittany, after sailing from Ireland for a day and a night. At all events, he left after twenty-eight days.[13] He was not even a priest at the time, let alone a saint.

Later, he was to be known and honoured, and his writings were to be known, and also works ascribed to him. The background of his cult in Brittany is not very clear, but it is unlikely to depend upon his visit. More probably, his cult spread because of his authority among monks. There used to be relics, but the evidence is so old and vague that I cannot tell whether the existence of these relics was the cause or consequence of the cult.

St Columban

St Columban also came to Brittany,[14] but only as a traveller, who had not come to stay. He must have landed at one point near Saint-Malo,[15] and we know that

Catholics. 12 Le Duc, 'Bretagne, intermédiaire'. 13 Galliou, *L'Armorique romaine*, p. 277; Kurzawa, *Petite vie*, pp. 68–9. 14 Jonas, *Vita Sancti Columbani*, I.4–5; *Sancti Columbani opera*, p. xix. 15 Merdrignac, 'Bretons et Irlandais', pp. 123–4, 133.

he experienced a shipwreck in an unknown places on the shores of Brittany.[16] In the latter case, it is evident that Brittany was not his goal: like many others, he expected to follow the coast before crossing the Channel, without any intention of landing except at Nantes.[17] He must not have been the only one to land in Brittany in this way.

It must be noted that he recruited several companions in Brittany, probably near Nantes. An incidental problem is posed by the circumstance of the monastery of Bobbio's owning salt marshes near Venice: a vexing puzzle, as early documents are lacking to explain the sharing of the techniques and vocabulary of salt production near Guérande and near Venice. It may well be that the twelve Bretons who accompanied Columban to Nantes were not only Christians, but also people with some knowledge of salt production.[18]

He might also have recruited Bretons near Saint-Malo, as Malo himself is said in his Life to have spent some time in Luxeuil.[19] But this may only reflect obedience to Columban's rule: as such, it would be no more than a marginal instance of Irish influence in northern Gaul in the fifth and sixth centuries – which is another subject.

St Brendan

Here the story is rather detailed than complicated; the implications of the evidence can be summarised fairly easily. According to his legend,[20] St Malo was the pupil of St Brendan, abbot in Llancarfan. It is clear that a legend of Irish origin – more precisely, of Kerry origin – was drawn upon here.[21] The text does not, however, say that Brendan came to Brittany. It is the Middle Irish version of the Life which states that he founded the city of Bleit, apparently in fact Alet; but this is probably inspired by the Life of St Malo.[22]

It is however quite probable that St Brendan acquired a cult near Saint-Malo in the ninth century.[23] Later, he was to replace St Brevalaire/Broladre/ Branwaladr, who was not Irish, but who was identified with St Brendan.[24]

IRISH SAINTS WHO CAME TO BRITTANY AND STAYED

St Budoc

Here we are in fact dealing with two or three characters with the same name.

16 Jonas, *Vita Sancti Columbani*, I.23; Walker, *Sancti Columbani opera*, pp. xxvii, xxxviii.   17 Le Duc, 'Bretagne, intermédiaire'; cf. Gougaud, 'Point obscur'.   18 Buron, 'Origine des marais', pp. 51–2.   19 *Vita Sancti Machutis* §46 (Le Duc, p. 131).   20 Ibid.   21 Merdrignac, *Vies des saints*; cf. Gw. Le Duc, 'Bretagne, intermédiaire', p. 184.   22 *Vita Sancti Machutis* §59 (Le Duc, pp. 185–6).   23 This is hinted at in the life of S. Malo, in which St Brendan bows to his pupil, or is rebuked by him: *Vita Sancti Machutis* §§12, 13, 16, 19, 23, 26.   24 Duine, *Mémento*, nr 99;

The first St Budoc: According to his legend he was born in a barrel and landed in Ireland, became an abbot, then fled and surfed back to Brittany on his sleeping-stone to live as a hermit; he later became bishop of Dol.[25]

In a way, he was Irish, but only barely. His name is Brittonic, he is of Breton descent. I do not think that it is legitimate to say that he was an Irish saint: his Life does not make this claim.

In fact, we may be dealing once again with two or three characters who have been brought together to form a nicer legend.

All of this affords good material for reflection, because it presents coincidences; but it is not evidence. We cannot say that this Budoc was Irish: he was never said to be.

Another figure with this name was St Gwennole's master on the island of Lavret.[26] Since Gwennole was 'a disciple of St Patrick',[27] it would seem logical that his master Budoc should be called Irish, out of generosity – but this is nowhere stated.

According to Leland, who quotes an otherwise unattested Cornish tradition, 'Budoc was an Irischman, and cam into Cornewalle, and ther dwellid'.[28] This could refer to yet another, third figure, but might explain the confusion.

St Castus

St Castus was said to be of Irish origin.[29]

The name is not even Celtic. We have no documents concerning him, and those which are said to have existed were not held in high esteem.[30] We can suppose that his Latin name points to a Breton origin, but there is no hope of getting any further than that. He was Irish because nothing was known about him – if he existed at all.

St Commeanus

This saint was a bishop of Vannes whose name is clearly Irish, not Brittonic. He was unknown to Le Grand, and also apparently to Colgan.

He is known from a list compiled probably in the twelfth century, at the beginning of the *Cartulary of Quimperlé*,[31] which we have reason to believe was

---

idem, *Bréviaires et missels*, pp. 73, 79, 227; Loth, *Noms des saints*; de Garaby, *Vies*, p. 552 (16 mai); Orme, *Roscarrock's Lives*, pp. 118–9; Lapidge and Sharpe, *Bibliography*, nrs 362, 385, 412, 441, 476; Doble, *Saints of Cornwall*, iv. 11–127.   **25** The Latin text is still unpublished, but the legend is available in French: Le Grand, *Vies des saints*, pp. 623ff. Le Grand also published this text separately in a rare book, *Providence de Dieu*. See further de Barthélemy, 'Légende de S. Budoc', and Le Menn, *Femme au sein d'or*.   **26** Simon, *Abbaye de Landévennec*, p. 39; *Vita Winwaloei*, I.19 (Latouche, 'Vie de S. Guénolé').   **27** *Vita Winwaloei*, I.23 (Latouche, 'Vie de S. Guénolé'). Cf. Duine, *Mémento*, p. 43 n. 5; Merdrignac, 'Bretons et Irlandais', p. 125.   **28** As cited by Orme, *Roscarrock's Lives*, p. 121.   **29** Duine, *Mémento*, pp. 94–5, nr 78.   **30** Ibid.   **31** Maître and de Berthou, *Cartulaire*, pp. 86–7. J.-M. Le Mené, however, indulgently ignores him (*Histoire*).

one of the numerous more or less clumsy forgeries which accompanied the creation of the abbey.[32] The catalogue as a whole is too short for some five centuries, what it says about the first bishop is certainly wrong, and the rest cannot be checked (though it is noteworthy that some names are doubled). In brief, the list is useless and unsupported – not even a decent forgery.

The problem however is that it incorporates an Irish name, St Commeanus. Although he is said to be a saint, he has no cult, appears nowhere in the calendar, and appears to have no site dedicated to him. We have, in fact, no reason to consider him a historical figure, no reason to think that he ever existed. This may be the oldest instance of a fabricated Irish saint; but it seems strange that the fabrication should be supported by what appears to be an authentic Irish name.

None of the Irish Cummeans known to me was a bishop, or had a connection with Vannes, or with a place which could have been confused with Vannes.

There is still the question why and how this Irish name was taken up. If we take it that this happened in good faith, the only possibility might be Cumméne Fota or Cummianus Longus. He composed a penitential using texts of Breton origin; but there is no known Breton manuscript of this work, and no reason to think that it was known in Brittany.[33] We must look for another solution.

If we are open to the possibility of deliberate fabrication, we can consider the possibility that the name was imported by someone who lived in the abbey of Quimperlé. This man, Iuthael filius Aidan, had a Brittonic name; but his father's name was clearly Irish.[34] Moreover, it is he who provided the genealogy of St Gunthiern at the beginning of the *Life of St Gunthiern*, composed together with the Life of St Ninnoc in the course of the eleventh century – quite probably to give more authority and venerability to the collection of forged charters which follows. (The genealogy is in fact Vortigern's, drawn from or inspired by *Historia Brittonum*.)

We know nothing about Commeanus or his Life. He appears in a list drafted or forged in the eleventh century, a document which is not even coherent. He probably never existed.

St Meldroc or Meldeoc

The same list contains another name which might be Irish. The form in the list is Meldrocus, identified with a St Meldeoc,[35] a saint who actually had a cult as he appears in the 1530 Vannes calendar.[36] As Loth has noted, Meldeoc might be an Irish name.[37] There seem to be two possibilities. Perhaps the name was

32 Guillotel, 'Sainte-Croix de Quimperlé'.   33 Bieler, *Irish Penitentials*, pp. 5–7, 108–35.
34 Maître and de Berthou, *Cartulaire*, p. 42; Uhlich, *Morphologie*, pp. 145–6, cf. p. 125.
35 Le Mené, *Histoire*, pp. 130–1.   36 26 June: S. *Meldoci episcopi Venetensis*.   37 Loth, *Noms des saints*, p. 91. He cites '*Felire Oengus*, fête le 11 Décembre'; cf. Stokes, *Félire Óengusso*, pp. 251, 258–9.

picked up at random, and no such saint ever existed. Or else he was an Irish saint who came to Brittany, lived as a hermit, died, and was held to be a saint, his name being eventually used in forging a list of bishops. The existence of a cult might support the latter possibility. Unfortunately (but of course) I have no legend for him.

I could not directly check the reading *Meldrocus*, as my microfilm is poor, but I find it suspect. I hope that it is not a misreading or a misprint, or indeed an interpretation. With regard to the third of these possibilities, the printed form might have been guided by a false hypothesis: Canon Le Mené thought (wrongly) that he was the eponym of Locmeltro – *Locmeltnou* in 1435.[38] If there existed a St Meldroc/Meldeoc/Meldoc, he has left no other trace; and we are not even sure that we are dealing with a single character.

Both Commeanus and Meldeoc have Irish names, but nothing in fact proves that they existed, and we have excellent reasons to believe that they were invented. In any case, no one knows anything about them.

St Efflam[39]

The Life of St Efflam states that he was born into a royal Irish family but despised worldly honours; even though he had just been married, he left Ireland secretly to land in Brittany. His wife Enora searched for him for a long time, before they were reunited and lived together in chastity. The themes of the 'pagan father' and 'exile to preserve chastity' occur in other Lives, casting strong doubts on the historicity of this story.

The name is not Irish, and can be readily explained as Brittonic *Eu-flam*,[40] 'good flame'. His wife Enora's name is not Irish either. We may note also that he fights a dragon which Arthur (not King Arthur, but a mere warrior) is unable to defeat. This would point to Wales or Cornwall, not to Ireland, as the story's probable place of origin.

The historical existence of an individual with this name is confirmed by his presence in two calendars (Tréguier and Vannes). But there is nothing apart from the Life which clearly and unambiguously confirms that he was Irish.

We have excellent reasons not to believe anything of what is said in the Life, and there is nothing else to indicate that he was Irish. Oral tradition also offers no help in this regard.[41] He might have been said to be Irish because nothing was known about him or his origins, or perhaps simply because such was the trend at the time.

---

38 Vallerie, *Diazezoù*, ii.105. The actual reading in the seventeenth-century edition is *Locmeltuou*.   39 Lapidge and Sharpe, *Bibliography*, nr 913; Duine, *Mémento*, p. 89, nr 67; Kenney, *Sources*, nr 38. De la Borderie, 'Saint Efflam'; cf. Le Grand, *Vies des saints*, pp. 82–8.   40 The form is *Euflamus* in ms. B.N. lat. 1148, *Legenda sanctorum Britanniae ad usum ecclesie Trecorensis*, s. XV, ff. 86–8. The letter groups -*uu*-, -*ff*-, -*uf*-, -*fu*- alternate freely in Middle-Breton spelling.   41 Cf. *Kannën neue*; *Buez sant Efflam*; Le Braz, 'Gwerz sant Efflamm', in 'Saints bretons', pp. 184–8. The influence of Le Grand's telling is however more than

It may be worth mentioning one further consideration, which may however be mere coincidence. The popular oral version of the story is preserved in *Gwerz Honora*, which was collected in the nineteenth century and subsequently: this appears to bring together elements from the Life of Efflamm and Honora on the one hand, and the legend of SS Azenora and Budoc, already mentioned, on the other.[42] The lack of agreement between oral vernacular tradition (which ignores Ireland) and learned Latin tradition provides us with another reason for suspecting that the latter invented Efflamm's 'Irishness'.

St Feock[43]

This saint is mentioned by Kenney, who for once gives a vague reference: 'Le Grand, *op. cit.*':[44] most annoying. He is the eponym of Feock in Cornwall. In fact, Le Grand does not seem to mention him: Kenney was in error in giving the impression that he was a Breton saint.[45] The corresponding form in Brittany, as M. Bourgès kindly reminds me, is *Mieuc, Maeoc*:[46] but the saint of this name is never said to have been Irish, and was not, like the Cornish saint, a lady.[47] A form in *f-* may be reflected in the Breton place name *Liffiac* (in Trégomeur).[48]

The name could in any case be Brittonic *Miocus*. We have the place names Plumieux and Saint-Mieu. I have no reason to propose an Irish origin for this saint. We have no Life.

Kenney made a mistake: that is all.

St Jaoua, bishop of Léon[49]

This is a tangle.

We have no Latin Life for this saint, apart from what is contained in the Life of St Pol.[50] According to Le Grand, he was Irish, uncle of St Tinidor, who was the father of St Tenenan.[51] His mother was St Pol's mother's sister. Called back to Ireland by his mother, he heard of St Pol's coming to Brittany and sailed over to join him.[52]

This does not agree with what we find in the Life of St Pol, nor with what Le Grand said of St Tenenan.[53] The sources are a breviary, now lost, and a

probable.   **42** The texts have been brought together by Le Menn, *Femme au sein d'or*, pp. 9–20; bibliography p. 145.   **43** Doble, *Saints of Cornwall*, iii.53–6.   **44** Kenney, *Sources*, p. 181, nr 38 (6).   **45** Perhaps quoted by Doble, who gives Irish *Fiacc* as an equivalent. **46** I thank him for this useful remark.   **47** 'I am not even sure whether S. Feock was a man or a woman', writes Canon Doble, noting that in the Middle Ages the saint was *sancta Feoca*, but was later represented as a man.   **48** But a saint's name would not appear in such a compound. I merely repeat this suggestion from the *Dictionnaire des saints bretons*, in which a saint is often created from a place name.   **49** Le Grand, *Vies des saints*, p. 102 (2 mars); Duine, *Mémento*, nr 48; idem, *Bréviaires et missels*, pp. 165, 167, 228; AASS Mart. I, p. 139; Loth, *Noms des saints*, p. 134; de Garaby, *Vies*, pp. 77–9; Tanguy and Daniel, *Sur les pas*; in particular, an Irien, 'Le culte', esp. pp. 98–9.   **50** A new edition by Fr. Kerlouégan is forthcoming. For the moment, we can refer to the edition by Cuissard, 'Vie de S. Paul', pp. 39–40.   **51** Le Grand, *Vies des saints*, pp. 52, 307.   **52** Ibid., p. 52.   **53** Ibid., pp. 307 sqq.

document compiled by Le Grand's great-uncle, who apparently never existed.[54] Why Jaoua is called an Irishman is by no means evident; but since he is said to be the uncle of Tinidor, who is Tenenan's father or Tenenan himself, this might have been enough to prompt Le Grand to make him an Irishman.

As for his name, the oldest form that we have is *Iahoueius*,[55] and he has been assimilated to St *Jaouenn*, whose name derives from Latin *Iouinus* (*Jouan* in French). On his grave, the form is St *Ioevin*.[56] I have no explanation for the name, which seems however to be Brittonic, as there is a very similar name in Welsh.[57]

St Tadec[58]

In the Life of St Jaoua we are told how Judulus, abbot of Landévennec, and Tadecq, another abbot, were killed by a local tyrant.[59] As Colgan had no other version of the Life of St Jaoua, he translated Le Grand's French into Latin.[60] In his notes Tadecq became Thadecus; and he added a note concerning St Taidecus, thus making the name Irish. He was obliged however to admit that Taidecus must have been someone else.[61]

The Irish origin of both saints is improbable and contrived, despite its endorsement by Colgan.

St Ké / Kenan / Colledoc[62]

Loth listed him among saints who he thought might have been Irish.[63] His reason for doing so was clearly the Irish appearance of the form *Kenan*.

The saint constitutes a thorny case, however: even in Brittany he has several names which are not etymologically or logically related, suggesting that he represents a conflation of several saints. In the earliest surviving legend concerning him he has only two: Ké and Colledoc – 'and also Kenan', adds Le Grand. Later variants are more numerous.[64]

Le Grand presents a St Quay/Ké or Colledoc as a saint born in Britain; but he also gives him the name Kenan, without relating him in any way to Ireland. Ké had a companion named Kerian (Querrien). Le Grand might have used a text of Cornish origin; at any rate, the author of the Latin work on which he drew knew Cornwall well.

54 Ibid., p. 56; Lahellec, 'Albert Le Grand'. After a careful examination of his genealogy, it is clear that Albert Le Grand never had a great-uncle called Tanguy. 55 *S. Iahouie* (vocative) in the Salisbury litanies, Salisbury Cathedral MS 180, f. 171vb. 56 Le Grand, *Vies des saints*, p. 57 (anonymous annotation). P. Guigon, 'Les sites religieux', i.341, 357. The grave is probably not earlier than the fifteenth century. I examined the cenotaph, and did not see any name on it. 57 Evans and Rhŷs, *Book of Llan Dâv*, p. 229: *Iohiu*. 58 Le Grand, *Vies des saints*, pp. 54–5. 59 Ibid., p. 53 §iv. 60 Colgan, *Acta sanctorum*, pp. 441–4. 61 Ibid., p. 443a n. 5. 62 An Irien, *Saint Ké*. 63 Loth, *Émigration bretonne*, p. 64. Loth considered the form *Kenan* only. 64 S. Ké, Quay, To-Cai, Quenanus, Kenan, Colledoc, Collodocus, Caledoc, Kecoledoc, Collezoc, Colledan, Collodan, Querian, Kieran, Queran,

At what time St Ké was identified with a St Kenan I do not know, but it happened before Le Grand. We are dependent on his (perhaps free) French rendering; but references to Modred and King Arthur make it quite certain that the Latin Life postdated *Historia regum Britanniae*, and that Ké had been confused with King Arthur's steward Kay. There may have been some contact with St Fingar, as King Theuderic or Theoderic is mentioned in both Lives. There may be a clue in a note attached to the Life by the three canons, which mentions dedications to St Ké at the chapel of Coat-Kénan in Plouguerneau, and a Languénan.[65] Here 'Kenan' might reflect *kin, ken-* (> *ker*) 'nice, handsome, beautiful', a Breton adjective and not an Irish name. *Languénan* can in fact be identified as *Languenan* (Dol), which was *Langanano* in the twelfth century, *Languennen* in 1251. It might be this dedication which inspired the merging of the names.[66]

On the other hand, St Jaoua had a companion named Kenan (not, however, stated to be Irish).[67] The name is known in Irish, but can also be explained in terms of Old Breton; or it could reflect Welsh *Cynan*. Le Grand kept these characters separate.

When Colgan took up the Life of St Jaoua, he wrote a long note speculating on the identity of St Kenan. He proposed three candidates: a confessor honoured on 29 November, an abbot honoured on 25 February, and a bishop honoured on 24 November, said to have come to France. He eventually picked the third as being most likely. Colgan eventually associated him with the St Ké, or Kenan, nicknamed Colodoc (Caledoc), in this following Le Grand; and he identified Kerianus with St Kieran, honoured on the same day as St Kenan (24 November). It is Colgan who first made one character of St Jaoua's companion and St Ké.[68]

Let me attempt to clarify matters. St Kenan the companion of St Jaoua is a separate character. There is no reason to believe that he was Irish: this is only Colgan's conjecture.

I do not think that we can retain him or them. As already noted, the name is known in Ireland, but could be Brittonic. As far back as we can check, confusions and assimilations have been numerous and intricate, and it does not seem that any of the sources is reliable.

St Ké, nicknamed Colledoc, seems to have been identified with St Kenan relatively early: since no legend is attached to the latter in early sources, I think that it is only the finding of a 'similar name' in the calendar which inspired or justified the assimilation.

Later, Dom Lobineau made one character of Ké and Kerianus.[69] Then Father Tresvaux in his reprint of Dom Lobineau took the notes regarding

---

Querrien (*Dictionnaire de saints bretons*, pp. 223–6, 228).   **65** Le Grand, *Vies des saints*, p. 567.   **66** Vallerie, *Diazezoù*, ii.93.   **67** Le Grand, *Vies des saints*, p. 567.   **68** Colgan, *Acta sanctorum*, p. 443 n. 11.   **69** Lobineau, *Vies des saints*, p. 26.

Kenan from Colgan's version of the Life of Jaoua, and used these to rewrite the legend of St Ké.

Later still, several saints were merged, without having been consulted. This is how we come to have a single legend for a so-called Irish saint, named St Ké, Quay, To-Cai (?), Quenanus, Kenan, Colledoc, Collodocus, Caledoc, Kecoledoc, Collezoc, Colledan, Collodan, Querian, Kieran, Queran, and so on.[70] We may note that St Quay was subsequently identified with St Caius, pope and martyr, and with St Guy;[71] and in 1687 St Querrien was assimilated to St Chéron, martyr in Chartres.[72] 'Kernan' has been seen as a survival of the Gaulish god Cernunnos.[73]

There is no Irish saint, only a chain reaction. Jaoua was Irish because of Tenenan; since Jaoua was Irish, so was his companion Kenan, who was identified with St Ké. His companion Kerian was therefore also Irish, and could be identified as Kieran.

Le Grand's source is a breviary, but his text is longer than any breviary's version. He also quotes a manuscript, now lost, written by his great-uncle; which would be nice if he had had such a great-uncle.[74]

St Leutiern[75]

For St Leutiern, we have nothing but the name, and even this is dubious: we also find Leuthern, bishop, and Leucern. He has been identified with St Leucher or Loucher of Dol, which is probably due to a resemblance between the names. We have no Life or documents concerning him, and he was not said to be Irish before the time of Canon de Garaby;[76] Father Duine later assimilated him to St Lughtiern, an Irish abbot named by Giraldus Cambrensis.[77]

His identification as an Irishman seems to have been exclusively due to the enthusiasm of nineteenth-century hagiographers who had nothing else to say about him. They simply pointed to a similar name.

St Maudetus[78]

St Maudetus is said to have been Irish – why, I do not know. His Life belongs probably to the eleventh or twelfth century, and does little to confirm the idea of his Irish origin.[79]

---

70 Cf. n. 64 above.   71 Pain, 'Actualisation des sources', p. 85; Doble, *Saints of Cornwall*, iii.100.   72 Doble, *Saints of Cornwall*, iii.96; Le Grand, *Vies des saints*, p. 567.   73 St Ké is admittedly portrayed with a deer at times (an Irien, *Saint Ké*, p. 21); but the name alone would be sufficient 'evidence' for any Celtomaniac. No one has yet made him into a fertility goddess (ibid., p. 29).   74 Cf. n. 54 above.   75 Duine, *Mémento*, nr 155.   76 de Garaby, *Vies*, p. 444 (28 avril).   77 This Lughtiern was a historical figure. See Uhlich, *Morphologie*, p. 274.   78 Duine, *Mémento*, pp. 97–8, nr 82; Orme, *Roscarrock's Lives*, pp. 151–2; BH L 5722; Kenney, *Sources*, nr 38 (ix).   79 De la Borderie, 'Saint Maudez', pp. 202–4, 210–7.

Even though his name has not been satisfactorily explained, it is evident that it is not Irish: the first element is probably *mau-* 'servant', the second possibly *-deth* 'day'.[80] This is a bad start. There is nothing else to prove his Irishness, except tradition. The names of his parents, *Ercleus* and *Gentusa* (*Herculeus* and *Getusa* in a later version), have not yet been explained.[81]

The tradition has drawn comfort from the fact that there still exists on the island of Lavret a small circular building called St Maudet's oven: this could have been the saint's cell, although it has evidently been rebuilt and repainted several times to serve as a bearing for local sailors and fishermen. This building has been described as a typical Irish monk's cell,[82] or the foundation of a round tower. This is very optimistic, to say the least. I have only seen photographs of the building, and archaeological reports: but there is no relationship between these and what I have seen of cells and round towers in Ireland.

St Maudet once seemed like the surest case of an Irish saint, because there was archaeological evidence and a Life in Latin. In reality, however, there is nothing worth taking into account.

It should be noted, however, that we know from the Life of St Gwennole that Irish merchants used to frequent the island.[83] Even if Maudez was not Irish, it is quite possible that he saw Ireland, and quite evident that he met with Irish people – whether saints, scholars, or more probably merchants. The occasional presence of Irish people on the island, and perhaps some knowledge of Irish, might explain his having been said to be Irish himself. He does not appear to have come from Ireland, but he might have visited there. *Vt pie creditur.*

I do not think that he can be retained as an Irish saint, if only on account of his name; but the island's clear Irish connections make it plausible that he actually went to Ireland, and that a nickname became an adjective. Another possibility is that he was, like SS Budoc and Gwennole, called a 'disciple of Patrick'.

St Mezeoc[84]

We know nothing concerning this saint. There is a place named Lan-Vezeoc, from which Loth deduces **Mezeoc*, which could be a form of *Mo-Seoc* (saint *Sioc*, *Sieu*).[85] There is also a corresponding Brittonic form in *To-seoc*, the name of a companion of St Pol.[86] I include him here because the prefix *Mo-* is usually Irish, while *To-* is usually Brittonic; but there is no other reason for doing so.

---

80 Loth, *Noms des saints*, p. 89.   81 The first thing to explain would be the circumstance of their having classical Roman names, albeit deformed ones. There might have been some twisted metaphor in an earlier (lost) text which was not perhaps the saint's Life. A guess is no explanation.   82 Guigon, 'Influences irlandaises', pp. 206–8, rightly destroys the myth. 83 *Vita Winwaloei*, I.19 (Latouche, 'Vie de S. Guénolé').   84 Loth, *Noms des saints*, p. 93. 85 Loth gives as a source the *Pouillé de Tréguier*, which I have not been able to trace, and de Courson, *Cartulaire*, CXCII: the correct reference is not to charter CXCII, which contains nothing of relevance, but to p. cxcii of de Courson's introduction, notes, col. 1.   86 Loth, *Noms des saints*, p. 113.

If an Irishman of this name ever existed, he has been forgotten as such. We know nothing of him beyond his name, which has had to be deduced and reconstructed. He appears in no calendar known to me. I do not want to forget him, but I don't want to invent him either.

St Ninnoc[87]

With regard to St Ninnoc, I cannot see why Kenney included her among Irish saints.[88] Perhaps he had in mind the Middle-Irish word *ninach*, of unclear meaning.[89] Perhaps he was misled by the fact that she was baptised by St Columbanus (*Columchille* in the *Vita*). Her Life is in any case a patchwork, clearly owing much to Welsh tradition but never mentioning Ireland. I would not have expected Kenney to invent an Irish saint, but he appears to have done so. The Welsh traditions used to write the Life might have been brought over by the son of an Irishman;[90] but St Ninnoc was not Irish.

Her original name, furthermore, was *Guengustle*, which is Brittonic. She is also said to have been one of the children of King Brychan.[91]

St Pompée[92]

St Tudual's mother was said to be Irish. She is still honoured as a saint, and her name is Pompée, Pompeia, which is Latin. We do not know much about her, except that she was of Irish origin and lived in Britain.

In Breton tradition, however, she is called *santez Koupaia*. The existence of a form with initial *K-* for what seems to be a normal Latin name could be sound evidence that Breton oral tradition has preserved that name's older form – not an Irish name, but apparently the Irish rendering of a Latin name.[93]

Granted that this represents a late, oral tradition, I am quite prepared to see it as very sound evidence that she really was of Irish origin. We do not know much about her, but since she had both a Latin and an Irish name, lived in Britain and married a Briton, she might have been one of the Irish settlers in Wales or Cornwall.[94]

I will keep her on the list, even though she appears to have been of Irish ancestry rather than of Irish birth.

---

87 Duine, *Mémento*, p. 101, nr 85. Her Life is in Maître and de Berthou, *Cartulaire*, pp. 55–68; cf. BHL nr 6242. 88 Kenney, *Sources*, p. 181, nr 38 (11). 89 Quin, *Dictionary*, fasc. N-O-P, col. 48. The name need not in any case be explained in terms of derivation from Irish, as it can be plausibly explained as based on Brittonic *nin* 'lord'. 90 Juthael filius Aidan; see note 34 above. 91 Dr Karen Jankulak very kindly gave me the probable origin of the mistake: there is a *S. Nennocae V<irginis>* 4. *Jun.*, not said to be Irish but mentioned in an Irish calendar (Fennessy, 'Printed Books', p. 114). If the manuscript was in Louvain, it might be expected that Colgan had made the mistake in the first place, but I did not find this in his book. This was also unpublished in Kenney's day. The date however is the same as that of the feast of St Ninnoc in Brittany. 92 Duine, *Mémento*, nr 180; Loth, *Noms des saints*, pp. 107, 137. 93 Le Duc, 'Bretons et Irlandais', p. 8. 94 John Carey, whom I thank, informs me that there is an inscribed stone in Margam with mutilated ogams and the Roman

St Ronan[95]

St Ronan is a very nice case. His name is clearly Irish. Even though it is sometimes (but not always) adapted into Breton as *Renan*, the onomastic evidence is sound and clear. His historical existence is not in doubt; the problem is rather that we have excellent reasons to see in him a seventh-century saint, and other excellent reasons to assign him to the ninth century. An interesting aspect of his legend is that he provoked both hostility and esteem. This could be explained as having been due to a problem of language, hence a reflection of his foreignness; but it must be admitted that it is also a recurrent motif in the Lives of saints, and especially of hermits.

The real problem is the *troménie*. This is a circuit, a walk which has to be made every sixth year, said by tradition to follow the route taken by the saint when he was going around his possessions. In fact the custom has been shown to have a calendrical basis, and to be rooted in pre-Christian tradition.

We can retain St Ronan as a specimen of an Irish saint, born in Ireland, who died in Brittany. The historical character however escapes us, and we still have to explain how he came to be involved in the survival of a pagan ritual.

St Sané or Senan[96]

This saint is the eponym of the parish of Plouzané. He is said to be Irish, and was identified by Le Grand with St Senán, bishop and abbot of Inis Cathaigh, and later archbishop of Armagh.[97]

It is clear however that Irish *Senán* cannot have become Breton *Sané*. The period when most *plous* were created (fourth-fifth century) would be quite early for an Irish saint, and the name would have become **Henan*. But it is clear that the Life which we have for St Sané is simply the Life of St Senán, from an Irish source, in which Le Grand incorporated local legends (in some cases perhaps his own fabrications) to explain his coming to Brittany.

The confusion of the two saints was not however created by Le Grand, for St Senan has been in the Tréguier calendar (for 6 March) since the fourteenth century. His Life is in the *Breviary of Léon*.[98] Le Grand also used 'un extrait authentique des Archives manuscrites de Nostre-Dame d'Inis-Kaha et

---

inscription PVMPEIVS CARANTORIVS (Macalister, *Corpus inscriptionum* nr 409 [I.387]). This refers to a man, but the presence of ogams confirms the possibility of Irish-Roman hybrid names.   **95** Cf. of course Duine, *Mémento*, p. 344, nr 87; Kenney, *Sources*, p. 182, nr 38 (13); Lapidge and Sharpe, *Bibliography*, nr 949; also, most recently, Laurent, *Saint Ronan*.   **96** Le Grand, *Vies des saints*, pp. 79–84; Colgan, *Acta sanctorum*, pp. 512–29 [numbered 602–11] (1 March); Duine, *Mémento*, pp. 345–6, nr 89; Grosjean, 'Trois pièces', pp. 222–30. Omitted by Kenney, and listed by Lapidge and Sharpe not as a Breton but as an Irish saint (nrs 378, 411, 480). A critical edition is available in Heist, *Vitae*, pp. 301–24.   **97** Le Grand, *Vies des saints*, pp. 79–84.   **98** It does not seem that the text has been published, except in the Gothic breviary of 1519, of which only one half of a single copy is known to have survived. A transcript is provided in Appendix I below.

Killsenan au territoire d'Aruest au comté de Kierri, Diocese d'Artfarten, province de Mommoine en l'Irlande, à moy transmis par le R.P. Frère Vincent Du Val de Saint-Marie, Vicaire provincial d'Hybernie, l'an 1629'. The text used by Le Grand seems to have been unknown to Colgan, who had to translate Le Grand's French.[99]

Who started it does not matter. On the one hand we have several saints called Senan, among them the one whose Life was used by Le Grand, and who may in reality have been called Senach:[100] a saint honoured on the same day as St Senán (8 March),[101] who never travelled to Brittany but was said to have had Roman pupils in Ireland.[102] On the other hand there is *Sanae*, who was not Irish and who is honoured on 6 March. It is clear that on the one hand an Irish name and a date were chosen, and on the other another Irish saint's Life.

I note that another St Senan, a bishop, was honoured on 1 March, the same day as St Jaoua; and that St Sezni is also honoured on 6 March.[103] This seems to be a coincidence. I note too that St Kieran's Life mentions St Senan. These associations may be coincidental, or contrived; in any case it does not matter.

We have in fact no reason to see St Sané as an Irish saint.

In Cornwall there is also a St Senan, who has been identified with St Senan the bishop, although in Cornish tradition she was a female saint. Clearly another character, but also a clear case of assimilation.[104] Finally, I may add that Senan had two companions called Tinnianus and Kieranus: this may have led to further assimilations.[105]

St Seznius or Sezni[106]

The only Life which we have for him is in French, first published by Le Grand in 1636. Le Grand's version is in fact a translation of an adaptation of the Life of St Piran of Cornwall, which itself copied the Life of St Kieran of Saighir.[107]

Colgan, who was short of a Latin text, translated Le Grand's version into Latin again, which prevented him from seeing that he had in fact already edited the same text or rather the same story twenty pages before (since St Kieran is honoured on 5 March).

---

99 Colgan, *Acta sanctorum*, pp. 542–4. [On 'Vincent Du Val de Saint-Marie' see Dumville, 'Seventeenth-Century Hiberno-Breton Hagiological Exchange' – Eds.]. 100 Ibid., p. 543. 101 Ibid., pp. 542b–543a. 102 Ibid., p. 533. 103 Ibid., p. 440. 104 Orme, *Roscarrock's Lives*, p. 173. 105 In the second Life of St Senán edited by Colgan, *Acta sanctorum*, p. 533, §xx. But Colgan translated this text from Irish; we must suppose that Le Grand obtained another translation himself. 106 Le Grand, *Vies des saints*, p. 391; Colgan, *Acta sanctorum*, p. 477; Duine, *Mémento*, nr 90; Orme, *Roscarrock's Lives*, pp. 172–3; Doble, *Saints of Cornwall*, ii.3–14. 107 The life of St Senan in the *Breviary of Léon* (1519) bears the following title (fo. 241 vb): *De sancto Pierano episcopo ... ix. lec. de communi. senani episcopi & confessoris*. It might be that two saints honoured on the same day were mixed up: but some deliberate manipulation must have been involved, if only to change the saint's name in the text.

According to Kenney,[108] Colgan wished to identify him with *Iserninus*, (*Esserinus/Isserinus*), who was a follower of St Patrick. In fact, Colgan was doing his best to identify him at all, not knowing that he was dealing with a forgery.

Le Grand quotes several sources, all of which are lost.[109] One of these he may have invented; another is known from brief extracts; one was seen and copied by the Benedictines, who strangely enough did not copy this text. If Le Grand had invented it all himself, I do not think that he would have multiplied references in this way. He would also not have bothered to mention a discrepancy: the saint he mentions is honoured on 19 September, and he notices that in Guissény he is honoured on 6 March. This difference however betrays the antiquity of the confusion.

I therefore conclude that the confusion and assimilation, whether or not they took place in good faith, are much earlier than Le Grand. The Life of Kieran was probably imported to Cornwall in the thirteenth century, to be used as St Piran's Life, because of a vague similarity of names (*P* in Brittonic corresponds to *K* in Goidelic, as everyone knows); and this entailed a modification of dates.[110] The Life of St Sezni known to Le Grand must be later than that.

We have no reason to keep it on our list, except in the category of saints who have been thought to be Irish for a very, very long time. This was due to a confusion, or rather a misidentification, which was in any case based on a series of clearly dishonest acts. The only Latin text which we have is Colgan's, and this is the translation into Latin of the translation into French of a text forged from another text forged from an Irish saint's Life.

The text is suspect, and the suspect is guilty.

Since more saints are involved, the whole question might however be worth studying as an episode in the intellectual traffic between Cornwall and Brittany. The Cornish side has been studied by Canon Doble; but more remains to be done on the Breton side before we will understand what happened in detail. I am only interested in the result.

I notice that in Cornwall there is a St Sethny.[111] Even if this is not the same saint, it is at least the same name; he is honoured on 15 April, not 6 March as in Guissény or 19 September as elsewhere. According to the editor of Nicholas Roscarrock's manuscripts the Life is inspired, like St Piran's, by the Life of St Kieran of Saighir. This we cannot check; but there might be a confusion with St Senan here. We must remember that in the Middle Ages Cornwall and Brittany certainly shared a tradition, and we may notice that the saint was said to be Irish on both sides of the Channel, and that on each side, but separately, Irish saints' Lives were freely used to provide a Life for St Sezni. Nicholas

---

108 Kenney, *Sources*, p. 182, nr 38 (14). 109 Le Grand, *Vies des saints*, p. 393 (19 septembre). 110 Orme, *Roscarrock's Lives*, pp. 172–3; Doble, *Saints of Cornwall*, iv.3–30. 111 Orme, *Roscarrock's Lives*, pp. 172–3.

Roscarrock actually wondered if he might be the same as St Senan; but he wisely refrained from asserting it.[112]

St Ténénan[113]

Another saint said to be Irish. Once again, however, this is not a simple case, as what we know about him is very limited and certainly confused.

He has two names, *Tenenan* (variant *Teneuan*) and *Tinidor*,[114] neither of which have I found in Irish sources; he is however said to be a former companion of St Patrick.[115] He also had to face the Normans when he came to settle in Brittany, which casts serious doubts on the veracity of anything which we can gather from his Life. In any case, there is nothing of the sort in the surviving fragments of his Latin Life.[116] On the contrary, it is clearly stated there that he was British, as he lived 'at that time when Britons held both Britains, in Great Britain which is now the Land of the Saxons'.[117]

As Tinidor he has a counterpart in Cornwall, St Enoder: all that is lacking is an initial *t-*, probably the characteristically Brittonic prefix *To-*.

As for *Tenenan*, the name is Brittonic: it represents *To-* + *Nenan*, a name known in the *Cartulary of Redon*.[118] There are variants *Telenan, Enenan, Elenan, Tenenar*, which might explain how he came according to Loth to be confused with the Irish saint *Ternan* (Tiernan). Loth observes that if *Tenenan* was not attested in early sources, we might postulate an evolution *Terenan* > *Tenenan*.[119] There was actually another confusion with another saint, Ternoc. Loth got it wrong simply because he seriously envisaged a linguistic link between forms which were only linked by a forced coincidence.

There used to be a St Tinnian, a companion of St Senán of Kilkenny.[120] But the text which refers to him could not have been known in Brittany, since it was originally in Irish (*ex Hibernico transumptum*). It might explain the presence of St Patrick in the legend, which however does not mention St Senan.

---

112 Ibid., pp. 113–4.   113 Le Grand, *Vies des saints*, pp. 307–14; Colgan, *Acta sanctorum*, pp. 441–4 (Life of St Jaoua); Kenney, *Sources*, p. 182, nr 38 (16); Duine, *Mémento*, p. 78, nr 54. Not listed by Lapidge and Sharpe, *Bibliography*.   114 In the Life of St Jaoua, for which our sole source is Le Grand (*Vies des saints*, p. 52), Tinidor is said to be Tenenan's father. 115 Le Grand, *Vies des saints*, p. 307. This was apparently suggested by a Life of St Senan; see note 105.   116 De la Borderie, 'Deux saints Caradec'. This version is a fragment of a Life of St Caradoc; another version is a seventeenth-century Benedictine copy, which awaits an editor. See Appendix II.   117 *Tenenanus qui & Tinidorus tempore quo Britones utramque Britanniam obtinebant in Maiori Britannia quæ nunc patria Saxonum a Britonibus appellatur extitit oriundus, diuina nobis iam tunc in eo prouidente misericordia.* 'Tenenan, also called Tinidor, at the time when Britons held both Britains, was born in Greater Britain which now is named Bro-Saoz (Country of the Saxons) by the Britons, divine mercy already providing for us through him.'   118 Courson, *Cartulaire*, Index generalis, p. 682. Cf. *nen* 'lord' in Williams, *Canu Llywarch Hen*, p. 35.   119 Loth, *Noms des saints*, p. 119.   120 Colgan, *Acta sanctorum*, p. 533a.

Let us consider what we know about him.[121] It is limited to a couple of passages from breviaries: one of these is lost, and known only through a seventeenth-century copy; while the other is an extract from the Life of St Carantoc,[122] which actually mentions one Teneuan as an Irishman who came over to Wales. This seems to be a different character; but the passage was known in Brittany. These sources do not agree with the Life in French, which reflects the combination of several traditions, some of them possibly Irish. De la Borderie recognizes three saints, who have been conflated to provide a nice story.[123] It is a complete mess; and if Le Grand had not known too much about Irish saints, and had not seized the first opportunity for connecting a Breton saint with St Patrick, Tenenan would not have been Irish.

Since Le Grand found that Jaoua was Tenenan's uncle, this might be why Jaoua is now an Irishman as well.

St Vougay or Vio[124]

St Vougay is said to have been an Irish archbishop of Armagh who came to Brittany to live as a hermit. The only Life which we have for him is a translation and/or adaptation by Le Grand of a Latin text which appears to be lost. This saint is not in the calendar. We have a most precious relic, said to be his mass-book, which is a twelfth-century manuscript.[125]

The name is not Brittonic, and is odd, for an initial *U-* should have evolved into *Gw-*. I prefer to follow Loth's explanation: that there existed a saint *Becheu(e)*, which might have given *Bec'heu* or *Beheu*, with initial mutation after *sant*.[126] We would therefore be dealing with a saint named Bec'heu, heard as *sant Veo/Vio*, honoured on 15 June, who was identified with an Irish saint named *Vouga* who was also honoured in June, but on the 7th.

Le Grand used 'les memoires authentiques d'Armacan en Yrlande, à moy transmis par le R.F. Vincent du Val-de Sainte Marie, de l'Ordre des frères prédicateurs, Vicaire provinciale d'Hybernie'. That is, he used a document from Armagh. I would rather not go on to express an opinion about this source before considering the point with some specialist in the history of Armagh. There used to be a St Vouga honoured in the parish of Carn, Co. Wexford.[127]

Two saints have been assimilated: Bec'heu who was a Breton and Vouga who was an Irishman – and St Vio because he was available. The Latin Life was seen

121 Le Grand, *Vies des saints*, p. 312.   122 *Breviary of Léon*, 1519, 16 May.   123 Le Grand, *Vies des saints*, pp. 312–4; de la Borderie, *Histoire de Bretagne*, i.496 n. 2.   124 Le Grand, *Vies des saints*, p. 222; Duine, *Mémento*, nr 95.   125 Deuffic, 'Missel de Saint-Vougay'. 126 Loth, *Noms des saints*, pp. 12, 126. S. Vio (Guiziau, Vizio, ibid. pp. 57–8, 125, 126) is another character; Le Grand brought them together because of the similarity in their names. 127 Loth, *Noms des saints*, p. 126, citing O'Hanlon, *Lives of the Irish Saints*, 7 June (a reference which I have not been able to follow up).

by Le Grand in the abbey of Saint-Matthieu. I wonder what it could have contained.[128]

We can tick St Vio off our list.

ANY OTHER METHODS?

I have relied mainly on onomastic evidence: even if the Lives are of historical interest, their value as historical documents is all too easily contested. Is this our only investigative tool?

It is quite possible – or at least imaginable – that some Irish saints are in fact Welsh or Cornish (i.e. Brittonic) saints who went to Ireland to pray or study, and then came or came back to Brittany. Some names could actually be cited, such as Harthian, Gildas, Idunet, Gwenaël – or even St Gwennole, who wished to do so. Actually, none of these was said to be Irish; on the contrary, even when St Malo and his thirty-three companions are given as St Brendan's pupils, St Brendan himself is said to be Welsh. In fact, I have found no case in which this explanation can be usefully or conclusively applied. It might have been true for St Maudez, for instance; but then we would have to add another chapter to his Life.

I have also conjectured that, if the adjective *scottus* could refer to an Irishman, a Welshman, or a Breton, this might be responsible for some of the confusion that is reflected in the sources. The only instance of this which I have found dates from the twelfth century: in the Life of Tudual, *scottigenus* is actually used as an insult – addressed to a Breton. Now, the saint's mother (Koupaia) may have been Irish, but St Tudual was not. The word *scottus* seems not to have been used in Brittany; and in fact I have been unable to find any example which could be explained in this way. I could be right or wrong; it scarcely matters, as there are no instances to interpret.[129]

I also envisaged that some saints with Brittonic names could have been linked to the Irish minority populations in Wales and Cornwall. This explanation may be correct in the case of St Pompeia/Koupaia; but she seems to be unique. St Fingar/Guigner may be another example, but I leave that to be determined by Dr Jankulak. If this explanation were correct, we would expect the difference to be clear and sharp, in Cornwall at least, when there are

---

128 I notice that Pierre Le Baud, who visited the abbey and took notes from the archives at the end of the fifteenth century, does not mention this. But the text would have been of little interest to him.   **129** The Life of St Senan opens with the words *Sanctus Senanus ex nobilibus christicolis parentibus de Scotia natus fuit, patre uidelicet Hercano et matre Cogella. Erat tunc temporis in insula Hybernensium quidam episcopus nomine Patricius opere et sermone prepotens* ... But this is not a confusion: the saint is Irish; and it is the Life, not the saint, which has been imported into Brittany.

dedications on both sides of the Channel. So far as I can tell, this is not the case. The problem, as with St Sethny/ Sezni, is rather to determine on which side of the Channel the confusion was first made.

At first it seemed that saints said to be Irish could be discarded if their names began with *S-*, as this should have been transformed or adapted to initial *H-* in Brittonic. But this simple rule does not work in practice. First, saints would have had to come before the sixth century, roughly, in order for their names to undergo this sound change. Second, there are several Breton names in *S-*, mostly borrowings from Latin. When we turn to our list we find that, for one reason or another, this phonetic criterion is of no use to our inquiry.

The honorific prefix *Mo-* is usually Irish, its counterpart in Brittonic being *To-*. This would seem to be a water-tight criterion, but it is seldom useful. I have invoked it once in the case of **Mo-Seoc*, but as the form itself is reconstructed from a place name it could be either an exception or an illusion.

The presence in saints' Lives of what are said to be 'typically Irish motifs' could also be mentioned. These are certainly alluring, but again there are problems. First of all, I do not think that motifs can be called 'typically Irish' simply because we find them in Irish literature, as with the Irish parallels for the stories of St Goueznou or St Hernin dragging a club and thereby creating a ditch, or the story of St Melor with his silver hand. At most, this suggests that an Irishman transmitted something, or perhaps even wrote the text which we have – but it does not prove it. In any case, these saints have never been said to be Irish, so that in fact there is no problem. The influence of extracts from the archives of Armagh on Le Grand's imagination is better documented.

Besides onomastics, other elements in the texts could suggest an Irish origin. But here too we are disappointed. We do have evidence of contacts between Brittany and Ireland; but when we find for example what might be the description of a curragh, it occurs in a text concerning a saint who evidently was not Irish.[130] And it is clear to me that the object itself was mere flotsam, with no significance for the natives.

---

130 It is S. Enora's boat: *Vt ad suum nouum opus decorio (sic) pararet nauigium ... corio se circundedit parato, et sic confidens in Domino vitam pelagi committit fluctibus;* when the boat is found by a monk in a fishery, *hic solum depositum inuenit, quod primo abhorrens, quia nunquam tale reperierat (Vita Sancti Euflami*, Ms. BN fr. 22 321, p. 706 [de la Borderie, 'Saint Efflam', pp. 15–6, 17 n. 2, 33]; cf. Fleuriot, *Origines*, pp. 210–1; and Merdrignac, *Recherches*, p. 66). The boat is probably known through flotsam, or hearsay, but is clearly foreign to the country. It might also be a learned invention, as Le Grand reveals in his adaptation (*Vies des saints*, p. 585): 'Elle fit équiper secrètement un bateau de cuir bien joint, cousu & poissé; car en ce temps-là les peuples septentrionaux, tant des Isles que de la terre ferme, usoient de cuir en leurs vaisseaux, au lieu d'aix & de planches, comme il se trouve par ce passage de *Sidonius Appolinaris*, en son *Panegyrique ad Avitum*: Quin et Aremoricus Pyratam Saxona tractus/Sperabat, cui Pelle salum sulcare Britannum/Ludus, etc.'.

I hesitate before introducing one last character: in the Life of St Hervé, we have a devil who is forced to acknowledge that he is Irish. This seems to be an element of Irish folklore, fortuitously preserved in Brittany; and the devil's name, Huccan, might in fact be the nickname of an Irish pagan god. It might also be an anti-Irish motif – the nationality of devils is not usually mentioned. But this occurs in the Life of St Hervé, who is not Irish, even if one of his masters is said to have studied in Ireland.[131]

In fact, there are not many sound criteria and methods. The study of the name is the soundest method, and anyway the only one which can yield results. Very ordinary, not to say elementary, historical criticism of the available evidence readily reveals confusions and forgeries; and this allows us to reach greater certainty.

WHY DID IT HAPPEN?

The reasons are clear: the need to have something to say about a saint; perhaps a taste for exoticism; or simply the application of the hagiographical principle expressed in the Life of St Fingar: *Spondet deuotio quod negat scientia* ('Devotion proposes what science denies').

WHEN DID IT HAPPEN?

There seems to have been a fashion in the twelfth century for assigning to saints an Irish nationality. This might have been the case in Brittany as much as elsewhere. But it is only a consideration of relevance to a few of the saints in our list: Maudet and Efflamm, for instance, because their Lives appear to have been written in that period; or Commean and Meldroc, because their names were used at that time in forging a list of bishops. For other texts, no date is available. It may also have been in precisely that period that several Irishmen came to Brittany. I could mention a 'Cornish package' involving SS Sané, Senan, Sezni, Piran, Kieran, Kenan; B. Merdrignac has suggested a 'filière trégorroise'.

Although I remain cautious on this point, these arrivals might have created a trend, bringing documents, tales, and legends. The Cistercians in particular might have played a role. But this is only a working hypothesis, not a conclusion.

Things become clearer with the first great collection of Breton saints' Lives, Albert Le Grand's work of 1636. He knew many sources which are now lost to us, and certainly added some of his own. It is in Le Grand that we find most of the earliest mentions of Irish saints. Le Grand says that he used documents of Irish origin; our problem is to identify these.

---

131 *Vita Sancti Hervei*, §10, variant (De la Borderie, 'Saint Hervé').

I am struck by the fact that in Le Grand's Lives, saints said to be Irish are all from the province of Ultonia, i.e. Ulster. He probably did not know where this was. His consistency in this respect leads me to suggest that he had access to some document of Ulster provenance. He quotes from documents sent to him by a Dominican residing in Ireland. He had documents concerning Armagh. We do not have them; nor have I been able to pursue the question of these sources in Brittany. In my opinion, Le Grand used those documents freely, identifying Irish and Breton saints whenever he could. This may seem bold – but he made even less fortunate assimilations elsewhere.

I have great esteem for Colgan's work, and I believe that this sentiment is general. For many reasons, he enjoys the status of an authority. It must however be noted that he unknowingly contributed to a vicious trend. Le Grand said that some saints were Irish. Consequently, Colgan included them in his *Acta sanctorum Hiberniae*. Sometimes he could supply a Latin text (as in the case of St Fingar); but, when better evidence was lacking, he contented himself with rendering Le Grand's French text into Latin. Eventually, the existence of a Latin text lent a semblance of authenticity to Le Grand's claims of Irishness.

Colgan did still more: he endorsed the Irishness of these saints, and at times added notes which lent more solidity to Le Grand's inventions.

Consequently, Kenney listed them among Irish saints in his bibliography. Kenney himself, I think, was responsible for the mistaken inclusion of St Feock and St Ninnoc.

Before Kenney, Loth had studied the names of Breton saints, and had already sorted out those who could be Irish. Unfortunately, although he was quite qualified to make a judgment in the matter, he did not question cases in which a saint's Irish background was supported by a legend. He should have been more critical.

Meanwhile, most nineteenth-century writers of saints' Lives and canticles simply drew their information from Le Grand. This is how many Breton saints came to be 'traditionally Irish': the tradition can be dated 1636.

Canon Garaby added more to the lot in 1839; but he never hesitated in creating new saints. Later in the same century, Dom Plaine acted with the same confidence.

The recent, and rightly anonymous, *Dictionnaire des saints bretons* has in its turn added everything up, reaching a yet higher total. Misunderstanding Loth's study, the author has created even more Irish saints whom I did not have the courage to add. In discussing the names of Breton saints, Loth often gave cognates in Welsh, Irish, and Gaulish; in the *Dictionnaire* this is fastened upon as evidence that the saint had an Irish name, and was therefore Irish. Some other saints have Gaulish names on the same principle. Most of the time, no evidence is offered: assertions are gratuitous, not to say scandalous.

Let us face facts. There are many saints concerning whom we know nothing, which is extremely frustrating. The temptation to grasp the first thing which looks like information is immense; and this temptation has always existed. If you don't know the origin of a saint, just say that he was Irish, and no one will raise his finger to contradict you.

That connections really existed between Ireland and Brittany is clear; but the number of Irish saints who came to Brittany and settled there has been grossly and unduly exaggerated, for various reasons and at different periods.

We could not really expect Brittany to be attractive to Irish students; nor would preaching have been easy, for linguistic reasons. Those of whom we find any mention landed there by accident, or by mere chance. In some cases, they fled from Ireland to avoid marriage; and it is striking that this theme recurs (Maudez, Efflamm, Tenenan). Their purpose was not learning, or preaching, or converting, but merely to go further than others had gone, or to live alone as hermits. This they would have done, had God not chosen to annoy them by revealing their sanctity. This is the general picture that we get; but if the saints in question were not Irish, then the picture's coherence is only an illusion.

Loth retained twelve saints who could be Irish. I have been obliged to shorten the list. Even if this represents some progress, I feel a bit sorry about it. In Brittany, quite certainly, people would have been disappointed or perhaps offended by what I have just said, and might have opposed the claims of *tradition*. But I have little choice: the only possible method is to go back to the sources and analyse what we have. Most of the time there is nothing, or very little, and that little is contradictory: the case is closed when I can explain the source of the misunderstanding. In most cases, Irish documents have been used in thoughtless ways.

To sum up: leaving aside St Briac and St Fingar, the only sound case of an Irish saint in Brittany is St Ronan. Two others, Commean and Meldeoc, have Irish names but are nothing more than ink on parchment. St Pompée may have been an Irishwoman, though she had a Latin name. All the others have Brittonic names; and if they are said to be Irish, it is in documents which are vague, unreliable, forged, or falsified – or else we do not even have evidence to criticise.

Later, the process of attribution went out of control, and any unknown saint could easily be labelled Irish. Is it a fib, is it a lie …? Well, it is a matter of opinion.

However disappointing this may seem, saints were always a minority. Reducing the number of Irish saints in Brittany does not mean denying that travel, trade, and exchange took place between Ireland and Brittany, less by saints than by virtuous individuals like scholars, merchants, and traders. Breton saints or holy people said to have gone to Ireland are more numerous, and they certainly brought something of Ireland home with them.

Out of this we get a highly satisfactory picture: our saints are Breton, the devil is Irish, and God is French.

APPENDICES

Appendix I: The Life of St Senan

The Life of St Senan, from the *Breviary of Léon* [*Breuiarium insignis ecclesiae Leonensis, pars hiemalis* (Paris 1516): Bibliothèque Municipale de Rennes nr 15 952]. Since one single copy is known, and as it has not been republished since, I offer a transcript.

This Life is a prose version, shortened, of the metrical Life of St Senan published by Colgan, *Acta sanctorum*, pp. 602 (read 512)-628 (read 529) (8 March); cf. Lapidge and Sharpe, *Bibliography*, nr 480, critical edition in Heist, *Vitae*, pp. 301–24. Several times, the use of identical wording in both texts betrays this version's origin.

folio 241vb

De sancto Pierano episcopo & confessoris. ix. lec. de communi. Senani episcopi & confessoris.

lectio prima

Sanctus Senanus ex nobilibus christicolisque parentibus de Scotia natus fuit, patre uidelicet Hercano, et matre Cogella. Erat autem tunc temporis in Insula Hybernensium quidam episcopus nomine Patricius opere et sermone prepotens, ydolatras ad fidem conuertens, qui interrogatus a populo quis esset sibi in episcopatus successurus, prophetizans respondit, quod Senanus nondum pro (folio 242ra) tunc genitus. Quod et ita secutum est, nam iuxta dicti Patricii uaticinia non multo post natus est Senanus omni uirtute preditus.

lectio ii

Cuius natiuitatis tempore lignum aridum quod eius mater manu tenebat confestim floruit quasi pronosticans quod puerulus qui nascebatur florere deberet in domo Domini sicut Cedrus Libani; quem immediate post ipsius natiuitatem parentes fecerunt baptizari ac ut Patricius predixerat Senanum nominari. De cuius ortu parentes et consanguinei immenso gaudio repleti sunt. Senanus ergo ablactatus cepit corpore, fide, et uirtutibus crescere. Ipse namque corpus suum abstinentiam macerans, quadam die matrem suam mane in ore cibos degustantem arguebat dicens, quod Deus certa tempora refectionis et certa tempora abstinentie constituit.

lectio iii

Processu uero temporis cum parentes eius locum habitationis sue mutarent nouumque habitaculum alibi construxerunt, beatus Senanus diuine contemplationi uacans aliis in edificando occupatis iuuare negligebat. Qui de hoc a matre acriter redargutus contemplatiuam orationem repetiit. Vnde contigit quod vtensilia suorum parentum in uilla prime mansionis dimissa ad locum in quo edificabant per miraculum allata sunt de quo dicti parentes Deo gratias egerunt.

Lectio iiii

Quadam tempestate dum parentes eiusdem cum (folio 242rb) ipso paruulo et familia hospicium peterent in quodam castello quod eis ab inhumanis habitatoribus dicti castelli denegatum est. Vnde mater eius immensa tristitia repleta est, et dictus paruulus matri compatiens eam consolari studuit, inquiens Dominum esse ultorem omnium malorum. Quo dicto plaga subsequens prefatum castellum cum habitatoribus et pertinentiis uniuersis abyssum indilate petiit a Deo ut ipsorum nulla uestigia remanerent.

lectio v

Sequenti uero tempore prefatus paruulus cum matre sua adiit maris ripam querens nauigium, quo mare transire posset. Quo non inuento exorauit creatorem celi et terre ut sibi prouideret de transitu quod ita factum est. Nam deinde ipse et mater sua ultra mare ad partes quas elegerant mirabiliter translati sunt.

lectio vi

Deinde factus episcopus inibi fontem dulcifluum a Deo precibus impetrauit in quo dum quedam mulier infantem suum incaute balnearet quidam monachus beati Senani discipulum Deum deprecatus est, ut prefatus infans subiungeretus (leg.: submergeretur) quod ita factum est. Mater uero pueri de eius submersionem ad beatum Senanum conquesta est de dicto monacho. Qui uocatus a beato uiro iussus est uel ut puerum a flumine eripiat uel cum puero se submergat.

lectio vii

Cum igitur monachus accessisset ad aquam uolens (folio 242va) cum baculo experiri aque profunditatem aqua se sibi prebuit calcabilem, et super aquam ambulans inuenit puerum quem estimabat mortuum in ea ludentem quem ad beatum uirum detulit, et ipsum matri uiuum restituit. De quo miraculo inter magistrum et discipulum talis fuit amicabilis altercatio sicut legimus olim fuisse inter beatum Benedictum et suum discipulum Maurum in ereptione pueri a fluuio liberati. Tu.

lectio viii

Nauigantes socios patrui sui submersos in equore ad deprecationem dicti patrui sui et aliorum amicorum suorum Senanus fusa oratione cum lachrymis uite restituit. Dicti uero resuscitati beato Senano supplicauerunt ut benedictione ipsius percepta permissu eius (sic, leg.: eis) liceret repetere gaudia superna. A quibus deprecatione ipsius ad uitam mortalem fuerant reuocati, quod ita factum est.

lectio ix

Post hec beatus Senanus obdormiuit in Domino; cuius corpus per octo dies sequentes inhumatum eius coepiscopi et abbates cum innumeris populis diuinis obsequiis insudantes dum honorifice sepelire satagunt corpus defuncti Senani feretro positum inibi resedit et spiritum resumpsit, ubi uir sanctus uerbis salutaribus secreta quedam reuelauit presentibus. Tunc maiores qui aderant rediuiuum interrogauerunt eum an in die obitus uel in octauis eius deinceps facerent eius memoriam. Qui respondit, die octaua hanc inquit annuatim colite, et tunc ualedicens his qui aderant se resedit exanimem. Cetera de communi unius confessoris et episcopi.

Appendix II:
The 'Life' of St Tenenan, or at least one of them: in fact a passage from a Life of St Caradoc, from the same Gothic breviary.

folio 266va

le.i.

Quodam tempore fuit uir nomine Ceretic, et hic uir habuit multos filios: quorum unus erat Karadocus nomine. In illis diebus venerunt Scoti et occupauerunt regionem britannicam. Ceretic autem erat senex: et dixerunt seniores. senex es tu non potes dimicare: debes unum ordinare de filiis tuis qui est senior. Dixerunt illi Karadoco, oportet te esse regem. Karadocus autem plus diligebat esse regem celestem quam terrenum: et post quam audiuit fugam iniit ne inuenirent eum. Accepit ergo Karadocus peram cum baculo et sacculo a quodam paupere et uenit in locum quod dicitur Guerith Karantoc et mansit ibi per aliquod tempus. Post multos autem dies uenit ad sanctum Karadocum uox de celo, precepitque ut quia hic latere non poterat et quo (leg.: quanto) ignotior et remotior a suis tanto fieret seruus Dei utilior: Patricium sequeretur in Hyberniam. Karadocus igitur descendit in Hyberniam et ibi incipit construere monasterium. Relatum erat Karadoco in partibus illis apud quemdam tyrannum Dulcemium nomine esse quandam arborem ornatam atque caram que patris sui fuerat. Venit Karadocus et petiit arborem. Vtrum melior es tu dixit tyrannus omnibus sanctis qui postulauerunt eam? Non sum dixit Karadocus.

le.ii.

(folio 266vb) Tyrannus dixit. Voca tamen deum tuum: et si modo ceciderit tua sit. respondit Karadocus: non est impossibile Deo quicquam: et hec dicens orauit Dominum, completa oratione cecidit arbor radicibus extirpatis et stabant attoniti infideles. Credidit ergo tyrannus et baptizatus est et omnes sui cum illo conuersi sunt ad fidem: et receperunt sacramentum. hoc lignum artifices portauerunt in crastino ad opus inchoatum: et scinderunt in quatuor bases. Quadam nocte uenerunt religiosi quidam aliunde ad locum et deerant ligna foco ad usum pernoctantium: tunc surrexit Karadocus ad unam basem de quattuor absciditque particulum ex illa. Artifex autem hoc intuens uehementer indignatus est: et decreuit abire et ait Karadocus fili mi: mane in hac nocte. Ille uero mansit inuitus. Sole autem orto surrexit ut abiret. et exiens circa ecclesiam uidit basem illam similem aliis basibus non habentem in se cissuram.

le.iii.

Erat illis diebus quidam sanctus in Hybernia nomine Teuenanus et hic erat leprosus. Venit igitur ad sanctum Karadocum: sed antequam uenisset nunciauit ei angelus uenturum ad se Teuenanum. Karadocus cum gaudio et exultatione preparauit balneum suo hospiti. Veniens ille cum exisset iam ecclesiam et orasset accurrit iste obuiam (folio 267ra) illi et osculati sunt inuicem benedicentes. Et ducto eo a monasterio ad refectorium cogebat enim oppido ut introiret lauachrum. Ille negabat et inueniebat causas satis ydoneas. Denique Karadocus ait. Si non intraueris non uiues in uita eterna. Cum hoc audisset Teuenanus coactus intrauit balneum. Accedebat iterum Karadocus ut lauaret eum. Animaduertens igitur Teuenanus quoniam ad se abluendum accederet dixit: non lauabis me in eternum. Respondit Karadocus: Nec tu uiues in eternum si non lauero te. Locus est itaque et statim ut tetigit eum Karadocus sanatus est a lepra. Et conquerebatur dicens: non bene fecisti in me frater: quia forte superbus fiam a modo et multum deceptus ero. Nequaquam ille ait sed pulchrior eris: et tua caro non erit fetida. Tunc sanctus Teuenanus ait. Ingredere et tu ut laueris. Adiuratus ipse ingressus est balneum. surrrxit (sic) Teuenanus ut faceret obsequia. habebat enim Karadocus septem cingula ferrea circa se et mox ubi tetigit ea Teuenanus fracta sunt omnia. Tunc ait Karadocus. Non bene egisti: tibi ueruntamen dampnum hoc uidetur reparabile. Ait Teuenanus. Nequaquam quia si uenerint omnes fabri: non poterunt (leg.: poterint) tibi fabricare cingulum. Et post hec uerba laudauerunt Deum: et facta est pax et unitas inter ipsos. Tu.

Fingar/Gwinear/Guigner:
An 'Irish' Saint in Medieval
Cornwall and Brittany

Karen Jankulak

The cult of St Fingar or Guigner (in Brittany) or Gwinear (in Cornwall) provides a reasonably representative example of a process of attribution of Irish identity to Breton or Cornish saints.[1] Yet this saint's Irishness is singularly paradoxical: although in the medieval period he is not in any significant fashion Irish, the most important thing anyone can say about the saint is that he is Irish. The cult of Fingar, Guigner, or Gwinear can be described as a 'composite' cult: one should in this case consider the whole as the sum of its parts. That is, the process of conflation here adds identifications to existing identifications; it is not really a question of a process of replacement, but of accumulation and even at times subtraction. Therefore the method of this paper will be to trace the whole of this cult (or, perhaps, cults) in order to establish a pattern of identification. Although the medieval and early modern hagiographers who interested themselves in this saint for the most part preferred circumlocutions to the use of one particular name, it is necessary to refer to the subject of this paper by some single designation. Thus where no specific area or aspect of cult is intended the saint will be referred to as 'Fingar', in part because this paper is mostly concerned with the saint's supposed Irishness, which is best represented by this name.

The composite Fingar's cult in Cornwall and Brittany can be traced through his *vitae*, feast days, church dedications, and place-names. A historiographical approach takes us from, at least in theory, the fifth or sixth century, the reputed *floruit* of the saint, to the seventeenth and eighteenth centuries, in which his character was firmly established. While one may consider aspects of the cult in

1 While this paper has benefited from the assistance of many people, whose contributions have been noted at the relevant points, I wish especially to thank Gwenaël Le Duc, Oliver Padel, and Bernard Tanguy for profound assistance, both for their generous discussion of this cult, as well as for the provision of many references and indeed inaccessible or unpublished material. Any errors which result, however, are solely my own. 2 Cf. Sharpe's comments in *Medieval Irish Saints' Lives*, pp. 89–90. One might, in addition, argue that this process has continued into the twentieth century, with even this paper merely a further attempt to define this saint.

isolation (the cult of Gwinear in Cornwall, for example, could be considered without reference to Ireland or Brittany), an essential first step is the consideration of the pattern of the whole, the enumeration of its constituent pieces, and, if possible, the separation of some of these pieces. The role of the early modern collectors and assemblers of the material, often viewed as purely mechanical, is of primary importance.[2]

One can usefully separate this cult into two main areas. First, there is a group of primarily hagiographical traditions concerning St Fingar. This aspect of the cult can further be divided into two main bodies of tradition. These correspond roughly to what will here be called the *Vita A* with its Parisian transmission,[3] and what will be called the *Vita B* of chiefly Breton transmission.[4] The two traditions, however, are closely linked, albeit in ways that are not always clear. The *Vita A* is the only Life of the saint to have survived in full: the *Vita B* is apparently merely a summary (and that perhaps mostly of the *Vita A*). A second main area, mainly hagiological and concerned with the Breton St Guigner and the Cornish St Gwinear, is represented by a group of dedications and feast days, as well as a third Life, the *Vita C* – the latter, however, known only from a passing allusion.[5] Not surprisingly, the hagiographical tradition concerning Fingar is far better represented in surviving records: the *Vita A* has become the main source of tradition for the composite cult. Yet the traditions of Fingar, Gwinear, and Guigner do interact, although at times obscurely. One of the strongest threads connecting these areas of cult is the attribution of an Irish origin to this saint or saints.

Seventeenth-century hagiographers, such as John Colgan and Thomas Messingham, are more or less responsible for rescuing Fingar from obscurity through the publication of his Life, the *Vita A*; Fingar was of interest to these precisely, and solely, because of his Irishness. As the saint's Irishness was in part bestowed upon him by the attention paid to him by such collectors, the process is visibly circular.

John Colgan's inclusion, in the seventeenth century, of Fingar's *vita* (here known as the *Vita A*) in his collection of Lives of Irish saints (*Acta sanctorum veteris et maioris Scotiae, seu Hiberniae sanctorum insulae*)[6] can be seen as a

---

3 This is BN ms. lat. 15005, ff. 68r–71v, nr 895 in Lapidge and Sharpe, *Bibliography*, which, however, has the manuscript as 'untraced' as well as erroneously giving the reference number to Plummer's 'Tentative Catalogue' as 254 rather than 252. The reference to Lucas's article there should also be disregarded. Gwenaël Le Duc is preparing an edition of the *Vita A*, newly collated against the manuscript, and I would here like to extend my deepest thanks to Professor Le Duc for allowing me to see this edition. 4 Le Grand, *Vies des saints*, pp. 703–4. 5 See below, note 70. 6 Louvain, 1645, pp. 387–91. This was the first volume, covering January to March, of a planned four-volume collection of Lives of Irish saints, arranged by feast day. Joep Leerssen has argued that a six-volume collection was envisaged, consisting of the *Annals of the Four Masters*, to serve perhaps as 'a general historical introduction to the actual lives of the saints', four volumes of *vitae*, and finally the *Trias thaumaturga* (which appeared in 1647), the latter an account of Ireland's three chief saints,

determining step in the establishment of the previously marginal and even somewhat dubious Fingar both as a significant saint and as a specifically Irish saint. Colgan's confirmation or even establishment of Fingar as an Irish saint can be seen as the logical outgrowth of what was arguably the primary impetus behind the project of collection of hagiographical documents undertaken by the Louvain Franciscans in the seventeenth century. This process of collection had many aspects: in its broadest sweep it grew from a desire to investigate and record early Christianity according to Protestant and Humanist standards of scholarship.[7] The desire to protect a threatened Catholic and native Irish culture also contributed.[8] Specifically, however, the Louvain hagiographical collection can be seen as a response to writings, promulgated by, among others, Thomas Dempster, claiming the early saints of the Scoti not for Ireland but for Scotland.[9] Thus for Colgan and his associates the specific connection of these saints with Ireland was the main point to be made.

Not surprisingly, as Canice Mooney has commented, Colgan's definition of both 'saint' and 'Irish' was broad, to say the least,[10] and certainly Colgan included in his *Acta sanctorum* many saints whose relevance to Ireland was (and has remained) at best debatable.[11] Fingar should probably be numbered among these: as with other medieval Cornish and Breton saints what one might term the historical character is unrecoverable, and one must look instead to a cult whose records significantly postdate the period of historical existence. While this is not to say that these men and, less often, women did not exist (and there is no reason at all to make this argument), an argument based on their actual characteristics or origins is useless and ultimately, therefore, irrelevant. It is enough to say for the moment that the saint's Irish origin is highly unprovable, and Fingar shows no sign of having left any trace in Ireland. Yet in the case of Fingar, Colgan's view of this saint as distinctly, even primarily, Irish, has prevailed, and it is through Colgan, arguably, that one can trace the inclusion of Fingar in subsequent treatments of Irish saints.[12]

Patrick, Brigit, and Columba. See Leerssen, *Mere Irish*, pp. 307–8; Cunningham, 'Culture and Ideology', p. 24.   7 Cunningham and Gillespie, '"Most Adaptable of Saints"', pp. 87–8.   8 Sharpe, *Medieval Irish Saints' Lives*, p. 40.   9 Mooney, 'Father John Colgan', pp. 17–8; Sharpe, *Medieval Irish Saints' Lives*, pp. 40–1; Leerssen, *Mere Irish*, p. 306. Note, in this connection, the full title of Colgan's *Acta sanctorum*, as well as that of a proposed work, 'De Monasteriis pro veteribus Scotis seu Hibernis per suae gentis viros sanctos … fundatis' (Historical Manuscripts Commission, *Fourth Report*, p. 609). But see Cunningham, 'Culture and Ideology', p. 28.   10 Mooney, 'Father John Colgan', p. 33.   11 See Bieler's terse comments on the inclusion by Colgan of several distinctly non-Irish saints: 'Colgan as Editor', pp. 19 (SS Maimbod and Gildas) and 22 (SS Frediano of Lucca and Cuthbert). See also a list of saints who were to be included in subsequent volumes of the *Acta* for similar examples: Fennessy, 'Printed Books', pp. 113–7, as well as the table of contents of Colgan's unfinished work on Irish–founded monasteries throughout Europe (above, note 9).   12 For example, O'Hanlon gives an extensive treatment of Fingar in his *Lives of the Irish Saints*, ii.672–81.

Colgan, however, was not the first to publish the *Vita A*; indeed he was not even the first to single out this *Vita* as the Life of a specifically Irish saint. Thomas Messingham, not a Franciscan but a secular priest who was rector of the Irish College in Paris,[13] was the first to publish the *Vita A* in a collection of Lives of Irish saints. Messingham should certainly be viewed as part of the general movement among Irish on the Continent to establish a canon of Irish saints and their associated materials within a historical framework, and indeed his *Florilegium insulae sanctorum* (1624) was published before the works of the better-known Franciscan project. Despite this, Messingham worked in relative isolation.[14] No doubt Colgan knew of Fingar through Messingham's *Florilegium*, although arguably he would have unearthed the *Vita A* without Messingham's edition, albeit with greater difficulty. Nevertheless, Colgan is clearly responsible for Fingar's henceforth secure Irish identity; Messingham's work was far less obviously influential,[15] and the much larger Franciscan project visibly super-seded the work of its predecessors.[16]

Messingham's legacy has perhaps also been depreciated because although he collaborated with some of the Franciscans (notably Fleming and Ward)[17] who were intent on uncovering previously unknown Lives, his *Florilegium* relied mostly on previously published materials,[18] and his undertaking has justly been characterised as 'for the most part ... a derivative compilation'.[19] The Life of St Fingar included by Messingham was no exception: it was taken from a published collection. That being said, Messingham did not obtain the *Vita A* from an obvious source. Messingham culled the *Vita A* not from a published collection of Lives of Irish saints, but from the published works of Anselm of Canterbury. The *Vita A* has a named author, Anselm, and its only extant manu-script is a Victorine miscellany; these two aspects of its history are probably linked.[20] Because of this, the *Vita A* was first published by Iohannes Picard, himself a canon of the abbey of Saint-Victor in Paris in whose library the

13 Boyle, *Irish College*, p. 5 and Document 2, p. 164.   14 Sharpe, *Medieval Irish Saints' Lives*, p. 40.   15 Messingham's *Florilegium*, however, was consulted by Ussher (Leerssen, *Mere Irish*, p. 305), to which we probably owe Ussher's notice of St Fingar in his *Britannicarum ecclesiarum antiquitates* (Dublin, 1639; see Elrington, Todd, and Reeves, *Whole Works*, vi.411 and 431). Albert Le Grand probably also consulted the *Vita A* in Messingham's collection (see below, note 38).   16 Cunningham and Gillespie, '"Most Adaptable of Saints"', p. 93. 17 Jennings, *Michael O Cleirigh*, p. 27. The collaboration between Messingham, Ward, and Fleming seems to have ended in some acrimony (Sharpe, *Medieval Irish Saints' Lives*, pp. 49–50).   18 Cunningham and Gillespie, '"Most Adaptable of Saints"', p. 90; Sharpe, *Medieval Irish Saints' Lives*, p. 46.   19 Sharpe, *Medieval Irish Saints' Lives*, p. 46.   20 Paris, BN ms. lat. 15005, ff. 68r–71v, possibly of thirteenth-century date: Fleuriot, *Origines*, p. 278; Loth, *Émigration bretonne*, p. 245; [Bollandists], *Catalogus codicum*, iii.284. Loth and Fleuriot erroneously give the shelf mark as 1505. Hauréau describes the manuscript as 'un assemblage de pièces qui n'ont rien de commun': *Notices et extraits*, iv.190.

manuscript resided, as part of his *Opera omnia Anselmi* of 1612.[21] Messingham extracted the *Vita A* from this collection, its first and at the time its only edition.

The *Vita A* is in some ways a strange text, containing no feast day for the saint, and using two names, *Fingar* (gen. *Fingaris*) and *Guignerus* (gen. *Guigneri*), to designate its subject.[22] The preface to the *Vita* presents an unnamed 'I' (in the conclusion named as Anselm) who states that he is expanding and more elegantly presenting brief notes kept by an unnamed 'you' ('quam prius brevibus notulis retinebas') concerning the holy martyr *Guigner* (ms. G.).[23] The preface deploys commonplace topoi (protestations of unworthiness to the task, for example), and its assertions that this was a commissioned work, or that it was expanded from brief notes, need not be read literally. Yet it is noteworthy that here the form of the name is Guigner rather than Fingar, and perhaps some meaning does attach to this.

The *Vita* proper begins in Ireland, where Patrick comes from Cornwall, *Cornubia*, to convert the pagan Irish. His arrival is foreknown, and a group of seven Irish kings with their retinues and pagan priests gather in an assembly. The resemblance to Patrick's meeting with Lóegaire at Tara is not accidental, and Fingar, predictably, is converted by Patrick in the same way as Erc son of Daig and later Dubthach maccu Lugair are in Muirchú's *Vita Patricii*, rising at Patrick's approach.[24] One king, 'nobilior … ac potentior omnibus' is named as Clito; he is given as Fingar's father. The saint himself is referred to in this section only once by name, but here the name used is *Fingar* (ms. Fingar).

The saint's father expels him and his companions from his kingdom, and these decide to go to Brittany ('minorem in Britanniam'). A Breton *iudex* (also variously described as a *dux*, and *dominus*), having foreknowledge of their arrival, greets them and endows them with land sufficient for sustenance. While in Brittany the saint miraculously elicits a spring from the earth, and decides to pledge himself entirely to God, after which he retires to a cave to live in isolation. The Breton lord, having anxiously sought the saint, finds him, grants land for the construction of an oratory and more fully endows land previously granted. In this Breton episode the saint is named four times; each time the name given is *Fingar* (ms. Fingarem, Fingarem, Fingar, Fingar).

The saint is then told to return to Ireland, which he finds to have been converted to Christianity. His father having died, he is asked to take up the rule of the kingdom, but refuses. He recommends one of the other nobles, and

---

21 Cologne, 1612.   22 The *Vita* is most easily accessible in the facsimile of Colgan's *Acta sanctorum*, pp. 387–91, as well as in PL clix.325–34. The title of the *Vita*, 'Passio SS. Guigneri sive Fingaris, Pialae et sociorum 777', is not in the manuscript, and would seem to originate with Picard's edition.   23 Here, uniquely, Migne's text differs from Colgan's: the former gives *Guinerus* while Colgan gives that appearing in the rest of the *Vita*, *Guignerus*. 24 Muirchú, I 17 (16) and I 19 (18) (Bieler, *Patrician Texts*, pp. 88 and 92).

further advises that the new king marry his sister Piala; she, however, refuses as she has pledged herself to Christ. The saint then leaves Ireland with seven hundred and seventy men, as well as seven bishops who had been consecrated by Patrick; among his companions is Piala.

The first two episodes of this *Vita*, which take place in Ireland and Brittany, show no geographical precision at all: Fingar is given no local or recognisable dynastic affiliation in Ireland,[25] and the location of his stay in Brittany is unspecified. However, this third episode, the saint's second stay in Ireland, is slightly fuller in this sort of detail, and subsequent episodes in Cornwall are very detailed indeed. Moreover, it is striking that here, at the second visit to Ireland, the name given to the saint changes, exactly at the point when the Life tells us more about his family. The saint is, in this second visit to Ireland, twice named as *Guigner* (ms. *Guigeri, Guigneri*), exclusively with reference to his sister Piala.[26] That is, the saint's name appears only in the phrase, which occurs twice, 'virgo Piala ... soror ... Guigneri'. This fuller description of the saint's family, as well as the change in name of the saint, occurs at the transition to the next portion of the *Vita* which will take place in Cornwall. However, the change in name is not at all straightforward, and Doble is mistaken in his comment that 'in the first part of [the *Vita A*] he [Anselm] calls his hero *Fingar*, and in the latter part always Guigner'.[27] Nevertheless the visible increase in incidental information – especially, in the Cornish portion, topographical and toponymic information – is surely significant. That being said, not all of these references are independently attested: while, for example, it is likely that Anselm or his source included Piala by name with reference to a particular local Cornish saint, St Piala is unknown outside the *Vita A*, and shows no cult in Cornwall or Brittany.[28]

At this point the *Vita* pauses for a moment, in order to introduce the crossing from Ireland to Cornwall of a rather better attested figure, a virgin Hya, or Ia. Like Fingar and his sister, Ia does not appear in any medieval or early modern Irish calendars or lists of saints; unlike Fingar and his sister, however, Ia was known to

---

25 *Clito* (here occurring twice in the genitive, *Clitonis*, and twice in the ablative, *Clito* and *Clitone*) is unknown as a medieval Irish personal name, much less that of a ruler. Gwenaël Le Duc (personal communication.) has ventured the plausible and suggestive theory that this name originated as the Latin *clito* (gen. *clitonis*), meaning 'prince'. Harvey, Devine, and Smith, *Archive*, s.v. *clito* shows only two occurrences of this word, both in a presumably Cornubo-Latin context, and it occurs otherwise in a mainly Anglo-Saxon or Anglo-Norman context: see Du Cange, *Glossarium*, s.v. *clitones*; Niermeyer, *Lexicon minus*, s.v. *clito*; Latham, *Word-List*, s.v. *clito*; idem, *Dictionary*, s.v. *clito*. **26** Bernard Tanguy has noted this correspondence: 'Cornou', p. 577 n. 21. I wish to thank Professor Tanguy for providing me with a copy of this article. **27** Doble, *Saints of Cornwall*, i.105. **28** St Piala was in the eighteenth and nineteenth centuries identified with the patron saint of the parish of Phillack, which is adjacent to the parish of Gwinear. However, as Lynette Olson and Oliver Padel note, the mistaken identification cannot have been made in the Middle Ages: Olson and Padel, 'Tenth-Century List', p. 49.

William Camden and hence appears in Henry Fitzsimon's early seventeenth-century *Catalogus praecipuorum sanctorum Hiberniae*. It isn't clear, however, what particular saint Fitzsimon may have had in mind: she appears in his *Catalogus* as either *Iia* or *Ita*, the latter perhaps by confusion with the well-known Irish saint Íte.[29] St Ia was also known to other antiquaries in Cornwall.[30]

St Fingar and his companions, the *Vita* continues, arrive in Cornwall, *Cornubia*, to find that Hya is already there. Doble has noted the appearance of geographical and toponymic details concerning western Cornwall, the area of Gwinear's cult, in the *Vita A*: they land at a port called Heul (Hayle, near St Ives), and proceed to *Conectonia* (Connerton, inland from Hayle). From this Doble conjectures, somewhat wistfully, that an unnamed site visited on the way, the *habitaculum* of a certain holy virgin, might represent the nearby site of a chapel of St Anta, attested in the fifteenth century.[31] While this is not at all supported by the text, other geographical details show both a knowledge of Cornish toponymy and a desire to include local features, as with SS Ia and (perhaps) Piala, and again it is fair to argue that either Anselm or his source had some specific site in mind for the holy virgin's abode.

The rest of the *Vita* is set in Cornwall, and vacillates between calling its subject Fingar and Guigner. The episodes in which the saint is named are, in order: the saint, *Guigner* (ms. Guigner*us*), briefly meets the unnamed virgin; the saint, *Fingar* (ms. Fingar), and his companions are miraculously fed by a woman, Coruria; the saint's companions, companions of *Guigner* (ms. Guign*ero*), are strengthened in their resolve. Finally the *Vita* describes the saint's martyrdom at the hands of the king of Cornwall, Theoderic: in this episode he is named only once, as *Fingar* (ms. Fingar). Five postmortem miracles are then related, all set in Cornwall as there is no hint that the saint's corpse or relics are anywhere other than in Cornwall. The saint is named only once, here as *Guigner*;[32] indeed, the *Vita's* circumlocutory fashion of referring to its subject

---

29 Grosjean, 'Édition du *Catalogus*', p. 368: 'Ita [or Iia] Virg. à qua S. Iuis Bay in Cornuallia. Camd. Subense. Mart.' See idem, p. 345 for *Martyrologium Subense*. See Stokes, *Félire Óengusso*, p. 43 for St Íte, whose feast falls on 15 January.   30 While the sixteenth-century antiquary Leland saw a Latin Life of the saint, it is no longer extant and such notices as are now devoted to St Ia are passages culled from the *Vita A* of Fingar (Colgan, *Acta sanctorum*, pp. 164–6; O'Hanlon, *Lives of the Irish Saints*, i.442–4; Doble, *Saints of Cornwall*, i.89, 94 and n. 13). Colgan's feast day for Ia, 25 January, is derived from the second edition of the *English Martyrology* ('J. Wilson', *English Martyrologe*; see note 77); in 1478 the feast at St Ives in Cornwall was observed on 3 February, and in the early twentieth century occurred on the Sunday after this date; the Bollandists give 27 October as the feast day, according to Doble on dubious authority.   31 Doble, *Saints of Cornwall*, i.81 n. 4. Doble's further argument, that as the *Vita A* stipulates that the saint found Christians on arriving in Cornwall one can see that Cornwall was already partly Christianised at this period (presumably that of the saint's lifetime) is untenable (ibid., p. 106).   32 The manuscript gives this as .*G*.

throughout, but especially in this section, is striking. Finally there is a short conclusion, in which the subject, as in the preface, is named *Guigner* (ms. Guigneri), and in which the author identifies himself as 'Anselm'.

The tradition of the *Vita B* is far less clear, as we only have extant Albert Le Grand's summary of his purported sources. Le Grand, a Dominican, published his *Vies des saints de la Bretagne armorique* in 1636.[33] This collection presents several Lives which are no longer extant, as well as notices which seem not to be based on *vitae* at all.[34] Le Grand's account of Guigner (Guiner as he spells it) is in part based on a lost 'vieil' legendary of Le Folgoët, which also supplied information or *vitae* for several other saints.[35] Yet Le Grand's account, a French summary of an apparently Latin text,[36] cannot be seen as representing a Breton tradition in isolation, even assuming that the tradition underlying his sources (here known as the *Vita B*) developed in isolation from that of *Vita A* – itself a highly debatable proposition.[37] Le Grand had recourse to Messingham's *Florilegium*,[38] and perhaps to another source (as suggested by the name Princius, for which see below). Although Le Grand refers in his title to the saint as '*Guiner* ou *Eguiner*', in his summary of his presumed source he refers to the saint either as *Guiner* or *Fingar*. Initially he calls the saint Guiner, and gives Fingar as a sort of patronymic or dynastic name,[39] but it becomes clear that Guiner and Fingar are, in his opinion, one and the same. The saint, expelled from Ireland, sets out for 'Bretagne Armorique'. The saint's father, in a rage, writes to Theodoric, 'prince de Cornoüaille Armorique', to warn him that his son and three hundred others were coming to wage war on him on behalf of Theodoric's uncle Macence, his territorial rival. Theodoric encounters the saint and his companions after they land in Cornouaille. In a dramatically presented

33 Or perhaps 1637. The edition most widely available, and that consulted for this paper, is the fifth edition, with annotations by A.M. Thomas and J.M. Abgrall, as well as P. Peyron (Quimper, 1901). 34 Bourgès, 'Archéologie du mythe', p. 11. 35 Bourgès, ibid., p. 14, suggests a date of the first half of the fifteenth century for this Legendary. 36 But see ibid., p. 23 n. 45, where he notes that when Le Grand summarises Latin texts he tends to keep Latin proper names; where the 'French' forms of these names appear Bourgès presumes a French exemplar. The proper names in Le Grand's account of our saint would seem to be French. 37 Indeed, the Breton tradition as a whole is arguably based either directly or indirectly on the *Vita A*: see, for example, the *Roman Breviary* in use in the diocese of Vannes in the nineteenth century which summarises the narrative of the *Vita A* more or less faithfully, but refers to the saint exclusively as *Guigner*: *Breviarum romanum*, p. 7. The Vannes missal of 1530 also, in its *proprium sanctorum*, contains a mass for St Guigner, 'which gives the story of the saint as in Anselm's *Vita Guigneri*': Doble, 'Mass at Vannes', p. 135. I wish to thank Gwenaël Le Duc for these references. 38 Deuffic, *Questions d'hagiographie*, p. 24. 39 'Saint Guiner, estoit gentil-homme Hybernois, lequel, estant de la maison du prince Fingar (fils aisné d'un Roy de l'une des provinces de ladite Isle, nommé Clyto), fut converty à la Foy, avec son maistre & grand nombres d'autres seigneurs, par la Predication de l'Abbé Princius, lequel, par commandement exprés du Ciel, à luy notifié par un Ange, avoit passé de la paroisse de Cambrie en Grande Bretagne, dans l'Isle d'Hybernie, pour y prescher l'Evangile.' Le Grand, *Vies des saints*, p. 703.

scene, Theodoric approaches the saint with a bloody sword, crying 'A mort, à mort, ces hypocrites'; the saint reproaches him for his bloodthirstiness, to no avail, and finally falls on his knees, encouraging his companions to be peaceful, as he stretches out his neck towards Theodoric, who duly slays him and his companions. Le Grand notes that several miracles were performed at the saint's tomb, but doesn't relate any.

There are several notable differences between the *Vita A* and the *Vita B*, although the main story is the same, and, like the author of the *Vita A*, Le Grand seems to prefer to refer to the saint by name as infrequently as possible. Rather than being converted by Patrick (who according to the *Vita A* came to Ireland from Cornwall), the subject in Le Grand's account was converted by 'l'Abbé Princius', who came to Ireland from 'la paroisse de Cambrie en la Grand Bretagne'.[40]

The chief difference between the *Vita A* and the *Vita B*, however, is entirely understandable: the *Vita B* locates the saint's martyrdom and burial, similar to that presented in the *Vita A*, not in Cornwall but in Cornouaille. Thus the saint makes only one trip from Ireland to Brittany in the *Vita B*, rather than one from Ireland to Brittany, another back to Ireland, and finally a third journey to Cornwall as in the *Vita A*. In fact, in the *Vita B* the saint never visits Cornwall at all.[41] This is clearly an adaptation of a tradition which spoke originally of Cornwall: the *Vita B* merely gives the vague 'Cornouaille' as the location of the martyrdom, without specifying any particular place, and gives no topographical information. This reticence is reminiscent of the portions of the Life which occur in Ireland, and argues against the inclusion of any local tradition. At any rate, there is no discernible local tradition commemorating this or a like-named saint in Cornouaille, as one would expect if a strong tradition located him there.[42]

Another reflection of this posited adaptation of a Cornish source to a superficially Breton context is the alteration of Theodoric (corresponding to 'Theoderic' in the *Vita A*). In the *Vita B*, as in the *Vita A*, Theodoric is a murderous lord or prince. Yet while this figure is familiar from other Cornu-Breton *vitae*, in these he is always presented as a Cornish, never a Breton, ruler.[43]

---

40 Gwenaël Le Duc and John Carey (personal communication) have pointed out that 'Princius' would seem to be a mistaken expansion of a contracted form of 'Patricius'. It is also suggestive, however, that in the English Martyrology of 1640 (see below, note 76) the name 'Patricius' is followed by 'Principisque'.   41 Thus, because the episodes introducing them have been omitted, there is no sign in the *Vita B* of the saint's sister Piala, nor of Ia. 42 The only occurrence of an actual location within Breton Cornouaille in the vast and diverse materials concerning this saint is the nineteenth-century *Vannes Breviary*'s naming of the unnamed Breton *dux* of the *Vita A* as Audren, 'king in the region of Quimper' (see above, note 37). Otherwise in all instances Cornouaille could be replaced with Cornwall (and 'Bretagne armorique' with 'Bretagne insulaire') without contradicting any other information furnished by the tradition.   43 The character appears in a Life of St Kea (which survives only in a summary by Le Grand) as well as that of St Petroc; Leland's notes from a Life of

In the *Vita B*, however, he is presented as a Breton ruler, and is curiously conflated with the benevolent Breton *iudex* of the *Vita A*. The *Vita B* as presented by Le Grand now presents a Theodoric who rather than being identified with the Cornish tyrant of folklore, has clearly been incorporated into a legendary tradition which is centred on figures mentioned by Gregory of Tours. According to the *Historia Francorum*, the Breton ruler Macliavus seized the patrimony of Theudericus, himself the son of another Breton ruler, Bodicus. Theudericus ultimately killed Macliavus and his son Iacob, leaving Macliavus' other son Warochus as ruler of a diminished portion of his father's land.[44] The various Lives of St Meloir, 'tissée de folklore et de pseudo-généalogies celtiques', weave the saint into this context, presenting him as the son of one of Budic's sons, Meliavus.[45] The Life given for this saint by Le Grand goes further: the Breton ruler Maxence seizes the patrimony of Theodoric, himself the son of another Breton ruler, Maxence's brother Budic. Theodoric successfully wages war against his uncle, but in the process massacres St Guigner and his companions, fearing that they had come from Ireland to assist Maxence. Because of this sin (which echoes exactly the tale told in the *Vita B* just where it seriously diverges from the *Vita A*), Theodoric loses his kingdom which then goes to his brother Meliau, the father of St Meloir.[46] These are clearly the same characters whom one sees in the *Vita B*, and it seems likely that Lives of different saints have affected one another: the *Vita B* provided a motive for Le Grand's account of St Meloir, and the Lives of St Meloir, as well as the *Historia Francorum*, provided a Breton context for the homicidal Theodoric, no longer the Cornish king of folklore but a historically or pseudo-historically attested Breton ruler. Yet these episodes of the *Vita B* have only been assimilated into the Breton context in the most superficial way, and no care has been taken to provide the saint with any local link to Cornouaille or to include any toponymic details.[47]

Theodoric's uncle of the *Vita B*, Macence, also provides suggestive analogues: he seems to hark back to the figure Maxen Wledic who is associated with the British settlement of Armorica in the Welsh tale *Breuddwyd Maxen*, as well as in various Welsh triads and genealogical traditions.[48] This Maxen also seems to have a reflex in King Massen of the Cornish play *Beunans Meriasek*,[49] and indeed, it has been argued that the *Vita* of Fingar might have inspired the addition of Cornish episodes to the tradition of Meriasek (or Meriadoc in

---

St Breage state that 'Tewder' slew some of Breage's companions. Doble has further noted that there is also in Brittany a St Teudar or Tuder. See Duine, *Memento*, pp. 189–90; Doble, *Saints of Cornwall*, iv.151–2 as well as ibid., i.106, 117; Orme, 'Saint Breage', p. 352. **44** Gregory of Tours, *Historiae* V.16 (Krusch, p. 214); Fleuriot, *Origines*, p. 240; Tanguy, 'Cornou', p. 577. **45** Duine, *Mémento*, pp. 99–100; Doble, *Saints of Cornwall*, iii.20–1, and now Bourgès, *Saint Melar*. See also appendix for P. Le Baud's contribution in this context. **46** Doble, *Saints of Cornwall*, iii.27. **47** While, for example, Le Grand says that miracles occur at Guiner's tomb, he doesn't say where this is located. **48** Bromwich, *Trioedd Ynys Prydein*, pp. 451–4. **49** Harris, *Life of Meriasek*, pp. 90–105.

Breton).[50] Meriadoc's *Vita* is set exclusively in Brittany,[51] but the saint's Cornish play contains significant visits to Cornwall, as well as characters resembling those of Fingar's *Vita*: Theodoric (*Vitae A* and *B*) and Massen (*Vita B*). However, it is worth restating that Theodoric in particular is well known to Cornish hagiographical folklore. Moreover, the episode of *Beunans Meriasek* in question has wider literary analogues;[52] only the name of the king, Massen, who is an entirely incidental character in it, gives one the least pause.

The names of the saint in the *Vita B* are only slightly different from those of the *Vita A*, although this may be less than significant if one considers that Le Grand was summarising a text or texts, one of which probably was Messingham's *Vita A*. Moreover, Le Grand may have confused his subject with another Breton saint, St Eguiner, the patron of Loc-Éguiner (Finistère). Doble noted that Le Grand describes the saint as patron of the *trève* of Loc-Éguiner and doesn't mention Pluvigner in Morbihan, St Guigner's most significant dedication. Thus, Doble argued, Le Grand seems to have been thinking of the subject of the *Vita B* as the patron of Loc-Éguiner rather than Pluvigner, and might have derived his spelling of the saint's name, Guiner, from this.[53] Such is Le Grand's influence that this confusion proved to be persistent.[54] Moreover, Le Grand's stated sources come from two locations: one, at Vannes cathedral, is in an area of Guigner's cult; the other stated source (for exactly what one is not sure) is at the collegiate church of Le Folgoët. Le Folgoët is in an area of Éguiner's cult alone – Guigner has no cult in Finistère. Le Grand himself seems to have been far more interested in (and inventive with) saints commemorated near his own place of origin, Morlaix, in Finistère;[55] hence his desire to combine Guigner and Eguiner?

However, even if, as seems likely, Le Grand had St (É)guiner[56] in mind rather than St Guigner, he nevertheless followed the same fashion as the *Vita A* in its form of reference to the saint: this supports the suspicion that Le Grand saw and used the *Vita A* as a source. Le Grand's introduction presents the saint

50 Murdoch, *Cornish Literature*, p. 102.   51 Doble, *Saints of Cornwall*, i.127.   52 Murdoch, 'Holy Hostage'.   53 Doble, *Saints of Cornwall*, i.108.   54 The notes to the fifth edition of Le Grand's *Vies* correct his omission of the dedication at Pluvigner and list dedications to St Guiner rather than Eguiner, but on the mistaken understanding that Eguiner and Guiner are the same saint; the annotator goes on to relate the story given by the *Vita A* in preference to that of the *Vita B*, describing its subject, however, as St Eguiner and contributing the otherwise unattested information that the saint was killed not because of his faith, but because of the hatred of the British for the Irish (Le Grand, *Vies des saints*, p. 704 n. 1). Duine, it should be noted, follows Le Grand in giving the name of the saint as Guigner or Eguiner in his heading, but in his text, which summarises the *Vita A*, he uses the names Fingar or Guigner (*Mémento*, pp. 126–7).   55 André-Yves Bourgès, personal communication The provision of a context in Cornouaille points somewhat to a Finistère saint, although Loc-Éguiner as a place-name is found in that part of Finistère which was in the Middle Ages Léon, not Cornouaille.   56 The exact form of the name is not entirely clear: see Tanguy, *Dictionnaire des noms … du Finistère*, p. 118.

as *Guiner* of the house of prince *Fingar*, and notes that he was converted along with his 'maistre'; this would almost seem to imply that Guiner was a minion of Fingar, the two being different people. Yet after this introduction, Le Grand presents a narrative in which the saint, clearly a single character, is called *Fingar* twice in the Irish portion of the Life, *Guiner* when he arrives in Brittany (and unambiguously presented as the same person as the Fingar of previous episodes), both *Guiner* and *Fingar* at the saint's martyrdom (again, with an ambivalent hint that there may be two characters at this particular point in the narrative),[57] and finally *Guiner* in his conclusion.

Philologically,[58] the Breton equivalent of Cornish *Gwinear* is *Guigner*, *Guinier*, or *Guiner*.[59] A species of hypercorrectness, no doubt, led Joseph Loth to differentiate, on a philological basis, between St Gwinear or Guigner, on the one hand, and Fingar, on the other; these two saints had previously been phonologically equated, even by Loth himself.[60] Bernard Tanguy followed Loth in separating SS Guigner or Gwinear from Fingar,[61] and argued further that the form Fingar was an Irish equivalent of the name of a different Breton saint, Guengar, reading Fingar as an eccentric translation of the Old Breton elements *win* ('pure', 'blessed') and *car* ('friend', 'parent') into Irish *finn* ('blessed') and *car* ('fond of', 'loving').[62] Yet despite the reservations of Loth and Tanguy, the form *Fingar* can be best explained as an Old or Middle Irish spelling of what would be in Modern Irish *Fionnghar, corresponding to Cornish Gwinear and Breton Guigner, composed of 'blessed' and an unknown *-gar*;[63] the Breton saint Guengar,

---

57 'Theodoric ... ayant aperceu le prince Fingar, avec 200 de ses gens, se rua sur eux, & les tailla en pieces. S Guiner qui, avec le reste, suivoit de loin, voyant ce massacre ...'   58 I would like to thank Máirín Ní Dhonnchadha for initially bringing to my attention the philological implications of the name Fingar, as well as for subsequent discussions; many others have generously discussed the Irish and Breton names with me as well, including John Carey, Gwenaël Le Duc, Kevin Murray, Oliver Padel, Paul Russell, and Jonathan Wooding. These can in no way be held responsible for such philological analysis as appears here, and I claim all errors as my own.   59 Tanguy, 'Cornou', p. 577 and n. 2, citing Loth, 'Noms des saints', p. 299 (original edition in *Revue celtique*).   60 Loth initially equated Fingar with an erroneous form *Gwincar* which he said was Cornish and saw as the same name as that represented in the Breton place-name Pluvigner (*Chrestomathie bretonne*, p. 129), in effect equating Fingar with Guigner, the eponym of Pluvigner. He later corrected the mistake, noting that Gwincar was a mistaken transcription for Gwinear, and had misled him into equating Fingar and Guigner. He then concluded: 'Les deux noms sont très differents: *Fingar* ne peut donner *Guigner*' (Loth, 'Noms des saints', p. 299). It is interesting to note that Loth's phrasing clearly shows his assumption that an Irish name was translated into a British form rather than vice versa.   61 Tanguy, 'Paroisses primitives', p. 142.   62 Tanguy, *Dictionnaire des noms ... du Finistère*, pp. 117–18; 'Cornou', p. 576 and n. 21. If one took Fingar as a compound name in Middle Irish composed of *finn* and *car* (Quin, *Dictionary*, s.vv. 1 *finn* and 5 *car*), one would expect a form such as **Fin(d)char*. The form *Fingar*, however, would necessarily imply nasalisation of the second element (*-car* to *-gar*), where one might expect lenition (*-car* to *-char*) in Irish.   63 Jackson, *Language and History*, pp. 436–9, especially 439.

despite some suggestive Cornish connections, must be left to one side.[64] Thus, in effect, the *Vita A* and the *Vita B* alternate between two different forms of its subject's name, Guigner or Guiner (corresponding to Gwinear) and Fingar.[65]

The name Fingar itself is unattested in medieval Irish sources: the closest form is *Finchar* or *Finecha(i)r* which would seem to be composed of *fin(e)*, 'kin' and *-char*, 'loving'.[66] This, however, is not the same name as Fingar. The Brythonic form is more securely evinced: it is attested in a ninth-century charter from the Book of Llandaf, as *Guiner* and *Guinier*.[67] The logical, if not provable, conclusion is that the Brythonic form gave rise to the 'Irish' form, and that this was done in the context of the composition or transmission of the *Vita A*.[68] The form Fingar suggests strongly that this is, dare one say, a learned invention; the author of the *Vita A*, or of his immediate source if indeed he had one, is its likely originator.[69] The contrast in the *Vita A* between the detailed account of events in Cornwall, including much local toponymy and the unconvincing or absent personal names as well as the vague settings for the Irish and Breton episodes, strongly suggests an immediate Cornish source or author. The fact of the saint's martyrdom in Cornwall (in the *Vita B* somewhat clumsily disguised as Breton Cornouaille) indisputably points to the primacy of the cult's association there for the author of the *Vita A*. The absence in the *vitae* of the saint's Cornish name, Gwinear, however, hints that this Cornish material might have been partially adapted into a Breton context: the *Vita A* would seem to have been either composed in Brittany (with Cornish materials, by a Cornish cleric?), or transmitted in the form in which we now have it there. Indeed, it is worth recalling that the sole extant manuscript of the *Vita A* has Paris as its provenance.

The *Vita C* is known only from one tantalisingly brief antiquarian note, which nevertheless strongly suggests that there was a significant local tradition

---

64 See appendix. 65 This is not, however, an example of a double-name formula such as Hywel Emanuel found in the Lives of St Cadog and St David ('Double-Name Formula'). Here Emanuel examined the use of the name 'Sophias' for St Cadog as well as Dewi for St David in these respective *vitae*; it should be noted, however, that as straightforward as Cadog-Sophias may be, in Lifris's *Vita Cadoci* Cadog begins life as Cadfael, and thus is endowed with three names, the switch from Cadfael to Cadog being accomplished without explanation: Wade-Evans, *Vitae sanctorum*, pp. 28, 32, and especially 34. 66 As found in various annals as well as *dindshenchas* from the Book of Leinster: J. Uhlich, *Morphologie*, p. 250. I wish to thank Kevin Murray for this reference. 67 Evans and Rhŷs, *Book of Llan Dav*, p. 174; Loth, 'Noms des saints', p. 299; Davies, *Welsh Microcosm*, p. 172. 68 One might also consider the suggestive example of the Life of St Idunet in the *Cartulary of Landévennec*: the scribe copied a Life of St Ethbin, replaced the name of the latter with that of the former in the first six instances, but then desisted, retaining the name Ethbin throughout the rest of the Life. See Guillotel, 'Origines de Landévennec', p. 102. 69 Oliver Padel has noted that the 'e' of the second syllable of the Brythonic form does not correspond to the 'a' of the second syllable of Fingar (personal communication); this would suggest that Fingar is a close rather than exact equivalent (hibernicisation?) of the name Gwinear.

concerning the eponymous patron saint of Gwinear. The sixteenth-century antiquary, John Leland, made a précis of a Life of St Breage which he found in Cornwall, in which he read (or perhaps noted), 'Barricus socius Patritij ut legitur in uita S. Wymeri [*for* Wynieri]'.[70] Doble and, later, Orme have pointed out that as the *Vita A* does not mention a Barricus, Leland or the author of the Life he saw must be referring to a Life of Gwinear which differed from, and was perhaps even independent of, the *Vita A*.[71] This is the only discernible reference to this *Vita*: other evidence for the saint's cult in Cornwall is either documentary rather than narrative, or refers clearly and it seems exclusively to the *Vita A*, in which case the saint is named Fingar rather than Gwinear. The record of this cult in Cornwall, as it appears in the admittedly sparse sources for medieval Cornish cults, is patchy: its earliest appearance occurs in the bishop's register of 1258 which mentions a church of *Sanctus Wynerus* (*Wynierus* in 1286).[72] A tenth-century list of what seem to be Cornish saints does not mention this cult;[73] William Worcestre's notes on the saints honoured at various local churches from his journey through Cornwall of 1478 fail to refer to the saint.[74] Nicholas Roscarrock, a seventeenth-century Cornish antiquary, apparently knew nothing of Gwinear until after he had completed his *Lives of the Saints*; he inserted references to Gwinear and his sister Piala, and augmented his discussion of Ia, only after seeing Picard's published edition of the *Vita A*. Thus Roscarrock refers to the saint not as Gwinear but as 'Guigner or Fingar'.[75]

The absence of feast days within either the *Vita A* or (as far as can be ascertained) the *Vita B* renders these Lives liturgically unsatisfactory, and complicates the separation of what are probably several cults. The hagiographical tradition surrounding Fingar, the product of the medieval Anselm as well as the seventeenth-century researchers, has attracted to itself one main feast day, which itself would seem to date only from the seventeenth century. The second edition of the English recusant *English Martyrologe* (1640) ascribes the commemoration 'in Cornwall' of St Fingar, spelled *Finguar* and clearly known from Messingham's *Florilegium*, to 23 March.[76] The first edition of this

---

70 Orme, 'Saint Breage', pp. 344 and 352. As Orme argues, 'The phrase "*ut legitur*" is not characteristic of Leland's note-taking in Latin. It is more likely to be a quotation from Breage's Life – a cross-reference by the author of that Life to other Lives that he knew – rather than a gloss added by Leland' (ibid., p. 344). 71 Ibid., pp. 344–5 and 351. Orme argues that as the *Vita C* seems not to have been known to Anselm, it might have been written after the *Vita A*; the use, or not, of the *Vita A* as a source for the *Vita C* is unprovable in any case. 72 Padel, *Popular Dictionary*, p. 93. 73 Olson and Padel, 'Tenth-Century List'. 74 Harvey, *William Worcestre*. 75 Orme, *Roscarrock's Lives*, pp. 77–8, 105, 135. Although Roscarrock was Cornish, he aspired to be, Orme stresses, a national rather than merely local historian (ibid., p. 17); and indeed his accounts of several Cornish saints show at times little local knowledge and a profound reliance on material previously collected, at times in contradiction of local information: K. Jankulak, 'Some Sources'. 76 I. W. P. [John Wilson, priest], *The English Martyrologe ... collected, reviewed, and much augmented* (1640),

martyrology, published in 1608 and signed by 'I.W. Priest', contains few
Cornish saints; this second edition, 'much augmented' with several Cornish
saints including Fingar and Ia, served as Colgan's source for the feast days of
these saints.[77] Colgan, however, gives Fingar's feast from this source as 23
February, whereas the Bollandists pointedly note that it gives the date as 23
March. This apparently innocuous error perhaps stems from Colgan's visible
frustration at his inability to find Fingar among the numerous Irish saints listed
in various and lengthy medieval and early modern lists of Irish saints. Having
searched the various Irish martyrologies for a suitable candidate under several
possible forms of the name Fingar or Guigner, Colgan settled upon *Finchan* or
Finchadhan 'of Ard' whose feast day is 23 February according to the martyrologies
of Gorman, Donegal, and Tallaght,[78] and identified the Fingar of the *Vita A*
with this saint. Colgan's desire to provide and enhance an Irish pedigree for this
saint led, arguably, to this substitution; Fingar's absence from the devotional
topography of medieval Ireland was indeed, for Colgan, a problem.[79]

In Brittany two feast days would seem to have been attributed to St Guigner,
as early as 1530. The Vannes Missal of this date gives only one feast day for St
Guigner (*Guinnerius*) in its calendar: this is 14 December. The *proprium
sanctorum* of the same Missal, however, has on this date merely a note referring
to May, where after the feast of St John *ante portam latinam* (6 May) there is a mass
for St Guigner (here *Guinnerus*) which gives a summary of the *Vita A*.[80] The 14
December feast day is that most often cited with reference to St Guigner, probably
because it is the date given by Le Grand. Yet while Le Grand clearly did not
invent it, one has to wonder if his embracing of the 14 December feast resulted
from his likely conflation of St Guigner with St Eguiner. One wonders further if
the subsequent prevalence of this feast day might not be chiefly due to the force
of Le Grand's influence. Certainly the early eighteenth-century *Martyrologe*

---

pp. 66–7: 'The same day [23 March] in Cornwall the commemoration of S. Finguar martyr,
sonne of Clito a king in Ireland, who converted to the Christian faith by S. Patricke, and
refusing the crowne and dignity of a prince after his father's death, came over into Cornwall,
to lead a solitary life where he was slayne in hatred of Christian Religion by Theodoricus
king of Cornewal about the year of Christ five hundred'. In the margin is 'D. Anselmus,
Florilegium SS. Hyberniae', a clear reference to Messingham.   **77** The first edition of this
martyrology has been reprinted as vol. ccxxxii of the series *English Recusant Literature
1558–1640*.   **78** Colgan, *Acta sanctorum*, p. 391.   **79** Interestingly, O'Hanlon ridicules
Colgan's emendation of Fingar's name and the identification with the saint commemorated
on 23 February, commenting that Colgan 'does not appear indeed to have been very happy
in his conjectures referring to our saint' in the case of the saint's name. However, in a
different footnote, concerning the two feast days, he merely comments that the Bollandists
have corrected Colgan's reading of his source from February to 23 March (*Lives of the Irish
Saints*, ii.673 nn. 8 and 11). As O'Hanlon follows Colgan in listing this saint under 23
February, presumably he does not connect the misreading of the saint's name to a possible
misreading of his feast day; alternatively, O'Hanlon, like Colgan, may be anxious to retain as
much of Fingar's Irish pedigree as possible.   **80** Doble, 'Mass at Vannes', p. 135.

universel of the Breton abbé Chastelain presents a composite of several saints, no doubt inspired mainly by Le Grand: he gives the feast day of St Eguiner, whom he describes as the brother of Piala, as 14 December.[81] Lobineau's *Les vies des saints de Bretagne*, which was published in 1725 but annotated in the 1830s, gives the same feast day; while he calls the saint Guigner or Fingar, never Eguiner, he lists Loc-Éguiner among the saint's dedications.[82]

If one looks to the Cornish parish named after and dedicated to a saint understood to be the same as the subject of the *Vita A* and *Vita B* (and whose toponymy corresponds to that of the detailed toponymy of the *Vita A* as the place of the saint's martyrdom) the matter is not entirely clarified. In England the standardised liturgical books of the Reformation left little room for the commemoration of local saints; increasingly a major parish feast could have little reference to the feast of the parish's patron saint.[83] Thus it is not necessarily informative that the only known reference to the parish feast of the Cornish parish of Gwinear states that it was held on the Sunday after the first Thursday in May.[84] However, the Cornish day is extremely suggestive in light of the date in May upon which, according to the Vannes Missal *proprium sanctorum*, Guigner's mass was to be celebrated. Moreover, St Guigner is the patron saint and eponym of the parish of Pluvigner (Morbihan);[85] this parish, which claimed from at least the eighteenth century to possess relics of its patron as well as of other saints,[86] celebrates its patronal feast, its pardon, on the third Sunday in May.[87] Arguably the May feast is more authoritatively connected to St Guigner than 14 December; it is reasonable as well to argue that SS Guigner and Gwinear are indeed the same saint.[88]

Thus if one looks at both the forms of the saint's name and his feast days, it seems increasingly reasonable to separate the saint's tradition into the tradition of the *Vita A* (and by extension, the narrative of the *Vita B*) which knows its subject mainly as Fingar; and that seemingly consistently independent of these Lives, which can be connected with the cult practices at Gwinear in Cornwall, perhaps Pluvigner in Brittany, and most likely with the lost *Vita C*. It is notable,

---

81 Vallerie, 'Références bretonnes', pp. 147 and 169. 82 Lobineau, *Vies des saints*, i.29. 83 Orme, *English Church Dedications*, pp. 42, 48. 84 Ibid, p. 85, on the authority of Boase's *Collectanea Cornubiensia* of 1890 and Doble, 'Mass at Vannes', p. 135, no doubt on the same authority. 85 Tanguy, 'Paroisses primitives', p. 142: *Pleguinner, Pleiguinner* in 1259, *Pleuvigner* in 1327. 86 This according to Lobineau (*Vies des saints*, i.31; cf. Duine, *Mémento*, p. 13); subsequently a description of the church's reliquaries, dated 1742, cites Lobineau's claim. This occurs in Cillart de Kerampoul's *Pouillé* (Archives Départementales du Morbihan, G 1118, p. 64), which is to be edited and published by Gwenaël Le Duc. As well, Guillotin de Corson's nineteenth-century account of the church mentions reliquaries holding relics not only of St Guigner but of several others: 'Pluvigner et son Pardon', p. 106. I wish to thank Gwenaël Le Duc for his provision of the latter two sources. 87 Guillotin de Corson, 'Pluvigner et son Pardon', p. 106. 88 Job an Irien sees the cult of Gwinear as an importation of that of Guigner from Brittany, possibly in the tenth century. This is a reasonable if unprovable argument: 'Saints du Cornwall', pp. 182 and 188.

for example, that the seventeenth-century *English Martyrologe*, while it refers explicitly to the saint's cult as evinced 'in Cornwall', refers to the saint by a form which seems to be a hybrid of the 'Irish' and 'Cornish' forms, the former predominating. Those occurrences of the saint's name in Cornwall which are not directly linked to the *Vita A* (and indirectly with the 23 February or March feast day) show it exclusively in the form *Gwinear*.[89]

The Cornish cult of Gwinear itself shows arguably legendary Irish accretions, although these are complex in their manifestations. A visible group of parishes in west Cornwall whose patron saints are credited with legendary and inter-related Irish origins has been the subject of much debate. Henry Jenner enthusiastically saw these as evidence of early medieval Irish settlement.[90] Charles Thomas jettisoned the hagiographical material but saw evidence for an Irish presence in western Cornwall which probably would have been less tempting without the discarded but still influential evidence of these church dedications; and indeed Thomas subsequently noted the connection between the picture presented by the traditions of the saints and various other types of evidence.[91] Some of Thomas's archaeological evidence for Irish settlement in western Cornwall has been questioned.[92] Most recently, Thomas has assembled most of his evidence for this Irish settlement (but, notably, not the more contentious archaeological material) and contrasted its implications with the suggestive if dubious hagiographical material (the latter 'included with every reserve') – leaving the reader to draw his or her own conclusions.[93] On the other hand, Doble and Orme have characterised the attributions of Irish origins to Cornish saints as a hagiographical fashion.[94] Irish attributions in the Breton hagiographical material have been similarly characterised.[95]

The attribution of Irish origins to some Breton and Cornish saints may or may not be without historical foundation; clearly, however, it is a distinctive and fertile hagiographical conceit. In the case of the saint under discussion, one must consider the absence of an Irish cult of Fingar as well as the *Vitae's* lack

---

89 With the dubious exception of Roscarrock's *Lives of the Saints*, for which see above. See, as well, the forms of the name of the patron saint of the parish of Gwinear listed by Orme, in which the name Fingar occurs only once and in a modern context: in 1925 the Cornish historian Charles Henderson listed the patron saint of the parish as Winierus or Fingar in his *Cornish Church Guide* (Orme, *English Church Dedications*, p. 85); here the form Fingar is derived from the *Vita A*.   90 Jenner, 'Irish Immigrations'.   91 Thomas, 'Grass-Marked Pottery', p. 328; idem, 'Irish Settlements'; idem, 'Irish Colonists', especially p. 7.   92 Ryan, 'Native Pottery', p. 630; Preston-Jones and Rose, 'Medieval Cornwall', pp. 175–6; Todd, *South-West to AD 1000*, p. 252.   93 Thomas, *Mute Stones*, p. 186 and fig. 11.1.   94 For example, Doble, *Saints of Cornwall*, i.110; Orme, 'Saint Breage', p. 349.   95 B. Merdrignac notes that Carolingian *vitae* of Breton saints often include a sojourn in Ireland by their subjects, while the 'cliché' of the Irish saint passing a period of exile in Brittany belongs more properly to post-Carolingian *vitae*: 'Perception de l'Irlande', p. 70 as well as 'Origines bretonnes', p. 298. See also the articles by Gwenaël Le Duc and A.-Y. Bourgès in the present volume.

of geographical or dynastic precision concerning Fingar's Irish context. In light of these circumstances, it looks very much as though a Brittonic speaker 'Hibernicised' the name of a Brittonic saint, apparently Guigner/Gwinear, into Fingar, a name unattested in medieval or modern Ireland, Cornwall, or Brittany except in connection with the *Vita A*. The author of the *Vita A*, whether in Cornwall or in Brittany (and both regions are subject to the hibernicising tendency) was probably responsible for installing the names in the forms in which we know them in the hagiographical canon of the composite cult; while the idea of an Irish origin or even of two names might have been implicit in the cult apart from the *vitae*, the *Vita A* seems to have authoritatively fixed the form Fingar. The name Fingar itself has left no reflex in the cults in Cornwall and Brittany apart from the *vitae*: it is arguably a literary fossil and seems connected to several feast days which themselves are literary fossils: 23 March in the British Isles and 14 December in Brittany. Nevertheless, the process of thus emphasising the saint's Irish origins belongs to an impulse similar to that which attributed Irish origins to various Breton and Cornish saints, at times at the level of local cult. This process of stressing this or that aspect of the cult of a saint through manipulation (in its least malicious sense) of *vitae*, dedications, and feast days, continued through the seventeenth century. Indeed, Fingar's pliability in this respect proved very convenient to his cult. In the seventeenth century Thomas Messingham and John Colgan merely extended a process which had its origins in the Middle Ages: they further consolidated the saint's Irish character. It is fitting that such breadth of reputation as the saint now enjoys is surely due to their efforts.

Appendix: St Guengar

According to a charter of 1133, a St Guengar was the patron saint of the parish church of Pierric (near Redon, in Loire-Atlantique).[96] The current dedication of the church, however, is to St Guénolé, a transformation which probably occurred in the nineteenth century – probably, Tanguy has argued, through confusion over various local pronunciations of Guengar's name.[97] The parish of Pierric would seem to have supplanted an older parish by the name of

---

96 Loth, 'Noms des saints', p. 294. St Guengar is in addition usually taken as the eponym of what in the Middle Ages was the parish of Languengar (now a sub-parish of Lesneven) in that part of Finistère which was Léon rather than Cornouaille: Largillière, *Saints et l'organisation*, p. 300; Loth, 'Noms des saints', p. 294; Pérennès, *Dictionnaire topographique*, p. 41; Tanguy, 'Cornou', p. 576, *Dictionnaire des noms … du Finistère*, pp. 117–8. This is rendered unlikely by the form of the place name: one would expect *Lawengar rather than Languengar, or even, as attested in 1420, Lagangar, which would seem to be an error for *Langangar, i.e. *lan* + *Kengar* (Gwenaël Le Duc, personal communication). Moreover, the local church (which is no longer extant) was dedicated not to St Guengar but to St Azenor (Tanguy, 'Cornou', p. 117). St Guengar's sole attestation is as patron of the medieval church of Pierric.   97 Tanguy, 'Cornou', pp. 575–6.

Cornou (mentioned in ninth-century charters) which had disappeared by about 870.[98] The name Cornou suggested to Fleuriot a reflex of the post-migration extent of 'Cornovia' or 'Cornouaille' over the whole of southern Brittany.[99] In the later sixth century Cornovia was divided into Bro-Erec (in the east, including the area of Cornou) and Cornouaille proper (in the west); Fleuriot saw the name Cornou as a reflex of a state of affairs before this division. Tanguy is noncommittal on this matter, but argues that the 'nom ethnique' of Cornou can certainly attest to the presence of 'Cornoviens' (immigrants from Cornwall) perhaps as distinct from the populace (?Bretons) of Cornovia proper. A perceived link between the cult of St Guengar and that of the Cornish saint Gwinear (through the form *Fingar*, which Tanguy saw as phonologically equivalent to Guengar but which is associated in the *vitae* with Gwinear) further supported this argument.[100] In addition, Tanguy noted that the characters named by Gregory of Tours in the creation of Bro-Erec (most notably Weroc or Waroc, from whom the name derives) resemble those found in the tradition of Fingar's *vitae*.

Interestingly, the fifteenth-century Breton historian, Pierre Le Baud, transcribed something which is clearly closely related to the *Vita A* for the most part (frequently echoing it exactly), but which contains additional material connecting the quotations, one piece of which is evidently related to the account found in the *Historia Francorum*. This additional material was presumably not composed by Le Baud himself[101] but appeared in his source, which he apparently found at Saint-Gildas-de-Rhuys.[102] Le Baud's account states that the saint (Vinerius or Vingnerus) came from Ireland 'in britanniam armoricam', specifically to 'Guerocus comes Venetensis' (further called 'rex britannie') who plays the role attributed in the *Vita A* to the unnamed Breton ruler. Gueroc is meant to stand for Gregory's sixth-century ruler Warochus. Le Baud's account otherwise clearly stems from the same source as the *Vita A* (the Cornish episodes, for example, take place in Cornwall rather than Cornouaille), but his invocation of Waroc hints that his source is very closely related to Le Grand's source; the legendary of the church of Le Folgoët, for example, was seen by both Le Baud and Le Grand.[103] Nevertheless one cannot make too much of the appearance of Gueroc: he occurs in several *vitae* of Breton saints and in several cases (the *vitae* of Guenhaël and Ninnoc)[104] he is merely, as Bernard Merdrignac describes him, a rather generic 'quelque puissant'.[105] Lest, however, Le Baud's (or

---

98 Ibid., p. 575.   99 Fleuriot, *Origines*, p. 240. The northern portion of Brittany was known as 'Dumnonia' or 'Dumnonée': Galliou and Jones, *The Bretons*, p. 134.   100 Tanguy, 'Cornou', pp. 576–7.   101 For it is in Latin; Gwenaël Le Duc, 'Évêché mythique', pp. 181–2.   102 Gw. Le Duc, personal communication.   103 Le Duc, 'Évêché mythique', p. 182; Bourgès, 'Archéologie du mythe', p. 15; I would like to thank Gwenaël Le Duc for allowing me to use his transcription of Le Baud's notes, from ms. 1 F 1003 of the Archives Départementales d'Ille-et-Vilaine, p. 177.   104 Lapidge and Sharpe, *Bibliography*, nrs 919 and 920 (Guenhaël) and 946 (Ninnoc).   105 Merdrignac, *Recherches*, ii.159; Duine, *Mémento*, p. 180.

his source's) invocation of Gueroc be seen as utter fanciful nonsense (Le Baud being, to my mind, an underrated historian),[106] it should be noted that only in his account does the landing of the saint in Brittany have any claim to geographical precision and accuracy, Vannes generally being the region in which one finds Guigner's cult.

Yet one might argue that the St Guengar associated with Cornou should not be seen as a Cornish saint: the link to the Cornish Gwinear, itself highly disputable, would have been indirect at best, and would have been made far later than the separation of Cornouaille and Bro-Erec. That is, if there were immigrants from Cornwall in Bro-Erec at an early date, they probably would not, on the evidence extant, have thought of Guengar as a Cornish saint. Certainly if the cult of Guengar was brought into Brittany with these 'Cornoviens' (as Tanguy's line of argument, if taken much farther than Tanguy does, would suggest), it has left absolutely no trace of its presumed origins in Cornwall. Even if the name Guengar were equivalent to the name Fingar, one cannot, and Tanguy would not, extend the identification between the composite Fingar/Guigner/ Gwinear and Guengar back into the sixth century. Having said this, the cult of Guengar in a location previously known as Cornou is suggestive – Tanguy will rightly say no more than this.[107] Yet the tradition of Fingar in particular seems dogged by suggestive coincidences. This may be yet one more.

---

106 See also Le Duc, 'Évêché mythique', p. 175.   107 Tanguy, 'Cornou', p. 578.

Une course en char dans l'hagiographie bretonne? Saint Samson contre la *Theomacha*

Bernard Merdrignac

Tout le monde s'accorde à reconnaître que la première *Vita* de saint Samson occupe une place stratégique dans l'hagiographie bretonne. Il serait toutefois présomptueux de ma part de prétendre rouvrir ce dossier alors que la réédition récente de ce document par le professeur Pierre Flobert[1] devrait enfin permettre de reprendre, sur des bases plus fiables, des débats chronologiques qui tournent en rond depuis un siècle faute d'avoir pu disposer, jusqu'à présent, d'un texte convenablement édité.[2] Il est donc prudent de fonder cette communication sur les données à propos desquelles un minimum de consensus devrait s'établir entre la plupart des chercheurs qui se sont intéressés à ce document. Quelle que soit la période de rédaction qu'on lui assigne (entre le VIIe siècle et la première moitié du IXe siècle),[3] la *Vita prima Samsonis* est sans doute le plus ancien document hagiographique de Bretagne continentale à nous être parvenu. Bien qu'il s'agisse d'une des lois du genre hagiographique, les prétentions de son auteur à s'appuyer une version antérieure (*Acta/Gesta S. Samsonis*, perdus) ne doivent pas être rejetées systématiquement, même si les opinions divergent sur la valeur de cette source 'fort possible'.[4] En préalable à toute discussion, voici la traduction que propose Pierre Flobert du passage du prologue de la *Vita prima* qui fait référence à cette source perdue:

> Avant toute chose, je veux que vous croyiez à mon sujet que ces propos n'ont été rassemblés ni d'après les divagations de mon imagination ni

---

1 Flobert, *Vie ancienne*.   2 Les deux éditions précédentes, celle de dom Jean Mabillon (*Acta sanctorum* I, pp. 165–85; reprise dans les AASS, Jul. VI, pp. 568–93) et celle de Robert Fawtier (*Vie de saint Samson*), comportent chacune des déficiences, voire des faiblesses, dont Flobert, *Vie ancienne*, pp. 59–61 fait sereinement état.   3 Cf. Flobert, *Vie ancienne*, pp. 102–111 qui propose une datation moyenne (milieu VIIIe s.). En faveur de la datation basse, voir Poulin, 'Dossier'; pour la datation haute, voir Guillotel, 'Origines du ressort', et Merdrignac, 'Première Vie'. Une *retractatio* de ma part (dont l'éventualité était déjà envisagée dans l'article cité précédemment, pp. 283–4) n'est pas à exclure, une fois posément pesés les arguments séduisants de Pierre Flobert.   4 Poulin, 'Dossier', p. 726.

d'après des rumeurs désordonnées et incohérentes, mais selon ce que j'ai appris d'un pieux et vénérable vieillard (*a quodam religioso ac uenerabili sene*)[5] qui menait, depuis près de quatre-vingt années, une vie catholique et pieuse dans son monastère fondé de l'autre côté de la mer par Samson en personne. Et à une date proche de l'époque du même Samson déjà nommé, la mère de celui-ci avait rapporté les faits à son oncle, un très saint diacre lequel était le propre cousin de Samson: voilà ce qu'il m'assurait véridiquement en me rapportant généreusement maints traits touchant ses actions prodigieuses. Ce n'est pas tout car il y a encore nombre de récits remarquables des actions prodigieuses qu'il accomplit merveilleusement de ce côté-ci de la mer en Bretagne et en Romanie qui furent emportés outremer par le saint diacre dessus-dit, appelé Henoc, écrits dans un style finement approprié, et le vénérable vieillard dont nous venons de parler et qui demeurait dans ce monastère en faisait la lecture sans cesse devant moi pieusement et scrupuleusement ... '[6]

On peut déduire de ces propos qu'une relation des *Acta* du saint a été rédigée sur le Continent, vers le troisième quart du VIe siècle, par le diacre Henoc, témoin direct qui avait accompagné son cousin durant une bonne partie de sa carrière insulaire ('au moins depuis la conversion de sa famille' et 'peut-être' dès l'épisode qui va nous retenir), puis qui l'aurait suivi en Bretagne armoricaine et en Romania. Il aurait par la suite emporté ces *emendatiores gestae* outre Manche.[7]

D'autre part, vu la propension au népotisme du monachisme celtique (mais que l'on retrouve ailleurs à la même époque), il est probable qu'Henoc a succédé à Amon, le père du saint fondateur, à la tête du monastère de Saint-Sampson-of-Golant (en Cornwall).[8] Le prologue de la *Vita prima* permettrait ainsi de reconstituer une amorce de liste abbatiale: Amon, le père de Samson, Henoc, cousin du saint (dont le nom, forgé sur la racine celtique *hen-*, signifie 'l'Ancien'), puis le neveu de ce dernier, le 'vénérable vieillard' (ou 'Ancien') dont l'auteur de la *Vita prima* se réclame de l'autorité.[9]

5 *Senex* ('l'ancien') constitue aussi un titre honorifique s'appliquant à un abbé (cf. Duine, *Origines bretonnes*, p. 63). Flobert, *Vie ancienne*, p. 143 n. 2–5, rappelle ce sens du terme *senex* et en relève des occurrences ailleurs dans *la Vita* (I.12, 18, 20, 21), mais il ne retient pas cette traduction dans la mesure où il est ici question du 'grand âge' de ce personnage.   6 *Vita prima* Prol. 2 (Flobert, pp. 140–3).   7 Poulin, 'Dossier', p. 719. Je ne suis pas ce chercheur lorsqu'il identifie le diacre Henoc et celui qui est mentionné au chapitre 25 du livre I. En effet, l'ordination au diaconat d'Henoc n'intervient, selon la *Vita prima* (I.52), qu'au moment où le saint se dispose à émigrer et confie sa fondation cornique à son propre père. Comme le remarque Pierre Flobert (*Vie ancienne*, p. 222, n. 52–1), il n'y a, avant ce dernier chapitre, 'presque rien dans le récit sur les cousins du saint' (I.30 et 45).   8 Merdrignac, 'Première Vie', p. 247. Voir aussi idem, 'Henoc', p. 169–70.   9 Le breton *hen est*, en effet, apparenté au latin *senex*, comme le rappelle Fleuriot, *Dictionary*, part I, p. 208. Cf. Merdrignac, 'Henoc', pp. 170–1.

Etant donné les divergences sur la portée historique de cette *Vita*, je me contente de récapituler ce qui ressort des propos de son auteur, sans préjuger de leur véracité. On doit sans doute comprendre (à la suite de F.C. Burkitt)[10] qu'il se présente comme un moine breton insulaire, ayant longtemps vécu à Saint-Sampson-of-Golant (plutôt qu'à Llantwit),[11] qui aurait été chargé de mettre à la portée de ses confrères de Dol (en Bretagne continentale) les traditions qui avaient cours outre-Manche dans les établissements contrôlés par la famille du saint fondateur.[12] Cette lecture du prologue de la *Vita prima* revient à considérer celle-ci avant tout comme un témoignage de la persistance des contacts entre les fondations samsoniennes de part et d'autre de la Manche (durant quelques générations ou sur plusieurs siècles, selon la perspective dans laquelle on se place). Par contre, les références que fait l'auteur à des témoignages oraux contemporains du saint sont, bien entendu, beaucoup plus difficilement contrôlables.[13]

Sans conteste, 'L'épisode le plus remarquable' sur le plan des rapports entre la tradition orale et l'écriture hagiographique est celui de la '*theomacha*-sorcière de la forêt' (I.26–7). Sans me poser en spécialiste de la recherche des éléments folkloriques dans l'hagiographie bretonne, je souhaite, dans la présente communication proposer une relecture du triptyque (I.22–36) dans lequel prend place cet épisode en soulignant d'emblée qu'il occupe une place centrale dans le premier livre de la *Vita*.

En voici tout d'abord une brève analyse. Tombé gravement malade, Amon, le père de Samson, fait appel à son fils, alors retiré au monastère de l'abbé Piro (Ynys-Pyr = Caldey Island; Pays-de-Galles). Après que le saint eut rencontré sur sa route et éliminé une *theomacha* 'maléfique', Amon confesse à Samson une faute qu'il a jusqu'alors tenue secrète et se voue à la vie religieuse ainsi que toute sa famille. Sur le chemin du retour au monastère, Samson extermine un 'serpent' que son père et son oncle qui l'accompagnent ont identifié par rapport à la tradition familiale. L'évêque Dubric, venu passer le Carême à Inis-Pyr, tire les conséquences de cette épreuve qualifiante en assurant la promotion de Samson à la charge de *pistor* ('cellérier'),[14] puis à l'abbatiat du monastère après la mort providentielle de Piro.[15]

A mon sens, la manière dont s'articulent dans ce récit les motifs traditionnels (sorcière/géante? serpent tutélaire? ...), les éléments liturgiques (viatique, Carême ...), les références scripturaires et les réminiscences des auteurs classiques et chrétiens n'apporte pas seulement des éclaircissements sur le mode de composition de la *Vita prima Samsonis*. Elle ouvre des perspectives sur l'organisation ecclésiastique des pays celtiques durant le haut Moyen Age.

---

10 Burkitt, 'Saint Samson', pp. 48–9. 11 Merdrignac, 'Première Vie', pp. 246–7.
12 Ibid., p. 250–1. 13 Cf le tableau suggestif (dans la perspective d'une datation haute) présenté par Thomas, *Mute Stones*, p. 226. 14 Flobert, *Vie ancienne*, p. 198 n. 34–1.
15 Pour une analyse plus détaillée, on se reportera avec profit à Flobert, ibid., p. 125.

I

Il convient d'abord de situer la rencontre de la *theomacha* dans son contexte narratif. C'est 'l'hiver' (*Quodam itaque tempore hiemis ...*). Le père de Samson est atteint d'une maladie qui paraît mortelle. Ses 'proches' (*suis uicinis*) l'incitent 'à recevoir, selon l'usage, le sacrement de la communion avant la mort de sa chair'. Le mourant insiste pour que l'on fasse venir à son chevet son fils aîné Samson, 'élu de Dieu', seul capable de lui rendre 'la santé du corps et celle de l'âme' (I.22).[16] Des messagers à cheval sont donc dépêchés à Inis Pyr, mais Samson fait des difficultés pour les suivre: 'Retournez en votre maison; en effet, si je ne m'abuse j'ai désormais quitté l'Egypte (*Aegyptum reliqui*); mon chemin n'y conduit pas; de fait, c'est Dieu qui a le pouvoir de guérir le malade' (I.24).[17] L'allusion à l'Egypte vaut d'être soulignée ici. En effet, on ne peut se contenter d'y voir une allusion passe-partout à la captivité des Hébreux en Egypte.[18] La réponse de Samson ne prend toute sa portée que par rapport à la communion que son père attend de lui en viatique. Dès le Ve siècle, l'usage est de ne pas refuser la dernière communion à un mourant, même coupable de fautes graves.[19] A Dieu de le juger! La comparaison entre la migration de l'âme du défunt et la sortie d'Egypte du peuple d'Israël est un thème fréquemment attesté à partir du VIe siècle (dans la *Vita* de Césaire d'Arles, par exemple) et le *Sacramentaire gélasien* ancien (vers 750) supplie le Seigneur d'accueillir 'avec douceur et tendresse' l'âme du défunt 'qui revient des régions d'Egypte'.[20] Bref, la mort qu'attend le père du saint est ainsi clairement assimilée à une Pâque personnelle, et l'on comprend que Samson, déjà mort à ce monde puisqu'il a opté pour la vie monastique, se refuse à retourner en Egypte en renouant avec sa famille charnelle.[21]

Aegyptum reliqui. Cette remarque est à mon avis essentielle pour interpréter l'épisode suivant. En effet, l'abbé Piro parvient à convaincre le saint de revenir sur sa position et de se rendre, par charité, auprès de son père en compagnie d'un jeune diacre qui va ultérieurement faire office de faire-valoir aux côtés du héros. Munis de la bénédiction de l'abbé, et après qu' 'un *uehiculum* eut été attelé à un cheval' (*impositoque in equum uehiculo*) les deux moines prennent la route. Chemin faisant, lors de la traversée d' 'une immense forêt' (*per uastissimam siluam*), ils rencontrent une '*theomacha* déjà vieille' (*theomacham ... iam uetulam anum*) qui se manifeste tout d'abord 'sur leur droite' par 'une voix sinistre' faisant 'un bruit terrifiant'. Saisi de peur, le diacre 'lâchant vivement le cheval qu'il tenait en main[22]

---

16 Cf. Flobert, ibid., p. 181 ; voir aussi la n. 22–1.　17 Ibid., p. 183.　18 Cf. Dt 5.15, 24.18; Hbr 11.27.　19 O Dwyer, *Célí Dé*, p. 90 n. 1 ; Treffort, *Eglise carolingienne*, p. 53. 20 Treffort, *Eglise carolingienne*, p. 53.　21 Cf. Flobert, *Vie ancienne*, p. 183, n. 24–1.　22 ... *equum quem in manu tenuerat uelociter dimittens*. Flobert, ibid., p. 185, traduit 'lâcha vivement le cheval qu'il tenait à la main'. Cf. César, *De bello ciuili* III.lxix.4: *equos dimittere*: 'mettre pied à terre'.

et jetant le *pallium* qui le couvrait' prend rapidement la fuite malgré les appels
au calme de Samson. Celui-ci, 'tenant solidement ses armes spirituelles
ordinaires et le bouclier de la foi, se retranchant sans cesse derrière le saint signe
de la croix', voit alors la *theomacha* 'qui survolait les vastes forêts d'une course
rapide et pourchassait le fuyard en ligne droite'. Avec intrépidité, le saint,
'tenant le cheval en main[23] et posant le *pallium* du fuyard sur le cheval, suivit
résolument le fuyard et sa poursuivante'. Un peu plus loin, il croise le diacre à
demi-mort et voit de loin la 'vieille *theomacha* qui courait'. Se rendant compte
qu'elle 'descendait déjà dans la vallée', il la défie, en des termes empruntés à
l'*Enéïde*:[24] 'Pourquoi fuis tu, femme?' La vieille ne s'arrête pas pour autant,
aussi le saint lui ordonne -t'il 'au nom de Christ' de ne plus faire un pas jusqu'à
ce qu'il la rejoigne et 'l'inculpe'.[25] A mon avis, le verbe *appellare* doit être pris
ici au sens fort, quasi-juridique, de 'porter plainte'. L'affrontement se termine
par la mort de 'cette femme malfaisante' qui s'écroule à terre en 'faisant un saut
brusque sur le côté gauche', de même qu'elle s'était manifestée préalablement à
la droite des voyageurs (I.26–7).[26] Hervé Martin vient de rappeler comment ce
genre d'oppositions structurelles élémentaires (droite bénéfique/gauche
sinistre) contribuait à opérer une mise en forme de la réalité de manière à
apporter une solution imaginaire à des contradictions fondamentales.[27]

A ma connaissance, aucun commentateur n'a remarqué que, curieusement,
la suite du récit ne fait plus intervenir ni le 'cheval', ni le *uehiculum* mentionnés
précédemment. Samson 'arriva' (*aduenit*) devant son adversaire avant de la sou-
mettre à un interrogatoire serré. Enfin, après qu'il eut ranimé son compagnon
mort de peur, tous deux 'poursuivirent leur voyage' (*iter perrexerunt*) pour
'parvenir' (*peruenerunt*), le troisième jour, à leur destination (*ad locum quo
tendebant*)' (I.29).[28] Tout se passe donc comme si le moyen de transport utilisé
par son héros était désormais devenu superfétatoire au propos de l'hagiographe.[29]
Pourtant, trois points doivent retenir l'attention. D'une part, avant de se lancer
à la poursuite de la *theomacha*, Samson se revêt d'une sorte de *lorica* spirituelle
qui suggère que cette course-poursuite doit bien être conçue comme un combat.
D'autre part, l'insistance sur la course 'en ligne droite', le choix du verbe *cernere*
('voir de loin', 'prévoir') et la descente de la *theomacha* dans la vallée évoquent
les trois qualités (*búada*) du cocher (de l'aurige), telles que les a dégagées
William Sayers à partir de certains récits irlandais (comme *Mesca Ulad* et *Táin
Bó Cúailgne*):

---

23 *equum in manu tens* … Flobert, *Vie ancienne*, p. 187 traduit 'tenant le cheval à la main
… '. **24** Kerlouégan, 'Auteurs latins', p. 187. **25** Flobert, *Vie ancienne*, p. 187, traduit
'jusqu'à ce que j'arrive et t'adresse la parole'. **26** Cf. Flobert, ibid., pp. 184–9. **27** Martin,
Mentalités médiévales, pp. 202–3. **28** Flobert, *Vie ancienne*, p. 189.

1. sighting along the goal (in order to hold the true course)
2. levelling obstacles, and
3. leaping gaps, i.e. travelling the shortest distance between two points.[30]

Ce chercheur propose, par ailleurs, un rapprochement suggestif entre les descriptions des chars de combat par les poètes irlandais et l'imagerie biblique que l'hagiographe samsonien avait sûrement présente à l'esprit ici: 'Préparez la voie du Seigneur. Tracez droit dans le désert un chemin pour notre Dieu. Que toute vallée soit comblée, toute montagne et toute colline abaissée … '.[31] Ces remarques autorisent-elle pour autant à affirmer que l'affrontement entre Samson et la *theomacha* transpose sur le mode hagiographique ces récits profanes de combats en char? Il faut convenir que le vocabulaire de ce chapitre est trop imprécis pour trancher catégoriquement. Le diacre 'tenait le cheval en main' avant de s'enfuir; Samson poursuit la *theomacha* 'en tenant le cheval en main'. On peut comprendre soit que l'un comme l'autre se déplacent à pied en tenant le cheval par la bride, soit que le diacre fait fonction d'aurige et que le héros doit prendre lui-même les rênes en main après que son compagnon lui eut lâchement fait défaut. La mention du *pallium* qui 'couvrait' le diacre (ou 'qui l'embarrassait': *quo indutus erat*) et dont il se débarrasse avant de s'enfuir[32] s'explique probablement aussi par l'arrière-plan biblique qui sous-tend l'épisode. Selon le Second Livre des Rois qui rapporte l'enlèvement d'Elie au ciel dans un char de feu, n'est-ce pas son disciple Elisée qui ramasse le manteau de son maître (IV Rg 2.1–14)? Le rapprochement est d'autant plus tentant que par la suite (I.28) Samson ressuscite le diacre en pratiquant un bouche à bouche 'selon l'autorité d'Elisée'.[33]

---

29 Le Dr John Carey me fait judicieusement remarquer que le char servait de moyen de transport aux guerriers celtiques plutôt que d'instrument de combat. C'est cette même fonction qu'il remplirait dans ce passage de la *Vita prima Samsonis*, si l'interprétation que je vais en proposer ici pouvait être retenue. **30** Sayers, 'Old Irish Chariot', p. 19. Cf. idem, 'Three Charioteering Gifts', pp. 163–7, que je n'ai pu consulter. Le Dr J. Carey a l'obligeance de remarquer que, dans ce contexte, 'the same three abilities are cited as the things "which qualify a charioteer" in the legal compilation *Bretha Nemed*: *IMorchur delend, foxal disligh, lem tar builg nemtiger aruid* (Binchy, *Corpus iuris*, p. 2219.40–1)'. Je le remercie vivement pour cette précision. **31** Is 40.3–4. **32** Samson prend soin de le 'poser sur le cheval' (in *equum imponens*) avant de se lancer dans sa course poursuite. Par lettre du 5 mars 1996, Pierre Flobert me fait aimablement remarquer que si Samson ne tenait pas le cheval par la bride, 'il jetterait le manteau du moine non sur le cheval, mais dans la carriole'. Je le remercie de cette mise en garde qui doit inciter à la prudence. **33** Flobert, *Vie ancienne*, p. 189 ; cf. IV Rg 4.34: le fils de la Sunamite. Je remercie J. Carey et R. Godding qui m'ont suggéré cette hypothèse au cours de l'International Conference on Hagiography de Cork. Dans *le De ratione temporum*, Bède se réfère à l'enlèvement miraculeux d'Elie pour situer chronologiquement le règne du roi Bladud, fondateur légendaire de Bath. Il n'est pas impossible que ce soit ce rapprochement qui ait conduit Geoffroy de Monmouth à développer dans son *Histoire des rois de Bretagne* (1136), la légende de 'Bladud, le roi volant' (voir Merdrignac, 'Fous volants', p. 143).

Le mot *uehiculum* employé par l'hagiographe n'est guère éclairant. Il s'applique
à tout 'moyen de transport', y compris le 'cheval' lui-même, par exemple dans la
vita de saint Colomban par Jonas.[34] Toutefois, le récit ultérieur des préparatifs de
Samson avant d'entreprendre sa pérégrination pourrait sans doute contribuer à
lever cette ambiguïté dans la mesure où une distinction s'établit nettement cette
fois entre, d'une part, la 'charrette' (*plaustrum*) destinée au transport des livres
et des objets cultuels et, d'autre part, 'son char' (*currus*) auquel sont attelés deux
chevaux (... *in duobus imponens equis*). La récente traduction de Pierre Flobert
permet de comprendre que c'est bien le 'char' que le saint a rapporté en
souvenir d'un séjour en Irlande![35] En tout cas, la confrontation de ces deux
chapitres de la *Vita* permet de considérer le *uehiculum* auquel est attelé un
cheval (I.26) comme le synonyme du *currus* que le saint utilise par la suite (I.47).
Louis Gougaud a souligné la tendance des moines celtes à voyager à pied par
esprit de pénitence.[36] L'érudit bénédictin a relevé, entre autres, à ce propos un
chapitre de la *Regula cuiusdam patris* ... (rédigée au VIIe s. dans les milieux
colombaniens)[37] qui interdit 'aux moines d'aller et venir en char ou à cheval à
moins d'être malades, et encore impotents et boiteux'.[38] Il est donc intéressant
de rapprocher cet épisode de la *Vita prima Samsonis* des textes hagiographiques
irlandais qui montrent leur héros se déplaçant en char. La *Vita* de sainte Brigitte
par Cogitosus et celles de saint Patrick par Muirchú et Tírechán se réfèrent à ce
moyen de déplacement. De même, selon Adomnán, alors que ses obligations
ecclésiastiques contraignent Colum Cille à parcourir un long trajet en Irlande,
celui-ci doit utiliser un char et c'est Colmán, fondateur du monastère de
Slanore, qui fait fonction d'aurige.[39] Le parallèle est intéressant puisque l'on
retrouve le couple formé par le héros et par son cocher, ce dernier se cantonnant
dans une fonction de faire valoir, comme l'aurige fait équipe avec le guerrier
dont il dirige le char de combat. Le texte de la *Vita prima Samsonis* est trop
allusif pour qu'il soit permis d'affirmer (dans l'état actuel de la recherche, tout
au moins) que l'affrontement du saint et de la *theomacha* se présente

---

34 Jonas, *Vita Sancti Columbani* II.5 (Krusch, p. 237): *uehicula quiete fouet* ('les bêtes de
somme, il les fait se reposer'); cit. par Niermeyer, *Lexicon minus*, s.v. *uehiculum*.   35 Flobert,
Vie ancienne, p. 215: ' ... *suumque currum in duobus imponens equis quem de Hibernia apud se
adportauerat*'; Flobert traduit ici *currum* par 'carriole'. Fawtier, *Vie de saint Samson*, p. 143,
n. 47–k, donne la leçon ' ... *quos de Hibernia secum adduxerat*' d'après un groupe de
légendiers tardifs – Cf. Duine, *Origines bretonnes*, p. 64.   36 Gougaud, *Chrétientés celtiques*,
pp. 208–10; idem, 'Anciennes traditions ascétiques'.   37 Pour la date, de Vogüé, *Règles
monastiques*, p. 56.   38 *Regula cuiusdam patris*, C. 20 ; cf. PL lxvi.991.   39 Adomnán, VC
II.43 (Anderson and Anderson, pp. 170–3). Sharpe, *Life of St Columba*, p. 344, n. 328
rappelle que Slanore (*Snám Luthir*) a été identifié à un 'townland' des environs de Kilmore
(Co Cavan) et propose (n. 329) un rapprochement avec un épisode analogue de 'the first life
of St Brigit' qui concerne l'évêque Conlaed (*Conlianus*). Cf. *Vita tertia S. Brigitae*, cap. 51,
dans Colgan, *Trias thaumaturga*, p. 532. (La *Vita tertia* de Colgan est aujourd'hui considérée
comme la *Vita prima*: cf., par exemple, Sharpe, '*Vitae S. Brigitae*', en particulier p. 83, n. 2).

incontestablement comme un combat en char. Il suffit pour mon propos d'envisager, à titre d'hypothèse, l'éventualité de ce que l'hagiographe ait pris en compte, à des fins édifiantes, certains motifs d'une tradition orale (pourquoi pas familiale) qui pouvait s'inscrire dans ce contexte de récits héroïques.[40]

II

Quoi qu'il en soit de cette hypothèse, la personnalité de la *theomacha* doit maintenant retenir notre attention. Robert Fawtier, suivi par la plupart des commentateurs,[41] comprend qu'il s'agit d'une vieille sorcière. En effet, la question de Samson qui somme celle-ci de s'identifier s'apparente à la démarche de l'exorcisme: il s'agit de contraindre l'adversaire à se nommer: 'Qui es-tu, mauvaise créature et de quelle espèce es-tu?' La réponse ne se fait guère attendre: 'Je suis une *theomacha* et il ne reste à présent personne de ma *gens* sinon moi seule. J'ai en effet huit soeurs et ma mère vit encore. Elles ne sont pas ici mais vivent dans une autre forêt'. R. Fawtier rapprochait judicieusement ces neuf personnages (var. *haec nouem sunt* ...) des neuf sorcières de Gloucester (*Caer Loyw*)[42] qui interviennent dans le *Peredur* gallois du XIIe siècle. Dans ce conte, le héros est accueilli dans un château par une 'grande et belle femme'. Son hôtesse lui déconseille cependant d'y passer la nuit: 'Il y a ici, mon âme, dit-elle, neuf sorcières avec leur père et leur mère. Ce sont les neuf sorcières de Caer Loyw. Au lever du jour, elles auraient tôt fait de nous tuer si nous voulions nous échapper (litt. 'nous serions plus près d'être tués que de nous échapper'). Elles ont réussi à prendre et à piller tout le royaume à l'exception de cette maison'. Peredur passe outre à ce conseil, et le lendemain matin il défait 'une sorcière en train de battre le veilleur'. Celle-ci lui déclare alors: 'Il est dans mon destin, j'en ai eu la vision, de souffrir une douloureuse épreuve de ton fait; quant à toi, tu dois me prendre un cheval et des armes. Tu resteras quelque temps avec moi pour que je t'apprenne à monter à cheval et à manier les armes'. Après avoir fait jurer à la sorcière de ne plus attaquer le domaine de son hôtesse, il l'accompagna ' ... à la cour des sorcières. Il y resta trois semaines de suite, puis il prit le cheval et les armes de son choix et reprit la route'.[43] On sait qu'à la fin du récit, Peredur apprend que ce sont ces sorcières qui ont tué le cousin dont la tête coupée lui a été présentée et qui ont estropié l'un des oncles

---

40 On sait, par exemple, que l'épisode crucial de la 'Razzia des Vaches de Cooley' (*Táin Bó Cúailnge*) est précisément le duel – en char – entre Cú Chulainn et son ami Fer Diad.
41 Flobert, *Vie ancienne*, p. 65 n. 90 soutient cette interprétation en écartant l'hypothèse que cette sorcière serait en même temps une géante proposée naguère dans Merdrignac, 'Saints et géants', pp. 23–5. L'argumentation de ce chercheur m'amène à reconsidérer la mienne.
42 Selon Lambert, *Mabinogi*, p. 78 n. 202, il s'agit de la forme galloise du nom moderne de Gloucester, latinisé en *Gleuum* à l'époque britto-romaine.   **43** Ibid., pp. 254–5.

maternels qui avaient pris en charge sa formation. Le combat décisif contre les sorcières s'engage alors avec l'appui d'Arthur et de ses guerriers. D'un coup d'épée, le héros fend la tête de l'une d'entre elles qui cria ' … aux autres sorcières de fuir en leur disant que c'était Peredur, l'homme qui avait appris l'équitation avec elles et qui était désigné par le destin pour les tuer. Arthur et ses guerriers frappèrent alors les sorcières, et toutes les sorcières de Caer Loyw furent tuées'.[44] Evidemment, la *Vita* se rapporte ici au même arrière-plan traditionnel. D'ailleurs, cette vieille et qui apparaît ensuite 'hirsute, chenue, vêtue d'une cape (*suis uestimentis birrhatam*) et tenant à la main un épieu à trois pointes (*trifulcatamque uenalem*)' et que le saint extermine sans pitié[45] est conforme au type littéraire de la sorcière qui court des *Satires* d'Horace (*Satire* I.8) aux *Odes* de Ronsard ('Contre Denise, sorcière …').[46]

Cependant, un sondage dans le vocabulaire des auteurs de l'Antiquité tardive dont s'inspire la *Vita* de saint Samson permet sans doute de préciser la personnalité de cette *theomacha*. Ce terme, démarqué du Grec, signifie littéralement 'ennemie de Dieu'. Il en découle une double conséquence. D'une part, F.C. Burkitt a suggéré que c'était sans doute la traduction latine par Rufin de l'*Histoire ecclésiastique* d'Eusèbe de Césarée (vers 400) qui avait fourni à l'hagiographe le nom et les éléments de description de la *theomacha*. Cet ouvrage en faisant allusion au verset de la Genèse (6.4) qui explique que les géants ' … en ces temps là (c'est à dire avant le Déluge) vivaient sur la Terre' rappelle que les premiers hommes sauvages ' … accomplirent entre eux des crimes abominables au point qu'ils en vinrent par une barbarie plus poussée à se dévorer les uns les autres. De là sont issues les THEOMACHIES et les GIGANTOMACHIES qui ont laissé au monde le récit de leur crimes'.[47] Un lien est ainsi établi entre l'Ecriture Sainte et les théogonies de l'Antiquité classique selon lesquelles titanomachie et gigantomachie (parfois confondues) préludent à la prise de pouvoir par Jupiter. D'autre part, à la suite de F.C. Burkitt, Hubert Guillotel a attiré l'attention sur l'emploi par Bède le Vénérable (+735) du mot *theomacha* (rare au féminin). En effet, en commentant un verset des Actes des Apôtres (5.39) 'Ne vous trouvez

---

44 Ibid., p. 281. Dans la n. 52, p. 396, Lambert signale l'ambiguïté du mot gallois *marchogaeth* qui signifie normalement 'fait de chevaucher' et qui peut désigner ici soit l'"équitation' soit la 'chevalerie'. 45 *Vita prima* I.26 (Flobert, pp. 184–7). Cf. Billaut, 'Vieille femme', pp. 34–5. 46 Ronsard, *Odes* 21 (22); 2 (14) dans l'édition définitive de 1584 (cf. Cohen, *Ronsard*, i.450, v. 19–24): ' … La Terre mère encore pleurante/Des Geans la mort violante/Brulez du feu des Cieux/Te laschant de son ventre à peine/T'engendra, vieille, pour la haine/Qu'elle portait aux Dieux … ' Ce ne serait pas le seul cas où le recours à un auteur de la Renaissance permet d'éclairer un texte du haut Moyen Age (cf. Merdrignac, *Vies de saints*, pp. 39–40). D'une part, la haine que la 'vieille' sorcière 'portait aux dieux', selon le poète du XVIe siècle, est comme la transposition, à peine paraphrasée, du terme *theomacha*. D'autre part, cette expression est ici explicitement associée au mythe des géants dont Ronsard fait les frères de la sorcière. 47 Schwartz et Mommsen, *Eusebius Werke*, p. 23. Cf. Burkitt, 'Saint Samson', p. 47. Voir, à présent, *contra*, Flobert, *Vie ancienne*, p. 65 et n. 90 qui suggéré plutôt un contact direct avec la *Retractatio Actum Apostolorum* de Bède.

jamais adversaires de Dieu … ', Bède développe: 'Là où nous avons *Deo repugnare* ou comme certains l'ont traduit *Deo repugnantes*, en Grec, on ne trouve qu'un seul mot, THEOMACHOI. J'ai jugé bon de le rappeler. En effet, comme nous trouvons dans des relations (*historiis*)[48] THEOMACHOS ou THEOMACHAM, nous pouvons connaître avec suffisamment de certitude la portée (*uirtutem*) du mot'.[49] Ce rapprochement présente d'importantes conséquences pour la datation de la *Vita prima Samsonis*. En effet, soit l'on souscrit à l'hypothèse d'Hubert Guillotel selon qui c'est directement à la *Vita prima Samsonis* que Bède se réfère quand il emploie ici la forme féminine du mot *theomacham* et l'on dispose d'un *terminus post quem* (715–731) bien assuré.[50] Soit l'on adopte le raisonnement inverse, et la fourchette chronologique de rédaction de la *Retractatio* fournit un *terminus a quo* si l'on considère, à la suite de Pierre Flobert, que l'hagiographe est sans doute ici le 'débiteur' de Bède, même si 'le sens particulier lui est propre'.[51] Le propos de la présente communication ne saurait être de trancher.[52] Toutefois, il me semble, contrairement à Pierre Flobert qui ne retient pas cette hypothèse, qu'une des clés de l'épisode réside dans le *Commentarius in Psalmum LXXXVII* de saint Jérôme (vers 391) dont l'auteur de la *Vita prima Samsonis* connaît sûrement, par ailleurs, les *Vitae* des ermites Paul et Hilarion.[53] En effet, en se référant à Symmaque, le docteur de l'Eglise glose ici le terme hébreu *raphaim* ('géants') par *theomachi*.[54] En tout cas, c'est bien ainsi que l'archevêque de Dol Baudri de Bourgueil (1107–30) interprète le mot *theomacha*. Lorsqu'il se charge de composer une réfection de la *Vita prima Samsonis*, cet illustre représentant de la Renaissance du XIIe siècle ne se prive pas de faire explicitement le rapprochement avec la *theomachia* ('combat des dieux contre les géants') de la mythologie antique. Dans cette version, encore en grande partie inédite, la *theomacha* se présente 'en faisant des pointes' comme l'a écrit, avec le sourire, l'abbé François Duine: 'A propos des *theomachae*, je suis une *theomacha*, si par hasard tu as entendu parler de la *theomachia*'.[55]

---

48 Guenée, *Histoire et culture*, p. 18, rappelle qu'*historia* peut désigner 'un récit qui s'attache essentiellement à dire la vie d'un saint et sert de base à la composition de *repons* qui seront dits à l'office de ce saint'. Il serait toutefois hasardé de prétendre interpréter ainsi le mot *historiis* dans la *Retractatio Actum Apostolorum* de Bède, puisque, selon Guenée, ce 'sens technique' n'est attesté, chez les liturgistes que depuis le IXe s.　**49** Merdrignac, 'Saints et géants', p. 24. Cf. Burkitt, 'Saint Samson', p. 47. Guillotel, 'Origines du ressort', pp. 43–4, n. 40, cite le texte de Bède, *Retractatio Actum Apostolorum*, d'après Laistner, *Expositio*, p. 116, v. 39. **50** Guillotel, 'Origines du ressort'. Poulin, 'Diocèse de Dol', p. 611, conteste à cette hypothèse un 'degré de probabilité suffisante', sans toutefois l'écarter catégoriquement. **51** Flobert, *Vie ancienne*, p. 65, et surtout n. 90.　**52** Ibid., pp. 98–9, Flobert propose d'autres rapprochements entre la *Vita* et l'oeuvre de Bède qui renforcent incontestablement sa position.　**53** Duine, *Origines bretonnes*, pp. 30–8; Kerlouégan, 'Auteurs latins', pp. 219–29; Flobert, *Vie ancienne*, pp. 95–6. **54** CCSL lxxii.222. Cf. Merdrignac, 'Saints et géants'. *Contra*, Flobert, *Vie ancienne*, p. 65, n. 90. **55** '*De theomachis una sum theomacha, si forte theomachiam audisti*; cf. Duine, *Notes*, p. 18. La *Vita Samsonis* par Baudri est encore en grande partie inédite. Mme Armelle Le Huërou en a entrepris, sous ma direction, l'édition

A l'arrière-plan de ces textes se situe une tradition exégétique développée par saint Augustin et reprise par Isidore de Séville. A propos du passage de la Genèse qui présente les géants antédiluviens (*nephilim*) comme issus de l'accouplement des 'fils de Dieu' avec les 'filles des hommes'(6.4) ces auteurs expliquent qu'il faut comprendre que ceux-ci descendaient de l'union entre les fils de Seth et les filles de Caïn. La Bible n'établit pourtant pas de lien entre le récit du meurtre d'Abel par son frère (4.8–16) et celui de la naissance des géants. Mais Augustin et Isidore à sa suite réagissent ainsi vivement contre une explication du texte biblique influencée par les apocryphes juifs qui faisait des 'fils de Dieu' de la Genèse des anges déchus ayant succombé aux charmes des 'filles des hommes'. L'auteur espagnol, avant de parler des cyclopes de la mythologie antique et après avoir donné l'étymologie grecque des géants (γηγενεῖς: 'né de la Terre'), dénonce explicitement les commentateurs qui ' … sans expérience des Ecritures saintes pensent que de mauvais (*preuaricatores*) anges ont couché avec les filles des hommes avant le Déluge. De là naquirent les géants, c'est à dire des hommes très grands et robustes qui remplirent la terre' (*Etymologiae* XI.iii.14). Cette lecture hétérodoxe de la Genèse[56] se retrouve dans le *Livre d'Enoch* qui rend compte ainsi du cannibalisme attribué aux géants.[57] Or il n'est pas impossible que des interprétations de la Genèse influencées par toute cette littérature apocryphe ait eu cours en Bretagne dès le haut Moyen Age. Mario Esposito a supposé que le récit de navigation des moines de Saint-Mathieu adapté par Geoffroy de Viterbe dans son *Panthéon* (XIIe siècle) pouvait remonter à une telle source.[58] Une confirmation indirecte de cette hypothèse est peut-être à rechercher dans le nom d'Henoc que l'auteur de la *Vita* de saint Samson donne comme celui du cousin de son héros, même si, cela n'exclut pas, comme je viens de le suggérer, une interférence avec le vieux-Breton *hen* ('l'Ancien').[59] A la lumière de cet arrière-plan culturel, si mon interprétation est recevable, l'épisode de la rencontre entre Samson et la *theomacha* prend toute sa portée. On peut comprendre ainsi la manière dont celle-ci se présente au saint: 'Je suis une géante adversaire de Dieu (*theomacham*) et effectivement jusqu'à présent mes aïeux (*gentes*) se sont dressés comme des traîtres à votre encontre' (I.27).

---

commentée dans le cadre d'une thèse d'histoire médiévale. Nul doute que ce travail apportera des éclaircissements à ce sujet.   **56** Merdrignac, 'Saints et géants', p. 25. Cf. Mellinkoff, 'Cain's Monstrous Progeny', Parts 1 et 2.   **57** Jack, *Beowulf*, p. 13.   **58** Esposito, 'Apocryphal Book', pp. 203–4; McNamara, *Apocrypha*, p. 24–7; Merdrignac, 'Désacralisation du mythe'. Le Dr J. Carey m'indique toutefois obligeamment que 'the apocryphal *Book of Enoch and Elias* postulated by Esposito is not the same as the so-called *Ethiopic Book of Enoch* in which the seduction of the "daughters of men" by angels (or vice versa) is described. That the relevant passage of the latter was known in early medieval Ireland may however be indicated by the preservation of the names which it assigns to the fallen angels in *Saltair na Rann*' (cf. Carey, 'Angelology'). Je le remercie vivement pour cette précision qui pourrait bien venir à l'appui de mon hypothèse.   **59** Cf. Merdrignac, 'Henoc', pp. 172–3.

Relevons au passage que le qualificatif *preuaricatores* (*preuaricatrices*) que l'hagiographe applique aux 'aïeux' de la *theomacha* est celui dont les *Etymologies* d'Isidore gratifient les mauvais anges séduits par les femmes. Quand Samson demande à son adversaire de rendre la vie à son jeune compagnon mort de peur, la géante en rajoute: 'Je ne veux ni ne peux m'améliorer, en effet je ne suis capable de rien faire de bien. Depuis mon enfance jusqu'à présent, j'ai toujours été exercée au mal'. De tels propos s'expliquent tout à fait si l'on veut bien admettre que dans l'esprit de l'hagiographe la *theomacha* descend des anges déchus. En effet, c'est, semble-t'il, à cette tradition hétérodoxe que se réfère ici la *Vita*. Il n'est sans doute pas indifférent que Samson pour arrêter la géante dans sa fuite lui crie: 'Je suis un être humain (*ego homo sum*) comme mon semblable que tu as terrassé … ' En effet, quelques chapitres plus loin, lorsque ses parents lui présentent ses cinq frères et sa jeune soeur qu'il destinent au monastère, le saint écarte celle-ci en prophétisant qu'elle est destinée aux 'désirs mondains'. Il n'en ajoute pas moins: 'toutefois, élevez-là, puisque c'est un être humain' (*quia homo est*; I.29). De même, quand le diacre Morin, possédé du démon, se confesse au saint avant de rendre l'âme, ses aveux font, presque mot pour mot, écho à ceux de la géante: 'depuis l'enfance jusqu'à présent j'ai été exercé au mal par les artifices de la magie (*philosophie machinatione*; II.8)'. Pourtant, cela n'empêche pas Samson de faire célébrer des messes jusqu'à sa délivrance (II.9).[60] Une seule conclusion s'impose: la *theomacha* n'est pas humaine! La prière finale du saint n'a donc rien d'impitoyable: 'Je supplie Dieu Tout Puissant que tu cesse de nuire et, comme il n'y a pas de remède (*dum inremediabilis es*), que tu meures à l'instant' (I.27). Le saint demande ainsi à Dieu d'actualiser le châtiment qui est déjà intervenu à l'occasion du Déluge.

Selon la Bible, les géants nés de l'union entre les 'fils de Dieu' et les 'filles des hommes', n'ont pas pu survivre au Déluge (Gn 7.17–24). Geoffroy de Monmouth a diffusé dans tout l'Occident l'idée d'un peuplement originel des Iles Britanniques par ces géants antédiluviens. A sa suite, dans le livre II de sa *Topographia Hiberniae* (1187) Giraud de Bari a expliqué, entre autres, que la 'Danse des Géants' (Stonehenge) avait été magiquement transportée en Grande-Bretagne par Merlin depuis l'Irlande 'où les géants l'avaient apportée du fin fond de l'Afrique'.[61] Toutefois, une enquête antérieure m'a permis d'établir que (sans être originale) cette conception était reçue bien avant le XIIᵉ siècle.[62] *Aegyptum reliqui?*

Cette association du motif du 'tombeau du géant' aux monuments mégalithiques explique sans doute, en dépit de Robert Fawtier qui écartait cette explication, la raison pour laquelle la géante qui a dû suivre son mari dans cette

---

60 Duine, *Saints de Domnonée*, p. 10, n. 20; Merdrignac, 'Première Vie', pp. 279–81; Vogüé, 'Grégoire le Grand', p. 299. **61** Giraldus Cambrensis, *Topographia Hiberniae* II.51 (Dimock, p. 100; O'Meara, p. 143). **62** Merdrignac, 'Saints et géants', pp. 25–8 ; idem, *Vies de saints*, p. 105–11.

solitude est contrainte d'y demeurer: 'Mon mari est mort et pour cette raison je ne peux pas quitter cette forêt'. Sans doute faut-il comprendre que si elle se trouve dans l'impossibilité de quitter les lieux, c'est qu'elle doit assurer le culte des morts sur le tombeau de son époux?[63]

Au détour d'une note, James Carney avait suggéré un rapprochement entre la *theomacha* et la mère du géant Grendel dans le *Beowulf*.[64] Cette hypothèse, qui, à ma connaissance n'a guère rencontré d'échos chez les chercheurs en hagiographie celtique, devrait être reconsidérée à la lumière d'une étude récente de Michael Lapidge qui met en évidence les rapports entre l'épopée anglo-saxonne et le milieu dans lequel a travaillé Aldhelm de Malmesbury.[65] Quelques remarques suffiront ici. Beowulf, bien entendu, ne combat pas en char. Grendel et sa mère, géants monstrueux, sont les descendants de Caïn (106–114) et se présentent sous forme humaine (*on weres woesmum*: 'in the form of a human being'; 1352). Doivent-ils pour autant être considérés comme des êtres humains?[66] La victoire du héros sur ses adversaires est inscrite dans la perspective de la 'finale rétribution' (*endelean*: 1692) des géants selon la Genèse (c'est à dire du Déluge: 7.17–24). Par contre, les origines du dragon que Beowulf doit par la suite affronter demeurent inexpliquées. Mais, par nature, il apparaît comme un 'gardien de trésor' sans qu'il soit diabolisé. Paradoxalement, des qualificatifs comme *féond mancynes* ('ennemi de l'humanité'; 164, 1276), *ealdgewinna* ('l'antique adversaire'; 1776) sont appliqués à Grendel, pas au dragon![67]

III

Sur le plan narratif, le récit du premier combat de saint Samson contre un dragon constitue le pendant de sa victoire sur la *theomacha*. L'épisode prend place sur le chemin du retour vers le monastère d'Inis Pyr 'par un chemin différent de celui de l'aller' précise la *Vita* (I.31). Amon, le père du saint, miraculeusement rétabli après s'être confessé à son fils, s'est voué à Dieu jusqu'à sa mort, sur l'injonction de son épouse. Celle-ci a fondé un monastère où elle s'est retirée. Pratiquement toute la famille du saint a opté pour la vie religieuse et les biens des parents du saint ont été, en grande partie, distribués aux pauvres ' … en ayant gardé un petit peu pour leur usage personnel, car ils possédaient beaucoup de ressources' (I.30). Amon et Umbraphel, l'oncle de Samson, ont décidé de le suivre au monastère. Chemin faisant, c'est Amon qui remarque le premier 'un sentier, puis autour du sentier des champs comme brûlés par le feu, une trace enfin comme si on traînait une poutre dans les herbes grillées. Il

---

63 Fawtier, *Vie de saint Samson*, p. 45, n. 1, rejette cette interprétation. Elle avait cependant retenu l'attention de F. Duine. 64 Carney, *Studies*, p. 124, n. 1 qui définit toutefois la *theomacha* comme 'hag-sorceress'. 65 Lapidge, 'Beowulf'. 66 Mellinkoff 'Cain's Monstrous Progeny', Parts 1 et 2. 67 Jack, *Beowulf*, p. 14.

commença évidemment par prendre peur et montra cela à son frère qui le suivait en disant: Regarde mon frère: le serpent dont nous avons entendu dire chez nos parents (*apud parentes nostros*; ou 'par nos ancêtres': *a patribus nostris*, selon un légendier de la fin du XIIe s.)[68] qu'il habitait dans cette forêt nous précède et, si je ne me trompe, il n'est pas loin de nous' (I.32). Les solitudes hantées par le serpent sont celles qui entourent le domaine familial que Samson et les siens viennent de quitter définitivement. Le reptile est d'ailleurs identifié immédiatement par Amon en se référant aux traditions de la famille. Si l'on suit le chanoine Raison du Cleuziou,[69] peut-être même est-il possible d'aller jusqu'à soupçonner un écho direct de la tradition orale dans la description de 'ce serpent à la crête flamboyante qui se voit de loin en train de serpenter dans les landes désolées' (*uidit a longe serpentem flammiuoma crista per uasta deserta serpitantem*). En effet, à la place de *flammiuoma crista*, certains manuscrits[70] portent la '*lectio difficilior*' *flammiuoma crepta* qui pourrait bien constituer un calque du vieux-Breton *cripeticion*.[71] Par ailleurs, l'archéologie a mis au jour en Grande Bretagne des figurations de tels serpents crêtés comme sur la stèle dite 'du serpent' à Maryport (Cumberland) ou sur la poignée d'un vase, peut-être à destination cultuelle, en provenance de Carlisle.[72] Dans la mise en forme de ce passage, à la suite de l'abbé Duine, le chanoine Raison du Cleuziou et François Kerlouégan, ont indépendamment reconnu des influences virgiliennes au niveau du vocabulaire[73] (*nidor, sibilum* à quoi peuvent s'ajouter *gyrum, septens*, ainsi que l'emploi simultané *d'anguis* et de *serpens* pour désigner l'animal), mais aussi au niveau de l'organisation du récit qui évoque le passage de l'*Enéïde* (V.72–103) dans lequel le héros, devant la tombe de son père Anchise, voit un énorme serpent en sortir pour consommer les libations. Le chanoine Raison du Cleuziou a même proposé (avec la prudence d'usage) un rapprochement entre le rituel antique de l'inhumation et le geste du serpent mordant le sol pour en arracher une motte de terre et la projeter à grand peine à la figure de Samson qui s'approche de lui.[74] Quant au réseau de citations du psautier qui sous-tend l'épisode, s'il souligne la foi en Dieu qui permet des merveilles, il n'implique aucune diabolisation de cette 'créature'[75] : 'Le Seigneur est ma lumière et mon

---

68 Fawtier, *Vie de saint Samson*, p. 129, n. 32–f: il s'agit du ms K, Namur, Fonds de la Ville 53 (Musée des Arts anciens) qui provient du monastère de Saint-Hubert. 69 Couffon et Raison du Cleuziou, 'Dragon', p. 17, n. 22. 70 Fawtier, *Vie de saint Samson*, p. 129, n. 32–x. Flobert, *Vie ancienne*, p. 194, qui retient dans l'apparat critique cette leçon du ms N: B.M. Rouen 1393, légendier du XIIIe s. originaire de Jumièges. 71 Cf. Fleuriot, *Dictionary*, s.v. 72 Ross, *Pagan Celtic Britain*, p. 345 et pl. 85. 73 Duine, *Origines bretonnes*, p. 15; Couffon et Raison du Cleuziou, 'Dragon', p. 17; Kerlouégan, 'Auteurs latins', p. 188. *Contra*, Poulin, 'Dossier', p. 722; Flobert, *Vie ancienne*, p. 101 qui note que Virgile n'a 'sûrement pas été lu' par l'auteur et que bien des rapprochements sont 'inopérants'. 74 Couffon et Raison du Cleuziou, 'Dragon', pp. 17–8. 75 C'est sans doute pourquoi l'auteur de la *Vita secunda* a éprouvé le besoin de modifier ce réseau de citations en substituant au Ps 135 l'Hymne des trois enfants dans la fournaise (Dn 3.57). Cf. Merdrignac, *Vies de saints*, p. 101, n. 2. Cette

salut ... ' (Ps 26.1); 'Plaçons notre confiance dans le Dieu des dieux ...' (cf. Ps 135.2). Le sermon qu'improvise Samson pour la gouverne de son père et de son oncle sur le thème 'ceux qui ont vraiment foi dans le Créateur ne doivent pas craindre une créature ...' s'inscrit dans la ligne des réflexions d'Augustin et d'Isidore de Séville pour qui le dragon n'a pas encore revêtu tout son symbolisme maléfique,[76] mais représente simplement 'le plus grand de tous les serpents et de tous les animaux de la terre' (*Etymologiae* XII.iv.4). C'est sans doute Isidore, 'le premier encyclopédiste du Moyen Age'[77] qui permet de comprendre l'inscription de la victoire du saint sur son adversaire dans 'le schéma de la croix allié au cercle'. Ce motif qui existait déjà à l'époque paléochrétienne est très fréquent du VIIe s. au IXe s., 'aussi bien dans l'art mérovingien que dans les oeuvres irlandaises dont les croix sont les plus célèbres exemples'. Toute une symbolique (Bède, Sedulius, un commentaire irlandais sur saint Marc du VIIe s.) inscrit la croix du Christ sur la terre dont elle détermine les quatre points cardinaux. Quant au cercle, il représenterait ici le cosmos.[78] Pour préciser cet arrière-plan, le mieux est, sans doute, de confronter le passage concerné de la *Vita* aux *Etymologies* d'Isidore de Séville: 'Quand le serpent vit que l'homme de Dieu venait avec confiance et surtout qu'il était entouré par la puissance de Dieu, il lance un formidable hurlement de sa voix affreuse[79] comme s'il était frappé par une épée, puis en tremblant, se roule vite en boule rongeant sa queue avec ses dents furieuses'. Si l'on en croit Isidore (*Etymologiae* XII.iv.4), le serpent se met déjà ainsi de lui-même hors d'état de nuire, dans la mesure où 'sa force ne réside pas dans ses dents, mais dans la queue'. Puis saint Samson 'continuant à chanter en lui-même son psaume habituel et préféré qui commence par "*Confitemini Deo deorum*",[80] traça résolument le signe du cercle contre le serpent qui jetait partout des regard affolés (corr. Pierre Flobert = *circumspectantem*; ou 'qui se lovait' = *circumseptantem*), puis faisant au dessus de lui le signe de la croix, il dit: "Ne vas que là où il t'est permis d'aller" ... ' Le saint invite alors ses compagnons à le rejoindre pour constater que 'le serpent qui se déroulait lentement rampait sur le sol, et s'étendait en rond jusqu'au cercle décrit par le bâton du saint, répétant sans cesse le même mouvement, mais sans pouvoir lever la tête au delà de la limite'. Le motif du cercle magique[81] se combine ici à celui du serpent enroulé.[82] Isidore connaît ces 'dragons annulaires' qui se mordant la queue figurent l'année (*Annus quasi anulus*). Pour notre propos, il semble pertinent de faire ressortir que les

---

réflexion m'avait été suggérée par le chanoine Jacques Raison du Cleuziou que je remercie vivement.　76 Cf. Le Goff, *Pour un autre Moyen Age*, pp. 246–9.　77 Ibid., p. 246.　78 Cf. Gousset, 'Jérusalem céleste', p. 54.　79 Flobert, *Vie ancienne*, p. 195, n. 4 relève ici l'influence de Rufin, *Historia monachorum* §1.　80 Ps 135.2. Flobert, *Vie ancienne*, p. 195, n. 5, remarque que le même psaume est repris en I.58 (expulsion du serpent de Pental).　81 Cf. Flobert, ibid., p. 195, n. 6.　82 Ibid., p. 195, n. 4, Flobert reconnaît ici le 'thème d'inspiration artistique (bracelets) du serpent qui se mord la queue'.

Etymologies (V.xxxvi.2) attribuent cette figuration du temps circulaire sous la forme d'un 'dragon se mordant la queue' aux anciens 'Egyptiens'.[83]

Aegyptum reliqui, s'était exclamé précédemment Samson (I.24). Ce n'est sans doute pas forcer le texte que d'interpréter la mort du serpent sur l'ordre du saint comme la rupture définitive avec le temps cyclique de l'éternel retour et le passage au temps orienté du christianisme. A la fin de la journée, sur l'ordre du saint, 'le serpent se dressant sur sa queue, élevant la tête et faisant stupidement un arc avec son corps, vomit tout son venin et mourut' (I.32). C'est donc bien le serpent tutélaire de sa famille que le saint extermine sans retour. J'ai collecté ailleurs plusieurs exemples (depuis la légende de Mélusine jusqu'au roman autobiographique de Camara Laye, *L'Enfant noir*)[84] de ces génies familiaux qui n'apparaissent dans la littérature écrite qu'au moment de leur disparition. Leur fonction de prospérité économique et de fécondité démographique est bien établie et confère toute sa cohérence à cet épisode de la *Vita*. A partir du moment où Amon se 'fait tondre la tête', où Anna 'reçoit l'ordre du veuvage', et où pratiquement tous leurs enfants et neveux ont opté pour le monachisme, la fonction démographique du serpent tutélaire n'a pratiquement plus de sens. Après le partage des biens familiaux, sa fonction économique de gardien de trésors est réduite à néant. Il n'a plus qu'à mourir sur l'ordre de Samson sous les yeux de son père et de son oncle, témoins consentant de la dissolution du clan.[85] Dès lors, le temps chrétien, axé sur la mort et la résurrection, se substitue au temps cyclique qui permettait les échanges entre les vivants et leurs ancêtres.

IV

C'est dans cette perspective qu'il convient de replacer la confession d'Amon à son fils qui constitue la scène centrale du triptyque dont l'épisode de la *theomacha* et celui du dragon représentent en quelque sorte les deux volets extérieurs.[86] Lorsque Samson et son compagnon parviennent auprès d'Amon, alors que les voisins entourent le lit du malade, celui-ci s'exclame: '"Voici la sauvegarde de mon corps et de mon âme que le Seigneur a daigné me montrer durant mon sommeil". Et bientôt, quand on eut fait sortir tout le monde, il ne resta plus que sa mère avec eux trois: Samson, le diacre, son père et sa mère. Aussitôt Amon révéla publiquement (*publicauit in medium*) en présence des trois personnes susdites, en leur demandant pardon et en les implorant humblement, le péché capital mortel qu'il avait caché en lui-même … ' (I.29).

---

83 Le Goff, *Pour un autre Moyen Age*, pp. 248–9.   84 Cf. Merdrignac, *Vies de saints*, p. 97; idem, *Recherches*, p. 140–3. L'amitié d'Hervé Martin me permet d'adjoindre à ce dossier le récit de la vision de Gontran d'après Paul Diacre, *Historia Langobardorum* III.34 (Bougard, 74–5). Voir surtout, Le Goff, *Pour un autre Moyen Age*, pp. 307–31.   85 Merdrignac, *Vies de saints*, pp. 97–8.   86 Cf. Couffon et Raison du Cleuziou, 'Dragon', p. 18: 'c'est le thème de

A l'issue d'une lecture croisée de cette scène et du récit de l'ultime confession du diacre Morin (II.8) l'abbé Duine avait proposé de situer la conception de la pénitence et de la réconciliation qui ressort de la *Vita prima Samsonis* dans le contexte de 'l'ancien régime pénitentiel', en précisant qu'il était possible de reconnaître dans cette combinaison 'd'éléments plus anciens et d'éléments plus nouveaux' un mélange assez caractéristique de l'époque de Grégoire le Grand.[87] Contrairement à la conclusion à laquelle j'avais abouti dans une précédente étude,[88] le père A. de Vogüé a établi que l'influence de Grégoire le Grand sur l'hagiographe est ici incontestable.[89] Après tout, une *retractatio* de ma part ne paraîtra pas incongrue dans le cadre monastique de la présente étude.[90] En fait, Grégoire continue de se situer dans le cadre de la pénitence antique, mais avec une claire conscience des problèmes qu'elle pose. Dans la mesure où la pénitence publique n'est pas renouvelable, elle n'est pratiquement plus administrée qu'aux grands malades et aux mourants. Les interdictions et les contraintes qu'elle faisait peser à vie sur le pénitent subsistent, mais l'état de celui-ci les rend en général inapplicables. Aussi l'accent est-il mis par Grégoire sur la confession et le rôle intercesseur du pasteur (qui n'est plus obligatoirement l'évêque, mais qui peut aussi être un prêtre; cf. *Dialogi* I.12). Si l'on suit les conclusions de Bruno Judic qui vient de rouvrir le dossier grégorien sur la pénitence, on doit constater que l'oeuvre de Grégoire permet de saisir 'le passage de la pénitence publique aux nouvelles formes du VIIe siècle autour des pénitentiels', puisque le pape était en relation avec les milieux colombaniens. La place que tiennent la pénitence et la confession dans la *Regula pastoralis* témoigne d'un 'type de mentalité qui va permettre l'accueil des pénitentiels. Cette mentalité peut se caractériser par le sens de l'énumération des péchés accompagné d'une classification'. De plus, cet accent mis sur l'aveu manifesterait l'introduction 'de pratiques monastiques dans la vie de l'Eglise en genéral'. Cette double tendance fait du pasteur l'intermédiaire entre les péchés des fidèles et l'absolution divine, entre la souillure et la pureté'.[91]

C'est peut-être la réflexion de Grégoire le Grand sur la pénitence qui permet de saisir pourquoi Anna reste présente durant la confession de son époux. Il faut remarquer que, pour l'hagiographe, celle-ci assiste à la scène en tant que 'mère' du saint et qu'elle n'est désignée comme 'épouse' d'Amon qu'une fois la faute avouée. En effet, probablement sous l'influence de la spiritualité monastique, la *Regula pastoralis* recommande aux 'directeurs' (*rectores*) de faire en sorte que 'les sujets ne rougissent pas de leur présenter même leurs actes cachés; que lorsque les plus petits subissent les flots des tentations, ils aient recours à l'âme du pasteur comme au sein d'une mère … (*Regula pastoralis* II.5)'. Un peu plus

---

la *donatio*'.　**87** Duine, *Saints de Domnonée*, p. 6, n. 6 et p. 10, n. 20; idem, *Origines bretonnes*, p. 37.　**88** Merdrignac, 'Première Vie', pp. 276–1.　**89** de Vogüé, 'Grégoire le Grand', p. 299 et n. 2.　**90** Poulin, 'Dossier', n'a pas retenu ces contacts qui sont pourtant, à présent me semble-t'il, solidement établis.　**91** B. Judic, 'Pénitence publique'.

loin (II.6), Grégoire conseille d'être comme une mère par la pitié et comme un père par la discipline.[92]

Paradoxalement, Anna ne redevient *uxor* pour l'hagiographe que lorsque son mari entre dans l'ordre des pénitents sur ses conseils: 'il s'engagea de tout son coeur à servir Dieu, de ce jour jusqu'à sa fin, à l'instigation particulièrement de sa femme, et sur l'heure il se fit tondre la tête d'autorité …'.[93] En effet, selon le rituel de la pénitence publique antique, le pécheur, le crâne rasé, revêtu d'un cilice, était contraint à la continence et à l'abstinence. Même une fois réconcilié, il restait soumis à certaines interdictions comme celles de se marier, d'ester en justice ou d'exercer des charges publiques. La sanction est particulièrement lourde pour Amon qui possédait, ainsi que son épouse, un riche patrimoine (I.30: *multarum facultatum*) et dont les parents avaient été *nutritores* royaux (I.1). En fait, le pécheur se voyait ainsi imposer les contraintes que les moines s'infligeaient en tant que pénitents volontaires.

C'est aussi en tant qu'"épouse' (*uxor*) qu'Anna suggère 'instamment' à Amon d'offrir à Dieu davantage qu'"il sied et qu'il convient' (*ut decet et convenit*), en lui offrant tous leurs descendants et tous leurs biens. A l'exception de la petite soeur du saint dont celui-ci prophétise qu'"elle a été destinée aux plaisirs de ce monde', en une même journée, tous se convertissent, imités par le frère d'Amon, Umbraphel, et par sa famille. *Aegyptum reliqui*: comme le baptême dont elle restitue la pureté au pécheur, la réconciliation solennelle du pénitent intervenait à l'occasion de la fête de Pâques. En commentant le verset des Actes des Apôtres (2.38) où Pierre dit: 'Faites pénitence et que chacun de vous soit baptisé', Grégoire le Grand rapproche la pénitence et le baptême (*Regula pastoralis* III.30).[94] L'un et l'autre sacrement revoient au schéma initiatique qui sous-tend le mystère pascal: la séquence mort/résurrection aboutit à la naissance d'un homme nouveau.[95]

Le dénouement s'inscrit dans cette dynamique pascale. En effet, au bout de trois jours de route, Samson et ses trois compagnons atteignent le monastère d'Inis Pyr. Ils y trouvent l'évêque Dubric qui venait de s'y retirer pour passer le Carême pascal.[96] La *consolatio* qu'il procure 'aimablement et cordialement' (I.33) à Amon et à Umbraphel doit sans doute se comprendre au sens spécifique de réconfort d'ordre religieux. Quant à cet usage porté par l'hagiographe au crédit de Dubric de 'passer presque tout le carême pascal dans une île (*insula*)' comme le monastère insulaire de l'abbé Piro, il est bien attesté dès l'Antiquité chrétienne. Il est question de la pratique de s'isoler dans une île durant l'Avent

---

92 Ibid., p. 50. 93 *Vita prima* I.29 (Flobert, 191). 94 Judic, 'Pénitence publique', p. 47. 95 Cf. Carozzi, *Voyage de l'âme*, pp. 130–3. On m'excusera de renvoyer à mon propre commentaire de 'la Vision de saint Fursy' d'après Bède, dans Arrignon et al., *Christianisme et Chrétientés*, pp. 24–36. 96 *quippe in sua domo commanebat.* … D'après Niermeyer, *Lexicon minus*, s.v., en latin ecclésiastique, le terme *domus* peut désigner le 'siège d'un évêché', une 'cathédrale', une 'abbatiale' ou un 'monastère'.

ou le Carême dans l'*Hexameron* de saint Ambroise (III.5) ou dans l'*Historia Francorum* de Grégoire de Tours (VIII.43) ainsi que dans la *Vita Marculfi* (cap. 12) rédigée au VIᵉ siècle. Fortunat (v.530–600), lui-aussi, aurait séjourné 'dans une île de l'Océan qui entoure la Bretagne'.[97]

Informé des épisodes précédents par le diacre dont il a suscité le témoignage, Dubric en tire les conséquences en promouvant, sur l'heure, Samson à l'office de *pistor*: 'Tous les biens qui, par le don de Dieu, abondent dans cette *cella*,[98] je t'enjoins de les administrer et je veux, avant tout, qu'ils soient distribués au nom du Seigneur par ton entremise'(I.34). Un miracle accompli par Samson dans l'exercice de cette fonction amène ensuite l'évêque à juger Samson 'digne de commander aux autres dans une charge plus élevée' (I.35). Bientôt la mort peu édifiante, mais providentielle de l'abbé Piro qui se noie, en état d'ébriété, dans le puits du monastère, permet l'élection abbatiale de Samson à l'instigation de Dubric (I.36).[99]

Il est séduisant de replacer ces événements dans la logique du don/contredon qui rend compte de nombreux traits des mentalités médiévales. N'est-ce pas dans la mesure où sa famille s'est vouée presque toute entière à Dieu avec tous ses biens patrimoniaux, au delà de ce qu'il 'sied et convient', que Samson se retrouve chargé d'administrer les biens du monastère puis d'en prendre la direction? En clair, l'hagiographe n'est il pas ici en train de justifier la fondation du réseau monastique samsonien dont il a été chargé de consigner les traditions? Ce passage à la vie religieuse d'une famille influente de la société profane s'inscrit dans une méditation sur le renoncement pénitentiel et l'ascèse monastique. A mon sens, ce n'est pas un hasard si le récit s'inscrit dans le temps liturgique du Carême: il faut quitter l'Egypte pour gagner la Terre promise, à laquelle c'est un lieu commun d'assimiler le monastère. Cette Pâque de l'Ancien Testament préfigure la fête de Pâques qui célèbre la mort et la résurrection du Christ selon le Nouveau Testament. Dans cette perspective la démarche pénitentielle d'Amon implique la rupture définitive avec le passé préchrétien que figure la géante condamnée à mort ainsi que la transposition sur le plan spirituel des liens familiaux qu'entérine l'extermination du serpent tutélaire désormais devenu inutile.

---

97 PL lxxxviii.43–4. Je suis redevable de ces exemples au chanoine J. Raison du Cleuziou que je remercie vivement. Cf. Merdrignac, 'Première Vie', p. 261. 98 Flobert, *Vie ancienne*, p. 199, choisit de traduire ici *cella* par 'cellier'. Niermeyer, *Lexicon minus*, s.v., donne, entre autres, le sens de 'monastère [...] subordonné à une église épiscopale' (' ... an episcopal see'). 99 Flobert, *Vie ancienne*, pp. 196–9.

Les origines irlandaises de
Saint Briac honoré en Bretagne:
Légende ou réalité

André-Yves Bourgès

Comme le faisait déjà remarquer dom L. Gougaud au début de notre siècle,[1] et comme l'a rappelé récemment le professeur P. Riché à propos de saint Maudez,[2] le nombre de saints irlandais que la tradition hagiographique bretonne armoricaine s'est appropriés, suite à leur installation dans la péninsule, est infiniment moindre que ceux des saints d'origine galloise ou cornique. Encore ce nombre, indiquait J. Loth, a-t-il été sans doute exagéré par les hagiographes tardifs qui auront 'transformé en Irlandais des saints dont ils ne connaissaient pas bien l'origine': d'après la forme de leurs noms, seraient incontestablement Irlandais huit saints seulement, dont saint Briac.[3]

Pour autant il ne faut pas minimiser les relations commerciales et donc culturelles au sens large, qui ont rapproché, très tôt et tout au long du Moyen Age, l'Irlande et l'Armorique, souvent par le biais de l'île de Bretagne, et dans lesquelles il semble que le Trégor maritime ait joué un rôle central.[4] Quant à la période à laquelle ces relations ont été les plus intenses, il est possible qu'elles soient seulement postérieures au premier tiers du Xe siècle et qu'elles aient été, pour une large part, la conséquence de la participation de moines irlandais à la

---

1 Gougaud, *Chrétientés celtiques*, p. 161. Dom Gougaud mentionne les seuls saints Fingar, Briac, Maudez, Vouga; cette courte liste est sans doute démarquée de celle donnée par J. Loth: voir ci-dessous n. 3. 2 Riché, 'Saint Maudez, irlandais'. 3 Loth, *Émigration bretonne*, p. 164. La liste complète (pp. 164–5) comprend Fingar alias Guigner, Briac, Maudez, Tenenan, Senan, Quenan, Ronan et Vouga. A ces noms dont la forme serait la garantie de leur origine irlandaise, J. Loth ajoute, d'après les bréviaires et légendaires, ceux des saints Sezni, Sané, Efflam, Kerrien et de sainte Osmane. 4 Sur ces relations directes ou triangulaires – via l'île de Bretagne – entre l'Irlande et la Bretagne continentale, voir dans Merdrignac, 'Perception de l'Irlande', en particulier pp. 70–2, l'hypothèse d'une 'filière trégoroise' qui aurait favorisé le passage et l'acclimatation en Bretagne armoricaine d'un certain nombre de traditions historico-légendaires venues d'Irlande. Nous avons reconnu à l'occasion de notre propre travail d'édition du dossier littéraire de saint Melar, martyr dont le principal lieu de culte est à Lanmeur dans le Trégor occidental, deux motifs qui sont très nettement empruntés à la mythologie irlandaise: Bourgès, *Saint Melar*.

reconstruction religieuse de la Bretagne armoricaine après les raids vikings qui avaient dévasté la péninsule pendant plus d'un demi siècle.[5]

I RAPIDE ÉTAT DE LA QUESTION ET PROBLÉMATIQUE

Saint Briac est donné, ainsi que l'indiquait en 1636 l'hagiographe dominicain de Morlaix, Albert Le Grand, comme originaire d'Irlande et plus précisément de la 'province d'Vltonie', notre moderne Ulster.[6] On a vu que les spécialistes comme J. Loth et dom L. Gougaud ont fait fond sur cette origine irlandaise que corroborait la forme du nom du saint; et le chanoine (anglican) G.H. Doble a même cru un moment devoir reconnaître saint Briac sous le voile virginal de sainte *Breaca*, comme l'avait fait en son temps l'évêque d'Exeter, John Bothe (1465–1478) qui appelle *Briacus* le patron de la paroisse cornique de Breage.[7] Les fragments conservés de la *Vita* de la sainte éponyme de Breage nous disent en effet qu'elle était originaire d'Irlande, et justement native des pays de Leinster et Ulster, *nata in partibus Lagonie et Vltonie*. N.I. Orme, à qui nous devons l'édition récente et largement commentée des fragments de cette *Vie* latine suggère lui-aussi, mais très rapidement et très allusivement, un possible rapprochement entre sainte *Breaca* et saint Briac.[8] Cependant, à l'occasion de son travail sur saint Brieuc, le chanoine Doble a émis une autre hypothèse et supposé que Briac était le même que Brieuc,[9] opinion depuis rappelée par L. Fleuriot.[10] Plus récemment encore, A.J. Raude a conclu que 'l'existence d'un *Briac* différent de *Brieuc* est douteuse. S'il avait été irlandais le nom aurait du être **Briach*'.[11]

La première interrogation concerne donc l'existence d'un saint du nom de Briac et sa différenciation d'avec un autre saint nommé Brieuc. Ensuite, si nous pouvons conclure de manière suffisamment formelle à la réalité hagiographique de saint Briac, la seconde interrogation portera sur sa prétendue origine irlandaise. Mais il sera nécessaire à cette occasion de procéder à une analyse discursive et comparative à partir des rares indices en notre possession.

II SAINT BRIAC N'EST PAS LE MÊME QUE SAINT BRIEUC

Brioc est une forme hypocoristique de *Briomaglus* (**Brimael*) et, au delà de petites confusions graphiques avec le nom *Briac* à l'occasion de la transcription

---

5 Merdrignac, 'Perception de l'Irlande', p. 72. Cet auteur fait écho en l'occurrence à une hypothèse déjà avancée par Couffon, 'Echos hagiographiques'. 6 Le Grand, *Vies des saints*, p. 650. 7 Doble, *Saints of Cornwall*, i.98. 8 Orme, 'Saint Breage'. L'édition des fragments de la *Vita Sancte Breace* figure à la p. 352; saint Briac est signalé à la n. 38, p. 349. 9 Doble, *Saints of Cornwall*, iv.94–5. 10 Fleuriot, *Origines*, errata et corrigenda, p. 348. 11 Raude, *Origine géographique*, p. 156.

plus ou moins tardive de certaines pièces d'archives,[12] les deux noms sont bien distingués, comme le sont également les deux personnages qui les portent. En effet, saint Brieuc ne partage pas avec saint Briac ses coordonnées hagiographiques d'ordre topographique et d'ordre chronologique, 'éléments simples mais nécessaires et suffisants pour identifier un saint', comme l'écrivait le promoteur de ce système, le père H. Delehaye.[13]

Ainsi Saint Brieuc était-il honoré principalement au chef-lieu éponyme du diocèse qui porte son nom, ainsi que dans le diocèse de Cornouaille, à Plonivel (**Ploe Brimael* > **Ploe Vrimael* > *Ploerimael* en 1338) à la date traditionnelle du 1er mai. Saint Briac quant à lui était honoré principalement à Bourbriac, dans le diocèse de Tréguier, à la date traditionnelle du 18 décembre attestée jusqu'au milieu du XVe siècle au moins. Cette date fut par la suite avancée au 17 décembre.[14] En outre, le culte de saint Briac était établi dès le début du XIe siècle: son nom et la date de son *festum*, mais aussi sa qualité de confesseur et le territoire où s'est exercé son apostolat font en effet l'objet d'une laconique mais précieuse mention dans un sacramentaire d'une église du nord de la France, repéré et daté d'après son écriture par l'abbé F. Duine.[15] Dans ce sacramentaire le nom de Briac figure en compagnie de ceux de saints 'bretons' beaucoup plus connus comme Samson, Malo et Magloire.

Un inventaire de l'abbaye Saint-Magloire de Paris daté 1319 mentionne la présence, entre celles de nombreux saints, de reliques de saint *Briachi*, regroupées avec celles de saint Léon pape, de saint Brice et de saint Méloire confesseur, sans que soient d'ailleurs précisées leur nature, ni leur quantité,[16] d'où l'on peut en déduire qu'il s'agissait vraisemblablement de fragments d'os assez insignifiants. Cet inventaire est en français, mais son auteur a conservé les formes anciennes des noms des saints les moins connus de lui que lui avaient sans doute procurées les authentiques attachées à ces reliques. C'est le cas pour *Briachi* (génitif de **Briachus*) dont la forme du nom peut aider à renforcer la conviction de l'origine irlandaise de celui qui le portait. Comme la présence de reliques de saint Briac à l'abbaye Saint-Magloire de Paris n'est pas attestée dans un inventaire plus ancien, rédigé vers 1138,[17] il faut donc en conclure qu'elles ont

---

12 C'est notamment le cas dans la transcription des statuts synodaux de Tréguier promulgués en 1450 et 1459 par les évêques successifs Jean de Ploeuc et Jean de Coëtquis, qu'a donnée dom Morice, *Mémoires*, respectivement col. 1523 et 1532: voir plus bas nn. 18 et 19. 13 Delehaye, *Cinq leçons*, p.13, cité par Dubois et Lemaître, *Sources et méthodes*, p. 16. 14 Saint Briac était fêté à Bourbriac au 17 décembre dès avant 1631 comme en témoigne Albert Le Grand. Nous ignorons la raison de ce changement, sinon peut-être pour favoriser la célébration au 18 du culte de saint Victor martyr, dont l'église de Bourbriac conservait également quelques reliques. 15 MS Paris, Bibliothèque nationale de France, fonds latin 11589. Voir Duine, *Inventaire liturgique*, notice 21, p. 23 et suiv.; p. 27: *In Britania Sancti Briaci confessoris*. On s'attendrait plutôt à avoir, puisqu'il s'agit de la Bretagne armoricaine, la formule *In Britania minori*. 16 Terroine et Fossier, *Chartes et documents*, p. 556. 17 Cet inventaire a été publié par Auvray, 'Catalogue'. Le document intitulé *Translatio sancti*

été amenées tardivement en ce lieu et sans doute en petite quantité comme dit plus haut. D'ailleurs en 1631, à l'époque de la visite d'Albert Le Grand à Bourbriac, les autochtones croyaient que les reliques de leur saint patron étaient toujours conservées sur place.

Au XVᵉ siècle, entre 1437 et 1450,[18] la fête de saint Briac avait été instituée dans le diocèse de Tréguier par l'évêque du lieu: *Item similiter* [*statuimus et ordinamus*] *festum beati Briaci; et hoc in parrochia de Burgobriaci die decima octava mensis decembris.*[19] Et en 1459, on rappellait la qualité de confesseur de saint Briac: *In mense decembri … Briaci confessoris.*[20]

Les différentes attestations du culte de saint Briac sont donc totalement indépendantes de celui rendu à saint Brieuc. En outre, même s'il ne peut être question de comparer l'ancienneté sinon la valeur des éléments biographiques rapportés d'une part dans la *Vita* de saint Brieuc, composée à Angers au XIᵉ siècle, d'autre part dans la *Vie* tardive de saint Briac par Albert Le Grand (composée entre 1631 et 1636 à partir d'une source manuscrite conservée à Bourbriac mais difficilement identifiable et de traditions orales également recueillies sur place), force est de constater que les deux récits n'ont aucun point de contact, ce qui constitue une forte présomption qu'il devait exister une tradition hagiographique relative à saint Briac au moins aussi ancienne que celle dont témoigne la *Vita* de saint Brieuc pour ce dernier. Sinon en effet la légende de celui-là aurait emprunté à la biographie de celui-ci des traits particulièrement remarquables. Ainsi, sans pouvoir affirmer avec une complète certitude que les deux personnages sont originellement distincts, il paraît possible de conclure provisoirement qu'ils ont été soigneusement distingués l'un de l'autre depuis l'époque de la première attestation du culte de saint Briac, au début du XIᵉ siècle.

III AUTOUR DE L'AN MIL

Le *terminus a quo* de l'An Mil est en lui même très intéressant et nous encourage à étendre notre réflexion relative au culte de saint Briac à celui d'un autre saint lui aussi présenté comme étant d'origine irlandaise, Efflam, ainsi qu'à l'époque et aux circonstances de l'invention des reliques de ce dernier.

Selon sa *Vita*,[21] le souvenir d'Efflam et celui de sa sépulture avaient fini par s'effacer presqu'entièrement après sa mort: *Hic longo tempore pretiosum corpus*

Maglorii et aliorum Parisius, dont l'original peut-être contemporain de l'exode des corps saints bretons a été interpolé par un moine maglorien qui connaissait l'inventaire rédigé vers 1138, ne mentionne pas non plus les reliques de saint Briac.   18 Morice, *Mémoires*, ii, respectivement col. 1280 et 1523.   19 Ibid., ii, col. 1523. Le texte en question porte les formes *Brioci* et *Burgobrioci*.   20 Ibid., ii, col. 1532. Le texte en question porte la forme *Brioci*.   21 *Vita Sancti Euflami*, ed. de la Borderie, 'Saint Efflam'; tiré-à-part, Rennes, 1892.

requieuit absconditum in corpore terrae; *cursu tempore labente, pene memoria eius de terris ablata est.*[22] Mais à la suite de la désignation miraculeuse de l'endroit de la sépulture oubliée, les fouilles ordonnées par l'évêque permirent la découverte du corps d'Efflam, avec une inscription – probablement gravée dans la pierre de son tombeau – qui renseignait sur l'identité du personnage, autant que sur son caractère de sainteté les nombreux miracles accomplis: *sanctum corpus inuenerunt et litteris secum inuentis crebris quoque miraculis dignoscitur.*[23] Ce fut alors prétexte à de grandes fêtes, avec l'assistance de l'évêque et de tout le clergé (*pontifex cum universitate cleri*) ainsi que du roi et de ses principaux seigneurs (*rex cum suis principibus*).[24]

L'époque à laquelle se sont déroulés ces événements pour lesquels Albert Le Grand donnait la date précise 994, a été déterminée par A. de la Borderie en son temps,[25] et les conclusions du célèbre historien breton sont toujours acceptées par la critique moderne.[26] La découverte des reliques de saint Efflam aurait eu lieu, selon toute vraisemblance, sous le règne du duc Geoffroy Ier, c'est à dire entre 992 et 1008, 'dans le contexte de relance de la vie religieuse qui constitue le point le plus positif de ce règne'.[27] Cette découverte s'inscrit également dans le contexte plus large d'invention généralisée de nombreuses reliques de saints que Raoul Glaber date de 'la huitième année après le millénaire de l'Incarnation du Sauveur' en nous précisant que ces reliques furent découvertes, sur la foi de divers indices, 'dans des lieux où elles étaient restées longtemps cachées'.[28] G. Duby nous fournit l'explication – déjà implicitement donnée par le chroniqueur médiéval – du phénomène: 'tout naturellement les terrassements préparatoires aux reconstructions d'églises mettaient au jour des sarcophages inconnus'.[29]

La spécificité de la Bretagne, comme l'a rappelé B. Merdrignac en rapprochant le cas de saint Efflam de celui de saint Ronan dont le culte a lui aussi connu un développement tardif,[30] c'est la pénurie locale de reliques. La plupart d'entre elles en effet étaient toujours conservées à l'époque dans les différents endroits où le clergé breton avait été accueilli pendant son exil, suite à sa fuite devant les incursions des vikings. Ce qui dès lors donnait, en Bretagne, une importance considérable à la découverte dans une église, une chapelle, voire un simple oratoire, de la sépulture d'un saint personnage, dont on ne savait en général presque (plus) rien – sauf peut-être son origine, car longtemps après sa disparition son souvenir avait pu se maintenir dans la mémoire populaire sous un sobriquet ethnique, comme c'est aujourd'hui encore souvent le cas dans nos campagnes quand il s'agit d'évoquer un 'hors venu'. Ou quelquefois même son nom que venait opportunément rappeler, sinon apprendre, aux découvreurs une inscription gravée dans la pierre du sarcophage.[31] Pour autant, il est logique de supposer

23 Ibid., § 22, p. 21 du t.-à-p. 24 Ibid., § 23, p. 22 du t.-à-p. 25 'Saint Efflam', pp. 35–7 du t.-à-p. 26 Merdrignac, 'Saint Ronan', voir en particulier p. 156. 27 Ibid., p. 156. 28 Voir Duby, *L'An Mil*, p. 427. 29 Ibid. 30 Merdrignac, 'Saint Ronan', p. 156. 31 Le risque d'une confusion était important quand le nom s'était effacé de la mémoire populaire.

que, si ces *reliques* n'avaient pas suivi le même chemin que celles dont les sanctuaires bretons étaient désormais privés, c'était sans doute pour une des trois raisons suivantes:

1) soit que le culte du personnage en question fût encore trop peu développé à l'époque des incursions des vikings et n'eût pas retenu l'attention du clergé, ni attiré celle des pirates;

2) soit que ce personnage ne fût pas revêtu d'un caractère éminent de sainteté, du moins à l'époque considérée;

3) soit enfin que son existence fût postérieure à l'époque des incursions des vikings et de la fuite du clergé breton; et qu'elle fût plutôt inscrite dans le contexte de la reconstruction religieuse de la Bretagne qui suivit cette période troublée.

Quoiqu'il en soit, il est à noter que plusieurs des saints bretons réputés avoir été d'origine irlandaise sont des personnages dont l'antiquité ne peut pas remonter au delà des dernières années du IXe siècle au plus tôt, ou plus sûrement encore au delà du premier tiers du Xe. Leur culte d'ailleurs, d'après les documents liturgiques ou para-liturgiques conservés, n'est pas attesté avant le début du XIe siècle. Quant à leurs vestiges onomastiques, ils se rencontrent essentiellement dans les strates toponymiques les plus tardives, notamment celles des noms de lieux en *loc-* et en *saint-*.

IV TOPONYMIE DE SAINT BRIAC ET LIEUX DE CULTE

Presqu'au centre géométrique du triangle Saint-Briac (actuelle commune d'Ille-et-Vilaine),[32] *Lopriac* (village de l'actuelle commune morbihannaise de Kervignac),[33] et *Lann-Briac* (toponyme en l'actuelle commune finistérienne de Taulé),[34] l'actuelle commune de Bourbriac, chef-lieu de canton des Côtes d'Armor, non seulement revendique elle aussi d'avoir saint Briac pour éponyme, mais surtout le vénère en qualité de patron de l'église paroissiale. En outre on prétend conserver en ce lieu même les vestiges de son monastère, son sarcophage, son tombeau, ses reliques enfin comme nous l'avons déjà dit. Une chapelle rurale, à

Dans le cas de saint Efflam (*Euflam*), le nom ne paraît pas d'origine irlandaise mais une explication par le brittonique n'est guère plus satisfaisante. En fait il s'agit peut-être des seules lettres déchiffrées de l'inscription qui figurait sur son tombeau. **32** Le toponyme *Saint-Briac* se retrouverait également aujourd'hui en l'actuelle commune d'Hénanbihen et autrefois en l'actuelle commune de Saint-Alban, toutes deux des Côtes d'Armor: voir Le Menn, *Grand choix*, p. 18. **33** Le toponyme *Lopriac* se retrouve également aujourd'hui dans une autre commune morbihannaise, en l'occurrence Langonnet: voir ibid. **34** Il faut interpréter ce toponyme comme 'la lande de (saint) Briac', étendue sacralisée par la présence d'un calvaire désigné *Croix-Briac*, lequel était situé sur le chemin du *tro-Breiz* entre Saint-Pol-de-Léon et Tréguier, via Morlaix.

quelque 3 km à vol d'oiseau au sud-est du bourg, porte encore le nom de *Pénity*. Cet endroit était connu d'Albert Le Grand qui écrit: 'Nos anciens Princes, tant Roys que Ducs de Bretagne, ont porté une singulière devotion à saint Briac, et ont donné droit de franchise ou azyle à son Hermitage, nommé communément *Peniti Sant Briac*, c'est à dire *Maison où Saint Briac a fait sa pénitence*'.[35]

On sait que les actuels territoires communaux de Bourbriac et de Saint-Adrien correspondent ensemble à peu près au finage d'une ancienne paroisse appelée au bas Moyen Age *Minibriac*, laquelle faisait alors partie du ressort d'une plus vaste châtellenie également appelée *Minibriac*, nom emprunté dans l'un et l'autre cas à une modeste circonscription monastique (le *minihi* ou la *monachia* de Briac) à l'entour de l'église actuelle de Bourbriac.[36] Rien n'oblige à faire remonter la fondation de ce *minihi* à l'époque des premières manifestations du culte rendu sur place à Briac et moins encore à celle du saint. Il faut plus vraisemblablement en rapporter l'origine à la donation du sanctuaire de Briac vers le milieu du XIIe siècle, par un *comes Britanniae* de la maison de Penthièvre, à l'abbaye Saint-Melaine de Rennes.[37] C'est peut-être d'ailleurs une donation similaire à l'abbaye Sainte-Croix de Quimperlé par le comte de Cornouaille qui est à l'origine du *minihi* de Locronan un siècle plus tôt.

La troménie briacine, *tro ar (m)vinihi*, 'le tour du *minihi*', que l'on appelle sur place *leo dro*, 'la lieue de tour', circuit rituel effectué annuellement le jour de l'Ascension et qui n'est pas sans rappeler la plus courte des deux troménies de Locronan, commémore sûrement les limites de la donation comtale que nous avons supposée. Comme l'avait souligné R. Largillière,[38] le territoire circonscrit par la *leo dro* ne contient pas la chapelle du *Pénity*, bénéficiaire de l'immunité accordée au lieu que sanctifia la pénitence de Briac. A l'inverse il s'y trouve les vestiges d'une motte féodale appelée *Coz castel*, 'le vieux château', dont il faut admettre qu'elle avait été aliénée par le donateur au moment de la donation ou/et qu'elle était déjà abandonnée à cette époque. En tout état de cause, les habitants de Bourbriac ont depuis longtemps associée la *leo dro* au souvenir de leur saint patron. En effet, selon Albert Le Grand qui nous a conservé l'état de la tradition locale en 1631 et qui nous renseigne également sur la prononciation du toponyme, 'Saint Briac avoit de coûtume de faire tous les ans une solennelle Procession le jour de l'Ascension, tout à l'entour des terres que le Roy Deroch avoit donné à son Monastère, en action de graces de ce qu'à tel jour il avoit fondé cette ceremonie qu'on a depuis observée tous les ans à pareil jour en la Paroisse de *Boulbriac*'.[39]

---

35 Le Grand, *Vies des saints*, p. 655. **36** Largillière, 'Minihys', en particulier pp. 190–6. Bourgès, 'Minihy-Briac'. **37** Dès 1158 les moines de Saint-Melaine possédaient l'*ecclesia de Minihy Briac*. Mais cette église n'est pas nommée dans deux actes de confirmation des biens de cette abbaye datés 1121 (bulle papale) et 1152 (charte comtale): voir Largillière, 'Minihys', p. 193 et n. 21. **38** Largillière, 'Minihys', pp. 191–2. **39** Le Grand, *Vies des saints*, p. 656.

Les moines de Saint-Melaine ne paraissent pas avoir conservé au delà de la fin du XIIe siècle leurs possessions dans une zone rurale qui ne présentait pas le même attrait, ni le même intérêt que les autres lieux où la grande abbaye rennaise implanta des prieurés (notamment à Lamballe, Moncontour, Châtelaudren, Guingamp, La Roche-Derrien, pour ne citer que les possessions situées dans la 'principauté' de Penthièvre). L'église du *minihi* ayant été sécularisée, le nom de *Minibriac* a rapidement passé à une vaste circonscription féodale connue dès 1205,[40] qui englobait les actuels territoires communaux de Bourbriac, Coadout, Plésidy, Magoar et Saint-Adrien. Les limites de la châtellenie de *Minibriac* avaient repris sensiblement, et sans doute fortuitement, celles beaucoup plus anciennes d'une *ploe*, grande paroisse baptismale des premiers temps de l'Armorique bretonne, dont le nom a été conservé dans celui de Plésidy (**ploe Seidi*).[41]

Mais l'apostolat de saint Briac et la fondation monastique que la tradition lui attribue n'ont peut-être pas eu pour seul cadre la **ploe Seidi*. En tout cas le souvenir du saint est au moins aussi anciennement attesté dans la *ploe* voisine, laquelle couvrait initialement un vaste territoire depuis divisé en des entités paroissiales plus petites, et de nos jours partagé entre les communes de Senven-Léhart, Saint-Péver, Saint-Fiacre, Boquého, Lanrodec, Saint-Jean-Kerdaniel, Châtelaudren (partie située sur la rive gauche du Leff), Plouagat enfin dont le nom conserve celui de l'ensemble primitif (**ploe Adgat*).[42] En effet, à relative proximité d'un établissement monastique attesté dès 1163 sous le nom de *Claustrum Briaci*[43] – aujourd'hui le village du *Cloître* en la commune de Saint-Fiacre où se voit encore la chapelle d'un prieuré alors dépendant de l'abbaye Saint-Jacut-de-L'Isle et qui malgré des vicissitudes diverses devait demeurer jusqu'à la fin de l'Ancien Régime possession foncière de cette abbaye – on relève le toponyme *Guerbriac*, village sur la limite communale entre Plouagat et Lanrodec, avec chapelle aujourd'hui disparue.[44] Il existait aussi en Boquého une chapelle placée sous l'invocation de saint Briac.[45] Ce sont là autant d'indices d'une imprégnation forte de ces lieux par la tradition relative à ce saint.

Surtout, il semble que l'église Saint-Fiacre – chef-lieu à partir du bas Moyen Age d'une paroisse qui avait été rattachée en qualité de succursale à celle de Plésidy dans des circonstances encore mal éclaircies – était en fait placée plus anciennement sous l'invocation de saint Briac, au moins depuis 1170, date à laquelle les moines de Saint-Melaine, déjà possesseurs comme on l'a vu de l'église du *Minihy Briac*, se font confirmer par l'évêque de Tréguier entre autres biens ce qu'ils détiennent dans celle de Saint-Briac (*quod in ecclesia de Sancto-Briaco habent*).[46] De même portait encore en 1330 le nom de saint Briac la

---

40 Maître et de Berthou, *Cartulaire*, p. 183.   41 Tanguy, *Dictionnaire des noms ... des Côtes d'Armor*, pp. 28 et 187.   42 Ibid., p. 201.   43 De Barthélemy et Geslin de Bourgogne, *Anciens évêchés de Bretagne*, iv.278.   44 Peyresaubes, 'Plouagat et ses chapelles'.   45 Le Menn, *Grand choix*, p. 18.   46 Barthélemy et Geslin de Bourgogne, *Anciens évêchés de Bretagne*, vi.135.

paroisse dont cette église était le chef-lieu. A cette occasion la *parrochia de Sancto-Briaco* apparaît comme nettement distincte et en même temps voisine de celle de *Minibriac*.[47] Au village du *Cloître*, appelé encore le *Cloaistre Briac* en 1574, le souvenir de son éponyme s'effaça au point d'être remplacé par saint Nicolas dans la chapelle du lieu, comme il l'avait été, dès cette époque, dans celle de Saint-Fiacre, par un saint qui, pour être lui aussi irlandais, n'avait d'autre lien avec lui qu'une vague analogie de nom.[48]

V ARCHÉOLOGIE DE SAINT BRIAC

Si les parties les plus anciennes de l'église Saint-Fiacre et de la chapelle Saint-Nicolas du *Cloître* ne remontent pas au delà du XVᵉ siècle, comme c'est aussi le cas pour la chapelle du *Pénity*, l'église de Bourbriac quant à elle présente en plusieurs endroits un caractère d'antiquité affirmé. De l'avis de P. Barbier, spécialiste de l'histoire monumentale du Trégor,[49] 'la crypte et le carré du transept appartiennent à l'art roman'.[50] En fait, pour ce qui est de la crypte, 'seule la partie centrale, couverte d'une voûte d'arêtes, date du XIᵉ siècle dans son état actuel, les deux nefs latérales ont été remaniées au XVIᵉ siècle'.[51] Cette crypte a vraisemblablement abrité le sarcophage hélas anépigraphe dit de saint Briac, remploi gallo-romain ou du haut Moyen Age, avant son transfert dans l'église supérieure. 'Le carré du transept est, comme à Notre-Dame de Guingamp, tout ce qui subsiste de l'église romane élevée dans la seconde moitié du XIIᵉ siècle'.[52] L'époque de cette construction correspondrait donc à celle de la possession du lieu par l'abbaye Saint-Melaine de Rennes.

Le tombeau du saint était situé, selon le témoignage d'Albert Le Grand, 'au milieu de la Nef près les pilliers du costé droit'. L'hagiographe dominicain le décrit 'beau et élevé, basty d'une pierre blanche retirant à l'Albastre, tout historié en relief des principales actions de sa Vie; et sur la table du tombeau est son Effigie couchée de son long, la Mitre Abbatiale en teste et la Crosse en main; le tout cerné d'une cloison de fer en forme de Chapelle'.[53] Un incendie en 1765 fit s'écrouler sur lui la nef. On construisit alors, en utilisant plusieurs vestiges de l'ancien, un nouveau tombeau à l'extrémité occidentale du bas-côté nord de l'église. Ces remplois sont du XVIᵉ siècle, qui est donc l'époque assignée au tombeau disparu. A ce sujet il faut remarquer que le tombeau de saint Efflam dans l'église de Plestin avait également été élevé au XVIᵉ siècle, en 1576, pour envelopper et décorer un monument considéré comme le tombeau primitif du saint. Peut-être en fut également de même à Bourbriac. Il est

---

47 De la Borderie, *Monuments originaux*, pp. 138–41. 48 Tanguy, *Dictionnaire des noms …
des Côtes d'Armor*, p. 281. 49 Barbier, *Trégor historique*. 50 Ibid., p. 346. 51 Ibid., p. 348.
52 Ibid. 53 Le Grand, *Vies des saints*, p. 656.

possible en tout cas que les bas-reliefs qui ornaient le tombeau de saint Briac, et qui ont disparu à l'occasion de sa reconstruction après 1765, aient pu largement inspirer le récit d'Albert Le Grand.

VI LES SOURCES D'ALBERT LE GRAND

Outre un éventuel recours à la statuaire et aux bas-reliefs, cet auteur cite des sources écrites pour sa *Vie* de saint Briac: les anciens 'legendaires manuscrits' de la cathédrale de Tréguier et 'un vieil mss jadis copié en l'Eglise de Boul-Briac'. Ce dernier document paraît irrémédiablement perdu et les fragments conservés ou recopiés des anciens légendiers de Tréguier ne contiennent pas d'élément hagiographique relatif à saint Briac. En ce qui concerne les sources orales, Albert Le Grand invoque, à propos de faits miraculeux récents, le témoignage de 'personnes dignes de foy' qu'il dit avoir rencontrées 'l'an 1631, au mois de May [qu'il fut] à Boul-Briac rechercher cette Histoire'. Mais s'il est évident que ces témoignages oraux ont pu s'étendre à bien d'autres épisodes de l'"histoire" en question, l'hagiographe ne nous en dit rien de plus précis. Enfin, le dominicain fait allusion aux 'legendes des Saints Tugduval et Guevroc'. Faut-il comprendre que la tradition orale relative à ces deux saints, telle qu'elle était connue d'Albert Le Grand, les associait dans des récits légendaires à saint Briac? Ou bien s'agit-il d'une référence qu'il faut alors qualifier de mensongère aux différentes *Vitae* de saint Tudual dans lesquelles on chercherait en vain le nom de Guevroc et celui de Briac?

En outre restent posés, d'une part, le problème des relations entre la tradition locale, écrite et orale, relative à saint Briac et les informations qu'avait pu recueillir par ailleurs Albert Le Grand; d'autre part, celui des rapports entre l'ensemble de ce *corpus* hagiographique briacin en Bretagne et la tradition cornique, écrite et orale, relative à sainte *Breaca*, notamment sa *Vita* composée au bas Moyen Age. Ainsi, et par exemple, N.I. Orme a montré que l'origine irlandaise, et plus précisément encore ulstérienne, de sainte *Breaca* telle que la rapportait l'hagiographe insulaire était extrêmement sujette à caution et avait été sans doute été déduite de la *Vita* de sainte Brigitte.[54] Mais rien ne s'oppose à ce qu'Albert Le Grand, qui admettait sans discussion l'origine irlandaise de saint Briac, très affirmée en Bretagne, ait emprunté à la tradition cornique relative à sainte *Breaca* la précision que Briac était né en 'Vltonie'; à moins évidemment que cette précision ne figurât déjà dans le vieux manuscrit de l'église de Bourbriac.

Il est bien difficile d'établir des certitudes sur Briac à partir de la confrontation aventureuse de sources qui ont disparu. Aussi, malgré l'impossibilité de tout

---

54 Orme, 'Saint Breage', pp. 346 et 350.

contrôle, c'est le texte d'Albert Le Grand lui-même qu'il faut finalement examiner pour en extraire ce qui peut confirmer ou infirmer l'origine irlandaise du saint. Comme nous l'avons dit à propos de la nette distinction entre saint Brieuc et saint Briac, il devait exister une tradition hagiographique ancienne relative à ce dernier. L'absence de véritable enjeu pour le religieux morlaisien, plus susceptible, on le sait, d'intervenir personnellement et d'affabuler quand il s'agit d'écrire la biographie des saints du diocèse de Léon, fonde avec suffisamment de force la présomption que l'hagiographe dominicain nous a assez fidèlement transmis cette tradition.

VII RÉSIDU HISTORIQUE DE LA VIE DE SAINT BRIAC COMPOSÉE PAR ALBERT LE GRAND

En dehors des précisions relatives à l'origine géographique du saint, deux autres éléments de sa tradition hagiographique telle qu'elle nous a été conservée dans sa biographie tardive doivent être signalés et pris en compte.

Tout d'abord saint Briac apparaît nettement comme un ouvrier zélé et efficace de l'évangélisation de la Bretagne armoricaine, et surtout comme un organisateur. Que, pour les hagiographes tardifs, cette caractéristique dût être rapportée à l'époque de l'immigration en Armorique des saints bretons fondateurs, tel saint Tudual, rien que de parfaitement compréhensible. Mais le contexte de la fondation monastique initiée par Briac, sous l'impulsion et de la volonté même du souverain qui régnait alors en Bretagne, peut s'entendre d'autres périodes de l'histoire de notre péninsule, en particulier de celle qui a immédiatement suivi le temps des incursions normandes.

Ensuite et surtout, il faut prendre en compte le voyage à Rome et le périple occasionné par ce pèlerinage *ad limina Apostolorum*. L. Fleuriot a écrit de Briac qu' 'il paraît en tout cas être l'un des plus nomades parmi les saints bretons, ce qui n'est pas peu dire'.[55] Curieusement L. Fleuriot n'a pas rappelé, peut-être parce qu'il ne croyait pas à la possible origine irlandaise de Briac, combien les insulaires furent justement de grands voyageurs, quelle attraction les Lieux Saints exercèrent sur leur imagination et comment 'Rome fut donc fréquemment visitée par les pèlerins irlandais'.[56] Albert Le Grand donne des détails sur le périple de Briac. Celui-ci voyage par terre depuis Bourbriac avec deux compagnons, qui ne sont pas nommés et dont rien n'indique qu'il s'agissait de religieux, jusqu'à la Provence où il rejoint un certain *Havre*. Briac embarque alors sur un caboteur à destination du port de *Gaïette* (Gaète). De là il rallie Rome où il est évidemment reçu par le pape 'qui l'enrichit de plusieurs précieuses Reliques'. Après avoir visité les Lieux Saints de Rome, le retour

55 Fleuriot, *Origines*, p. 270.   **56** Gougaud, *Chrétientés celtiques*, pp. 202–3.

s'effectue à nouveau par Gaète où Briac embarque sur un vaisseau qui le ramène à Marseille. Après un court séjour dans la cité phocéenne, il va visiter l'archevêque d'Arles qui le retient par amitié auprès de lui pendant deux ans.[57] Finalement Briac prend congé de son hôte et rentre en Bretagne, à Bourbriac, non sans aller faire son rapport à l'évêque de *Lexobie* et à l'abbé du monastère de *Val de Trecor* (**Nant Trecor* > *Lantreger* en 1267> *Lantreguier* ou *Treguier* en 1394 >Tréguier).

Si, comme nous l'avons supposé, ces précisions appartenaient déjà plus ou moins à la tradition hagiographique connue à Bourbriac et transmise à Albert Le Grand par diverses sources locales (monumentales, orales, écrites), lesquelles avaient elles mêmes relayé des témoignages plus anciens, nous disposons alors d'un dossier qui permet de poursuivre, sinon d'achever, le travail de nomenclature – entamé par P. Ó Riain[58] – des différentes représentations de l'Irlandais telles qu'elles ont été fixées et propagées au Moyen Age par les hagiographes continentaux. A l'Irlandais-type de l'hagiographie mérovingienne (VIIe siècle), ascète et éternel voyageur, à celui de l'hagiographie carolingienne (IXe siècle), pèlerin régulier à Rome en même temps qu'érudit, prototypes qui aboutissent finalement au XIIIe siècle, dans la *Vita* de saint Ronan, à l'Irlandais né natif de 'l'île des saints' et donc prédestiné à la sainteté, il faut sans doute ajouter un type intermédiaire incarné par saint Briac: pèlerin à Rome et artisan actif d'une véritable organisation religieuse des campagnes bretonnes. Cette représentation pourrait avoir été particulièrement répandue au XIe siècle dans le Trégor où, comme nous l'avons dit, l'influence irlandaise fut sans doute plus marquée qu'ailleurs. Ainsi l'auteur de la *Vita* moyenne de saint Tudual et qui lui aussi attribue à ce dernier une origine 'scotique' – l'hagiographe évoque la 'terre natale' de son héros, *terram natiuitatis suae, Scothiam uidelicet* – non content de rappeler le zèle pastoral dont fit preuve le saint en Armorique, inclut dans son récit l'épisode du séjour à Rome de Tudual, lequel serait alors devenu pape sous le nom de *Leo britigena* et aurait même effectué durant son pontificat un pèlerinage à Jérusalem.

VIII CONCLUSION PROVISOIRE ET SUBJECTIVE

Il n'est guère possible d'aller plus loin. Peut-être même avons nous déjà dépassé la limite que nous imposait l'état de notre documentation, en accordant un crédit qu'ils ne méritent pas toujours aux travaux d'Albert Le Grand, ou en sollicitant au delà de ce qu'ils peuvent réellement donner les matériaux

---

57 Il n'y a pas apparemment de traces au moins très visibles du séjour et de l'apostolat de Briac en Arles comme nous l'a fait savoir sur notre demande Monsieur F. Debost, maire-adjoint délégué aux affaires culturelles et au patrimoine par lettre du 8 octobre 1996.
58 Ó Riain, 'Saint Ronan', en particulier pp. 157–9.

onomastiques (anthroponymie et toponymie), topologiques et archéologiques. Le nom de Briac, l'attestation relativement tardive de son culte dans la liturgie et dans la toponymie, sa notoriété essentiellement locale, la conservation sur place de ses reliques, certains éléments de la tradition orale et écrite que nous a transmise son hagiographe du XVIIe siècle, sont autant de facteurs qui autorisent une origine irlandaise pour ce saint.

Nous conjecturons que Briac a débarqué en Bretagne continentale vers la fin des années 30 du Xe siècle. Pendant quelques années, une dizaine, une quinzaine, il a oeuvré dans un terroir sylvestre, non loin de la source du Trieux, sur les deux rives de ce petit fleuve. Son apostolat lui a valu l'estime de l'évêque (d'Alet ? de Léon ?) dont dépendait cette zone forestière et surtout de l'abbé du grand monastère de Tréguier pour le compte duquel il s'est rendu à Rome (dans le cadre d'une mission relative à l'érection d'un évêché à Tréguier ?) Mort dans l'un de ses ermitages, petites cellules construites au milieu des populations civiles qu'il pouvait ainsi mieux encadrer, Briac fut ensépulturé à proximité, dans l'un des oratoires qu'il avait fondés. Après deux générations, son nom et son souvenir avaient presque disparu quand, à la faveur du renouveau religieux qui suivit l'An Mil, on fit la découverte de son sarcophage. Aussitôt tenues pour celles d'un saint, ses reliques firent l'objet d'un culte qui prit rapidement de l'ampleur, en particulier dans les lieux que Briac avait marqués de sa forte empreinte et dont la dimension monastique fut encore renforcée par l'implantation postérieure des abbayes de Saint-Jacut et de Saint-Melaine, respectivement fondatrices des petits établissements de *Claustrum Briaci* et de *Minihi Briac*.

St Cathróe of Metz and the
Hagiography of Exoticism

David N. Dumville

St Cathróe[1] was one, perhaps the leader, of a group of thirteen Insular ecclesiastics who undertook perpetual exile for God's sake, arriving on the Continent within (and possibly early within) the period 941 x 946 (the dates derive from information about Cathróe's travels through England).[2] His group went first from Boulogne to pay their respects to the church of St Fursa at Péronne in Picardy, where Cathróe enjoyed a vision of the patron. A noblewoman,

---

1 The saint's name has proved to be strikingly troublesome. The forms known from the Life of St Cathróe (as printed by Colgan, *Acta sanctorum*, in 1645: cf. 5, below) are all treated as indeclinable in Latin (references are to §§ of the text): Cadroe (heading); Kaddroe (I, VI, VII); Cathroe (XI, XIII, XIV, XVI, XVII³, XVIIII², XX, XXI, XXII², XXIII, XXIV², XXV, XXVII, XXIX, XXXI³, XXXII³, XXXIV, XXXV); Cothroe (XXI); Catthroe (XXVI). According to the author of the Life of St Cathróe, the name meant *bellator* (§VI). Colgan (*Acta sanctorum*, p. 503 n. 45) further noted that 'In MS Cod. aliquando *Caddroe*, aliquando *Cadroe* legabatur; sed vtrumque mendosè: author enim indicat nomen hoc iuxta suum etymon significare *bellatorem*: *Cath* autem Hibernis idem sonat, quod *bellum* vel <*p*>*rœlium*; et *roe* idem quod *agon*, seu locus certaminis; vel si *Cathroe* legatur *Cathoer*, deriuatur similiter a *bellando*, et idem est quod *bellator*, estque nomen perfrequens hodiè et olim inter Hibernos'. The second name mentioned by Colgan is presumably earlier *Catháer/Catháir* and is highly unlikely to have been the saint's name, on the evidence of the forms in the Life. The Gaelic name Cathróe is attested in the early middle ages: see, for example, CGH, pp. 452 (Cathrae), 537 (Cathráe, Cathróe); AU, pp. 242/3 (786.7: Cathrue, king of Mugdorna). For the second element, see Vendryes et al., *Lexique*, fasc. RS, pp. 38–9 s.v. 'róe'. The name as a whole means 'battlefield'. The forms used at Metz (the centre of the cult of St Cathróe) seem to have been *Cadroe, Kadroe* (see below, n. 4; cf. n. 63). It has been suggested that St Cathróe was a Briton – see Anderson, *Early Sources*, i.lxxiii and 432 n. 2 – and the name should therefore be explicable in terms of Brittonic philology. *Cad-, Cadd-, Kadd-* would all be explicable as Old Cumbric *Cat-* (with the same meaning as Irish *cath*), but the spelling would be that of a foreigner hearing the name. But it is unclear how the second element of the name would be explained in a Brittonic context. The Bollandists (n. 5, below) wrote that the name-form was 'in his actis semper *Kaddroë*' (p. 475 n. c). According to the Life, his brother, born after him, was called *Mattadan* (§IX). This is a well attested Gaelic name, Old and Middle Irish *Matudán*: see, for example, CGH, p. 698 (cf. p. 482); AU, pp. 310–11 (851.5: *Matodhan*), 314–15 (857.3: *Matudhan*), 382–3 (933.3), 395–6 (949.1), 408–9 (970.3). Anderson, *Early Sources*, i.434 n. 1, offered a Gaelic etymology. This therefore reduces further the possibility that *Cad(d)roe* is a Brittonic name. It could conceivably be hybrid: cf. n. 34, below, for comparanda. 2 See below, pp. 176–7.

Hersendis, who owned property not far away, asked Cathróe's group to settle at her church of Saint-Michel en Thiérache. The group decided to elect Cathróe as their *dominum et patrem*, but on his refusal one Machalanus/Malchalanus[3] was chosen instead. After some time Hersendis despatched Machalanus to Gorze and Cathróe to Fleury for monastic training, and on their return she added another site, at Waulsort, where Cathróe was made first prior and then, at the petition of Abbot Machalanus and on the authority of King Otto I, abbot. Monastic life flourished at these two locations, attracting local adherents, and Cathróe's renown grew. As a result, Adalbero I, bishop of Metz 929–62, appointed Cathróe to revive a monastery dedicated to St Felix (later called Saint-Clément) at Metz.[4] In that office he remained until his death in his seventieth year, in the thirtieth year of his pilgrimage, therefore in the period 971 × 976. It is consequently evident that he was born in 901 × 906 and undertook his pilgrimage in his fortieth year.

This whole narrative I have drawn from the Life of St Cathróe (BHL 1494)[5] allegedly written at Metz in the early 980s (and therefore within at most a dozen years of Cathróe's death);[6] the dedicatee was Immo, abbot of Gorze (an abbey praised in this Life) from 982 until about 1016, and it seems likely that the author was a monk of Gorze.[7] This Life seems to have survived by a slender

---

3 The forms of this name in the Life of St Cathróe (as printed by Colgan, *Acta sanctorum*) are *Machalanum* (§§XX, XXI), *Machalanus* (§§XXI, XXII), and *Malchalanus* (§XXII). Although in a note Colgan (*Acta sanctorum*, p. 504 n. 67) gave another slightly variant form (*Malchallanum*), he offered no further information, merely cross-referring to a life of St Machallanus/Machallinus at 21 January: there (pp. 152–3) we find a biography constructed by Colgan himself from various sources ('De B. Malcallanno abbate. Ex diuersis'). Quoting the Life of St Cathróe, he gave forms in the order *Malcallanum* (§XX), *Malcalanum* (§XXI), *Malchalanus* (§XXI), *Malcallanus* (§XXII²). Clearly this does not inspire confidence in his handling of names. The Bollandists (n. 5, below), in their edition of the Life, consistently printed *Machalanus, -um*. Colgan wrote (*Acta sanctorum*, p. 153 n. 2), 'Quidam scribunt Maccallinum, quidam Malcallinum, alij et rectiùs Malcallanum, nisi et rectiùs Malcallannum'. The necrology of Gorze has useful information, calling him *Marcolanus*: Parisse, *Nécrologe de Gorze*, pp. 17, 19, 44, 65, 103. Furthermore, Colgan confused this abbot with another (see below, n. 86), thus rendering the name-form yet more uncertain. Attested names are *Mac Cuilind* (CGH, p. 482, s.v. 'Meic-Cuilind', and 681) and *Máel Calland* (ibid., p. 686; AU, p. 374 [921.9: Mael Callann]).   4 De Gaiffier, 'SS. Clément de Metz et Caddroë'.   5 Twice edited: by John Colgan in 1645, *Acta sanctorum*, pp. 494–507; by G. Henschenius in 1668, AASS, Martii I.474–81 (introduction on pp. 469–74), from which derives the text printed in 1685 'Ex Martio Bollandiano' by Mabillon, *Acta sanctorum*, v.489–501. Cf. BHL, i.223–4, nr 1494. Both editions are stated to depend on a manuscript of the monastery of Saint-Hubert (see below, n. 8). In 1967 de Gaiffier ('SS. Clément de Metz et Caddroë', p. 32 n. 1) stated that this manuscript was lost. 6 Despy, *Chartes*, i.7, 32–6; de Gaiffier, 'SS. Clément de Metz et Caddroë', p. 32 and n. 1. Cf. Misonne, 'Charte de Raoul de Laon', p. 305; Dierkens, *Abbayes et chapitres*, pp. 161, 167–8, for the date 982 × 983.   7 Despy, *Chartes*, i.7, 32–6; Dierkens, *Abbayes et chapitres*, p. 167. Immo died on 21 August: Parisse, *Nécrologe de Gorze*, pp. 32, 37, 84, 102. For the status of the author in relation to Abbot Immo, see §I, *Cum me tibi, Pater, obedire sponderem*,

thread, namely a manuscript of the abbey of Saint-Hubert in the Belgian Ardennes, now lost like most of that church's books, but printed in the seventeenth century, principally in John Colgan's *Acta sanctorum Hiberniae* (1645) and in the Bollandists' *Acta sanctorum* for 6 March (1668). No extant mediaeval manuscript is known to scholarship.[8]

Although St Cathróe is best known to Insular scholarship in connexion with the abbey of Waulsort,[9] it is worth stressing that he was abbot there but briefly and not its first, that his Continental career was spent mostly at Metz, and that his Life has no particular connexion with Waulsort. In the first half of the twelfth century it was not known at Waulsort and was only acquired or reacquired during the writing of a house-history after 1150.[10]

The Life is a remarkable specimen of its genre. It begins with a prologue opened by a salutation addressed to Immo who has apparently commanded the author's services.[11] The author claims to write from hearsay rather than personal knowledge of the saint,[12] but in defending himself against possible charges of geographical ignorance invites the critic to read unspecified *historias*.[13] The first few chapters, after a long paragraph of pious reflections, are designed (albeit without any statement to that effect) to place Cathróe's family and place of origin in the broadest possible context.[14] It was in Greek Asia Minor that the process began which ultimately brought settlers to Ireland.[15] Their landing was near Cruachan Feli, *montem Hiberniae*.[16] There they found the *gentem Pictaneorum*

'When I promised my obedience to you, Father'.   8 Despy, *Chartes*, i.33; de Gaiffier, 'SS. Clément de Metz et Caddroë', p. 32 n. 1. In AASS (as n. 5), there is reference to a Reims manuscript (p. 475, n. a, in connexion with the name Fochertach, §4, p. 474).   9 Kenney, *Sources*, pp. 608–10 (nrs 425–9). For the history of Waulsort, see in particular Despy, *Chartes*, i.1–75; Misonne, *Eilbert de Florennes*, pp. 1–44; Dierkens, *Abbayes et chapitres*, pp. 149–96. 10 Despy, *Chartes*, i.32–6, especially 35–6; p. 56 n. 1; p. 58 n. 1; p. 61.   11 My quotations from the Life of St Cathróe are all taken from Colgan, *Acta sanctorum*, pp. 494–507. §I: 'Venerabili in Christo patri Immonio + Ousmanno + omne bonum in summo bono. Cum me tibi, Pater, obedire sponderem tale quid imposuisti quod nisi ad ultima quaeque promisissem digne recusarem.'   12 'Iussisti enim ut aliquid de actibus felicis uiri Kaddroe describerem, quasi aut disciplinarum quippiam consecutus sim aut ita uiro illi familiaris fuerim; cum neque ingenium suppetat, neque gestorum eius aliquid sciam praeter audita.'   13 'Si autem [schedula] incurrerit manus aliquorum, stilum excusabit materia, quae licet inter aemulos sicuti forte fuerint omni carebit inuidia cum et ipse bono animo acceperim, si quis eam in melius commutatam augmentauerit. Caeterum in situ insularum et nomine regionum minus nos reprehendat ne inertiam alterius monstrando suam insipientiam ostendat. Legat potius historias ut nos uera dixisse cognoscat.'   14 §§II–V (pious reflections in § II.1). The whole section was omitted by the Bollandists, with the comment (p. 474 n. b), 'Nempe descripturus Scotorum origines fabulosas hæc sibi præfanda credidit: nos eam laciniam hinc rescidimus, quam apud Colganum legat, qui volet'.   15 §II.2 begins: 'Pactolus igitur Asiae fluuius Choriam Lydiamque regiones diuidit, super quem Choriscon urbem manus antiqua fundauit, cuius incolae, lingua et cultu nationeque Graeci, multimodi laboris negotiis seruiebant'.   16 §III. Having left the Mediterranean, 'Hinc illius affrico uento exergente post immensa pericula in Tyle ultimam detorquentur'. 'Tunc quo uenissent quia nesciebant

whom they fought through province after province – from Clonmacnoise to Armagh, from Kildare to Cork, *Muminensium urbem*, and at length to Ulster's Bangor.[17] Some while later they invaded Britain, taking first Iona, then the *urbes* of *Rigmonath* and *Bellathor*.[18] At length, after their Spartan commander Nel or Niul's Egyptian wife, Scota, they called their new territory Scotia.[19] Eventually, through St Patrick, they received christianity.[20] This rather remarkable and very

aliquantisper recreati aliquando refectis nauibus ut gentiles se fortunae uela uentis classem Neptuno committunt et Deo iubente tandem prospero cursu iuxta Cruachan Feli montem Hiberniae applicuerunt.' This is of course Cruachan Éli (Croagh Patrick, Co. Mayo), famous in Patrician hagiography: it is found in Tírechán's *Collectanea*, written in the late seventh century (§§15, 38, as *Cróchan Aigle* and *montem Egli*) and in Lives derivative of it (*Vita tertia*, *Vita quarta*, and Probus's *Vita S. Patricii*); see Bieler, *Patrician Texts* and *Four Latin Lives of St Patrick*. A form approximating to that in the Life of St Cathróe first appears in *Historia Brittonum*, Harl. §§47–9, written in Wales in AD 829/30: Dumville et al., *Saint Patrick*, pp. 224–5 (*Cruachan Eile*). **17** §IV: 'Cloin urbs est antiqua Hiberniae super Synam fluuium: huius habitatores aduenientium naues succendere uolentes, mox armis deuicti priuati sunt. Post uero Chorischii, uidentes terram lactis et melle fertilem, frequenti congressione insulanos illos debellantes, Artmacham metropolim totamque terram inter lacus Erne et Ethioch inuaserunt; longe lateque diffusi, Celdar ciuitatem Corach quoque Muminensium urbem ceperunt. Iamque confortati Benchor Ullidiae, urbem obsessam, intrauerunt.' The place-names are sometimes corrupt but are always recognisable. *Muminenses* for the people of Munster is standard Hiberno-Latin. **18** §V: 'Fluxerunt quot anni, et mare sibi proximum transfretantes Eueam insulam – quae nunc Ioua dicitur – repleuerunt. Nec satis, post pelagus Britanniae contiguum perlegentes, per Rosim amnem Rossiam regionem manserunt. Rigmonath quoque Bellethor urbes a se procul positas petentes, possessuri uicerunt.' For discussion, see Skene, *Celtic Scotland*, i.319–20. The naming of what are otherwise known as *Cennrígmonaid* and *Cinnbelathoir*, the latter attested in reference to AD 862 as a Pictish palace in the 'Chronicle of the Kings of Alba' from which it is alone otherwise known, bespeaks significant Scottish knowledge: see Anderson, *Kings and Kingship*, pp. 249–53 (Chronicle), and 'St Andrews before Alexander I'. For a recent edition and translation see Hudson, 'Scottish Chronicle', especially p. 153 n. 13. Cf. Dumville, 'Chronicle of the Kings of Alba'. The author's subsequent (§VI) explanation of St Cathróe's name as *bellator in castris Domini* (for the wording, but hardly the context, cf. Dt 2.14) seems to me to be unlikely to be unconnected with the place-name *Cinnbelathoir*. Was that where Cathróe's parents lived? **19** §V: 'Sicque totam terram suo nomine Chorischiam nominatam post cuiusdam Lacedemonii Aeneae filium nomine Nelum seu Niulum, qui princeps eorum fuerat et olim Aegypti<c>am coniugem bello meruerat nomine Scottam, ex uocabulo coniugis patrio sermone deprauato Scotiam uocauerunt.' Nél or Niul is known as a figure in the Gaelic national origin-legend: see, for example, CGH, p. 712; for comment, see Van Hamel, 'On Lebor Gabála', pp. 143–4 (a reference for which I am indebted to John Carey). The Egyptian lady Scotta had only relatively recently made her appearance in the origin-legend, where she was the wife of that Pharaoh with whom Moses contended: see Contreni, *Carolingian Learning*, chapter XVII (and additional notes, p. 7). **20** §V: 'Atque post annorum curricula per beatum Patricium armis induti fidei Christo domino colla submiserunt. Quorum multi fuere qui legitime in stadio fidei decertantes aeternae remunerationis palmam adepti in sacrario diuinitatis laureati Christo assistunt. Sed quia beati eorum actus proprias repleuerunt paginas, ne alieno labori oneri simus quae nota sunt supersedenda iudicauimus.' As far as I know, no Patrician hagiography of the middle ages went so far as to attribute the conversion of Scotland as well as Ireland to St Patrick: on the historical dimension, see Dumville et al., *Saint Patrick*, pp. 183–9.

ecclesiastically oriented rewriting of the Gaelic national origin-legend[21] then suddenly gives way to the usual stuff of hagiography.

St Cathróe was born into a royal family as a result of the prayers directed by barren parents to St Columba.[22] His father, having promised him to the Church, reneged, only to be bought off by a holy man, Beán or Beoán,[23] whose prayers provided the parents with another son, Matudán,[24] to take Cathróe's place in secular life.[25] Eventually, Cathróe was sent to study at Armagh, *Hiberniae metropolim* (the second time it is called *metropolis* in this work),[26] whence at length he returned by sea to *Scotia*.[27] Only at this point does it become apparent that *Scotia* is in Britain, and is neither Ireland nor the Gaelic world at large, and that Cathróe's family lived in Scotland where his early life was spent.[28] He now became the father of the *Scoti*: for, we are told, they have (note the tense) many thousands of teachers but not many *patres*.[29]

The next stage in Cathróe's development followed a vision given to his tutor Beoán: Cathróe must go through three stages, voluntary loss of possessions, departure from his native land, and practice of the monastic life.[30] Then God commanded Cathróe as he had Abraham, *Exi de terra tua*, etc.[31]

There now follows a remarkable narrative of Cathróe's journey through Britain, a veritable court-crawl from north to south.[32] First he was with Constantine, king of *Scotia*.[33] Then he was conducted to the land of the *Cumbri*

---

21 On that subject see Carey, *Gaelic National Origin-legend*.   22 §§VI–VII. The parents are named as Faiteach or Fothereach/Fochereach (supposedly for Fochertach: see above, n. 4) and Bania. St Columba is here referred to as *beatus Columbanus* (§§VI, IX): for discussion see Boyle, 'St Cadroe in Scotland', p. 4. With this story, one may compare that of the barrenness of Hersendis, Cathróe's Continental patroness, in §XX.   23 Both forms appear in the text: *Beanus* (§§VIII, X[2], XII, XIII); *Beoanus* (§X). In the Bollandists' text he is consistently Beanus (§§6–12). As Pádraig Ó Riain has pointed out to me, an Irish bishop called *Beoanus* appears in both *Vita I* (§3, where he appears with one Meldanus) and *Virtutes* (§19, where Patrick himself also occurs) of St Fursa (who himself occurs later in the Life of St Cathróe in an important role: §XVIIII): Krusch, *Passiones*, pp. 435–6, 447; cf. Ó Riain, 'Vies de saint Fursy', pp. 406–9. For discussion of a Scottish Beán, see Anderson, *Early Sources*, i.433 n. 1, and Boyle, 'St Cadroe in Scotland', pp. 4–5.   24 On this name see above, n. 1.   25 §§VII–X.   26 §XI; cf. §IV (n. 17, above). However, for *metropolim* in §XI the Bollandists' text has *mittit qui* (§10); theirs is not a witness to §IV (cf. n. 14, above). In any technical sense, this term addresses ecclesiastical issues. By the tenth century Armagh had a long-standing claim (by virtue of being held to be the principal foundation of the apostle of Ireland) to be the metropolitan seat of the whole Irish Church: see Sharpe, 'St Patrick and the See of Armagh', and 'Armagh and Rome'. However, the term came to be used of Dublin: see Gwynn, *Irish Church*, pp. 69, 75–7.   27 §XII: 'aequore remenso ad Beanum rediit'. Cf. also 'nullus sapientium mare transierat, sed adhuc Hiberniam incolebant'.   28 It can be seen, once this point has been absorbed, that the author always made a clear distinction between *Hibernia* and *Scotia*.   29 §XII: 'Licet enim Scoti multa millia paedagogorum habeant, sed non multos patres'.   30 §XIII: 'primus itaque rerum est spontanea amissio, secundus patriae relictio, tertius monasticae uitae exercitatio'.   31 §XIV: Gn 12.1; cf. Act 7.3. §§XIV–XV deal with Scottish reaction to Cathróe's decision to go into religious exile abroad.   32 §§XVI–XVIII.   33 Constantine began to rule in 900; the date of the end of his reign is uncertain (but not

(Strathclyde) where he met King Douenaldus, his *propinquus*.[34] From there he was accompanied to Leeds,[35] a border-town of the Cumbri and the *Normanni*, Northmen,[36] whence he was taken by an aristocrat called Gunderic to York,[37] to the court of King Eric (Bloodaxe) whose wife was a *propinqua* of Cathróe.[38] Thence he continued to *Lugdinam ciuitatem* (taken by Colgan to be London)[39] where he was received by one Heyfrid.[40] A miracle worked there brought him to the attention of King Edmund at Winchester to whom he was summoned.[41] Eventually, accompanied by Archbishop Otto (Oda of Canterbury, 941–58, that is, not of Winchester as in the text),[42] he travelled to Lympne (Kent) where he took ship for the Continent.[43]

---

before 940), for he appears to have abdicated to enter religion. For legends about him see Dumville, 'Cusantín mac Ferccusa', for the bibliography. Since Cathróe was *regii sanguinis* through his father (§VI), Constantine was presumably a relative. It is in Constantine's reign that we first find the abandonment of Pictish nomenclature and the use of the name *Alba* for his kingdom: see Dumville, *Churches of North Britain*, pp. 34–6.   **34** §§XVI–XVII. *Cumbri* was the usual term for the Strathclyders: cf. Modern Welsh *Cymry*, Old English *Cumbras*. Old Welsh *Dumn(a)gual* and Old/Middle Irish *Domnall* were used to represent the same name in a bilingual context: for examples of Gaelic-Brittonic interchange, see Dumville, 'Celtic Latin Texts', especially pp. 22–4, and 'Eastern Terminus'. That *Douenaldus* was a relative of Cathróe has given rise to much speculation. There are various ways to explain it, depending on whether *Douenaldus* was a Briton, a Gael, a Pict, or of mixed blood, and on the types of marriage-custom followed. *Douenaldus* is a 'Continentalised' and latinised form: cf. further Dumville, 'Chronicle of the Kings of Alba', pp. 82–3.   **35** *Loidam ciuitatem* (§XVII). The suggested counter- identification of this place as Carlisle – by Smyth, *Scandinavian York*, ii.181 and 189 n. 107; cf. p. 295 n. 30 – is unacceptable in terms of palaeography, philology, and political geography. It has been repeated with approval by Woolf, 'Erik Bloodaxe', p. 193 n. 18.   **36** One might have expected *Nordmanni* (or *Nortmanni*) as the commoner and earlier form for 'Northmen'.   **37** *in Euroacum urbem* (§XVII). The usual form was *Eboracum*.   **38** On Eric (here *regem Erichium*; Old Norse Eiríkr, Old English Yric/Yryc/Hyryc), see Smyth, *Scandinavian York*, ii.155–70, 172–5, 178–83, 185–9, *et passim*; Sawyer, 'Last Scandinavian Kings' (who has argued that Eiríkr reigned at York 950–2); Woolf, 'Erik Bloodaxe' (who has argued that Eiríkr reigned at York in 936 x 940 also – but the evidence is the Life of St Cathróe). Eiríkr had a Scottish wife: 'Rex habebat coniugem, ipsius domni Cathroe propinquam' (§XVII); this presumably resulted from King Constantine's policy of anti-English alliance with Scandinavian rulers. See also discussion by Anderson, *Early Sources*, i.441 n. 6; cf. pp. 455–9, 462.   **39** Colgan, *Acta sanctorum*, p. 504 n. 60: 'Hodiè Lundinum, priscis Lugdina, Lundonia, Lundoniæ, &c.'. For Celtic *Lug*-place-names (and for London, which is not one such), see Rivet and Smith, *Place-names of Roman Britain*, pp. 396–8, 401–2 (for the unidentified *Lugudunum*, in what is now northern England, see also pp. 208–9). The form in the Bollandists' text is *Lungdinam* (§16), a step nearer to London but perhaps under the influence of Colgan's identification.   **40** 'a quodam sene Heyfrido nomine susceptus' (§XVII). The Bollandists' text has *Hegfrido* (§16). The name is presumably Old English *He(a)hfrith*. No Heahfrith is known who convincingly meets the chronological requirements, unless the beneficiary can be rescued from a forged Winchester diploma dated 939: Sawyer, *Anglo-Saxon Charters*, p. 157, nr 351.   **41** §§XVII–XVIII. Winchester: *in Uindecastræ ciuitate* (§XVIII). Edmund: *Hegmundum nomine* (§XVIII). Edmund I ruled 939–46.   **42** *archiepiscopum eiusdem urbis Otthonem nomine* (§XVIII). Here Old English Oda has been replaced by German/Latin *Otto*. In the reverse

There follow the Continental adventures which I summarised at the outset. But one intervening episode deserves mention. On the first attempt at the Channel, the ship was forced back to shore by a storm. Cathróe received a vision that this whole party could not make the journey: his nephew and some others were to be sent back to Scotland, leaving the lucky (or, rather, holy) number of thirteen persons who then sailed to Boulogne.[44] There is a parallel in Adomnán's Life of St Columba,[45] but I am reminded particularly of comparable episodes in the *immrama* and other Gaelic stories of holy navigation.[46]

Numerous questions arise even from this selective retelling of the Life. Here I can address only a few most relevant to my theme. But let me begin by observing that the Continental history of Cathróe and his companions, their monasteries of Thiérache, Waulsort, and Metz, and the Life itself have in the last century and more become surrounded by a mountain of scholarship because of the relationship of their careers to monastic reform and its patronage in tenth-century Lotharingia.[47] In all that, two elements of the Life have remained largely unexamined. The Insular content has attracted remarkably little attention, in spite of its many rich possibilities. And no one has sought to examine the author's intentions and to assess the sources used: students of tenth-century Lotharingia have accepted it unquestioningly,[48] seeking merely to refine the late tenth-century dating, establish the place of composition, and identify the dedicatee.

Cathróe's journey through Britain can be placed in the period 941 x 946, limited by the accession of Archbishop Oda in the former year and the death of

situation, members of the tenth-century German royal family who were called Otto, the 'Anglo-Saxon Chronicle', s.a. 982 C, has Old English *Odda* (apparently a different name from Oda), continuing a tradition begun earlier in that century: Keynes, 'King Athelstan's Books', pp. 147–9 and Plate II. In that text, s.a. 887 and elsewhere, we find Old English *Oda* used for West Franks/Frenchmen/Normans called Odo, and after the Norman conquest of England Odo written for Oda (s.a. 961 A, addition). In a south German confraternity-book (Pfäfers, AD 941 x 946) we find *Odo* used for Oda of Canterbury: Keynes, 'King Athelstan's Books', p. 201 and plate XVI.   43 *portum … qui Limen dicitur* (Bollandists); cf. *Hymen* (Colgan, §XVIII). The identification as Lympne was made by Anderson, *Early Sources*, i.442 n. 6. For such a crossing in the opposite direction by vikings see the 'Anglo-Saxon Chronicle', s.a. 892; cf. Smyth, *Scandinavian York*, i.31. For the Romano-Celtic background, see Rivet and Smith, *Place-names of Roman Britain*, pp. 386–7.   44 §XVIIII. Boulogne is *portum Boloniensem*. The number thirteen emerges in the course of §XX.   45 VC I.6. 46 Dumville, '*Echtrae* and *Immram*', pp. 75–6, 78.   47 Sackur, *Die Cluniacenser*, especially I.181–6; van der Essen, *Etude critique*, especially pp. 111–42; Fuhrmann, *Irish Medieval Monasteries*, p. 80 (with hesitation); Kenney, *Sources*, pp. 605–6, 608–13; Hallinger, *Gorze-Kluny*; Parisse, *Lorraine monastique*, chapters I–II; Dierkens, *Abbayes et chapitres*, especially pp. 332–49; Heuclin, *Origines monastiques*, pp. 67–88, 115–92; Kottje and Maurer, *Monastische Reformen*; Iogna-Prat and Picard, *Religion et culture*; Parisse and Oexle, *Abbaye de Gorze*; Flachenecker, *Schottenklöster*, pp. 47–50.   48 This remains true even of the most impressive recent pieces of research, for example, Dierkens, *Abbayes et chapitres*.

Edmund I, king of England, in the latter.[49] The narrative is not without its question-marks, but it could hardly have been constructed long after the event or by one with no knowledge of mid-tenth-century British politics. The names of persons (and to some extent places) outside *Scotia* are not in forms native to the region in question, being either Continentalised (for want of a better expression) or later in character.[50]

We are left in no doubt, however, of Cathróe's high-born Scottish origin or of the Scottish provenance of the rest of his party. One of his monks whom he cured on the Continent was *Lasarus Scottigena*.[51] And this Scottishness gives a futher twist to the charters which Waulsort attracted early in its history. We read in a spurious charter that Cathróe's successor-but-one there, Forannán (Forondanus),[52] abbot by June 946 (and dead by 981), lived there as abbot of a community comprising *non pauca Scottigena atque Francigena*.[53] In September 946 King Otto I provided that the foundation, to be known henceforth as *monasterium peregrinorum*, should be ruled only by members of the original foundation, as long as they lived: 'semper in ditione Scottorum permaneat,

---

49 Dumville, *Wessex and England*, pp. 173–84; on p. 180 n. 51, I observed that the journey 'should be placed in 941 x 943, if we allow that Eric has supplanted in the narrative one of his less famous predecessors'.   50 *Douenaldus, Gunderico, Erichium, Euroacum, Lugdinam, Heyfrido* (§XVII); *Uindecastræ, Hegmundum, Otthonem* (§XVIII). Cf. Dumville, 'Chronicle of the Kings of Alba', pp. 83–4.   51 §XXIX. This is presumably derived from Old and Middle Irish *Laisre*, perhaps with the Biblical Lazarus in mind. Irish *Las(s)a(i)r* is a female name.   52 For the name (Old Irish *Forindán*, Middle Irish *Forannán*), see Ó Máille, *Language of the Annals of Ulster*, pp. 17, 23, 105–10, 193; it seems not to be attested in Irish chronicles in annals later than the mid-ninth century, except for an instance at AU 951 recording the death of one Gúaire úa Forannáin (Gúaire's grandfather presumably died in the second half of the ninth century). However, there are a good many examples of *Forannán* attested in the twelfth-century genealogical collections in CGH, pp. 654–5 (as also of the presumptively radical form *Forand*, ibid., p. 654). I am not aware of any other examples of the form *Forondán* which is attested (latinised) in the charter of 946 (see next note), but it is a theoretically possible form, with -*o*- as a spelling for the weakened vowel usually represented by -*a*- in the medial syllable. *Fairennán* (with palatal -*r*-) is also found: CGH, p. 135.   53 This is a charter of Robert, count of Namur, ostensibly issued at Namur on 2 June 946 (it survives as an apparent original without seal), by which a property was given to the abbey *sub regula beati Benedicti* at Waulsort under Abbot Forondanus. For the text see Rousseau, *Actes des comtes de Namur*, pp. 3–8 (nr 1), and Despy, *Chartes*, i.324–5 (nr 2), and cf. ibid., i.84, 173–5, 291–3; both editors considered it genuine. However, very varying opinions have been expressed about its authenticity; if it is, as probably, a forgery, the intention was presumably to show that the community had been Benedictine and the abbot Forannán from the first: 'cuique preesse uenerabilis abbas Forondanus dinoscitur ac prodesse, olim a sua pro Deo exulans patria, cum non pauca Scottigena atque Francigena, quam ipse in Christi famulatu educauit monachorum sub regula almi patris Benedicti degencium turmula'. For specific discussions of this document, see Ballon, 'Acte de donation' (with facsimile); Misonne, 'Éloge de Forannan' (including an edition of the text).

et quamdiu aliquis illorum uixerit nullus alius fiat abbas nisi unus ex ipsis'.[54] No *Scottigena* is however known to have ruled after 980.[55]

Normally in the context of Insular *peregrini* on the Continent, one would treat any manifestation of the word *Scottus* or its relatives as relating to Ireland, or otherwise to the Gaelic world at large. It is a commonplace of our studies that the Latin words *Scotia* and *Scotti* began to be employed in the tenth century in relation to Scotland rather than Ireland,[56] but examples have been much harder to find than those of the Old English words *Scotland* and *Scottas* in such usage.[57] Here we have a text whose author seems positively to have insisted upon this particular specificity. Was he or his source of information precocious in this regard? The Life of a bogus Irishman, St Plechelm of Mont-Saint-Odile (in northern Belgium),[58] also displays the distinction between *Scotia* and *Hibernia*: it too has been dated to the end of the tenth century.[59]

We should perhaps think further about the origin-legend which prefaces the hagiographical narrative. The Greeks who invaded Ireland found *Pictanei* there, whom they conquered.[60] Indeed, the story seems something of a mixture of the Pictish and Gaelic origin-legends.[61] Its focus is in any case remarkably on Scotland and Scottish concerns.

Cathróe's Scottish party enjoyed a significant role in tenth-century Lotharingian Church-history. To its members can be attributed a series of refoundations which penetrated to the heart of the region's ecclesiastical structures.[62] At Metz Cathróe's successor Fíngen was given the task of

---

54 Otto's diploma is dated at Reims on 19 September (no single sheet survives); it refers to 'quosdam Dei seruos peregrinationis gratia a Scotia uenientes et sub regula sancti Benedicti uiuere cupientes' and recites the lands held by Waulsort Abbey at this date: for the text see Sickel, *Diplomata*, i.160–1 (nr 81); Despy, *Chartes*, i.325–7 (nr 3), and cf. ibid., pp. 160–1; Ballon, 'Acte de donation', pp. 46–7. Again (cf. n. 53, above), various views have been expressed about this diploma's authenticity. 55 A Continental abbot was in office by 981: Despy, *Chartes*, i.7–8, 9–10. 56 Skene, *Celtic Scotland*, i.1–7, 115, 259 (n. 52), and ii.441 n. 39; Plummer, *Venerabilis Baedae opera historica*, ii.11–12, 126, 172, 186; Esposito, 'Conchubrani Vita Sanctae Monennae', p. 203, and 'Sources of Conchubranus' Life of St. Monenna'; idem, 'Notes on a Latin Life of Saint Patrick', pp. 66–8. For a rather different approach, see Carney, *Studies*, pp. 402–7, and *Problem of St. Patrick*, pp. 49–52. Sharpe, *Medieval Irish Saints' Lives*, p. 41, has approached the question from the other end in writing of '*Scotia*, a word which meant Ireland until the twelfth century', but the formulation is misleading: *Scotia* was used in reference to northern Britain in our late tenth-century text and in various eleventh-century texts. 57 On Old English usage, see Dumville, 'Britain and Ireland', pp. 181–3. 58 BHL 6867. 59 Snieders, 'Influence de l'hagiographie irlandaise', pp. 849–50. 60 If we were to allow ourselves to equate Latin *Pictanei* with Irish *Cruithni*, we could find Irish pseudohistorical texts which saw them as the predecessors of the Gaels. Cf. MacNeill, *Phases of Irish History*, pp. 58–60, 62–5, 66, 74, and *Celtic Ireland*, pp. 58–9, 93; O'Rahilly, *Early Irish History and Mythology*, pp. 15–16, 34–6, 84, 98, 101, 163, 341–52, 444–52; Byrne, *Irish Kings and High-kings*, pp. 8–9, 39, 108, 200, 236–7. Furthermore, for the Gaels as Greeks, see Carey, 'Ancestry of Fénius Farsaid'. 61 On the Pictish origin-legend see in particular Miller, 'Matriliny by Treaty', and Mac Eoin, 'Origin of the Picts'. 62 On the first, Saint-Michel, see Misonne, 'Charte de Raoul de Laon': the

reforming a second abbey, that of St Symphorian, and again the Gaelic (and now presumptively Scottish) character was institutionalised.[63] It seems that the tenth-century monastic history of Lotharingia gives another twist to the well

document in question is known only from a thirteenth-century cartulary; there are various opinions about its authenticity but the reference to *quidam homines hibernicae regionis* seems, in the present context, rather damaging. In general, see Semmler, 'Iren in der lothringischen Klosterreform', and Bulst, 'Irisches Mönchtum'. 63 For Fíngen as Cathróe's successor see Sickel, *Diplomata*, ii.791–2 (nr 362), an originally undated apparent original – with date, 991, added much later, on which see Kehr, *Urkunden Otto III.*, p. 253(–4) n.1 –: 'nos ob petitionem domni Fingenii uenerabilis abbas suo monasterio ad honorem beatissimi confessoris Felicis constructo iuxta Metensem urbem sito nostra imperiali auctoritate confirmamus ... qualem noster bone memorie pater Otto inuictissimus cesar tempore sancte memorie Cadroelis abbatis iam dicto monasterio concedere dignatus fuit'. The diploma of Otto II does not seem to survive. Another diploma of Otto III, dated 25 January 992 at Frankfurt but not surviving in any mediaeval manuscript (Sickel, *Diplomata*, ii.493, nr 84), reports the petition of Bishop Adalbero II (984–1005) and the Empress Adalheid that the Emperor confirm the possessions of the abbey of St Symphorian, which the bishop had restored. According to the diploma, the Emperor did so 'ut abbas primus nomine Fingenius hyberniensis natione, quem ipse praelibatus episcopus nunc temporis ibi constituit, suique successores hybernienses monachos habeant, quamdiu sic esse poterit et, si defuerint ibi monachi de Hybernia, de quibuscumque nationibus semper ibi monachi habeantur'. This diploma must lie under a heavy burden of suspicion, but that Bishop Adalbero II did refound Saint-Symphorien and give it to Abbot Fíngen is made quite clear by the metrical *Vita S. Clementis* (BHL 1860f; cf. de Gaiffier, 'SS. Clément de Metz et Caddroë'), written at Metz *c.* AD 1000 by a member of the community of Saint-Félix (later Saint-Clément). For the text, see Strecker, *Ottonenzeit*, pp. 109–45. The lines in question are 1057–68 (ibid., pp. 144–5): 'Iste (*sc.* Alter Adalbero [line 1043]) uirum sobrium Fingenum namque uocauit, / Qui fuit excellens meritis animique uirilis, / Presbiter eximius Scottorum semine cretus, / [1060] Kadroe consimilis actis ac moribus equus, / Prudens ac iustus nec<non> et corpore castus / Hicque locum sancti construxit Symphoriani / Atque gregem Christi lucratus pastor et abbas / Adsciuit socios monachos tunc ac peregrinos. / [1065] Presul Adalbero Fing(n)eno contulit ipse / Namque locum dictum firmatum duplice carta: / Primam nam cartam firmauit papa Iohannes, / Rex magnus Otto dictauit et ipse secundam.' The papal bull is lost; and the royal diploma is no doubt not nr 84 (as Strecker, ibid., p. 145). The author appears to name himself as Carus (lines 960, 992: ibid., pp. 141–2 and notes). Strecker (ibid., p. 110) took him to be a Gael: 'Der Verfasser hat seiner hexametrischen Darstellung an einigen Stellen rhythmische Stücke ... eingefügt, die in der Handhabung der Versschlüsse usw. einem Charakter tragen, wie er um 1000 eigentlich nur einem Iren zuzutrauen ist'. Kenney, *Sources*, p. 613 (nr 437), thought that 'It was probably written by an Irishman at Metz in the eleventh century'. It does not appear to have been listed by Lapidge and Sharpe, *Bibliography*. In view of the evidence collected here, it is likely that the author, if Insular, was Scottish rather than Irish. Furthermore, Fíngen seems to have become abbot of Saint-Vannes, Verdun, on the evidence of the necrology of that house: 'VIII. Id. Oct. Anno Domini .m°. quarto obiit dominus Fingenius abbas huius loci' (Sackur, 'Handschriftliches aus Frankreich', p. 131). It is not clear whether he held his abbacies in plurality. Fíngen died on 8 October, 1004 (Parisse, *Nécrologe de Gorze*, p. 19); he was succeeded by one Siriaudus (whom Parisse, ibid., pp. 13 and 19, thought Irish, presumably mistakenly taking his name to be so; cf. Semmler, 'Iren in der lothringischen Klosterreform', p. 952 n. 102), and a Constantinus, a monk of Gorze (Parisse, *Nécrologe de Gorze*, p. 80; cf. pp. 13–14, 19), but the details of the transmission of the abbacies remain unclear. Constantine's name makes one

known and notoriously tangled story of the *Schottenklöster*.[64] At Saint-Michel en Thiérache, at Waulsort, and at Metz the Scots were there first! What we do not know, of course, is whether they were followed there by more Scots or by Irish or by both.

This greater precision in the history of Gaelic-speaking *peregrini* on the Continent in the post-carolingian era coincides with other changes in our perception of ecclesiastical events and persons in the same time and place. Most histories of monastic reform in Lotharingia, and particularly of its Gaelic dimension, have given a significant place to that Bishop Israel who was once vainly offered as author of *Nauigatio Sancti Brendani*.[65] Israel, however, has recently been deprived of his Gaelic origin and retired to Brittany, the origin which contemporary sources attribute to him but which modern scholarship had allowed to be overlaid by later attributions of Gaelic origin.[66] I shall return to this theme.[67]

We can approach the Lotharingian monastic reform and its Scottish dimension afresh by closer consideration of the message offered by the author of *Vita Sancti Cathroe*. It is clear that the monastic houses ruled by Cathróe and his companions lived by the Rule of St Benedict. Looked at through Insular eyes, this has sometimes seemed strange.[68] But the Life makes both the history and the ideology of tenth-century Lotharingian reform fairly clear.

I have already drawn attention to Beoán's vision which prepared for Cathróe's departure from Scotland.[69] Cathróe and his companions would have to leap three mighty leaps to attain salvation: voluntary loss of possessions (already

think of the royal dynasty of Alba in Scotland (cf. n. 33, above) and that he might therefore be one of the Scots of Metz (but the name was used on the Continent); he survived until 1024. In the 1010s he wrote a Life of Bishop Adalbero II: Kenney, *Sources*, p. 611 (nr 432).
64 On Scots, Irish, and *Schottenklöster*, see Gwynn, 'Some Notes'; cf. Binchy, 'Irish Benedictine Congregation in Medieval Germany'. See now Flachenecker, *Schottenklöster*.
65 Selmer, 'Israel'; on the much earlier origin of that text, see Dumville, 'Two Approaches'.
66 Lapidge, 'Israel the Grammarian'; cf. his 'Schools, Learning and Literature', pp. 968–71. The attribution of Gaelic origin remains unexplained: Lapidge declined to consider the possibility that Israel came from Strathclyde, which might have allowed either attribution; or Israel's interest in the work of Iohannes Scottus Eriugena (and the Greek language) may have made him seem like an Irishman. A comparable (but ninth-century) case of a British bishop and monk resident in Francia where he was subsequently remembered as an Irishman is that of Marcus of Soissons: see Dumville, *Historia Brittonum*, iii.26–7. 67 See below, pp. 186–8.
68 For discussion of Benedictine monasticism in Ireland see first Gougaud, *Christianity in Celtic Lands*, pp. 405–6, and then de Varebeke, 'Benedictines in Medieval Ireland'; I have not seen de Moreau, 'L'Irlande et le monachisme'. De Varebeke's statement (p. 93) that 'the text of Benedict's Rule was known through Ireland in the seventh and eighth centuries' is not substantiated: references to Warren, *Antiphonary of Bangor*, ii.xv, xviii, 59, 98, are not material, while Warren's information on ii.81–2, 90, is not necessarily to the point. The best (perhaps only) evidence comes from an Hiberno-Latin exegetical text probably of the later seventh century: Hellmann, 'Pseudo-Cyprianus De duodecim abusivis saeculi', pp. 4–5, 32 (line 10), 34 (lines 3–4). For a Benedict in an undated inscription at Clonmacnoise, see Macalister, *Corpus inscriptionum*, ii.62–3 (nr 781). 69 See above, p. 176.

achieved), departure from their native land (which followed immediately), and finally the practice of monastic life. In a normal Insular hagiographic narrative of *peregrinatio*, the *peregrini* are already monks.[70] From that context one might be lulled into thinking that Beoán's disciples were so too. Our author has a different message, however.

When Cathróe and his party accepted land from the noblewoman Hersendis,[71] they established a communal way of life at Saint-Michel en Thiérache (not later than the beginning of February 945)[72] under the headship of Machalanus. But the hagiographer would allow no loose definition of monasticism. He wrote, 'As the desire for *deuotio* grew, the group began to aspire to *monasticae religioni*'.[73] Therefore their patroness sent Machalanus to the Lotharingian reform-monastery of Gorze under the discipline of Abbot Agenald,[74] but Cathróe went to far-distant Fleury, on the Loire, the Frankish reformed house specifically associated with the Transalpine cult of St Benedict of Nursia.[75] The two Scots were professed as monks at their adoptive houses, the very day of Cathróe's profession at Fleury being recorded.[76] Having at length returned to Hersendis, Machalanus *monasticum ordinem instituit*.[77] The reform-message is very clear. However holy (or apparently monastic) may be a group of *Scotti* turning up in Lotharingia – and pilgrim *Scotti* had a long-established reputation for holiness[78] –, no one would be accepted in reforming circles as having monastic status without being professed in a Benedictine monastery. Gorze trained the new abbot of Saint-Michel and Waulsort, and Cathróe is seen there paying his respects to Abbot John.[79] The importance of Gorze for the author is clearly established thus.

---

70 For discussion of Insular *peregrinatio*, see Plummer, *Venerabilis Baedae opera historica*, ii.126, 170–1; Jones, 'Celtic Britain and the Pilgrim Movement'; Hughes, 'Changing Theory and Practice'; Angenendt, *Monachi Peregrini*, pp. 124–75; Charles-Edwards, 'Social Background'. Cf. Etchingham, 'Idea of Monastic Austerity'. See also Albert, *Pèlerinage à l'époque carolingienne*, pp. 49–99, and Dumville, *Three Men in a Boat*.   71 Life of St Cathróe, §XX. On Hersendis, see Misonne, 'Charte de Raoul de Laon', and *Eilbert de Florennes*, pp. 8–21, 43–4.   72 For the date, see Misonne, 'Charte de Raoul de Laon', subject to the caveats in n. 62, above.   73 §XXI: 'Interea deuotionis crescente, monasticæ religioni coeperunt aspirare'.   74 §XXI: 'domina illa Machalanum Gorsiam scilicet disciplinatui uenerabilis Agenaldi … direxit'. On Gorze, see Sackur, *Die Cluniacenser*, i.150–6, 161–74; Hallinger, *Gorze-Kluny*; Parisse and Oexle, *Abbaye de Gorze*. For the rule of Abbot Agenald/Einold (933–966 x 968: Parisse, *Nécrologe de Gorze*, pp. 31–2, 37, 84, 94), see Sackur, *Die Cluniacenser*, i.112 n. 1, 141–86, 224, 368–70; Parisse and Oexle, *Abbaye de Gorze*.   75 §XXI: 'domina illa … Cathroe uero Floriacum, ubi Erchembaldus uir magnae religionis præerat, direxit'. On Fleury, reform, and the cult of St Benedict, see most recently Nightingale, 'Oswald, Fleury and Continental Reform'. Cf. John, 'Sources of the English Monastic Reformation'; Leclercq, 'Réforme bénédictine anglaise'. See also Berland, 'Nécropole'.   76 §XXI: 'Ambo ergo quod cupierant assecuti, Machalanus apud patrem Agenaldum monachum professus est, Cothroe uero die conuersionis Pauli apostoli apud Florianum coram domino Erchembaldo habitum et animum monachilem induit'.   77 §XXII.   78 Cf. n. 70, above.   79 §XXXI, towards the end of the Life. Abbot John is given a handsome eulogy: Cathróe went there, hearing of John's grave illness, and by his

Cathróe had however gone to Fleury to train, and we are left to wonder why. There is no doubt about its growing importance as a reform-minded source of Benedictinism in this period:[80] but why did not Cathróe go to Gorze like Machalanus? I offer one speculation. If we were able to eavesdrop on the conversation of Cathróe and Archbishop Oda as they travelled together across southern England from Winchester to Lympne,[81] we might find an answer. Oda had himself visited Fleury and was a professed monk.[82] A decade later he would send there his nephew Oswald, the future archbishop and saint.[83] The currents of Benedictine reform-ideology had begun to run in England by the 940s, indeed already in the previous decade or two.[84] One can imagine that Oda had recommended to Cathróe that, if circumstances permitted, he should travel to Fleury.

A further connexion has been sought for Machalanus. The last annal of the continuation of the Chronicle of Flodoard of Reims is devoted to an account of the death in 978, on the vigil of the feast of St Vincent, of *uir Domini Malcallan(n)us natione hibernicus*, abbot of the church of the Blessed Archangel Michael.[85] No location is stated for this monastery, but it has been supposed by some to be that of Saint-Michel en Thiérache where our Machalanus presided.[86] However, a charter of Rorico, bishop of Laon, dated 1 October 961, tells us that Rorico had summoned from Fleury *uenerabilem ... Melchalannum* with twelve monks to be the reform-community of Saint-Vincent de Laon.[87] There is some confusion, to be sure, but it seems more likely to be within this

---

example persuaded the ascetic abbot to eat some meat for his health's sake. John of Vandières was abbot from 967/8 or 973 until his death on 25 March, 976: Parisse, *Nécrologe de Gorze*, pp. 32, 37. On John, see Leclercq, 'Jean de Gorze'; Barone, 'Jean de Gorze'. See also Parisse and Oexle, *Abbaye de Gorze*. 80 Cf. n. 75, above. See also Bredero, 'Cluny et le monachisme carolingien'. 81 §XVIII. 82 The source is Byrhtferth, *Vita S. Oswaldi* (Raine, *Historians*, i.413): 'Praecepit pater uenerandus [Oda] ut [Osuualdus] ad beatissimi et luculentissimi confessoris atque abbatis Benedicti properaret arcisterium, ex quo idem pontifex suscepit monasticae religionis habitum'. On Oda see Robinson, *St. Oswald*, pp. 38–51; Darlington, 'Ecclesiastical Reform', pp. 386–7; John, *Orbis Britanniae*, pp. 158–9, 161; Brooks, *Early History of the Church of Canterbury*, pp. 222–37; Dumville, *Wessex and England*, pp. 164–5, 175–6, 183–4, 202–3; Bullough, 'St Oswald', especially pp. 4–8. 83 For Oswald's sojourn at Fleury see Byrhtferth, *Vita S. Oswaldi* (Raine, *Historians*, i.413–9); cf. Bullough, 'St Oswald', pp. 5–7. 84 For discussion, see Dumville, *Wessex and England*, chapter VI (cf. chapter V), and idem, *English Caroline Script*, especially chapters II and V. Cf. Leclercq, 'Réforme bénédictine anglaise'; John, 'Sources of the English Monastic Reformation', especially p. 198; Wormald, 'Æthelwold and his Continental Counterparts'. 85 Flodoard, *Chronicon* (Lauer, p. 164 and n. t). 86 See, for example, Lauer's difficulties and confusions, ibid., nn. 4 and 5. The confusion goes back to Colgan (*Acta sanctorum*, pp. 152–3) and beyond. 87 Poupardin, 'Cartulaire de Saint-Vincent', pp. 184–6 (nr III): 'Euocatis igitur a monasterio sancti Benedicti supra Ligerim sito duodecim monachis, uenerabilem eis Melchalannum prefeci abbatem ... '. Máel Callann was still abbot in 966 x 969 (nr V, pp. 188–90: 'monachi et eorum abbas Melcalannus') and in 973 (ibid., pp. 186–8, nr IV: 'Melcalannus uenerabilis abbas monasterii sancti Vincentii').

annal, between dedication and feast. This Máel Callann of Laon is he to whom the late Heinz Löwe attributed in 1961 a *Dialogus de statu sancte ecclesie*[88] – with, alas, no more plausibility or evidence than his earlier attribution of the *Cosmographia Ethici* to Virgil of Salzburg.[89] In sum, rather than suppose that Machalanus of Thiérache disappeared to Fleury and Laon for many years before resuming office (and dying) as abbot of Thiérache in 978, we should do better to suppose the existence of an Irish Máel Callann at Fleury and then Laon in the years from before 961 until 978,[90] and a Scottish Machalanus in Lotharingia from the 940s.

The question has also been put whether or not we should see Cathróe and his friends as culdees.[91] To do so certainly puts us, at least in theory, in a suitably ascetic context – but to what extent the culdee-movement had retained its radical character by the first half of the tenth century is far from clear.[92] Probably, in any case, the question has arisen because of the culdees' reputation in the last generation's scholarship as monastic reformers, prompting the thought that this prepared them admirably for a role in Lotharingian reform. This is, however, a mirage, for the culdees of the late eighth and early ninth centuries – the only ones whom we can see clearly – were by no stretch of the imagination reformers, but rather a strict-régime ascetic movement with no evident political agenda.[93]

I turn last to the question of exoticism. Foreigners and unusual behaviour have been the stuff of ascetic sanctity in the West since Sulpicius Severus wrote his hagiography of St Martin at the end of the fourth century.[94] By this criterion perpetual exiles for Christ might naturally present themselves as candidates for sanctity – and in tenth-century Latin Europe, as for some centuries, Gaels were prominent among such pilgrims. It is a question to what extent Cathróe's hagiographer chose exoticism as a means of defining his subject's sanctity. Certainly the prefaced national origin-legend creates a remarkably exotic atmosphere, but it seems strangely unintegrated with its surroundings.[95] More

---

88 Löwe, 'Dialogus'. Cf. Lapidge and Sharpe, *Bibliography*, p. 195, nr 725. 89 Löwe, 'Literarischer Widersacher'. Cf. Lapidge & Sharpe, *Bibliography*, pp. 169–70, nr 647. 90 This name (cf. n. 3, above) is attested in tenth-century Ireland: 'Mael Callann, princeps Dísirt Diarmata, quieuit' (AU, pp. 374–5 [921.9]). 91 For the culdees (*céli Dé*, 'dependants/clients of God') see Gwynn et al., *Ireland's Desert-Fathers*. For Cathróe in this context, see Skene, *Celtic Scotland*, ii.324–6. 92 For the later history of the culdee-movement, see the very fine work of Reeves, *Culdees of the British Islands*. The Scottish dimension was long treated by scholars with excessive imagination: see Ebrard, *Iroschottische Missionskirche*; and Skene, *Celtic Scotland*, ii, chapters 6 and 8; see now, instead, Barrow, *Kingdom of the Scots*, pp. 190–1, 212–32, and Cowan, *Medieval Church in Scotland*, pp. 3–4, 7, 15, 31, 33, 36, 98–9, 116, 158. 93 For a full exposition of this view, see Gwynn et al., *Ireland's Desert-Fathers*, pp. xi–lxxvi. 94 For this hagiography see Fontaine, *Sulpice Séuère*; and Halm, *Sulpicii Severi libri*. For a complete English translation of the hagiological writings, see Hoare, *Western Fathers*, pp. 1–144. 95 Colgan's §I is the author's prologue. §II

particularly, the narrative of Cathróe's early life, while more or less unremarkable in a Celtic hagiographical context, might have raised some eyebrows outside that world.[96] Furthermore, the names, the visit to Ireland, and the travels through Britain would all have impressed a Lotharingian readership by their foreignness. However, the author seems remarkably at home with these foreign elements, and Gaelic names appear to be reasonably well transmitted. If the author was not a Gaelic-speaker and/or if he wrote substantially after the late tenth century, it would, I think, be necessary to hypothesise a tenth-century written source or sources to account for the Insular elements of the Life. The question of possible non-contemporaneous elements in the Life is one of the most necessary tasks of criticism. Until a case for later composition or rewriting has been established, however, it seems to me that an author must be hypothesised who was steeped in the lore of Cathróe's community, having access to information deriving from stories of the saint's youth and travels and capable of reflecting effectively his group's sense of their Scottish identity. For his Life presents a construction not only of sanctity and of a reforming, ascetic Benedictine monasticism but also of Scottishness. If the author was a Continental who did not know Cathróe and indeed relied on hearsay,[97] he did a remarkable job.

As is well known, the hagiographical process of attributing Gaelic origins to saints became popular in the central middle ages. In England, for example, it affected St Modwenna whose hagiography embodies substantial Irish and Scottish elements.[98] In Italy the patron of Lucca, St Frediano, was deemed to be Irish and we owe to that the survival of important evidence for the hagiography of St Finnian of Movilla which was pillaged for St Frediano's benefit.[99] What is

contains a series of pious reflections by the author, both general and particular, ending 'If we cannot do him [St Cathróe] justice, then we may provide subject-matter for those who one day can and will'. The pseudohistory then begins (in the middle of Colgan's §II) with the transition rather absurdly made by *igitur*. It finishes (at the end of Colgan's §V), with a brief notice of St Patrick's conversion of the Gaelic world, that there were many christians who followed. 'Sed quia beati eorum actus, proprias repleuerunt paginas, ne alieno labori oneri simus, quæ nota sunt supersedenda iudicauimus.' Colgan's §VI opens: 'Quoniam uero in ignem semel manum externæ gentis uiros describendo, misimus ab eis minus recedentes, licet inculto sermone filium ecclesiæ, nouellam oliuam, ortam in campis syluæ statuere promisimus'. (At this point the Bollandists resumed their printing of the text, having already – p. 474 n. b – made this withering observation: 'Nempe descripturus Scotorum origines fabulosas hæc sibi præfanda credidit: nos enim laciniam hinc rescidimus, quam apud Colganum legat, qui volet'. The narrative of the Life of St Cathróe then begins, once again with *igitur* as a bizarre marker of transition. Were the pseudohistory not so well in tune with the Scottish ethos of the text, one would think it an interpolation. **96** For example, the exchange by which Cathróe's entry to religious life was achieved (§§VIII–IX; cf. §§VI–VII for his parents' original understanding with God and St Columba). **97** For hearsay, see §I: *neque gestorum eius aliquid sciam præter audita,* 'and I know nothing of his actions beyond what I have heard'. **98** On Modwenna see Kenney, *Sources*, pp. 366–71 (nrs 160–1); Esposito, 'Conchubrani Vita Sanctae Monennae', and idem, 'Sources of Conchubranus' Life of St. Monenna'. **99** On Frediano and Finnian, see Kenney, *Sources*, pp. 184–5 (nr 40), and Hennig, 'Note on the

less well known is when and where that process of gaelicisation of foreign saints got under way. Ninety years ago Léon van der Essen, in a fundamental study, showed the importance of eleventh- and twelfth-century Lotharingia in this process.[100] While the activities of Irish *peregrini* in Francia in the merovingian and carolingian periods provide the undoubted backdrop, one may wonder whether it was not the Gaelic presence in Lotharingia from the tenth century which was decisive in this development. After all, the Irish presence in Francia before 900 is notorious for not having created either institutional or ethnic continuity at the churches which *peregrini* founded or with which they were associated.[101] It was the Lotharingian monastic reform which was to change that fact.

We may examine this hagiographical process through writing associated directly with Waulsort. When Cathróe arrived on the Continent he made at once for Péronne, his Life tells us, where he successfully beseeched St Fursa to find a place which he and his companions could settle.[102] The memory of the seventh-century Irish saint is here deliberately cultivated. Fursa at once validates Cathróe and is validated by the Scotsman's devotion. Fursa had a longer reach (or more tentacles), however. From the late tenth century derive two other local specimens of hagiography, one of them written at Waulsort, which partake of a wholly different character.

The Life of St Eloquius (BHL 2315) purports to tell the story of an Irishman of that name who in 656 arrived from Ireland with a group of fellow-exiles: they established themselves at Lagny under Fursa's direction. Eventually Eloquius moved to Grigny-sur-Oise where he died on 3 December in an unspecified year. At his tomb two centuries later there were numerous miraculous cures in the reign of Charles the Bald, but it was destroyed by vikings at the end of the ninth century. Later, Hersendis, the noblewoman who was to become Cathróe's patroness, translated the relics to Waulsort where miracles resumed. It was there that Cathróe's monastery would be founded.[103] That relics were there by 946 is confirmed by charter-evidence.[104]

Traditions'. For the relevant texts, see Colgan, *Acta sanctorum*, pp. 633–51; and Zaccagnini, *Vita Sancti Fridiani*. Liam Naidoo (Girton College, Cambridge) is undertaking a thorough study of the interaction of the cults of the two saints.   **100** Van der Essen, *Étude critique*.
101 For discontinuity at Sankt Gallen, for example, see Duft and Meyer, *Irish Miniatures*; cf. Bischoff, *Latin Palaeography*, pp. 88, 94, 119, 198–9, 212. The situation at Bobbio in North Italy was similar: Engelbert, 'Zur Frühgeschichte'; cf. Bischoff, *Latin Palaeography*, pp. 88–9, 102, 191–2. In general, cf. Dumville, *Palaeographer's Review*, i.109–10.   **102** §XVIIII; cf. n. 23, above.   **103** Misonne, 'Sources littéraires', where an edition is to be found on pp. 358–65. Cf. idem, *Eilbert de Florennes*, pp. 74–80.   **104** As long, that is, as one finds the form and content of the charter acceptable: cf. n. 53, above. The text tells us, in words attributed to Robert, 'Inueni namque quoddam monasterium in comitatu meo Walciodorum nomine, dicatum in honore prefate matris Domini in pago Lomacinse, in quo almificus confessor Christi Eloquius pausat corpore, ubi multorum sanctorum condite noscuntur reliquie ...': cf.

The *Vita breuior Sancti Mononis* was written in this region at the same time. St Mono was, according to this Life, a colleague of Eloquius.[105] These imaginary Irishmen derive authority from Fursa, but they do so at around the presumed date of composition of the Life of St Cathróe and after about a half-century of experience of holy Scots and Irishmen as a reforming and refounding monastic presence in the region.

These supposedly seventh-century saints, whether wholly fictional or not, certainly came to derive a significant element of their holy authority from their exotic origin. They were followed by a long list of others, both in Lotharingia and farther afield, but the history of the attribution of Gaelic origins to diverse saints in the eleventh and twelfth centuries awaits its own chronicler and interpreter.[106] My contention is that realities of the tenth-century Lotharingian monastic reform provide the backdrop for the development of such exotic fantasies, which constitute a sociological as well as a literary phenomenon.[107]

Misonne, 'Éloge de Forannan', p. 53.   **105** BHL 6005–7; the feast-day is 18 October. The shorter and older Life has been dated to 980 x 1000, the longer and later Life to the first half of the eleventh century. The latter shows confusion between *Hibernia* and *Scotia*: Snieders, 'Influence de l'hagiographie irlandaise', p. 854 n. 4. Cf. van der Essen, *Étude critique*, pp. 144–9.   **106** For some aspects of the hagiography and cult of these others, see Snieders, 'Influence de l'hagiographie irlandaise', pp. 853–7 (on *Vita S. Liuini*, of the second half of the eleventh century: cf. BHL 4960–3; the feast-day is 12 November; for the distinction of *Scotia* and *Hibernia* see Snieders, p. 854 n. 4, but cf. p. 856 n. 1), and pp. 857–8 (on *Vita SS. Luglii et Lugliani*, said to be of the ninth century: cf. BHL 5061–3; the feast-day is 23 October). Cf. van der Essen, *Étude critique*, p. 195, on the English and Irish origins claimed for saints in the hagiography of the twelfth and thirteenth centuries. Cf. also St Plechelm: see above, nn. 58–9. It seems to me that *Vita S. Liuini* would particularly repay study.   **107** I am greatly indebted to the organisers of the *Naomhsheanchas* conference, who have mutated into the editors of this book, both for the initial invitation to speak (subsequently complicated by the unforeseen necessity for me to travel to Cork from Berkeley, California, where I was Visiting Professor of Mediaeval Studies in the Department of History) and for much editorial faith and encouragement. I am also obliged to Walter Berschin, József Nagy, and Jean-Michel Picard who all offered helpful observations at the conference, and to my colleagues Geoffrey Koziol (Berkeley) and Neil Wright (Cambridge) who provided help in areas where my own knowledge was inadequate.

Jonas's *Life of Columbanus* and his Disciples

Clare Stancliffe

Jonas's *Life of Columbanus and his Disciples* is a remarkable work of hagiography. It occupies some 90 pages in the large, quarto, edition of the Scriptores Rerum Merovingicarum series, or 150 pages in the ordinary format of the Scriptores Rerum Germanicarum;[1] and although it has its share of miracle stories, inaccuracies, and omissions, it contains a wealth of detail unusual for a saint's Life, naming many nobles and their families who came into contact with Columbanus or became converts to his monasticism. In some ways, the sheer length and wide range of this Life have inhibited study of it as a whole. Many people consult it for its account of the life of Columbanus, the great Irish ascetic who left his native island *c*.591 to travel to the Continent, where he founded the important monasteries of Luxeuil in Francia and Bobbio in Lombard Italy. But how many continue to read right through the second book of the Life, where Jonas continues his story with accounts of Columbanus's disciples at Bobbio, Luxeuil, and Faremoutiers? And yet we should not use a hagiographical work as a historical source unless we have first studied it in its own right, in order to gain understanding of what its author was seeking to do: for a hagiographer, even one writing close enough in time and place to his subject to be reliably informed, selects and presents his material with specific aims in mind; and these are not the aims of a disinterested historian.

In the last twenty years this Life has begun to attract the serious study which it merits. The path was blazed by Ian Wood in a perceptive and wide-ranging study.[2] This has been followed by a French translation with excellent introduction by Adalbert de Vogüé, some pages in Walter Berschin's history of medieval biography, and a recent article by Christian Rohr, to mention but the principal studies.[3] The present paper builds on these foundations. It is not primarily concerned with this work as a historical source, though it is to be hoped that it may indirectly contribute to a better understanding of the events which Jonas describes. Instead it seeks to study the Life in its own right, the

---

1 Jonas, *Vita Columbani* (Krusch, *Passiones* and *Ionae Vitae*). All references are to the latter edition unless the earlier is specified.　2 Wood, '*Vita Columbani*'.　3 De Vogüé, *Vie de S. Colomban*; Berschin, *Biographie*, ii.26–41; Rohr, 'Hagiographie'.

starting point being to investigate why Jonas wrote in the unusual form of a two-book Life, with the first book devoted to Columbanus himself, the second to his disciples. First, however, we will look briefly at the author and the background to his composition of this work.

Jonas was born at Susa in the southern foothills of the Alps, which at that time lay within the (Frankish-ruled) kingdom of Burgundy.[4] He entered the monastery of Bobbio, in the Appenines north-east of Genoa, shortly after Columbanus had died there in November 615.[5] He remained a monk at Bobbio for at least ten years, and was able to gather information in Italy and Francia from many who had known Columbanus personally. These included Athala, Eustasius, Chagnoald and Gall, who had all been monks under Columbanus, and were close to him. Athala had come to Columbanus after becoming disillusioned with the once great monastery of Lérins, and was probably his personal assistant for a time.[6] Columbanus entrusted him with leading the community at Luxeuil when he himself was sent into exile in 610;[7] but he must shortly have rejoined his master, for after Columbanus's death he succeeded him as abbot of Bobbio. Eustasius was also Columbanus's personal assistant for a time. Compelled to stay at Luxeuil when Columbanus was exiled, he appears to have become his effective successor there.[8] Chagnoald was the son of a nobleman whom Columbanus had visited at Meaux *c*.610, and brother of the virgin Burgundofara, whose double monastery of *Evoriacas* (Faremoutiers) was to figure prominently in Jonas's Life. Chagnoald too served as Columbanus's personal assistant, while he was at Bregenz in the Alps *c*.612. He helped in the early stages of the establishment of Faremoutiers, but by 626 or 627 had become bishop of Laon.[9] Gall appears in Jonas's narrative only in the context of a fishing miracle in the vicinity of Luxeuil; but if we can trust the later Lives of St Gall, he was one of the original band of Irish monks who had come with Columbanus all the way from Bangor to the Continent, remaining in the Bregenz area when Columbanus left for Italy.[10]

These details about Jonas's sources are given not simply because they reveal the quality of the information available to him about Columbanus's life, but also because they provide part of the context for his work. Jonas, in turn, had

---

4 Bullough, 'Career of Columbanus', p. 1 n. 1.   5 De Vogüé argues (*Vie de S. Colomban*, p. 19) that he had entered by February 617, little more than a year after Columbanus's death. See also Rohr, 'Hagiographie', pp. 230–1. On the date of Columbanus's death see Jonas, *Vita Columbani* I.30, and Krusch's note, ibid. p. 223 and n. 1.   6 Jonas, *Vita Columbani* II.1: 'suo ministerio iunxit'. So interpreted by de Vogüé, *Vie de S. Colomban*, p. 19.   7 *Epistula* IV (Walker, *Sancti Columbani opera*, pp. 26–37).   8 Jonas, *Vita Columbani* I.20 and 30 (and cf. 27) (Krusch, pp. 196, 222, 215).   9 Jonas *Vita Columbani* I.26–8; II.7 and 8; De Vogüé, *Vie de S. Colomban*, p. 35 n. 2; Guerout, 'Fare', cols 520–1.   10 Jonas, *Vita Columbani* I.11 (Krusch, pp. 171–2). On Gall, see the references in Bullough, 'Career of Columbanus', pp. 20–1; cf. below, p. 204.

become Athala's assistant or secretary at Bobbio, which means that he became very close to the man whom Columbanus had chosen to lead his monks at a critical time;[11] and after Athala's death, Jonas fulfilled the same function for his successor, Bertulf,[12] who was the abbot who originally commissioned Jonas to write Columbanus's Life. However, we do not know how long Jonas remained as Bertulf's secretary at Bobbio: his regular domicile during the 630s is obscure, but he was certainly able to meet and talk to various disciples of Columbanus in Francia, as well, presumably, as Gall in the Alps. His conversations with Eustasius of Luxeuil are relatively easy to account for, as links were very close between Bobbio and Luxeuil, and Jonas may well have accompanied Athala on his visit there.[13] More intriguing is the fact that Jonas appears to have been visiting Burgundofara's monastery of *Evoriacas*, east of Paris, around the time of the nun Gibitrude's death – an event which may well have taken place *c*.633–4.[14] This could have been a visit made on behalf of his abbot; but it could equally indicate that, as early as this, Jonas's base had shifted from Bobbio to north Francia. Jonas was certainly back at Bobbio *c*.639 when Abbot Bertulf and the monks asked him to write the Life of Columbanus, but the wording of Jonas's text seems to imply that he was then 'staying' rather than 'living' there.[15] Light may be shed on this by the fact that during the three years it took to produce the Life, Jonas was helping Amand with his missionary work in the far north of Francia around Amand's monastery of Elnon (later Saint-Amand). This lay near the confluence of the Scarpe and the Escaut, just south of the modern French-Belgian border. The link here was probably through the bishop of Noyon and Tournai, Acharius, who was himself a former Luxeuil monk.[16] It is, of course, possible that Jonas had gone to Acharius to interview him as a source of information for his work, and so found himself drawn into helping Amand; but equally, the link with Amand and that part of the world might well have been of longer standing. Jonas's future appears to have lain in Francia rather than in Italy, and he may have ended his days as abbot of Marchiennes, a predominantly female community founded in 647 near Saint-Amand.[17] We should thus think of Jonas not so much as a Bobbio monk, but rather a Columbanian monk.

---

11 Jonas, *Vita Columbani* II.2 (Krusch, p. 232); Columbanus, *Epistula* IV (Walker, *Sancti Columbani opera*, pp. 26–37).   12 Jonas accompanied Bertulf to Rome in this capacity in 628: Jonas, *Vita Columbani* II.23 (Krusch, p. 282). Cf. Rohr, 'Hagiographie', pp. 230–1. 13 Jonas, *Vita Columbani* II.23 (Krusch, p. 281); de Vogüé, *Vie de S. Colomban*, p. 35 n.2; Rohr, 'Hagiographie', pp. 231–2.   14 This date rests on the plausible but unproven assumption that Burgundofara's grave illness, mentioned in the Gibitrude story, was the occasion for Burgundofara to draw up her will, which is dated to the fifth year of Dagobert's reign: see Guerout, 'Fare', col. 524.   15 Jonas, *Vita Columbani*, prefatory letter (Krusch, pp. 144–5): 'Cum apud eos [Bertulf and the brothers] Appenninis ruribus vagans in Ebobiensem cenobium morarer'.   16 Jonas, *Vita Columbani*, prefatory letter, and II.8 (at end) (Krusch, pp. 145–6). So de Vogüé, *Vie de S. Colomban*, pp. 20–1.   17 De Vogüé, *Vie de S. Colomban*, pp. 21–3; cf. the caution of Rohr, 'Hagiographie', pp. 233–4.

I THE STRUCTURE OF THE LIFE

That a monastic founder as important as Columbanus should have a *vita* composed in his honour is readily understandable. The form which this Life takes, however, is interesting. It consists of two lengthy books, the first devoted to Columbanus, the second to his disciples. As published by Krusch, the Life comprises a dedicatory and prefatory letter addressed to Waldebert and Bobolenus, the current abbots of Luxeuil and Bobbio; a list of chapter headings for the first book; a separate preface to the Life of Columbanus, which forms the first chapter of Book I; some verses on Ireland, probably by another author, reproduced here by Jonas; and then a chronological account of Columbanus's life running from his pregnant mother's vision of his future greatness right through his youth in Ireland, his entry to the religious life, his *peregrinatio* to Gaul, foundation of monasteries in Burgundy, eventual exile on command of King Theuderic, his lengthy journeying across the breadth of Francia to Nantes and then back eastwards into Austrasia and up the Rhine to the area of Bregenz, followed by his crossing of the Alps into Italy, reception by the Lombard king at Milan, and settling at Bobbio, ending with his death there. Then follow a poem (*Clare sacerdos*) and hymn (*Nostris sollemnis*), both on Columbanus, which conclude Book I. Book II has its own list of chapter headings, but no separate preface. It consists of six chapters on Athala, Columbanus's successor as abbot of Bobbio, which effectively form a brief Life of Athala running from his conversion to death. Then come four chapters on Eustasius, Columbanus's successor at Luxeuil. These are concerned only with the years of Eustasius's abbacy, and are dominated by the story of the monk Agrestius's rebellion, though Eustasius's death is also covered. Next, Jonas gives a long section of twelve chapters on *Evoriacas* or Faremoutiers, the double monastery presided over by Burgundofara, which had been founded under Eustasius's inspiration. This is almost entirely taken up with narrating miracles associated with the deaths of individual nuns, while Burgundofara herself scarcely figures. Finally Book II returns to Bobbio, with a long chapter on Abbot Bertulf's life covering his conversion and abbacy (but not death), followed by two chapters on miracles wrought by various Bobbio monks during the abbacies of both Athala and Bertulf.

What is striking about this Life is the contrast between, on the one hand, the conscious artistry that Jonas shows in placing his work in a hagiographical tradition, together with his skill and care in constructing an impressive Life of Columbanus in Book I, and, on the other hand, an apparent lack of care over the construction of Book II. This has no coherence. Ordinary miracle stories illustrating command over nature or the abbot's powers of healing jostle beside stories of monastic rebellion. Worse, the Faremoutiers material, which forms a sizable block of twelve chapters, is repetitive and not integrated into the whole, and the work ends with a series of rather ordinary miracles wrought by a number of Bobbio monks. In other words, Book II is a ragbag. It is not even a monastic account of previous abbots and abbesses, for the Faremoutiers material is quite out of place, focusing, as it does, on the deaths of several individual nuns, and scarcely mentioning the abbess at all. Thus, whereas the rest of the work uses a biographical framework for organising the material, in the Faremoutiers section the link is purely thematic, and the passages which might have provided a biographical focus on Burgundofara are instead scattered elsewhere in Jonas's work.[18] The same also applies, on a small scale, to the last two chapters of the whole work concerned with miracles performed by a number of Bobbio monks, though here there is no connecting theme of any kind apart from the general focus on the miraculous.

Several scholars have recently devoted themselves to the questions posed by the structure and content of the *Vita Columbani discipulorumque eius*. There can be little doubt that it is all the work of Jonas;[19] but various scholars have recently questioned whether he deliberately composed it in the form in which Krusch presented it in his editions. The reasons for their doubts are twofold: on the one hand, the unsatisfactory nature of Book II, particularly its lack of homogeneity; on the other, the absence of any manuscript which gives the entire contents of Book II in the order in which Krusch prints it. The Italian scholar, Michele Tosi, who in 1965 edited a version of the Life given in a ninth-century manuscript that lacked the Faremoutiers material, suggested that this latter section might originally have formed a third book. Jonas's Book II would thus have consisted solely of the Lives of Athala, Eustasius and Bertulf, together with the following miracles of the Bobbio monks.[20] In 1988, Walter Berschin went so far as to hypothesise that the Life might well never have existed in the form in which we now have it. He appears to envisage Jonas completing and circulating Book I, the Life of Columbanus himself, and then adding on an Athala section for Bobbio, a Eustasius section for Luxeuil, and so on.[21] The

---

18 Jonas, *Vita Columbani* I.26, II.7 (Krusch, pp. 209, 241–3).   19 Jo Ann McNamara is a dissenting voice here, suggesting that the first person plural passages in the Faremoutiers section might indicate that this had been sent to Jonas by a nun of that community. She presumably regards it as having been incorporated bodily by Jonas: McNamara and Halborg, *Sainted Women*, p. 160. But the same concerns, and even the same idiosyncratic expressions, are found throughout the work, including this section: e.g. in the Gibitrude chapter, where the first person plural is used, the typical 'saecularibus ... faleramentis': Jonas, *Vita Columbani* II.12, and cf. I.10 ('faleramenta saeculi'); I.14, II.1, II.9 (Krusch, p. 260, and cf. pp. 169, 176, 230, 246). Cf. also 'cum iam nox atra inruisset' in II.13 with 'iam atra nox inruerit' in II.23 (Krusch, pp. 263–4, 283).   20 Tosi, *Vita Columbani*, pp. xxvi–vii. 21 Berschin, *Biographie* ii.38, and cf. p. 26 n. 59. Krusch himself suggested that Book I might have been published on its own by Jonas in 641, and republished the following year complete with Book II and the addition to Book I of the passage on Columbanus and the squirrels (Krusch, *Ionae Vitae*, pp. 58–9, 113–14); but there is no real evidence for Book I having originally been published separately from Book II. See below, n. 42.

most recent author to have addressed the question, Christian Rohr, appears to hesitate between one or other of these approaches. He feels either that Jonas might have originally composed the sections on Athala, Eustasius and Bertulf, with the Faremoutiers material and the two final chapters on Bobbio monks as later additions; or else that particular versions of the Life circulated for each Columbanian monastery.[22] Only Adalbert de Vogüé, writing in 1988, appears to have accepted the structure of the Life as Krusch prints it, and based his analysis on that.[23]

Our first task, then, is to try to discover how Jonas originally conceived his work. Our arguments will be based on the evidence afforded us by Jonas's actual text, together with that of the manuscript tradition.

The evidence of Jonas comprises both the Life itself, and the prefatory letter in which he sets out his own intentions. If one simply reads straight through the Life, the sections on Athala and Eustasius follow quite smoothly after the account of Columbanus's death, and close, as Rohr noted, with a similar formula to that coming after Columbanus's death at the end of Book I: Eustasius has reached the heavenly kingdom under the leadership of Christ, 'unto whom is power and honour, world without end. Amen.'[24] The transition to the Faremoutiers material at this point does seem somewhat abrupt, despite the fact that Jonas is careful to link it in: 'I should like the reader to remember that I promised above to relate miracles about Burgundofara's monastery, already mentioned ...' He has indeed told us earlier that he will be coming back to Burgundofara, both in the Columbanian section in Book I, and in the Eustasian section in Book II.[25] In fact, she is the only person to whom there are such forward references: Jonas could have included one to Eustasius in Book I; but, for whatever reason, did not.[26] Jonas also explicitly gives reasons to justify his inclusion of Faremoutiers material and of the miracles wrought by Bobbio monks, arguing that these miraculous accounts will have a beneficial effect on his readers.[27] This suggests that he was aware of a lack of coherence in his narrative, and also, perhaps, of problems posed by bringing his narrative up to the present and writing of people who were still alive. Nonetheless, it was his decision to do so, seemingly so that the current generation of Columbanian monks and virgins might be stimulated to keep to the extraordinarily exacting standards of the ascetic and spiritual life which we glimpse both in the *vita* and in Columbanus's own writings.[28]

---

22 Rohr, 'Hagiographie', pp. 242–4. Confusingly, he also suggests (p. 242) that the prayer at the close of the Eustasius section might have marked the intended end of Book II. 23 De Vogüé, *Vie de S. Colomban*, pp. 35–50 ('Le dessein de Jonas'). 24 Jonas, *Vita Columbani* II.10 (Krusch, p. 257). Cf. Rohr, 'Hagiographie', p. 242. 25 Jonas, *Vita Columbani* I.26, II.7 (Krusch, pp. 209, 243). 26 Jonas, *Vita Columbani* I.20; cf. also I.27 and 30 (Krusch, pp. 196, 215, 223). 27 Jonas, *Vita Columbani* II.16, 22, 23, 25 (Krusch, pp. 266, 277, 280, 291–2, 294). 28 Explicit in Jonas, *Vita Columbani* II.11 (at end) (Krusch, p. 259); cf. de

Further light is shed by Jonas's dedicatory letter to abbots Waldebert and Bobolenus. Here we learn that Bertulf, seconded by the Bobbio monks, had asked Jonas for a Life of Columbanus, and that it was apparently Jonas's own decision to extend this brief to include the Lives of Athala, Eustasius, and 'a great many, whose excellence made them worthy of memory'; that he was including only true and well attested information; and that, to prevent readers becoming bored by his mass of material, he had divided it into two books: 'the first book tells in brief the deeds of the blessed Columbanus, the second one sets out the life of his disciples Athala, Eustasius, and others whom we remember.' He further invites the abbots to examine his work carefully and approve it, so that it may dispel any uncertainty from 'everyone else'.[29] We will return to this passage later. For now, we need to note only that it was Jonas's initiative to add the contents of Book II; and that even if he did expand his ideas about what to include as he worked, the formal terms in which he here talks of dividing his material into two books and seeking the abbots' approval show that we are dealing with what he conceived of as a finished work. This consisted of two parts, of which the second included the Lives of Athala and Eustasius and of 'many others'.[30] This implies more than just the Lives of Athala, Eustasius and Bertulf, which Rohr suggests. Indeed, it would fit the Life as Krusch has edited it. Thus, while our conclusions about the precise contents of Book II must await our examination of the manuscript evidence, we can here and now reject the hypothesis that there was no 'finished' form of the Life, but simply a core Book I and a fluid Book II, the precise contents of the latter varying according as to whether the manuscript copy was destined for Bobbio, Luxeuil, or elsewhere. Jonas had already taken thought of what to include and what to exclude. He had composed a literary work of some pretensions, and he sent this finished work to the abbots of both major Columbanian houses for their *imprimatur*.

It remains, then, to discover what comprised this finished work in two books; and here we must obviously consider the manuscript evidence. It is a remarkable fact that no manuscript contains all the material in the order in which Krusch presents it in his two editions. The chief problems arise with Book II. Some manuscripts omit this book altogether, while others divide it into two books, so yielding a three-book Life. Since Jonas himself states that he has divided his material into two books, we can disregard both these variants. Even if we restrict ourselves to those manuscript families which give two books, however, there is still much variety. Several manuscripts omit specific sections

Vogüé, *Vie de S. Colomban*, pp. 27–30. **29** Jonas, *Vita Columbani*, prefatory letter (Krusch, pp. 145, 147). Cf. de Vogüé, *Vie de S. Colomban*, p. 36; below, p. 218. On Jonas's use of 'life' rather than 'lives' of Columbanus's disciples, cf. Gregory of Tours: 'It is better to say "life" rather than "lives" of the fathers, because, although there may be a diversity in merit and virtue, nonetheless one bodily life nourishes all in the world': *Vita patrum*, preface (Krusch, p. 212). **30** 'Plerumque': see de Vogüé, *Vie de S. Colomban*, p. 94 and n. 4.

of Book II, while the only one to contain the entire work, Turin Biblioteca
Nazionale, MS F.IV.26, from Bobbio, gives the contents of Book II in a
different order from Krusch's edition.[31]

In his first edition in 1902, Krusch discussed some forty-one manuscripts.
Simultaneously a study by Lawlor of the manuscript sources for Jonas's Life,
published in 1903, brought several new manuscripts to light;[32] and in 1905
Krusch published a new edition in the Scriptores Rerum Germanicarum series
which took these into account. He there listed 114 manuscripts. Finally another
early manuscript of the Life was rediscovered in the Bibliothèque du Grand
Séminaire at Metz in 1954, and its text was published separately by an Italian
scholar, Michele Tosi.[33] Although the Metz manuscript is of interest, its
discovery and publication have not superseded or invalidated Krusch's 1905
edition, which remains the basis for any serious discussion of Jonas's text. Both
Krusch and Lawlor recognised the excellence of St Gall Stiftsbibliothek MS
553 (original hand), now accepted as a ninth-century manuscript. This, Krusch's
A1a, together with the former Bobbio manuscript, now Turin F.IV.26 (Krusch's
B1a), were rightly regarded by Krusch as the foundation stones for the
establishment of Jonas's text.[34]

Krusch assigned the extant manuscripts of the *Vita Columbani discipulorumque
eius* to two classes, A and B, the latter comprising an 'Italian' class. He further
subdivided class A into various families; but of those manuscripts studied by
Krusch, only those in his A1 and A2 families contain Book II, and so concern
us now. The contents of Book II as given in the most significant manuscripts of
these two families are tabulated in Figure 1, together with the evidence from the
ninth-century manuscript published by Tosi, a manuscript which he plausibly
suggests is the archetype of Krusch's class A3 manuscripts.[35] As the table
demonstrates, there is considerable variety as to which blocks of material
individual manuscripts omit: St Gall, Stiftsbibliothek MS 553 contains only
Bobbio material; Brussels, Bibliothèque Royale MS 8518–20 contains everything
except for the six chapters on Athala of Bobbio, whereas The Hague, Koninklijke
Bibliotheek MS X.73 contains everything except for the four chapters on
Eustasius, and so on. What is striking, however, is that every single manuscript in
Class A contains its selections in the same order: Athala, Eustasius, Faremoutiers

---

31 It omits only the second hymn, *Nostris sollemnis*, and the chapter headings; cf. below.
32 Lawlor, 'Manuscripts'. 33 Tosi, *Vita Columbani*. For a description of the manuscript
and its contents see Leclercq, 'Recueil'. It had been known to James Ussher in the
seventeenth century: ibid., p. 196 n. 2. Bernard Bischoff has assigned the manuscript to
Rheims under Hincmar (Archbishop 845–82): thus Leclercq in Tosi, *Vita Columbani*, p. xv.
34 See Krusch, *Ionae Vitae*, pp. 60–3, 104, 120, 121, 135; cf. Lawlor, 'Manuscripts', p. 128.
The dating of St Gall, Stiftsbibliothek MS 553, to the second quarter of the ninth century,
rests on Bischoff's authority: Berschin, *Biographie*, ii.26 n. 59.   35 Below, p. 220. Tosi, *Vita
Columbani*, p. xxx. Its shelfmark is Metz, Bibliothèque du Grand Séminaire MS 1.

miracles, Bertulf and the Bobbio monks. This must mean that they derive from an original which contained them in this order, the order in which Krusch printed them; for, if we were dealing with individual scribes or monasteries making their own selection from a number of *vitae* circulating as individual booklets, we would surely see more variety in the order.

Such variety does, it is true, occur in the chief representative of the Italian (or B) class of manuscripts, Turin, Biblioteca Nazionale, MS F.IV.26. This groups the Bobbio material at the beginning, so assigning Bertulf and the Bobbio monks to second place immediately after Athala, before continuing with Eustasius and the miracles of Faremoutiers. However, a little thought will reveal that, faced with the choice of adopting the order of class A or class B manuscripts, Krusch made the right decision. First, this order is indicated by all branches of class A manuscripts – and significantly, on the evidence of the Metz manuscript, we can now include family A3, which in many respects is closer to class B manuscripts than to those of A1 and A2. Contrariwise, the evidence of the B manuscript, Turin F.IV.26, stands on its own.[36] Secondly, Jonas's own words in his prefatory letter imply that he planned to include the Lives of Columbanus, Athala, Eustasius, and others, in that order.[37] Finally, since Turin MS F.IV.26 was copied at Bobbio, its decision to group the Bobbio material together at the beginning, relegating the Luxeuil and Faremoutiers material to second place, is readily explicable; but there is no such explanation at hand to account for the order of material in class A manuscripts.

As for the precise contents of Book II, the manuscripts do, indeed, present bewildering variations; but Jonas's own prefatory letter makes it clear that it contained accounts of several others as well as Athala and Eustasius. This must mean, at the very least, that either the Faremoutiers block, or the chapters on Bertulf and the various Bobbio monks, were originally included, and very possibly both of them. This would rule out one of Rohr's suggestions, that Book II might originally have contained only the Lives of Athala, Eustasius and Bertulf (without the following chapters on the Bobbio monks). The only evidence in favour of this hypothesis is the late-seventh-century preface to the *Passio Praeiecti*, which includes a reference to Jonas's 'vitam beati Columbani et discipulorum eius Athale, Eustasi et Bertulfi.'[38] The manuscript evidence, however, shows that the account of Bertulf and the following two chapters on various miracles wrought by Bobbio monks were always copied together. The

---

36 Turin Bib. Naz. MS F.IV.12, another Bobbio manuscript representing class B, is independent for Book I of Jonas's Life; but Book II was copied at a later date from Turin Bib. Naz. MS F.IV.26: Krusch, *Ionae Vitae*, pp. 104–5. There are no other relevant manuscripts in class B.   37 'Primus [libellus] beati Columbae gesta perstringit, secundus discipulorum eius Athalae, Eusthasii vel ceterorum quos meminimus vitam edisserit' (Krusch, *Ionae Vitae*, p. 147).   38 Cited by Rohr, 'Hagiographie', p. 243 n. 68. For the date of the *Passio Praeiecti* see Fouracre and Gerberding, *Late Merovingian France*, pp. 254–70.

words of the *Passio Praeiecti* should therefore not be interpreted too literally as excluding these additional Bobbio chapters. As for the hypothesis that the Bertulf and Bobbio chapters were a later addition, and that Book II originally contained only the account of Athala, Eustasius, and the Faremoutiers miracles, this has nothing to commend it. The *Passio Praeiecti* evidence tells against it, as does the internal evidence of Book II. For the last words of the Faremoutiers block would make a most implausible ending, whereas the last paragraph of the Bobbio material does provide a possible ending. Conversely, since Bobbio originally commissioned the work, since readers there were in the forefront of Jonas's mind as he was writing,[39] and since the dedicatory letter was addressed jointly to the abbots of Luxeuil and Bobbio, all the Bobbio material is likely to have formed part of the finished work that Jonas presented to Waldebert and Bobolenus for their approval.

A somewhat stronger case exists for envisaging the original Book II as containing only the Athala, Eustasius, Bertulf and Bobbio chapters, and regarding the Faremoutiers material as a later addition. One can very plausibly cut from the end of the Eustasian section to the beginning of the Bertulf chapter; and Tosi has also advanced an argument in support of this hypothesis: that in the Eustasian section, Jonas declares his intention of documenting the miracles occurring at Faremoutiers if he should live long enough. This, Tosi argues, is an odd expression if he actually intended to tackle them only four chapters later.[40] This argument is, however, very weak. The thinking behind Jonas's expression, 'si vita comes fuerit', would have been a commonplace for Jonas, reared on Columbanus's teaching that a monk should live as though he died daily;[41] and I regard it as more justifiable to stand this argument on its head, and point out that already, in the Eustasian section, Jonas was planning to include material on the Faremoutiers miracles. It is perhaps worth mentioning that to omit the twelve Faremoutiers chapters would destroy the present balance between Book I's twenty-nine chapters (73 pages) and Book II's twenty-five chapters (64½ pages). A more significant point is that if Jonas had added the Faremoutiers material later, after completing the two-book work which he sent to the abbots of Luxeuil and Bobbio, one might expect this to have left a clearer trace on the manuscript evidence. As it is, only the Metz manuscript fully suits this hypothesis, whereas the evidence of various manuscripts tells against it: the A1b, c and d manuscripts, and even the A2a manuscript, where Bertulf and the Bobbio monks as well as Faremoutiers are relegated to a third book. Thus, although I would accept that one cannot be absolutely certain of the contents of Jonas's original Book II, I regard it as highly likely that Krusch's

---

39 De Vogüé, *Vie de S. Colomban*, p. 50.   **40** Tosi, *Vita Columbani*, p. xxvii, citing Jonas, *Vita Columbani* II.7 (at end) (Krusch, p. 243).   **41** Columbanus, *Instructio* III.3; cf. *Instructiones* VIII.2 and IX.2 (Walker, *Sancti Columbani opera*, pp. 76, 96, 100).

edition prints Jonas's composition by and large as he wrote it,[42] and that Krusch himself provided the correct explanation for the absence of any complete manuscript in the correct order. This occurred because Book II was concerned with so many different figures, living in places which were widely separated from each other, that copyists belonging to different houses preferred to select only what interested them, and thus the unity of Book II was lost.[43]

If, then, we are to assume that Jonas wrote the *Life of Columbanus and his Disciples* in two books as Krusch prints it, we need to consider why he chose to construct it like this. In the separate preface to Book I, Jonas names the saints and their hagiographers in whose tradition he is setting his own composition: first Athanasius's Life of Antony, Jerome's Lives of Paul, Hilarion 'and others', and 'Postumianus, Severus and Gallus' on St Martin.[44] These are the Lives of the founding fathers of the ascetic and monastic tradition. In the second place Jonas names those 'columns of the church', Hilary, Ambrose and Augustine, who had kept the true faith from harm amid the storms of the heretics. These are the three western bishops prominent as church fathers and as opponents of the Arian and Donatist heresies in the fourth and early fifth centuries. Jonas is thus ambitiously setting Columbanus in the tradition both of the great monastic exemplars, and equally of those who had written theological, exegetical, and apologetic works, and had striven against Arianism and other heresies. The relevance of the former tradition is obvious, and the relevance of the latter is acceptable if we recall Columbanus's attempts to promote catholic Christianity against Arianism in northern Italy, together with the fact that he is known to have written a commentary on the Psalms and a book against Arianism, although neither of these survives.[45] Columbanus's letter to Pope Boniface certainly witnesses to his concern to promote unity amongst the antagonistic,

---

42 Apart from the Faremoutiers section, which I regard as part of Jonas's original work, but where I recognise that an element of doubt must remain, there is one significant passage in Book I where Krusch's ordering of the text should be questioned. This is the passage about Columbanus's relationship with wild animals, including the detailed description of his playing with squirrels (*incipit* 'Cui sic bestiae ... ', or in Class A MSS 'Nam et Chagnoaldum ... '). Krusch prints this at the end of I.17, on the evidence of Class A1 and A2 manuscripts. The passage is omitted from Class B manuscripts, while Class A3 manuscripts place it at the end of chapter 15. Since it fits better at the end of chapter 15, and this placing now receives added confirmation from the rediscovered ninth-century Metz manuscript, I am inclined to regard this as its correct, original place. There is then no need for Krusch's theory that it was a late addition by Jonas to Book I – something which seems improbable, given that it was told on the authority of Chagnoald who had been dead for some six years by the time Jonas was writing. Cf. Krusch, *Ionae Vitae*, pp. 113–14, 179, 185–6; Tosi, *Vita Columbani*, pp. xxviii–xxix, p. 48 and n. 50. 43 Krusch, *Ionae Vitae*, p. 59. 44 This last denotes Sulpicius Severus's *Dialogues*, and probably includes his *Vita Martini* as well: cf. Prete, 'Vita S. Columbani', pp. 106–9. 45 Jonas, *Vita Columbani* I.3, 30 (Krusch, pp. 158, 221). Columbanus also wrote a book on the Easter question (Columbanus, *Epistula* II.5: Walker, *Sancti Columbani opera*, p. 16). But Jonas's silence about this is deliberate: cf. below, pp. 215–16.

but doctrinally orthodox, church groupings in northern Italy, in order to present a united front against the Arians;[46] and Bobbio's anti-Arian concerns are well brought out in Jonas's Book II.[47]

The precedents which Jonas invokes in this prefatory chapter are thus precedents for Columbanus's significance as an ecclesiastical figure, as Jonas sees it, not precedents for the type of saint's Life which he proposes to write. The structure of this Life appears to be Jonas's own creation. Of those Lives which he alludes to, only Venantius Fortunatus's Life of Hilary of Poitiers is a Life in two books;[48] and there the parallel with the *Vita Columbani discipulorumque eius* ends, for Fortunatus devoted his second book to Hilary's posthumous miracles, whereas Jonas focused on Columbanus's disciples. At one level, there is a ready explanation for Jonas's divergence which has been well brought out by Ian Wood: a monastic community would have suffered disruption if a tomb within the monastic precincts had become the centre of a thaumaturgical cult, attracting numerous lay visitors. Instead, Jonas was concerned to produce a Life that was intended 'to be edifying to ascetics. Here was the Rule in action.'[49] This provides a plausible explanation for the lack of posthumous miracles. Wood also comments on the way in which monastic *vitae* 'could almost become lengthy commentaries on the regular life of a community.'[50] This, as we shall see, has its relevance for Jonas's Life of Columbanus. The fact remains that although 'communal biographies' such as the *Life of the Jura Fathers*, or Gregory of Tours's *Vita patrum*, or Gregory the Great's *Dialogues*, already existed, and the last of these at least was known to Jonas,[51] none of them provided him with a real model. His dedicatory epistle, followed by a first chapter which serves as a preface, in fact recalls none of these works, but rather Sulpicius Severus's *Vita Sancti Martini*.

Thus Jonas's decision to write a second book devoted to the doings of Columbanus's disciples cannot be set down either to Abbot Bertulf's original request, or to Jonas's adoption of any model; rather, it appears to be entirely his own, original choice.[52] Why he should have made this decision is at first sight surprising. His attempt to write about Columbanus's successors in different monasteries provided him with a major challenge as to how to structure his work – a challenge which, as we have seen, he was not altogether successful at meeting. True, some of the material which he included would, he thought, be beneficial for contemporary monks and nuns. But do the contents of Book II,

---

46 Columbanus, *Epistula* V (Walker, *Sancti Columbani opera*, pp. 36–57). On the interpretation of the latter, see Gray and Herren, 'Three Chapters Controversy'. **47** Jonas, *Vita Columbani* II.23, 24 (Krusch, pp. 282–3, 286–9). **48** Sulpicius Severus's *Dialogues* were also (originally) written in two books. But the *Dialogues* scarcely form a 'Life' of Martin – rather they supplement Sulpicius's *Vita Martini*, which had already been published: Stancliffe, *St Martin*, pp. 80–5, 103–7. **49** Wood, '*Vita Columbani*', pp. 67–8. **50** Ibid., p. 66. **51** De Vogüé, *Vie de S. Colomban*, p. 32; Vogeler, 'Exkurs'. **52** Cf. Berschin, *Biographie*, ii.27–8.

taken as a whole, contribute greatly to their moral edification in a way which was not already provided for by Book I? In one key respect one could argue the opposite: whereas in Book I, Jonas had, with success, avoided portraying internal ecclesiastical dissension, Book II is full of the unedifying spectacle of monastic rebellions and sharp divisions within the church. This surprising contrast merits closer examination.

II JONAS'S TREATMENT OF INTERNAL ECCLESIASTICAL DISSENSIONS

As has long been recognised, Jonas's account of Columbanus's own life in Book I is wrong or misleading in certain respects: the age at which Jonas portrays Columbanus leaving Ireland, the name of the king who first welcomed him to Francia, and the way in which he passes over how Columbanus brought on himself the antagonism of the bishops. Instead, Jonas presents Columbanus's problems in Francia as stemming solely from Queen Brunechild and her son, King Theuderic. It is this last which concerns us here. We are fortunate in that six of Columbanus's own letters survive, and provide us with strictly contemporary evidence for his life. From these letters, we know that Columbanus's adherence to the Irish reckoning of Easter and his scathing opinion of Victorius of Aquitaine's Easter cycle, then normative in Gaul, had already prompted him to write (*c*.600) to Pope Gregory the Great for support.[53] The following years saw him writing and sending to the pope a lengthy work on the Easter question, while also sending a brief pamphlet on the same subject to Aridius, metropolitan bishop of Lyons. (That was the same Aridius to whom Athala had once been entrusted by his father, only to abandon him for Lérins, 'seeing that he was gaining nothing of use.')[54] In 603/4, Columbanus was summoned to appear before a synod of bishops meeting at Chalon because of his refusal to abandon his Easter reckoning.[55] Lying behind this summons may also have been his refusal to submit to Gallic episcopal jurisdiction. Columbanus excused himself from attending the synod in person, lest, he explained, he should find himself sucked into unChristian quarrelling; but as regards the Easter question, he

53 Columbanus, *Epistula* I. For its date, see Walker, *Sancti Columbani opera*, p. xxxvi. On the Easter question see Charles-Edwards, *Early Christian Ireland*; for elucidation of Columbanus's Easter reckoning, see McCarthy, '*Latercus* Paschal Cycle', pp. 38–9. 54 Columbanus, *Epistula* II.5 (Walker, *Sancti Columbani opera*, pp. 14–6); Jonas, *Vita Columbani* II.1 (Krusch, p. 230). 55 Columbanus, *Epistula* II. Cf. Walker, *Sancti Columbani opera*, p. x n. 7; Bullough, 'Career of Columbanus', pp. 13–14. Although Columbanus's monasteries were probably in the diocese of Besançon, the one-time metropolitan see for the province of Maxima Sequanorum, by this date the areas linked together in ecclesiastical synods tended to reflect political entities; and it was normal for those of Burgundy to meet under the presidency of the metropolitan bishop of Lyon.

appealed to the authority of Anatolius (commended by Jerome), and moreover of
the Bible. It is a remarkable letter for someone in Columbanus's position to send
to a synod of bishops, before whom he stood accused. He bases himself
unequivocally on the teaching and example of Christ, who was poor, humble,
and resolute in preaching the truth in the face of persecution from men: an
implicit rebuke to the aristocratic lifestyle of the bishops. Indeed, Columbanus
is also not afraid to needle them over their failure to enforce canonical norms.
Columbanus was probably thinking of New Testament teaching, and such
contemporary breaches as simony and bishops continuing to have marital
relations with their wives after consecration;[56] but it came well from one who
'broke every Gallic conciliar decree on the right relationship of monks with
diocesans.'[57] Columbanus called upon the bishops to join him in living out the
'canons' of Jesus Christ, and, invoking Jerome's authority, he held up parallel
courses for bishops and clergy on the one hand, and monks on the other, both
parties looking to Christ as their leader.[58] Thus the authority Columbanus recognised was that of Christ, not the bishops. His audacious stance is remarkable:
from paragraph seven it appears that he had already been threatened with
exile.[59] Even more remarkable is the fact that although the synod of Chalon did
depose and exile Bishop Desiderius of Vienne at the instigation of Brunechild
and Bishop Aridius,[60] Columbanus's pleas to be left in peace were heeded. The
support afforded him by King Theuderic of Burgundy was presumably the
chief reason,[61] and it was only when he lost that support that he was driven into
exile in 610.

The point that is relevant for us here is that although Columbanus was
evidently in serious trouble with the Gallic bishops for a period of many years,
Jonas breathes not a word of this. If we had only his *Life of Columbanus* to go
on, and Columbanus's letters had been lost, we would know nothing of the
long-running dissension between him and the bishops. Jonas has skilfully told
the story in such a way that Columbanus's rebuke to Theuderic about his
mistresses and refusal to bless his bastards are portrayed as the sole reasons for
his falling out of favour with Brunechild and Theuderic, who then stir up more
general opposition to his religious practices and Rule, and exile him.[62]

56 Columbanus, *Epistula* II.1–3; *Epistula* I.6 (Walker, *Sancti Columbani opera*, pp. 12–4, 8).
57 Wallace-Hadrill, *Frankish Church*, p. 66. On the context of Columbanus's *Epistula* II, see
N. Wright, 'Columbanus's *Epistulae*', pp. 61–9, 71–2, 76–8.   58 *Epistula* II.5, 6, 8 (Walker,
Sancti Columbani opera, pp. 14, 16–18, 20).   59 *Epistula* II.7: 'si ex Deo est, ut me hinc de
loco deserti ... propellatis ... ' (Walker, *Sancti Columbani opera*, p. 18).   60 Fredegar, *Chronicon*
IV.23 (Wallace-Hadrill, *Fourth Book*, p. 15). For the political background, see Wood,
Merovingian Kingdoms, pp. 131–4.   61 Cf. Jonas, *Vita Columbani* I.19, with its reference to royal
'largitatis ... munera et solaminis supplimentum' (Krusch, p. 190). Note also that Columbanus
again appealed to the papacy with his *Epistula* III (Walker, *Sancti Columbani opera*, pp. 22–5; cf.
p. xxxvii, also Bullough, 'Career of Columbanus', p. 14).   62 Jonas, *Vita Columbani* I.18–19
(Krusch, pp. 189–90 and note). Note the way that Jonas portrays Brunechild as responsible

Columbanus thus appears in the praiseworthy guise of a righteous prophet
speaking out against corrupt royal morals, while responsibility for his exile is
pinned entirely onto Brunechild and her son Theuderic. The story betrays
exceedingly skilful shaping in the hands of Jonas. By the time he was writing,
Brunechild and her family had been overthrown, and their actions denounced
by the rival branch of the Merovingians who supplanted them, namely
Chlothar II and his descendants. Jonas was thus able simultaneously to scapegoat
Brunechild's branch, to justify Chlothar's seizure of power (shown as prophesied
by Columbanus), and to cover up a serious rift between Columbanus and the
Gallic bishops.[63]

A different kind of ecclesiastical dissension is revealed by Columbanus's
fourth letter, written in 610 to Athala and his monks left in Burgundy after he
had been forcibly plucked from them and sent into exile. This letter reveals that
there were major dissensions amongst Columbanus's own monks. Columbanus
stresses the importance of unanimity. He appoints Athala as leader in his stead,
and advises him to depose his opponents, albeit in agreement with the Rule.
However, he is also aware that Athala may not be strong enough to rule the
monks in his absence. He orders those who are rebellious, and will not abide by
the strictness of the Rule, to depart; but by the end of the letter he is foreseeing
the possibility that his own loyal following amongst the monks might not
succeed in maintaining his traditions in the face of opposition, in which case he
advises them to unite with their brethren then accompanying him 'in the
neighbourhood of the Bretons'. Possibly he even envisaged them having to
settle in Brittany.[64] The two issues which are causing dissension are the Easter
question, and the strictness of his Rule; but the matters are treated in different
paragraphs, and the dangers may not lie in quite the same place. Addressing
Athala, he writes:

> If you see danger, come thence. By danger, I mean the danger of dissen-
> sion; for I fear lest, there too, there should be dissension over Easter, lest
> perhaps, through the devil's wiles, they might wish to cast you off, if you
> do not maintain peace with them. For you are seen to be weaker now,
> without me.[65]

Who are the 'they' in this passage, who have the power to cast off Athala? It
seems most likely to be the bishops and their allies amongst the local nobility,

---

for stirring up the nobles and courtiers, and for influencing the bishops to attack
Columbanus's religious witness and his rule. **63** See Wood, *Merovingian Kingdoms*,
pp. 140–3, 194–6. **64** Columbanus, *Epistula* IV.2–4 and 9 (Walker, *Sancti Columbani opera*,
pp. 26–31, 36–7). **65** *Epistula* IV.3 (Walker, *Sancti Columbani opera*, p. 28): 'Timeo enim,
ne et illic propter Pascha sit discordia, ne forte, diabolo insidiante, vos alienare velint, si cum
eis pacem non teneatis.'

perhaps aided by the royal family. It might also be a portion of Columbanus's monks, probably in alliance with one or both of these, but that is perhaps less likely. Let us turn now to consider those with different opinions on the strictness of the Rule. The subject matter would initially suggest that we are here dealing simply with some of the monks. However, Jonas's account of Brunechild and Theuderic's machinations against Luxeuil makes it clear that Columbanus's Rule was also under attack from them, and from the bishops.[66] One further pointer is that (according to Jonas) Eustasius's uncle Mietius, bishop of Langres, was responsible for forcibly separating Eustasius from Columbanus when the latter was exiled.[67] It looks, then, as though we have a very complex situation, with certain aspects of Columbanus's practice, notably his Easter observance and Rule, being simultaneously attacked by the royal family, bishops, and probably nobles from without,[68] and at the same time being to some extent undermined from within by some of Columbanus's Continental recruits, who would have found his Rule harsh, and would have lacked his instinctive and natural loyalty to the Irish position on Easter. This opposition was to surface again during Eustasius's abbacy, as we shall see. In the meantime, however, let us note simply that Jonas's narrative gives no hint that there were any internal dissensions amongst Columbanus's monks, while the antagonism of the nobles and bishops is ascribed solely to Brunechild's influence.[69]

A third occasion when Jonas appears to stay silent about an internal ecclesiastical dissension concerns the quarrel between Columbanus and his disciple, Gall. This occurred in the Bregenz area of the Alps, where Columbanus and his followers had settled after the failure of his attempted deportation from Francia. According to the later Lives of St Gall, Columbanus and his companions ran into trouble with the local population, and were told to leave. But, just at the time that Columbanus decided that they would set out for Italy, Gall was struck down by a fever, and told Columbanus that he would not accompany him. At this, Columbanus excommunicated him (according to the earliest, late-eighth-century Life), or at least forbade him to celebrate mass during Columbanus's lifetime (according to the ninth-century Lives).[70] Now, although this story is first attested about a century and a half after Jonas wrote, it is very probably true in its basic outlines. It can scarcely have been the invention of a St Gall hagiographer, who would have wanted to present his hero in a favourable light; conversely, we can readily understand why Jonas should have omitted it from his own work. It is a credit neither to his own hero, Columbanus, nor to Gall,

---

66 Columbanus, *Epistula* IV.4 (Walker, *Sancti Columbani opera*, pp. 28–30); Jonas, *Vita Columbani* I.19 (Krusch, pp. 189–90).   67 Jonas, *Vita Columbani* I.20 (Krusch, p. 196). 68 See Prinz, *Frühes Mönchtum*, pp. 147–8.   69 Jonas, *Vita Columbani* I.19 (Krusch, pp. 189–90).   70 *Vitae Galli vetustissimae fragmentum*, cap. 1; Wettinus, *Vita atque virtutes beati Galli*, I.9, 26; Walahfrid, *Vita beati Galli*, I.9, 26. All three Lives are edited in Krusch, *Passiones*: see pp. 251–2, 261–2, 270–1, 291, 304–5.

whom he knew personally. On the other hand, it is entirely in keeping with a story included elsewhere in Jonas's Life, which tells how Columbanus, arriving at Luxeuil at a time when its inmates were stricken with various diseases, commanded the monks to rise from their beds and thresh the grain. Obedience was required, even under such circumstances.[71]

We thus have evidence for three cases where Jonas has passed over an internal ecclesiastical dissension in silence: between Columbanus and the Gallic bishops over the Easter question; within Columbanus's own body of monks; and, probably, between Columbanus and Gall. In itself, there is nothing surprising about this. A hagiographer's job was to present his hero as a saint, and normally he also sought to show the church in a favourable light, rather than weaken it by revealing its quarrels and imperfections.[72] What is odd, however, is the very different way in which Jonas handles ecclesiastical dissensions in Book II of the Life, where they figure prominently. The very first chapter of Book II, on Athala, goes into some detail about a monastic rebellion amongst the Bobbio monks against the harshness of Athala's rule. Jonas portrays 'the serpent' as stirring up some of the monks, 'who said they could not bear the authority of an excessive zeal, and were not capable of supporting the weight of the harsh discipline.'[73] When Athala proved unable to pacify them, he allowed the most recalcitrant ones to leave. They 'separated' themselves from him – perhaps broke off communion with him; and some were received 'marinis sinibus' – perhaps into existing monasteries – while others opted for hermitages. Subsequently, however, the fates that befell various of their number prompted first one group, and then the rest, to make their peace with Athala and be received back into the monastery.

The second case of monastic rebellion was even more serious: that of Agrestius against Eustasius of Luxeuil. The story is a dramatic one, told at some length by Jonas in two long chapters amounting to ten pages of text.[74] It completely dominates his account of Eustasius's abbacy, if not Book II as a whole. Here, I give only an outline, which can serve as a basis for further discussion below. Agrestius was well born and well connected. He had had a secular career as a notary under King Theuderic of Burgundy, and so presumably acquired court contacts, before Eustasius's preaching fired him to abandon all and become a monk at Luxeuil. But all too soon, before he was anything more than a beginner (in Eustasius's eyes), he wrung permission from his reluctant abbot to go and

---

71 Jonas, *Vita Columbani* I.12 (Krusch, pp. 172–3).   72 An example occurs in the earliest Class B manuscript, where Jonas's wording in I.5 has been altered so that the poor state of Gallic Christianity is blamed not on the church leaders (*praesules*), but on the secular leaders (*prisci principes*) (Krusch, pp. 112, 161).   73 'Se aiebant nimiae fervoris auctoritatem ferre non posse et arduae disciplinae pondera portare non valere': Jonas, *Vita Columbani* II.1 (Krusch, p. 231). Cf. de Vogüé, *Vie de S. Colomban*, p. 64 and n. 75.   74 Jonas, *Vita Columbani* II.9–10 (Krusch, pp. 246–56).

try his hand at evangelising the Bavarians. Achieving little there, he went to Aquileia in north-east Italy, and there joined their schismatic church. This, though doctrinally orthodox, was in schism with the papacy as a result of divisions in the Italian church known as the 'Three Chapters' controversy. The latter stemmed from Justinian's attempts in the previous century to promote church unity by getting the 'Three Chapters' – works of a Nestorian leaning – condemned. In the west, Justinian's move had been seen as a threat to the faith as defined at the council of Chalcedon. Pope Vigilius had assented to Justinian's demands only under duress, and his actions were widely repudiated in the western church, leading to schism. Since these events in the mid-sixth century the papacy had made up much ground. But in northern Italy, particularly in the patriarchate of Aquileia, opposition to the condemnation of the Three Chapters remained, resulting in continued schism with the papacy. Columbanus himself had had much sympathy with the arguments of the non-papal party, which had been powerfully represented at the Lombard court by Queen Theudelinda and her confessor when he first entered Italy. Nonetheless, his own loyalty to the papacy had kept him from joining the Aquileian party in opposition to the papacy.[75]

Now, however, Agrestius joined them. He sent a 'poisonous' letter to Athala of Bobbio, and then turned his attention to Luxeuil. Having returned there, he sought to persuade Eustasius to join the Aquileian party and break off communion with Rome. Eustasius spent much time in discussion with Agrestius; but, finally, he broke off communion with him. It was at this point, according to Jonas's narrative, that Agrestius turned to launch a wide-ranging attack on Columbanian monasticism in an attempt to win highly-placed supporters for his cause. He attacked Columbanus's religious practices (*religio*) and his Rule, and was able to win the support of powerful backers. These included a number of bishops, first and foremost Abelinus of Geneva, who was a close relative. They also included the most powerful man in Burgundy, Warnachar, who was the Burgundian mayor of the palace and a long-standing enemy of Eustasius. Agrestius's party further attempted to win over Chlothar II. At the king's direction, a synod was held at Mâcon in 626 or 627,[76] and there Agrestius accused Columbanus and his monasticism of being heretical. Fortunately for Luxeuil, Warnachar died shortly before the synod met, and Eustasius's defence was listened to. Although Jonas presents the outcome as positively as he could, there was no real victory for Eustasius. In fact, reading between the lines, it looks as though he was compelled to abandon the most controversial aspects of Columbanus's inheritance, the Irish Easter and

---

75 Columbanus, *Epistula* V (Walker, *Sancti Columbani opera*, pp. 36–56).   76 Warnachar died just before the synod met (Krusch, p. 249); and his death is assigned to the forty-third year of Chlothar's reign by Fredegar (*Chronicon* IV. 54; see Wallace-Hadrill, *Fourth Book*, p. 44).

tonsure.[77] Peace was patched up between Eustasius and Agrestius, but it did not last; for Agrestius continued to undermine Eustasius's position, winning over Romaricus and Amatus of the Luxeuil-affiliated monastery of Remiremont. He even attempted to gain the support of Burgundofara, head of Faremoutiers, but she spurned his advances. In the event Remiremont did not long remain in schism with Luxeuil, for a series of terrifying deaths, culminating in that of Agrestius himself, readily lent themselves to interpretation as 'acts of God' in punishment for their action. So Amatus and Romaricus were led to make their peace with Eustasius, who at this point was probably prevailed upon to modify the austerity of the Rule.[78] The general outcome, as Jonas records it, was a strengthening of Columbanian monasticism, with several bishops now founding monasteries under Columbanus's Rule.

A third case of internal dissension is Jonas's account of the rebellion of some of the Faremoutiers nuns, who tried to flee the monastery under cover of darkness.[79] An initial attempt by a group of nuns was foiled. It would appear to have coincided with a thunderstorm which awoke others in the monastery, rendered the escapees highly visible, and terrified them. They returned and confessed their sins. A second attempt, undertaken by two different women, was successful in that they succeeded in escaping back to their own families; but they were then pursued and forcibly brought back to the monastery. However, they never confessed and mended their ways, and finally they were stricken and saw 'Ethiopians' coming to carry them off as they lay dying. They were buried outside the bounds of the monastic cemetery, and screams from their infernal torments were heard around their graves for some three years. Jonas explicitly comments on how this was specially designed to strike terror into the remaining sisters, to prevent them becoming lukewarm in their religious practice.

The final case of ecclesiastical dissension is Jonas's account of how Abbot Bertulf fought off the bishop of Tortona's attempt to assert his jurisdiction over Bobbio, which lay within his diocese.[80] This occurred in 628, early in Bertulf's abbacy. One can but speculate as to whether there was any connection with the recent council of Mâcon. Although Bobbio lay in the Lombard kingdom, and Luxeuil in Burgundy, the two monasteries remained closely linked; and it may be that the compromise which the Burgundian bishops had forced on Eustasius emboldened the bishop of Tortona to seek control over Bobbio. The bishop of Tortona had canon law on his side. He was able to win the support of neighbouring bishops, and he made a direct appeal to the Lombard king Ariowald. Fortunately, however, a courtier told Bertulf what was afoot, and with royal support, and accompanied by Jonas, he travelled to Rome to appeal in person to Pope Honorius. Honorius enquired carefully after

---

77 See further below. 78 See below, pp. 213–14. 79 Jonas, *Vita Columbani* II.19 (Krusch, pp. 271–5). 80 Jonas, *Vita Columbani* II.23 (Krusch, pp. 281–3).

Bobbio's monastic practices; and, according to Jonas, he was impressed by what he heard about their religious life and practice of humility. But in fact the pope kept Bertulf some time in Rome, urging him to take the gospel to the Arian Lombards. Eventually he granted Bobbio exemption from the supervision of its diocesan bishop, putting it directly under the papacy.

That, in outline, is all that Jonas tells us. Almost certainly, however, the Irish calculation of Easter will also have been one of the subjects which came up for discussion. For Honorius is known to have written to the Irish, urging them to conform to the Continental calculation of Easter, and his letter can reasonably be assigned, on quite independent grounds, to 628/9.[81] Since the papal privilege for Bobbio is dated to 11 June 628,[82] it is a reasonable inference that it was Pope Honorius's enquiries into Bobbio's practices that alerted him in the first place to the fact that the Irish calculated the date of Easter according to different criteria from the Victorian or Dionysian ones favoured on the Continent.[83] Given the line taken by Honorius's letter to the Irish church, we can be sure that one of the preconditions for his taking Bobbio under papal jurisdiction was that it conformed over Easter. Honorius would have been particularly concerned about this since Bobbio's catholic witness against the Lombard Arians, which Jonas tells us was explicitly urged by Honorius, would have been seriously impeded if Bobbio kept a different Easter from other catholic churches.[84]

How should we interpret Jonas's handling of ecclesiastical dissension? It is certainly highly selective; and a basic distinction appears to lie between Book I, where Jonas passes silently over Columbanus's dispute with the Burgundian bishops and over the painful divisions within Columbanus's own monastic community, and Book II, where he narrates Bertulf's conflict with the local bishop together with monastic rebellions at Bobbio, Luxeuil and Faremoutiers in considerable detail. How should we account for this contrast?

Two suggestions can be made, which, taken together, at least help to account for Jonas's apparent inconsistencies. The first is that Jonas was happy, if not eager, to include stories of such dissensions provided that the outcome showed God's judgement being visited on the wicked, that is, on the enemies of Columbanian monasticism. His view of moral edification embraced the wretched ends of evil-doers as readily as a happy outcome for the righteous. This explanation certainly fits Jonas's treatment of the rebel nuns at Faremoutiers well. It does not, however, apply to the story of Bertulf and the bishop of Tortona (who simply fades out of the story, rather than being visited with

81 See Walsh and Ó Cróinín, *Cummian's Letter*, pp. 4–6. 82 Krusch, *Ionae Vitae*, p. 283 n.1. 83 On this, see Charles-Edwards, *Early Christian Ireland*. 84 Columbanus's *Epistula* V is forceful testimony to the harm done to the catholic witness against Arianism by divisions within the catholic fold over the Three Chapters controversy. Honorius, aware of this still unresolved problem, would have been anxious to avoid yet another division within the catholic fold in northern Italy.

divine judgement); and even in the case of the rebellious monk Agrestius, where the theme of divine judgement is very prominent, one might question whether the damaging detail about Agrestius's accusation of heresy against Luxeuil did not constitute an 'own goal', outweighing any likely gain.

The second suggestion is that Jonas was able to stay silent about the opposition during Columbanus's own lifetime because it had happened sufficiently far in the past. This allowed him to recast the story in such a way that blame accrued only to Brunechild and her descendants, and not to bishops and monks, without his contemporaries being aware of anything untoward in his presentation. On the other hand Agrestius's rebellion, which led to the important synod of Macôn, had occurred only some fifteen years previously, and could not have been passed over without people being aware of distorting omissions in the history of Columbanian monasticism. Initially, this approach has much to commend it; but its weakness lies in the fact that, if adopted, it leads one inexorably to pose the obvious question we have already considered: why, in that case, did not Jonas opt to write simply a Life of Columbanus himself, rather than deciding to cover the entire history of Columbanian monasticism down to the present?

In addition to the inadequacies of these suggestions, one further point will not have escaped the reader: Jonas was still 'shaping' (or distorting) his account of events of the comparatively recent past, as we have seen with our discussion of the synod of Macôn and of Pope Honorius's response to Abbot Bertulf of Bobbio. Perhaps, then, the contrast between Book I and Book II of Jonas's Life is to some extent more apparent than real. Jonas has recast both the more distant and the more recent past, where it seemed advisable and possible to do so; but whereas Columbanus's own letters enable us to see at least some distortions of his Book I very clearly, the lack of such independent evidence for most of the events covered by Book II makes it seem as though Jonas was presenting these more faithfully. In reality, however, Jonas was creatively rewriting his entire account of the story of both Columbanus and his disciples. Let us therefore explore the background against which Jonas wrote in more detail, to see if we can understand what, precisely, he was doing in his *Vita Columbani discipulorumque eius*.

III JONAS'S TASK AND ACHIEVEMENT

One significant point to emerge from our previous discussion is the serious and long-lasting nature of the opposition to Columbanus and his followers. From the time of our earliest evidence, Columbanus's epistle 1 addressed to Gregory the Great *c*.600, we see Columbanus's poor opinion of those Gallic bishops guilty of simony or continuing sexual relationships with their wives. Meanwhile, judging from his appeal to the pope over the errors of Victorius's Easter cycle,

Columbanus had already been criticised by them because of his adherence to the Irish mode of reckoning Easter. Columbanus's second letter, to the bishops at the council of Chalon (603/4), brings this mutual antagonism into the open. By the time of his expulsion from Luxeuil in 610 there were significant pressures from within his community to relax his rigorous monastic Rule, as well as continuing pressure from without to conform on the Easter question. After Columbanus's death, Athala survived a monastic rebellion in a way that looks extraordinarily like the scenario that Columbanus had sketched in this earlier letter.[85] The fact that the rebellious monks opposed his harsh discipline, that Athala had earlier abandoned the laxity of Lérins for Luxeuil, and that he had been Columbanus's own trusted successor, all imply that there was no relaxation of the strictness of the Rule at that time.[86] This long-standing opposition to Columbanian monasticism culminated in Agrestius's attack and the subsequent synod of Mâcon. This linked together the internal rebelliousness of some of the monks with external attacks from leading nobles and bishops of the Burgundian kingdom. The personalities as well as the issues involved connect the earlier and the later opposition. On one side stood Columbanus and his disciples Athala and Eustasius. On the other stood Aridius, metropolitan bishop of Lyons and a political ally of Brunechild, who had presided over the synod of Chalon, and been abandoned by the young Athala; his suffragan Mietius, bishop of Langres and uncle of Eustasius, whom he sought to part from Columbanus when the latter was exiled; and Warnachar, the Burgundian mayor of the palace. Although by the time of Agrestius's attack Columbanus and Aridius were dead, continuity of factions is implied by Eustasius and Athala on the one hand, and on the other by Warnachar, a long-standing enemy of Eustasius by the time of the Mâcon synod.[87]

Thus the first decade after Columbanus's death did indeed see continuity in the issues that divided his followers from a powerful Burgundian group of bishops and aristocrats in his own lifetime. By the time that Jonas was writing, however, there had been significant changes. Jonas himself came to accept the Easter reckoning of Victorius of Aquitaine: he cited it openly at the beginning of his Life of John of Reomé, written in 659. Also, as we have seen, there are good reasons to think that Bobbio had changed its Easter reckoning many years previously, in 628, while Luxeuil had probably conformed on Easter as a result of the synod of Mâcon.[88] The second major change is that at some point the monastic Rule according to which Luxeuil and Bobbio lived was altered. Whereas originally it was that composed by Columbanus himself,[89] Eligius's

85 Cf. Columbanus, *Epistula* IV.2–4 (Walker, *Sancti Columbani opera*, pp. 26–30); Jonas, *Vita Columbani* II.1 (Krusch, p. 231).   86 See below, pp. 213–14.   87 Prinz, *Frühes Mönchtum*, pp. 147–8.   88 *Vita Iohannis abbatis Reomaensis*, edited in Krusch, *Ionae Vitae*, p. 326. Above, p. 208; below, p. 213.   89 Jonas, *Vita Columbani* I.10 (Krusch, p. 170). It is not clear

charter for Solignac, dated to 632, implies that by then Luxeuil had adopted the mixed Rule of Benedict and Columbanus. The same or a similar mixed Rule was in place in Bobbio by 643, when it is mentioned in a papal exemption.[90] Now there is reasonable evidence for arguing that Columbanus himself had been somewhat influenced by the *Rule of St Benedict* when he composed his *Regula monachorum*. He appears to echo it at the beginning (though a common parallel with other, earlier Rules complicates the matter), again in his placing a section on the virtues of obedience and silence immediately following on one another, and finally in the very idea of composing a Rule which succinctly outlines the chief monastic virtues.[91] The general tenor of his *Monks' Rule*, however, with its emphasis on total obedience to an abbot, its heavy burden of psalmody in the night offices, and its uncompromising high standards, is very different from Benedict's Rule 'for beginners', which explicitly seeks to avoid any harshness.[92] Thus Benedict's Rule was known in Columbanus's monasteries in his own lifetime, but did not at that period have extensive influence on Columbanian monastic life.

The date at which Columbanus's Rule gave way to the mixed Rule in Columbanus's monasteries has been much discussed, but the most plausible hypothesis is that it occurred about a year after the synod of Mâcon.[93] As we have seen, opposition to Columbanus's Rule was one of the points which consistently recurred, in Burgundy in 610 and the preceding years, at Bobbio early in Athala's abbacy, and around the time of the synod of Mâcon. The opposition from Columbanus's monks in 610 and those who rebelled against Athala *c.*616 was directed at aspects which weighed harshly on those living under the Rule. On the other hand, the criticisms of King Theuderic in the

whether Jonas was referring to Columbanus's *Regula monachorum* or *Regula coenobialis*, or both. The two are complementary; see Stevenson, 'Monastic Rules', pp. 206–7. 90 See Prinz, *Frühes Mönchtum*, p. 268 and n. 13, p. 146 and n. 130; de Vogüé, *Vie de S. Colomban*, pp. 67–9. For the Solignac charter see Krusch, *Passiones*, pp. 746–9, esp. p. 747. That for Rebais-en-Brie (635) mentions only Benedict (Prinz, *Frühes Mönchtum*, p. 125)! 91 De Vogüé, *Règle de saint Benoît*, i.163–6; idem, *Colomban: Règles*, pp. 42–3, 47–8, 53–5. For the text of Columbanus's *Regula monachorum*, see Walker, *Sancti Columbani opera*, pp. 122–40 (note that §10 is a later addition). The verbal parallel with the *Rule of St Benedict* near the beginning of Columbanus's section on obedience is complicated by parallels with Basil and with the *Rule of the Master*, though the *Rule of St Benedict* is marginally closer. 92 *Rule of St Benedict* prologue, and cap. 73. On the contrast between Columbanus's insistence on obedience to the abbot, as opposed to the *Rule of St Benedict*'s emphasis on obedience to the Rule, see Guerout, 'Fare', col. 522. 93 See below; cf. Krusch, *Ionae Vitae*, p. 38. Prinz's objection, that the introduction of the mixed Rule as a result of the synod of Mâcon would imply that the *Rule of St Benedict* was already in general use in Burgundy (*Frühes Mönchtum*, p. 287), carries no weight. The synod of Mâcon might have criticised certain Columbanian practices; and in response Eustasius might himself have decided to modify Columbanian practices by making large-scale adjustments, using the *Rule of St Benedict*, already known there, as his model.

period leading up to Columbanus's exile were that Columbanus differed from
the customs of Gallic monasteries, and would not allow all Christians into the
inner parts of his monasteries.[94] Given that this comes in the context of
Brunechild stirring up the bishops by attacking Columbanus's *religio* and *regula*,
it may well be that what we have here is an oblique reference not just to
Columbanus's refusal to allow non-religious into the inner bounds of the monasteries, but also to his refusal to accept any form of episcopal supervision. It can
also be plausibly suggested that Jonas's reference to an attack on Columbanus's
religio may be a coded way of referring to an attack on his Irish Easter.[95]

Many years later, Agrestius also attacked Columbanus's *religio* and his *regula*,
and won over several bishops.[96] In Jonas's account of the synod of Mâcon, the
criticisms to which he devoted most space were ones which Eustasius had no
difficulty in refuting: blessing spoons with the sign of the cross before eating
with them, making the sign of the cross when coming and going, and the
multiplication of prayers at the liturgy. Agrestius's accusation of heresy, and his
criticism of the Columbanian tonsure, which might also have ranked as a major
issue, are both slipped in by Jonas in a way that does not attract attention.[97] The
Easter question is conspicuous by its absence. After Eustasius had challenged
Agrestius to judgement at the hands of God, peace was made between them,
and the synod concluded. But Agrestius subsequently went to Romaricus and
Amatus at the recently founded monastery of Remiremont, which was affiliated
to Luxeuil. Amatus had been sent here by Eustasius to teach the Rule, but
Agrestius struck a sympathetic chord with him through his tempting suggestions;
for both Romaricus and Amatus were exasperated at having recently been
upbraided by Eustasius 'for neglecting certain things'. They were therefore
ready to receive Agrestius's 'poisoned words' and 'to propagate his madness in
contempt of the Rule of the blessed Columbanus'.[98] After a series of disasters
befell the inmates of Remiremont, including rabid wolves, a suicide, twenty
deaths resulting from a lightning strike, and concluding with Agrestius's own
violent death, Amatus and Romaricus made their peace with Eustasius. Jonas
immediately follows this statement with the information that after this,
Abelenus and the other Gallic bishops sought to strengthen Columbanus's
instituta, and he acclaims the number of monasteries which were now founded 'out
of love for Columbanus and his Rule.' Those named included Solignac, where, as
we have seen, the Rule prescribed was that of Benedict and Columbanus.[99]

---

94 Jonas, *Vita Columbani* I.19 (Krusch, p. 190).   **95** Charles-Edwards, *Early Christian
Ireland*.   **96** Jonas, *Vita Columbani* II.9 (Krusch, p. 248).   **97** Jonas, *Vita Columbani* II.9
(Krusch, pp. 249–51). In England the tonsure does not seem to have been a major issue *c*.603,
but it was by 664: cf. Bede, *Historia ecclesiastica* II.2 and III.25–6 (Colgrave and Mynors, pp.
134–6, 138 and 296–8, 308). In general see James, 'Tonsure Question', esp. pp. 95–8.
98 Jonas, *Vita Columbani* II.10 (Krusch, pp. 252–3).   **99** 'Amatus vero ac Romaricus
venerabilis Eusthasii conibentiam postulantes recipiunt atque, desidia submota, fruuntur.

Now, Abelenus of Geneva was a relative and partisan of Agrestius. What had happened to make him and the other bishops change from opposition to promotion of Columbanian monasticism?

We should note two points about Jonas's account of the actual synod of Mâcon. First, the only substantial matters raised by Agrestius, those of heresy and of the tonsure, receive no justificatory answer from Eustasius. Secondly, the Easter question is conspicuous by its absence – unless it is covertly alluded to in the heresy accusation, which may well be the case.[100] Given Jonas's readiness to pass over Columbanus's summons to the synod of Chalon without a word, his silence here certainly does not mean that the Easter question was not raised.[101] Rather, Krusch must be right in arguing that the bishops would never have made peace with Luxeuil unless it had first conformed on Easter – and perhaps, we should add, on the tonsure too.[102]

Krusch also thought that the Columbanian Rule was emended at the same time.[103] In view of Agrestius's behaviour after the synod of Mâcon, however, it appears more likely that, for all his attacks, the Rule was not changed at Mâcon itself, but shortly afterwards, presumably at the time when Amatus and Romaricus made their peace with Eustasius. For it is at this point in the story, and not at the synod, that Jonas places the approbation of Abelenus and other bishops for Columbanus's *instituta*. This would have occurred about a year after the synod of Mâcon;[104] and it may be that there was some form of (episcopal?) mediation between Eustasius, on the one hand, and Amatus and Romaricus, on the other, which has gone unmentioned by Jonas, but which led Eustasius to modify the severity of Columbanus's Rule by admixture with that of Benedict. Perhaps Jonas's use here of the word *instituta*, rather than the more precise *regula*, was carefully chosen in order to convey the general impression that Columbanus's monasticism was approved, while still allowing for it being a modified Rule that won this approbation.[105] One factor which might explain

---

Abelenus vero vel ceteri Galliarum episcopi post ad roboranda Columbani instituta adspirant. Quam multi iam in amore Columbani et eius regula monasteria construunt, plebes adunant, greges Christi congregant. Inter quos inluster tunc vir Elegius ... iuxta Lemovicensem urbem monasterium nobile Sollemniacum nomine construxit ... ' (Jonas, *Vita Columbani* II.10 [Krusch, p. 255]).   100 Wood appears to interpret Agrestius's heresy accusation as arising from his pro-Three Chapters, and so anti-papal, standpoint: *Merovingian Kingdoms*, p. 196. But if that had been the case, Jonas would surely have put a pro-papal refutation into Eustasius's mouth. The fact that no such refutation is given suggests that the accusation could not easily be gainsaid; and the Irish Easter and tonsure are probable butts for such an accusation.   101 So, naively, Walker, *Sancti Columbani opera*, p. xxxiii n. 2.   102 Krusch, *Ionae Vitae*, p. 38.   103 Loc. cit.   104 Eustasius challenged Agrestius to undergo God's judgement 'within a year', and he met his end thirty days before the year was up. Jonas then passes immediately to Amatus and Romaricus making their peace with Eustasius: Jonas, *Vita Columbani* II.10 (Krusch, pp. 251, 254–5).   105 Cf. de Vogüé, *Vie de S. Colomban*, pp. 66–7. *Instituta* was skilfully chosen, as it recalls Cassian's work, a major influence on Columbanus.

Eustasius's willingness to make this concession a year after Macôn is the death around this time of Athala, probably on 10 March 626.[106] In Jonas's account, Athala comes across as an unflinching proponent of the most exacting standards, in the same mould as Columbanus;[107] and he may well have held out against any relaxation of the Rule. Since Jonas specifically mentions the unanimity between Eustasius and Athala, and the freedom with which monks could transfer from one monastery to the other,[108] it may be that Athala stiffened Eustasius's resolve against any compromise in his lifetime, but that after his death Eustasius was more willing to modify the Columbanian Rule. In some ways, changes in the monastic Rule may have been less complicated than we might think. At this period, much was governed by the abbot and by tradition, rather than by a written Rule, and much of the *Rule of St Benedict* is taken up with issues which Columbanus did not cover in either of his Rules.[109] Thus, on the one hand, the abbot would have the power to introduce many changes which involved no alteration to the written Rule, since they had always been regulated by unwritten custom.[110] On the other hand, there were many respects in which the *Rule of St Benedict* could be used alongside Columbanus's Rules to complement, rather than replace, their provisions. These factors, taken together with Columbanus's own (albeit limited) use of the *Rule of St Benedict*, would have eased the transition for Columbanian monasteries.

Nonetheless, some explanation is required to account for the fact that the bishops, after fifteen years of hostility to Columbanus's Rule, are now found promoting it; and the obvious explanation is that this was the period which saw the Columbanian monasteries paying some heed to the bishops, modifying the austere Columbanian Rule, and introducing provisions from the *Rule of St Benedict* on a large scale. Fortunately this change can be dated independently to Eustasius's abbacy (615–29). For Eustasius was responsible for sending Chagnoald and Waldebert to teach the Rule to Burgundofara's monastery of Faremoutiers, and this Rule has survived and been identified. It is a mixed Rule, approximately three quarters Benedictine to one quarter Columbanian – and this despite Jonas's claim that Faremoutiers lived according to the Rule of Columbanus![111] Although this Rule is now generally attributed to Waldebert, whose role in the diffusion of the mixed Benedictine and Columbanian Rule is elsewhere attested,[112] it was

---

106 See Krusch, *Ionae Vitae*, p. 240 n. 1, and p. 286 n. 1. Cf. de Vogüé, *Vie de S. Colomban*, p. 19. 107 Jonas, *Vita Columbani* II.1, 6 (Krusch, pp. 230–1, 238–40); cf. above, n. 73. 108 Jonas, *Vita Columbani* II.23 (Krusch, p. 281). 109 Cf. Charles-Edwards, *Early Christian Ireland*; de Vogüé, *Colomban: Règles*, pp. 32–3. 110 Cf. Moyse, 'Monachisme et réglementation', p. 6. 111 Jonas, *Vita Columbani* II.7, and cf. II.11 (Krusch, pp. 243, 257). See Guerout, 'Fare', cols 520–1; Guerout and Chaussy, 'Faremoutiers', cols 535–6; Toucas, 'Regula Waldeberti', col. 1603. The *Regula cuiusdam patris ad virgines* was identified by Gougaud, 'Inventaire', pp. 326–31. 112 *Vita Sadalbergae abbatissae Laudunensis*, cap. 8: ed. Krusch and Levison, *Passiones*, p. 54. But this Life is 'of uncertain worth': Wood, *Merovingian Kingdoms*, p. 187.

Eustasius who sent Waldebert to Faremoutiers. Presumably, then, Waldebert was acting in accordance with Eustasius's wishes; and this implies that Luxeuil itself had by now modified its own Rule. As we have seen, the foundation charter for Solignac of 632 confirms that, by that date, Luxeuil was living according to the mixed Rule.

This complex background shows that Jonas faced an unusually delicate task in seeking to write the Life of Columbanus. He, and the communities for whom he wrote, genuinely wanted to honour their founder. At the same time he had to be extremely careful. He could not afford to be too open about the accusations which had been made against Columbanus, for the latter had in fact been accused of heresy at the synod of Macôn, probably because of his Easter reckoning. He may also have been similarly accused by the Gallic bishops in his own lifetime. What is more, Columbanus's communities had in a sense recognised that their founder was at fault, for they had changed their Easter reckoning and modified their founder's Rule. At least two of the abbots concerned with Jonas's writing of the Life, Bertulf and Waldebert, had themselves been involved in these changes; and as a result of them, several bishops who had formerly opposed Columbanian monasticism were now prepared actively to support it. Jonas's readership might well have included some of these bishops, as well as the abbots and inmates of Columbanian monasteries. So how was Jonas to handle this explosive brief: honouring Columbanus, but in a way that did not reflect badly on his episcopal opponents or his monastic successors, who had broken with some of his deeply cherished practices?

Jonas's consummate skill as a hagiographer emerges from the way in which he responded to this challenge. First, he told the story of Columbanus's life, omitting any reference to the major issues on which, in many people's eyes, Columbanus had been heretical. He also omitted the fact that Columbanus's earliest and most persistent critics were the Gallic bishops. Instead he pinned responsibility for the opposition to Columbanus entirely onto Brunechild and Theuderic, whom he portrayed as reacting indignantly against Columbanus's righteous outspokenness on royal immorality. This was brilliant propaganda. There was good hagiographical precedent for portraying a holy man upbraiding a king, and suffering because of it. Jonas was particularly fortunate in that he was able to blacken Brunechild and Theuderic as much as he wished, since he was writing at a time when a rival branch of the Merovingians was in power in Francia.

Secondly, Jonas skilfully fudged the issues on which Columbanus had been attacked. In his account of the great monastic founder, he never let on that Columbanus himself had been branded as heretical, or that his Easter and tonsure had come in for criticism. In Book II he did admit to dissension in the Columbanian monasteries; but here he portrayed it either as rebellion against the rigours of a strict Rule, or, in the case of Agrestius's attack at the synod of Macôn, as focused largely on inessentials, such as the frequency with which the sign of the cross was made or the additional prayers in the liturgy. This meant that, never having admitted that Columbanus had been attacked on the Easter question, and giving no space in his account of Macôn to the issues of heresy or the tonsure, he never had to admit that Columbanus's successors had changed these.

Thirdly, he sought to deflect attention from Agrestius's criticisms by slipping in the important ones in places where they would receive little attention, and simultaneously by seeking to discredit Agrestius. Just as Brunechild is cast as a Jezebel figure,[113] and made the scapegoat in Book I, so Agrestius is cast as a Judas figure, and fulfils the same role in Book II. At the beginning of the story Jonas portrays Agrestius as being stirred up to opposition by the devil, who sought to bring forth another Cain to slay his brother, or another traitor to destroy his master's teaching – the latter presumably a reference to Judas.[114] At the actual synod of Macôn, Agrestius is portrayed as speaking 'with trembling lips' – a phrase which may deliberately echo that used by Sulpicius Severus when describing an outrageous attack on St Martin by his disciple Brice, another Judas-like figure.[115] Jonas follows this up by portraying God's vengeance falling on Agrestius in a spectacular way. After Agrestius had made his accusation about the Luxeuil tonsure differing from that used elsewhere, Jonas has Eustasius submit these accusations to the judgement of God:

> 'In the presence of these bishops, I, the disciple and successor of him whose teaching and Rule you condemn – I challenge you to the divine tribunal to dispute with him within the course of the present year, so that you may feel the sentence of the just judge, whose servant you seek to stain with your evil speaking.'[116]

Agrestius – again like Judas – feigned peace with Eustasius, but then proceeded to tempt Romaricus and Amatus to join him; and this is followed by an extraordinary sequence of events, designed to show God's judgement being visited on Agrestius and his associates. Rabid wolves, suicide and lightning strike the unhappy inmates of Remiremont who are seduced by Agrestius's teaching; and finally, just before the year was up, Agrestius himself was killed by a servant. Jonas draws the moral explicitly: 'The just sentence of the divine

---

113 See Nelson, 'Queens as Jezebels', pp. 57–9.   114 Jonas, *Vita Columbani* II.9 (Krusch, p. 246).   115 'At ille *trementibus labiis* … ': Jonas, *Vita Columbani* II.9 (Krusch, p. 249). Cf. Sulpicius Severus, '*trementibus labiis* incertoque uultu decolor prae furore rotabat uerba peccati … ': *Dialogus* III.xv.4 (Halm, *Sulpicii Severi libri*, p. 214); the parallel with Judas Iscariot is explicitly drawn in II.xv.7. For Jonas's knowledge of Sulpicius's work, see above p. 199 and n. 44. However, Jonas used exactly the same phrase, 'trementibus labiis', when describing a virtuous young virgin of Faremoutiers who deserved to see the heavens open (Jonas, *Vita Columbani* II.15 [Krusch, p. 266, lines 7–8]), so we should not put too much emphasis on his use of the phrase here.   116 Jonas, *Vita Columbani* II.10 (Krusch, p. 251).

judgement did not delay striking him at this point, in order to show his supporters that they should shun attacking the servants of God, and also so that Agrestius should expiate his contumacy by receiving the vengeance he deserved.'[117]

Jonas had a further stratagem for deflecting attention away from areas where Columbanus had been sharply criticised and his successors had made changes, this time with reference to his Rule and practice of monasticism. Here, as we have seen, Jonas never admits that the Rule had come under criticism from some of Columbanus's monks within his lifetime;[118] but after his death, the theme of monastic rebellion looms large. In Jonas's account, however, opposition to the Rule from within the monasteries is always portrayed as the act of rebellious spirits who are either brought to their senses and repent, or, if they persist in their rebellious frame of mind, are doomed to retribution in this world or the next. There is never any admission that the rebels had a case, and never any admission that Columbanus's original Rule was softened under his successors. On the contrary – and here Jonas's skill emerges – Jonas subtly goes out of his way to emphasise elements of continuity between the monasticism of Columbanus and that of his successors. He is particularly eloquent in this respect about Eustasius, his successor at Luxeuil: 'When he [Eustasius] was regarded favourably by all, one who was steeped in Columbanus's teaching, so that no one lamented the loss of the blessed Columbanus, especially when they saw the *instituta* of the master remaining in the disciple ... '.[119] If we recall that it was seemingly under Eustasius that the austerity of Columbanus's Rule was mitigated by admixture with the *Rule of St Benedict*, then this passage appears disingenuous. It is an example of the preacher's legendary rubric: 'argument weak: shout.' Besides this particular passage, continuity of monastic practice is also affirmed by the way in which common themes are emphasised in both Book I and Book II: the most obvious are those of 'the medicines of penance', and of obedience,[120] both of which were acceptable to the bishops at the time that Jonas was writing.

Thus, what Jonas is doing in his *Vita Columbani discipulorumque eius* is presenting us with a skilfully doctored version of the story of Columbanus and his monastic successors. It is certainly meant to serve the obvious hagiographical functions of portraying Columbanus and his abbatial successors as holy men, preserving their memory, and of fostering the monastic movement which they had established. Equally, however, it is an attempt to come to terms with the controversies which had dogged so much of their past; and here, we should

---

117 Jonas, *Vita Columbani* II.10 (Krusch, p. 254).   118 On the contrary, cf. Jonas, *Vita Columbani* I.10 (Krusch, p. 170): 'mente una et cor unum'.   119 Jonas, *Vita Columbani* II.9 (Krusch, p. 246).   120 For references see de Vogüé, *Vie de S. Colomban*, pp. 55–6, 58–9; Wood, '*Vita Columbani*', pp. 73, 66–7.

ponder a passage in Jonas's dedicatory letter to the current abbots of Luxeuil and Bobbio:

> We have included those things which we know, through true statements, were accomplished; and we have decided to omit those things – and many are omitted – which we cannot remember in full, and which we have definitely decided not to write in part. I have divided the material set down into two short books, in order to avoid boredom for those reading one long volume: the first book tells in brief the deeds of the blessed Columbanus, the second one sets out the life of his disciples Athala, Eustasius, and others whom we remember. We think that these things ought to be weighed in your balance, so that having been approved by you in a searching examination, they may drive out uncertainty from everyone else. For if anyone should find things not strictly clear and carefully corrected, he will judge that they should be rejected – especially if, endowed with the eloquence of learned men, he abounds in knowledge.[121]

Jonas's Latin is here at its most obscure: perhaps deliberately so. The initial sentence makes it clear that he has been selective in his choice of material. But the most interesting passage is that where Jonas asks abbots Waldebert and Bobolenus to vet his work, so that his account can be 'approved' by them, and 'drive out uncertainty from everyone else'.[122] When set against the long history of opposition to Columbanus and his monasticism, discussed above, the full import of this sentence begins to emerge. It looks as though Jonas has taken on the task of producing an 'official' version of the story of Columbanus and the monastic movement that he founded, and that he here seeks the approval of the current abbots of Luxeuil and Bobbio for his selective and skilfully slanted account. Other versions of the story (which might, for instance, have cast Agrestius as a figure with some points in his favour) are to be displaced. The reference to Jonas's version driving out uncertainty from *ceteris* perhaps implies that the ructions of past disputes were still reverberating. Jonas has thus tried to retell the story in a way that brings together, into a common enterprise, both Columbanus, and many of those who had originally opposed him.[123]

Once we realise this, we are able to perceive the reason for the two-book structure of the Life adopted by Jonas. Book II was an essential part of Jonas's

---

121 Jonas, *Vita Columbani*, prefatory letter (Krusch, p. 147). I am grateful to Richard Sharpe for help with this translation.   122 'Ea ergo vestro libramine pensanda censemus, ut a vobis sagaci examinatione probata, a ceteris ambiguitatem pellant; nam si quippiam aliquis non rite distincta ac de industria correcta reppererit, reicienda iudicabit, praesertim si doctorum facundia fultus, affatim scientia oppletus habundet.'   123 There is a parallel here with the scenario which has recently been argued for the production of the late seventh-century *Passio Praeiecti*: Fouracre and Gerberding, *Late Merovingian France*, pp. 255–67, esp. 266–7.

design, for he was not simply producing a worthy Life of their founder. He was also concerned to do justice to those who had opposed and changed Columbanus's own practices in certain areas while nonetheless cherishing the tradition that he had founded. Somehow, Jonas had to find a way of including the *rapprochement* between Luxeuil and the bishops, which had come out of the synod of Mâcon or the subsequent reconciliation between Luxeuil and Remiremont the following year. This meant that the story of Agrestius had to be told, albeit in a partisan way; and one reason for giving such prominence to Burgundofara's religious community may have been to provide a counterweight to this. Whereas Agrestius had been able to win over Romaricus and Amatus at Remiremont, he was roundly repulsed by Burgundofara.[124] By including the section of miracles from her monastery of Faremoutiers, Jonas was illustrating the living out of the reformed Columbanian monasticism in a house with an unimpeachable record. It was important for Jonas to include the Columbanian monasticism of his own day, because that at least could be held up as exemplary to his contemporary audience, whatever doubts there might have been about some of Columbanus's own practices.

* * *

This paper has concentrated on two specific areas of Jonas's *Vita Columbani discipulorumque eius*: the two-book structure of the Life, and its handling of dissension. It makes no pretence at being a full, rounded study; different aspects have been fruitfully discussed by other scholars. Nonetheless, exploration of the topics addressed here has led us to think more deeply about the circumstances which lay behind the writing of the Life, and Jonas's intentions in writing; and these must lie at the heart of any attempt to understand a hagiographer and his work. In addition to contributing to our understanding in these areas, it is perhaps worth drawing out two more general points which emerge from this study.

The first is that we have to be exceedingly careful when we are using Jonas's Life as a source of historical information. The individual stories he relates are probably based on actual happenings; but sometimes matters of the greatest significance are merely hinted at; and we absolutely cannot trust his silences. This means, for instance, that we should not assume that Columbanus did not run into trouble with the Gallic episcopate on account of his infringements of episcopal rights and refusal to be subject to his diocesan bishop, just because Jonas says nothing of this. Jonas could well have suppressed information on this point, and Columbanus's own correspondence is demonstrably incomplete. More generally, it is theoretically possible that there were Irish traits in Columbanus's living out of the ascetic life, which have gone unrecorded by

---

124 Jonas, *Vita Columbani* II.10 (Krusch, pp. 252–3).

Jonas.[125] Of course Jonas presents him as being in the same mould as St Martin and other Continental saints: that is what we should expect. But we must be very careful not to make deductions from Jonas's silences.

The second point to emerge from this study is Jonas's skill as a hagiographer. The task that he undertook was a formidable one, and there are undeniable weaknesses in the structure of Book II. However, the Life served its apologetic purpose superbly: it was able to forge an identity for the modified Columbanian monasticism of Jonas's day, while still preserving its links with their founder, whom it honoured in exemplary fashion. It is a measure of Jonas's skill as a hagiographer that we, as historians, are still attempting to penetrate the truth lying behind his carefully chosen words.

Figure 1. The Contents of the Main Branches of Krusch's Class A
Manuscripts Containing Jonas's Book II.

Krusch's Sigla	Manuscript	Jonas Bk I Columbanus	Clare sacerdos	Nostris sollemnis	Bk II, 1–6 Athala	Bk II, 7–10 Eustasius	Bk II, 11–22 Faremoutiers	Bk II, 2 Bertulf Bobbio monk
A1a	St Gall 553	————————————————————						———
A1b	Brussels, BRoy, 8518–20	————————————			————————————			
A1c	Würzburg, Universitätsbib. M.P. Th. F.139	—————————————————————						
A1d	Trier, Dombibl. 5	———			———————————————			
A2	Paris, BN lat. 5600	———			———————————————			
A2a	The Hague, Kon.Bib.X.73[126]	————————————————————					———	
[Tosi, A3]	Metz, Bib. Gr. Sém. 1	————————————————————————				———		

125 Contrast Wood, '*Vita Columbani*', pp. 71–6, 80.   126 This MS begins a Book III with Faremoutiers, comprising Jonas II.11–25. Additional texts, including Jonas's chapters on Eustasius (albeit now defective) were subsequently prefixed to this MS: Krusch, *Ionae Vitae*, pp. 85–6.

The Cult of Columba in Lotharingia (9th–11th Centuries): The Manuscript Evidence

Jean-Michel Picard

In spite of its importance for the modern hagiographer, Adomnán's *Vita Columbae* (VC) had a relatively small circulation in the Middle Ages and survives in few manuscripts. The total amounts to only 28 manuscripts including versions derived from Adomnán's original text, such as the Lives by pseudo-Cumméne (BHL 1884–5) and from the *Codex Salmanticensis* (BHL 1890). In their *Bibliotheca Hagiographica Latina*, the Bollandists listed three recensions of Adomnán's *Vita Columbae*:

- The first recension, BHL 1886, is the long version edited by Reeves and the Andersons, based on the famous Schaffhausen manuscript written in Iona by Dorbbéne (died 713), and on three manuscripts derived from an exemplar written in Scotland in the twelfth century.[1] Three other manuscripts originating in France also belong to this recension.[2]
- The second recension, BHL 1887, is the abridged version published in Migne's *Patrologia Latina*. It originated in the Bodensee region in the ninth century, and from there spread throughout Germany and Austria to become the most widely known version during the Middle Ages. It has survived in 13 manuscripts.[3]
- The third recension, BHL 1889, has never been published and is the subject of this talk. The text originated in Upper Lotharingia and more precisely in the area of the city of Metz. This recension is a short version of the *Vita Columbae* which is roughly one sixth of the length of the full version and

---

1 Anderson and Anderson, *Life of Columba*, pp. 3–18; Sharpe, *Life of St Columba*, pp. 235–7.
2 Metz, Grand Séminaire, 1 (s. IX) < Saint-Mihiel de Lorraine; Florence, Biblioteca Medicea Laurenziana, Ashburnham 58 (s. XI–XII); Paris, Bibliothèque Nationale, lat. 5323 (s. XII) < Western France; in these last two manuscripts, Adomnán's phraseology has been substantially modified. 3 PL lxxxviii.725–76; see list of manuscripts in Brüning, 'Adamnans Vita Columbae', pp. 220–1. Two other manuscripts must be added to Brüning's list: London, British Library, Add. 19726 (s. XI) < Bavaria; and Klosterneuburg, Augustinerkloster, 707 (s. XII).

consists of only one preface, the first chapter of book one and the last eight chapters of book three. It has survived in two manuscripts both of which originated in the Metz region: Paris, Bibliothèque Nationale de France, lat. 5308 (s. XII) ff. 287v–292 and Paris, Bibliothèque Nationale de France, lat. 5278 (s. XIII) ff. 393–399. A third and older manuscript – Metz, Bibliothèque Municipale, 523 (s. XI) ff. 51–65 < Saint-Arnoul, Metz – contained the same text but was destroyed at the end of the second World War. Fortunately this manuscript had previously been studied by Krusch, Brüning and Levison.[4]

Like the second recension (BHL 1887), the Metz document is an abridgement of Adomnán's original text, but the approach of the redactor was different. In recension II, the overall structure of the work is preserved, but the episodes which are specific to the Irish context were excised, especially those referring to kings and named laymen. The manuscript St Gall 555 (s. IX), which is the oldest witness of the second recension, clearly shows the process of the redaction. In the chapters which were retained for their universal appeal, the Irish proper names which had been dutifully copied by the scribe were deleted at the correction stage (see plate, and note the marginal gloss, *mac . filius*, explaining the text which was subsequently erased).

In the Metz version, the phraseology of Adomnán is more closely adhered to, but the scope and structure of the work is totally changed. The original structure, which is seen in the first and second recensions, was based on the Hellenistic tripartition found in the *Vita Martini* and consisted of three parts clearly defined at the end of the second preface: 'These things will be more fully disclosed below, divided into three books: the first will contain prophetic revelations, the second divine miracles worked through him and the third angelic apparitions and phenomena of heavenly light seen above the man of God'.[5] The outline of the work is again stated at the end of the first chapter of book one, which is a digest of Columba's miracles: 'These stories about the miraculous powers of the holy man have been related here so that the more eager reader may savour, as a foretaste of sweeter delicacies, these brief notes which will be developed more fully, with God's help, in the three books which follow'.[6]

However, the redactor of the Metz version was only interested in the supernatural phenomena of the third book and declares his intention to the

---

4 Krusch, *Ionae Vitae*, p. 97; Brüning, 'Adamnans Vita Columbae', p. 222; Levison, 'Conspectus codicum hagiographicorum', pp. 535–6, 614.　5 VC, *praefatio secunda*: ' ... quae tamen inferius per tris diuisa libros plenius explicabuntur, quorum primus profeticas reuelationes, secundus uero diuinas per ipsum uirtutes effectas, tertius angelicas apparationes contenebit et quasdam super hominem Dei caelestis claritudinis manifestationis'. On the significance of this passage and on the structure of Adomnán's *Vita Columbae*, see Picard, 'Structural Patterns', pp. 74–9.　6 VC I.1: 'Haec de sancti uiri hic ideo enarrata sunt uirtutibus ut auidior lector breuiter perscripta quasi dulciores quasdam praegustet dapes quae tamen plenius in tribus inferius libris Domino auxiliante enarrabuntur'.

Plate 1: MS St. Gallen, Stiftsbibliothek, 555 (s. IX) p. 10
Adomnán, *Vita Columbae*, praef. 2, 9

chaffhausen, Stadtbibliothek, MS Gen. 1 (s. VIII in.) p. 4a: 'Sanctus igitur Columba nobilibus fuerat
ndus genitalibus, patrem habens Fedilmithum filium Ferguso, matrem Aethneam nomine, cuius
r latine filius nauis dici potest, scotica uero lingua mac Naue. Hic anno secundo post Cule
inae bellum, aetatis uero suae XLII, de Scotia ad Brittanniam pro Christo perigrinari uolens
igauit.'

reader. At the end of the long first chapter of Book I – an interesting item *per se*
since it is missing from the second recension – the Metz text differs from
Adomnán's original and reads: 'These stories about the miraculous powers of
the holy man have been related briefly so that the eager reader may taste some
of the sweeter extracts. However, we have added stories which are taken from
the third book of his life and are found written in Irish script: they show on the
one hand the angelic visions by which he was honoured during his life and on
the other hand they present a complete account of his holy departure from this
world'.[7] The rest of the work follows closely the third book of Adomnán's *Vita
Columbae* from chapter 16 to the end. Throughout the work the saint is called
Columba but in the Incipit, the Explicit and in one instance in chapter three, he
is referred to as Columbanus.[8]

7 *Vita Columbae* (BHL 1889): 'Haec de sancti uiri breuiter dicta sunt uirtutibus ut diligens
lector dulciores aliquos degustaret flosculos. Quae uero subicimus ex libro tertio uitae eius
assumpsimus, quae scottice scripti extant, demonstrantes ex parte quibus uisionibus angelicis
honestatus sit in sua uita, manifestantes simul et eius adplenum sanctum ex hoc mundo
egressum'.   8 *Vita Columbae* (BHL 1889), Prol.: 'Sanctus Columbanus, de nobilissima
Scottorum ortus progenie, uolens exulare propter Deum in Brittanniam transnauigauit, ubi

The use of 'Columbanus' for Columba is not a scribal error and represents a genuine confusion. Columbanus, the founder of Luxeuil and Bobbio, was undoubtedly more famous than Columba in Lotharingia. On his way to Saint-Gall and Bobbio in 610, Columbanus had stayed in Metz with king Theodebert, who had warmly welcomed him in his capital city.[9] In the generation following the death of Columbanus in 615, the same region saw the foundation of several monasteries connected directly or indirectly with him or with Luxeuil: Remiremont, founded in 620 by the young aristocrat Romaric, where Arnulfus (died 640), bishop of Metz and ancestor of the Carolingians, spent the last years of his life; Saint-Dié founded by Deodatus; and Saint-Martin, built against the wall of the fortified city of Metz and supported by King Sigibert III (died 656). But, while the fame of Columbanus is well attested in Lotharingia from the seventh century, there is no evidence for the commemoration of Columba before the ninth century. The oldest document attesting devotion to the saint is a copy of the full version of Adomnán's *Vita Columbae* (BHL 1886) in a manuscript now kept at the Seminary in Metz.[10] This *libellus* contains only the *Vita Columbae* and the Lives of Columbanus and his disciples by Jonas of Bobbio, appropriately called here Jonas Elnonensis, i.e. Jonas of Saint-Amand.[11] It formerly belonged to the abbey of Saint-Mihiel, which was moved in 815 by abbot Smaragdus from Castellio to its present site on the Meuse. Although it has been suggested that Smaragdus was Irish, there is no evidence that this was so, although he was certainly acquainted with Insular circles.[12] While it is commonly referred to as the Metz manuscript, it was copied by a scribe from the school of Reims at the time of bishop Hincmar (845–82).[13] In the ninth and tenth centuries, Reims attracted pupils from a wide area between the Marne and the Rhine. It had close relations with Metz and monks from Murbach, a monastery with Insular connections, are also known to have studied there. The copy of VC is derived from the Schaffhausen manuscript but the compiler was clearly a Continental scholar. Although interested in the edificatory content of VC, he was not interested in the Irish context and suppressed most of the proper names and geographical data included by Adomnán.

By the mid-ninth century, there was so much circulation of Irish texts and persons in Lotharingia that it is impossible to know by which channels VC reached Saint-Mihiel. If the filiation of the text of Jonas's *Vita Columbani*,

paganum usque tunc temporis Pictorum populum per suam industriam diuinis uirtutibus et maximis prodigiis roboratam Domino lucratus seruus fidelis adeptus est'; Explicit: 'Explicit uita sancti Columbani abbatis'; III.16: 'Nam cum idem Osuualdus rex esset in procinctu belli castrametatus, quadam die in sua papilione super puluillum dormiens, sanctum Columbanum in uisu uidet forma choruscantem angelica, cuius alta proceritas uertice nubes tangere uidebatur'. 9 Jonas, *Vita Columbani*, I.27 (Krusch, p. 211). 10 Metz, Grand Séminaire, 1 (s. IX) fol. 1–79. 11 On the career of Jonas in Flanders after 639, see de Vogüé, *Vie de S. Colomban*, pp. 19–23. 12 See Kenney, *Sources*, pp. 542–4. 13 Leclercq, 'Recueil d'hagiographie', p. 194, n. 4, quoting a letter from B. Bischoff.

which is in the same manuscript, can be used as an indication, the two texts could have come originally from the Saint-Amand/Nivelles/Fosses region, where interaction between the Irish from Péronne and the Frankish monastic circles inspired by Columbanus took place in the preceding centuries.

However, this can only be a suggestion as we do not know exactly where and when the Schaffhausen manuscript travelled to the Continent. It is reasonable to assume that it was between 713 (when the scribe Dorbbéne died) and 802 (when Iona was burnt by the Vikings).[14] The manuscript does not seem to have reached the Bodensee before the 850s. Walahfrid Strabo (died 849), who became abbot of Reichenau in 838, shows no acquaintance with Adomnán's text in his writings, although he knew about Columba and had direct contacts with monks from Iona. His poem on the death of Bláthmac shows not only first-hand knowledge of the sack of Iona by the Vikings in 825, but concern about the relics of Columba and even an interest in Irish proper names since he quite accurately renders the name Bláthmac *pulcher natus*.[15] In contrast, Notker Balbulus (died 912), monk of Saint-Gall, clearly displays his knowledge of VC in the martyrology which he wrote in the last decade of the ninth century.[16] The manuscript written by Dorbbéne was certainly in St Gall some time between 841 and 872 when it was used for compiling the short version found in Saint-Gall 555. The existence of the Saint-Mihiel manuscript is evidence that, before reaching the Rhine valley, the Schaffhausen manuscript was in Lotharingia, and that the commemoration of Columba existed there before 850 in connection with the cult of Columbanus. This would explain why in the Metz Legendaries Columba is celebrated not on 9 June, as in the British Isles and in other parts of the Continent, but on 23 November which is the feast day of Columbanus. The confusion between Columba and Columbanus is also found in the *Vita Cadroe* written in Metz by a monk of Saint-Félix at the end of the tenth century.[17] The initial chapters of this Life are set in Scotland and Ireland and several visits to the tomb of St Columba are referred to, but in each instance the saint is called Columbanus.[18]

---

14 AU s.a. 712 (=713): 'Dorbeni kathedram Iae obtinuit et V mensibus peractis in primatu V Kl Nouimbris die sabbati obiit'; AU s.a. 801 (=802): 'I Columbae Cille a gentibus conbusta est'.   15 Walahfrid Strabo, *De beati Blaithmaic uita*, lines 28–9 (Duemmler, p. 297): 'cuius honorandum nomen sermone latino/pulcher natus adest ...'   16 Notker Balbulus, *Martyrologium*, cols 1101–3. On Notker's uses of VC see Picard, 'Adomnán's *Vita Columbae*', p. 9 and appendix, pp. 22–3.   17 On the *Vita Cadroe* and its author see de Gaiffier, 'SS. Clément de Metz et Caddroë'.   18 Hermann of Saint-Félix, *Vita Cadroe* (AASS, Mart. I), cap. 6: 'Unde post multa sanctorum suffragia quae ad piissimas Dei omnipotentis aures admouerat Beati Columbani cum uiro suo adiuit merita nec suo uoto est frustrata; namque cum ad sepulchrum eius cum ieiuniis et orationibus pernoctassent ... et ecce uir praeclari habitus apparuit'; and cap. 9: 'Tandem uero illachrymans licet intuitus cum matre pergans ad tumulum Beati Columbani, infantem Deo qui petebat afferens, seni praedicto nutriendum tradidit'.

In the Lotharingian version of VC, the confusion between Columba and Columbanus can be attributed to a Continental redactor who compiled the collection of the *Legendarium Mettense* in the eleventh century.[19] However, the main body of the text was the work of an Irishman and this can be seen in the treatment of the proper names. This recension differs notably from other Continental versions in that it follows Dorbbéne's text very closely. Mistakes in the Schaffhausen manuscript were corrected and often correspond to the text of the Scottish manuscripts (the B family in the Andersons' edition) but the possibility of influence from the B family has to be ruled out since BHL 1889 contains words of Adomnán which are not found in the B family. The proper names, which in other Continental versions were deleted, are retained and Dorbbéne's spelling is usually followed.[20] However, in several instances the form of proper names has been changed to reflect a more modern usage. The following forms deserve to be commented upon:

Schaffhausen (BHL 1886)	Metz (BHL 1889)
I.1 Ossualdus,	5–8 Osuualdus
I.1; III.23 Adomnanus	3,9; 11,50 Adamnanus
III.17 Comgellus mocu Aridi	5,1 Comgellus macchoi Aridi
III.17 Cainnechus mocu Dalon	5,1 Cainnechus macchui Thalann
III.17 Brendenus mocu Alti	5,1–3 Brendenus macchui Eltai
III.17 Cormac nepos Leathain cf. I.6 nepote Lethani	5,1 Cormac nepos Liathain
III.19; III.23 Virgnous, Virgnoum Virgnoui, Virgnouo	7,1–6; 11,47–9 Fergnaus, Fergnaum, Fergnai, Fergnao
III.20 Colgius filius Aido Draigniche	8,1 Colgius filius Aida Draigniche
III.20 de nepotibus Fechreg	8,1 de nepotibus Fiachrach
III.22 mocu Blai	10,2 macchui Blai
III.23 Lugudius filius Tailchani	11,43 Luguidus filius Tailchain
III.23 in Muirbulc mar	11,48 hiMuirbulc Mar
III.23 Ernene mocu Fir Roide	11,50 Ernene mocchui Fir Roide
III.23 in ualle fluminis Fendae	11,50 in ualle fluminis Bo<i>nne

19 On the *Legendarium Mettense* see Levison, 'Conspectus codicum hagiographicorum', pp. 535–6. 20 For example (the first set of chapter numbers refers to the Schaffhausen manuscript, the second set to the Metz MSS): *Patricius*, Praef. 2 = Praef. 5; *Maucteus* Praef.2 = Praef. 5; *Culedrebinae*, Praef. 2 = 1, 1; *Findbarrus*, I.1 = 3, 1; *Catlon*, I.1 = 3, 5–8; *Failbeus*, I.1 = 3, 9; *Segineus*, I.1 = 3, 9; *Cnoc angel*, III.16 = 4, 7; *Baitheneus*, III.18 = 3–4; *Berchanus*, III.21 = 9,1; *Diormitius*, III.23 = 11, 9.

- *Osuualdus* and *Adamnanus* instead of *Ossualdus* and *Adomnanus* are found in the Continental manuscripts of VC, but they were also the forms used in Ireland from the tenth century onwards. *Cormac's Glossary* gives the form as *Adamnan* and interprets it as a diminutive of the name Adam.[21]
- The correction of Latin forms into Irish forms in *Tailchain* for *Tailchani* and *hiMuirbulc* for *in Muirbulc* clearly shows the Irish origin of the redactor. There seems to have been confusion as to the exact nature of the *in* before *Muirbulc mar*. For Adomnán it was probably a Latin preposition: when writing an Irish form, he normally used the pre-tonic *hi-* as in *hiClochur* or *hiTeilte*.[22] But Dorbbéne understood it to be Irish since the whole expression *in Muirbulc mar* is surmounted by four dashes which, as elsewhere in the Schaffhausen manuscript, are marks of italicisation indicating an Irish form. In that case the *n* of *in* would not have been pronounced since nasalized /m/ and radical /m/ have the same pronunciation. The Metz redactor improves on the reading of Dorbbéne by supplying a form which is unambiguously Irish.
- Archaic old Irish *é* has been replaced by the diphthong *ia* in *Fiachrach* and *Liathain*. The forms with long *é* – *Fechreg*, *Fechureg*, *Fechrach* – were used in the seventh century and are found both in VC and in the *Collectanea* of Tírechán.[23] They were still acceptable to Ferdomnach, who wrote the Book of Armagh around 800. However the change had already started at the end of the seventh century with the use of the intermediary form *éa*, which is seen here in *Leathain* and which also appears in the Book of Armagh.[24] The process was complete by the end of the eighth century, and remained stable afterwards.[25]
- The genitive in *-o* in *filius Aido Draigniche* has been replaced by the form in *-a*, which is more common in later texts as the genitive of *Áed*.
- The spellings *Virgnous* and *Virgnouus* in VC, referring to the fourth abbot of Iona, Fergnae, have already been commented upon.[26] The existence of the forms *Fergnoi* and *Fergnouo* in VC shows that around the year 700 the sound /w/ had already changed to /f/ and the letters v and f probably represented the sound /f/. *Fergna* was the most common form of this name in the eleventh and twelfth centuries, as can be seen in the Irish annals and genealogies.[27] In our text only the form *Fergna* is used with Latin inflectional endings added.

---

21 Meyer, 'Sanas Cormaic', p. 1: 'Adamnan .i. homunculus .i. disbegat anma Adaim'. 22 VC II.5: 'quae inhabitauerat *hiClochur*'; II.12: 'aquam cessat amaram exinanire *hinin glas*'; III.3: 'hoc famen factum est *hiTeilte*'. On the use of Old Irish prepositions in Hiberno-Latin see Picard, 'Celticismes', p. 360. 23 Tírechán, *Collectanea* §14(2) (Bieler, *Patrician Texts*, p. 134): 'Endeus filius Amolngid sum ego filii Fechrach filii Echach'; VC I.17: 'De Colcio Aido Draigniche filio a nepotibus Fechureg orto'; ibid. III.20: 'quidam de fratribus, Colgius nomine filius Aido Draigniche de nepotibus Fechreg'. 24 Tírechán, *Collectanea* §46(2) (Bieler, *Patrician Texts*, p. 158): 'et fecit aeclessiam iuxta Druim Leas'. 25 Thurneysen, *Grammar of Old Irish*, pp. 36–7. 26 The most recent assessment is Harvey, 'Retrieving the Pronunciation', pp. 59–61. 27 AU s.aa. 556 (=557): 'Mors Fergna (uel Fiachrach) nepotis

- The genitive *Alti* written by Dorbbéne is generally given as *Altai* in later sources.[28] The same ending is found here in the form *Eltai*, but the initial *A* has been changed to *E*. This shift is consistent with Middle Irish usage: other examples are *Alpae* > *Elpa* (as in *Slíab nElpa*, the Alps), *Aquitania* > *Equitáin* (as in *Equitáin mór* 'great Aquitaine' in the Book of Leinster) or the doublet *esbal* which is found for *apstal*.[29]
- *Dalon* is generally written *Dálann* in the genealogies, as in Corcco Dálann. Lenition was expected after *moccu* (cf. *mocu Fir Roide* in the Schaffhausen MS) or after *uí*. Here, the spelling *Thalann* reflects not only the Middle Irish ending in *-ann* but the rendering of the dental spirant /ð/ by *th*, a hyper-archaism which shows that the writer was able to differentiate between lenited and unlenited sound.
- In the Metz manuscripts the form *macchui* always replaces the archaic form *mocu* used by Dorbbéne. Family names containing the word *moc(c)u*, equivalent of Latin *gens*, were common in the seventh century but disappeared during the eighth.[30] Subsequent texts render the obsolete *moccu* as *mac hui*.[31] The chronicler Máel Brigte (died 1082), who wrote in the second half of the eleventh century, translates *moccu* by *filius nepotis*, which is an exact calque of *mac uí*.[32] Known as Marianus Scottus in Continental circles, Máel Brigte is commemorated in the necrology of Metz.
- The transformation from *Fendae* to *Bo<i>nne* completes our list of linguistic items. It is found in a passage where Ernéne, a monk of Drumhome, tells of the vision he had of a great pillar of fire shooting up into the sky on the night St Columba died. He would seem to have been fishing on the lower Foyle, as the large number of fishermen involved in the fishing operation implies.[33] The term *Fenda*, which Adomnán uses, is generally identified with the River Finn in county Donegal, but it can also refer to the Foyle, which is

Ibdaig, regis Uloth'; 581 (=582) and 582 (=583): 'Mors Fergna mic Caibleine'; 622 (=623): 'Obitus Fergnai abbatis Iae'; Mac Airt, *Annals of Inisfallen* s.a. 557: 'Mors Fergnai, ríg Ulad'; 582: 'Mors Fergnai m. Aibléni'; 624: 'Quies Fergnai, abb Iae'; O'Brien, *Corpus genealogiarum*: 'Fergna' (pp. 186, 259, 278); 'mac Fergnae' (pp. 83, 158, 228); 'mac Fergnai' (pp. 175, 226, 261, 364); 'ingen Fergna' (p. 341). **28** O' Brien, *Corpus genealogiarum Hiberniae*, pp. 287, 319; O Riain, *Corpus genealogiarum sanctorum Hiberniae*, pp. 22, 165. **29** Best et al., *Book of Leinster*, iii.531, line 16408; Quin, *Dictionary*, s.v. 'esbal'. **30** Quin, *Dictionary*, s.v. 'maccu'. **31** For example Stokes, *Annals of Tigernach*, p. 149 (=AD 570): 'Aennu mac húi Laigse, ab Cluana maic Nois'; p. 168 (=AD 609): 'Quies Lugdach .i. mo Lua, maic hui Oche'; p. 198 (=AD 663): 'Quies Segain maic hui Chuind'; p. 199 (=AD 665): 'Ulltan mac húi Cunga ab Cluana hIraird'; p. 204 (=AD 678): 'Dairchill mac hui Rite, espoc Glíndi da lacha'. **32** Marianus Scottus, *Chronicon* (PL cxlvii.715 = Vatican, Pal. Lat. 830 (s. XI) fol. 138): 'Sanctus quidem Patricius uenditur ad regem nomine Miluc, filius nepotis Buain in aquilone Hiberniae cuius porcorum pastor erat Patricius'. Cf. Tírechán, *Collectanea*, §1(2) (Bieler, *Patrician Texts*, p. 124): 'et empsit illum unus ex eis, cui nomen erat Miliuc maccu Boin magus, et seruiuit illi septem annis omni seruitute ac duplici labore, et porcarium possuit eum in montanis conuallibus'. **33** VC III.23: 'ego et alii mecum uiri laborantes in captura

the name the river Finn takes between its confluence with the river Mourne near Strabane and the estuary at Derry. The Metz redactor was evidently not from Donegal and must have misunderstood *Fenda* as the other river Finn (now called Blackwater) which flows from Slieve Gorey in County Cavan to meet the Boyne at Navan; or he may have assumed a corruption of the word *Bóend* (< *bó* 'cow' + *find* 'white'), the Old Irish name of the famous river Boyne. The lenited *f* had already disappeared by the Old Irish period, and the forms *Boend*, *Board* and *Boind* are found in seventh-, eighth- and ninth-century texts.[34] The ingredients of the compound were still remembered in the twelfth century when the *Dindshenchas* was copied in the Book of Leinster, but the meaning of the name was not clear to the redactors: they understood the form *Bóend* as the amalgam of the names of the two rivers which meet at Navan to form the lower Boyne, the Bó and the Find.[35] The Metz redactor correctly uses the form *Bóinne*, the genitive of *Bóinn* most commonly used in the Middle Irish period, as a genitive of apposition.

The treatment of the proper names in the BHL 1889 version of VC allows us to get closer to the time and circumstances of the redaction. As the linguistic evidence points to the Middle Irish period (tenth-twelfth centuries), and the oldest manuscript dates from the eleventh century, the tenth century is the period which we should explore. As it happens, this was a time of intense Irish activity in Lotharingia and especially in Metz.[36] Following the death of their patron Charles the Bald in 877, the Irish seem to have been less prominent in ecclesiastical circles on the Continent. However, from the 940s, a new generation of Irishmen began to attract the attention of chroniclers and hagiographers. Lotharingia had been taken over and attached to Germany in 925 by the Saxon Henry the Fowler, father of Otto the Great. Otto succeeded his father in 936 and appointed his younger brother Brun as chancellor of the kingdom in 940. Brun had been a pupil of Israel Scottus and throughout his career was a patron of the *Scoti*, a term which Continentals applied to Irish, British and Breton *peregrini* alike. One of Brun's functions as administrator was to consolidate Ottonian power in Lotharingia, a task which he conducted successfully from the archbishopric of Cologne where he was installed in 953.

---

piscium in ualle piscosi fluminis Fendae ... sed et alii multi piscatores qui sparsim per diuersas fluminales piscinas eiusdem fluminis piscabantur, sicut nobis post retulerant, simili apparatione uisa magno pauore sunt perculsi'. **34** Vendryes et al., *Lexique*, fasc. B, p. 62; Quin, *Dictionary*, s.v. 'Boänd, Bóinn'. **35** Best et al., *Book of Leinster*, iv.861 (= Gwynn, *Metrical Dindshenchas*, iii.32–3): 'Nó Boand Bó acus Find/do chomruc na da ríglind/ in t-uisce a sléib Guaire gle/7 sruth na sidise' ('Or, Boand is Bo and Find/from the meeting of the two royal streams/the water from bright Slieve Gorey/and the river of the *síd*s here'). **36** For previous research on this topic see Kenney, *Sources*, pp. 605–13; Gougaud, *Christianity in Celtic Lands*, pp. 154–7; Gwynn, 'Irish Monks'.

In Upper Lotharingia, Otto was supported by the bishops of Metz, Adalbero I and Thierri I. Adalbero I (929–958) came from a powerful family in Lotharingia: his father was Wigeric, the Count of the Palace, and his brothers were counts at Verdun, Luxemburg and Bar-le-Duc. After an initial period of rebellion, he collaborated with Otto from 939. Bishop Thierri I (965–984) was a first cousin of Otto and had a prominent role at the imperial court, especially in the period of expansion following the coronation of Otto as Roman Emperor in 962. With territorial possessions extending far beyond the limits of its diocese into Champagne, Alsace and Flanders, Metz was one of the richest ecclesiastical centres in the Empire.[37] In such a climate, the Irish are found contributing once again to the establishment of the new structures of a rising power, just as they had done under the early Carolingians.

During his episcopacy, Adalbero fostered a strong movement of ecclesiastical reform, equivalent to that of Odo of Cluny (926–942) in Burgundy, and Gerard of Brogne (died 959) in Northern France. The centre of the reform movement in Lotharingia was the monastery of Gorze where in 933 Adalbero had installed John of Vandrières, a former monk of Saint-Mihiel, and Einold, archdeacon of Toul. Soon afterwards, Irish monks became involved in the new movement. By then the monastery of Waulsort, originally founded by the local magnates Eilbert and Hersende for Irish pilgrims, was under the influence of the king and the reformers, who acknowledged the legitimacy of the Irish presence, but insisted on a strict adherence to the Benedictine rule. A charter dated 19 September 946 and signed by Otto and Brun confirms that Waulsort was founded by Hersende for Irish monks who followed the Benedictine rule, and stipulates as the condition for the patronage of the king that it should always remain under the authority of the *Scoti* and that if no Irish abbot could be found, an abbot following the rule should be elected.[38] The insistence on the Benedictine rule is important in the context of the activities of the three Irishmen connected with Waulsort: Máel Callann (died 21 January 978),[39] Cathróe (died 6

37 For the history of the period see Wattenbach and Holtzmann, *Deutschlands Geschichtsquellen im Mittelalter*; Hampe, *Germany under the Salian and Hohenstaufen Emperors*; Parisse, *Histoire de la Lorraine*; Le Moigne, *Histoire de Metz*.   38 Sickel, *Diplomata*, i.160–1: '... in loco qui dicitur Walciodorus ubi iam dictus uir et uxor sua Heresuindis in religione feruentissima susceperant quosdam dei seruos peregrinationis gratia a Scotia uenientes et sub regula Benedicti uiuere cupientes.' Ibid.: ' ... decreuimus ut illud monasterium perpetuo in usus peregrinorum et pauperum stabiliatur firmetur atque corroboretur et semper in ditione Scottorum permaneat et quamdiu aliquis illorum uixerit nullus alius fiat abbas nisi unus ex ipsis, post decessum uero illorum alius Deum diligens amator sancte regule efficiatur abbas.' 39 Called *Machalanus* in later sources, he is called *Malcallanus* in the contemporary continuation of Flodoard's *Chronicon* (ed. Pertz) for AD 978: 'Vir Domini Malcallanus natione Hibernicus in uigilia sancti Vincentii leuitae et martiris, uitam transitoriam quam habebat exosam deseruit, et cum Deo uiuo cui indesinenter dum adhuc uiueret seruiuit uiuere feliciter inchoauit. Qui praefatus abbas in corpore humatus quiescit in aeclesia beati Michaelis archangeli cuius abbatiam dum corporaliter in hoc seculo uiuens mansit pio

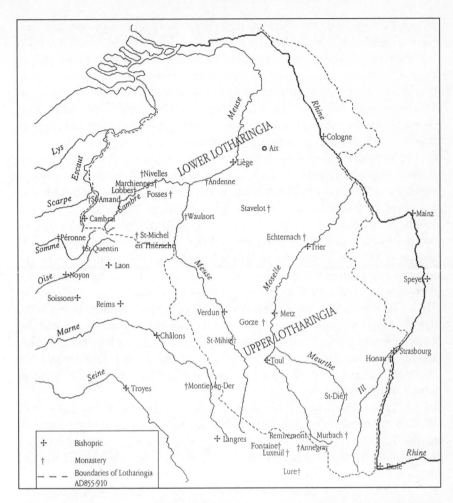

March 978), and Forannán (died 982).[40] According to the *Vita Cadroe*, written by Hermann of Saint-Félix in 982/983, Máel Callann had to undergo training at Gorze before he was given the charge of abbot at both Waulsort and Saint-Michel en Thiérache. Cathróe was sent to Fleury-sur-Loire which was considered a model of reformed observance on the fringes of the Cluniac movement.[41] The details found in our documents may be historically inexact, but they clearly

moderamine rexit'. The name Máel Calland is attested in the Irish genealogies among the Dál Messin Corb in Leinster, and in Ulster among the Uí Néill (O'Brien, *Corpus genealogiarum Hiberniae*, pp. 39, 134, 167). **40** Most of the information concerning these three saints is found in the following sources: John of Saint-Arnoul (died 980), *Vita Iohannis abbatis Gorziensis* (ed. Pertz); Hermann of Saint-Félix (fl. 980x1015), *Vita Cadroe* (ed. AASS); *Historia Walciodorensis monasterii* (s.XII–XIII) (ed. Waitz); Robert of Waulsort (s. XII), *Gesta Forannani* (ed. AASS). **41** *Vita Cadroe*, §§21–2.

reflect the opinion of the tenth-century redactors as regards the function and place of the Irish monks. They are praised for their asceticism, their holy life, and their organisational skills, but they are not credited with introducing any form of 'Celtic' monasticism. They belong to a large reform movement, where they play a critical but not leading role. The model of asceticism is John of Vandrières and the rule is firmly Benedictine. Cathróe must have fulfilled his duties at Waulsort in a satisfactory manner as he was invited to Metz *c*.950 by bishop Adalbero I to take charge of the monastery of Saint-Félix.

The work of Adalbero was continued by his successor, Thierri I. The *Vita Cadroe* portrays Thierri as fond of Cathróe's company and as a generous benefactor of Saint-Félix.[42] According to the *Chronicle of Waulsort* he also held Forannán in high esteem.[43] Thierri certainly reorganised the structures of Waulsort: he attached to it the nunnery of Hastières, founded in the seventh century by St Glossinde, and transferred the joint property to the cathedral church of Metz under his own authority. The official document confirming the transfer is a charter dated 16 December 969 and signed by Otto the Great. Although it recalls that Waulsort was originally founded by Eilbert and Hersende, it does not mention any *Scoti* nor any of the stipulations found in the 946 charter.[44] This does not mean that the Irish were no longer there (Máel Callann, Cathróe and Forannán were still alive in 969), but it reminds us that the control of Waulsort was really in the hands of the bishop of Metz and that the Irish, as vassals or clients of Thierri, did not have to be mentioned in administrative transactions.

The aggrandisement of Metz as an episcopal city continued under Thierri's successor, Adalbero II (984–1005). Adalbero II also belonged to the imperial family. He was the son of Frederic, nephew of Brun and Duke of Upper Lotharingia since 959, when, at the instigation of Brun, Otto the Great had divided Lotharingia into two duchies. Beatrix, mother of Adalbero, was the sister of Hugues Capet, the future king of France. Adalbero II invited the Irishman Fíngen (died 1005) to succeed Cathróe as abbot of Saint-Félix.[45] The arrival of Fíngen corresponds to the time when the name of the monastery gradually changed from Saint-Félix to Saint-Clément. It is likely that, as part of Adalbero's rebuilding of Metz in the new Ottonian architectural style, renovation work took place at the abbey of Saint-Félix/Saint-Clément. In 992, Adalbero invited Fíngen to take charge of the abbey of Saint-Symphorien. The charter, dated 25 January 992 and signed by Otto III, mentions Fíngen by name

---

42 *Vita Cadroe*, §32.   43 *Historia Walciodorensis monasterii*, §18–19 (ed. Waitz).   44 Sickel, *Diplomata*, i.522–3.   45 The career of Fíngen is known from several eleventh- and twelfth-century sources: Constantine of Saint-Symphorien, *Vita Adalberonis II Mettensis episcopi* (AD 1012×1017); *Gesta episcoporum Virdunensium* (*c*.1050); *Vita Richardi abb. Sanvitonensis* (s. XII in.); Hugo of Flavigny, *Chronicon Flaviniacense seu Virdunense* (AD 1090×1102); *Carmen Mettense* (s. XI); see Kenney, *Sources*, pp. 611–3, nrs 432, 434, 435, 436, 437.

and stipulates that the abbey should receive Irish monks for as long as possible.[46] This stipulation, which recalls the Waulsort charter of 946, also reflects the personal interest of the regent queen Adelaide of Burgundy, whose admiration for Cathróe is recorded at the end of the *Vita Cadroe*.[47] Otto III was a boy of eleven, and his grand-mother Adelaide had taken over the regency after the death of his mother Theophano in 991. The charter makes clear that she was the main instigator of the royal donation.[48] Saint-Symphorien had been in a state of ruin and Adalbero must have asked Fíngen to organise a new monastic community in a newly reconstructed building. Metz in the era of Thierri I and Adalbero II was described by Sigibert of Gembloux as a thriving city, well supplied by the rich surrounding countryside, well defended by strong walls, adorned with beautiful churches which held the relics of famous saints, renowned for its markets and the richness of its religious ceremonies. With the reopening of Saint-Symphorien, the total of reformed Benedictine monasteries in Metz was brought to four: Saint-Arnoul and Saint-Félix/Saint-Clément, reformed by Adalbero I; Saint-Vincent, reformed by Thierri I; and Saint-Symphorien. Irishmen had been put in charge of two of these, and not the least important since Saint-Félix/Saint-Clément and Saint-Symphorien housed the two martyria of Metz, where all the bishops of Metz were buried, except for Arnulfus, who had died as a monk in Remiremont and whose relics were transferred to the church called Saint-Arnoul after him (see map).

The choice of Irishmen to be caretakers of the *martyria* may not be fortuitous as they had acquired a reputation as mediators with the next world. The visions of Fursa were well known in Lotharingia and there are several tenth-century manuscripts of the *Vita Fursei* which come from that kingdom.[49] The readers of the *Vita Geretrudis*, another popular text in Lotharingia, also knew that Ultán, Fursa's brother, could foresee the future and had predicted the exact date of Gertrude's death on St Patrick's day.[50] The link between Fursa and Cathróe is clearly shown in the *Vita Cadroe*. Hermann relates that, on his way to the Meuse valley, Cathróe stopped in Péronne where he saw Fursa in a vision.[51] Cathróe was also able to foretell his own death away from

---

46 Sickel, *Diplomata*, ii.493: ' ... ea uidelicet ratione ut abbas primus nomine Fingenius Hyberniensis natione quem ipse praelibatus episcopus [Adalbero] nunc temporis constituit, suique successores Hybernienses monachos habeant quamdiu si esse poterit et, si defuerint ibi monachi de Hybernia de quibuscumque nationibus semper ibi monachi habeantur ... '. 47 *Vita Cadroe*, §34–6. 48 Sickel, *Diplomata*, ii.493: 'Nos uero ob interuentum dilectae auiae nostrae Adalheidis uidelicet imperatricis augustae piae petitioni illius benignum assensum praebentes eidem abbatiae sancti Symphoriani omnia loca ... regia denuo nostra munificentia donamus atque confirmamus ... '. 49 Paris, Bibliothèque Nationale de France, lat. 5568 (s. X) < Saint-Amand; Brussels, Bibliothèque Royale Albert I, 7984 (s. X) < Wissembourg; Cambrai, Bibliothèque Municipale, 865 (s. X–XI) < Cambrai; The Hague, Koninklijke Bibliotheek, 71 H 66 (s. X); see Krusch, *Vita uirtutesque Fursei*, pp. 423–34. 50 Krusch, 'Vita Geretrudis', pp. 462–3. 51 *Vita Cadroe*, §18.

Metz and to organise the return of his own body to Saint-Clément.[52] In nearby Toul, bishop Gerardus (963–994) was also a patron of the Irish. According to Widric, abbot of Saint-Èvre at Toul, who wrote the *Vita Gerardi* in the first half of the eleventh century, the Irish community at Toul lived on funds provided personally by the bishop.[53] Widric tells of the prophetic powers of an Irishman who announced the death of Gerardus on 23 April 994 as revealed to him by the Lord in a vision.[54] Tenth-century Lotharingia was also an important centre for the spread of the legend of St Brendan's journey to the *terra repromissionis*.[55] In the late tenth century, the tradition of Irish visions corresponded to the cultural and mental context of the time. The Ottonian period is characterised by an increase in hagiographical production and by a general interest in visionary material.[56] These facts are well known and seventy-five years ago Wilhelm Levison pointed out the function of vision literature in the politics of the Carolingian and Ottonian rulers.[57]

I would suggest that the general context of hagiographical production in late tenth- and early eleventh-century Lotharingia was the ideal climate for the redaction of the BHL 1889 version of VC. Unlike the short version which circulated in Germany and Austria, the Metz redaction was not just an abridgement of VC, but reflects a deliberate choice of chapters dealing with supernatural encounters. As stated above, there are countless channels by which VC could have arrived in Lotharingia, but the devotion of Cathróe to St Columba is a factor which on its own would explain the renewal of interest in the saint of Iona. What is interesting is that the exemplar used was not the ninth-century Continental copy belonging to Saint-Mihiel de Lorraine, but a manuscript written in Irish script and containing readings identical with those of Dorbbéne. It may have been an early copy made in Péronne or Fosses, but it is more likely to be the Schaffhausen manuscript, which by then was either at Saint-Gall or at Reichenau. The readings found in the Metz recension are too close to the text of Dorbbéne to allow several intermediary copies. In spite of the political divisions into kingdoms and duchies, scholars and books travelled freely in the former Carolingian empire. Pierre Riché has shown that the links between monasteries and between cities were especially close in tenth-century

52 Ibid., §34–5.   53 Widric, *Vita Gerardi* (Waitz, p. 501): ' ... coetum quoque Graecorum ac Scotorum agglomerans non modicum, propriis alebat stipendiis commixtum diversae linguae populum ... '.   54 Ibid., p. 503: 'Die nono Kalendarum Maiarum, quidam boni testimonii ex Scotis quos alebat, primo surgit diluculo urbis plateas circuit eiulando, clamans ac protestans patrem ac dominum suum, sanctum uidelicet episcopum, eximendum a saeculo, idque certo uisionis signo praemonstratum sibi a Domino. Corda percellit omnium hoc flebile indicium sed tristis rerum exitus dat Scoto testimonium.'   55 Selmer, *Nauigatio*, pp. xxviii–xxxi.   56 Corbet, *Saints ottoniens*. A collection of 23 visions available at the time is found in the *Liber uisionum* written in the eleventh century by Otlohus, monk of St Emmeram at Ratisbonne (Migne, PL cxlvi.341–88).   57 Levison, *Politik in den Jenseitvisionen*.

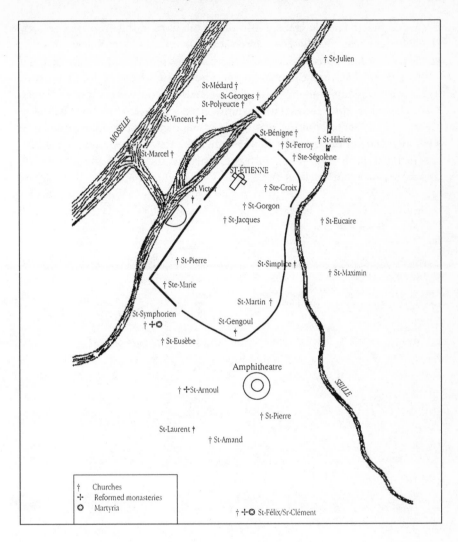

St-Julien †

St-Médard †
St-Georges †
St-Polyeucte †
St-Vincent † +

MOSELLE

St-Vincent † +

St-Bénigne †
† St-Ferroy † St-Hilaire
† Ste-Ségolène

St-Marcel †

ST-ÉTIENNE

St Victor
†

† Ste-Croix

† St-Gorgon
† St-Jacques

† St-Eucaire

† St-Pierre

St-Simplice †
† St-Maximin

† Ste-Marie

St-Martin †

St-Symphorien
† + ☉

St-Gengoul
†

† St-Eusèbe

Amphitheatre

† + St-Arnoul ◎

SEILLE

† St-Pierre

St-Laurent †
† St-Amand

†	Churches
+	Reformed monasteries
☉	Martyria

† + ☉ St-Félix/Sr-Clément

Lotharingia.[58] The library of Saint-Gall was famous and scholars came from far and wide to consult or to borrow books. Thierri I, bishop of Metz, had been a pupil of the scholiast Gerald at Saint-Gall.[59] Irishmen were still living in Saint-Gall in the tenth century as is attested by the poem written by Dubdúin in the manuscript Saint-Gall 10.[60] The Irish redactor of the Metz recension had

58 Riché, *Écoles et enseignement*, pp. 163–9. **59** Ekkehard IV, *Casus S. Galli, continuatio prima*, §103 (Haefele, *Ekkehard IV*, pp. 208–10): 'Thietericus uero Metensis episcopus adolescens, Kerhaldi nuper in loco discipulus, regulae librum manu gerens apertum ... '. **60** Saint-Gall 10 (s. X–XI) p. 3, ed. Strecker, *Ottonenzeit*, p. 527. This MS begins a Book III

perhaps a better knowledge of Latin than Dubdúin, as the improvements on the Dorbbéne readings show, but even though he tried to adapt Adomnán's text to the taste of his contemporaries, his recension never travelled further than the Metz region. However, he contributed to a better knowledge of Iona's founder saint, who was less known beyond Irish circles than were Patrick, Brigit, Columbanus or Fursa outside monasteries closely associated with Irish circles. Thanks to his work, Columba was formally commemorated in the capital city of Lotharingia in the eleventh century when the rewritten version of his Life was included in the *Legendarium Mettense* between the Life of St Columbanus and the *Passion of St Cecilia*.

with Faremoutiers, comprising Jonas II.11–25. Additional texts, including Jonas's chapters on Eustasius (albeit now defective) were subsequently prefixed to this MS: Krusch, *Ionae Vitae*, pp. 85–6.

Patterns of Hypocorism in
Early Irish Hagiography

Paul Russell

The assumption that certain personal names which occur in early Irish hagiographical texts are related to each other hypocoristically is widespread and is frequently employed with relatively little explanation or justification. The framework of this assumption seems, as far as I can tell, to go back to a series of discussions by Heinrich Zimmer and Kuno Meyer which were themselves based on, what was at the time, ground-breaking work by Classical scholars on Greek personal names.[1] There remains much of value in this work but even so it still seems to me high time that we re-considered these assumptions about the formation and status of hypocoristic names. It would seem to be a useful exercise not least because in recent years Pádraig Ó Riain has argued for the original identity of certain saints, notably Colum Cille and Cainnech, and Finbarr, Finnian, and Finnio/Uinniau.[2] Much of the argument focuses on the association of cults but part of it is an assertion that these names are somehow formally related. Further aspects of these arguments are also worth considering; Ó Riain has claimed that Adomnán's treatment of Cainnech and Columba as separate individuals was because Adomnán did not recognize the particular pattern of name formation involved: 'By Adomnán's time a hypocorism differing significantly from its radical form would probably have been unrecognizable as such'.[3] Several aspects of this claim are worth exploring in greater detail, notably what counts as a significant difference and what is meant by a radical form. In short, then, what follows offers some brief and preliminary thoughts on the nature of hypocorism in the context of early Irish ecclesiastical naming patterns.

---

1 Zimmer, 'Keltische Studien 10'; K. Meyer, 'Zur keltischen Wortkunde I–IX' [herafter *Wortk.* (references by continuous paragraph numbering)]; cf. Fick, *Griechischen Personennamen*. For a brief discussion, see Russell, *Celtic Word-Formation*, pp. 16–21. I am grateful to Pádraig Ó Riain for his helpful comments on an early draft of this paper.   2 Ó Riain, 'Towards a Methodology'; idem, 'Cainnech *alias* Colum Cille'; on *Uinniau* etc., see Ó Riain, 'St Finbarr', idem, 'Finnian or Winniau', idem, 'Finnio and Winniau'; Fleuriot, 'Winniau'; Dumville, 'Gildas and Uinniau'; and most recently, Ó Riain, 'Finnio and Winniau: a return to the subject'. 3 Ó Riain, 'Cainnech *alias* Colum Cille', p. 31.

It may be helpful to begin with a definition or two, and in particular to consider the potentially confusing distinction (or rather the lack of one) between hypocorisms and diminutives. Essentially a hypocorism is a form of a personal name used in an affectionate context; its form is often related formally in some way to the basic or radical form.[4] For example, among modern English naming patterns, we find sets of the type *James*: *Jim, Jimmy*; *Samuel* : *Sam, Sammy*; *Robert* : *Rob, Bob, Robby, Bobby*. The usual understanding of such groups is that someone familiarly or affectionately called *Jim* or *Jimmy* would in more formal contexts be called *James*. However, the relationship can break down in a number of ways. The formal connection can remain but simply not operate in a particular case; that is, someone called *Jim* may not have been christened or otherwise formally named *James*. Conversely, there may be a hypocoristic relationship between two names which in synchronic terms are formally unrelated (whatever the historical origins of the link), e.g. *Richard* : *Dick(y)*, *Elizabeth* : *Betty*, in Scotland *George* : *Doddie*. Such forms differ both from formally related hypocoristic forms of names and from nicknames, such as *Curly, Fatty*. Whereas the latter, in addition to connotations of familiarity and affection, carry a semantic load arising from some identifying feature (or perhaps the complete lack of it, such as calling a bald person *Curly*), the former are both formally unrelated and semantically empty (insofar as names can be said to be semantically empty), but still retain some affectionate and familiar sense. Some forms can be ambiguous; for example, in Welsh it is relatively common to find suffixed hypocoristics based on one of the elements of a compound name, e.g. *Cynog* : *Cynfael, Maelog* : *Maelgwn, Briog/Tyfriog* : *Briafael* (cf. Irish *Finnian* : *Findbarr, Bairre* : *Barrfhind*). Since the suffix was also used to form adjectives, *Cynog*, for example, could operate as a nickname, but if *Cynog* can in any given case be regarded as a hypocoristic version of *Cynfael*, it is not clear that at the same time it can mean 'dog-like' or 'possessing hounds'.[5]

A related issue is the terminological confusion between hypocorism and diminutive. It is common to see these terms used interchangeably and the problem is exacerbated by the fact that in many languages the same markers, whether prefixes, suffixes, or vowel-changing, can be used both hypocoristically and diminutively; for example, as is well known, Irish *-án* and *-óg*, and Welsh and Breton *-ig* are used in both senses. It crucially depends on whether the base of the derivative is a personal name or a common noun: if the former, it would

---

4 An issue which is rarely raised with regard to the use of hypocoristic names in the early Irish ecclesiastical context is why they are so widespread. Clearly it is impossible to reconstruct the precise connotations of these hypocorisms, but perhaps a modern analogy is relevant: one aspect of modern evangelism is the rapid, often immediate use of first names and familiar forms of names between the evangelist and the audience in an attempt to develop a closer spiritual relationship. This may provide a plausible scenario for early Ireland too. 5 On the adjectival use of *-og*, see Russell, *Celtic Word-Formation*, pp. 32–60.

be hypocoristic; if the latter, probably diminutive. In broad terms, *Johnny* would be primarily affectionate, though it may secondarily say something about his size (in that such a term may often be applied to a child). On the other hand, a diminutive with the sense 'little boat' probably says nothing affectionate but everything about its size. Identification, therefore, of the first element as a personal name is vital in interpreting the whole as a derived hypocorism. This view presents a different definition of hypocoristic and diminutive from that adopted by O'Brien in his discussion of Old Irish personal names:[6] he makes a formal distinction characterizing forms which show shortening, doubling of consonants and prefixation as hypocoristic and those with suffixation as diminutive. It is easy to see how the distinction came to arise since his hypocoristic category largely contains ecclesiastical names (where in theory the pattern of derivation may be more discernible), but it is not clear that there is any real distinction here. It may arise out of statistical variation where certain suffixes, e.g. Irish *-ín*, may be more often found with a common noun base rather than a personal name base, but that does not stop *-ín* functioning as a hypocoristic marker in the appropriate derivational context. It is not clear that in the case of personal names the distinction between hypocoristic and diminutive can be clearly and consistently maintained. My preferences would, therefore, be to make a functional distinction between 'hypocoristic' applied to personal name formation (however it may be marked) and 'diminutive' applied to common noun formation.

On the other hand, O'Brien is surely right in his contention that the picture in Irish is particularly confused because of British influence, such as the introduction of the *-óc* suffix and the use of pairs of markers, one British and one Irish, to create hybrid forms:[7] a particularly good example of this hybridisation of names is the different versions of the name, *Uinniau* (British), *Finnio* (hybrid), *Finnian* (Irish).[8] In the context of this argument, it may be worth speculating whether the hypocoristic use of *-ach*, which is anomalous among the usages of this suffix, may not be a Hibernicisation of *-óc*. In addition to *-óc*, the otherwise inexplicable voicing in forms like *Báetán* /baida:n/, Ogam *BAIDAGNI* (: *báeth*); *Túatán* /tuada:n/ (: *túath*); *Tecán*, Ogam *TEGANN* (:*tech/*étig* 'ugly'; cf. Welsh *teg*), may also reflect the importation of British sound patterns.[9] As the Ogam forms show, they do not simply reflect (expressive) gemination but also voicing. Whether *-ucán*/*-acán* can be explained in the same way as derived from

6 O'Brien, 'Old Irish Personal Names', pp. 220–1.   7 On *-óc*, see Russell, *Celtic Word-Formation*, pp. 108–16. Cf. also Ó Riain's important distinction between British influence on name formation and British origin of the saint so named ('Finnio and Winniau'); his contention is that evidence for the former is often thought to imply the latter.   8 See Dumville, 'Gildas and Uinniau', pp. 205–10.   9 McManus, *Guide to Ogam*, p. 179 n. 36. The voiced dental may also be reflected in *Buite*/*Buíte* (in *Mainister Buite*/*Buíte*, Monasterboice) if this is connected with *Báetán*.

-ach (+ *-án*) is open to doubt; they probably reflect re-marking of derivatives in
-uc, which, as I have suggested elsewhere, was the earlier borrowing of the
British suffix -/o:g/ before the reduction of Irish unstressed long vowels and
which was subsequently replaced by *-óc*.[10]

That, in theory, is how things would seem to operate but, as is usual, all is
not as clear as it might be. A clear-cut distinction between personal name and
common noun bases is all very well but specifically Irish factors can muddy the
waters. For example, in the modern dialects the suffixes *-óg*, *-án* and *-ín* can still
retain a diminutive sense when added to a common noun, but frequently they
do not, especially when the base is not in common use in the dialect; in such
cases the derivative takes on the basic semantic load and no more.[11] This loss or
perhaps non-existence of a diminutive sense when the base form is not attested
has its parallel in early Irish personal names and it is a point which has not
always been clearly recognized. Just as the diminutive sense of a derivative in
-ín or *-án* or the like is dependent on its semantic relationship to a base form, so
the hypocoristic function of a personal name in *-án* or *-óg* is dependent on a
presumed or assumed link with a basic form of the name. The problem in the
early history of the Celtic languages is having enough evidence to establish that
two names refer to the same person, and then, if they do, being sure that the
two names are formally related and not just two separate names for the same
person. The former is a problem of evidence, the latter a linguistic problem.

There is plenty of evidence for individuals having different names at
different stages of their lives, names which can in no way be claimed to be
formally related.[12] The most famous example of this is probably Patrick's four
names: *Sucaid ainm baisdi Padraic, Codraidi a ainm a ndairsine, Mogomius a ainm
aca foglaim, Patricius a ainm ac Romanchaib* (§654).[13] But there are plenty of
other cases to show that this is not an isolated example: *Crimthand ainm Coluim
Cille* (§703.1; cf. §661), *Oengus ainm Meic Nisi Condere* (§703.2), *Cunnid ainm
Meic Culind Lusca* (§703.3), *Gnia ainm Muru Othna Moire* (§703.6, but cf. §658:
Dima ainm baisdi Muru m. Deaga), *Tairchell ainm Molling* (§703.12), *Moninni –
qui Darerca prius dicebatur – ingen Mochta* (§98.1; cf. §703.8), *Nem mac Ua Birn:
Nem tribus nominibus uocabatur .i. Nem Púpu Cailbe. Nem primum nomen a*

---

10 Russell, *Celtic Word-Formation*, pp. 15–6. See also Uhlich, *Morphologie*, pp. 195–7.
11 See Lucas, *Grammar of Ros Goill Irish*, p. 208; de Bhaldraithe, *Gaeilge Chois Fhairrge*, p.
250; idem, 'Diminutive Suffix *-ín*'.   12 In what follows, the primary source of evidence is
Ó Riain, *Corpus genealogiarum sanctorum Hiberniae* (CGSH), and in particular the text called
'Aliases of saints' (§703). In many cases this evidence is itself derived from other
hagiographical texts, but these versions do at least provide a convenient collection of
material. Paragraph numbers without any further indication of source refer to this work.
13 For earlier forms of the names, see Bieler, *Patrician Texts*, pp. 62–3 (Muirchú: *Sochet,
Mauonius, Cotrice* (?), *Patricius*), pp. 124–5 (Tírechán: *Succetus, Magonus, Patricius,
Cothirthiacus*). On *Sucaid*, see *Wortk.* §87; also Guyonvarc'h, 'Celtique commun *Letavia*'.
Note also *Bablóir ainm do Pátraic* (Meyer, 'Sanas Cormaic', §117).

parentibus. Pupu apud Scottos, id est Papa; eo quia cathedram Petri petiuit .i. Cailbe .i. cáel beo, eo quia homines mirabantur eum uidere … (§735). The example of Librán in Adomnán's *Vita Columbae* (VC) is particularly striking since it shows the process in action: he is given the name *Librán* because, as Columba tells him, he is now free, *liber: Tu Libranus uocaberis eo quod liber sis.*[14] The idea that a different name from the one given at birth could be acquired during one's lifetime is familiar. The cases above exemplify that pattern in Irish. In a number of cases it would seem that the later a name was acquired the more perspicuous it is likely to be. In Irish terms that often means the more prone it is to be etymologised; the case of Nem's names *Púpú* (: *papa*) and *Cailbe* (: *cáel béo* 'thin living') is a good example of this process.[15]

The evidential problem occurs because we are not always clear that a particular hypocoristic form presupposes the radical form of the name. Hypocoristic versions of a radical form can be multiplied endlessly without necessarily assuming that the person who used a particular hypocoristic form had the original form in mind rather than another hypocoristic form. The point is that a hypocoristic form only carries affectionate and familiar connotations in relation to some other form, whether the radical form or not. If, then, the connections are broken, obscured by sound changes or lost through time, the hypocoristic connotation will vanish and the form will become a simple personal name. If a hypocoristic form of that name is then required, some other additional marking will be needed, and so cumulative hypocorism develops.[16]

So far these remarks have been intended to set the rest of the paper in some sort of methodological framework. Patterns of hypocorism in the ecclesiastical context of early Ireland provide at once a full and diverse range of material and certain difficulties. We may begin with the evidence itself. Two observations are worth making at this stage. First, that the Irish themselves were aware of different naming patterns is clear from the fact that they had different terms for different types of name:[17] *ainm ndíles* 'first name, Taufname';[18] *lánainm* 'full name, Vollname';[19] *forainm* 'nickname, agnomen, Übername';[20] *ainm báide*

---

14 VC ii.39. If we are to take *Librán* as associated with Latin *līber* with /i:/ rather than from *liber* 'book', then we perhaps ought to be spelling the derivative as *Líbrán*. Note that *Liber* functions as a wholly native name from which the hypocoristic *Molippa* probably derives. 15 Cf. the etymologies offered on the names of Patrick; references in n. 13 above. 16 The difficulties have afflicted early studies of Celtic names in a major way. For example, d'Arbois de Jubainville in several places claimed that the Irish personal name *Senach* was a hypocoristic version of a compound name corresponding to Gaulish names in *Seno-*, without ever attempting to provide evidence for identity between an individual named *Senach* and someone with a name beginning **Sen-*; see d'Arbois de Jubainville, 'Noms hypocoristiques'. Note that Jürgen Uhlich's study of compound personal names in Old Irish, *Morphologie*, contains no examples of compounds beginning with *sen-*. 17 See *Wortk.*, §33 n. 4; in what follows the German terms are Meyer's. 18 E.g. Stokes, *Calendar of Oengus*, p. clxix: *Aed … ainm díles Chumin.* 19 E.g. Book of Leinster, fol. 324b 14 (Best et al., vi.1401): *Ailill Basscháin a lánainm dó.* 20 E.g. Best and Bergin, *Lebor na hUidre*, line 6847: *forainm for*

'affectionate name, Kosename';[21] *comainm* 'cognomen(tum)'.[22] Some of these terms may have arisen under Latin influence, in particular, *comainm* and *forainm* which may well be calques on *cognomentum* and *agnomen* respectively. The following passage of Isidore may well have been influential:

> *Species propriorum nominum quattuor sunt: praenomen nomen cognomen agnomen. Praenomen dictum eo quod nomini praeponitur ... Nomen quia notat genus ... Cognomen quia nomini coniungitur ... Agnomen uero quasi accedens nomen, ut 'Metellus Creticus' quia Cretam subegit. Extrinsecus enim uenit agnomen ab aliqua ratione.*

> There are four kinds of proper name: forename, name, *cognomen* and nickname. The forename is so-called because it is placed before the name ... Name because it notes the family ... *Cognomen* because it is joined to the name ... Nickname indeed as if it modifies the name, e.g. *Metellus Creticus* because he subdued Crete. For the nickname comes from some other factor external to the name.[23]

For our purposes, the most striking feature is that at least by the period of *Cormac's Glossary* (late ninth/early tenth century), there was a term for a hypocorism, namely *ainm báide*, which Cormac applies to the name *Munda*.[24]

Secondly, patterns of hypocorism are not restricted to ecclesiastical contexts, though there is significant variation in the distribution of different formations. The figures presented below are simply a count from the indices of CGSH of the individuals having names formed with these particular suffixes or prefixes:

	Saints (41 pp.)	Others (39pp.)
-án	106	130
-íne/-éne	23	28
-óc	49	1?
Mo-/To-/T-	99	0
[Totals	277	159]

cach Mani .i. Mani Athremail ... **21** E.g. Meyer, 'Sanas Cormaic' §878: *Munda .i. mó a finda .i. ainm báide.* **22** E.g. CGSH, §735: *Nem macc ua Birn, brathair gle, dian chomainm Pupu Airne Nem* ' ... whose *cognomen* is P. A.' **23** Isidore, *Etymologiae* I.vii.1–2. **24** Note that the corresponding version at CGSH §630 has *baiste*. All versions of Cormac have *báide*. For the background details, see Stokes, *Félire Oengusso*, p. 226, which does does not contain the phrase in question. It is striking that the *Félire* note explains the identity of Fintan and Munnu/Munda as involving name-swapping *in commemoratione societatis* and does not envisage any possibility that the names are formally related, as indeed they are (*Munnu < *Mo-finn-*).

While *-án* and *-íne/-éne* names are common in all types of name, forms in *-óc* or *Mo/To-* are strikingly ecclesiastical. In other words, within the broad range of hypocoristic patterns available in early Irish, the last two were markedly ecclesiastical; on the other hand, no formant was markedly secular. These figures are useful as a guide to where we should look for ecclesiastical naming patterns, but they do not give much help by themselves. They indicate which are the productive patterns but they do not tell us how they are formed, i.e. from what base forms they derive. Early Irish hagiography does, however, provide quite a lot of evidence as to how hypocoristic names were thought to be related. We have already considered the evidence for individuals having different names; set out below is a range of material where individuals with different but formally related names are identified. In other words, what this material supplies is what is so often missing from discussions of hypocorism, namely evidence that a given individual had more than one name and that those names could be formally related. The evidence is divided into two groups: the first contains material where there is identification between the owner of a radical personal name and the owner of a hypocoristic version of it; the second where there is identification between two hypocoristic versions of a name without any apparent reference to the radical form. Each group is sub-divided depending on whether all the information is presented in a single entry or whether it has to be pulled together from separate entries or there is textual variation between different versions of the same entry.[25]

A. Hypocoristic form derived from radical form:
   (i) identification within one entry:
      CGH 122bb 10: *Midsuí/Midnúa .i. Mo Medóc*
      CGH 121a 42: *Díarmait mac Siabair m. Dalláin in suí .i. Mo Dimmóc Glinni Uissen*
      CGSH §242.1: *Momedoc Feda Duin – Aed proprium nomen*
         §703.4: *Carthach ainm Mochutu Lis Moir*
           .5: *Moeca ainm Fechin Fabuir*
           .7: *Dachua ainm Dachualen*
          .16: *Aed ainm Moedoc Ferna*
          .17: *Lasren ainm Molassi*
          .18: *Finnbarr ainm Finnen Maige Bile*
          .20: *Diarmait ainm Modimoc*
        §660: *Fintan ainm baisde Munnu m. Tulchain* (cf. Cormac Y 878)
   (ii) individuals in separate entries identifiable by regional affiliation or patronymy:

CGSH §285: *Aed Clúana Mór m. Eogain m. Bruidgi* = §498 *Maedoc Clúana Mór m. Eogain m. Bruide*
> §43: *Aedgen ... m. Lugair* = §662.113 *Aedhan mac Lucchair*
> §241: *Colum apstal Tiri Da Glas m. Nannida* = §457 *Colmán m. Nindeada*

(iii) textual variation within a single entry:
CGSH §129: *Malán m. Sinell* = §722.22 *chóic mac Sinell .i. ... Malach* (*Malán* BLc1M)

B. Identification made between two hypocoristic forms:
(i) identification within one entry:
Rhigyfarch, *Life of St David*, cap. 42: *Maedoc qui et Aidanus ab infantia*
CGSH §224: *Mothemnioc* (.*i. Temnén* added above line in La1) *m. Corbbain*
> §707.946: *Ultán Tech Tultóc*

(ii) individuals in separate entries identifiable by regional affiliation or patronymy:
CGSH §129: *Mobaí ... m. Sinill m. Nadfraich* = §132.1: *Baetán Clúana Andobair m. Sinill m. Nadfraich.* Cf. §369: *Baedan .i. Mobeoc macua Lada o Chlúain Abannabair ...*
> §181: *Cóemán Enaig Thruim* = §707.732: *Mochoemóc Enaig Truim*
> §236: *Gobban Find m. Lugdach* = §707.811: *Mogobboc Find.* Cf. *Vita S. Albei cap.* 45: *misit cum eis cocum ... scilicet Mogoppoc ... cocus eorum Gopbanus mortuus est.*[26]

(iii) textual variation within a single entry:
> §242.1: *Momedoc Feda Duin ...* (*Momaedhoc* B(LbM), *Mochoimoc* LC, *Maedog* R1)
> §302: *Mac hÍ – .i. Colmán .i. Conna – m. Amargin* (.*i. Conna* above line L, .*i. Colmaet* BLc, .*i. Conna* om. Lb, *m. Conna* MHH1, .*i. Colmán* om. H)

There are three questions which may usefully be distinguished about this material. The first has to do with how the system developed. The second concerns the perceived synchronic patterns of hypocorism at the time when the system was in full flow. The third has to do with how the jigsaw puzzle of names was reconstructed by subsequent generations. The evidence presented above probably has more to do with the last question than the first two. Yet if we are to say anything sensible about when and how they began to fail to understand the relationship between these names, then we ought to begin with the evidence for how the system arose and how it worked.

26 See Heist, *Vitae*, p. 128.

The most perspicuous part of the pattern was obviously the *Mo-/To-* prefix, often with the suffix *-óc* added to a (short) form of the full name (a pattern familiar from Wales as well as Ireland), e.g. Irish *Dochonna/Mochonna, Dobeóc, Docholmóc, Mochóemóg* (explained as *meus pulcer iuuenis*, VSH ii.167), *Moernóc/Mernóc*, Welsh *Teilo : Eliud, Teleri/Meleri : Eleri, Tyfaelog : Maelog, Mwrog : Gwrog*. This type has been discussed frequently and it does not figure greatly in what follows, except that we may note that this prefix can be combined with most of the other suffixed patterns except the *-ach* suffix.[27] Apart from the prefix pattern, the most common pattern involves suffixation. The most common native suffix in Irish is *-án* along with *-íne* and *-éne*. In British *-awc*, and its forerunner, were very common, e.g. *Maelog, Cadog* (though clear examples of hypocoristic and full form in Welsh are virtually non-existent), and this suffix was borrowed into Irish as *-óc*.[28] The cognate suffix in Irish to British *-awc* was *-ach*. However, it does not figure widely in hypocoristic usage, though in other functions it is extremely common. There are, however, some cases, the most well known of which is *Cainnech*, and it is possible that such cases represent a Hibernicisation of the *-óc* pattern.[29] In other respects, the processes of prefixation and suffixation are relatively clear except that it is not always clear on what stem a hypocoristic has been built. A full compound name consists of two elements and it would appear that either element could be pressed into service as the stem of the hypocoristic derivative.[30] What is less clear is what is going on with other aspects of the process, for example, the apparent doubling of consonants and palatalisation which also occurs in such forms. Gemination of consonants is a regular feature, e.g. *Luiccín* (: *Lóchán*), *Molaisse* (: *Laisrén*), *Gobbán / Mogobbóc* (cf. *gobae* 'smith'); the voicing of consonants may reflect British influence.[31] There are some forms, e.g. *Dimma* < *Díarmait, Comma* < *Colum* (or perhaps *Colmán*), where a development of a central cluster of liquid + nasal gives a double nasal. The formation seems to involve the first syllable to which is added a vowel, usually *-a*. Such developments are not unfamiliar; similar things seem to happen in Old English, e.g. *Irmin : Imma, Truma- : Tumma*. A further development seems to involve the palatalisation of this geminate cluster, e.g. *Lóchán : Luiccín, Énna : Éinne, Molaisse : Laisrén*. The creation of formations containing geminates and front vowels is very common across a wide range of languages and is not restricted to the Indo-European group though they are common there.[32] The rise of front vowel

---

27 See Evans, 'Comparison', p. 426 n. 16 (with detailed references); also Vendryes,'Sur les hypocoristiques celtiques'; Baumgarten, 'Syntax'; Russell, *Celtic Word-Formation*, pp. 111–2; Uhlich, *Morphologie*, p. 18. **28** Russell, *Celtic Word-Formation*, pp. 108–16. **29** See above, p. 239–40, on Hibernicisation and the influence of the British sound system on name forms. **30** See Russell, *Celtic Word-Formation*, pp. 16–23. **31** See above, p. 239–40. **32** See, for example, the two essays: Langdon, 'Sound Symbolism in Yuman Languages', and Ultan, 'Case of Sound Symbolism in Konkow', pp. 296–8. I am indebted to Joshuah Katz for these

suffixes in Irish, i.e. *-ín*, *-íne*, *-éne*, may be part of this trend. In general terms, none of this is surprising; it is a universal feature of hypocoristic patterns that they involve gemination and front vowels, hence the *Sammy*, *Robby* pattern in English.

There was, then, a range of different hypocoristic patterns available in early Irish. Some go together, such as *Mo-/To-* with *-óc* or with gemination, e.g. *Mochonna*. However, those aside, it would be reasonable to suppose that at any given moment only one marker of hypocorism would have been necessary. This takes us back to the earlier point that hypocorisms are relative; they only have hypocoristic status in relation to another form. Thus, *Colmán* may be regarded as a hypocorism of *Colum*; but, if in a particular instance an individual's name becomes fixed as *Colmán* and the link with *Colum* is lost or at least weakened, then how would a hypocorism based on *Colmán* be formed? Perhaps by the process of gemination and addition of a final vowel, thus *Comma* or perhaps *Conna*; certainly with *Conna* it is unlikely that a direct link with *Colum* would have been widely perceived, since at least one intermediate form containing *-n-* would seem to be required to generate the geminate *-nn-*. A form like *Conna* could be re-marked as a hypocorism by the addition of a suffix, thus *Conóc*, or by palatalisation, thus *Cainne*. And all of these could be prefixed by *Mo-/To-*. The palatalised form could also be suffixed (thus *Cainneóc* in the Martyrologies of Gorman and Donegal corresponding to *Cainnech* elsewhere), and also prefixed (thus the local name *Port Do Chaineóc* on the Shannon near Clonfert). It might also have been suffixed by what may be the Irish version of *-óc*, namely *-ach*, thus *Cainnech*.[33]

The scheme outlined in the preceding paragraph focuses very much on the creation of the system which seems to have been preceded by a process of what might be called 'proximate' hypocorism; that is, a personal name has something added to it to produce a hypocoristic form, and, when in turn that was treated as a simple personal name, it was again re-marked as a hypocorism. Schematically, we would have something like this:

$$
\text{Colum} > \text{Colmán} > \begin{cases} \text{Conna} > \text{Cainne} > \text{Cainneóc/Cainnech} \\[1em] \text{Comma} > \text{(Mo) Chommóc} \end{cases}
$$

references.   33 In passing we may note a further point about this form. We are assuming a form /caN'əχ/ with palatalisation, and that is what is indicated in the Latin Life of Cainnech in the *Codex Salmanticensis* (Heist, *Vitae*, pp. 182–98) and in the A text (Schaffhausen) of Adomnán. But it is worth pointing out that in the B text (reconstructed from the three British Library manuscripts) a spelling *-ai-* regularly represents a diphthong /ai/ while palatalisation is not marked, thus *Mailodran* and *Oingus* with diphthongs but *Elni* (*Eilni* A), etc. where palatalisation is not indicated. In B *Cainnech-* is regular with two examples of *Cannech-*. There seems then to have been some confusion over the spelling of this form, perhaps reflecting a primarily written tradition of the name.

We may now return to the distinction between the creation of the system, the subsequent interpretation and use of the system (i.e. what these individuals called each other), and finally the later perception of these patterns. The evidence tends to point us towards the last of these, since it is clear that the commentators were not always able to relate well evolved hypocorisms to their base forms. If the patterns developed 'proximately' in the way suggested above, then it is hardly surprising that they would have found difficulty in relating 'non-proximate' names, if they did not understand the system of generating the names. Moreover, once the system was up and running, the synchronic perception of it may well have been as a series of networks of names in which it would be possible to relate different forms of the basic name without any reference to the base name at all. Moreover, separate churches might have preferred different hypocristic forms of some saints' names. The following network may serve as an example:

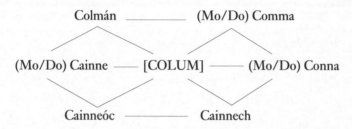

At that stage it may well have been perfectly possible for *Cainnech* to have been understood as a hypocorism of *Colum* without presupposing the intermediate stages. But it could equally well have been related to, for example, *Conna* without any reference to *Colum* at all; this would be the situation with the second block of material presented above in which hypocorisms were connected with other hypocorisms. Alternatively, *Cainnech* could have been regarded as totally unrelated to any of these forms, especially as the *-ech* formant is relatively rare in these schemes. The synchronic perception of this network would still require some understanding of what counted as an acceptable hypocorism, if only to exclude unacceptable patterns. But once understanding of some of these patterns was lost, then the full system, as outlined above, would distintegrate, and names could 'float' off and their formal connections be lost.

We can perhaps gain some insight into the difficulties confronting Adomnán with regard to these names by considering the entries in the *Annals of Ulster* for the period spanning his lifetime.[34] The following list presents all the hypocoristic names from the entries in the *Annals of Ulster* between 640-720 (secular names are in square brackets):

---

34 Mac Airt and Mac Niocaill, *Annals of Ulster*, pp. 120–75.

643	Crónán
645	[Lóchéne]
650	Crónán of Mag Bili
651	[Oiséne]
652	Ségéne
	Mainchéne
	[Cuiléne]
654	Colmán
	Oiséne Fota
	Dochua Lóchre
656	Mochoémóc (H2 add)
657	[Cellchéne]
658	[Tomán]
659	Dímma Dub
	Cuiméne
660	Finnán
	Colmán
661	Toiméne
662	Cumméne Fota
663	Ségán moccu Cuind
	Tu Énóc
	Dímma
664	Comgán moccu Teimni
	Báetán moccu Cormaicc
665	Manchán
	Colmán Cas
668	Colmán
669	Cuiméne
	Mochua m. Cuist
676	Colmán
	Fínán
687	Dochuma Conóc
	Oiséne
688	Segéne
689	Dochinne
690	Dobécóc
691	Crónán maccu Cúailne
696	Lóchéne Menn
	Moling
706	Dochonna Daire
711	Dicolán
	Ultán moccu Min
713	Doirbéne
718	Crónán

What emerges is that Adomnán would have been reasonably familiar with the *Mo-/To-* type names and those containing the suffixes *-án*, *-ín*, *-íne*, *-éne*, but the names involving gemination and palatalisation seem to have already vanished from the record as a productive pattern, leaving forms such as *Cumméne*, *Dímma*, *Toimméne* relatively isolated. That is not to say that he was familiar with all the nuances of the derivational patterns which resulted in the *-án*, *-ín*, *-íne*, *-éne* type. But the important point is that names created by these derivational patterns seem to have survived into this period, even if understanding of the patterns had not. On the other hand, even the names themselves which were generated by gemination and palatalisation do not seem to have been common in this period, at least in the *Annals of Ulster*. It would appear, then, that there was some kind of chronological distinction between these naming patterns. In this context, then, it would hardly be surprising if Adomnán failed to identify Cainnech with Columba (irrespective of their original identity or not).

The aim of this paper has not primarily been to examine the case for the identity of pairs of saints such as Columba and Cainnech, but rather to reconsider the linguistic aspects of the discussion. In passing, we have observed that *Cainnech* could be derived from *Colum* within the acceptable parameters of hypocoristic formation, though it is not a 'proximate' form and it does involve the relatively rare hypocoristic suffix *-ech*. That is not the same as saying that they are related; that depends on the much more significant non-linguistic evidence. More importantly, it has been possible to develop some views about how the system of hypocorism arose and also how it then came to decay and thus become incomprehensible to later hagiographers.

The Genealogies of Leinster as a Source for Local Cults

Edel Bhreathnach

The rich corpus of Irish genealogies remains one of the least exploited sources of information about medieval Ireland. Despite the valiant efforts of scholars such as Séamus Pender and M.A. O'Brien,[1] much material is unedited and detailed analysis has been sporadic. Yet it is clear that whenever genealogies are examined they are likely to reveal insights into many aspects of the period, whether regional polities or dynasties, centres of scholarly activity, echoes of mythological beliefs, topographical details or manuscript traditions. The importance of the genealogies as a source for Irish hagiography was recognised probably as far back as the seventeenth century, when the Four Masters compiled their work *Seanchas Riogh Ereann: Genealuighi na Naomh nEreannach*, now better known by its published title *Genealogiae regum et sanctorum Hiberniae*.[2]

In the past twenty years, quarrying of the genealogies for ecclesiastical and hagiographical information has advanced to some extent. Donnchadh Ó Corráin, in a paper published in 1981,[3] alluded to the importance of references in the genealogies to the hundreds of small churches throughout Ireland and to the families who owned them. Pádraig Ó Riain's monumental *Corpus genealogiarum sanctorum Hiberniae* made saints' pedigrees accessible to scholars, while his observations elsewhere have emphasized the significance of genealogical material when plotting the progress of a saint's cult.[4] He has proposed an argument similar to Ó Corráin's, that in its original milieu each saint's pedigree represented a document of title, insofar as title to office and property was transmitted by the founder to his or her family group.[5] Whereas Ó Riain has concentrated primarily on saints' pedigrees, Máire Herbert's comments in a review of the final volume of the diplomatic edition of the Book of Leinster, and in a more recently published paper on aspects of hagiography, have sought to establish the relevance of secular genealogies to hagiography.[6] She takes the

---

1 Pender, 'Guide to Irish Genealogical Collections'; O'Brien, *Corpus genealogiarum Hiberniae* (hereinafter CGH). 2 Walsh, *Genealogiae regum et sanctorum*. 3 Ó Corráin, 'Early Irish Churches', p. 337. 4 Ó Riain, *Corpus genealogiarum sanctorum Hiberniae* (hereinafter CGSH); Ó Riain, 'Irish Saints' Genealogies'. 5 Ó Riain, 'Conservation', p. 360. 6 Herbert, Review, pp. 167–8; eadem, 'Hagiography'.

view that 'saints' pedigrees have a contextual significance in secular genealogical tracts which they lack in the secondary corpus of genealogies of saints' and, therefore, that

> explicit demonstration in the secular tracts of the dynastic links between the powerful in church and state seems to mirror the Irish social situation, particularly from the eighth century onward.... The proposition remains to be scrutinized ... that the Irish saint's genealogy helps to plot the progress of his cult, and the pattern of succession in his churches.[7]

The view that hagiographical material preserved in secular genealogies reflects dynastic and ecclesiastical circumstances at various times and in different geo-graphical locations, depending on its context and origin, is central to this present study. In sum, the following analysis of the secular genealogies of pre-Norman Leinster attempts to demonstrate what detailed scrutiny of the genealogies of a small number of population groups in a relatively well-defined geographical area might add to the understanding of the origin and extent of a saint's cult and to the function of a saint's genealogy in a secular and ecclesiastical milieu.

We are fortunate in Ireland that an extensive corpus of genealogies survives in manuscripts dating from the early decades of the twelfth to the seventeenth century. Much of the material in these manuscripts pre-dates the twelfth century, in some instances possibly extending as far back as the seventh century. The periods at which the secular genealogies were shaped into a coherent structure have yet to be conclusively determined, though clues in the texts themselves, corroborated by other sources, suggest nodal points in the eighth century, the tenth century and the twelfth century, when shaping and re-appraisal took place. A high concentration of information about the dynasties of a particular area, or the inclusion of information additional to the genealogical lists, reflect the interests of these dynasties and probably of the churches or learned schools in which the material was collated and committed to writing. Allusions in the genealogies to particular saints' cults and to the dynastic and ecclesiastical interests of certain churches undoubtedly reflect claims which influenced the content of the secular genealogies.[8] By intensifying the examination of such components our understanding of the origin and structure of the secular genealogies will advance, with consequent benefits to the study of the dynastic and ecclesiastical polity of early medieval Ireland.

This paper deals with information provided in the secular genealogies with regard to the ecclesiastical rights of population groups dominating, settled in or maintaining interests in the geographical area of east-central Ireland. This is an area bounded to the east and south by the sea, extending to the Slieve Bloom

---

7 Herbert, 'Hagiography', p. 88.   8 Bhreathnach, 'Killeshin'; Mac Shamhráin, *Church and Polity*, pp. 13–18.

Mountains, and penetrating northwards into the modern counties of Meath and Westmeath. In genealogical terms the population groups inhabiting this region in early medieval Ireland were generically known as Laigin. The earliest surviving genealogical collections provide the basis of this study, namely, those preserved in Rawlinson B 502,[9] a codex compiled in Leinster *circa* 1130[10] and in the Book of Leinster,[11] a codex primarily compiled by Áed mac Crimthainn in the mid- to late twelfth century.[12] The main body of genealogical material relating to the Laigin, in line with other population groups, consists of pedigrees of dynasties, some powerful until the twelfth century and beyond, others of little consequence by the twelfth century. Interesting extraneous information is also recorded, including anecdotal evidence about saints, churches and ecclesiastical families associated with many of these dynasties. This evidence is most effectively evaluated by comparing it with information found elsewhere, in hagiographical texts, martyrologies, saints' pedigrees, post-Norman charters, land grants and ecclesiastical taxation documents. Its significance is further enhanced by using it as the basis for topographical and distributional analyses of churches associated with specific population groups. This is rendered possible by accurate mapping, insofar as place-names can be identified, and by correlation with archaeological monuments. Archaeologically many of the sites are similar, at least on superficial inspection, incorporating a church, graveyard, enclosure(s), mound, holy well, crosses or cross-slabs and post-Norman monuments such as a castle, settlement and earthworks.

The genealogies of the Laigin examined in this paper are those of the Uí Garrchon, the Uí Labrada (part of Dál Cormaic Loisc), Dál Messin Corb, the Uí Bairrche, and to a lesser extent – and following the pattern evident from the secular genealogies themselves – the Uí Chennselaig and the Uí Dúnlaing.

Part of the introductory section of the Laigin genealogies[13] is prefaced by comments which lay down the framework adhered to by the compilers. According to these, there were four primary kindreds (*prímshlointi*) of the Laigin:[14]

  (i)   Dál Niad Cuirp from whom are descended the sons of Catháir Már. The
        Uí Dúnlaing and the Uí Chennselaig belong to this group;

 (ii)   Dál Messin Corb whose status is that of *tánaisi ríg*;

---

9 CGH, pp. 24–86.   10 For arguments in favour of Glendalough as the location where Rawlinson B 502 was compiled see Ó Riain, 'Book of Glendalough'; idem, 'NLI G2'; idem, 'Rawlinson B 502' (responding to Breatnach, 'Rawlinson B 502').   11 Best et al., *Book of Leinster*, vi.1331–65.   12 O'Sullivan, 'Script and Make-up'.   13 Charles-Edwards (*Early Irish and Welsh Kinship*, p. 118) distinguishes two strata in the Leinster genealogies, Leinster A and Leinster B. He dates Leinster A to the twelfth century and Leinster B to the mid-tenth century. I concur with the general schema proposed by Charles-Edwards, although it might be altered somewhat by more detailed consideration of specific genealogies. For the purposes of this paper, the material under consideration is that of Leinster B.

(iii) Dál Cormaic Loisc whose segments are the Uí Labrada, Uí Gabla, Uí Chuilind and Cuthraige;

(iv) Dál Cairpri Loingsig Bic to whom the Araid Chliach belong.

This provides the order in which the genealogies are presented as is clear from the statement in Latin that ends the version of the preface preserved in Rawlinson B 502,[15] referring to the four sons of Cú Chorbb, in ascending order, as Coirpre Crúaid or Loingsech Bec, Cormac Losc, Mess(in) Corb and Nio Corb.

Within this overall structure a secondary format is used at certain junctures in the detailed genealogies of specific population groups, and this is particularly relevant to the hagiographical elements of the genealogies. The structure of the format may be summarized as follows:

(i) A list of saints belonging to the population group is prefaced by the phrases *is iat a nnoíb*, 'these are their saints'; *Y a quo X*, 'X [the saint] descended from Y [an ancestor]'; *Is díb X*, 'X [a saint] belongs to them'.

(ii) The pedigrees of the various segments of the group.

(iii) A component which details either the limits of a territory or the ecclesiastical and secular interests of the population group prefaced by the phrase *It é ranna Z*, 'These are the divisions of Z'; *is leo ó A co B*, 'They own from A to B'; *Z ó A co B*, 'Z from A to B'.

This format is most strikingly illustrated by specific examples from the Rawlinson B 502 version of the genealogies.[16] The section dealing with a segment of Dál Niad Cuirp, the Uí Lúascán, begins by explaining that they comprise four main segments (*cethri prímshlointi*): Uí Lúascán Midbine, Uí Lúascán Chrúaich, Uí Lúascán Trosca and Uí Lúascán Scuirri. This is followed by detailed pedigrees into which are inserted the topographical details of each segment's territory. Uí Lúascán Midbine's territory was from *Grellach Boair* (?Grallagh, barony of Balrothery West, Co. Dublin) to Áth mBithlann (Belan, barony of Kilkea and Moone, Co. Kildare). Uí Lúascán Chrúaich extended from *Toithi* or *Toichi* (unidentified) to Eiscir (Esker, barony of Newcastle, Co. Dublin) and from *Sceith Chruaich* (?Cruagh, barony of Uppercross, Co. Dublin) to *Féith nEchaille* (unidentified). The territory of Uí Lúascán Trosca is not mentioned. Uí Lúascán Scuirri extended from *Belach Echla* (?Ballaghaclay, barony of Rathvilly, Co. Carlow) to *Móen in Ibair* (?Monure, barony of Slievemargy, Co. Laois or Monatore, barony of Narragh and Reban,

---

14 Rawlinson B 502, f. 118b 35–45 (CGH, pp. 24–5); Book of Leinster, f. 312a 1–16 (Best et al., vi.1331–2). 15 Rawlinson B 502, f. 119a 6–7 (CGH, p. 26). The text includes the comment: *In genealogia .iiii. istorum filiorum ordo ascensionis ab inferioribus ad superiora ascendens.* 16 E.g. the section on the Uí Lúascán on ff. 120b 54–121a 19 (CGH, pp. 42–4).

Co. Kildare) and from *Ibur Brechmaige* (unidentified) to *Cluain Caín* (?Clonkeen, barony of Carbury, Co. Kildare). In their heyday, which would seem to be reflected in this text, the Uí Lúascán were powerful in an area extending from north of the Liffey through the Wicklow mountains as far as Áth mBithlann (Belan, close to Maistiu, Mullaghmast, Co. Kildare, one of the royal assembly sites in Leinster) and possibly westwards towards Slievemargy, Co. Laois. The section dealing with the Uí Lúascán ends by listing their saints and their churches, whose distribution accords well with their territory at its most extensive:[17]

> *Téora nóebhuaga Húa Lóscán: Cercc hóg hi Cnoitti, ⁊ Tailech máthair Finnia moccu Tellaich ⁊ Rígnach hi Cill Rígnaige hi Fothartaib Mara.*

The three holy virgins of the Uí Lóscán: Cercc the virgin in *Cnoitte* [?Nutstown, barony of Balrothery West, Co. Dublin], Tailech mother of Finnia moccu Tellaich and Rígnach in Cell Rígnaige [Kilrane, barony of Forth, Co. Wexford] in Fotharta Mara.

An alternative and more expansive secondary format is used in the section concerning the pedigrees of the Uí Bairrche. This begins with the declaration:[18]

> *Dáre Barrach mac Catháir a quo Húi Bairrche, is iat a nnóeb: Tigernach Cluana Euis et Fiacc ⁊ Fiachra(ich) hi Sléibti, Mac Táil Cille Cuilind ⁊ Mac Cuill hi Manaind et Émíne hi Letha; Diarmait mac Siabair m. Dalláin in suíi .i. Mo Dímmóc Glinni Uissen.*

Dáre Barrach mac Catháir *a quo* Uí Bairrche, these are their saints: Tigernach of Clúain Eois [Clones, barony of Dartree, Co. Monaghan] and Fíacc and Fíachra in Sléibte [Sletty, barony of Slievemargy, Co. Laois], Mac-Táil of Cell Chuilind [Old Kilcullen, barony of Kilcullen, Co. Kildare] and Mac Cuill in Mana [Isle of Man] and Émíne in Letha,[19] Díarmait son of Síabair son of Dallán the sage, namely, Modimmóc of Glenn Uissen [Killeshin, barony of Slievemargy, Co. Laois].

This statement is followed by the detailed pedigrees of the Uí Bairrche where allusion is often made to saints and ecclesiastical families of particular segments. The section closes with the *It é ranna* formula which concentrates on ecclesiastical connections:[20]

---

17 Rawlinson B 502, f. 121a 17–9 (CGH, p. 44).   18 Rawlinson B 502, f. 121a 39–42 (CGH, p. 46).   19 Letha is usually identified as Rome (Latium), but the reference here may be to Émíne of Ros Glais (Monasterevin, Co. Kildare) who is described in CGSH as *Émíne Bán Uissenaig* (p. 173, §722.34). This may denote a link with *Glenn Uissen*, which probably originates from **Uise*, the river or valley itself (see de hÓir, 'As Cartlann na Logainmneacha'). 20 Rawlinson B 502, f. 122bb 3–7 (CGH, p. 54); see also Ó Corráin, 'Early Irish Churches', p. 337.

It é ranna Húa mBairrchi la Laigniu .i. Cluain Conaire ⁊ Cell Auxilli ⁊ díb in Cróebán cita-conagab in cill ⁊ atát díb fine ocon chill .i. Húi Laigéni hi Caisse ⁊ Húi Duib-cillíne ⁊ is díb Húi Mátaid la Hú Enechglais Maige ⁊ is leo ó Áth Truisten cosin nÁth i Cill Corpnatan.

These are the portions of the Uí Bairrche amongst the Laigin: Clúain Conaire[21] and Cell Auxailli [Killashee, barony of Naas South, Co. Kildare] and that Cróebán who first founded the church is of them and they have kindred at the church i.e. Uí Laigéni in Caisse and Uí Duib Cillíne and the Uí Mátaid beside Uí Enechglais Maige and they own from Áth Truisten to the ford at Cell Chorpnatan.

The concept that secular genealogies consist of documents of title or at least of an attempt to define the rights and interests of a kindred is borne out in many instances by the genealogies of the Laigin. While it might be too bold to represent the genealogies as charters, some do record – in a less formulaic manner than either classically defined charters[22] or British-Latin charters[23] – the confirmation of property rights, privileges and other issues likely to cause disputes or involve legal transactions. It seems plausible to regard the formulae embedded in the secular genealogies as having been originally the type of traditional lore (*senchas*) of the historians (*senchaid*) consulted as part of legal proceedings. This is otherwise known from legal texts such as that concerning the seating arrangements in a law-court.[24] The formulae might also be equated with the written evidence relating to two churches disputing a piece of land such as that referred to in the *Collectio canonum Hibernensis*:[25]

> *Sinodus: Ager inquiratur in scriptione duarum ecclesiarum; si in scriptione non inveniatur, requiratur a senioribus propinquis, quantum temporis fuit cum altera ...*
>
> A synod: The land should be looked up in written evidences of the two churches; if not found there, inquiry should be made of elders neighbouring [on the property] as to how long it has been held by the present holder ...

---

21 This is either of two churches of that name, Cloncurry, barony of East Offaly, Co. Kildare or Cloncurry, barony of Ikeathy and Oughterany, Co. Kildare. 22 For discussions of the many categories of documents used to settle disputes see Davies and Fouracre, *Settlement of Disputes*. 23 Davies, 'Latin Charter-Tradition'. 24 Kelly, 'Old-Irish Text on Court Procedure', p. 85, §3. The *senchaid* sat in the side court (*táebairecht*), according to the text, *fo bith is fri senchus na senchad ⁊ is fri rellad na sencad dobeir int airecht taeb* 'because it is on the lore of the custodians of tradition and the clarification of the custodians of tradition that the court relies'. 25 *Collectio canonum* XXXII.24, XLII.8 (Wasserschleben, pp. 117–8, 163–4). See also Sharpe, 'Dispute Settlement', p. 183.

If these formulae in the secular genealogies reflect in some abbreviated form the model documents that were used either to confirm property transactions and inheritance rights or legal precedents, then perhaps they offer an Irish equivalent – albeit in the vernacular and less elaborate in the formulaic use of language – to Anglo-Saxon and Continental models.

The next section of this paper discusses in detail the hagiographical information extracted from the secular genealogies of each population group known as Laigin. As previously noted, this information is often accompanied by phrases such as *is iat a nnoíb* 'these are their saints'; *Y a quo X* 'X [the saint] descended from Y [an ancestor]'; *Is díb X* 'X [a saint] belongs to them'.

I UÍ GARRCHON CHURCHES AND SAINTS

Although the Uí Garrchon are normally regarded as part of or related to the Dál Messin Corb, their saints, churches and ecclesiastical families are listed separately in the secular genealogies.[26] If one follows the genealogical tract and distinguishes the Uí Garrchon from the other Dál Messin Corb saints and churches, an important pattern emerges. Five churches are mentioned, four of them associated with Uí Garrchon families, and one with saints. These are the seven bishops of Druimm Aurchaille (Dunmurraghill, barony of Ikeathy and Oughterany, Co. Kildare), together with the ecclesiastical families of the Uí Báethallaig described as the *fine* (kin-group) of Cell Bicsige (Kilbixy, barony of Moygoish, Co. Westmeath), the Uí Draignén of Fobur (Fore, barony Fore, Co. Westmeath), the Uí Inmete of Conull (Old Connell, barony of Connell, Co. Kildare) and Cenél Nath Í of Cell Éogain in Mag Ailbe (Killogan, barony of Carlow, Co. Carlow).[27] While the number of churches mentioned is small, their geographical extent is nonetheless noteworthy. They are all located inland, with two churches, Cell Bicsige and Fobur, located in the north midlands, and not in the eastern coastal area to which the Uí Garrchon were confined from the ninth century, if not much earlier. This pattern corroborates the view, derived from information in the annals and in the Lives of Patrick, that the Uí Garrchon ruled much of north Leinster at the height of their power in the sixth century with the focal point of their kingship located at Naas or Ráith Inbir.[28] As to noteworthy details concerning hagiographical material in the Uí Garrchon section of the secular genealogies, Bicsech of Cell Bicsige introduces a recurring phenomenon: that of the extent of minor cults. The saints' pedigrees

26 Rawlinson B 502, f. 118b 24–9 (CGH, p. 24). 27 On the identification of Killogan and its proximity to Clonmelsh, see Fanning, 'Some Field Monuments', and Nicholls, 'Charter of John', p. 199. 28 On the territory of the Uí Garrchon and the identification of Ráith Inbir, see Smyth, *Celtic Leinster*, p. 51; Nicholls, 'Land of the Leinstermen', pp. 543–6; Byrne and Francis, 'Two Lives of Saint Patrick', pp. 87–8.

do not identify Bicsech's genealogy[29] nor does this secular genealogical tract claim that she was of the Uí Garrchon. Dedications to Bicsech are dispersed as far apart as Cell Bicsige (Kilbixy, barony of Moygoish, Co. Westmeath), Cell Bicsige (Kilbixy, barony of Arklow, Co. Wicklow)[30] and Imlech na Lega (possibly in Lége, barony of Portnahinch, Co. Laois).[31] Ailbhe Mac Shamhráin, in his study of the monastery of Glendalough, recognizes the close association between Bicsech's dedications, Dál Messin Corb segments and 'locatable' Brigidine dedications.[32] That the Uí Báethallaig were *fine Cilli Bicsige*, according to the secular genealogies, suggests that they may have been the *fine érlama* 'family of the founder-saint'.[33] Whether Bicsech was genuinely of the Uí Garrchon is unknown. She was certainly claimed by them. Another metaphor for the claims of the founder saint's family is used in connection with the Uí Garrchon sub-segment, Cenél Nath Í of Cell Éogain. Of them it is said *is leo grian na cille* 'they own the church's land (glebe land)', which, on the evidence of the laws and of other hagiographical texts,[34] is equivalent to holding the rights of the *fine érlama*.

II DÁL MESSIN CORB

The Uí Garrchon were part of Dál Messin Corb, but lists of Dál Messin Corb saints in the secular genealogies and the saints' pedigrees have a different context to the material discussed specifically in relation to the Uí Garrchon (section (i) above). Dál Messin Corb churches, ecclesiastical families and saints mentioned in the secular genealogies are best summarized as follows:

Church	Family	Saint
Cell Garraisc (?Kilkerris, Ballymore Eustace)	Síl Conaill (a quo Uí Bróccéni)	Téora ingena Éogain meic Conaill
Glenn dá Locha (Glendalough, Co. Wicklow)	Uí Náir	Cóemgen
Ard Sratha (Ardstraw, Co. Tyrone)	Uí Náir	Éogan

⟶

29 CGSH, p. 109, §663.10; p. 116, §670.22.   30 Price, *Place-names of County Wicklow*, vii.474–5.   31 CGSH, p. 113, § 670.22; p. 325.   32 Mac Shamhráin, *Church and Polity*, pp. 185–6 (Figure 6D).   33 Ó Riain, 'Conservation', pp. 359–60.   34 Meyer, *Betha Colmáin maic Lúacháin*, p. 38, lines 1–3: *Táncatar malle dochum Colmáin 7 dorónsat a manchine dó eter bás 7 bethaid 7 a ferann ar bithdílsi co bráth, conid síatt is fine Griein [leg. griein] ac Laind ósin*

Continued

Church	Family	Saint
Cell Manach Escrach (Kilnamanagh, Co.Dublin)	Uí Náir	Lóchán 7 Énna
Mugna Moshenóc (Dunmanoge, Co. Kildare)	Uí Náir	Moshenóc
Tír dá Glas (Terryglass, Co. Tipperary)	Uí Náir	Mochóeme
Enach Truim (Annatrim, Co. Laois)	Uí Náir	Cóemán
Cell Lainne (Killenny, Co. Kilkenny)	Uí Náir	Petrán
Clúain Fota Báetáin Aba (Clonfad, Co. Westmeath)	Uí Náir	Éitchén mac Maine écis
Cúl Fothirbi (?Merrion, Co. Dublin)[35]	Uí Náir	Nath Í mac Senaich
Tech Tacru (Saggart, Co. Dublin)	Uí Náir	Moshacru mac Senáin
Cell Dara (Kildare)	Uí Náir	Conláed
Senchill (Shankill, Co. Dublin)	Uí Náir (Uí Amsáin)	Berchán
Cell Adgair (Killegar, Co. Wicklow)	Uí Náir (Uí Chonnois)	Findbarr
Cell Rannairech (Kilranelagh, Co. Wicklow)	Síl Senaig (Uí Loppéni)	Nath Í of Cúl Fothirbi Conláed of Kildare belonged to this family[36]

alle ('They both together came to Colman and granted him service both in death and life, and their land to be his own for ever. And from that time onward they have been the family of the glebe land in Lann'). **35** Price, 'Antiquities and Place Names of South County Dublin', p. 130: O'Brien, 'Churches of South-East County Dublin', p. 519. **36** Rawlinson B 502, f. 120b 45–6 (CGH, p. 42); Book of Leinster, f. 313b 7–8 (Best et al., vi.1339).

When this list of Dál Messin Corb saints preserved in the secular genealogies – both the Rawlinson B 502 and Book of Leinster versions – is compared with the lists in the corpus of saints' pedigrees[37] and in the text known as the Litany of Irish Saints,[38] it is evident that the list in the secular genealogies is not as extensive as the other two. With the exceptions of Éogan of Ard Sratha (Ardstraw, barony of Strabane, Co. Tyrone), Mochóeme of Tír dá Glas (Terryglass, barony of Ormonde Lower, Co. Tipperary) and Cóemán of Enach Truim (Annatrim, barony of Upperwoods, Co. Laois), all the saints are associated with places known to have been under Dál Messin Corb authority at various periods up to the ninth century, which suggests that this list was compiled prior to that date. The concentration of saints in an area north of the Wicklow Mountains (Cell Manach Escrach, Tech Tacru, Senchill and Cell Adgair), the survival of interest in a midland church (Clúain Fota Báetáin Aba) and in a church in the Nore valley (Cell Lainne),[39] and the emphasis on the origins of Conláed bishop of Kildare (?died 520) and his family's link with the early church at Cell Rannairech are testimony to the earlier glory of Dál Messin Corb when their kings claimed the kingship of Leinster.[40] The interests of the *paruchia* or of *familia Coemgeni* at Glendalough are less to the fore in the secular genealogical list than in the other lists of Dál Messin Corb saints. While Glendalough's interests are probably reflected by the inclusion of outliers such as Cóemán of Enach Truim, the territorial interests of the Dál Messin Corb dynasties predominate in the secular genealogies. Ailbhe Mac Shamhráin notes with regard to the tract on the *familia Coemgeni*, preserved in the Litany of Irish Saints, that, whereas a few individuals mentioned seem to have been associated historically with Glendalough, this list is more likely to represent a catalogue of churches subject to the *comarba* at Glendalough.[41] He also comments on the geographical extent evident in the Litany's list in which several members are associated with the midlands, with northern and eastern Munster and north-east Ulster. In political terms, he surmises that this distribution suggests a combination of factors, namely, the ambitions of early Laigin overkings in Munster, the survival of Laigin segments in the midlands and a consistent relationship with the ruling dynasties of the Ulaid.[42] In all versions of the Dál Messin Corb list, the majority of saints belong to the Uí Náir, a segment of Dál Messin Corb which, unlike the related Uí Garrchon and Uí Nastair, did not figure as a politically important dynasty in the historical period. They exercised power through ecclesiastical connections, and most especially by claiming that Cóemgen of Glendalough belonged to them.[43]

37 CGSH, pp. 30–1, §181.   38 Book of Leinster, f. 373b 40–55 (Best et al., vi.1698–9): see also Plummer, *Irish Litanies*, pp. 54–7.   39 Note the existence of a sub-segment of the Uí Náir in this area, *Síl Cruachéne for Gabraun* (Rawlinson B 502, f. 120b 36 [CGH, p. 41]).   40 Smyth, 'Húi Néill', pp. 130–7.   41 Mac Shamhráin, *Church and Polity*, pp. 114–19.   42 Ibid, p. 227.   43 Ibid, pp. 111–13.

III DÁL CORMAIC LOISC: UÍ LABRADA

The hagiographical material in the secular genealogies concerning Dál Cormaic Loisc, and most specifically the Uí Labrada, differs somewhat from that relating to other population groups. There are few references to specific churches, those mentioned being *Tech Midnann* and *Cell Chlochair*[44] (unidentified), Killeshin[45] and Cell Chonaich[46] (Kilkenny West, Co.Westmeath). Three saints are claimed by them: Abbán moccu Cormaic, whose cult was extensive in Leinster,[47] and the duo known as *in dá Shinchell*, Sinchell mac Cenannáin and Sinchell or Sen-Shinchell mac Corcáin,[48] both of whose pedigrees are incorporated into the Uí Labrada genealogies. Despite the existence of two saints known as Sinchell with distinct pedigrees, it is possible that this is an instance of duplication or of one person being a disciple of the other, and hence the adoption of the terms *sen-* and *óc-*. One of them was a renowned, and allegedly severe, *magister* of an ecclesiastical school, if the forbidding tract in the corpus of saints' pedigrees known as *Teist Chóemáin Chluana meic Threóin* is to be believed.[49] Though they are not associated with any church in the secular genealogies, the corpus of saints' pedigrees links these two saints with Cell Achaid (Killeigh, barony of Geashill, Co. Offaly), *Cell Shinchill* (unidentified) and *Domnach Sinchill* in Uí Máil (unidentified).[50]

The ecclesiastical connections of Dál Cormaic Loisc, as related in the secular genealogies, depended much on saints' mothers. The mothers of Colum mac Crimthaind of Terryglass, of Modimmóc of Killeshin and of Mochua mac Lonáin of Timahoe, Co. Laois, are claimed in Rawlinson B 502 to have belonged to various segments of Dál Cormaic Loisc.[51] The Book of Leinster adds that Coímell mother of Cóemgen of Glendalough was also of Dál Cormaic Loisc.[52] Connections with churches through a maternal lineage undoubtedly offered a population group an opportunity to hold an office and perhaps to enjoy other privileges in a particular church. Dál Cormaic Loisc claimed an interest in important churches through maternal connections: Terryglass, Glendalough, Killeshin and Timahoe. As I have demonstrated elsewhere,[53] Killeshin – whose founder Díarmait was claimed by the Uí Bairrche on the paternal side and by Dál Cormaic Loisc on the maternal side – was situated on a boundary between Dál Cormaic Loisc and Uí Bairrche.[54] Dál Cormaic Loisc, in the guise of one segment, the Uí Máeluidir, controlled the

---

44 Rawlinson B 502, f. 119b 42 (CGH, p. 33).   45 Rawlinson B 502, f. 120a 9 (CGH, p. 35).
46 Rawlinson B 502, f. 120a 11 (CGH, p. 35).   47 Ó Riain, 'St. Abbán'.   48 He is called Óc-Shinchell or Sinchellus Iunior in CGSH (for variants see ibid., p. 265).   49 Meyer, *Hibernica minora*, pp. 41–2; CGSH, p. 167, §719.   50 Mac Shamhráin, *Church and Polity*, pp. 73, 133.   51 Rawlinson B 502, f. 120a 4–10 (CGH, p. 351).   52 Best et al., *Book of Leinster*, vi.1336, line 29.   53 Bhreathnach, 'Killeshin', pp. 34–6.   54 Rawlinson B 502, f. 120a 1–2 (CGH, p. 34).

church at Killeshin from at least the mid-ninth to the early eleventh century, providing eight abbots, one bishop and one *airchinnech*.

With regard to Cóemgen of Glendalough's mother, Coímell, she appears less credible than the other mothers referred to in the Dál Cormaic Loisc genealogies. Her name is a compound of the element *Cóem-*, so prevalent in Cóemgen of Glendalough's alleged family.[55] In the pedigrees of saints Coímell is listed as one of the saints of Dál Messin Corb: *Coimell ⁊ Trenan Drui i nImgan.*[56] The Book of Leinster's list of the mothers of Irish saints names Coímell as mother of Cóemgen of Glendalough, of Cóemán Santlethan of Ardcavan (barony of Shelmaliere East, Co. Wexford), of Nadchóeme of Terryglass and of Cóemóc.[57] The last of these is listed in the saints' pedigrees as Cóemgen's sister and is also given the alternative name Coímell.[58] Mac Shamhráin observes that the use of the element *Cóem-* as a 'genealogical contrivance' was an attempt 'to band together a group of foundations which retained some recollection of a common origin but had in fact diverged through local fragmentation of the cult of Cóemgen'.[59] This concept of 'genealogical contrivance' applies very much to Dál Cormaic Loisc saints. Such genealogical connections enhanced Dál Cormaic Loisc, and more specifically Uí Labrada, claims to many churches from the east coast to the Shannon. If genuine, in a pattern similar to the material concerning Dál Messin Corb saints in the secular genealogies, they preserve a memory of a period when Dál Cormaic Loisc's power was much more extensive prior to the rise and expansion of the Uí Dúnlaing in Leinster.[60]

IV UÍ BAIRRCHE

The Uí Bairrche were a population group whose influence in the early historic period is believed to have extended into the east midland area as far as Tara.[61] Their ever-shrinking authority in the early medieval period was concentrated in the Barrow valley area.[62]

Whereas Dál Messin Corb had Cóemgen of Glendalough and the *familia Coemgeni*, the Uí Bairrche claimed no monastic *paruchia*. The ecclesiastical influence of the Uí Bairrche was exercised in important churches such as Killeshin and Leighlin and through association with a far-flung company of prominent saints, Tigernach of Clúain Eois, Fíacc of Sléibte, Mac Táil of Cell Chuilinn, Mac Cuill of Mana (probably Maughold, Isle of Man), Émíne *hi Letha*, Díarmait *alias* Modímmóc of Glenn Uissen and Magister of Cell Magistrech.[63] When Tigernach and Mac Cuill, whose churches lay outside Uí

---

55 Mac Shamhráin, *Church and Polity*, p. 180. **56** CGSH, p. 31, §181.15. **57** Book of Leinster, f. 372a 40–2 (Best et al., vi.1692). **58** CGSH, p. 30, §181.1. **59** Mac Shamhráin, *Church and Polity*, p. 180. **60** Ibid, p. 82. **61** Byrne, *Irish Kings and High-Kings*, pp. 136–7. **62** Nicholls, 'Some Place-names from *Pontificia Hibernica*', pp. 86–7. **63** For identifications

Bairrche territory, are excluded and the churches of the Uí Bairrche as listed in
the secular genealogies are plotted, their extent corresponds to the area subject
to that population group's influence when the Uí Dúnlaing and Uí Chennselaig
increasingly pushed them further west towards the Barrow valley in the late
seventh and early eighth century. According to the genealogies, Cell Chuilind,
Clúain Conaire, Cell Auxailli and Cell Chorpnatan (?Kill, Co. Kildare) either
had an Uí Bairrche founder saint or were in the hands of Uí Bairrche families.
Further afield the Uí Boíth who were part of Uí Meic Barddíne, a segment of the
Uí Bairrche who held interests in Tech Moshacru or Tech Tacru (Saggart, barony
of Saggart, Co. Dublin), retained possession of the church at Banba Mór
(Bannow, barony of Bargy, Co. Wexford).[64] According to the secular genealogies,
Robartach mac Elgusa of the Uí Boíth was *princeps* of Banba Mór.[65]

The importance of Díarmait of Killeshin, to the compilers of the Uí
Bairrche pedigrees at least, is underlined by the references to him on three
occasions in this section of the secular genealogies. Ó Corráin first noted that to
'the monastery of Glenn Uissen we no doubt owe the Uí Bairrche genealogies
with their detailed listing of churches and church families'.[66] The inclusion in
the Rawlinson B 502 text of Dál Cormaic Loisc genealogies of Flann Fili mac
Máelmáedóc's family, the Uí Máeluidir, and of their close relatives, as well as
the fact that the family's pedigree ends with Flann himself (died 979), suggests
that he was involved in their compilation in the mid-tenth century.[67]

One interesting legendary anecdote relates to Mac Cuill of Mana. In a
lengthy narrative in Muirchú's *Life of Patrick*,[68] Mac Cuill moccu Greccae –
regarded in the Life as belonging to the Greccraige and not to the Uí Bairrche
as suggested by the secular genealogies – was a wicked ruler in the territory of
the Ulaid *ut cyclops nominaretur*. He set a trap to kill Patrick but was outwitted
by the saint. He repented but Patrick, rather harshly since Mac Cuill had
agreed to be baptized, ordered him to go down to the seashore unarmed and to
leave that part of Ireland:[69]

> *nihil tollens tecum de tua substantia praeter uile et paruum indumentum quo*
> *possit corpus tantum contegi, nihil gustans nihilque bibens de fructu insolae*
> *huius, habens hoc insigne peccati tui in capite tuo, et postquam peruenias ad*
> *mare conliga pedes tuos conpede ferreo et proiece clauim eius in mari et mitte te*
> *in nauim unius pellis absque gubernaculo et absque remo, et quocumque te*

of these churches see page 254 above. On the identification of Cell Magistrech see Nicholls,
'Charter of John', p. 254. **64** Nicholls, 'Land of the Leinstermen', pp. 557–8.
65 Rawlinson B 502, f. 121b 14–8 (CGH, p. 48). **66** Ó Corráin, 'Early Irish Churches',
p. 331. **67** For further arguments in favour of this supposition see Bhreathnach,
'Composition of the Leinster Genealogies' (forthcoming). **68** Bieler, *Patrician Texts*,
pp. 102–7. **69** Ibid, p. 104, lines 21–9.

duxerit uentus et mare esto paratus et terram in quamcumque defferat te diuina proudentia inhabita et exerce ibi diuina mandata.

... taking none of your property with you except one paltry short garment which just barely covers your body, neither eating nor drinking anything that grows in this island, with this emblem of your sin on your head and when you have come to the sea, fetter your feet with an iron chain, throw its key into the sea, board a small boat made of a single hide, without rudder or oar, and be ready to go wherever the wind and the sea shall carry you; and on whatever shore divine Providence may land you, dwell there and practise the divine commandments.

This is the well-known punishment of being sent adrift. Having survived his punishment, Mac Cuill landed on the Isle of Man and, as Muirchú declares:[70]

Hic est Maccuill di Mane episcopus et antestes Arddæ Huimnonn.

This is Mac Cuill, bishop of Mane and prelate of Ardae Huimnonn [Isle of Man].

That the Uí Bairrche connection with Mac Cuill is not alluded to by Muirchú is not altogether unusual. The Latin Life of Tigernach of Clúain Eois, which reflects the interests of Clúain Eois (Clones, Co. Monaghan) and not those of the Uí Bairrche, makes much of his mother's kin, the Airgialla, but simply refers to his father as being a noble, *Laginensem genere, nomine Corbreum*,[71] despite Tigernach's prominence in the Uí Bairrche genealogies.

The final sentence in the Uí Bairrche section of the secular genealogies states:[72]

Cormac [mac] Diarmata ro idpair Imblech nEch do Chomgall Bendchuir, is leo ó Beluch Forcitail co Bannai.

Cormac mac Diarmata [a seventh-century Uí Bairrche king] granted Imlech nEch to Comgall of Bangor. They own from Belach Forcitail to the Bann.

This reference adds to the ample evidence for a connection between Bangor and Leinster, and specifically between Bangor and the Uí Bairrche.[73] The particular grant to Bangor is referred to in the Latin Life of Comgall.[74] Cormac mac Díarmata, styled incorrectly as a king of Leinster of the Uí Chennselaig,

---

70 Ibid., p. 106, lines 16–7. **71** VSH ii.262, cap. 2. **72** Rawlinson B 502, f. 122bb 8–9 (CGH, p. 54). **73** Byrne, *Irish Kings and High-Kings*, pp. 136–7, 145–6; Mac Shamhráin, *Church and Polity*, p. 122. **74** VSH ii.16, cap. 42.

offered himself and three strongholds (*cum tribus castellis*) in the territory of the
Laigin to God and to Comgall. The three forts were at Cetharlach (*super ripam
fluminis Berba positum*), Foibran [?Foyran, barony of Fore, Co. Westmeath] and
Ard Crema.[75] One might speculate that Imblech nEch of the genealogies is an
alternative or earlier name for Cetharlach [Carlow] and is not the same as
Imblech Equorum apud Ciarrige Connact mentioned in the *Additamenta* to the
Book of Armagh, which Bieler identified as Emlagh, Co. Roscommon.[76]

V UÍ LÚASCÁN

The structure of the section in the genealogies dealing with the Uí Lúascán
segment of Dál Niad Cuirp has been mentioned in the earlier part of this paper.
In ecclesiastical terms, the Uí Lúascán are credited with three holy virgins, two
of whom are associated with churches: Cercc Óg of Cnoitte, Tailech mother of
Finnio moccu Tellaich and Rígnach of Cell Rígnaige in Fotharta Mara.[77] The Uí
Lúascán origin of Finnio moccu Telduib, founder of the monastery of Clonard,
was their greatest claim to influence in the church.[78] Tailech was Finnio's mother,
while Rígnach was his reputed sister. Rígnach was further claimed to be the
mother of the fourth abbot of Clonard, Colmán moccu Telduib (died 654) and
also of Fintan Fochlae and Garbán of Cell Garbán (?Kilmagarvoke, barony of
Tullowphelim, Co. Wicklow) near Achad Aball (Aghowle, barony of Shillelagh,
Co. Wicklow).[79] While chronologically unlikely,[80] Rígnach's relationship with so
many ecclesiastics not only reflects the persistent interests of the Uí Lúascán, but
once more underlines the usefulness of women to those intending to preserve or
to accentuate the reputation of a people in decline. Rígnach is commemorated in
churches as far apart as Kilrane, Co. Wexford, Kilrainy (barony of Carbury, Co.
Kildare) and Templerainy (barony of Arklow, Co. Wicklow).

VI DOUBLE INTEREST AND PATRICIAN CHURCHES

As pointed out by Ó Corráin, families of quite different origin could have
property rights in the same church, though it is not clear whether they were

---

75 Unidentified. This church is also mentioned in the Life of Munnu (ibid., ii.231, cap. 14)
as being *inter nepotes Barraidh* [Uí Bairrche] and *iuxta mare*, which might suggest a location
on the south Wexford coast.   76 Bieler, *Patrician Texts*, pp. 168 (lines 23–4), 260. Later
evidence supports this suggestion: in a charter dated to *c*.1200 John Comyn, Archbishop of
Dublin during a vacancy in the see of Leighlin, instituted Thurstin of Hampton to the
moiety of a number of churches in the lands of John de Clahalla, one of them being the
church of St Congall of Catherloc (St John Brooks, *Knights' Fees*, pp. 56–7).   77 Rawlinson
B 502, f. 121a 17–8 (CGH, p. 44).   78 Byrne, 'Community of Clonard', pp. 158–60.
79 Best et al., *Book of Leinster*, vi.1697, lines 18–20.   80 Byrne, 'Community of Clonard',

simultaneous owners or whether one displaced the other.[81] Five examples of what might be described as 'double interest churches' can be deduced from the secular genealogies relating to the Laigin, not all examples of the same type of overlapping interest. Killeshin was dominated by Dál Cormaic Loisc for a lengthy period through their domination of many ecclesiastical offices, while the Uí Bairrche dominated it politically. The church was situated on a border between these two population groups, at the time of its foundation at least.[82] Tech Tacru's founder saint, Moshacru mac Senáin, was claimed by Dál Messin Corb, while the Uí Rónáin, a segment of the Uí Bairrche, claimed privileges there.[83] Fothairt and Uí Bairrche families had interests at Cell Auxailli,[84] while the Uí Bairrche and the Uí Dúnlaing, in the guise of a segment known as Uí Fhínáin, are mentioned as connected with Cell Chorpnatan.[85] The situation in this church was replicated elsewhere, in that the authority of an earlier dominant power was superseded or had to accommodate a rising or later power. Kildare is the prime example of levels of authority in one monastery,[86] a case also reflected in the secular genealogies. The opening section of the Fothairt genealogies leaves us in no doubt as to whom Brigit, the reputed foundress of Kildare, belonged. The poem *A Eochaid Airtt Fuath arafalnather iath anéoil* foretells the arrival of Brigit: *bid ala Maire márChoimded máthair*, 'she will be the second Mary, the mother of the great Lord'.[87] As noted in the section concerning Dál Messin Corb, Conláed bishop of Kildare, was claimed by them. The genealogies of the Uí Dúnlaing make many claims on their own behalf regarding Kildare. Clann Bruidge, of whom the Uí Fhínáin of Cell Chorpnatan were part, also boasted Áed or Máedóc úa Dúnlaing of Cluain Mór (Clonmore, barony of Rathvilly, Co. Carlow) and Brandub mac Fíachrach, a seventh-century abbot of Kildare. Elsewhere, it is noted in the secular genealogies that Óengus mac Áedo Find, Brandub's possible successor as abbot of Kildare, and Áed Dub mac Colmáin, *rígepscop Cilli Dara* (?died 639), were of Uí Dúnlaing stock.[88] The situation of other churches subject to similar intrusions can be deduced also from the genealogies. The Book of Leinster genealogies provide ample evidence that Uí Fhailge families took possession of Cell Achaid, the church of the two saints called Sinchell, who were of the Uí Labrada.[89] Achad Aball, a church in origin associated with the Uí Lúascán, succumbed to the Uí Fhelmeda, a sub-segment of the Uí Chennselaig, as proven by the pedigree of Mithigén mac Coscraig, a tenth-century abbot of Achad Aball.[90] The Annals of

p. 160, §4. 81 Ó Corráin, 'Early Irish Churches', p. 337. 82 Bhreathnach, 'Killeshin', pp. 35–6. 83 Rawlinson B 502, f. 121b 15 (CGH, p. 48). 84 Rawlinson B 502, ff. 122b 3, 126a 2 (CGH, pp. 54, 82). 85 Rawlinson B 502, ff. 122bb 7, 124b 29 (CGH, pp. 54, 74). 86 Ó Riain, 'Pagan Example'; Mac Shamhráin, *Church and Polity*, p. 72. 87 Rawlinson B 502, f. 125b 19 (CGH, p. 80). 88 Book of Leinster, f. 316a 22–6 (Best et al., vi.1356). 89 Book of Leinster, f. 314d 1, 19, 39, 45–6 (Best et al., vi.1348). 90 Book of Leinster, f. 317c 22 (Best et al., vi.1365).

the Four Masters record the death in 1018 of his son Cormac, also an abbot of Achad Aball.

Patrick and churches either dedicated to him or associated with him pervade the ecclesiastical matter of early Ireland. That is not the case in secular genealogies of the Laigin. The only direct reference to St Patrick is the sentence in the Book of Leinster section of the Uí Chennselaig pedigrees which reads: *Is é Crimthann ro chreit do Patric i rRaith Bilig 7 foracaib bennachtain fair co brath*, 'It was Crimthann [son of Énna Cendselach] who believed Patrick in Ráith Bilig [Rathvilly, Co. Carlow] and he [the saint] left blessings upon him forever'.[91] Although it is not apparent from the genealogical tracts, some churches mentioned are known from Patrician texts to have been subject at certain periods to Patrician influence. The most renowned case was that of Sléibte, whose bishop Áed, at whose request Muirchú wrote his Life of Patrick, offered his church to Armagh in the late seventh century. Three other churches in north Leinster are recorded by Tírechán in his *Collectanea* as having submitted to Patrick: Druimm Aurchaille, Cell Auxailli and Cell Chuilinn:[92]

> *Et perrexit ad fines Laginensium ad Druimm Hurchaille et posuit ibi Domum Martirum, quae sic uocatur, quae sita est super uiam magnam in ualle et est hic petra Patricii in uia. Exiit ad campum Lifi et posuit ibi aeclessiam et ordinauit Auxilium puerum Patricii exorcistam et Eserninum et Mactaleum in Cellola Cuilinn.*

> And he proceeded to the territory of the Laigin, to Druimm Aurchaille, and established there the House of Martyrs, as it is now called, which is situated on the great road in the valley, and there is Patrick's Rock on the road. He went out to Mag Lifi and established there a church and ordained Auxilius, a pupil of Patrick, an exorcist and Eserninus and Mac Táil in Cell Chuilinn.

None of this material is included in the genealogies. But why should the compilers of tracts on the pedigrees of the Laigin acknowledge that any of its saints or churches owed their origins to Patrick's mission? The focus of the genealogies was more local or regional, the compilers' aims being to establish the secular and ecclesiastical interests or rights of particular population groups and dynasties. Although worthy of much greater notice than can be given here, it is nonetheless important to record that two types of genealogical compiler seem to have existed, local or regional and provincial or national. The latter fitted the work of the former into a greater schema. In the case of the Laigin, Flann mac Máelmáedóc belonged to the first category, while Áed mac Crimthainn worked on the more extensive schema of genealogies.

91 Book of Leinster, f. 316c 10–1 (Best et al., vi.1359). 92 Bieler, Patrician Texts, p. 162, lines 25–9.

In conclusion, I return to Professor Herbert's comment referred to at the beginning of this paper, in which she supposed that saints' pedigrees had a contextual significance in secular genealogical tracts. When compared to other sources relating to saints, these tracts contain remarkably little hagiographical information about the saints mentioned because the primary focus is not on the saint's life, but on the kin-group to whom he or she belonged. The material concerning saints, churches and ecclesiastical families in the secular genealogies of the Laigin would appear to confirm this opinion. Saints and their churches and cults are used as confirmation of rights to property and also as memories of or testimonials to influence in territories which have succumbed in many instances to the authority of other population groups. The dating of this material is vital to providing a chronological framework for the corpus of Laigin genealogies. On the basis of this critique of the hagiographical material, the 'geo-political' image conveyed by the ecclesiastical and hagiographical information in these tracts suggests an early origin for the material. While the compilation of the material into a coherent genealogical schema for the Laigin (as the material survives today) dates possibly to the tenth century, the hagiographical and ecclesiastical elements in the secular genealogies would suggest that the sources for these compilations may date to as far back as the seventh century.

ACKNOWLEDGEMENTS

I wish to thank Professor Pádraig Ó Riain and Mr Raghnall Ó Floinn for comments on earlier versions of this paper.

The Study of Folk-Motifs in Early Irish Hagiography: Problems of Approach and Rewards at Hand

Dorothy Ann Bray

The study of early Irish hagiography has in the past been dominated by textual and philological concerns, and by other concerns of history – the date and provenance of the texts, ecclesiastical and political issues related to the provenance of the texts, and the social and religious worlds which the texts might reveal. Such concerns rule the field even to this day. In the sphere of folklore and literature, the Lives of the early Irish saints have always been a rich mine of material yet, also, a rich minefield. The problems of authorship and dates, while not the main interest of the folklorist, nevertheless circumscribe any folkloristic study. A literary analysis of the Lives is similarly circumscribed, and all too often falls into literary judgements: that the Lives at their best are good folklore; at their worst, they are bad literature and even worse history.

Dáibhí Ó Cróinín makes no bones about his views of hagiographical texts: 'Most of these Lives are less than edifying, being little more than a catalogue of miracles and wonders, some of them amusing, most of them ridiculous.'[1] ' ... With few exceptions, the saints' Lives are a dismal swamp of superstition and perverted Christianity, dreary litanies of misplaced reverence and devotion.'[2] The Lives of the saints, to Ó Cróinín, have 'little claim to strictly historical importance' except for incidental information on contemporary social and economic conditions. But what of his comment regarding the genre itself 'There is no development in the genre; seventh-century texts are practically indistinguishable from twelfth-century ones, and the same tedious formulae recur time after time, often borrowed shamelessly from one Life to another'?[3] Such a view is less than helpful in analysing the Lives of the saints, and ignores certain aspects of just what it is that constitutes literary development and change in a genre that is, admittedly and unashamedly, formal and formulaic, yet by no means homogeneous over a range of five centuries.

In a paper presented in Montreal in May of 1996, Professor Claude Poulin of the Université de Laval reviewed the various methodologies used in the

1 Ó Cróinín, *Early Medieval Ireland*, p. 210.   2 Ibid., p. 211.   3 Ibid., pp. 210–1.

study of hagiography and called for a broadening of perspectives, especially in the light of the new technological and cross-disciplinary resources now available to researchers in medieval history and literature. Professor Poulin reminds us that medieval hagiographical sources are, like all other historical sources, 'des construits et non des données' and pertain to other spheres of medieval life and culture, not just the religious.[4]

Speaking as an historian, he pointed out the limitations of a folkloristic approach to the study of hagiographical literature:

> La difficulté reste de s'entendre sur la notion de folklore en sortant du raisonnement circulaire habituel:
> – ce qui est folklorique a été revelé par S. Thompson;
> – si c'est dans la répertoire de S. Thompson, c'est folklorique.[5]

Such a summation is, unfortunately, too often true. It is also too often true that scholars of hagiography rarely look beyond an approach other than the textual, philological or historical. But Professor Poulin goes on to say: 'Même si une oeuvre hagiographique est entièrement constituée d'extraits tirés de documents préexistants, elle possède une légitimité entière aux yeux de l'historien.'[6] And hagiography possesses that legitimacy also in the eyes of the folklorist. For it is precisely that shameless borrowing, that so-called tedious recurrence of formulae, that seeming lack of development in the genre which are of interest to the student of folklore and literature.

This paper attempts to address the problems of a folkloristic study in medieval hagiography, in the analysis and classification of motifs according to the grand master, Stith Thompson, and in the light of the new resources mentioned by Professor Poulin. Current research in various fields, and the new computer technology, are now allowing the 'inter-' in 'interdisciplinary' to become more meaningful. Such a study should demand that the literary and the folkloristic be tackled with an awareness of the historical dimension, even while maintaining their own principles. Yet for Thompson and his follower in the area of Irish literature, Tom Peete Cross, this was not the case.

The validity of a literary and folkloristic interpretation of medieval hagiography is not in question – not to folklorists and students of literature, at any rate – but the problem is how to resolve that circular thinking with regard to folklore in the Lives. It is taken as a given that a medieval hagiographical text is a literary construct, composed according to narrative conventions similar to those of folktales: the structure is formalistic, the characterization is simple, the plot is linear. The episodic structure most favoured in hagiography reveals no sub-plots or secondary narratives, and in this again resembles the traditional

---

4 Poulin, 'Méthodes de recherche', p. 8.   5 Ibid., p. 5.   6 Ibid., p. 8.

folktale. The focus, too, is always on the expression of the saint's sanctity, as Père Delehaye laid down in his seminal study on saints' legends.[7]

What, then, can a folkoristic study of medieval hagiography reveal? The standard reply to such a question invariably involves notions like 'folk belief in saints', 'popular religion', 'the image of the saint in popular religion'. But it must be kept in mind that most *vitae* are literary creations produced in a literate and monastic milieu, for the purpose of reading; and such narratives follow certain 'compositional principles', similar to the folk narrative, however rudimentary they may seem, within a literate milieu. The use of a particular canon of motifs is one of those compositional principles, and folkloristic studies turn on the examination of the recurrence of these motifs in both Judaeo-Christian and native Irish tradition.

It is often taken as a given, too, that saints' lives have had an oral existence prior to their being consigned to parchment and ink, largely on the evidence of the folk motifs we find in these Lives. Even such a literary text as Adomnán's *Life of Columba*, within its tripartite form, follows the episodic convention found in other *vitae* which do not have such a well-documented literary pedigree, and relates numerous miracles of the saint which can be found in Thompson's *Motif-Index of Folk Literature*.[8] Therefore, following the argument described by Poulin, it is folklore. Yet, although oral sources relating to Columba no doubt reached Adomnán's ears,[9] his work, it must be remembered, is not a record of an oral tradition, but a literary shaping of that tradition – 'un construit, pas une donnée'. As such, to try to extract from medieval hagiography the medieval popular imagination and folk beliefs regarding saints becomes a risky business, although it is certainly not without interest and profit.

However, much of the problem of a folkloristic study lies with Stith Thompson and that circular reasoning of folklorists: if it is folklore, it is in Thompson; and if it is in Thompson, it is folklore. Stith Thompson's monumental compilation and classification of motifs, in his *Motif-Index of Folk Literature*, all six volumes of it, is both a triumph of scholarship and a tribulation to researchers. It cannot be ignored, yet its use is curtailed by the fact that Thompson's interest in folklore was geographical not historical; his concern was to provide a tool for the folklorist, an encyclopedia of reference. The Index was meant to be a statistical scientific classification of folklore material, not an analysis of motifs in their context nor a discussion of their significance.[10] For this reason, his references are not, for the most part, to primary texts. Furthermore, his

---

7 Delehaye, *Légendes hagiographiques*.   8 Thompson, *Motif-Index*; cf. Bray, *List of Motifs*, pp. 50–2.   9 By his own admission Adomnán learned several stories 'from the lips of certain informed and trustworthy aged men' (VC, *Praefatio secunda* [Anderson and Anderson, p. 6]). See also Ó Riain, 'Towards a Methodology', for a discussion of the orality of the *vitae*. 10 Thompson, 'Narrative Motif-Analysis'.

classification and numbering system is frequently confusing, owing to a logic which is often not immediately apparent.

An example of a single motif and its classification will illustrate the problem: the motif of wild deer who plough for a saint (in the Lives of Saints Berach (BNE 18), Déclán (VSH ii.29), Finnian (BL 2552), Mochua (VSH ii.7), Mochuta (BNE 9; VSH ii.25), Rúadán (BNE 14, VSH ii.19). The motif is readily found under B256.9: '*Stags plough for saint*', classified under the major category of B. *Animals*, sub-category B250: *Religious animals*. (Logically speaking, all animals which interact with the saints might be considered Religious Animals – and indeed, most are thus classified). There is as well B292.4: '*Stags plough for man*. Also draw chariot, bear burdens and allow saints to use their horns as a book rest.' This, curiously, is all listed under one motif, and is not separated into four discrete motifs or sub- motifs.

These numberings are as they appear in the 1955–8 version of Thompson's *Motif-Index of Folk Literature*, which had supposedly been coordinated with Cross' 1952 *Motif-Index of Early Irish Literature*.[11] Cross does not have a number B256.9: '*Stags plough for saint*'; but he does have B292.4, and beneath it, B292.4.1 '*Wild oxen (deer) plow for man (saint)*'. Thompson, under B292.4 '*Stags plow for man*' has cross-referenced B188 '*Magic deer*'. This is where it appears in Cross, but in Thompson, it appears as B184.4 '*Magic deer.*' B443.1 '*Helpful deer*' appears as B445 '*Helpful deer (stag, doe)*' in Cross.

This may simply be a case of lack of coordination and human error, but it does create a dilemma – does the researcher follow Cross or Thompson? Does the stag plough for a man or for a saint? And what does one do with the motif of the saint's book resting on the stag's horns or the deer drawing the saint's chariot, both of which have little to do with ploughing? Or is the main focus the deer, and are they Magic or Helpful or Religious animals?

Cross's classifications are marginally more logical than Thompson's, perhaps because he was dealing with a more specialized corpus, but it, too, suffers from some of the same drawbacks as Thompson's *Motif-Index*. Nevertheless, Thompson's system of classification has stood since its publication as the standard reference work. The availability now of Thompson's *Motif-Index* on CD-Rom will undoubtedly make searching easier: one can use a word search instead of having to rely on Vol. 6, the index to the Index (which is where most people learn to start, before attempting a major search). But the logic of his classification system still creates problems, and the discrepancies with Cross will still cause the researcher in early Irish literature to stumble.

In my own preliminary effort to compile a motif index for the Lives of the early Irish saints – and it was and still is only preliminary – I had tried to get around some of the confusion by creating more inclusive categories, then

---

11 Cross, *Motif-Index.*

dividing them into more specific ones, in order to make cross-referencing easier, and to get out of the circular reasoning described by Poulin.[12] Thompson is also looked to for the definition of a motif in folklore, as well as the types of motifs to be found – that is, the smallest recurrent element in folk narrative. But what of motifs which often recur together in a stable pattern? What of incidents which do not appear in Thompson's list, but which might be considered motifs with regard to the saints? These are only two of the problems I encountered when I first embarked on this project.

The corpus of material was defined as *vitae*, Lives of saints, specifically, rather than other material such as martyrologies, annals, hymns, and so on. The initial corpus was further refined to include a representative sample rather than the entire hagiographical corpus, hence the perceived gaps in the list of texts. These other materials were (and are) to be added in the next stage. The sample was selected for a study in depth, rather than in breadth. As in any experiment, the sample was subjected to scrutiny as to its content in order to isolate and record what were determined as motifs. My admiration for Thompson grew the more I pursued this idea – as did my exasperation with his system of classification.

It seemed then that a less complex, numerical system of classification was in order, if only to sort out the kinds of motifs found in the Lives and to begin a rough analysis of their occurrence. Without consciously trying to imitate the structure of Adomnán's work or the *Tripartite Life* of St Patrick, I developed a three-part division in my list of motifs, partly to aid in cross-referencing and partly to experiment in showing the links between individual motifs, motifs which seem to form a 'motif cluster'. An example is the motif of the saint's staff, which when planted in the ground often produces a fountain in a desert, this fountain then usually having healing powers (attested in the Lives of Ailbe, VSH i.16; Brigit, B.Br. 15; Colmán Elo, VSH i.7; Fínán, Fin. 556; Moling, BLSM 69; Rúadán, BNE 16, VSH ii.11; Senán BL 2179). This cluster of motifs has obvious parallels to a miracle of Moses (a prefiguration of Christ), and the 'cluster' (for lack of a better word) has a considerable frequency in the Lives (seven instances so far, with or without the healing element).

But first, what did this study reveal? In the broad classifications which were used (based on the studies of Thompson and others), it became clear on a purely statistical basis that miracles of healing, of raising from the dead, and of the provision of food provide the motival basis for the majority of narrative episodes in each saint's Life. While specific incidents do vary (which only proves that Irish hagiographers were not lacking in imagination when they drew upon oral and native tradition and 'shamelessly' reproduced miraculous events), in the general sphere such miracles reflect the major preoccupations of life in early Ireland: the maintenance of good health and of the food supply for

12 Bray, *List of Motifs*.

survival. But more to the point, several miracles of the Irish saints have their precedents in the Scriptures, frequently in the gospel Lives of Christ, whose most important miracles were those of healing, provision of food, and resurrection of the dead.

It does not take much effort in narrative study to observe in the episodic structure of the saints' Lives an imitation of the gospel Lives of Christ, particularly Matthew and Luke, with regard to form and structure – that is, the narrative composition, the generic construct. The lives which the saints try to lead have their model in the life of Christ, but the model is not an *imitatio* in the strictest sense; the literary gospel Lives of Christ provide a kind of prototype, rather than a rigid template, of the writing of the Lives of the saints, which then become modified to suit the cultures and conditions in which they are composed.

One of the most prevalent diseases in the Lives is leprosy, which makes several appearances in Biblical texts as well. This is not to deny that leprosy (or some similar disease) existed in early Ireland, as did paralysis, deafness, blindness, and broken limbs (which are the next most popular ailments). The point is, these afflictions also appear in the Scriptures and provide instances of divine punishment or miracles of healing as they do in the *vitae*. To take the Lives as historical evidence of a prevalence of leprosy in Ireland can therefore only be undertaken with great caution, although the attitudes and concerns of a society with only basic medical knowledge are readily detectable in such episodes.

Angelic visions and the appearance of heavenly light also form a large group within the Lives, and with them prophecies. The saint's prophetic powers are emphasized in numerous ways, including instances of 'second sight'. While the gift of prophecy belongs to both the Christian and native traditions, it is perhaps safer to say that the saints' prophetic powers owe as much to the Judaeo-Christian tradition as to the native pre-Christian. The gift of 'second sight' invariably enhances the sanctity of the holy man or woman, as does the visitation of angels and the phenomenon of divine light about the saint. The fact that the power of prophecy was familiar in native tradition serves to enhance the saint's image, in his own land, even further.

All this is well known and often goes without saying. However, what of the interpretation of these motifs? It is in the miraculous elements of the Lives that the analysis of 'folk beliefs' and the 'popular image of the saint' has its foundation – the saint as holy magician, as inheritor of druid tradition (suitably Christianized) or *filid* tradition;[13] or else, on a historical level, the saint is seen as a political force in the community, interceding with petty kings, opposing

---

13 See especially Plummer in VSH i.cxxix–clxxxvii. However, for a more recent point of view, see Ford, *Celtic Folklore and Christianity*, which presents a collection of articles with an expanded idea both of the saint and of folklore in the *vitae*.

tyrants, exacting tribute, and, by the by, acting as a spiritual figure. This recalls the aforementioned example of a motif cluster – the saint's staff and the healing fountain can be construed as an imitation of the miracle of Moses, the prefiguration of Christ, in whose name the people were baptized in the waters of life. The connection is subtle, yet discernible.

Motifs which cannot be related to Christian tradition, but rather to Irish tradition, have been given attention precisely for being non-Christian, for possibly pointing to an older stratum of beliefs, folktales, myths, and so on. Dan Melia, for example, has examined the motif of fasting against God in Irish hagiographical literature in light of pre-Christian practices in Ireland (the *troscad*) as an example of the accommodation of native values to Christian, and vice versa.[14] On another level, the mention of white, red-eared cows, especially in the early Lives of St Brigit, such as the *Vita prima* – but not in the Life by Cogitosus – appears also to point to an older, native tradition.[15] The birth of St Brigit in the *Vita prima* seems almost self-evidently to stem from an older pre-Christian tradition: the child is born of a nobleman and a slavewoman at dawn on the threshold of the dairy, an event with strong links to secular saga material.[16] St Brigit's feast day, 1 February, supports this interpretation: it is the pre-Christian festival associated with Brigit the goddess. The infant saint is raised in a druid's household, thus associating her further with pre-Christian beliefs; she cannot eat his food but must have the milk of a white, red-eared cow, of the breed belonging to the fairy folk.

B251.2.10.1. (under the sub-category of B250. *Religious animals*) is listed in Cross under B259.11.1. '*Brilliantly white cow comes to be milked for infant saint*' (in Thompson, there is also B531.2 '*Unusual milking animal*', which is not in Cross). It is marked in Cross as a distinctively Irish motif, although he records only two instances of it. B259.11, in Cross, is '*Cow gives twelve measures of milk for the Twelve Apostles of Ireland*', another distinctively Irish motif, recorded in one instance, according to Cross, in the *Félire Óengusso*[17] – the cow in question is the famous Dun Cow of St Ciarán of Clonmacnoise. I am certain that someone will at some point make a connection with the twelve portions of butter which the young Brigit was wont to make for the poor, which is a feature (not a distinctive motif, although it could come under V401. *Charity of saints*) shared by the *Vita prima* and the Life by Cogitosus.[18]

The use of this native Irish motif, undoubtedly borrowed from a secular, story-telling tradition, shows the ingenuity on the part of the hagiographer in both christianizing what appears to be a pre-Christian homegrown Irish feature, and in hibernicizing a Christian literary genre.[19] The milk of the brilliantly

---

14 Melia, 'Law and the Shaman Saint'.   15 See Connolly, '*Vita prima Sanctae Brigitae*'; also Sharpe, '*Vitae S. Brigidae*' and *Medieval Irish Saints' Lives*.   16 See McCone, 'Early Irish Saints' Lives', pp. 35–6.   17 Stokes, *Félire Óengusso*, p. 203.   18 Connolly, '*Vita prima Sanctae Brigitae*', p. 17; Connolly and Picard, 'Cogitosus' *Life of St Brigit*', p. 13.   19 See

white cow, milked by a pious Christian virgin, is the only food the infant saint will take, not the druid's. The brilliantly white cow must therefore be touched by the Lord, who feeds the holy infant with the milk of his wisdom, as in I Pt 2.2 – 'Like newborn babes, long for the pure spiritual milk, that by it you may grow up to salvation'. However, I would maintain that the occurrence of such a motif in any saint's *vita* is not a good enough indicator of the date of its composition, nor is the number of identifiable 'folk motifs' to be found in any *vita*.

There are, as well, motifs which are neither identifiably Christian (i.e. through Scriptures, apocrypha, etc.), nor native Irish (through saga material). For example, again from Brigidine tradition, the anecdote of the silver brooch found in the body of a fish; this appears both in Cogitosus's Life[20] and in a variant form in the *Vita prima*.[21] A nobleman entrusts a brooch to a chaste woman after whom he lusts; thinking to reduce her to being his slave, he steals the brooch and throws it into the sea. When he demands the brooch, the woman flees to Brigit for safety; at that moment, a fisherman brings a fish to the saint, in which the brooch is found. In the *Vita prima*, a stolen lunula, thrown into the sea, is recovered in the innards of a fish. Cross offers the following classifications: N211.1. '*Lost ring found in fish*'; N211.1.0.1.* '*Lost articles found in interior of fish through virtue of saint*'; N211.1.5.* '*Brooch lost by saint found in fish*'.

The story is clearly a variation on the Classical story of the ring of Polycrates, an ancient Indo-European tale, but why this motif should appear in Irish hagiography, in the Life of St Brigit, is a question which remains unanswered. James Carney traces this motif in *Táin Bó Fraích* and *Vita Kentigerni* in a discussion of the connection between the two texts. He concludes that *Táin Bó Fraích* borrows the motif from the incident of Rhydderch's Ring in the Life of St Kentigern, and that it enters Irish literary tradition ultimately from the *Vita prima* of St Brigit. This would indicate that the motif in its earliest manifestations in Irish literature was considered appropriate hagiographical material,[22] which was later incorporated into a secular tale; but the sacred association itself remains unexplained.

Nevertheless, the motif's occurrence does demonstrate the saint's divine power, which is the main point of the anecdote, as well as the fact that the tale had reached Ireland by this time. It is worth noting that Cross indicates that its use in a saint's Life is distinctively Irish, although he cites only a single reference in Plummer's Introduction to the *Vitae sanctorum Hiberniae*.[23]

---

especially Ó Riain, 'Pagan Example', for a superb discussion of this aspect of the subject. **20** Connolly and Picard, 'Cogitosus' *Life of St Brigit*', pp. 21–2. **21** Connolly, '*Vita prima Sanctae Brigitae*', p. 46. **22** Carney, *Studies*, pp. 35–56. My sincere thanks go to Dr John Carey for reminding me of Carney's discussion and also for his kind suggestions regarding the rest of this paper which have saved me from my more egregious errors. Those which remain are all my own. **23** VSH i.clxxxv. The motif does crop up in other saints' Lives, such as the Life of St Cainnech, ibid. i.15.

The discussion now leads back to the question: What does a systematic classification of motifs in the Lives of the early Irish saints reveal? That the Lives share compositional features in common, in creating the images of Christian virtue which they wish to promote, and that such compositional features are stable and conservative (revealed in the perceived lack of development in the genre) seems to be reasonably clear. But such features need also to be read in context, with an eye to their meaning in hagiography. A motif index is thus a useful reference point, a foundation for the interpretation of the Lives as hagiographical literature, rather than as strictly historical or philological sources.

The classification of motifs also reveals the kind of imagery that was used to portray the saints, the miracles which not only placed them in the Scriptural narrative tradition of Christ and his apostles, the patriarchs and the prophets, but also in the native storytelling tradition of Irish heroes – the champions and protectors of their respective groups – and the prophetic druids and poets. The gift of foresight, even in hindsight, is a crucial attribute for the virtuous saint, through whom the power of God must flow in order to interpret God's signs to the laity and to mediate between God and man.

The motifs reveal major concerns both of the Church and of the laity; among them are the maintenance of the food supply, the prevalence of disease and the consequences of debility (such as poverty, starvation, homelessness and loss of status), the concern for property rights, the clash of secular and ecclesiastical law (especially in the case of criminals and captives in whom the saints took an interest). And it is in hagiography especially that we may see, if we look through the appropriate interpretative lens, just how native traditions were adapted to the Christian agenda.

It is clear that Thompson's *Motif-Index*, as grand and breathtaking as it is, needs some modifications: a more rationalized numerical classification; standardized descriptions of motifs using identifiable keywords; a better and more coordinated cross-referencing of the motifs. The CD-Rom version should make some of these modifications feasible, as well as an update of the entire work. In the meantime, instead of working against Thompson, it is necessary to work with him, so to speak, and the project of defining and classifying motifs in the Lives of the Irish saints continues, using both Thompson and Cross as a basis. Where a motif does not have a classification in either, Thompson's system has the advantage of being flexible enough for the creation of new numbers; for, even if it is not in Thompson, it just might be folklore, as Thompson himself would have agreed.

Whether or not this project is successfully or satisfactorily completed remains to be seen. However, the attempt itself and what may already be construed from such an ambitious overview have raised questions, in my mind at least, regarding not only the classification of motifs but the very definition of a motif. There is also the matter of recurrent motif 'clusters' or sequences –

those tedious formulae so shamelessly borrowed from one Life to another – which current motif-indices cannot adequately underscore, but which a study aimed more at the literary elements may yet disclose. Such a study may also lead to a further assessment of the compositional principles which define hagiography as a literary genre, and, in conjunction with linguistic studies, to a further understanding of the genre's development through an examination of those motival formulae and thematic preoccupations in the Lives.

And an overview of motifs in the Lives of the saints may eventually reveal that which is, or which is meant to be, edifying in those catalogues of wonders and miracles – that which gives meaning to the Lives of the saints and makes a saint a saint in the value and belief system of the early Irish Church. Having celebrated the anniversary of the death of St Columba of Iona, 1400 years ago, we should remind ourselves that we know him through his hagiographers, who range through the best and worst examples of the genre. But he does not seem to have suffered too badly at their hands.

The Reproductions of Irish Saints

Joseph Falaky Nagy

In the pre-Norman Latin Lives of Brigit we are introduced to a female disciple of the great saint's, named Darlugdach.[1] This young woman, our sources tell us, falls in passionate love with a young man in a moment when she lets her guard down. The feeling is reciprocated, and they arrange to meet. The night she is supposed to go to her beloved, however, Darlugdach happens to be sleeping with Brigit in the same bed. Feeling hopelessly torn between staying in bed with her teacher and joining the young man in his, the girl prays to God for deliverance and receives it in the form of the prescription that she should fill her shoes with hot coals and then try to walk away from her bed. Darlugdach takes the divinely-transmitted advice and finds that the pain which she experiences in her feet blots out all desire, and so she goes back to bed still a virgin. The next morning she confesses to Brigit, who, in fact, had been awake during her bedmate's trials. The saint commends Darlugdach for having resisted temptation – and heals her feet. Subsequently, so close does the bond between teacher and pupil become, that shortly before Brigit's fated hour Darlugdach asks if she herself may die at the same time. Brigit refuses, but promises that Darlugdach will be her abbatial successor, and that she may have the privilege of passing away a year from the day of her own, Brigit's, death, so that they may enjoy the same feast day.[2]

What is perhaps most remarkable about this legend is the way that Darlugdach in the coda to the story of her great temptation draws closer and is almost assimilated to the figure of her saintly mentor Brigit. Darlugdach's death will replicate that of her role model, and from the perspective of posterity it will be hard to keep the dates of their deaths, or feast days, apart. It is as if the virgin, having finally refused to go down a path leading to sex and possible reproduction, had opted for another kind of affiliation, leading to an altogether different sort of reproduction: namely, becoming virtually a *Brigida secunda*. Notably, the course of Darlugdach's career as a woman saint is determined by Darlugdach herself. Even though Brigit is awake and could have intervened in

---

1 *Vita prima Sanctae Brigitae*, AASS, Februarii I, pp. 32–3 (trans. Connolly, pp. 43–4); *Vita quarta*, ed. Sharpe, *Medieval Irish Saints' Lives*, pp. 197–8. 2 AASS, Februarii I, p. 134 (trans. Connolly, p. 48); Sharpe, *Medieval Irish Saints' Lives*, p. 207. Darlugdach is mentioned for 1 February in Best and Lawlor, *Martyrology of Tallaght*, p. 14.

the young girl's crisis of conscience, she does not – specifically, the text says, in order to test Darlugdach's resolve.

Of course, as much as Darlugdach desires to be with Brigit through both life and death, she cannot simply be a clone of Brigit's, with the details of her own experience erased from the hagiographic record. Darlugdach carelessly catches sight of a man who arouses desire in her, while Brigit is never said in our sources to have been guilty of such a lapse. The pupil is given by God, and successfully undergoes, the notable cure by 'hot-footing', resembling nothing experienced by her teacher, who is rarely associated with such rigorous asceticism in the stories told about her. And while they may ultimately share the same feast day, Darlugdach is still Darlugdach, and Brigit is still Brigit.

There is another legend preserved in early Brigidine hagiography that features not a would-be Brigit but another woman actually called Brigit.[3] The latter invites the more celebrated Brigit to a meal. While they are eating, the saint eyes something intently on the serving dish. Hostess Brigit asks guest Brigit what is wrong, and she explains that she is watching a demon perched on the plate. Blessed with an inquiring mind, the hostess asks if she could partake of Brigit's vision. After her eyes are signed with the cross, she too sees the monstrous demon. Like any good Irish saint, who will not let a supernatural being manifest itself without interrogating it, Brigit proceeds to engage the demon in conversation. He reveals that he arrived in the company of a virgin who came to visit or dwell in the same house, and who is guilty of the sin of laziness. This woman is summoned, she too is shown the demon, and her laziness becomes a thing of the past.

The virgin afflicted by the demon is not the same person as Brigit the hostess, but what they have in common also separates them both from the saint. This is the same difference that comes between Brigit and Darlugdach: namely, a difference in perspective. Darlugdach allows her eyes to roam, and to see what Brigit would shun, and so Darlugdach ends up conflictedly in love. Although Brigit the hostess may be a holy woman, she cannot see what the 'real' Brigit sees, without the latter's guidance. Of course, the unseeing Brigit does finally share in the vision, as does even the lazy girl who brought the devil in the first place. It is no small matter for a saint to share her or his sight with another: it is a sign of intimacy and privilege. Just as Darlugdach makes the decision to stay in bed with Brigit and later requests to share the same death with her, so too Brigit's namesake is not forced to share in the horrid vision of the demon, but asks if she may do so. In both stories, saint and devotee draw closer together with mutual consent, not as the result of the saint's power to impose her will.

Clearly, then, Brigit can remake willing women in her image. What can she do with her male devotees? Not surprisingly, the results in this case of what I

---

3 AASS, Februarii I, p. 121 (trans. Connolly, pp. 20–1).

would call *saintly reproduction* are different, but Brigit transforms and leaves her mark upon men, too. An example of how the division and subsequent merger between identities, saintly and secular, can operate over the boundary of gender is to be found in the story of Conall mac Néill's makeover at the hands of Brigit.[4] This member of the dynastic family of the Uí Néill asks her to bless his military expedition, to the undertaking of which he and his men are compelled by the *stigmata* they wear. These are the notorious *signa diabolica* originally noted by Richard Sharpe, mysterious native symbols that in the setting of a saint's Life cry out to be dismantled, just as their bearers cry out to be converted.[5] In this replay of a common hagiographic scene, Brigit's response includes not only a blessing on Conall and his men but also the expression of the wish that they put these *stigmata* aside as soon as possible. Brigit then creates a wholly illusory experience for the warriors, replete with phantom battle, phantom victory, and even phantom trophies. Again, what separates saint from devotee is *vision*, in this case a false vision fabricated by the saint and inflicted upon the devotee for his own sake. Once the latter is let in on the vision, or on the illusion, as Conall and his men are when they realize that no mayhem took place, the relationship between saint and devotee grows stronger, and the 'family resemblance' between them increases. This development can be seen in the sequel to this episode, in which Conall, engaged in further acts of marauding, declares his dependence on Brigit for his deliverance from his enemies when trapped with his men in a house in enemy territory. Through the saint's miraculous intervention the scouts of the advancing hostile forces, who come upon Conall and his men in the house, see monks poring over their manuscripts instead of the warriors drinking amidst severed heads. Thus camouflaged, Conall and his men escape detection and return home safely.[6] True, Conall's tonsure and turning to books are fleeting illusions, but for a magical moment the princeling is transformed into the monastic male counterpart of Brigit. Its being so artificial a moment makes the saintly compulsion to reproduce underlying this episode all the more apparent.

While the compulsion is particularly acute in these stories from early Brigidine legend, I would propose that it is typical of Irish saints as they are represented in their Lives. This is not to say that the reproductive urge is unique to Celtic hagiography. Indeed, here is another example of how the early Irish church shared the concerns that characterized late antique and early medieval Christianity in general. For, as Peter Brown has noted, a fascination with the prospect of nonbiological reproduction emerged in Christian thought in conjunction with the rise of the cult of the saint, a teacher and model by

4 AASS, Februarii I, p. 127 (trans. Connolly, pp. 31–2); Sharpe, *Medieval Irish Saints' Lives*, pp. 180–2. 5 Sharpe, 'Hiberno-Latin *Laicus*', pp. 82–4. The *stigmata* have been more recently discussed by Connolly, pp. 10–1. 6 AASS, Februarii I, p. 127 (trans. Connolly, p. 32); Sharpe, *Medieval Irish Saints' Lives*, pp. 181–2.

whose power the identity of both the community and the individual could be profoundly transformed and revalidated.[7] Speaking of the Gnostics and other, more mainstream thinkers of second-century Christianity, Brown has said:

> [They] contributed directly to the spinning of one fine strand in the sensibility of continent Christians of all shades of opinion. ... [They] presented the intimate passing on of an irreplaceable, saving wisdom as the truest form of procreation. Teaching and baptism, and not the begetting of children, made the best provision for the future. Natural, social man gained continuity through physical intercourse; but such intercourse produced only fodder for death. Truly lasting continuity came through spiritual birth, due to spiritual intercourse ... Marriage was a dark and shadowy affair compared with the intimate and insubstantial moment when, through invitation after long teaching, the initiate joined his or her spirit to the angel guide on their spiritual marriage bed of baptism. Through teaching and through solemn baptismal initiation, the Christian church as a whole – and not only the sheltered study-groups within it – had found a strange, high-arched means of continuity that could look past both marriage and the grave. ... Through the efforts of a generation of great teachers, the Christian church had become, in effect, an institution possessed of the ethereal secret of perpetual self-reproduction.[8]

The key to that 'secret' is the figure of the saint, him/herself a reproduction of Christ, of other Biblical paradigms, and of other saints, but a reproduction possessing distinguishing characteristics, such as attachment to a particular place and people, particular saintly characteristics, and the particular agenda of those who fostered the saint's cult. The saint as a figure mapped out and defined in hagiography, and as an institution in a particular social, political, and cultural context, performs a delicate balancing act between sameness and difference, between a concept of reproduction as a return to, or maintenance of, a 'given', and a concept of reproduction as a building upon and away from that 'given'.

As the saint is him/herself reproduced, so (s)he reproduces. These reproductions, like the saint, point in the direction of their origins and destinations. In other words, they are *signs*, as reflective of power as the miracles (often called *signa*) which saints perform. Moreover, Brigit and her saintly colleagues are, as it were, semioticians, negotiating on their devotees' behalf the distance between signifier and signified, between shadow and substance. As we read through the considerable body of saints' Lives that has been left to us by Irish hagiographers from the period between the seventh and the sixteenth centuries, we find holy men and women making and remaking signs, and leaving traces of all makes

---

7 *Cult of the Saints*, pp. 50–68. 8 *Body and Society*, pp. 119–20.

and models: saints' wells and other monuments, ecclesiastical institutions, and sacred relics. And yet the kind of semiotic production that is valued most highly in these Lives is the transformation, not of things, but of people, and of what they 'stand for', in other words, the process of conversion, which entails both assimilation (the convert becomes like those already converted) and differentiation (the convert is a new person, different from those among whom he previously blended in). Having been transformed by the saint, the willing subject becomes a significant object, caught up in a double move, both toward newly kindred spirits and away from erstwhile associates. In Christian hagiography, which wholeheartedly subscribes to the trope of similarity as a potential mode of representation, the convert can and often does serve to represent or replace the saint who converted him/her.

This knack the saint has for converting – for turning people away from evil or from old ways and investing their persons and lives with new significance – is a part of the hagiographic hero(ine)'s dossier that we tend to overlook, focused as current scholars are on the saint as wonderworker or politician or cultural innovator. No matter what the social or even cosmic repercussion of the saint's actions, these are usually predicated on the saint's tendency to seek people out, or on people's tendency to seek the company of saints, and to enjoy some kind of personal and dialogic relationship with them. The Irish saint is often presented in the Lives as a paradigmatic *anmcharae* 'soul-friend' with whom the disciple or devotee can engage in free and liberating conversation, just as the saint can converse with his/her own 'soul-friends', a select circle which usually includes angels as well as other saints. Conversion comes via such conversation, as the following examples from Adomnán's *Vita Columbae* (VC) show.

These three episodes all hinge on the magnetism of Columba's *praesentia*, the term used by Peter Brown to designate the saint's function as common denominator in a social context, and as a sanctifying mnemonic device for the individual. The saint's presence, whether operating centrifugally or centripetally, allows for the manifestation of his *potentia* with which he can create signs and wonders, and recreate lives in his/her own image. In the typical Columban legend as recounted by Adomnán, the saint is stationary, exiled on an island and waiting for something to happen – usually, for someone to approach him, drawn across the waves in search of a word with Columba. I note in passing that such 'staging' contrasts dramatically with that to be found in the Lives of Patrick, whose *praesentia* operates centrifugally, perhaps as a result of his role as missionary saint. Patrick perennially moves away from the centres he establishes, in order to track down the 'voice of the Irish' that has drawn him into his mission.[9]

---

9 Patrick's mystical experience of this voice is described in his *Confessio* (Howlett, p. 66). See also Bieler, *Patrician Texts*, pp. 72 (Muirchú), 134 (Tírechán).

Columba, a saint for a different era and a different purpose, goes on no such quest for dialogue. He is himself the object of quests, most of which he miraculously anticipates. One such approaching seeker, whose arrival Columba predicts, is Fíachnae, a *sapiens*, coming to perform penance for grave sins. Columba actually meets him part-way, coming down to the harbour. Here, Fíachnae throws himself at the saint's feet and confesses all. As moved to tears as the sinning *sapiens* himself, Columba tells him that his sins are forgiven.[10] The saint sympathetically joins the sinner in an outpouring of emotional contrition, a scene not unlike the cathartic merging of identities that we have witnessed in previously discussed acts of conversion. In this dialogue with a visitor from across the waters, as in so many others featured in Adomnán's work, we wonder whether its strong impact upon the saint does not stem at least in part from the visitor's being an aspect of Columba's own past come back to confront him or to be reconciled with what Columba has become. No man, not even Columba, is an island. He too was once a sage of Ireland, but then, according to a story only vaguely adumbrated by Adomnán but fleshed out in later sources, he was compelled to leave in the wake of actions that, at least in the eyes of some of his saintly contemporaries, were gravely sinful.[11] Do we then have here the hint of the young Columba meeting and confessing to the old?

In another episode of predicted encounter, the visitor is far more removed from Columba and undertakes a much more epochal sea-voyage than that of Fíachnae, who is a literate, Christian contemporary of the saint's. The conversion of this other visitor is therefore all the more remarkable. An old pagan warrior named Artbranán comes to the saint on the island of Skye (as foretold by Columba). Through an interpreter he listens to what Columba preaches, embraces the new faith, and subsequently dies. The river that supplied the waters of Artbranán's baptism still bears the convert's name, Adomnán pointedly concludes.

There is some question about the meaning of the designation for this old warrior, *Geonae primarius cohortis*,[12] and the need for a translator shows that Artbranán was probably Pictish. Nevertheless, it is arguable that here we have the makings of Columba's own *Acallam na Senórach*, fully equipped with open-minded, big-hearted veteran and similarly endowed cleric, a premise for dialogue, and a substantial item of *dindshenchas*. As for this last component, Sharpe points out that its inclusion is rather striking for the Life, since neither the body of water nor the place where the baptism occurred is invested with ecclesiastical significance by Adomnán, and the only link between the placename and the cult of Saint Columba is the figure of Artbranán himself.[13]

10 VC I.30 (Anderson and Anderson, pp. 56–8). 11 See Adomnán's text, VC I.7, III.3 (Anderson and Anderson, pp. 30, 184); and Sharpe's discussion of traditions concerning Columba's leaving for exile in *Life of St Columba*, pp. 12–5. 12 VC I.33 (Anderson and Anderson, p. 62); see Dumville, '"Primarius Cohortis"'. 13 Sharpe, *Life of St Columba*, p. 294.

If, however, the convert is a reproduction of the converter, a signifier to his signified, then the link is strong indeed.

In our third Columban example of the relationship between saint and devotee, the one seeking after Columba is not in search of forgiveness or religious conversion. Rather, it is another warrior or brigand, but one with murder on his mind. Complicating the situation even further is the presence of a third party, a complication in the equation of conversion that we have been examining. Columba, upon excommunicating a renegade branch of the Dál Ríata ruling family, is set upon by one of its supporters, Lám Dess, who is described in terms that clearly make him a colleague of Conall mac Néill and other dangerous figures featured in hagiography. Columba, however, is saved from the warrior's spear by one of his monks, Findlugán, who stands between the saint and his would-be slayer. Fortunately for Findlugán, he is wearing Columba's cowl, and this protects him miraculously from the spearthrust. Lám Dess, thinking he has slain Columba (having mistaken Findlugán for the saint), runs away. One year later Columba announces that it is now time for Lám Dess to die – and die he does, the sole casualty in a battle where he is felled by a spear thrown by a warrior calling upon the assistance of Columba.[14]

Two relevant observations can be made about this story. One is that here we have a genuine 'devil's man', a *díberg(ach)* or *fénnid*,[15] who confronts a saint and stays in character, who is neither desirous of a blessing, like Conall, nor inquiring after a new religion, like Artbranán, but who recognises the saint as posing a threat. This is not just the threat of a revolutionary creed or worldview that will not brook acts of violence; for the saint may be seen to render the *fénnid* obsolete in the matter of semiotics. The *fénnid* is essentially a hunter, a tracker of traces, a reader of signs, and a producer of signs himself. This affinity may bring saint and brigand together in mutual quests for meaning, but it can also make them into ruthless, competitive enemies. In this Columban legend the saint may not be able to convert the incorrigible Lám Dess, but in a mordant way he can stage a death for this figure that indexes what would have been Columba's own: the failed assassin is singled out to be slain with a spear thrown by Columba's proxy on the day that *would* have been Columba's feast day. This situation bizarrely parallels Brigit's modification of Darlugdach's request that she die on the same day as her beloved saint.

Another observation to be made about this episode in VC is that here we have yet another hagiographic sacrificial victim to add to our file of figures such as Patrick's charioteer (who in various sources and scenarios takes a spear meant for Patrick, sometimes even wearing his clothes), Brendan's *crosán* (who sacrifices himself to man-eating mice in order to save Brendan and his crew),

---

14 VC II.24 (Anderson and Anderson, p. 128).   15 The pioneering work on this figure in early Irish literature is Sharpe, 'Hiberno-Latin *Laicus*'; see also McCone, 'Werewolves'.

and Columba's monk Odrán (who in the Middle Irish Life of the saint plays the key role in a foundation sacrifice).[16] There is, however, a problem with the fate of Findlugán, whose name of course virtually invites mythological speculation. He does *not* die but survives the attack, thanks to the talismanic power of Columba's clothing. We could ascribe this plot twist to Adomnán's artistic license in handling the hagiographic story pattern, but perhaps it would be closer to the mark to suggest that in this case the theme of reproduction overwhelms that of sacrifice. In other words, the hagiographer is emphasizing the productive resemblance of devotee to saint, and the protection such resemblance affords.

To complete the 'Thaumaturgic Triad', I turn to a legend about the reproductive powers of the missionary Patrick. A pagan named Éogan, after having strenuously opposed the new faith, is finally won over by the power of Patrick's preaching. Right away he complains about his ugliness (*étche*), or he actually requests of Patrick that it be removed. Patrick asks Éogan what or whom he wishes to look like, and Éogan chooses the young man (*ócl&aech*) carrying Patrick's book satchel. The saintly prescription for Éogan's transformation consists of his sleeping in the arms of the satchel-bearer under a single cloak for one night. Éogan does as directed, and as a consequence he comes to look so much like his model that no one can tell the two apart, except for the difference in their haircuts.[17]

That profound issues of cultural identity underlie this story becomes clear when we examine the details. Éogan is a son of Níall and thus a brother of Conall, whom we met in a Brigidine context above, and of Lóegaire, the putative king of Ireland in the Patrician Lives. Éogan's conversion represents not only the breakdown of the resistance offered by the pagan status quo to Patrick's missionary efforts but also a convergence, on political and literary levels, of the agenda of Patrick's successors and those of Níall's descendants. Moreover, the companion of Patrick, to whose appearance the convert Éogan aspires, is identified by way of the book satchel (*tíag*), a metonym for the new written and writing culture that Christianity introduces to Ireland, and part of the new religious 'load' now shouldered by Éogan.

So we see that Patrick and his fellow saints can not only turn people into signs even while making their dreams come true, but they can reveal people to be signs that stand in or stand for other signs, all of them pointing toward the social and cultural denominators that both shape individual identities and establish the basis for shared, collective identity. In making it possible for Éogan

16 These and other 'necessary sacrifices' featured in saints' legends are examined in Nagy, *Conversing with Angels and Ancients*, pp. 199–286. 17 Mulchrone, *Bethu Phátraic*, pp. 92–3; Bieler, *Four Latin Lives of St. Patrick*, p. 104 (*Vita quarta*). After changing his appearance, Patrick makes Éogan taller as well, per request.

to look exactly like the Christian book-carrier, Patrick, or more accurately the hagiographic tradition that produced this story, has once again enriched our sense of both the equivalence and the multivalence that obtains among signs.

The saint's drive to produce signs and to reproduce him/herself, as well as the ease with which saints lend themselves to reproduction, gives new meaning to much of what we see happening in the world depicted in Irish saints' legends, a confusing world rife with overlapping and redundant traditions. This proliferation is the product of shifting historical circumstances, as Pádraig Ó Riain has taught us,[18] but also the product of the semiotic fecundity I have described. In this legendary milieu, individual saints rarely remain in the singular. They bifurcate and multiply, so that we have a situation in which both medieval hagiographers, and modern-day scholars trying desperately to keep track of what those hagiographers have wrought, talk of two or more Patricks, two Brigits, any number of Finnians, and individual saints sporting multiple, and sometimes serial names. We also find spin-off cults, including the oft-encountered situation of multiple saints bearing the same name and seeming suspiciously similar, except for their being associated with different places. There are even to be found in this world of celebrated Irish holy men and women feeble emanations of saints that barely have a historical or legendary leg on which to stand.

I conclude with a brief consideration of a particular example of saintly reproduction that opens up compelling questions about the nature of the relationship between the saint and the saint's designated institutional successor. The importance of the latter figure or role extends beyond the context of the hagiographic narrative, reflecting as it does upon the site of the production and dissemination of the saint's legend, namely, the church or monastery where the Life was produced, and where the person in charge was traditionally referred to as the 'heir' of the founder-saint. The epigonal figure to whom we turn is Benignus (Benén), Patrick's chosen successor in the episcopal see of Armagh. Here is Tírechán's account of the first meeting of Patrick with his favorite protégé and perennial companion:

> In the evening Patrick came to the estuary of Ailbine to a certain (naturally) good man and baptized him. Patrick met the man's son, who pleased him and whom he named Benignus, for he would cling to Patrick's feet, holding them between his hands and his chest, not wishing to sleep anymore with his father or mother, and weeping if he were not allowed to sleep with Patrick. The next morning they arose, and Patrick, having given a blessing to Benignus's father, started to climb into his

---

18 See for example his study of the 'hiving-off' of a saint's cult, 'Cainnech alias Colum Cille'.

chariot. With one of Patrick's feet in the chariot and the other still on the ground, Benignus grabbed the foot outside the chariot with both hands and cried out: 'Allow me to stay with Patrick, my real father'. Said Patrick, 'Baptize the boy and lift him into the chariot, for he is the heir to my kingdom'. And so this is who became Bishop Benignus, Patrick's successor in the church of Armagh.[19]

In a celebrated incident recorded by Patrick's other seventh-century biographer Muirchú as well, Benignus actually serves as Patrick's 'body-double' in a life-endangering test. This is the trial by fire that Patrick proposes in the court of the still-unconverted Lóegaire, who is weighing the competing authorities of foreign Christian holy man and native *magus*. Patrick arranges the following: the chief druid and a person from Patrick's party (identified by Muirchú as Benignus) enter a house with the druid wearing Patrick's clothing and the Christian representative wearing the druid's, the house is set on fire, and the onlookers are to see which man, or religion, survives. Of course it is Benignus, minus the druid's (burnt-off) clothing, who emerges unscathed, even though he was put in the dry part of the house, as opposed to the wet part in which the druid faced the trial by fire. Nothing survives of the druid, but Patrick's vestments are left undamaged.[20] It is puzzling in this story of druidic downfall that Patrick is given the option of sending a substitute into the burning house, an option not afforded the druid, and that a demonstration of Patrick's own doubtless imperviousness to flames is thereby avoided. In light of what we have discovered in this study, that a saint's power, his/her religious and cultural value, lies in the ability to reproduce and to be reproduced, the nature of Patrick's triumph becomes clearer. Perhaps even more important than the saint's own indestructibility, and more impressive to the witnesses of this miracle, is the ability to invest such indestructibility in those who wish to be close to and to be like the saint – the ability to manufacture and send forth into the world doubles or shadow figures, who can extend and even complicate the saint's cult.

Adomnán's *Vita Columbae* (specifically, the second preface) observes that, while the words or names 'Jonah', 'Peristera', and 'Columba' all come from different languages and do not at all sound the same, each refers to the same thing, namely, the dove: a reality and/or concept that, as Adomnán proceeds to show, itself plays signifier to various signifieds, such as the Holy Spirit and the qualities of meekness and simplicity.[21] There is, however, nothing simple about the semantic 'house of mirrors' that Adomnán evokes in this observation, which applies as well to the cultural edifice of saints' cults and Lives as it does to the weave of languages and their correspondences. Devotees, as different and

---

19 Based on Bieler's edition and translation, *Patrician Texts*, pp. 126–7. 20 Ibid., pp. 94 (Muirchú), 130 (Tírechán). 21 VC, *Praefatio secunda* (Anderson and Anderson, pp. 2–4).

as diverse as they are, refer to their saints, while saints in turn refer to each other and to their Scriptural models. This welter of cross-reference is not an accidental by-product but precisely what the community of saints as it evolved in Christendom and took root in Ireland is supposed to engender. This is how saints, saints' Lives as a literary genre, and the social institutions patronized by saints multiply, forming genealogies every bit as nuanced and tempered by sameness and difference as any population formed by biological means of reproduction.

Irish Hagiography in the *Acta sanctorum* (1643–1794)*

Robert Godding

The Jesuit, Heribert Rosweyde, who was born in Utrecht, published his *Fasti sanctorum quorum vitae in belgicis bibliothecis manuscriptae* in 1607. This modest little work outlines the plan and principles of what was to become the *Acta sanctorum*.[1] And although Rosweyde, already then fourteen years dead, did not participate directly in the preparation of the first volume of *Acta* published in 1643, before his death he had collected an impressively large number of Lives of saints towards the fulfilment of his project, not only from Belgian but also from foreign libraries.

For Rosweyde's heirs and fellow Jesuits, Bolland and Henschenius, who really inaugurated the publication of the *Acta sanctorum*, Irish hagiography was to be a particularly sensitive area. For one thing, there was the heuristic problem of finding materials. Although copies of Lives of Irish saints who had worked on the Continent were available in libraries of the Netherlands, France and Germany, the latter two of which were soon visited by Henschenius and Papebroch, Lives of those who stayed at home could rarely be discovered in this way. Besides, among the peculiarities of Irish hagiography is a particular interest in the miraculous, and on this point the hagiographers of Antwerp, habitually severe as to the historical value of the texts they published, were forced to take a stand. These, then, are the two main divisions of my paper: (1) What sources of Irish hagiography were used by the Bollandists? and: (2) What was their attitude to this literature? I shall conclude by attempting to judge what they achieved in this, for them, quite unfamiliar area.

I should make clear that my study is limited to the volumes of the *Acta sanctorum* published by the early Bollandists, up to the end of the eighteenth century, and that it bears only on the Irish saints of Ireland, to the exclusion, therefore, of such Continental saints of Irish origin as Fursy and Columbanus. The assembly of texts concerning these latter saints posed no specific problems to the Bollandists.

* It is a pleasure to thank Professor Pádraig Ó Riain for translating my text into English and for suggesting some improvements.   1 Cf. Delehaye, *Oeuvre des Bollandistes*, pp. 11–16.

I THE SOURCES

Despite the inherent difficulty of finding Irish *vitae,* in this regard Bolland and his successors had extraordinary good fortune, in the form of the *Codex Salmanticensis.* Together with the collections known as *Insulensis* and *Kilkenniensis,* this fourteenth-century manuscript represents one of the great medieval collections of Irish saints' Lives.[2] In the very early seventeenth century it belonged to the Irish Jesuit College in Salamanca, whose rector between 1613 and 1631, Father Thomas Bryan, at a date yet to be established gave the book as a gift to his Belgian colleague Father Gilles de Smidt, who in turn handed it over to Rosweyde.[3] Through their possession of this most important of witnesses to Irish hagiography, with its no fewer than forty-eight unedited *vitae,* the task of the Bollandists was greatly simplified.[4]

Having noticed that, according as the *Acta sanctorum* progressed from month to month, the *Codex Salmanticensis* came to be described in an increasingly precise way, Paul Grosjean began to wonder whether the earliest Bollandists might have been deliberately discreet about their custody of the manuscript, lest it be reclaimed by a new rector in Salamanca. Grosjean could find no mention of the *Codex* as a source in the first two January volumes of the *Acta,* except in relation to the Life and miracles of St Fursy where reference is made to it, very discreetly, as *ex ms. hibernico.*[5] In fact, however, there is already an explicit reference in the second January volume to an old codex received from the Irish Jesuit College in Salamanca.[6] The still greater detail of later volumes, including a reference to the shelf number of the manuscript in the *Museum Bollandianum,* was simply due to an increasing tendency towards prolixity in the successors of Bolland and Papebroch.[7]

2 Cf. Sharpe, *Medieval Irish Saints' Lives,* pp. 6, 228–46. Ó Riain, 'Codex Salmanticensis', O'Sullivan, 'Waterford Origin'.   3 'Codicem hunc Rector Collegii Salmanticensis Hibernici Societatis Iesu dono dedit nostro Patri Aegidio de Smidt qui eundem donavit P. Heriberto Rosweydo' (manuscript note of Papebroch's on fol. 2 of the *Codex*). The *Codex Salmanticensis,* which carried the shelf-number P MS 11 in the *Museum Bollandianum,* is now preserved in the Bibliothèque Royale in Brussels (MS 7672–74). It has been edited in full by De Smedt and De Backer, *Acta sanctorum Hiberniae* and, with the omission of the non-Irish Lives, by Heist, *Vitae.*   4 By reference to a letter from Hugh Ward to Bolland, Grosjean ('Soldat de fortune', p. 427) has shown that Ward was still unaware of the existence of *Salmanticensis* by October 1634, which probably means that by then Bolland had taken little cognizance of it.   5 Grosjean, 'Soldat de fortune', pp. 419–20, at n. 8.   6 AASS, Ian. II, p. 1111.   7 Cf AASS, Febr. I, p. 102; Iun. II, pp. 24, 236; Aug. III, p. 736; IV, p. 625; VI, p. 489 (the fullest notice); Sept. I, p. 664; III, p. 732; IV, p. 643. In the fifth October volume (p. 643), published in Brussels in 1786, the manuscript is numbered 167. Having been forced by the Austrian authorities to leave their novitiate in Antwerp, and having seen their *Museum* reduced to a bare minimum, the Bollandists reorganised their collections (cf. Delehaye, *Oeuvre des Bollandistes,* p. 120).

To have had access to the *Codex Salmanticensis* in this way was indeed a stroke of good fortune, but not the complete answer to Bolland's lack of material on the Irish saints. Access to other collections of Irish Lives came via a network of personal relations which was to prove very valuable. The time was particularly propitious. As is well known, during the first few decades of the seventeenth century Ireland was witnessing an extraordinary upsurge in hagiographical research. Whether it be the Jesuits, Henry Fitzsimon and Stephen White, the secular priest, Thomas Messingham, the lay scholar, Philip O'Sullivan Beare, the Anglican archbishop of Armagh, James Ussher, or the Irish Franciscans of Louvain, Hugh Ward, Patrick Fleming and John Colgan, all of these individuals were feverishly assembling manuscripts and publishing Lives of the early Irish saints. A major influence on this research was exerted by the publications of the Scottish Catholic, Thomas Dempster, who claimed for Scotland all the saints of ancient *Scotia*, a name that had been used of Ireland up to the twelfth century.[8]

In their search for texts, first Rosweyde, then Bolland and, to a lesser extent, Henschenius and Papebroch, corresponded with Irishmen, soliciting texts from them. Most texts came from the Franciscans of St Anthony's College, Louvain, whose enthusiasm for the study of Irish hagiographical texts is well attested. An initial period of cooperation between the Franciscans, Patrick Fleming and Hugh Ward, and the secular priest, Thomas Messingham, was followed by a decision to pursue on their own the scheme for the collection and publication of the hagiographical remains of their country which culminated in the publication by John Colgan of *Acta sanctorum Hiberniae*.[9] Had it survived, this correspondence between the Franciscans of Louvain and the Jesuits of Antwerp, which many indications show to have been substantial, would be a most valuable subject of study. Unfortunately, however, only scattered fragments have been preserved.

One of the few letters that does survive, from Bolland to Hugh Ward, dated 26 July 1634,[10] one year before Ward's death and nine years before the publication of the first two volumes of the *Acta sanctorum*, refers to a recent previous letter.[11] Ward's reply, also extant and dated 7 October 1634, speaks of a pending visit by Bolland to the Irish friary in Louvain, which shows how seriously Ward took the requests made of him by the Bollandists.[12] One need

---

8 Cf. Sharpe, *Medieval Irish Saints' Lives*, pp. 46–61. 9 Colgan, *Acta sanctorum*. Cf. idem, *Trias thaumaturga.* 10 MS Boll. 141, fol. 336 contains the rough draft of a letter, or rather note, from Bolland to Ward. It has been edited by Grosjean, 'Soldat de fortune', p. 428. 11 'Cum nuper ad reverentiam vestram scriberem … '. Bolland presents himself here as an intermediary acting on behalf of his colleague, Fr Chifflet, who was looking for information concerning Columbanus's letters on the Easter controversy. This letter, preserved at St Isidore's in Rome, has been edited by Jennings 'Miscellaneous Documents', pp. 188–9; and by Hogan, 'Irish Historical Studies', p. 68, n. 1. This is the edition reproduced by Grosjean, 'Soldat de fortune', pp. 423–4. 12 'Ex litteris vestris heri mihi traditis et gratissimis intelligens optatum vestrum adventum in hanc urbem, in eum plura quae scribenda

but consider the number of *vitae* sent by Ward to Rosweyde and Bolland, no fewer than twenty-two, which makes Ward by far the most valuable collaborator of the Bollandists concerning Irish materials, to realise how intense and cordial their relations were.

The collaboration continued under J. Colgan. However, in his case also, only one letter survives, from Henschenius and dated 28 August 1638, to bear witness to his good relations with the hagiographers of Antwerp. In it Henschenius asked Colgan to examine what he had written on *S. Beandanus seu Blandanus*, concerning whom he had been unable to find any early documentation. Henschenius referred in the same letter to a martyrology lent to him by the Irish Franciscans which he wished to keep a while longer so that it could be examined and a copy made of it by a colleague.[13] Requests for information, the sending of copies of texts, the lending of manuscripts, these services were mutually provided by Louvain and Antwerp. The contribution of the Irish Franciscans is acknowledged several times in the *Acta sanctorum*.[14] Colgan's copies of texts from the *Codex Salmanticensis*, for example, originated with the Bollandists, who had presented them to Hugh Ward, as Colgan gratefully acknowledges.[15] He refers in one passage to Bolland as *doctissimus*,[16] and on Bolland's death in 1665 the Franciscans of Louvain sent a letter of condolence from which Henschenius was prepared to include an extract in the biography of Bolland published in the preface to the March *Acta*. The Franciscans claimed to have celebrated a solemn mass in memory of Bolland, and expressed their debt to him as follows:

> This is indeed the least we could do for a man who has earned high regard, through his writings, from the Catholic Church and especially from our Island; but it is also to be admired how much he has deserved from our house through his good deeds, obtaining for it more than once the resources it needed in its poverty.[17]

Bolland, whose generous nature is well known, would doubtless have offered books to the Franciscan college whose beginnings were marked by great poverty.[18]

The last Irish Franciscan at Louvain interested in hagiography was Thomas Sheerin (Sirinus). A letter of his has survived addressed to Papebroch, thanking the Bollandist for a copy sent of the Life of St Ibar, which had been made from a manuscript of Henry Fitzsimon's.[19] And as he explains in another letter, dated

---

offerebantur remitto' (Grosjean, 'Soldat de fortune', pp. 424–7).   13 Jennings, *Louvain Papers*, p. 127, n. 173.   14 Thus, in reference to an explanation given them by 'vir doctissimus Ioannes Colganus, ex ordine S. Francisci Sacrae Theologiae professor, qui de sacris patriae suae Hiberniae antiquitatibus plura brevi editurus est' (AASS, Ian. II, p. 1111). 15 Colgan, *Trias thaumaturga*, p. 320.   16 Colgan, *Acta sanctorum*, p. 227.   17 AASS, Mart. I, p. x.   18 Cf. Jenning, *Louvain Papers*, p. v.   19 Cf. Grosjean, 'Deux textes inédits'.

25 April 1670, to a fellow friar named Francis Harold, Sheerin, who had experienced difficulty in getting four or five copies of his edition of Fleming's *Vita Columbani* to Rome, turned for help to the 'fathers continuing the works of Bolland' in the hope that he might gain a place for the volumes in a consignment of *Acta sanctorum*. But the next volume of *Acta* was not due out for four or five years and the Bollandist printer in any case had no Italian trade connexions. The Bollandists recommended an Antwerp merchant involved in consignments to Rome, but his rates proved too exorbitant for the Franciscan.[20]

With Sheerin gone, the Louvain house had no more great hagiographers to show for itself. We can scarcely make an exception of a curious return to former custom in January 1686, when Fr Francis O'Donnochu sent Papebroch a panegyric on St Brigit composed by himself.[21] In doing so, however, he availed of the opportunity to remind the Bollandists of the kindness they had earlier shown to the Franciscans.[22] For their part, according as the *Acta sanctorum* progressed, the Bollandists made use of the materials on Irish saints already available to them, which had mostly come from Ward. From time to time, however, the Bollandists wrote to Louvain, looking for a text or verifying the existence of a martyrology. At this stage they were no longer consulting specialists but custodians of manuscripts. Thus, when about to publish the Life of St Declan in 1727, Fr Boschius became worried about an entry in the Martyrology of Donegal, which Colgan, whose plans were interrupted by death, had hoped to publish in the July volume of his own work. We may note with some surprise that the Bollandists had neglected to obtain a full copy of this martyrology in the first place. In any case, it was Francis Friell who responded from Louvain, sending Boschius a copy of Míchéal Ó Cléirigh's version of St Declan's Life (BHL 2116). As it happened, the Bollandists had already received a copy of this text several decades earlier from the Louvain Franciscans.[23] Indeed, they had even sent this copy to St Isidore's in Rome to be collated with another copy by Francis Harold, who had duly returned it to them in 1679.[24]

---

20 Jenning, *Louvain Papers*, p. 229 n. 333.   21 Several panegyrics of this kind are now preserved among the F manuscripts at the Franciscan Library, Killiney, Co. Dublin.   22 'Ob vestram quam semper geritis erga nostros hic benevolentiam, quae primo in P. Bollando piae memoriae initium sumpsit, magnumque deinceps progressum in reverenda admodum paternitate vestra' (Jennings, *Louvain Papers*, p. 270, n. 382).   23 Cf. AASS, Iul. V, pp. 590–1, 593.   24 Ibid., p. 593. The important correspondence between Papebroch and Francis Harold from 1665 to 1690 concerns almost entirely Italian Franciscan saints. In one letter, however, Papebroch expresses his opinion of Irish hagiography: 'Nam quod dolemus, mirum in modum vacillant Hibernica. Ipsi Patricio quis credat? – ex cuius aetate omnis fere pendet sanctorum Hibernorum historia, annos plerique quadraginta quinquaginta alii supra verum adiiciunt, et actuosissimum virum triginta ac pluribus annis prorsus sic relinquunt desidem ut nihil egerit quod in actis quantumcumque prolixis meruerit commemorari. Dicere vix possim quanto mihi labore steterit illas plusquam cymmerias tenebras utcumque illustrare modica illa quam adferre potui luce.'

In addition to the aid they received from the Franciscans of Louvain and Rome, Rosweyde and Bolland were also assisted by two Irish Jesuits, Henry Fitzsimon and Stephen White.[25] A count of the references to him as source in the *Acta sanctorum*, taken together with a number of surviving copies, shows that Fitzsimon, author of the *Catalogus praecipuorum sanctorum Hiberniae*,[26] supplied Bolland with at least fourteen Lives, and probably with many more. As for White, who was already corresponding with Rosweyde in 1615,[27] he supplied many important texts from libraries in Germany.[28] Moreover, the Bollandists had two other works from his hand that were never used for publication.[29]

From among Bolland's Irish collaborators mention must also be made of Philip O'Sullivan Beare, an Irish émigré in Spain who was more a polemicist than an historian. Having learned of the Antwerp Jesuit's project, O'Sullivan Beare sent him in 1633, through an intermediary named Thomas (possibly Thomas Bryan, former rector of the Jesuit college in Salamanca), a Latin translation of the Life of St Ailbe of Emly, urging him to open the *Acta* with it, on three grounds. First, the name of the saint began with A; second, Ailbe's feast-day was 1 January; third, Ptolemy began his description of the world with Ireland! Not content with this proposal, O'Sullivan Beare added to his consignment of material to Bolland a polemic entitled *Animadversio in Vitas universorum Iberniae divorum*, which set out to prove that, despite the Scottish historian Thomas Dempster, the ancient name of Ireland was *Scotia*.[30] O'Sullivan Beare urged Bolland to publish this under his own name, but Bolland refrained. In the *Praefatio generalis*, which opens the *Acta sanctorum*, he alluded to the problem but, stating that he loved Ireland and Scotland equally, prudently declined to support either side.[31] Six months after this first consignment O'Sullivan Beare forwarded to Bolland, this time through Fr Paul Sherlock rector of the Irish Jesuit college in Salamanca, a list of Lives he had translated from Irish into Latin, which he was prepared to place at the Antwerp Jesuit's disposal.

The great scholar James Ussher, Anglican archbishop of Armagh, was also in communication with the Bollandists. Not directly, of course, in view of the politico-religious situation, but Grosjean has shown that, through the good offices of the Catholic bishop of Ossory, David Rothe, who went under the pseudonym of Nicolas Laffan, and with the aid of Christopher Talbot who acted as 'post box', Ussher obtained a copy made by Rosweyde of a pseudepi-

---

25 For these, see Sharpe, *Medieval Irish Saints' Lives*, pp. 41–6. **26** For a critical edition, see P.Grosjean, 'Édition du *Catalogus*'. Cf. Sharpe, 'Origin and Elaboration'; Ó Riain, '*Catalogus*'. **27** Cf. AASS, Iul. II, p. 487. **28** For example, the Latin Life of St Cáemgen (BHL 1868), from a manuscript in the Jesuit college at Ingolstadt (cf. Grosjean, 'Notes d'hagiographie celtique 20'). **29** Cf. Grosjean, 'Soldat de fortune'; pp. 437–40 (Appendix: Sur quelques pièces imprimées et manuscrites de la controverse entre Écossais et Irlandais au début du XVIIe siècle). **30** For an account of all this, see Grosjean, 'Soldat de fortune', pp. 418–36. **31** *Praefatio generalis in Vitas Sanctorum*, cap. 2, § VI: AASS, Ian. I, pp. xxx–xxxi.

graphical poem addressed by S. Livinus to S. Florbert from a manuscript kept at Corsendonch.[32] Papebroch described Ussher as *rerum hibernicarum peritissimus et Archiepiscopus (si sic nominare eum fas est) Armacanus atque Hiberniae primas.*[33] Another correspondent of Bolland's on Irish matters, the martyrologist John Wilson, informed him, inaccurately, that St Finbarr was commemorated on 20 September.[34]

What remains today of the many copies of texts made for the Bollandists by their Irish correspondents? We know that these, like all other texts, were grouped together in the order of the calendar in bound volumes at the beginning of the last century. These *Collectanea Bollandiana* are now divided between the Bibliothèque Royale in Brussels and the present Bollandist library. Following a systematic examination both of the *Acta sanctorum* (up to Oct. V) and of the catalogues of manuscripts in the Bibliothèque Royale and Bollandist library, I have prepared a summary table listing the Irish saints included in the *Acta*, the Lives of Irish saints published or mentioned in them, the provenance of the manuscripts used and, where known, their present whereabouts.[35]

What emerges from this examination? Alas, the principal conclusion is that very little has survived, and the almost systematic absence of copies of Lives of Irish saints suggests that the Irish material was brought together in one volume, now lost. This was probably MS 167 of the *Museum Bollandianum*, which is regularly cited in the *Acta sanctorum* under the title of *Collectanea nostra MSS de Sanctis Angliae, Scotiae et Hiberniae, sub involucro +Ms 167.*[36] Included in this lost volume was a number of Lives provided by Henry Fitzsimon. Thus, when discussing the dossier of St Lugidus, Boschius mentioned a Life of this saint contained in *Ms. non admodum antiquo P. Fitz-Simonii nostri signato + Ms 167.*[37] This composite manuscript – the word *involucrum* denotes a casing or wallet – also contained other materials, according to a reference in the first September volume of the *Acta* to *catalogis quibusdam mss sanctorum Hiberniae, quos habemus sub involucro +ms 167.*[38] The systematic catalogue of the former *Museum Bollandianum*, to which I shall return later, includes under shelf-number 167 fifteen *Sancti et kalendaria*, together with a list of counties and dioceses. And, although this precious volume has since been lost, another, so similar in content that it received the designation MS 167 A (later corrected to 131a), is still extant under the shelf number MS 8530–34 of the Bibliothèque Royale. Among other texts, this includes an index of Irish saints and *Collectanea quaedam de rebus hibernicis.*[39] The old catalogue of the *Museum Bollandianum* likewise alludes to

---

32 Grosjean, 'Vies de S. Finnbarr'. Cf. Sharpe, *Medieval Irish Saints' Lives*, pp. 65–6. 33 AASS, Apr. III, p. 579.   34 AASS, Iul. II, p. 4, where Finbarr is included among the *praetermissi* of the 4 July. According to that notice, he is also mentioned under 20 Sept. in 'Sheerin's papers', but his more usual date is 25 Sept.   35 See Appendix 1 below.   36 For example, AASS, Aug. VI, p. 488.   37 AASS, Aug. I, p. 342.   38 AASS, Sept. I, p. 662. 39 Van den Gheyn, *Catalogue des manuscrits*, p. 476 (n. 3473).

three other manuscripts: 167 B, which comprised *Vitae aliquot breviores* collected by Stephen White, 167 E which included material on the theme of *Hibernia Scotorum antiquorum patria*, and 167 F, which related to *Historia ecclesiastica praecipue de sanctis*. The former Bollandist manuscript 168 (later 131b), also relating to Ireland, has been partly preserved at the end of MS 8590–98 of the Bibliothèque Royale, where we find some offices of Irish saints.[40]

Judging by the above mentioned reference to his copy of *Vita S Lugidii*, most of the Lives sent by Fitzsimon would appear to have formed part of MS 167, which would explain why only two of the fourteen Lives mentioned in the *Acta sanctorum* have survived in manuscript. Three others, not used by the Bollandists because they concern saints commemorated in November and December, have been discovered here and there among the *Collectanea Bollandiana*. Two of these have since been edited by Grosjean, and the third by K. Hughes.[41] Much the same fate has befallen the copies of texts provided by other Irish correspondents. Thus, of the copies of Irish Lives made for the Bollandists by Hugh Ward, twenty-two of which are cited in the *Acta sanctorum*, eight only survive. Similarly, of the four copies supplied by Stephen White, two are extant. Ironically, no fewer than seventeen copies of texts from the still extant *Codex Salmanticensis*, made to be used for purposes of collation with other manuscripts or for printing, have been preserved in the collections of the Bollandists.

Copies of Lives to be published seem to have constituted the major part of the documentation collected by the Bollandists. But there was much else. For example, copies of martyrologies and of other texts concerned with the feast-days of the saints, although less numerous, were also crucial to their researches. In the *Praefatio generalis* of the first January volume of the *Acta*, Bolland enumerated the works of this kind then in his possession. Those relating to Irish saints were the two editions (1608, 1640) of John Wilson's *Martyrologium anglicanum*, the *Liber de Scotorum pietate* of David Camerarius (1631), and, most important of all, Henry Fitzsimon's *Catalogus praecipuorum sanctorum Hiberniae*. References to this latter text in the volumes of the *Acta* that followed were to the first edition of 1611, but the Douai edition of 1615 was also cited, as was the augmented and revised edition published at Liège in 1619.[42] Bolland also drew martyrological information from Adam King's *Kalendarium scoticum*,[43] and in his preface to the February volume, he explained how he had sought to persuade Colgan to publish the martyrologies, of which he claimed to

---

40 Ibid., pp. 482–3 (n. 3477).   **41** Grosjean, 'Vie de Saint Secundinus', idem, 'Antiquitates de Jacques Ussher'; Hughes, 'Offices of S. Finnian'. Doubtless these Lives had been separated from the remainder of Fitzsimon's collection with a view to their future publication.   **42** For an account of the various editions, see Grosjean, 'Édition du *Catalogus*'; Sharpe, 'Origin and Elaboration'; Ó Riain, '*Catalogus*'.   **43** AASS, Ian. I, p. liii.

have a large number, before all else, but in vain.[44] Instead, Colgan arranged for him to have copies of the contents of Gorman and Tallaght relating to February, which are extensively quoted in the volume. To these two may be added *Calendarium Casselense*, the Martyrology of Donegal and the copy of the Martyrology of Óengus made for Cathaldus Maguire, of which the Bollandists possessed either full or fragmentary copies.[45] Besides those obtained from the Louvain Franciscans, the Bollandists also received some martyrological texts from Stephen White. Thus, in the first August volume of the *Acta*, published in 1733, Boschius cited 'handwritten catalogues of Irish saints, collected for our use in the last century by Fr Stephen White, himself an Irishman'.[46]

In his previously mentioned *Praefatio generalis* to the January volume of the *Acta*, Bolland also discussed breviaries and propers of the saints. For office texts concerning Irish saints he depended on a 1620 edition of *Officia propria aliquot sanctorum Hiberniae*, which was possibly Messingham's volume of offices published in Paris in that year.[47] Subsequently, the *Breviarium Aberdonense*, published in Edinburgh in 1509, of which the Bollandists had a manuscript copy, was also cited.[48] And, from the month of August onwards, a *Missae propriae sanctorum patronorum ac tutelarium Franciae et Hiberniae*, published in Paris in 1734, is mentioned several times.[49]

In addition to these diverse, mostly manuscript, sources, the Bollandist hagiographers consulted numerous scholarly printed works, most of whose

---

44 'Sunt quidem a Ioanne Colgano Sacrae Theologiae professore ex Ordine Minorum, edi promiscue coepta Sanctorum Hibernicorum, etiam qui fere sola in patria noti sunt, Acta, labore immenso: haud adhuc constat, an pari apud exteros fructu, propterea quod his ignota sunt, quibus illorum sanctitatem ac dies iis dicatos adstruit, Martyrologia et alia quae sequi se profitetur documenta. Suasimus aliquando, ut haec prius vulgaret: nam cum ea amatores antiquitatis probassent, futurum ut firmiori deinde gradu ad Vitas ipsas progrederetur. Aiebat autem se complura habere Martyrologia, quaedam ante annos DCCC ab sanctis et doctis viris concinnata: Concilia item Hibernica, poëmata scriptaque alia mirae antiquitatis: et nobis pro sua humanitate duorum eiusmodi Martyrologiorum ecgrapha ad Februarium spectantia communicavit: unum compositum aiebat a B. Mariano Gormano Abbate Lugmudensi circa annum MLXXI, alterum a S. Enguso Episcopo, qui seculo octauo vixerit, asseruatumque in Tamlachtensi monasterio: iis nos haud raro usi sumus. Verum quod ei fideliter dabamus consilium, ei tunc sese acquiescere negabat posse: sive quod amici ac praesides vulgari prius Vitas mallent, seu quia fortassis in iis Martyrologiis aliqua reperiebat, quae minus probatum iri nasutis censoribus putaret, cum ipse quaedam posterius adiecta videri fateatur. Deo tamen supplicamus, ut ad opus de Sanctis, ut inchoauit, perficiendum, vires ei subsidiaque alia largiatur' (AASS, Febr. I, p. xvii). 45 AASS, Mart. III, pp. 32, 268; Iun. II, p. 182. 46 'Mss catalogi sanctorum Hiberniae, quos praeterito saeculo ad usum nostrum concinnavit P. Stephanus Vitus noster, Hibernus ipse, et, cum Theologiam Dilingae traderet, antiquitatum patriae sacrarum indagator assiduus' (AASS, Aug. I, p. 341). 47 The full title of Messingham's book was *Officia S.S. Patricii, Columbae, Brigidae, et aliorum quorundam Hiberniae sanctorum.* 48 'Breviarium Aberdonense anno 1509 typis editum, cuius exemplar MS in Museo nostro habemus' (AASS, Sept. VI, p. 643; cf. Febr. III, p. 16; Mart. II, p. 64). 49 AASS, Aug. VI, p. 488; Sept. I, p. 662; III, p. 371; IV, p. 27; VII, p. 143; Oct. V, p. 643.

authors we have already met, viz. Colgan, Ussher, Messingham, Sheerin, O'Sullivan Beare, and David Rothe. The most frequently cited author is James Ware, both for his *Commentarium de praesulibus Hiberniae* and for his *De scriptoribus Hiberniae*. Other authors cited in connexion with Irish saints were Camden, Francis Porter, Hector Boethius, John Leslie, Louis-Augustin Alemand, George Buchanan, George Con, and John Spotswood. The *Museum Bollandianum* was particularly rich in learned printed works, as its catalogue, now in the Bollandist library, shows.[50]

II ATTITUDE OF THE BOLLANDISTS TO IRISH HAGIOGRAPHY

In the *Praefatio generalis* to the January volume of the *Acta*, Bolland characterised Irish hagiography, like that of the Scots, Britons and Bretons, as 'full of the marvellous and interlaced with almost incredible miracles'.[51] He repeated that judgement in relation to the first Irish Life he edited, that of Mochua, saying: 'it contains many astonishing prodigies which, as is apparent from the acts of other saints, were normal in the view of this holy and simple people'.[52] Some of these traits may indeed have been due to unscrupulous copyists, as, according to Bolland, Fitzsimon maintained. But, as Bolland further said:

> What may be additions of this kind is difficult for us to judge, ignorant as we are of the secular history of Ireland. It is sufficient therefore to alert the reader to the need to read discerningly those passages which commemorate prodigious deeds and like miracles, unless they be reported by serious authors. As for us, we have decided to subtract nothing, unless it involve faith or morals, or a passage of a kind which we can refute with evidence.[53]

This was a wise principle, which Rosweyde had already adopted. The whole text ought to be published, subject to an introductory warning to the reader

---

50 Appendix 2 below contains an edition of the systematic part of this catalogue devoted to the subjects *Hibernia* and *Scotia*. Mentioned there are not only works dealing with Ireland but also parts of more general works, including specific pages of the *Acta sanctorum*! 51 'Hibernorum, Scotorum, Britannorum tam qui Albionem, quam qui Armoricam Galliae oram incolunt, plane portentosae sunt Sanctorum Vitae, atque ex miraculis fere incredibilibus contextae' (AASS, Ian. I, p. xxxiv). 52 'Multa continet admiranda portenta, sed usitata apud gentem illam simplicem et sanctam, ut ex aliorum actis sanctorum patet' (ibid., p. 45). 53 'Sunt tamen fortassis nunnulla imperitorum librariorum culpa vitiata aut amplificata. Quod in gentilium suorum rebus gestis animadverti oportere nos docuit Henricus Fitzimon Societatis nostrae Theologus, egregio rerum usu praeditus. Quae tamen sic adiecta censeri debeant, nobis profanae Hibernorum historiae ignaris non facile est statuere. Satis est lectorem monuisse ut cum discretione ea legat quae prodigiosa, et crebro similia miracula commemorant, nisi ab sapientibus scripta auctoribus sint. Nobis tamen nihil expungere constitutum est nisi rectae fidei aut bonis moribus repugnet, aut sit eiusmodi ut clare id possimus refutare' (ibid.).

concerning the credibility of this or that passage. But, if a text seemed seriously laden with errors, then a decision not to publish it was to be taken.

This was not the position adopted by Colgan, who proposed to publish all the texts at his disposal. For example, the *Vita Cuannathei*, preserved in the *Codex Salmanticensis*, was published by Colgan but rejected by Bolland, because its chronological terms of reference do not agree among themselves. Although he had the *vita* near at hand in his library, the hagiographer refused to publish it, going so far as to relegate Cuannatheus to the *praetermissi*.[54] The same fate was in store for St Fínán of Cenn Eitig in the first April volume of the *Acta*. Its editor, Henschenius, wrote:

> His Life, which we have in our Salamancan manuscript, has been written solely from tradition, with little judgement. We shall postpone, therefore, its publication until some more light is thrown on his acts, and until his cult is supported by more evidence.[55]

Even where not relegated to the rank of *praetermissi*, many Irish saints were given synoptic historical treatment only, with no edition of the texts concerning them. Gerald of Mayo, who is noticed in the second March volume, is a case in point. Bolland had obtained a copy of his Life from Ward and, at 20 January, in a note to his commentary on St Fechinus, he had announced that he would publish it at the 13 March. When the time came, however, the new editor, doubtless Henschenius, wrote:

> Having examined the text, we deem it sufficient that it has been edited in *Acta sanctorum Hiberniae* by John Colgan, lest, by multiplying editions of it, one would diffuse a work which contains in its first and principal part as many errors, some of them very serious, as paragraphs; so that if there be any hidden grain of truth, it is impossible, with so much dross, to distinguish it from the rest.[56]

More surprisingly, perhaps, even St Brendan is subjected to an historical commentary only, bereft of edited texts, although Henschenius refers to a Life *ex ms. hibernico apud nos servata*.[57] He also had a copy to hand of the celebrated *Nauigatio*, but renounced its publication entirely because of its 'apocryphal absurdities', a judgement he borrowed from Vincent of Beauvais.[58]

However, the general tendency of the first generation Bollandists was to publish texts, subject to the provision of a warning about their veracity. The problem was, of course, that these warnings were seldom read. In the second

---

54 AASS, Febr. I, pp. 447–8.   55 Ibid., Apr. I, p. 656.   56 Ibid., Mart. II, pp. 289–93.
57 Ibid., Maii III, p. 600.   58 Ibid., p. 602.

March volume of the *Acta*, as part of an *Appendix de S. Patricio*, Henschenius launched an appeal for order:

> We would welcome it greatly if those who happen on *Acta* of this kind would also read Chapter 4 of the General Preface for January, or that they would at least not neglect the introductory commentaries, where they will learn of our judgement concerning such *Acta*.[59]

In effect, since the commentaries often made for arduous reading, more so in any case than the texts themselves, it often happened, for example at readings during mealtimes in the monasteries, that only the texts were read. This could mean that, if the text were of a fabulous variety, then the good name of the *Acta sanctorum* as a whole might be compromised. It was again Henschenius who recalled the principles that should be adopted:

> The *Acta* that we consider to be fabulous, we have not published any of them. If more authentic *Acta* are lacking, we have not hesitated to publish in full those that seem probable, even if they also contain less likely elements. In this way, satisfied with having warned the reader, we abstain from removing from the documents whatever there may be of this kind, even if there be just cause for doing so. In effect, this procedure reflects the consensus among scholars of this century. We believe, however, that we do not displease if, having regard to the infirmity of the weak, we expurgate from the text some really offensive elements and reproduce them in the commentaries, where they can be safely either read or skipped. We have sometimes deemed it our duty to avail of this liberty in these *Acta*, and we wish, reader, to alert you to this.[60]

This is certainly one of the clearest statements of the policies followed by the editors of the *Acta sanctorum*.

These criteria changed in nuances only over the course of 150 years. All of Bolland's successors were in agreement concerning the fabulous character of

---

59 'Vehementer sane optaremus, ut, qui in huiusmodi Acta incidunt, Praefationis generalis ad Ianuarium mensem caput prius quartum legissent, vel saltem non negligerent commentarios praevios, ex quibus nostrum de iis iudicium discerent ... ' (AASS, Mart. II, p. 584). 60 'Quae fabulosa iudicabamus Acta nulla dedimus; quae probabilia videbantur, si quidem certiora deficerent, non subterfugimus dare integra etsi quaedam minus probanda continerent: dandum hoc antiquitati existimantes, ut contenti lectorem admonuisse de vitio, manum ceteroqui abstineremus ab eiusmodi monumentis ulla, quamvis iusta ex causa truncandis: propterea quod ita faciendum suaderet eruditorum omnium communis hoc seculo sensus. Quia tamen non omnibus displiciturum credimus, si imbecilliorum infirmitati consulentes, pauca quaedam certo offensura tollamus e textu, atque ad commentarios referamus, in quibus innoxie possint vel legi vel praetermitti: hac nobis libertate iudicavimus in hisce Actis aliquoties esse utendum, de quo hic te monitum, Lector, volumus' (ibid.).

Irish *vitae*. However, the editorial decisions that followed this judgement might vary. One of the most interesting and, in some ways, one of the most modern comments was made by F. Baert, who discussed five Irish saints, including Colum Cille, in the June volumes of the *Acta*. In 1695, and again in 1698, he hesitated greatly before publishing the Lives of Kevin and Colman. He decided finally to do so, but not without prefacing the texts with such eloquent titles as *Acta suspecta* and *Acta fabulosa*, descriptions designed to put on their guard those responsible for mealtime readings in monasteries, and to encourage them to read the *commentarius praevius*. Of Colman's *Acta* Baert wrote:

> Doubtless, a certain number of people will consider that *Acta* of this kind ought to be suppressed and not published. This was also my view. However, having considered in the meantime that no other *Acta*, not to mention authentic ones, existed for the majority of Irish saints, I came to believe that it would not be without value for the public if hitherto unpublished *Acta*, which no one else might ever edit, were to be placed before the curious reader, especially in view of the fact that the compiler of the *Breviary of Aberdeen* drew lessons for the divine office from them, and that they are also often quoted by Irish historians who have scarcely any other documents at their disposal concerning the affairs of their country.[61]

An excellent reflection of an historian, brought to fruition by the scruples of a man of religion anxious to avoid scandal. However, one cannot but notice that, according as the calendar year progressed, Irish saints became much rarer in the *Acta sanctorum*. Thus, although present in every volume from January to April, their initial eclipse can be noticed in May, where only two of seven volumes take any account of them. In June, they are absent from Volumes IV to VII, and there are only two Irish entries for the whole of July, divided between two of seven volumes. August and September are marked by a slight improvement, but, by now, the Lives published are taken almost exclusively from the *Codex Salmanticensis*. Ward, Colgan and Fitzsimon are no longer there to supply alternative documents.

What were also evolving in the course of a century and a half of Bollandist history were the mentalities. What could be more natural? Although they were examiners of witnesses to the past, the Bollandists were also men of their own

---

61 ' ... et fortassis erit non nemo, qui iudicet, convenientius eiusmodi Acta in hoc opere supprimi, quam vulgari. Idem et meum erat iudicium. Sed interim considerans plerorumque Hibernorum Sanctorum, nec exstare alia, nec certiora, credidi non omnino inutile futurum publico, si hactenus inedita, et a nemine forsan edenda, curioso proponerentur lectori: praesertim cum Breviarii Aberdonensis collector, ex iis lectiones pro Divino Officio desumpserit, saepiusque citentur ab Hibernis Historicis, quibus vix alia suppetunt rerum patriarum monumenta' (ibid., p. 25).

time. In the middle of the eighteenth century C. Suysken was by no means impervious to the influence of the Enlightenment – or perhaps he was trying to escape from the taunts of the *Philosophes*. In any case, in the third September volume of the *Acta* he refused to edit the *Vita S. Kierani*,[62] and, in the following volume, he took the same decision in regard to the *Vita S. Albei*, a text for which he could not find words harsh enough:

> The longer Irish saints' Lives are, the more they contain of fables, thus obscuring the authentic acts of the saintly prelate with a huge number of fictions and enormous anachronisms. In a word, they are nothing but a farrago of fictions that excite equally both laughter and irritation in the reader.[63]

Arriving at St Finbarr in the sixth September volume, Suysken entitled the second paragraph of his commentary *Vitae eius fabulosae nec edendae*.[64] Suysken went on to discuss five dossiers of Irish saints and, although he subjected them all to long commentaries, he did not edit a single text.

Only one Irish dossier was to follow, that of St Canice in the fifth October volume, the last but one volume of *Acta* before the Bollandists were suppressed. In the dramatic circumstances of the period, one cannot reproach J.B. Fonsonus, when stating his intentions concerning Canice, for having copied word for word the paragraph in which Suysken announced his reasons for not publishing the Life of St Kieran.[65]

CONCLUSION

What conclusion is to be drawn from this long odyssey of a century and a half, and what traces of it still survive? Some figures may prove more eloquent than a long discussion. By the end of the eighteenth century 117 Latin hagiographical texts concerning Irish saints had been published, either fully or in part, in separate collections, including *Acta sanctorum* and *Acta sanctorum Hiberniae*. Of these, 52 had been published in their entirety in the *Acta sanctorum*, together with fourteen fragments of texts. And of the 66 texts published in this way, 22 – 14 from the *Codex Salmanticensis*, 8 from other manuscripts – could not be consulted anywhere else in print before the end of the last century or, in some

---

62 Ibid., Sept. III, p. 372.   63 '… sed, quod in aliis etiam Sanctorum Hiberniae Vitis crebro contingit, quo ampliora sunt, eo plures fabulas continent, eoque pluribus fabellis et enormibus anachronismis vera sancti Antistitis gesta obscurant. Verbo, non sunt, nisi quaedam figmentorum farrago, quae risum pariter ac stomachum lectori moveant' (ibid., Sept. IV, p. 27).   64 Ibid., Sept. VI, p. 144.   65 Ibid., Oct. V, p. 643.

cases, before the beginning of the present century. Indeed 4 of the 22 have yet to be subjected to new editions.

Remarkable as the contribution of the Bollandists to Irish hagiography may have been, it by no means exhausted the documentation assembled by them. They could have published much more. Texts translated from Irish into Latin, for instance, found little favour with them; I have discovered four only of which two derive from the *Acta sanctorum Hiberniae*. The risk of duplicating John Colgan's contemporary project must have had some influence. He would have been seen as being better prepared for the task, and as having access to more sources. His scheme, although dependent on the work of his predecessors, especially on that of Hugh Ward, remained the achievement of a single scholar. His death effectively marked the end of the *Acta sanctorum Hiberniae*; a projected third volume, although allegedly ready for the press, was never published.[66] Bolland's achievement, on the other hand, was to have known how to transform his project into an institution within the Belgian Jesuit Order, which ensured its continuity. A considerable amount of work could thus be accomplished in a century and a half, even in the particularly inaccessible area of Irish hagiography.

APPENDIX I

The first three columns contain the names of saints, references to the commentaries on them in the *Acta sanctorum* and, where known, the authors of these commentaries.(The commentaries in the January and March volumes are anonymous). In the next column each text is identified by its number in the *Bibliotheca hagiographica latina* (BHL); if printed in **bold**, this number shows that the text in question has been published in the *Acta*; if printed in *italics*, this shows that the text is only mentioned in the *Acta*; and, if printed in roman letters, this shows that the text is not mentioned in the *Acta*. The letters 'IRL' denote a text written in Irish. The fifth column shows whether the text had been edited previous to its mention in the commentary of the *Acta* and the use here of bold letters means that the *Acta sanctorum* took their text directly from this edition. Should a text have been taken from the *Codex Salmanticensis*, this is indicated by an 'EX' in the sixth column; the existence of a copy of a text in the same manuscript is denoted by 'COP'. The seventh and last column shows the provenance of the manuscript copies used in the *Acta*; if this still survives, then the current shelf-number of the manuscript containing it is shown in bold.

---

66 Mooney, 'Father John Colgan', p. 24.

Saints	AASS	Author	BHL	Previous Edition	COD SALM EX	COP	Provenance of the Manuscript
Mochua ab. of Tech Mochua	Ian. I, 45–7		Bolland **5977**				Ward
Mochua (Cronan) ab. of Balla	Ian I, 47–9		Bolland **IRL**				O'Sullivan Beare
Ita (Itta, Mida) v. of Clúain Credail	Ian. I, 1062–8		Bolland **4497**				Colgan (ex Kilkennensi codice pervetusto)= **BR 7569**, 263–70
			?				Ward (ex Ms Insulae Sanctorum in lacu Rivensi)
Blaithmac of Iona	Ian. II, 236–8		Bolland **1368**	Canisius			
Fechinus ab. of Fobar	Ian. II, 329–33		Bolland **2845**	**Hymnus**			Ward Fitzsimon
							Ward
Maedoc (Aidus, Aidanus) ep. of Ferna	Ian. II, 1111–20		Bolland **185**				Ward (ex vetustis codicibus Kilkenniensibus)
			186		x	x	
			187	Capgrave			O'Sullivan Beare

Saints	AASS	Author	BHL	Previous Edition	COD SALM	Provenance of the Manuscript
Brigida v. Kildariae	Feb. I, 99–185	Bolland	1455	Colgan (copy of White sent by Bolland to Ward: quod Colganus cum Ms. Atrebatensi S. Autberti, et Hibernico monasterii Insulae Sanctorum alioque Carthusiae Coloniensis collatum edidit, testatus aliud exemplar extare in monasterio Dunensi Brugis).		White (ex veteri Ms. Ecclesiae S. Audomari, diligenter collata cum ea, quam ex antiquo codice monasterii Ripensis, sive *am Hof* S. Magno dicati, in suburbio Ratisponensi ad pedem pontis, sua manu descripserat olim, miseratque Heriberto Rosweydo)= **BR 7763**, 113–34.
			1457	Canisius, Surius, Messingham, Colgan		Rosweydus (e vetustissimo codice D. Preudhomii Canonici Atrebatensis: quam contulimus cum Mss monasteriorum S. Maximi Treviris, Wiblingensis in Suevia, Bodecensis in Westphalia; cumque editionibus H. Canisii e Ms. Aistadiano, et

Saints	AASS	Author	BHL	Previous Edition	COD SALM	Provenance of the Manuscript
			1458	Colgan		Ioannis Colgani ex Mss S. Huberti ac S. Amandi).
			1460	Colgan		Ward
			1461	Colgan	x	
			1462			**BR** 4241, 32–4.
			IRL	Colgan		
Cuannatheus (Cuanna) ab. Lismoren.	Feb. I, 447–8	(Praeterm.)	1996	Colgan	x=	**BR** 7763, 135–8
Tarahata (Attracta) of Cell Sáile	Feb. II, 296–300	Henschen	7986	**Colgan**		
Berachus ab. of Clúain Coirpthe	Feb. II, 832–9	Bolland	1168	**Colgan**		Ward (ex ms. membranaceo coenobii canon. regular. Insulae omnium SS. ad lacum Rybhium in Connacia)= **BR** 8964, 118–25
			IRL	**Colgan**		
Fintanus ab. of Clúain	Feb. III, 16–21	Henschen	2993	Colgan	x	x(collatum cum ms. Kilkenniensi ut puto R. P. Hugonis Vardei)= **BR** 7763, 191–200 →

Saints	AASS	Author	BHL	Previous Edition	COD SALM	Provenance of the Manuscript
Senanus of Inis Cathaig	Mart. I, 760–79	?.	7573	Colgan	x	x(collato cum ms. R. P. Vardei)= **BR** 3196–203, 415–30
Ciaranus (Keranus, Piranus) ep. of Saigir	Mart. I, 389–99	?.	**IRL**	Colgan Hymnus	x	Ward= **BR** 3196–203, 431
			4658			
			4657	**Colgan**		
			4659	**Capgrave**		
Constantinus mon. of Raithen	Mart. II, 64–5	?.	1932	Brev. Aberdonen.		
Mochoemoc (Pulcherius) ab. of Liath Mochoemoc	Mart. II, 280–8	?.	5975	Colgan		Ward (ex cod. Kilkenniensi)= **BR** 3196–203, 399–410
Geraldus ab. of Magh Eo	Mart. II, 288–93	?.	*3416*	Colgan		Ward (ex ms. Insulae omnium Sanctorum)= **BR** 7812, 85–90
Finanus ab. Surden.	Mart. II, 444–7	?.	2992			Fitzsimon (in cod. chartaceo, non illo quidem admodum vetusto, sed quem ex alio vetustiori ante annos paullo plus centum →

Saints	AASS	Author	BHL	Previous Edition	COD SALM	Provenance of the Manuscript
						transcriptum esse satis apparet)
Patricius ep.	Mart. II, 517–92	Henschen (cfr Maii, III, 375)	6492			André Denys, S. J. (ex ms. antiquissimo codice in bibliotheca celeberrimi Nobiliacensis Monasterii S. Vedasti Atrebati)
			6493			Id.
			6513	C. Hugo, Messingham, Colgan		
			6504			White (ex antiquo ms.)= **BR 3196–203**, 347–54; Unknown Provenance = **Ibid.**, 368–74
			6506			* White (ms. of the Jesuits of Ingolstadt)= **BR 3196–203**, 467–72; **Boll.** 121, 78.* Fr. Baltazar Bisscot, S. J. (e libro ms. Patrum S. J. Duacensium)= **BR 4241**, 176–80.

Name	ALISS	Author	BHL	Previous Edition	COD SALM	Provenance of the Manuscript
Lactinus of Achad Úr	Mart. III, 31–3	?	6507			P. J. Gamans (ex Bodecensis monasterii diocesis Paderbornensis passionali pergamento manuscripto)= **BR** 3196–203, 355–63
			6511			(ex ms. S. Maximini Treveris) = **BR** 3196–203, 379–87
Endeus ab. of Aran	Mart. III, 267–74	?	4669			(ex ms. nostro Dublinensi)
			2543	Colgan		Ward (ex ms. Insulae Omnium Sanctorum) = **BR** 3196–203, 120–30
Fingar	Mart. III, 455–9	?	2988			(ex ms. Parisiensi S. Victoris, cod. 975)
Tigernachus of Clúain Eois	Apr. I, 401–4	Henschen	8287		x	Ward Fitzsimon
				Hymni		Ward
Finanus ab. of Cenn Etigh	Apr. I, 656	(Praeterm.)	2979		x	x= **BR** 7773, 466–74
Ruadanus ab. of Lothra	Apr. II, 382–6	Papebroch	7349		x	
Lasreanus (Molaisse) ab. Lethglinnen.	Apr. II, 543–7	Papebroch	*7426*		x	x= **BR** 7773, 397–400
			7427			Fitzsimon
Ibarus ep.	Apr. III, 173–4	Henschenius	4140m			Fitzsimon= **BR** 7773, 550–1
Cronanus ab. of Ros Cree	Apr. III, 579–83	Papebroch	1995		x	Sheerin

Saints	AASS	Author	BHL	Previous Edition	COD SALM	Provenance of the Manuscript
Comgallus ab. of Bennchor	Maii II, 579–88	Henschen	**1909**		x	Fitzsimon Ward
			1910	Fleming (ed. Sheerin)		(ex aliquo codice Hiberno)
Mochuda (Carthach) ep. of Les Mór	Maii III, 375–88	Henschen	**1623**		x	Fitzsimon
			1624	Colgan		(ex antiquo codice Hibernico)
Brendanus ab. of Clúain Ferta	Maii III, 599–603	Henschen	**1440**		x	
			1442			(ex vetustissimo ms. monasterii Aquicinctensis in Belgio)= **BR 4241**, 243–64
			1438		x	
Coemgenus ab. of Glenn dá Loch	Iun. I, 310–22	Baert	**1866**			Ward
			1868			*White (copy of a twelfth-century manuscript preserved by the Jesuits of Ingolstadt, now Munich Univ. 20312)= **Boll. 121**, 78–79.* (Ex ms. historico latino Biblioth. Caes. [=Vienna] signato num. 23 supra 3 infra) = **Ibid.**, 87. →

Saints	AASS	Author	BHL	Previous Edition	COD SALM	Provenance of the Manuscript
			?			Fitzsimon
Colmanus ep. Drumoren.	Iun. II, 24–9	Baert	1867		x	x= **Boll. 121**, 80–5
			1878		x	
			1879	Brev. Aberdonen.		
Columba ab. Hien.	Iun. II, 180–236	Baert	1885	Colgan		*Miraeus (ex Belfortii manuscripto)* Museum Bollandianum P 159 (ms. from Vaucelles, later transferred to Balthasar Moretus in Antwerp) = **BR 7400**, 167–9
			1886	Canisius, Messingham, Colgan	x	White (ex ms. Augiae-divitis [Reichenau])
			1890	Colgan	x	
Baithinus ab. Hien.	Iun. II, 236–8	Baert	896		x	
Moling (Dairchellus) ep. of Tech Moling	Iun. III, 406–10	Baert	5988		x	
			?			Fitzsimon
Moninna (Moduenna, Darerca)	Iul. II, 290–312	Pinius	2095		x	

Saints	AASS Manuscript	Author	BHL	Previous	COD SALM	Provenance of the Edition
			2096			Irish Franciscans of Louvain: 'in Mss postumis Sirinianis' (ex cod. Ms. Bibl. Cottonianae, sub effigie Cleopatrae A.2)
			2100			
Declanus ep. of Ard Mór	Iul. V, 590–608	Boschius	2116			Ms. of Irish Franciscans of Louvain, collated by Fr. Harold, OFM, with a manuscript kept at St Isidore's College, Rome.
Lugidus seu Molua ab. of Clúain Ferta Moluae	Aug. I, 339–52	Boschius	5058		x	
			5059	Fleming (ed. Sheerin)		
			5060 ?		x	Fitzsimon (in Ms. non admodum antiquo signato + Ms 167)
Maccartinus ep. Clogheren.	Aug. III, 208–10	Boschius	5105	Colgan	x	
Daigeus ep. of Inis Cáin Dega	Aug. III, 656–62	Pinius	2119		x	x= **Boll. 128**, 217–23
Mochta ep. Lugmaden.	Aug. III, 736–47	Pinius	5976		x	x= **Boll. 114**, 22–8
Eugenius (Éogan)	Aug. IV, 624–7	Cuperus	2677		x	

Saints	AASS	Author	BHL	Previous Edition	COD	SALM Provenance of the Manuscript
Flannán of Cell Dalua	Aug. VI, 488–91	Pinius	3024		x	x= **Boll. 128**, 338–64
Mac Nisse (Áengus) ep. Conneren.	Sept. I, 662–6	Veldius	**5125**		x	x= **Boll. 137**, 216–9
Ciaranus (Kyaranus, Queranus) ab. of Clúain meic Nóis	Sept. III, 370–83	Suyskens	4654			
			4655		x	x= **Boll. 140**, 123–8
Lasrianus (Molaisse) ab. of Daminis	Sept. IV, 2	(Praeterm.)	4725			Ward (not mentioned in the AASS)= **Boll. 141**, 221–6
Albeus (Helveus) archiep. of Imlech	Sept. IV, 26–31	Suyskens	197		x	x Ward= **Ibid.**, 353–69
			198			Ward (ex ms. Inisensi)= **Ibid.**, 344–52
			199			Ward (ex ms. Kilkenniensi) = **Ibid.**, 276–91
Adammanus ab. Hien.	Sept. VI, 642–9	Suyskens	69			
Findbarrus (Barrus)	Sept. VII, 142–51	Suyskens	2984			Ward= **Boll. 150**, 1–8
			2985			B. Medus= **Ibid.**, 120
			2987			Fitzsimon
Cainnicus (Cainnech) ab.	Oct. V, 642–6	Fonsonus	1519		x	x = **Boll. 148**, 51–72
			1521	Brev. Aberd.		

APPENDIX 2

Systematic Catalogue of the former *Museum Bollandianum* (Ms. Boll. 22, 23)

(The Catalogue is divided into sections headed *Hibernia* and *Scotia*. Capital letters and numbers denote bookshelves. Manuscripts are indicated by the siglum + Ms.)

HIBERNIA

Hiberniae Antiquitates et memorabilia per Iac. Waraeum. Lond. 1654. – V 78

Gentis origo, mores etc. per Thom. Carve. Solisbaci 1666. – V 59

Pro Hibernis Alithinologia per Eudoxium Alithinologum. 1664. – V 54

Hibernia resurgens Donati Roirk *adversus Thom. Dempsterum.* Rothom. 1621. – V 80

Vindicata adversus eumd. Dempsterum. Antv. 1621. – V 81

Defensa contra Giraldum a Gratiano Lucio. 1662.

Item a P. Vito – + Ms. 158. p. 306

Item Vindiciae mss. Stephani Viti S. J. – + Ms. 158

Hibernia Scotorum antiquorum Patria – + Ms. 143. p. 20 + Ms. 167. E – *Item* Cod. 43 p. 108

Hiberniae comitatus et episcopatus – + Ms. 167

Praesules commentario illustrati per Iac. Waraeum. Dublinii 1665. – V 35

Hiberniae historia antiq. et Nov. gallice per Ma-Geoghegan. tomi 3. Parisiis 1758 – V 42 b et seqq.

Hiberniae historia monastica. Par. 1690. – V 84

Item Ecclesiastica praecipue de Sanctis – + Ms. 167. f

Sancti Patroni

Sanctorum Acta per Ioan. Colganum. 1645. – V 3

Vitae aliquot breviores collectae a Steph. Vito S. J. + Ms. 167. B

Sancti et Kalendaria – + Ms. 167 – O 43. p. 83

Item Sancti per Messinganum. Par. 1624. – V 42

Sanctorum Officia propria – + Ms. 168

Item propria. Par. 1620. – * X 96

Scriptores per Iac. Waraeum. Dublinii 1639. – M 106

Epistolarum veterum Sylloge per Iac. Usserium. Dublini 1632. – V 73

De Sanctis Hiberniae Ms. Salmanticense – P Ms. 11

Hiberniae SS. Patronorum et Titularium Missae propriae – V 42.a

Hiberniae brevis notitia et incolarum constantia in fide catholica – V 74. p. 47

Annales ab an. 1162 ad 1421 apud Cambdenum – P 54. p. 794

Hiberniae et Angliae Bibliotheca ms. Oxoniae. 1697 – M 6.a

Coenobii Bancorensis Antiphonarium antiquissimum, in quo sancti plures memorantur – Z 76. p. 119

Aliquot episcopatus et coenobia per Waraeum latine – V 76

Topographia per Giraldum Cambrensem – V 15. p. 692

Aliquot coenobia – V 22. p. 1019

Annales Ecclesiastici per Porterum – V 48

Archiepiscopatus, provinciae, coenobia etc. – V 48. p. 160

Sanctorum catalogus recognitus a Fitz-Simon – V 81. p. 83

Hibernia caret veneno – Tom. 2. Mart. pag. 585 et seqq.

Quamdiu nomine Scotiae sit appellata. – Tom. 2. Maii pag. 301

Hiberni artem scribendi a S. Patricio primum didicerunt – Tom. 2? Mart. pag. 517
  et seqq.

Hiberni Belgii apostoli per Vernulaeum – B 169

Hiberni orant, ut plebs per pestem minuatur, probante S. Fechino – Tom. 2? Ian.
  pag. 332

Hibernorum SS. stupenda et incredibilia miracula – Tom. 1? Ian. in praef. pag.
  xxxiv – Tom. 1? Ian. pag. 45, 47 – Tom. 2? Ian. pag. 1112

Hibernorum SS. Acta, Martyrologia, Lites cum Scotis etc. – Tom. 1 Feb. in praef.
  pag. xvi et seqq.

Sanctorum Catalogus editus a Portero – V 48. p. 129

Hibernicum Missale, sive de SS. Hibernis missae propriae. Par. 1734. – V 42.a

Hibernensium Canonum Capitula Selecta – Z 3. p. 492 – Z 66. p. 1

Eorum Supplementum – Z 19. col. 1

Hibernicarum rerum defensio contra Giraldum – * V 40

Hibernicarum rerum Polychronicum a O. C. ad sec. XIV per Higdenum – V 20. p.
  179

Hibernica Martyrologia qualia sint, quibus usus sit Colganus ipse explicat tom. 1.
  SS. Hibern. p. 4. – V 3

Hibernicarum Vitarum origo ac de iis iudicium. – Tom. 1 Martii. pag. 390

SCOTIA

Scotiae Historia. Per Georg. Buchananum. Edimburgi 1582. Item Ultraiecti
  1707 – V 37 – V 77

Ad illam Apparatus Dempsteri. Bon. 1622. – SS 8

Gentis Origo et Gesta per Io. Leslaeum. Romae 1578. – V 47

Regum Catalogus, dies natales et mortuales, Item Sepulturae ex Boetio – L 117. p.
  401

Historia ecclesiast. per Spotswood. Londini 1655. Angl. – V 31

Scriptores per Dempsterum. Bonon. 1627. – V 55

Leges Veteres Scotorum per Skenaeum collectae – V 38

Religio per Conaeum. Romae 1628. – V 50

Haeresis Origo et Progressus. Item Virtutes per Camerarium. Par. 1631. – V 49

Patroni Sancti – * O 26. p. 46

Sancti. 1689. Per Dempsterum – SS 8

Sancti vindicati per Eumd. – V 83

De Iure Regni apud Scotos Dialogus Buchanani. Ultraj. 1707. – V 77

Apologia pro Sanctis hodiernae Scotiae contra Hibernos. – + Ms. 158

Scotiae Sancti ex Breviario Aberdonensi – + 167

Scotiae Reges per Schmidium – L 165

Scriptores vetustiores. Heidelbergae 1587.

Scriptorum 1603 *Nomenclatura* per Dempsterum – SS 8

De Scotorum Antiquorum Patria Hibernia, Dissertatio – + Ms. 143. p. 20

Alia eiusdem Argumenti. – + Ms. 167. E

Item alia per Thom. Sirinum. Post *Vitam S. Rumoldi* – * V 58. p. 88

Scoto-hibernica historia – + Ms. 167. E

Scotiae antiqui episcopatus – Tom. 2 Junii pag. 534 et seqq.

Scotorum historia per Fordin – V 20. p. 565

Scotia an Hiberniae nomine fuerit appellata – Tom. 2? Maij pag. 311

Scotiae et Angliae mulieres illustres – O 62

Scotiae aliquot monasteria – V 22. p. 1051

Scotorum Historia Auctore Hectore Boethio – V 28

Scotorum antiqua Religio Christiana Auctore Thomsono – V 28 in fine – V 57

Scotorum Historia per Jo. Majorem – V 52

Scotiae genuinae investigatio in Vita S. Rumoldi – V 58

Scotiae gentis antiquitas contra Usserium ulterius defensa Ms. – V 45.a

Regum Prosapia et Antiquitas Mackenzie – V 80.a

Scotorum lites cum Hibernis circa patriam quorumdam Sanctorum – Tom. 1? feb. praef. pag. xvii – Tom. 1? jan. praef. pag. xxx

Scoti de suis Sanctis narrant stupenda et incredibilia – Tom. 1 jan. in praef. pag. xxxiv et pag. 816

Scotorum peregrinationes et varia monasteria in Germania – Tom. 2. Feb. pag. 361 et seqq.

Scotici schismatis circa celebrationem Paschae causa et finis – Tom. 2. jun. pag. 190 et seqq.

Scotorum aliquot regum Genealogia – Tom. 2. jun. pag. 322 et seqq.

Scotorum et Pictorum limites ac conversio ad fidem – Tom. 2. jun. pag. 533.

Vita Sancti Carthagi in the Seventeenth Century

D.J. Thornton

The first half of the seventeenth century was an active period for Irish hagiography. The contributions of the Irish Jesuits Henry Fitzsimon and Stephen White, the Bollandists, the Dublin scholars Ussher and Ware, and the Irish Franciscans of St Anthony's College Louvain are well known.[1] These people were all aware of each other's activities and, despite their religious differences, there was a great deal of mutual cooperation as material was copied and exchanged between those working in Dublin, Louvain, and Antwerp. Much work has been done on the sources that were available at that time and on the transmission of information between the different centres. In particular, there appears to be general agreement about the routes by which material from the three major collections of Irish saints' Lives in Latin – the *Codex Salmanticensis*, the Dublin collection represented by Marsh's Library MS Z 3.1.5 and TCD MS 175, and the Lives from the Rawlinson MSS B 485 and B 505 – travelled from one project to another.[2] Nonetheless, one seventeenth-century witness to the Latin manuscript tradition, Maynooth MS RB201, appears to have been overlooked or, rather, dismissed. This paper will look first at the relationship of the Maynooth MS RB201 copy of the Life of St Carthage, or Mochuta, patron of Lismore, Co. Waterford, to other copies of his Life. It will then consider the transmission of the longer Latin version of Carthage's Life between Dublin and the Continent. Before concentrating on these two questions, however, it might be useful to provide a broader view of the Life.

---

1 Sharpe, *Medieval Irish Saints' Lives*, pp. 39–74, provides a full account of the seventeenth-century scholars and collectors. 2 Sharpe, *Medieval Irish Saints' Lives*, pp. 39–74 and 75–90, provides a comprehensive review of the work of his predecessors before presenting his own conclusions.

I THE LONGER LATIN LIFE OF ST CARTHAGE

The Lives of St Carthage, or Mochuta, can be arranged in four groups:

1. The longer Latin Life (LLatin): four examples and fragments, fifteenth and seventeenth century.[3]
2. The shorter Latin or Office Life (Office): two examples, early fourteenth and seventeenth century.[4]
3. The late Middle Irish Life (LMI): two examples, both seventeenth century.[5]
4. The early Modern Irish Life (EMI): seven examples, eighteenth and nineteenth century, and a fragment dated to the seventeenth century.[6]

Although the longer Latin Life is the subject of this paper, evidence provided by the Office, LMI, and EMI versions will be used in Part IV to explain the later stages of LLatin.

LLatin is represented by four full texts, manuscript and printed. These are: *M*, Marsh's Library MS Z 3.1.5, ff. 94rb–99vb; *T*, Trinity College Dublin MS 175 (formerly E.3.11), ff. 60vb–66rb; *B*, the second of two Lives of Carthage edited by the Bollandist Godefridus Henschenius and published in 1680 in Maii III of the *Acta sanctorum*, pp. 378–88; and *A*, Maynooth MS RB201 (formerly 3G1), pp. 23–35.

In addition to these four copies, excerpts from what is clearly an example of LLatin are found in Patrick Fleming's *Collectanea* (F) and in John Colgan's *Acta sanctorum Hiberniae* and *Trias thaumaturga* (C).[7] Finally, MS F2 in the Franciscan Library, Killiney, consists of two pages that contain the opening chapters of LLatin 'ex codice Kilkenniensis', written in what appears to be Colgan's hand; their format suggests that they were part of a copy prepared for printing.[8]

---

3 See below for details of copies.   4 Brussels Bibliothèque Royale MS 7672–7674 (*Codex Salmanticensis*), ff. 192b–194d, and *Acta sanctorum*, Mai III (1680), pp. 375–8.   5 Brussels Bibliothèque Royale MS 2324–2340, ff. 151a–157b, and Royal Irish Academy MS 968 (formerly A.iv.1), pp. 18–40.   6 Royal Irish Academy MS 1008 (formerly 23 M 50), pp. 77–108; Maynooth MS M39 (formerly 3 E 5), pp. 67–105; National Library of Ireland MS G 656, pp. 64–123; Royal Irish Academy MS 810 (formerly 3 B 7), ff. 57r–104r; Kings Inns Library MS 19, pp. 569–626; British Library Additional MS 39665, ff. 124v–136r; Royal Irish Academy MS 661 (formerly 24 A 27), pp. 283–8, 313–58; and Brussels Bibliothèque Royale MS 5057–5059, ff. 48r–51v.   7 Colgan, *Acta sanctorum*, pp. 250–2 (De S. Cuanna), p. 475 (De S. Carthagio), p. 301 (De S. Cronano), pp. 560–2 (Vita S. Cataldi), p. 631 (De S. Gobbano); idem, *Trias thaumaturga*, p. 459; Fleming, *Collectanea sacra*, pp. 314, 337–8. 8 F2 may be the fragment noted by Kenney, *Sources*, p. 452 n. 256. I am indebted to Pádraig Ó Riain for making this MS known to me, for offering his opinion on the hand, and for providing a copy.

M and T: The Lives of the Dublin Collection

Marsh's Library MS Z 3.1.5 and Trinity College Dublin MS 175, sister manuscripts dated on palaeographical grounds to the late fifteenth century, have been
carefully studied.[9] Their respective copies of *Vita Sancti Carthagi*, *M* and *T*,
are remarkably similar; the differences are few and minor, usually involving
onomastic variations and slight changes in word order or vocabulary. In each
copy the Life of Carthage has suffered some loss. *M* is missing the end of the
Life owing to the cutting away of f. 100. *T* has lost f. 65; and the top corner of
f. 66, with loss of text affecting the first twelve lines of the outer column, is also
lacking. Fortunately, the two MSS have not lost exactly the same text and each
for the most part covers the deficiencies of the other. The history of Marsh's
Library MS Z 3.1.5 remains unclear for the period before the end of the
sixteenth century; that of TCD MS 175 is unknown before the 1630s. It is
generally accepted that both MSS were known and accessible to Archbishop
Ussher, and that Marsh's Library MS Z 3.1.5 was in his possession by 1626.[10]
In a recent article, Pádraig Ó Riain has argued that Marsh's Library MS Z 3.1.5
was used before 1604 in the compilation of recension C of the *Catalogus
praecipuorum sanctorum Hiberniae*.[11] Ó Riain has also shown that the same MS
was used by Meredith Hanmer for his Chronicle of Ireland, compiled between
1591 and 1604.[12]

B: The Second Bollandist Life

The Bollandists published two Lives of Carthage in the *Acta sanctorum*. The
first is an example of the Office Life.[13] Concerning the second Life, the LLatin
copy, the *Acta sanctorum* introduction states: 'But the following Life, broadly
drawn, has been copied for us from an old Irish codex. James Ussher frequently
cites both [i.e., the Office and LLatin Lives] in his *Britannicarum ecclesiarum
antiquitates*. Moreover, John Colgan has published miscellaneous pieces from
the second Life in the *Acta sanctorum Hiberniae* for the months of January,
February, and March.'[14]

---

9 See Sharpe, *Medieval Irish Saints' Lives*, pp. 94–111, for full description, dating,
relationship, and bibliographical references for these MSS. 10 The evidence for both MSS
is summarised in Sharpe, *Medieval Irish Saints' Lives*, pp. 63, 98–108. It seems that Ussher
may have had access to the Marsh's Library MS as early as 1619. See Ó Riain, *Beatha
Bharra*, p. 102 n. 30. 11 Ó Riain, '*Catalogus*', pp. 400–1. I am grateful to Pádraig Ó Riain
for allowing me to read this article in draft. 12 *Beatha Bharra*, pp. 103–4. 13 See above,
n. 4. This was edited from the two copies, one in the *Codex Salmanticensis* and the other
provided by Henry Fitzsimon, which were in their possession. 14 'At posterior, late
deducta, nobis ex antiquo codice Hibernico descripta est. Utramque saepius allegat Iacobus
Usserius in suis Britannicarum Ecclesiarum antiquitatibus. Ioannes autem Colganus varia ex
secunda Vita edidit in Actis Sanctorum Hiberniae mensium Ianuarii, Februarii & Martii'
(*Acta sanctorum*, p. 375).

A: Maynooth MS RB201, pp. 23–35

Maynooth MS RB201 is a paper MS, consisting almost entirely of Lives of Irish saints. It is believed to have been written by Dr Thomas Arthur in Ussher's library in Drogheda in 1627.[15] Scribe, date, and place of writing are given in two colophons. The first, on one of the front flyleaves in what appears to be a different hand from that of the MS, reads: 'Vitae Sanctorum Hiberniae. Ex libris D[r]. Thomae Arthurij philosophiae et medicinae doctoris qui omnia quae in eo continentur propria manu transcripsit ex vetustissimo codice membraneo inter libros D[r]. Jac. Ussherij primatis Armachani et in eiusdem bibliotheca extante Pontanae anno domini 1627.' The second, in the hand of the MS, is on p. 230: 'Anno domini 1627. Haec per D[r]. Thomam Arthurium philosophie et medicinae doctorem transcripta sunt ex MS codice Bibliothecae D[r]. Jacobi Usheri archiepiscopi Ardmachani totius Hiberniae Primatis, ...' Two other notes on the front flyleaves appear to provide information about the later history of Maynooth MS RB201: one reads 'ex Bibliotheca Chandosiana'; the other, directly above the flyleaf colophon quoted, is a note in Irish stating that the MS had been bought by Charles O'Conor in Dublin in 1770.[16] Laurence Renehan, president of St Patrick's College Maynooth from 1845–1857, has written that this MS, of which he made a detailed description, was one of three documents lent to him by Hugh MacDermot, a student of Achonry in Maynooth College, in Holy Week, 1856.[17]

The colophons and flyleaf inscriptions would appear to indicate that the Lives in Maynooth MS RB201 are copies made in 1627 by Dr Thomas Arthur from a vellum manuscript in Ussher's library;[18] that the MS later became part

---

15 I am indebted to Dr Thomas Kabdebo, Librarian, Maynooth, and Ms Penny Woods of the Russell Library, Maynooth, for allowing me access to this MS and for arranging for photographs to be made of the relevant pages. 16 The fullest description of the MS is in Paul Grosjean, 'Catalogus codicum ... Dubliniensium', pp. 116–18. Grosjean tentatively suggests that entry 3852 in the catalogue of the Chandos sale might refer to Maynooth MS RB201. William O'Sullivan has however pointed out to me (personal communication) that the MS referred to in this entry has been identified as Rawlinson B 485, and that he has so far not succeeded in locating Maynooth MS RB201 in the Chandos sale catalogue. He has also found several examples of Ussher's hand in the margins of Maynooth MS RB201. I am indebted to Mr O'Sullivan for several helpful discussions. 17 Maynooth MS R49 (formerly 4G5). This entry is in the last pages of an unpaginated notebook. Hugh MacDermot, described by Renehan as 'eldest son and heir to the hereditary estate and style of the lords of Moylurg and Princes of Coolavin', appears to have been Hugh H. O'R. MacDermot (1834–1904), who went on to have a distinguished legal career. He was a great-great-grandson of Charles O'Conor. I am grateful to William O'Sullivan for drawing my attention to Hugh MacDermot's later history. 18 This is usually taken to have been Marsh's Library MS Z 3.1.5. See for example Sharpe, *Medieval Irish Saints' Lives*, pp. 96, 100. Maynooth MS RB201 includes Lives for most of the Irish saints found in Marsh's Library MS Z 3.1.5; it does not contain the Lives of Lawrence, Malachy, Louis, Anthony, or Fintan of Taghmon. Present in Maynooth MS RB201 but not in either Marsh's Library MS

of the Chandos collection; and that after the Chandos sale in 1747 it made its way back to Ireland, where it was bought in Dublin by Charles O'Conor of Belanagare in 1770.[19] Renehan's note suggests that the MS passed to the MacDermots of Moylurg, relatives and neighbours of the O'Conors of Belanagare, from whom it came into the possession of the Maynooth Library at some time between 1856 and 1910: at that time James MacCaffrey, in a review of Charles Plummer's *Vitae sanctorum Hiberniae*, appears to have been the first person to refer to it in print.[20]

F, K, C: The Louvain Excerpts
Carthage's feast day is 14 May; his full Life would have appeared in the second volume of Colgan's *Acta sanctorum Hiberniae* but, although there is evidence that preparations for this volume were well-advanced, it was never published and most of the material appears to have been lost.[21] However, as witnesses to the Louvain copy of LLatin there remain *K, F* and *C*.[22] *K* consists of §§1–8 of the Life; *F* and *C* between them provide part, or, rarely, all of §§1, 2, 9, 10, 12, 13, 15, 20, 34, 35, 36, 39, 42, 43, 51, 63, 65.[23]

II THE RELATIONSHIP OF THE TEXTS OF THE LONGER LATIN LIFE

Plummer made use of *M, T,* and *B* in his VSH edition of *Vita Sancti Carthagi*.[24] He chose to publish *T*, which he had collated with *M*. He also used *M*, supplemented by *B*, to supply the text lost with *T* f. 65.[25] Of *B* itself Plummer writes that it 'seems to be based chiefly on M, as B generally agrees

---

Z 3.1.5 or TCD MS 175 are Lives of Livinus, Attracta, Bega, Laisrén of Leighlin, a piece about St Cuthbert, Gilbert of Limerick's *De statu ecclesiae*, to which the colophon on p. 230 (noted above) is attached, and an untitled text that is called by James MacCaffrey from its opening line *Norma anchoritalis vitae* ('Lives', p. 339 n. 1). I have not been able to identify this text, which begins: 'Incipit vita vel norma anchoritalis vitae perfectorum Christi militum salubris ordo dilectione Dei et proximi contractor quae charitas nuncupatur.'   19 The reliability of this evidence has yet to be established. In a personal communication, William O'Sullivan has pointed out the possibility that the colophon on p. 230 may in fact refer only to *De statu ecclesiae*, to which it is attached, and that the colophon on the flyleaf may be a roughly expanded copy of this, mistakenly applied at a later date to the whole MS. O'Sullivan's argument is supported by the fact that the internal colophon goes on closely to paraphrase the note on sources given by Ussher for his own edition of *De statu ecclesiae* (Ussher, *Whole Works*, iv.510). The problem of the Chandos note has been mentioned above, n. 16.   20 'Lives', p. 339 n. 1.   21 Jennings, *Michael O Cleirigh*, pp. 179–82; Mooney, 'Father John Colgan', p. 24; MacDonnell, 'Notice', pp. 371–5.   22 See notes 7 and 8 above. 23 All numbering follows Plummer's edition in *Vitae sanctorum Hiberniae*, i.170–99, which is divided into 69 chapters.   24 VSH i.170–99.   25 VSH i.xlv–xlvi. Plummer dealt with the loss of the upper corner of *T* f. 66 by re-translating from Early Modern Irish into Latin.

with M against T where these differ; but T must also have been used for the later sections which are not in M; and B omits the second half of §67 which is mutilated in T.' In a footnote attached to this section, Plummer adds: 'The fact that B has §64 complete, whereas part of it is now missing both in M and T might only mean that the mutilation of one or other of these MSS. was subsequent to Fitzsimon's time. The fact, however, that the text of the earlier part of this section in B varies somewhat considerably from that of M makes it probable that the editor had some other source than transcripts of M and T.'[26]

Plummer, who had been unaware of the existence of Maynooth MS RB201 until MacCaffrey's review, examined it in 1923 and dealt with it briefly in *Miscellanea hagiographica hibernica*. He gives only a very general description of the MS but does make several points which appear to have had considerable influence: ' ... Dr. Mac Caffrey cites an Irish note from a flyleaf of the MS., stating that it was purchased at Dublin by Donough [sic MacCaffrey] O'Conor in 1770; and another note stating that it was copied by Thomas Arthur in 1627 from an old vellum MS. belonging to Ussher. (These notes I omitted to record.) The lives are of the M type, and it is certain that Ussher used a MS. of that type, if not M itself. But the scribe has edited the texts after his own fashion.'[27] He concludes by commenting that 'the MS. has a certain value as illustrating the interest taken in Irish Hagiography in the 17th century, but for critical purposes it is obviously worthless, and no account is taken of it in the fifth section of this Catalogue, which deals with Latin Lives.'[28]

The Louvain excerpts of Carthage's Life all show a close relationship to *M*, *T*. It would be strange if they did not, since it has been shown that Fleming, Ward and Colgan all made use of the transcript of a source called both the *Codex Ardmachanus vel Dubliniensis* and *Codex Kilkenniensis*, made during the period 1626–7 when, at the behest of those working in Louvain, Francis Matthews, at that time Minister Provincial of the Franciscans in Ireland, commissioned transcripts of at least two other manuscripts: a vellum MS containing Lives in Irish; and the MS usually called by Colgan *Codex Insulensis*.[29] William Reeves has shown that Fleming's *Codex Ardmachanus vel Dubliniensis*,

---

26 VSH i.xlvi–vii. I do not understand Plummer's reference to Fitzsimon here; he seems to be implying that Fitzsimon had some part in providing *B* to the Bollandists, but this is not specified.   27 Plummer, *Miscellanea*, p. 178.   28 *Miscellanea*, p. 178. Despite this pronouncement, Plummer might well have made use of *A* had he known of it when he was editing *Vita Sancti Carthagi*. He certainly made use of texts published by the Bollandists and Colgan, even though he classified them as editions rather than primary sources in his *Miscellanea*.   29 Both transcripts survive: the former, copied by Domhnall Ó Duinnín, is now Royal Irish Academy MS 968 (formerly A iv I); the latter was copied by Fr. John Goolde of Cashel and is now MS F1 in the Franciscan Library, Killiney. See Sharpe, *Medieval Irish Saints' Lives*, pp. 53, 99–100. For Colgan's *Codex Insulensis* see Ó Riain, *Beatha Bharra*, pp. 104–13.

a transcript of which Fleming states that he obtained from Francis Matthews 'circa annum 1626', refers to Marsh's Library MS Z 3.1.5.[30] Plummer then went on to gather textual evidence to demonstrate that the *Codex Kilkenniensis* was Marsh's Library MS Z 3.1.5, a view that has come to be generally accepted.[31] Since Fleming, Ward, and Colgan were thus all referring to the same collection of Lives, it is likely that all three were taking their material from the transcript supplied by Francis Matthews. A transcript of the *Codex Kilkenniensis* is listed as being amongst the materials in Colgan's study after his death but this is now lost.[32]

In turn, the Franciscans in Louvain were cooperating with the Bollandists in exchanging information and copies of texts and in lending manuscripts.[33] Ward is known to have provided copies of twenty-two Lives of Irish saints, a service acknowledged by the Bollandists in the introductions to a number of the Irish Lives published in the *Acta sanctorum*.[34] In addition to the donor, the sources of the Lives are often mentioned, and it is generally assumed that the Bollandist *Codex Kilkenniensis* and *Codex Insulensis* Lives provided by Ward are copies taken from the Matthews transcripts made in 1626–7. Thus Plummer writes in his introduction to the Life of Mochóemóc: 'The Bollandists say that their text was taken from Codex Kilkenniensis (i.e. M), furnished by Hugh Ward, and compared with Colgan. Fleming is much nearer to the MS. than Colgan, while the Bollandists generally follow the latter. There are, however, places in which all three editors agree against M; and the explanation probably is that they all worked from the same transcript of M which had already departed somewhat from the original, much as F has departed from R2'.[35] Neither donor nor source is named in the introduction to the Life of Carthage quoted above. However, the references to Ussher and Colgan and the evidence of the Life itself would all suggest that *B* came to Antwerp by way of the *Codex Kilkenniensis* transcripts sent by Matthews from Dublin to Louvain.

On the basis of the findings presented above concerning the relationship of Marsh's Library MS Z 3.1.5 and TCD MS 175; Plummer's conclusions about the relationship of *M*, *T* and *B*; the evidence that both *Codex Ardmachanus vel*

---

30 Reeves, 'Manuscript Volume'; Sharpe, *Medieval Irish Saints' Lives*, pp. 99–101. 31 VSH i.xii–iv; Sharpe, *Medieval Irish Saints' Lives*, pp. 93–4 and n. 3. 32 Gilbert, 'Manuscripts', p. 612a. 33 Cf. Robert Godding's contribution to this volume, above. 34 Ibid. 35 VSH i.lxxix. Richard Sharpe obviously agrees with Plummer's conclusions: 'The fact, noted by Plummer, that there are points in the text where all three editions [here Sharpe is referring to the Plummer passage quoted above] agree on a reading different from that of M does not undermine Reeves's identification of the *Codex Ardmachanus* with M but demonstrates that Fleming, Ward, Colgan, and the Bollandists all worked on the transcript originally supplied by Matthews' (*Medieval Irish Saints' Lives*, pp. 100–1 and n. 31). I am assuming that Plummer and Sharpe both mean here that the Bollandists worked from copies of the Matthews transcript, made for them on the Continent, rather than directly from the Matthews material.

Dubliniensis and *Codex Kilkenniensis* refer to a transcript of Marsh's Library Z 3.1.5 commissioned by Francis Matthews for the Franciscans in Louvain; the common view that a copy of this transcript is likely to have been sent to the Bollandists in Antwerp; and Plummer's verdict that the Lives in Maynooth MS RB201 are probably freely edited copies of Lives in Marsh's Library Z 3.1.5, one might draw up the following stemma for the longer Latin Life of Carthage:

STEMMA I

δ = common exemplar, Dublin Collection
γ = transcript supplied by Matthews
χ = unknown source posited by Plummer
β = transcript supplied to Bollardists

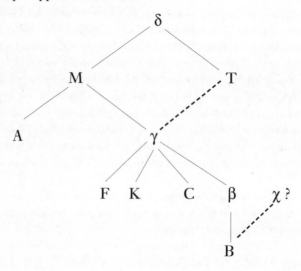

III. A: THE STEMMA REVISITED

Based on the evidence of the notes on the flyleaf, his own observations, and the conventions of textual criticism, Plummer's pronouncement that Maynooth MS RB201 was worthless for critical purposes is not surprising. Whatever Plummer's intention, his remarks give the impression that this MS is the free copy by an idiosyncratic scribe of a surviving exemplar.

However, in 1928 Paul Grosjean published a description of Maynooth MS RB201 as part of his catalogue of Latin hagiographical material in Dublin.[36] Grosjean's interest was strictly hagiographical, and he did not mention *De statu*

36 'Catalogus codicum … Dubliniensium', pp. 116–18. 37 Ibid., p. 118.

ecclesiae and *Norma anchoritalis vitae*, noting only 'pag. 227–240 nonnulla complent a re nostra aliena, ...'.[37] He seems to have examined the MS carefully: he attempted to identify the sources for the Lives not included in Marsh's Library Z 3.1.5 or TCD 175, suggested a very tentative identification for the MS with an item listed in the catalogue of the Chandos sale, and also commented on the collection as a whole:

> One would have believed this to be a transcript, altered now and again in style and with the Irish genealogies from the margins inserted into its Latin Lives, of Codex Z 3.1.5 of Marsh's Library, which we know to have belonged to Ussher, more complete than it now is, were it not that here and there (for example the beginning of the Life of S. Carthage or Mochuta p. 23ff.) it agrees more with the codex E.3.11 of Trinity College, which also we know to have been Ussher's at that time. But it appears to have the greatest resemblance to those Lives which John Colgan writes that he had taken from that Codex Kilkenniensis of his. Was this Chandos codex or one similar the transcript for Colgan of the Kilkenny volume? But we will perhaps go into greater detail on these matters sometime, when there is more time in Maynooth available.[38]

Unfortunately, Grosjean did not find the time to expand on his observations, although he does refer to Maynooth MS RB201 again in an article on Ussher's sources.[39]

It would appear that Plummer's judgement on Maynooth MS RB201 has become the general view, and that Grosjean's comment that the Lives of this MS resemble most closely those of Colgan's *Codex Kilkenniensis* has never really been investigated – although Ludwig Bieler, perhaps reading into Grosjean's remarks more than their author had intended, did write: 'The comprehensive manuscript collections of Vitae Sanctorum Hiberniae are not yet fully exhausted. MS. Maynooth 3.G.1 (written in A.D. 1627), a copy of the Kilkenniensis collection which is possibly independent of the Marsh manuscript, should be fully collated ... '.[40] Nonetheless, since that time Maynooth MS RB201 appears

---

38 'Credideris hoc apographon esse, mutato subinde stilo genealogiisque hibernicis e marginibus in ipsas Vitas latine inductis, codicis Z.3.1.5 bibliothecae Marshianae, quem saec. XVII in. apud Usserium fuisse novimus, pleniorem quam nunc est; nisi hinc inde (exemplo sit initium Vitae S.Carthagi seu Mochutu, p. 23 sqq.) cum codice E.3.11 Collegii Sanctissimae Trinitatis magis consonaret, quem etiam Usserii fuisse tunc temporis non ignoramus. Sed maxima similitudo haberi videtur cum eis quae ex illo suo Kilkenniensi Iohannes Colganus se deprompsisse scribit. Hicne Chandosianus vel similis codex fuerit Colgano Kilkenniensis libri apographon? Sed haec aliquando forsan elaborabimus, ubi plus otii apud Maynooth suppetierit, ('Catalogus codicum ... Dubliniensium', p. 117). 39 Grosjean, 'Antiquitates de Jacques Ussher', pp. 161–2. 40 Bieler, 'Recent Research', p. 232. Not mentioned by Plummer or Grosjean is a note pasted on the inside front cover of

to have been treated as a curiosity, useful mainly as a witness to the ownership of Marsh's Library Z 3.1.5 and to the contents and location of Ussher's library in 1627.[41]

However, as part of a thesis examining the different Lives of Carthage and their relationship to one another, I made a complete collation of all the surviving examples of LLatin, including *A*, *K*, *F*, and *C*. This had an unexpected result: *A* was revealed to be closely related to *B* and the Louvain excerpts. There are numerous instances where *A* and *B* (and *F*, *C*, or *K*, when present) share a reading that differs from the reading of *M*, *T*. Moreover, not only do *A* and *B* contain the same text for the lines lost between the end of *M* f. 100 and beginning of *T* f. 66, they continue to agree with each other in some passages even when the material covered by *T* f. 66 is available. This *A*, *B* agreement is most striking towards the end of the Life, where longer passages are involved – these will be discussed in Part IV – but examples are distributed throughout the text:

§4. utero *A*, *B*, *K*] ventre *M*, *T*
§13. institutor *A*, *B*, *C*] nutritor *M*, *T*
§13. generatione tua *A*, *B*, *C*] genere tuo *M*, *T*
§21. & ait *A*, *B*] om. *M*, *T*
§21. est bonus hic fructus qui *A*, bonus est hic fructus qui *B*]
        bona est hec virtus que *M*, *T*
§32. stridentem *A*, *B*] se ridentem *M*, *T*
§36. exposuit *A*, *B*] *om. M*, *T*
§55. dolebant *A*, *B*] dicebant *M*, *T*
§69. fratres cenobij sui *A*, fratres sui coenobii *B*] ce[no]bium suum *T*
§69. antistes *A*, *B*] episcopus *T*

Thus it does not appear that *A* could have been copied directly from *M* or from *T*. This indicates that *A* can no longer be isolated in the stemma as an independent copy of *M* but must instead be considered as part of the line of transmission leading to Fleming, Ward, Colgan, and the Bollandists. Of course, these findings apply only to the Life of Carthage. However, if Plummer and

Maynooth MS RB201: 'To the interest of future students, I note here that the lifes [sic] of the Irish saints, the pedigrees of whom are given in Irish, have been taken from the Codex Kilkenniensis, a copy of which is in Marsh's Library, Dublin. The immense advantage of the present MS. is that it is written in full whereas the marsch's [sic] library copy is full of contractions.' It is initialled TLS(f?). **41** See especially Sharpe, *Medieval Irish Saints' Lives*, p. 100 n. 28. The existence of Maynooth MS RB201 is well known and it has been frequently mentioned since MacCaffrey's note. See Kenney, *Sources*, p. 306 n. 56; Ó Fiaich, *Má Nuad*, p. 91; Ó Riain, *Beatha Bharra*, pp. 6n, 102n, 229. Kenney cites Plummer; Ó Riain cites Plummer and Sharpe.

Sharpe, among others, are correct in believing that the Franciscans of St Anthony's College and the Bollandists used material derived from the same transcript supplied by Francis Matthews to the Louvain project, then it is clear that other Lives in Maynooth MS RB201 need to be examined in order to find out how they are related to their *Codex Kilkenniensis* counterparts in Louvain and Antwerp.

Accepting that the source of the Louvain and Bollandist texts was the transcript, designated γ, commissioned by Matthews, there would appear to be three choices for explaining the relationship between *A* and *B*:

1. γ descends from A.
2. *A* and γ descend from a common exemplar which is not *M* (or *T*).
3. *A* descends from γ.

Taking the simplest case (1) first, *A* could not have been the source of γ. A number of readings shared by *M*, *T* and *B* are either absent or differ markedly in *A*:

§14. apertionem] ampnem *M, T, B*
§15. ad te iuvenis et sanctus] presbyter iuvenis et sanctus ad te *M, T, B*
§27. revertens] redeuntes *M, T, B*
§32. *om.*] in regione *M, T, B*
§45. *om.*] post eum *M, T, B*
§53. sponte suscepit] accepit sponte *M, T, B*
§53. *om.*] stabat enim ipse in vestibulo chori *M, T, B*
§53. *om.*] cum tuis *M, T, B*
§57. diem Domini] iudicium Dei *M, B*
§69. pater] noster patronus Mochutu *T, B*
§69. erecta] sancta *T, B*

It is possible that both A and γ descend from a common exemplar (choice 2). In addition to readings in which *A, B* agree against *M, T* and readings in which *M, T, B* agree against *A*, examples of which have been listed above, there are also numerous readings in which *M, T, A* agree against *B*:

§8. intente aspicis omni nocte *M, T, A*] attente tota nocte audis *B*
§20. parrochiam suam, it est regionem *M, T, A*] regionem eius *B*
§29. sanctus Carthagus ad sanctum Colmanum *M, T, A*] ad eum S. Carthagus *B*
§32. illis artificibus *M, T, A*] artificibus dispiciens *B*
§36. semitipso et tota sua parrochia *M, T, A*] semet & sua familia *B*
§39. sanctus ipse antistes Mochudu *M, T, A*] ipse S. Carthagus *B*
§51. cum torce *M, T, A*] *om. B*

§58. et respexit rex. Dixitque ei sanctus: Nec terram *M, A*] om. *B*
§61. causa pudicicie *M, A*] caussa voluptatis *B*
§65. benedicens pontifex cum ceteris sanctis illum agrum *T, A, C*] loco
benedicens sanctus pontifex cum ceteris sanctis *B*
§65. atrium erit, sed magnum *T, A*] sed magnum erit *B*

The large number of independent *B* readings, some quite garbled, would suggest that *B* is several removes from *M, T*, as one would expect were the Bollandists working from a transcript of γ.

The final choice (3) is the least amenable to testing. In this stemma *A* and the Louvain excerpts *K, F* and *C* would be sister texts at two removes from *M, T* while *B* would be at three removes. One would not expect *A* to agree with *M, T* against two or more of *K, F, C, B*. There are, however, several examples of this agreement. It must be kept in mind that only *B* is a full text; omission of one or more of *K, F, C* means that that source is not available for comparison:

§2. predixit] praedixerat *K, F, B*
§4. in utero tunc] tunc in utero *K, B*
§6. obviavit] obviabat *K, B*
§7. et amabilis] *om. K, B*
§8. castris] castellis *K, B*
§13. multis prodigiis in eo] in eo multis prodigiis *C, B*
§63. obtulit (*M*)] *add.* S.Carthago *C, B*
§65. in illa (*T*)] illic *F, C, B*

Collation of *K*, the longest continuous excerpt, with the four full texts *M, T, A, B* shows *K* agreeing most often with *B* against *M, T, A*; agreeing frequently with *A, B* against *M, T*; and in only one instance, §8 *Aeda Bennáin*, agreeing with *A* against all others. If *A*'s exemplar was the Matthews transcript made in Ussher's library, then *A* must have been made before that transcript, said by Fleming to have been made 'around the year 1626', was sent to Louvain.[42]

Although the evidence suggests that A is more likely to have shared an exemplar with γ than to have been copied from it, one must remember that the stemmata choices presented above were the simplest possible. Much depends on the way the Franciscans in Louvain and the Bollandists used their respective texts. Did Ward and Colgan work from γ or did they make their own transcripts? Colgan, despite his stated principles, is known to have taken liberties with his texts.[43] In several instances, the same passage from Carthage's Life was quoted more than once in the *Acta sanctorum Hiberniae* or *Trias thaumaturga*; and these

42 Fleming, *Collectanea sacra*, p. 431; cited in Sharpe, *Medieval Irish Saints' Lives*, p. 99.
43 Bieler, 'Colgan as Editor'; Ó Riain, *Beatha Bharra*, pp. 44–5.

passages, compared, are not absolutely identical. If and when the Franciscans sent a copy of *Vita Sancti Carthagi* to Antwerp, did they go back to γ to make a transcript or did they use a later copy? The Bollandists are known to have had the transcripts they received recopied.[44] It seems almost certain that more copies were involved – and more opportunity for interference with the text – than can be shown in the stemma. In addition, the possibility that A was collated with M cannot yet be rejected. Marginalia found in Marsh's Library Z 3.1.5 have been copied into the margins of Maynooth MS RB201 in what appears to be the hand of the MS. None of these is attached to A – in any case the marginalia in M serve to locate names and incidents in the text rather than to provide information or comment – but their presence in Maynooth MS RB201 does suggest that they were either copied directly from the corresponding Lives in Marsh's Library Z 3.1.5 or carried over from that MS into Maynooth MS RB201's exemplar(s).[45]

IV THE TRANSMISSION OF *VITA SANCTI CARTHAGI*: THE EVIDENCE OF THE OFFICE, LMI, AND EMI LIVES

It is clear that the LLatin stemma must be adjusted to indicate the relationship between A and B. However, the addition of A to the Continental line of transmission does not, on its own, do anything toward explaining why A and B take the form that they do. At this point it is worth asking whether the other versions of the Life have anything to contribute to a better understanding of LLatin.

All copies known to me of the Office, LMI, and EMI Lives have been collated and the variant readings for each version arranged in an *apparatus variorum*. Comparison of the four existing versions suggests that all descend from a LLatin original. This, on the basis of the concerns expressed in the surviving copies of LLatin, was probably composed shortly before 1215, when, in the course of the fourth Lateran Council, Pope Innocent III made a definitive pronouncement on the case of the long-running dispute between the dioceses of Lismore and Waterford. By finding in Lismore's favor in the

---

44 Grosjean, 'Antiquitates de Jacques Ussher', p. 178; Sharpe, *Medieval Irish Saints' Lives*, pp. 70–1.   45 Marsh's Library MS Z 3.1.5 marginalia are found attached to Maynooth MS RB201's Lives of Declan, Ailbe, Rúadán, Cíarán of Saighir, Colmán, and Abbán. The note at Maynooth RB201 p. 42 (Declan) is particularly noteworthy. This corresponds to a note in Marsh's Library MS Z 3.1.5 f. 103v, written in a hand recently identified by Pádraig Ó Riain as that of Henry Fitzsimon and corrected, with addition, by Ussher. See also Sharpe, *Medieval Irish Saints' Lives*, p. 102 and note. There is a puzzling reading in §65: *T* has 'in quo loco monasterium sanctimonialium est hodie in civitate Less Mor'. This is missing in *C*, *B* while *A* has 'in quo loco' with a line drawn through the words: the scribe evidently began to copy the clause, then decided to omit it.

presence of so many of the Irish bishops, and by imposing perpetual silence on the question thereafter, the Pope hoped to put an end to the attempts by successive bishops of Waterford to absorb Lismore.[46] The Office and LMI Lives can be shown to be independent reworkings of a LLatin exemplar; although both are considerably abbreviated in comparison with LLatin, there is no evidence that they derive from exemplars substantially different from the fifteenth-century copies M and T that now survive. The Office Life was in existence by the time of the compilation of the *Codex Salmanticensis*, recently re-dated to the early fourteenth century.[47] LMI now survives only in two seventeenth-century copies, but is likely to reflect the fifteenth-century fashion for writing in Irish that produced the saints' Lives in the Book of Lismore, Laud 610, and the Book of Fermoy.[48] The earliest complete copy of EMI, which is a very close translation of LLatin as we now have it, is dated 1741 but an abbreviated and incomplete copy dated to the seventeenth century survives in Brussels Bibliothèque Royale MS 5057–5059. If it is the case that all surviving versions descend ultimately from a common original, it should be possible to bring the shared evidence of the Office, LMI, and EMI Lives to bear, with caution, on the problems presented by three passages that are missing or mutilated in M and T.[49] These losses have already been mentioned briefly above; it will now be necessary to describe them in detail.

Both M and T are faulty: the end of M, from what would have been the ninth line of §64, is missing owing to the cutting away of f. 100. T has lost f. 65, which contained the material from approximately the middle of §56 to ten lines before the end of §64. M and T almost cover each other's deficiencies, but not quite. The last line of f. 99vb in M reads: '–aribus. Et tunc mallina implevit alveum fluminis. Sanctique'. The first two lines of T f. 66ra read: 'per divisi ponti arida, et revolute in latus geminum aque ad instar muri dextera et leua steterunt, nudataque telus spoliatur aquis cognotis'. It is clear that something has been lost.

In addition, the outer top corner of T f. 66 is defective: this comprises a triangular section affecting the first 8 lines of f. 66rb and a further narrow strip missing on the margin, affecting the final 3–4 letters of lines 9–12. The chapters in question are §67 and §68.

Although it could well be that the loss of T f. 65 was accidental, since together with the missing f. 72 it formed the outer leaf of a gathering, Plummer believed that the loss of the cut-away M f. 100 and the mutilation of the upper

---

46 Detailed argument for this date will be presented elsewhere. For an account of Lismore's difficulties with Waterford see Dunning, 'Waterford-Lismore Controversy'.   47 Ó Riain, 'Codex Salmanticensis'; O'Sullivan, 'Waterford Origin'.   48 Ó Riain, *Beatha Bharra*, p. 41.   49 Editions of all three versions have been published: the Office in Heist, *Vitae*, pp. 334–40; LMI in Plummer, BNE i.291–9; EMI in Power, *Lives of SS. Declan and Mochuda*.

outer edge of *T* f. 66 were deliberate. In both MSS the Life of Carthage is followed immediately by the Life of Declan, beginning somewhere on *M* f. 100 and at the bottom of *T* f. 66rb. Declan's Life opens with an account of triple incest and Plummer felt that the mutilations were made in an attempt at censorship.[50] If this was the case, and Sharpe seems to find this conjecture reasonable,[51] there is little evidence for the date of the mutilations. Grosjean, in his edition of the *Catalogus praecipuorum sanctorum Hiberniae*, suggested that the S. Mulronus assigned to the Life of Carthage might be a corruption of the S. Molua found in the LMI, Office, and EMI versions of §64, thus indicating that f. 100 was still present in Marsh's Library Z 3.1.5 when the index for the *Catalogus* was made.[52] However, it is clear that f. 100 was missing when Ware quoted the incipit and passages from *Vita S. Carthagi* in BL MS Add.4792.[53] To my knowledge, no attempt has been made to date the loss or mutilation of ff. 65 and 66 in *T*.

Even when one has the use of both *M* and *T*, a hiatus remains in §64; there are as well a number of truncated lines in §67 and §68. Nonetheless, *A* and *B* offer a full text: the break in §64 has been filled and §67 and §68 read smoothly. Plummer's statement that *B* appeared to be based on *M*, with horizontal transmission from *T* or an unknown source, has been quoted above.[54] His explanation begs several questions about the manuscript transmission between Dublin and the Continent, scribal practice, and the copies and versions of the Life of Carthage available to the copyist whose transcript was the basis of *B*. Even so, Plummer has set out the relationship, awkward as it is, and *A*'s new position in the stemma compounds rather than resolves the problem. However, if one can consult the corresponding passages in the Office, LMI, and EMI versions as witnesses to LLatin, I believe that an explanation can be proposed.

§64: CARTHAGE CROSSES THE BLACKWATER

In this episode, Carthage and his eight hundred and sixty-seven followers reached a ford on the river Blackwater in the last stage of their journey to Lismore. Unable to cross by any of the usual methods, Carthage caused the waters to be divided and the company, Carthage last of all, crossed dryshod. This is likened to Joshua's crossing of the river Jordan. There is a detailed description of the tides and currents on the Blackwater.

---

50 VSH i.198 n. 1; ii.32 n.2.   **51** *Medieval Irish Saints' Lives*, p. 106.   **52** 'Édition du *Catalogus*', p. 378 n. 516; Sharpe discusses this point in *Medieval Irish Saints' Lives*, p. 106 and n. 51.   **53** The last section quoted is from §63, after which Ware comments that the end is wanting. In a marginal note, Ware quotes from §69 'ex al. ms'. That the first copy was *M* is very clear: *M* is the only copy of LLatin that begins 'Gloriosus Christi' rather than 'Gloriosus episcopus'. See also VSH i.xiv n. 5.   **54** pp. 321–2.

In the Office, LMI, and EMI versions, two saints not previously mentioned, Molua and Colmán, have an active part in the crossing of the Blackwater. These saints do not appear in any of the four LLatin copies: they are not named in *M* before the end of f. 99, they are not named after *T* takes up the narrative again on f. 66, and they do not appear in *B* or *A*. Nonetheless, when taken in conjunction with *sanctique*, the last word in *M*, and *Et post sanctos turba pedestris intrat*, line 3 in *T* f. 66ra, the agreement of the Office, LMI, and EMI versions would suggest that Molua and Colmán belong in this chapter.

EMI and *M* agree very closely as far as the end of *M*; EMI is in close agreement with *T* once it is again available for comparison. *B* and *A*, while in close agreement with each other, show minor differences with *M* in word order and vocabulary, though not sense, until they reach the final *M* line *Et tunc mallina implevit alveum fluminis*. *Sanctique*, which they replace with a longer passage. Moreover, in the section between the end of *M* and the reappearance of *T*, for which *B* and *A* are the only LLatin witnesses, there is an almost total lack of agreement between the Office, LMI, and EMI Lives on the one hand and *B* and *A* on the other. *B* and *A* share a second long addition following the first two lines in *T* on f. 66ra. From *Et post sanctos* to the end of §64, *B* and *A* agree as closely with *T* as they had earlier agreed with *M*. The passages shared by *B* and *A*, particularly the passage that fills the hiatus between the last surviving line of *M* and the reappearance of *T*, are not in agreement with the manuscript tradition as a whole.

§67: CARTHAGE, THE POOR MAN, AND THE MIRACULOUS FOUNTAIN

Carthage was approached by a poor man who requested both beer and milk. The saint blessed a nearby well and it promptly became a fountain first of milk, then of beer, and finally of wine. The poor man was invited to take his fill. The remainder of this episode is mutilated but from the fragments remaining it appears that the fountain remained until Carthage did something to it, that the well was in the sanctuary of Lismore, and that someone said that the grace of healing illness was connected with something.

Chapter 67 is the more severely affected of the two chapters mutilated by the loss of text at the top of f. 66rb. The first 4½ lines of this chapter are at the bottom of f. 66ra, the remaining five at the top of 66rb. Less than half of each of these five lines remains. *B* and *A* lack all text affected by the mutilation in *T*; both end with the last complete sentence at the bottom of 66ra: *Et iussit illi homini ut tolleret quantum vellet*. EMI agrees closely with *T*, including the detail that the poor man asked for beer and milk but was offered beer, milk and wine, as far as *ut tolleret quantum vellet*. It goes on to tell that the fountain remained until Carthage changed it back and that an angel of the Lord told the saint that this and all other wells blessed by him would have healing power. LMI, although much abbreviated, includes the poor man; the transformation of the nearby well to give beer, milk, and wine; and the restoration by Carthage of the well to its former state once the poor man had had his fill. This episode is not in the Office Life.

§68: CARTHAGE AND THE MONASTERY OF LISMORE

In *T*, there remains of the opening of this episode only ... *bus diversas edes monasterii fortiter et incessa* ... The chapter then goes on to tell how Carthage began to suffer great weariness because of the din of something and that his strength was failing because of work and old age. As a result, he received permission to withdraw from the monastery to a secluded place nearby where for a year and six months he lived an eremitical life. There, because of his wise teachings, he was much visited by members of the Lismore community.

Chapter 68 covers 12½ lines of f. 66rb. The first 1½ lines are badly affected, i.e., the opening words and at least half of the first full line of the chapter are missing. The next line lacks 8–10 letters, the following five lines lack 3–4 letters, and the last five lines are complete. Comparing *B*, *A* with *T*, one finds considerable verbal agreement with *T* combined with re-arrangement of the text in the sections affected by mutilation; from the beginning of the first complete line of text there is again a close correspondence between *B*, *A* and *T*. However, there is nothing to correspond to the opening fragment in *T*. The din responsible for Carthage's weariness is attributed to the crowds flocking to him from all sides. The Office and LMI Lives are too abbreviated to be of use here but EMI, which again agrees closely with what remains of *T*, tells us that Carthage's weariness was caused by the construction of the buildings of the monastery.

On the basis of these three passages, I would suggest that we must consider the possibility that *B* and *A* are witnesses to the work of a seventeenth-century editor. Someone wanted to make a transcript of *Vita Sancti Carthagi*. This person had access to two copies, *M* and *T*, so similar to each other that he might well have seen no reason to distinguish between them. He most likely prepared his version based on *M*, since Marsh's Library Z 3.1.5 appears to have been the more accessible of the two MSS,[55] but took readings from *T* when he felt this to be appropriate.[56] From §56 to the beginning of §64, his only source was *M*;

---

55 Hanmer, Fitzsimon, Ussher, and Ware all are known to have used Marsh's Library MS Z 3.1.5; evidence for use of TCD MS 175, especially as the primary source, is much more limited.   56 Examples of *B*, *A*'s agreeing with *T* when *M* is available are infrequent and usually very minor. However, as Grosjean observed ('Catalogus codicum ... Dubliniensium', p. 117), a few are quite striking: §1. episcopus *T, A, B, K*] Christi *M*; §3. solemnitate *T, A, B, K*] nativitate *M*; §28. ducis *T, A, B*] om. *M*; §54. subiit *T, A, B*] sibi *M*.

from the middle of §64 to the end in §69 he had only *T*. When he reached §64, he realized that there would be a break before *T* was available again. Nonetheless, the sense of the missing section was fairly obvious: Carthage was going to divide the waters of the river Blackwater so that he and his company could cross. Thus, any narrative coincidence in this section between *B*, *A* and the Office, LMI and EMI versions is due to the demands of the storyline and the conventions and models of miraculous crossings rather than to shared history. But, this hypothetical editor knew nothing of the part played by Molua and Colmán. Their names occur in the very section missing from both *M* and *T*. Thus, he was left with *sanctique*, the last word in *M*, and the phrase *Et post sanctos* in *T* with no indication of who these saints were. However, he rose to the occasion. Omitting *sanctique*, he re-wrote the preceding sentence to expand the description of the state of the river and to bring Carthage into position at the ford. He composed a brief section in which the waters are divided. He took up *T* as soon as he could but added a sentence after *telus spoliatur aquis cognotis* to explain the *Et post sanctos* of the following sentence. In *B* and *A*'s §64 we have evidence that the editor had access only to *M* and *T* and that *M* f. 100 and *T* f. 65 were already missing.

In §67, the editor was faced with a short episode combined with considerable loss of text. Using EMI Plummer was able to complete the mutilated lines very convincingly, but without EMI I think that it would now be difficult to guess what was supposed to be happening in the second half of the chapter. Since the text as far as *vellet* could stand, awkwardly, on its own, the editor simply omitted all of the section affected by mutilation. Thus the upper corner of *T* f. 66 was already missing.

On the other hand, most of the losses in §68 involved single words or even letters and the editor was able to get some feel for the sense of the chapter. Working in as much of the vocabulary of his exemplar as he could, he re-wrote the opening in order to give a reason for Carthage's exhaustion and rearranged the remainder of the section affected by the mutilation.

One copy of this edited version of Carthage's Life, which, if one may rely on the colophons in Maynooth MS RB201 and the evidence for the copy commissioned by Francis Matthews, is likely to have been in Ussher's library, found its way to Louvain, where only fragments of it were used, and thence to the Bollandists, whose printed text of course survives in the *Acta sanctorum* although the transcripts from which they worked have been lost. Another copy was made by Dr Thomas Arthur, perhaps for his own use, and survives in Maynooth MS RB201.[57]

---

57 Thomas Arthur, 1593–1674, was a successful medical doctor. Member of a family long settled in Limerick, almost certainly a Catholic, he was educated in Bordeaux and Paris, and had a degree from the university in Reims. On his return to Ireland in 1619, he practised first in Limerick before expanding his practice to Dublin in 1624. In addition to his medical work,

STEMMA 2

From the point of view of the manuscript evidence, this explanation has several advantages: it explains §64, §67, and §68; it explains why B, A sometimes agree with M and sometimes with T without demanding yet another exemplar; it explains the variant readings in §64 and §68 without requiring another copy of the text other than those known to have been in Ussher's library. Thus, the stemma is simplified by the substitution of α, a lost copy within the line of transmission, for χ, a lost copy belonging outside the existing main line of transmission.

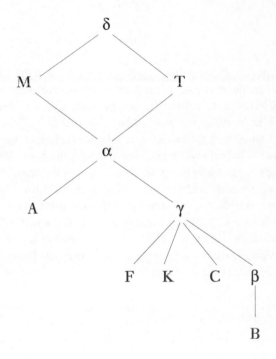

he was much involved in property speculation and he gathered a large personal library. His diary, now British Library Additional MS 31885, contains a list of his patients, together with their ailments and the fees paid, from 1619–63. His patients included the most prominent members of the Irish establishment, Catholic and Protestant, among them Ussher and James Ware. See Hayes, 'Limerick Doctors'; MacLysaght and Ainsworth, 'Arthur Manuscript'. *Dictionary of National Biography* entries for Arthur and Ussher suggest that Arthur was treating Ussher in 1626, and since Ussher was known for his generosity in making his library available to scholars, it is likely that Dr Arthur would have had access, had he wished. Ian Doyle, who has compared the hand in Arthur's diary with that of A, sees no reason to doubt that Arthur was the copyist of the Carthage Life. I am grateful to Dr Doyle for his examination.

Although this explanation would answer some questions about the seventeenth-century copies of *Vita Sancti Carthagi*, it leaves others open. Why was an edition made? By whom? Did the original editor give any indication that his was a conflation rather than the true copy of a single text? Did he mark his own insertions and emendations? It is hard to believe that the Bollandists, had they known that they were dealing with an edited text, would have published their version without comment – the Netherlands were a center of Classical scholarship at this time and the Bollandists would have been well aware of current practice – but it is also not always clear from their introductions in the *Acta sanctorum* just how they dealt with their own texts.[58]

CONCLUSIONS

In retrospect, very little that is actually new has been presented here. Although Plummer made no use of *A*, his view of the relationship between *M*, *T* and *B* requires adjustment rather than correction. Grosjean's observations are, of course, even more to the point. Had either of them had the opportunity to collate *A* with *M*, *T* and *B*, he would have recognized immediately what had happened. What this paper does show, I think, is that more needs to be known about the editorial practice of those engaged in the study of Irish hagiography in the seventeenth century and that, particularly now, when the process of transmission itself has become an interesting topic, no manuscript should be rejected before it has been examined. Only the collation of all the Lives in Maynooth MS RB201 will allow the question put by Fr Grosjean in 1928 – 'Hicne Chandosianus vel similis codex fuerit Colgano Kilkenniensis libri apographon?' – to be answered.[59]

58 Sharpe, *Medieval Irish Saints' Lives*, pp. 70–4, discusses this problem. **59** I am indebted to John Barry, John Carey, Helen Davis, Pádraig Ó Riain, and William O'Sullivan for reading and commenting on earlier drafts of this paper. FLK MS F2 is cited with the permission of the Librarian, Franciscan Library Killiney, Marsh's Library MS Z 3.1.5. with the permission of the Governors and Guardians of Marsh's Library, and TCD MS 175 with the permission of the Board of Trinity College Dublin.

Problèmes et premiers résultats d'une histoire générale de la littérature hagiographique

Guy Philippart, François De Vriendt et Michel Trigalet

I   POUR UNE HISTOIRE GÉNÉRALE DE LA LITTÉRATURE
HAGIOGRAPHIQUE

Il est rare, dans nos disciplines, que nous ayons la possibilité et la chance de faire une recherche commune, qui aille de la conception à la réalisation, voire à la rédaction finale d'un rapport. C'est d'une de ces entreprises collectives, conçue, discutée, élaborée en communauté scientifique, que je suis aujourd'hui le rapporteur. François De Vriendt et Michel Trigalet la conduisent avec moi depuis plusieurs mois. À Michel Trigalet, qui prépare une thèse sur le sujet de ma communication, nous devons en particulier et notamment toute la conception informatique du programme[1].

Étudier les œuvres hagiographiques? Supposons que les érudits aient accompli leur immense travail, qu'elles soient toutes datées, que de chacune on connaisse l'auteur ou du moins le milieu de provenance et la patrie, qu'on ait identifié les sources, caractérisé le style, les conceptions historiographiques, l'idéologie, compris ou au moins éclairé les fonctions dans la société, l'histoire de la littérature hagiographique serait-elle pour autant achevée? Non, parce qu'il y a place pour une histoire spécifiquement générale de la littérature hagiographique, qui porte non sur les œuvres individuelles comme telles, mais sur leurs données comparables, promues au rang d'objet spécifique du savoir.

Pour entreprendre une histoire spécifiquement générale de la littérature hagiographique latine en tant que telle, nous nous fixons quelques principes :
1) le saint sera considéré comme un personnage littéraire, un 'Papierheiliger';

---

[1] Les définitions et les problèmes critiques sont constamment l'objet de débat dans le groupe. Tel qu'il est présenté ici, le rapport n'engage donc que le directeur du projet et conférencier de Cork, Guy Philippart. De leur côté François De Vriendt et Michel Trigalet ont présenté nos recherches sous le titre 'L'indexation informatique de la *Bibliotheca hagiographica latina*'. Voir aussi Philippart, 'Pour une histoire générale'.

cette histoire ne sera donc ni une histoire biographique des saints, ni une histoire [socioculturelle, politique, économique ou autre] du 'Sitz-im-Leben' des saints, ni une histoire [socioculturelle ou autre] des cultes et des pratiques extra-littéraires; 2) la littérature hagiographique sera étudiée en tant que telle, dans sa *genèse*, ses *œuvres*, sa *diffusion* [à l'époque de l'*'édition manuscrite'*], son *utilisation*; 3) l'outil de la recherche sera comparatiste; 4) la matière s'inscrira dans la longue durée, en l'occurrence des origines à la renaissance; 5) la matière couvrira un vaste espace, en l'occurrence la chrétienté latine.

Immense travail. Il suppose en effet d'innombrables études d'érudition, sans lesquelles les idées générales sont inconsistantes. Et nous ne prétendons pas le mener à terme: simplement, notre objectif oriente et détermine nos travaux. Il nous a fait concevoir une stratégie avec ses buts et ses moyens successifs. C'est dans cette stratégie que s'inscrivent nos travaux en cours à l'université de Namur. À savoir, d'une part, une étude statistique et sérielle des données comparables des œuvres hagiographiques latines de l'antiquité et du moyen âge, et, d'autre part, une étude statistique et sérielle des exemplaires manuscrits de ces œuvres hagiographiques. Ces enquêtes sont coordonnées d'une part à l'*Histoire internationale de la littérature hagiographique* en cours de parution[2] et à la Typologie des sources du moyen âge occidental[3], en concertation avec son directeur, René Noël, professeur aux universités de Namur et de Louvain.

Nous présenterons brièvement ici les deux études statistiques et sérielles. Et d'abord celle relative aux données comparables des œuvres hagiographiques.

L'ÉTUDE STATISTIQUE ET SÉRIELLE DES DOSSIERS HAGIOGRAPHIQUES

a. Les dossiers du corpus hagiographique latin dans son ensemble
Pour arriver à nos fins, nous avons d'abord voulu prendre les mesures de notre corpus, du moins du corpus conservé[4]. Comment se distribue dans le temps et

---

2 Publiée par l'éditeur Brepols, dans le cadre du *Corpus Christianorum*. Le premier volume a paru en 1994, le second en 1996; le troisième est en cours d'élaboration. L'ensemble comprend seize sections, la première consacrée à l'antiquité, les quinze autres à des aires géographiques, distinguées essentiellement sur base de critères linguistiques, à savoir: Italie, Espagne et Portugal, Orient latin, Hongrie, Croatie et Slovénie, Bohême et Moravie, Pologne, Gaule et Germanie précarolingiennes, aire germanique, aire française, aire néerlandaise, Angleterre et Pays de Galles, Écosse, Irlande, Scandinavie. On notera que parmi les matières déjà traitées les littératures vernaculaires occupent une place importante: ainsi, celles des domaines allemand, anglais, danois, français, hongrois, portugais et suédois. 3 L'hagiographie narrative y a déjà été abordée indirectement ou partiellement dans quatre volumes: ainsi, dans les fascicules consacrés aux légendiers (24–5, 1977), aux martyrologes (26, 1978), aux translations de reliques (33, 1979), aux lectures liturgiques et à leurs livres (64, 1992). 4 Peut-on estimer ce que représente le corpus conservé par rapport à tout de

dans l'espace le corpus hagiographique latin des origines à 1500 environ? Les questions critiques abondent aussitôt: la principale étant de savoir ce que nous allions mesurer et comment.

De manière empirique, nous sommes partis des données déjà mises à notre disposition dans la *Bibliotheca hagiographica latina antiquae et mediae aetatis* et dans son *Novum supplementum* (BHL)[5], qui forment ensemble notre 'répertoire canonique'. Pour rappel et en bref, il nous documente

- sur les 'dossiers littéraires'. On appelle ici 'dossier' l'ensemble des pièces littéraires placées dans la BHL sous une même *rubrique* hagiographique; ainsi, par exemple, le dossier 'Kiaranus ab. in Clonmacnois, + 548';
- sur les saints, identifiés et qualifiés sommairement dans les rubriques de la BHL;
- sur les 'légendes', c'est-à-dire sur les œuvres et leurs variantes. Cette formule cache pudiquement un des problèmes majeurs de l'histoire de la littérature hagiographique et en particulier de la qualification et, partant, de la classification des textes, à savoir le problème de l'identification de l'œuvre hagiographique: à partir de quand les différences entre deux états d'un texte sont-elles suffisantes pour qu'on puisse parler de deux œuvres distinctes? Il n'était pas dans l'intention des créateurs de la BHL de qualifier de ce point de vue chacune des pièces de tous les dossiers. Ils ont néanmoins fait un bon bout de chemin dans cette direction et tenté de regrouper sous un même code alphanumérique, à l'intérieur d'un dossier, les 'variantes' d'une même légende. Un seul exemple. Dans le dossier 'Patricia v. Cpolitana [sic], culta Neapoli, saec. IV/VII', dont la rubrique même indique déjà la complexité, les bollandistes ont distingué trois 'légendes': la première (code: 1) est anonyme et connue par l'édition des *Acta sanctorum*; la seconde (code général: 2), attribuée au prêtre Léon, est connue sous trois 'variantes' (codes: 2a, 2b, 2c); la troisième (code: 3) est constituée d'une collection de miracles. En première approximation, dans nos évaluations, nous retiendrons que le dossier comprend trois légendes, même si l'alphanumérotage général des 'objets textuels' (voir ci-dessous) va de 6483 à 6491, en ce compris un 6484b[6].
- sur les 'objets textuels'. Faisant abstraction ici du statut textuel ou littéraire des *œuvres*, nous appelons 'objets textuels' les entités littéraires de tous niveaux – œuvres originales complètes, récritures de différents types[7], parties

qui a été écrit? En d'autres termes, avons-nous des critères qui nous permettent d'évaluer les pertes? Nous avons tenté de répondre à ces deux questions symétriques lors d'un colloque de l'Associazione Italiana per lo Studio della Santità, dei Culti e dell'Agiografia, qui s'est tenu à la Terza Università di Roma du 24 au 26 octobre 1996. Michel Trigalet aura à traiter de cette question dans sa thèse.   **5** Nous utiliserons le sigle BHL aussi bien pour le *Novum supplementum* que pour l'édition originelle.   **6** À dix codes correspondent donc seulement trois légendes.   **7** Ce concept sert à désigner toutes les formes de manipulation des textes.

d'œuvres – qui ont eu la bonne fortune d'être dotées d'un code propre dans la BHL (BHL 1455, 1456, 1456a ...); c'est uniquement cette donnée 'accidentelle' qui les définit. Ces 'objets' forment donc un ensemble, exclusivement 'formel', parfaitement hétéroclite et ne constituent pas en soi un objet spécifique d'histoire;
– sur les hagiographes;
– sur les éditions imprimées.

Peut-on donner une idée du nombre total d'œuvres hagiographiques latines conservées? À l'heure actuelle, ce serait illusoire. Proposer une évaluation fondée sur l'addition des codes utilisés dans la BHL? Mais ces codes désignent, nous venons de le rappeler, non pas spécifiquement des œuvres mais des 'objets textuels' hétéroclites. En outre, quantité de légendes seraient exclues du compte, du fait qu'elles ont été enregistrées dans la BHL sans code, notamment sous le titre général d'*Epitomae*[8]. On ne peut donc rien tirer du chiffre total des 13 568 'objets textuels' pourvus d'un code dans la BHL: soit 9031 'objets textuels' dans la BHL proprement dite numérotés de 1 à 9031; et 4537 autres dans le *Novum Supplementum*, désignés cette fois, le plus souvent, par des nombres accompagnés de lettres (par exemple 6250d, 6252b, 6252c ...).

Le travail statistique sur les 'dossiers littéraires' conservés est plus significatif. Il porte d'abord sur le nombre brut de dossiers, qui nous servira de terme de comparaison pour les autres calculs. Il y en a 3 321, dont quelque 10% consacrés à plus d'un seul saint: comme, par exemple, les dossiers de *Cosmas et Damianus*, ou *Cyprianus et Iustina*.

Il porte ensuite sur l'ampleur des 'dossiers'. En attendant une analyse rigoureuse de chacun d'entre eux, nous pouvons déjà, sans trop de risques d'erreurs graves dans l'ordre de grandeur, les distribuer selon leur importance quantitative, soit à partir du nombre de leurs 'objets textuels', soit, moins mal, à partir du numérotage interne de chacun des dossiers[9]. Travaillant sur la seule BHL originelle, c'est-à-dire sans le *Supplementum*, nous constatons d'abord que pas loin de la moitié de ces 3 013 dossiers n'ont qu'une seule légende[10]; à l'autre bout du spectre, 80 – soit moins de 3% de l'ensemble – en ont au moins 10.

8 389 dossiers, soit près de 12% de l'ensemble, ne sont représentés que par des 'epitomae' ou légendes brèves sans codes alphanumériques; il en va ainsi, par exemple, pour le dossier 'Felix I papa, + 274', qui compte cinq 'légendes' brèves. Parmi les 2 932 autres dossiers, un très grand nombre comptent outre des légendes dotées de codes alphanumériques, des 'epitomae' qui en sont dépourvus. Un exemple pris au hasard: dans le dossier 'Odo ab. Cluniacensis, + 942' où deux légendes brèves ou 'epitomae', à savoir celle de Pierre de Natalibus et celle de Hilarion de Milan, sont dans ce cas. 9. Ce numérotage ne permet pas de déduire le nombre exact de légendes distinctes de chacun des dossiers, mais donne une première idée de l'ampleur de chacun d'eux. 10 C'est leur nombre hors *Supplementum*.

Dans la BHL, les dossiers les plus volumineux sont ceux de Jésus (65), de Marie (58), de Thomas Beckett (39), de Dominique, de François, de Laurent et de l'apôtre Pierre (27), de Charlemagne (26), de Martin (23), de Denis (22), de Marie Madeleine et de Nicolas (21), de Patrick (20). Rappelons que ces chiffres n'ont qu'une valeur indicative.

Des mesures peuvent aussi être prises à partir du traitement des 'rubriques', à savoir des titres des 'dossiers'. Encore que ce traitement soit parfois, ici encore, problématique. D'abord parce que les bollandistes ont rédigé leurs rubriques dans un but pratique: permettre une identification claire et non ambiguë du saint. Ils ont, pour ce faire, considéré et caractérisé les saints tantôt à partir de la légende, tantôt à partir de traditions tardives, éventuellement non littéraires, tantôt à partir d'un travail de reconstitution historique. Ils n'avaient pas, comme nous, l'intention de dresser des statistiques avec des données *de même valeur*, sur les seuls 'saints de papier'. Il y a bien sûr des qualités ou des qualifications peu contestables: le sexe[11] et le 'type' hagiographique par exemple. Les quelques cas ambigus en matière de type hagiographique ne viennent pas troubler l'évaluation générale. Deux exemples de ces ambiguïtés. Un hagiographe audacieux n'a-t-il pas fait de Martin de Tours un martyr (voir BHL 5666m)? Plus classique le cas de Magne de Trani: selon l'état sans doute le plus ancien de sa légende (BHL 5167), le saint meurt au cours d'une persécution, mais sans avoir été torturé et après avoir échappé miraculeusement à l'exécution capitale. Dans la variante BHL 5171d, le saint échappe à l'exécution mais subit des sévices avant de mourir à l'abri des bourreaux. Dans une autre variante de la légende (BHL 5168), les soldats furieux que le saint leur ait échappé décapitent le cadavre[12]: voilà un martyr posthume. Un hagiographe enfin le fait mourir dans les supplices: *milites comprehenderunt eum et variis suppliciis interfecerunt*; c'est cette récriture (BHL 5169) qui a été canonisée par les *Acta sanctorum* et explique la rubrique de la BHL: *Magnus ep. Tranensis m.* En dépit de ces cas, nous pouvons estimer sans crainte que notre répartition entre 'confesseurs' (71% des dossiers) et 'martyrs' (29%) est très fidèle à la réalité.

De même la répartition entre dossiers d'un saint (83%) et dossiers d'une sainte (15%)[13]. Retenons cette proportion générale de 15%. Elle noie bien des différences, chronologiques et géographiques. Anticipons quelque peu en examinant en particulier la distribution entre hommes et femmes parmi les 'Irlandais', au sens où nous les définirons, plus loin. Cette fois, les dossiers féminins ne représentent plus que 6% du total. Dans l'aire des anciens Pays-Bas, ils forment 35% de l'ensemble! Ces chiffres devraient être analysés et expliqués.

---

11 Encore que nous ayons quelques anges. 12 Voir Simonetti, 'Sulla tradizione agiografica', p. 109. M. Simonetti est revenu deux ans plus tard sur le dossier de Magne de Trani: 'Un testo inedito'. 13 2% des dossiers sont mixtes, comme dans le cas de *Cyprianus et Iustina*.

Le traitement des 'fonctions' ou des 'états' des saints n'est pas assez avancé pour que nous puissions vous proposer des statistiques analogues sur les répartitions entre clercs et laïcs, religieux et séculiers, membres des différents ordres sacrés (acolytes, exorcistes, lecteurs, portiers, sous-diacres, diacres, prêtres, évêques), titulaires des diverses fonctions civiles ou religieuses, catégories de l'état-civil (veuves, enfants …). Encore que tout soit déjà possible. Les chercheurs pourraient en effet trouver dès à présent dans notre banque une liste bien utile des saints enregistrés dans la BHL sous un type donné: rois, empereurs, comtes, princes ou chevaliers, par exemple.

Le traitement des 'lieux' nous a davantage retenus. Voyons avec un peu plus de détails les problèmes qu'ils posent. J'en relève cinq, liés à la conception même des rubriques. À savoir: 1) La polyvalence sémantique des mots géographiques ou topographiques. Ils désignent des 'lieux' de types divers: le lieu du martyre: *Maimbodus martyr in territorio Vesontionensi*; le lieu d'exercice d'une fonction: *Magnus abbas Faucensis*; le lieu de culte principal pour les saints d'origine inconnue: *Magnus cultus Collebecae in Saxonia*; le lieu de résidence ou de provenance: *Marcella vidua Romana*; le lieu quasi patronymique: *Margarita de Cortona*; le lieu d'origine nationale ou ethnique: *Maria Aegyptiaca*. 2) La pluralité des lieux; pour un même saint, deux lieux, ou davantage encore, de valeur distincte ou non, peuvent être attribués, comme dans les cas suivants: *Marcus ep. Lucerinus, patronus Bovini; Margarita de Faventia abbatissa Ordinis Vallumbrosani, Florentiae; Maurus Afer m. Romae, cultus Parentii, Floriaci, Fundis; Mathildis praeposita Diessensis, abbatissa Oetilstetinensis*. 3) L'extension géographique des mots: villes, bourgs ou églises; pays, régions, provinces … : *Ludovicus IX rex Francorum; Maxellendis v. m. in Pago Cameracensi; Tigernacus ep. in Hibernia*. 4) L'inégalité des informations; ici, la BHL donne des informations, là elle les tait, empêchant tout rapprochement: Aemilianus de Faventia est dit Scotus; Columbanus est simplement dit *abbas Luxoviensis et Bobiensis*. 5) L'absence totale d'information explicite: *Marcus evangelista; Schetzelo seu Gisilenus; Scariberga uxor S. Arnulfi martyris*.

Le traitement statistique, on le voit, implique beaucoup de recherches. Elles doivent obéir à notre règle d'or. Porter non pas sur les saints historiques, mais sur les saints de la légende, les 'saints de papier'. Peu importe qu'Aemilianus soit ou non un *Scotus*, l'essentiel est que la littérature l'ait placé dans le panthéon des saints *scoti*.

Mais une fois ce travail achevé, il faut encore traduire ces mots dans des réalités comparables. Pour les 'sites', nous avons choisi les références des divisions administratives contemporaines, en dépit de certaines incohérences, dont le cas irlandais est un des exemples les moins douteux. Les paradoxes de ce choix peuvent être réduits grâce à des correctifs multiples au gré des utilisateurs. Mais que faire des saints désignés seulement par une appartenance nationale ou ethnique? Des *Scoti*, bien sûr, mais aussi de tant d'autres: *Afri, Angli, Aquitani, Armeni, Franci, Gothi, Hebraei, Hiberni, Romani* …

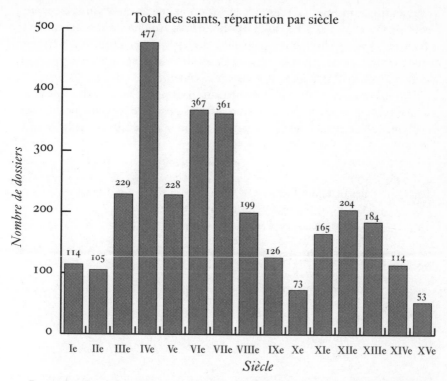

Total des saints, répartition par siècle

Le traitement des données chronologiques, bien que sensiblement plus facile, ne va pas non plus sans peine. Pour désigner les époques, les auteurs de la BHL ont eu recours à divers critères. En voici quelques exemples: *Scholastica + 543, Siviardus + 604 vel 683 vel 729, Sixtus I + 126 (?), Sollemnis + ante 511, Speciosus, saec. VI, Spyridon, saec. IV ineunte, Susanna martyr sub Diocletiano, Swibertus apostolus Fresonum + 713/715, Swibertus ep. Bethleemitanus (saec. VI extremo), Symeon Achivus saec. IX (?), Symeon Seleuciae, circa medium saeculum IV, Theodorus ep. Sedunensis, + post 390 (alias saec. IX)*.

Mais très souvent, ils n'ont tout simplement pas fourni de données chronologiques, soit qu'elles manquaient, soit qu'elles étaient évidentes: *Tancha v. m. in agro Trecensi, Tarasius erem. prope Constantinopolim, Thecla discipula Pauli apostoli, Theodorus ep. Veronensis, Trophima v. m. in Sicilia*.

Il nous a fallu donc traiter du point de vue de l'espace et du temps chacune des rubriques de la BHL. Dans l'état actuel de notre travail, nous pouvons déjà tirer quelques conclusions provisoires fiables. Commençons par les époques.

L'histogramme que vous avez sous les yeux est sans doute trompeur. La lecture spontanée qui en est faite est 'réaliste'. Les apparentes tendances de la sainteté réelle ou canonisée semblent d'autant plus convaincantes qu'elles sont régulières. Mais nous devons être sur nos gardes. Nous avons mêlé ici de nombreux phénomènes: nos saints du IVe siècle peuvent aussi bien être

d'authentiques martyrs de la grande persécution que de purs 'saints de papier'
créés de toutes pièces à l'époque carolingienne. Aux saints fondateurs de la
première mission chrétienne, peuvent s'être joints des créations littéraires
tardives commandées par une propagande locale. Notre histogramme piège sans
doute du réel, mais il faudra l'isoler soigneusement.

Pour les espaces, toutes les combinaisons sont possibles. En voici une assez
sommaire, suffisamment éloquente pour faire apparaître le poids considérable
de l'Italie [dû en particulier à ses martyrs des premiers siècles] et de la France :

Italie	1057
France	939
Îles britanniques	322
Méditerranée orientale et Moyen Orient	320
Allemagne, Suisse, Autriche	265
Belgique, Pays-Bas, Luxembourg	150
Péninsule ibérique	141
Europe non 'romaine'	59
Aires non intégrables ici	57
Europe latine de l'Est	47
Indéterminé	38
Afrique latine	35
Scandinavie	27

Mais, rappelons-le, chacun peut, à partir de la base, créer des aires 'historiques'.
Des exemples? Reconstituer le territoire du saint empire romain de la nation
germanique; les pays de langue d'oïl; les pays celtiques; la province ecclésiastique de Reims, etc.

b. Les dossiers du corpus 'irlandais'

Tentons maintenant un exercice un peu plus complexe avec l'Irlande et les
Irlandais. 'Complexe' c'est peu dire, 'périlleux' serait plus juste, pour qui n'est
pas solidement initié à l'hagiographie irlandaise. Il faudrait distinguer: les saints
du terroir et qui ont accompli leur vie dans l'île (*Coemgenus, al. Caimginus;
Keivinus, ab. Glendalochensis* ...), les saints de la *Britannia* ou du continent
venus faire carrière en Irlande (*Patricius episcopus apostolus Hibernorum; Ethbinus
monachus, discipulus S. Winlawoei*, venu, selon sa légende, vivre et mourir en
ermite en Irlande, pour échapper aux envahisseurs *Franci* ...), les *Irlandais*
d''Écosse' (*Columba abbas Hiensis* ...), les missionnaires ou *peregrini*,
authentiques ou littéraires, du continent (*Columbanus abbas Luxoviensis et
Bobiensis; Aemilianus episcopus [Scotus ?] cultus Faventiae; Disibodus ep. saec. VII
[?]*, dont Hildegarde de Bingen n'hésite pas à faire un Irlandais ...).

En ouvrant largement notre inventaire à tous ceux qui sont dits 'de
Hibernia', 'Scoti', ou qui, immigrés, ont fait leur carrière en Irlande, nous

dénombrons 113 dossiers hagiographiques latins, soit 3% de l'ensemble. Sur ces 113 dossiers, 44 concernent aussi d'autres pays, à savoir: les très nombreux dossiers d'Irlandais émigrés, y compris les moines d'Iona, les quelques dossiers d'étrangers immigrés en Irlande.

Nombre de dossiers latins 'irlandais' par pays

Autriche	2	Italie	6
Belgique	3	Grande Bretagne	10
Suisse	3	France	16
Allemagne	4		

La distribution des dossiers irlandais selon les époques 'littéraires' des saints réservera peu de surprises aux spécialistes:

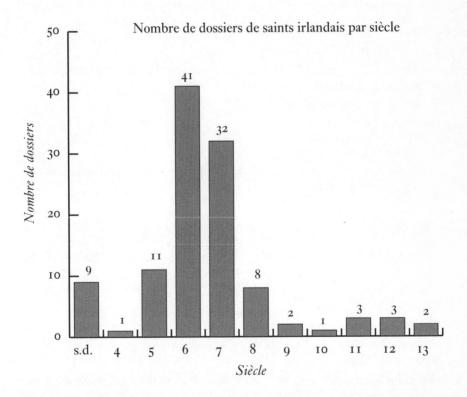

Nombre de dossiers de saints irlandais par siècle

Elle présente évidemment un profil singulier par rapport à la distribution générale des dossiers latins.

L'ÉTUDE STATISTIQUE ET SÉRIELLE DES ŒUVRES

Ces quelques réflexions, ces quelques données, vous auront éclairés sur les principes de notre banque et sur la multiplicité des problèmes qu'elle pose. Les chiffres bruts, comme toujours, suscitent des questions et appellent de nouvelles recherches. De plus, rappelons-nous que le travail sur les 'rubriques' ne constitue qu'une étape préliminaire. Si nous voulons atteindre nos objectifs d'analyse de l'espace hagiolittéraire et des tendances dans la longue durée, c'est au niveau des textes eux-mêmes qu'il faut descendre. Pour cela il nous faudra caractériser et qualifier les quelque 13 500 'objets littéraires' de la BHL et de son *Supplementum*. La tâche est immense, non seulement parce que les travaux à consulter sont innombrables, mais aussi parce que les études érudites sont encore largement insuffisantes. Dans notre programme, nous avons prévu de commencer par exploiter les résultats consignés dans *l'Histoire internationale de la littérature hagiographique* en cours de parution. Pour chacun des textes traités, une fiche d'identité sera dressée, qui pourrait comprendre les données suivantes:

– code de la BHL,
– auteur: nom ou, en cas d'anonymat, qualification plus abstraite (par exemple, 'moine', 'chanoine' ...),
– provenance géographique,
– époque,
– forme littéraire: prose, vers ... ,
– genre littéraire: miracula, passio, vita, translatio ... ,
– niveau d'originalité : œuvre originale, récriture, paraphrase, abrégé, plagiat ...
– longueur du texte en nombre de mots,
– éléments: lettre d'envoi, prologue, épilogue ...

Nous serons alors, on le voit, au cœur de la problématique littéraire, et aurons à affronter les difficiles problèmes de la définition de l'œuvre littéraire, des formes et des genres. Au terme de ces analyses, nous pourrons cartographier l'histoire de la littérature hagiographique et en saisir la distribution dans le temps et dans l'espace.

II L'ÉTUDE STATISTIQUE ET SÉRIELLE DES EXEMPLAIRES

Mais la littérature n'est pas que création littéraire, elle est aussi communication. Elle se transmet, se lit, s'écoute. Par la grâce de l'écriture, elle est sur les rayons des bibliothèques, dans les armoires des sacristies ou des infirmeries, sur les pupitres des salles de lecture, des réfectoires, des églises, dans les sacs des voyageurs, entre les mains des lecteurs. Et ces oeuvres connaissent des sorts contrastés: les unes restent confinées dans la bibliothèque du monastère où elles ont été conçues, au risque de disparaître au moindre incident; d'autres se répandent, se multiplient, se lisent dans toute une province, voire dans toute la chrétienté latine[14].

Nous avons donc conçu et lancé le projet d'une étude de l'édition manuscrite des textes hagiographiques, des origines à la renaissance. Une étude, ici encore, statistique et sérielle, qui aurait pour ambition de travailler sur la totalité du corpus des manuscrits hagiographiques latins médiévaux. Ambition démesurée et irréaliste, sauf, à nouveau, si le projet sert principalement à définir un but et aide à concevoir les stratégies qui permettraient de l'atteindre. Dans les faits, nous allons le voir, notre banque aura deux fonctions: heuristique et historique. Heuristique, car elle va faciliter pour tous la recherche et l'identification des exemplaires d'une œuvre. Historique, car elle va, par elle-même, éclairer immédiatement le passé et fournir les critères permettant d'expertiser les pièces singulières.

Commençons par préciser quelques concepts. Par 'codex' ou 'manuscrit', nous désignons le volume dans son état actuel, généralement relié et doté d'une cote dans une bibliothèque. Par 'édition', la pratique qui détermine la diffusion d'une œuvre. Par 'section éditoriale' d'un volume, la partie d'un volume qui relève d'un programme éditorial propre; une section éditoriale peut être distinguée d'un point de vue matériel (codicologique) et/ou d'un point de vue paléographique. Par 'légendier', nous désignons la collection des textes hagiographiques; on peut utiliser le mot soit pour désigner le codex, soit, de préférence, pour désigner une section éditoriale. Par 'dossier', nous désignons, dans un légendier, l'ensemble des textes qui se suivent et se rapportent à un saint, ou un groupe de saints, ou à une fête. Par 'légende', l'œuvre hagiographique, identifiable comme unité littéraire, soit à partir de l'exemplaire, soit à partir de critères modernes. Par 'exemplaire' d'une œuvre, l'œuvre elle-même telle qu'elle est connue par le travail d'un scribe; le mot 'exemplaire' a été préféré à celui plus traditionnel de 'copie', en raison de sa plus grande extension; l'autographe aussi est un exemplaire.

Nous avons commencé par circonscrire dans la masse des manuscrits hagiographiques ceux qui figurent dans les catalogues dressés par les bollandistes. Cela fait en tout quelque 4 000 manuscrits. Et, avec une moyenne de 11 ou 12 textes ou légendes par manuscrits, cela fait plus de 40 000 exemplaires, essentiellement médiévaux, d'œuvres hagiographiques. Nous avons presque achevé l'enregistrement des données des catalogues bollandiens. Répartis dans le temps, ces manuscrits, ou plutôt les 'sections éditoriales', toutes catégories confondues, se répartissent chronologiquement comme suit:

---

14 Ces phénomènes font l'objet spécifique de nos recherches; voir par exemple sur les lieux de conservation et l'usage des manuscrits hagiographiques Philippart, *Légendiers*, pp. 112–17; Mise à jour parue en 1985, pp. 25–8. Sur la problématique de la diffusion des textes, voir idem, 'Hagiographies'.

Sections éditoriales Nombre par siècle 13/04/97

Siècle	Nombre de manuscrits	Pourcentage		Siècle	Nombre de manuscrits	Pourcentage
s.d.	24	0,57%		12	771	18,40%
5	1	0,02%		13	544	12,98%
6	2	0,05%		14	588	14,03%
7	2	0,05%		15	921	21,98%
8	20	0,48%		16	247	5,89%
9	127	3,03%		17	185	4,41%
10	257	6,13%		18	33	0,79%
11	465	11,10%		19	4	0,10%

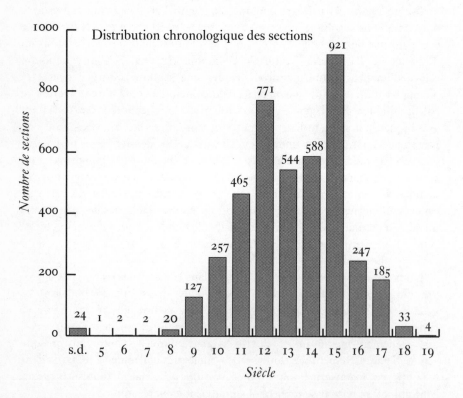

Grâce à notre banque, nous pourrions produire des catalogues de manuscrits enrichis des données empruntés aux divers fichiers de notre banque. Ils sont évidemment réservés aux bollandistes, qui décideront de leur usage. Nous pouvons aussi dresser un index cumulatif de tous les exemplaires de tous les textes hagiographiques, que les bollandistes publieront. En voici un échantillon:

Adalbertus diac. Egmondae in Hollandia
0033
– Köln, HA, W. 164 (103r–107r)
0036e
– Trier, SB, 1271 (726) (010v–012r)
Adalbertus 01
– Trier, Sem, 033 (R.I.8) (030r–031r)
Adalbertus ep. Pragensis
0037
– Bruxelles, BR, 09290 (3223) (090v–096r)
– Wien, OB, (9394) (087r–095r)
0037b
– Roma, Bibliotheca Alexandrina, codex 092 (alias I.g.7.8) <b> (657–663v)
– Roma, BN, Codices Sessoriani, codex 049 (alias XXI) <a> (053v–064)
Adalbertus 02
– Bruxelles, BR, 00409 (3135) (212v–216r)
Adalgisus presb. in Picardia
0057
– Mons, BU, 030, 196, 8439 (031v–036v)
Adalhardus ab. Corbeiensis
0058
– Douai, BP, 858 (146r–164v)
0060
– Bruxelles, BR, 08646–08652 (3210) (001r–022v)
– Douai, BP, 151 <c> (186r–187r)
– Douai, BP, 858 (146r–164v)
0061
– Bruxelles, BR, 08646–08652 (3210) (022v–031v)
– Douai, BP, 858 (165r–173v)
0062
– Bruxelles, BR, 08646–08652 (3210) (031v–038v)
– Douai, BP, 858 (173v–179v)
Adalheida imperatrix
0063
– Bruxelles, BR, 07460 (3176) (163v–166v)
– Douai, BP, 838 (181r–183r)
– Douai, BP, 855 (260v–272v)
– Trier, Sem, 005 (R. II. 1) <a> (128r–133r)
– Würzburg, UB, MP.TH.F. 034. <g> (147v–153v)
0064
– Bruxelles, BR, 07460 (3176) (166v)
– Trier, Cath, 093A <a> (070v–086r)
0065
– Trier, Cath, 093A <a> (070v–086r)

– Trier, Sem, 005 (R. II. 1) <a> (128r–133r)
Agalheidis abb. Vilicensis
0067
– Bruxelles, BR, 00098–00100 (3132) (220r–223v)
Adelphius ab. Habendensis
0073
– Paris, BN, 05308 (029v–030v)
– Trier. Sem, 035 (R.I. 11) (070v–071v)
Adventor, Octavius et Solutor m. leg. Theb
0085
– Milano, BA, D. 022 (111v–112v)
– Roma, Bibliotheca Alexandrina, codex 091 (alias I.g.4–6) <a> (527–258/259r–259v)
– Torino, BN, I.I. 03 (007r–022v)
– Torino, BN, K. II. 24 (110v–112r)
0086
– Torino, BN, I. I. 03 (059r–071v)
Aegidius Assisinas
0089
– Den Haag, KB, 73 H 35 (075r–089v)
– Trier, SB, 0644 (128) (170r–181v)
– Trier, SB, 0735 (468) (003v–010v)
0090
– Den Haag, KB, 73 H 35 (075r–089v)
Aegidius 01
– Rouen, BP, A 564 (186v)
Aegidius ab. in Occitania
0093
– Arras, B, 14(23) (050v–053r)
– Arras, B, 344 (961) (125r–127v)
– Bourges, BM, 28 (151v–153v)
– Bourges, BM, 31 (092v–093v)
– Bruxelles, BR, 00098–00100 (3132) (168v–170v)
– Bruxelles, BR, 00197 (3131) (047v–051r)
– Bruxelles, BR, 08059 (060r–062v)
– Bruxelles, BR, 08223 (3193) (116r–122r)
– Bruxelles, BR, 08675–08689 (3212) (076v–083r)
– Bruxelles, BR, 09290 (3223) (178r–180v)
– Bruxelles, BR, 09368 (3225) (089v–093v)
– Bruxelles, BR, 09742 (165v–169v)
– Bruxelles, BR, 11550–11555 (3233) <a> (134r–136v)
– Bruxelles, BR, 18108 (3239) (069v–074r)
– Bruxelles, BR, II. 1151 (3300) [Phillipps n° 47]

Mais notre but final n'est pas de produire des outils heuristiques. Nous traitons la matière pour en tirer des informations d'ordre historique. Voici, choisis parmi d'autres, deux types d'enseignement que nous pouvons obtenir: sur les pratiques de l'édition manuscrite, d'une part, sur les œuvres elles-mêmes d'autre part.

Prenons d'abord les livres hagiographiques comme des objets archéologiques ou matériels. Nous avons enregistré quelques données fondamentales de type codicologique. De quoi suivre par exemple l'évolution des formats des manuscrits :

Nombre de manuscrits dans l'échantillon : 679   Résultats au 28 février 1995

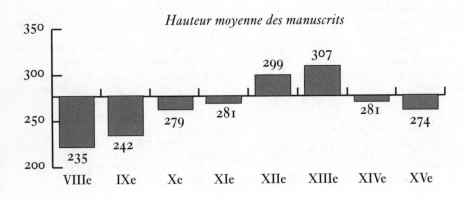

Hauteur moyenne des manuscrits

Tableau d'ensemble qui devrait être remplacé par une série de tableaux selon le support (papier, parchemin), les types de manuscrits (légendiers et livrets, par exemple), les régions. Toutes ces opérations sont déjà possibles. Les données italiennes notamment méritent un traitement particulier, les grands légendiers de la péninsule étant d'un format exceptionnel. Sur les 57 légendiers de notre corpus qui ont au moins 52 cm de haut, 55 sont conservés en Italie et quasi certainement originaires d'Italie. Ceci dit, à considérer le seul format, le chercheur se donne des critères qui lui permettent de repérer les pièces exceptionnelles ou de préciser dans quelle mesure elles le sont. Il suffit pour cela de connaître la hauteur moyenne générale des légendiers ou mieux la moyenne à l'intérieur d'un siècle, en attendant des comparaisons qui prennent en compte également la provenance et le type.

Un des bénéfices majeurs de nos travaux concerne sans doute l'étude des succès littéraires. Bien sûr, notre échantillon n'est pas encore parfaitement représentatif, pour diverses raisons qu'il serait trop long de préciser ici[15], et les chiffres devraient donc être discutés, mais, tels quels, ils indiquent des tendances. Passons en revue quelques-uns des résultats bruts. Quels sont les dossiers hagiographiques les plus fameux, à travers les âges, toutes périodes confondues.

1.	Iesus	379	18.	Laurentius	203
2.	Maria	372	19.	Agatha	195
3.	Martinus	324	20.	Paulus Thebaeus	191
4.	Petrus ap.	286	21.	Thomas ap.	191
5.	Hieronymus	280	22.	Antonius in Thebaide	186
6.	Nicolaus	272	23.	Bartholomaeus	182
7.	Benedictus	250	24.	Augustinus	179
8.	Patrum Vitae	242	25.	Dionysius	179
9.	Stephanus	239	26.	Clemens papa	173
10.	Andreas ap.	235	27.	Ambrosius	171
11.	Gregorius	230	28.	Lucia	170
12.	Iohannes ap.	228	29.	Marcus	170
13.	Vincentius	222	30.	Matthaeus	170
14.	Agnes	221	31.	Caecilia	168
15.	Iacobus Maior	219	32.	Philippus	163
16.	Sebastianus	207	33.	Georgius	162
17.	Silvester	206	34.	Mauritius	162

Trois observations, parmi beaucoup d'autres : 1) Les saintes sont peu représentées; 2) chez les hommes, les saints confesseurs occupent un rang honorable, Martin en particulier; 3) les apôtres sont relativement bien placés mais distribués dans la série.

Ce classement global devrait bien entendu être analysé siècles par siècles et provenances par provenances. Donnons en exemple le tableau du XVᵉ siècle, dans lequel les noms des saints qui ne figuraient pas dans la liste précédente sont en lettres grasses :

---

15 La principale est que les catalogues publiés par les bollandistes concernent principalement la Belgique, la France septentrionale, l'Italie; selon des chiffres un peu vieillis, voici dans l'ordre croissant comment se répartissaient, d'après les bibliothèques où ils sont conservés, les 3 457 manuscrits que nous avons analysés: Grande Bretagne (4), Autriche (29), Pays-Bas (36), Irlande (54), Allemagne (361), Belgique (453), France (724), Vatican (867), Italie (929). Le chiffre pour la France a considérablement augmenté depuis, en raison notamment du fait que, à l'époque où ces calculs ont été faits, nous n'avions vu qu'une partie des manuscrits de la Bibliothèque Nationale de Paris.

1. Hieronymus	119	19. Iohannes ap.	27
2. Maria	84	20. **Marcella**	27
3. Paulus Thebaeus	57	21. **Paula vidua**	27
4. Antonius in Thebaide	50	22. Agnes	26
5. Iesus	47	23. Andreas ap.	26
6. Martinus	44	24. **Asella**	26
7. **Malchus**	43	25. **Lea**	26
8. **Catharina**	41	26. **Blaesilla**	25
9. **Franciscus**	38	27. **Fabiola**	25
10. Nicolaus	37	28. **Bernardus**	24
11. Patrum Vitae	37	29. **Maria Aegyptiaca**	24
12. Petrus ap.	34	30. **Maurus discipulus S.**	
13. **Barbara**	33	**Benedicti**	24
14. Augustinus	31	31. **Ursula**	24
15. **Hilarion**	31	32. Benedictus	22
16. **Nepotianus**	28	33. Thomas ap.	22
17. **Elisabeth landgravia**	27	34. **Thomas Cantuariensis**	22
18. Gregorius	27		

La sélection et l'ordre, on le voit, diffèrent profondément. Faisons ici encore quelques observations. 1) Plus de la moitié des saints, soit 18 saints sur 34 ont disparu. 2) Jérôme occupe la tête, très loin devant tous les autres; un tel succès littéraire est surprenant, même pour ceux qui n'ignorent pas l'intérêt qu'ont voué au saint philologue et ermite les humanistes et les artistes de la renaissance. 3) D'ailleurs les saints dont Jérôme a écrit la vie ou l'éloge sont surreprésentés: Malchus, Hilarion, Nepotianus, Marcella, Paula, Asella, Lea, Blaesilla, Fabiola. 4) Les saints hommes confesseurs ont plus de succès que les martyrs; parmi eux les saints ermites. 5) Les martyrs ne sont plus guère représentés que par les apôtres. 6) La proportion de saintes femmes a considérablement augmenté. 7) Le remarquable succès de Catherine d'Alexandrie et de Barbe n'étonnera pas les historiens du Quattrocento.

Chaque dossier peut être examiné dans la durée. Une première présentation graphique a été conçue à la hâte; elle devrait être revue. Voici comment se présente celle du dossier de S. Jérôme. Les nombres absolus et le pourcentage par rapport au nombre de manuscrits conservés sont notés[16]:

---

16 Se référer au tableau 3, ci-dessus.

Nombre total d'attestations du dossier au moyen âge 245　　　Résultats au 22 octobre 1996

Évolution du succès éditorial d'un dossier　　　(3865cm : 3878n)

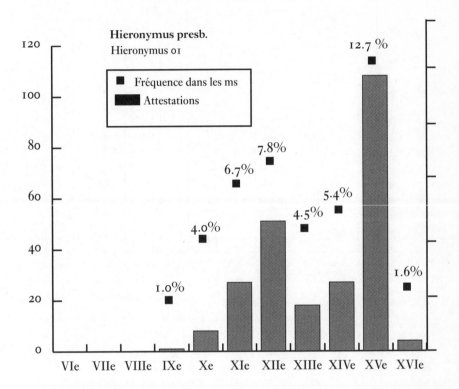

Terminons par les dossiers 'irlandais' de notre banque. Dix d'entre eux se détachent du lot:

Furseus	76	Brandanus	35
Brigida	65	Malachias	35
Columbanus ab. Luxoviensis	65	Kilianus	25
Patricius	44	Foillanus Fossis in Belgio	16
Gallus ab. in Alamannia	43	Frigdianus ep. Lucensis	15

Aucun des autres n'est attesté plus de huit fois.

L'étude diachronique comparative des dossiers doit être d'autant plus prudente que, dans les cas irlandais, elle porte sur des nombres peu élevés. Voyons d'abord l'évolution du nombre d'exemplaires par siècles pour l'ensemble des dossiers 'irlandais', puis l'évolution équivalente pour les dossiers de Brigide et de Patrick :

Nombre total d'attestations du dossier au moyen âge 364   Résultats au 7 Avril 1997

Évolution du succès éditorial des dossiers des saints irlandais

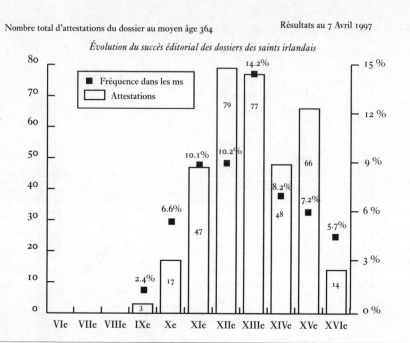

Nombre total d'attestations du dossier au moyen âge 65   Résultats au 7 Avril 1997

Évolution du succès éditorial d'un dossier   (1455 : 1462b)

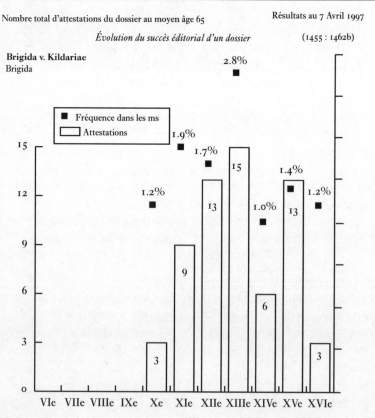

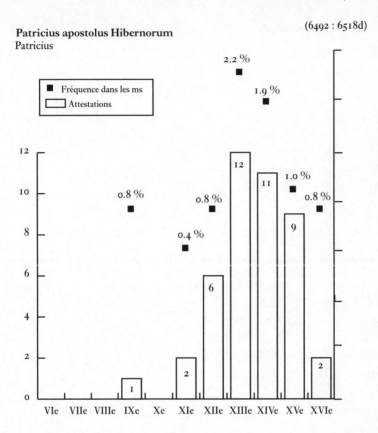

Patricius apostolus Hibernorum
Patricius

(6492 : 6518d)

Nous avons pris les mêmes mesures simples que pour Jérôme, qui ne permettent guère de constatations fermes mais suggèrent des hypothèses. Une singularité 'irlandaise': les dossiers n'ont pas au XVe siècle le succès qui se constate ailleurs, puisqu'ils ne sont présents que dans 7,2% des exemplaires, contre 8,2% au XIVe. Pour Brigide au contraire, une observation semble recouper ici un constat plus général: l'amélioration des scores des dossiers féminins au XVe siècle. Mais, à regrouper les exemplaires des deux derniers siècles médiévaux, le XIVe et le XVe s., c'est plutôt le contraire qui apparaît: le dossier de Patrick jusqu'alors moins attesté que celui de Brigide désormais l'emporte. On supposera sans grand risque d'erreur que le 'Purgatoire' a valu à Patrick ce relatif 'succès' tardif sur le continent. Comme on pouvait s'y attendre, tous nos chiffres bruts renvoient à des enquêtes nouvelles, d'ordre qualitatif cette fois.

'Il n'y a de science que du caché', dit l'adage. Nos recherches n'ont pas pour but final de produire des chiffres et des graphiques mais de faire apparaître, par leur intermédiaire, des phénomènes cachés qui devraient poser aux historiens des littératures hagiographiques des questions nouvelles. Nous espérons y être parvenus.

Bibliography

PRIMARY SOURCES

Adomnán, *Vita Sancti Columbae*, ed. A.O. and M.O. Anderson, *Adomnán's Life of Columba* (rev. ed. Oxford 1991).

Adomnán, *Vita Sancti Columbae*, ed. W. Reeves, *The Life of St Columba, Founder of Hy, written by Adamnan* (Dublin and Edinburgh 1857).

Adomnán, *Vita Sancti Columbae*, trans. R. Sharpe, *Adomnán. Life of St Columba* (Harmondsworth 1995).

Anderson, A.O., trans., *Early Sources of Scottish History AD 500 to 1286*, 2 vols (Edinburgh 1922).

Augustine, *De ciuitate Dei*, ed. B. Dombart and A. Kalb, 2 vols (CCSL 47–8; Turnhout 1955).

Augustine, *De doctrina christiana*, ed. J. Martin (CCSL 32; Turnhout 1972), pp. 1–167.

Auvray, L. 'Catalogue des reliques de Saint-Magloire', extract from 'Documents parisiens tirés de la bibliothèque du Vatican (VII–XIII siècles)', *Mémoires de la société de l'histoire de Paris et de l'Ile-de-France* 19 (1892), pp. 21–33.

Avienus, Rufus Festus, *Ora maritima*, ed. and trans. J. Murphy (Chicago 1977).

Baudonivia, *Liber II Vitae S. Radegundis*, ed. B. Krusch, MGH, Srm 2 (Hannover 1888), pp. 377–95.

Bede, *Opera historica*, ed. C. Plummer, *Venerabilis Baedae Opera historica*, 2 vols (Oxford 1896).

Bede, *Retractatio Actum Apostolorum*, ed. M.L. Laistner, *Expositio Actum Apostolorum et Retractatio* (Cambridge 1939).

Bede, *Vita S. Cudbercti*, ed. and trans. B. Colgrave, *Two Lives of Saint Cuthbert* (Cambridge 1940).

Bede, *Historia ecclesiastica gentis Anglorum*, ed. and trans. B. Colgrave and R.A.B. Mynors (Oxford 1969).

Beowulf, ed. G. Jack, *Beowulf. A Student Edition* (Oxford 1994).

Best, R.I., O. Bergin, M.A. O'Brien and A. O'Sullivan, eds, *The Book of Leinster formerly Lebar na Núachongbála*, 6 vols (Dublin 1954–83).

Best, R.I., and O. Bergin, eds, *Lebor na hUidre: Book of the Dun Cow* (Dublin, 1929).

Best, R.I., and H.J. Lawlor, eds, *The Martyrology of Tallaght* (London 1931).

Bieler, L., ed., *Four Latin Lives of Patrick* (Scriptores Latini Hiberniae 8; Dublin 1975).

Bieler, L., ed., *The Irish Penitentials* (Scriptores Latini Hiberniae 5; Dublin 1963).

Bieler, L., *The Patrician Texts in the Book of Armagh* (Scriptores Latini Hiberniae 10, Dublin 1979).

Binchy, D.A., ed., *Corpus iuris hibernici*, 6 vols (Dublin 1978).

Bourgès, A.-Y., *Le dossier hagiographique de saint Melar. Textes, traduction, commentaires*, (Britannia monastica 5; Lanmeur 1997), pp. 171–3.

Breuiarium insignis ecclesie Leonensis, pars hiemalis (Paris 1516); Bibliothèque Municipale de Rennes n° 15 952.

Breviarium romanum ex decreto ... S. Pii V. ([Vannes] 1877).

Bromwich, R., ed. and trans., *Trioedd Ynys Prydein* (2nd ed. Cardiff 1978).

Buez sant Efflam, prinç a Hiberni, ha Patron Plestin, ha buez santez Henori (Morlaix 1819).

Bulst, W., ed., *Hymni latini antiquissimi* (Heidelberg 1956).

Byrhtferth, *Vita S. Oswaldi*, ed. J. Raine, *The Historians of the Church of York and its Archbishops*, 3 vols (London 1879–86) i.399–475.

Caesarius of Arles, *Sermons*, trans. M.M. Mueller (Fathers of the Church 31, 47, 66; New York 1956–73).

Cahill, M., ed., *Expositio Evangelii secundum Marcum* (Scriptores Celtigenae 2, CCSL 82; Turnhout 1997).

Cahill, M., trans., *The First Commentary on Mark* (New York and London 1998).

Carey, J., ed. and trans., 'Scél Tuáin meic Chairill', *Ériu* 35 (1984), pp. 93–111.

Cicero, *De senectute, De amicitia, De divinatione*, ed. and trans. W.A. Falconer (Cambridge, MA 1923).

Cogitosus, *Vita Brigitae*, trans. S. Connolly and J.-M. Picard, 'Cogitosus's *Life of Saint Brigit*', *Journal of the Royal Society of Antiquaries of Ireland* 117 (1987), pp. 5–27.

Cogitosus, *Vita Sanctae Brigidae*, ed. J. Bolland, *Acta Sanctorum* Feb. I (Antwerp 1658), pp.135–41; PL lxxii.775–90.

Colgan, J., *Acta sanctorum veteris et majoris Scotiae seu Hiberniae ... sanctorum insulae*, I (Louvain 1645; repr. Dublin 1947).

Colgan, J., *Triadis thaumaturgae seu divorum Patricii, Columbae et Brigidae, trium veteris et maioris Scotiae seu Hiberniae, sanctorum insulae, communium patronorum acta* (Louvain 1647; repr. Dublin 1997).

Collectio canonum Hibernensis, ed. H. Wasserschleben, *Die irische Kanonensammlung* (Leipzig 1885).

Conchubranus, *Vita Sanctae Monennae*, ed. M. Esposito, 'Conchubrani Vitae Sanctae Monennae', *Proceedings of the Royal Irish Academy* 28 C (1910), pp. 202–51.

De Courson, A., ed., *Cartulaire de l'abbaye de Redon en Bretagne* (Paris 1863).

De la Borderie, A., *Monuments originaux de l'histoire de saint Yves* (Saint-Brieuc 1887).

De la Borderie, A., 'Saint Efflam : texte inédit de la *Vie* ancienne de ce saint avec note et commentaire historique', *Analecta Bollandiana* 7 (1892), pp. 279–312; separatum, Rennes, 1892.

Delehaye, H., 'Passio Sancti Mammetis', *Analecta Bollandiana* 58 (1940), pp. 126–41.

De Smedt C., and J. De Backer, eds, *Acta sanctorum Hiberniae ex codice Salmanticensi nunc primum integre edita* (Edinburgh, London 1887).

Despy, G., ed., *Les chartes de l'abbaye de Waulsort*, I (Brussels 1957).

Deuffic, J.-L., ed., 'Le Missel de Saint-Vougay (Archives départementales du Finistère 4 J 96)', *Britannia Christiana* 2 (1982), pp. 19–40.

De Vogüé, A., ed., *Saint Colomban: Règles et pénitentiels monastiques* (Bégrolles-en-Mauges 1989).

De Vogüé, A., ed., *La Règle de Saint Benoît*, 2 vols (Sources Chrétiennes 181–2; Paris 1972).

De Vogüé, A., *Les règles monastiques anciennes (400–700)* (Turnhout 1985).

Dicuil, *Liber de mensura orbis terrae*, ed. and trans. J.J. Tierney (Scriptores Latini Hiberniae 6, Dublin 1967).

Diodorus Siculus, *Historical Library*, ed. and trans. C.H. Oldfather and F.R. Walton, 12 vols (London 1933).

Dumville, D.N., ed., *The Historia Brittonum*, III (Cambridge 1985).

Eusebius of Caesarea, *Onomastikon der biblischen Ortsnamen*, ed. E. Klostermann (Leipzig 1904).

Evagrius, *Vita Antoni*, ed. PL lxxiii.125–70.

Félire Óengusso Céli Dé, ed. W. Stokes (London 1905).

Flacius Illyricus, M., *Historia ecclesiastica Christi, septima centuria* (Basel 1564).

Flodoard, *Chronicon*, ed. P. Lauer, *Les Annales de Flodoard* (Paris 1906). Flodoard , *Chronicon*, ed., G.H. Pertz, 'Annales Flodoardi', MGH, Srg 3 (1839), pp. 363–408.

Ford, P.K., ed., *Ystoria Taliesin* (Cardiff 1992).

Giraldus Cambrensis, *Topographia Hiberniae*, ed. J.F. Dimock, in *Giraldi Cambrensis Opera*, 8 vols (London 1861–91), v.3–204.

Giraldus Cambrensis, *Topographia Hiberniae*, ed. J.J. O'Meara, '*Giraldus Cambrensis in Topographia Hibernie*: The Text of the First Recension', *Proceedings of the Royal Irish Academy* 52 C (1948–50), pp. 113–78.

Gregory the Great, *Dialogi*, ed. A. de Vogüé, *Grégoire le Grand, Dialogues*, 3 vols (Sources Chrétiennes 251, 260, 265; Paris 1978–80).

Gregory of Tours, *Historiae*, ed. B. Krusch, MGH, Srm 1 (1884–5).

Gregory of Tours, *Historiae*, trans. R. Latouche, *Grégoire de Tours. Histoire des Francs* (Paris 1995).

Gregory of Tours, *In gloria confessorum*, ed. B. Krusch, MGH, Srm i.2 (Hannover 1885), pp. 364–6.

Gregory of Tours, *Vita patrum*, ed. B. Krusch, MGH, Srm, i.2 (2nd ed. Hannover 1969).

Grosjean, P., ed. and trans., 'S. Columbae Hiensis cum Mongano heroe colloquium', *Analecta Bollandiana* 45 (1927), pp. 75–83.

Grosjean, P., ed. and trans., 'A Tale of Doomsday Colum Cille Should Have Left Untold', *Scottish Gaelic Studies* 3 (1929–31), pp. 73–83.

Grosjean, P., 'Addenda et Corrigenda to *SGS* III.73ff.', *Scottish Gaelic Studies* 3 (1929–31), pp. 188–9.

Grosjean, P., 'Édition du Catalogus Praecipuorum Sanctorum Hiberniae de Henri Fitzsimon', in Ryan, *Féil-sgríbhinn Eóin Mhic Néill*, pp. 335–93.

Grosjean, P., 'Une vie de Saint Secundinus disciple de saint Patrice', in *Analecta Bollandiana* 60 (1942), pp. 26–34.

Grosjean, P., ed., 'Trois pièces sur S. Senán', *Analecta Bollandiana* 66 (1948), pp. 199–230.

Grosjean, P., 'Les Vies de S. Finnbarr de Cork, de S. Finnbarr d'Écosse et de S. Mac Cuilinn de Lusk', in *Analecta Bollandiana* 69 (1951), pp. 344–6.

Grosjean, P., 'Deux textes inédits sur S. Ibar', in *Analecta Bollandiana* 67 (1959), pp. 427–9.

Gwynn, E.J., ed. and trans., *The Metrical Dindshenchas*, 5 vols (1903–35, repr. Dublin 1991).

Gwynn, E.J. and W.J. Purton, ed. and trans., 'The Monastery of Tallaght', *Proceedings of the Royal Irish Academy* 29C (1911), pp. 115–79.

Gwynn, E.J., et al., ed. and trans., *Ireland's Desert-Fathers: the Culdees* (Cambridge 2000).

Haefele, H.F., ed., *Ekkehard IV, St. Galler Klostergeschichten* (Darmstadt 1980).

Halm, C., ed., *Sulpicii Severi Opera* (Corpus Scriptorum Ecclesiasticorum Latinorum 1; Vienna 1866).

Harris, M., trans., *The Life of Meriasek* (Washington 1977).

Hegesippus, *Historiae*, ed. V. Ussher (Corpus Scriptorum Ecclesiasticorum Latinorum 66; New York and London 1932).

Heist, W.W., ed., *Vitae sanctorum Hiberniae e codice olim Salmanticensi* (Subsidia Hagiographica 28; Brussels 1965).

Hellmann, S., ed., 'Pseudo-Cyprianus De duodecim abusivis saeculi', *Texte und Untersuchungen zur Geschichte der altchristlichen Literatur* 34 [3rd series, 4] (1909–10), Heft 1, pp. 1–62.

Herbert, M., and P. Ó Riain, ed. and trans., *Betha Adamnáin. The Irish Life of Adamnán* (London 1988).

Hermann of St. Félix, *Vita Cadroe*, ed. AASS Mart. I, pp. 468–81.

Hoare, F.R., ed. and trans., *The Western Fathers* (London 1954).

Hudson, B.T., ed. and trans., 'The Scottish Chronicle', *Scottish Historical Review* 77 (1998), pp. 129–61.

Hughes, K., 'The Offices of S. Finnian of Clonard and S. Cíanán of Duleek', in *Analecta Bollandiana* 73 (1955), pp. 342–72.

I.W.P. [John Wilson, priest], *The English Martyrologe conteyning a summary of the Lives of the glorious and renowned saintes of the three kingdomes, England, Scotland and Ireland. By a Catholicke Priest* (St Omer 1608), repr. as vol. 232 in D.M. Rogers, ed., *English Recusant Literature 1558–1640* (1975).

Isidore of Seville, *Etymologiae*, in W. Lindsay, ed., *Isidori Hispalensis episcopi Etymologiarum siue Originum libri XX*, 2 vols (Oxford 1911).

Jennings, B., *Louvain Papers 1606–1827* (Dublin 1968).

Jerome, *Commentarioli in Psalmos*, ed. G. Morin, *S. Hieronymi Opera exegetica* (CCSL 72; Turnhout 1959), pp. 163–245.

John Cassian, *Conlationes*, ed. E. Pichery, *Jean Cassien. Conférences*, 3 vols (Sources Chrétiennes 42, 54, 64; Paris 1955–9).

John Cassian, *De coenobiorum institutis*, ed. J.-C. Guy, *Jean Cassien. Institutions cénobitiques* (Sources Chrétiennes 109; Paris 1965).

John of St-Arnoul, *Vita Iohannis abbatis Gorziensis*, ed. G.H. Pertz, MGH, Srg 4 (1841), pp. 337–77.

Jonas of Bobbio, *Vita Columbani abbatis discipulorumque eius*, ed. Krusch, *Passiones*, pp 337–77.

Jonas of Bobbio, *Vita Columbani abbatis discipulorumque eius*, ed. Krusch, *Ionae Vitae*.

Jonas of Bobbio, *Vita Columbani et discipulorum eius*, ed. M. Tosi, with Italian translation by E. Cremona and M. Paramidani (Piacenza 1965).

Jonas, *Vita Sancti Columbani et discipulorum eius*, trans. A. de Vogüé, *Vie de S. Colomban et ses disciples* (Bellefontaine 1988).

Joynt, M., trans., *The Life of St Gall* (London 1927).

Justinian, *Digesta*, trans. C.F. Kolbert, *Justinian. The Digest of Roman Law* (London 1979).

Kannën neue sant Efflam é Parrèz Kervignac (1889, repr. 1952), facsimile in *Hor Yezh* 203/204 (1996), pp. 113–6.

Keil, G., ed. *Grammatici latini*, 7 vols (Leipzig).

Kelly, F., ed. and trans., 'An Old-Irish Text on Court Procedure', *Peritia* 5 (1986), pp. 74–106.

Krusch, B., ed., 'Vita Geretrudis', MGH, Srm 2 (1888), pp. 445–74.

Krusch, B., ed., *Passiones vitaeque sanctorum aevi merovingici*, MGH, Srm 4 (Hannover and Leipzig 1902).

Krusch, B., ed., 'Vita uirtutesque Fursei', MGH, Srm 4 (Hannover and Leipzig 1902), pp. 423–49.

Krusch, B., ed., *Ionae vitae sanctorum Columbani, Vedastis, Iohannis*, Srg in usum scholarum ex MGH separatim editi (Hannover and Leipzig 1905).

Krusch, B., and W. Levison, *Passiones Vitaeque Sanctorum Aevi Merovingici*, MGH, Srm 5 (Hannover and Leipzig 1910).

Lambert, P.-Y., trans., *Les Quatre Branches du Mabinogi et autres contes gallois du Moyen Age* (Paris 1993).

Le Braz, A., 'Saints bretons d'après la tradition populaire: Gwerz sant Efflamm', *Annales de Bretagne* 11/2 (1896), pp. 184–8.

Le Grand, A., *La Providence du Dieu sur les justes, en l'histoire de saint Budoc Archevesque de Dol, et de la princesse Azenor de Léon sa mère, Comtesse de Treguer & de Goëlo* (1640).

Le Grand, A., *Les Vies des saints de la Bretagne Armorique* (Nantes 1636, 5th ed., Quimper and Rennes 1901).

Liber de ordine creaturarum, ed. M.C. Díaz y Díaz, *Liber de ordine creaturarum. Un anónimo irlandés del siglo VII* (Santiago de Compostela 1972).

Liber Landavensis, ed. J.G. Evans and J. Rhys, *The Text of the Book of Llan Dâv reproduced from the Gwysaney Manuscript* (Oxford 1893, repr. Aberystwyth 1979).

Lucan, *Pharsalia*, ed. and trans. J.W. Duff (London and New York 1969).

Mabillon, J., *Acta sanctorum ordinis Sancti Benedicti*, 9 vols (Paris 1668–1701).

Mac Airt, S., ed. and trans., *The Annals of Inisfallen (MS Rawlinson B.503)* (Dublin 1951).

Mac Airt, S., and G. Mac Niocaill, ed. and trans., *The Annals of Ulster (to AD 1131)* (Dublin 1983).

Macalister, R.A.S., ed. and trans., 'The Life of Saint Finan', *Zeitschrift für celtische Philologie* 2 (1899), pp. 545–65.

Macalister, R.A.S., ed., *Corpus inscriptionum insularum celticarum*, 2 vols (Dublin 1945–9, vol. 1 repr. Dublin 1996).

Mac Mathúna, S., ed. and trans., *Immram Brain: Bran's Journey to the Land of the Women* (Tübingen 1985).

Maître, L., and P. de Berthou, eds, *Cartulaire de l'abbaye de Sainte-Croix de Quimperlé* (2nd ed. Rennes and Paris 1904).

Marianus Scottus, *Chronicon*, PL cxlvii.623–796.

Meehan, D., and L. Bieler, eds and trans., *Adamnan's De locis sanctis* (Scriptores Latini Hiberniae 3, Dublin 1958).

Messingham, T., *Officia S.S. Patricii, Columbae, Brigidae, et aliorum quorundam Hiberniae sanctorum* (Paris 1620).

Meyer, K., ed. and trans., *Cáin Adamnáin. An Old-Irish Treatise on the Law of Adamnan* (Oxford 1905).

Meyer, K., ed. and trans., *Betha Colmáin maic Lúacháin: Life of Colmán son of Lúachán* (Todd Lecture Series 17; Dublin 1911).

Meyer, K., ed., 'Sanas Cormaic (Cormac's Glossary)', *Anecdota from Irish Manuscripts* 4 (1912).

Mulchrone, K., ed., *Bethu Phátraic. The Tripartite Life of Patrick* (Dublin and London 1939).

New Jerusalem Bible (London 1985).

Notker Balbulus, *Martyrologium*, PL cxxxi.1025–1164.

O'Brien, M.A., ed., *Corpus genealogiarum Hiberniae*, 1 (Dublin 1962).

O hAodha, D., ed. and trans., *Bethu Brigte* (Dublin 1978).

O'Kelleher, A., and G. Schoepperle, ed. and trans., *Betha Colaim Chille* (Chicago 1918).

Ó Riain, P., ed., *Cath Almaine* (Dublin 1978).

Ó Riain, P., ed., *Corpus genealogiarum sanctorum Hiberniae* (Dublin 1985)

Ó Riain, P., ed. and trans., *Beatha Bharra: Saint Finbarr of Cork. The Complete Life* (Dublin 1994).

Ó Riain, P., '*Catalogus praecipuorum sanctorum Hiberniae* of Henry Fitzsimon', in A.P. Smyth, ed., *Seanchas. Essays Presented to Francis J. Byrne* (Dublin, 2000), pp. 396–430.

Ovid, *Metamorphoses*, ed. and trans. F.J. Miller, 2 vols (3rd ed. Cambridge, Massachusetts and London 1977).

P. de Ronsard, *Oeuvres complètes*, ed. G. Cohen, 2 vols (Paris 1950).

Parisse, M., ed., *Le nécrologe de Gorze. Contribution à l'histoire monastique* (Nancy 1971).

Passio S. Mennae, ed. B. Mombritius, *Sanctuarium* 2 (Paris 1910), p. 287.

Patrick, *Confessio* and *Epistola*, ed. and trans. A.E.B. Hood, *St. Patrick. His Writings and Muirchú's Life* (London 1978).

Patrick, *Confessio* and *Epistola*, ed. and trans. D. Howlett, *The Book of Letters of Saint Patrick the Bishop* (Dublin 1994).

Paulus Diaconus, *Historia Langobardorum*, trans. F. Bougard, *Histoire des Lombards* (Turnhout 1994).

Pender, S., 'A Guide to Irish Genealogical Collections', *Analecta Hibernica* 7 (1934).

Pliny the Elder, *Naturalis historia*, trans. H. Rackham et al., 10 vols (London 1942–62).

Plummer, C., ed., *Vitae sanctorum Hiberniae*, 2 vols (Oxford 1910, repr. 1968).

Plummer, C., ed. and trans., *Bethada Náem nÉrenn. Lives of Irish Saints*, 2 vols (Oxford 1922, repr. 1968).

Plummer, C., ed. and trans., *Irish Litanies* (London 1925, repr. 1992).

Plummer, C., ed., *Miscellanea hagiographica hibernica* (Subsidia Hagiographica 15; Brussels 1925).

Plummer, C., and J. Earle, eds, *Two of the Saxon Chronicles Parallel*, 2 vols (Oxford 1892).

Power, P., ed. and trans., *Lives of SS Declan and Mochuda* (London 1914).

Robert of Waulsort, *Gesta Forannani*, ed. AASS, April. III, cols 816–23.

Roseman, C.H., *Pytheas of Massalia; On the Ocean* (Chicago 1994).

Rousseau, F., ed., *Actes des comtes de Namur de la première race, 946–1196* (Brussels, 1936).

Rufinus of Aquileia, *Historia ecclesiastica*, ed. E. Schuartz and T. Mommsen, *Eusebius Werke – Die Kirchengeschichte – Die lateinische Übersetzung des Rufinus* (Leipzig 1903).

Russell, N., trans., *Lives of the Desert Fathers* (Oxford and Kalamazoo 1981).

Sawyer, P.H., ed., *Anglo-Saxon Charters* (London 1968).

Selmer, C., ed., *Navigatio Sancti Brendani Abbatis* (Notre Dame 1959).

Sickel, E., ed., *Diplomata regum et imperatorum Germaniae* pars I (Hannover 1879–84, repr. Munich 1980).

Sickel, E., ed., *Diplomata regum et imperatorum Germaniae* pars II (Hannover 1893, repr. Munich 1980).

Sidonius Apollinaris, *Poems and Letters*, ed. and trans. W.B. Anderson, 2 vols (London 1936–65).

St. John Brooks, E., ed., *Knights' Fees in Counties Wexford, Carlow and Kilkenny* (Dublin 1950).

Stokes, W., ed. and trans., *The Tripartite Life of St Patrick with Other Documents Relating to that Saint*, 2 vols (Rolls Series 89; London 1887).

Stokes, W., ed. and trans., 'On the Calendar of Oengus', *The Transactions of the Royal Irish Academy*, Irish Manuscript Series 1 (1880), pp. 1–32, i–ccclii.

Stokes, W., ed. and trans., 'The Voyage of Mael Duin', *Revue Celtique* 9 (1888), pp. 447–95; 10 (1889), pp. 50–95, 265.

Stokes, W., ed. and trans., *Lives of the Saints from the Book of Lismore* (Oxford 1890).

Stokes, W., ed. and trans., 'The Voyage of the Húi Corra', *Revue Celtique* 14 (1893), pp. 22–69.

Stokes, W., ed. and trans., 'O'Davoren's Glossary', *Archiv für Celtische Lexikographie* 2 (1904), pp. 197–504.

Stokes, W., ed. and trans., *The Birth and Life of Saint Moling* (London 1907).

Stokes, W., ed. and trans., *The Annals of Tigernach*, 2 vols (repr. Lampeter 1993).

Strabo, *Geographica*, ed. and trans. H.L. Jones, 8 vols (New York and London 1917).

Sulpicius Severus, *Vita Sancti Martini*, ed. J. Fontaine, *Sulpice Sevère. Vie de S. Martin*, 3 vols (Sources Chrétiennes 133–5; Paris 1967–9).

Terroine, A., and L. Fossier, eds, *Chartes et documents relatifs à l'abbaye de Saint-Magloire de Paris*, 2 (Paris 1966).

Thurneysen, R., ed. and trans., 'Die drei Kinder, die gleich nach ihrer Geburt sprachen', *Zeitschrift für celtische Philologie* 20 (1935), pp. 192–200.

Ussher, J., *Britannicarum ecclesiarum antiquitates* (Dublin 1639), repr. in C.R. Elrington, H. Todd and W. Reeves, eds, *The Whole Works of the Most Reverend James Ussher*, 17 vols, (Dublin 1847–64).

Varro, *On the Latin Language (De lingua latina)*, ed. and trans. R. Kent, 2 vols (London and Cambridge, Mass. 1938).

Venantius Fortunatus, *Vita S. Radegundis*, ed. G. Palermo, *Venanzio Fortunato: Vite dei santi Ilario e Radegonda di Poitiers* (Rome 1989).

Venantius Fortunatus, *Vita S. Radegundis*, ed. B. Krusch, MGH, Srm 2 (Hannover 1888), pp. 364–77.

Vendryes, J., ed., *Airne Fíngein* (Dublin 1953).

Vita prima Sanctae Brigitae, trans. S. Connolly, *Journal of the Royal Society of Antiquaries of Ireland* 119 (1989), pp. 5–49.

Vita prima Sancti Mauditi, ed. A. de la Borderie, 'S. Maudez', pp. 202–17.

Vita prima Sancti Samsonis, ed. P. Flobert, *La Vie ancienne de saint Samson de Dol* (Sources d'Histoire Médiévale; Paris 1997).

Vita prima Sancti Samsonis, ed. R. Fawtier, *La Vie de saint Samson. Essai de critique hagiographique* (Paris 1912).

Vita prima Sancti Winwaloei, ed. R. Latouche, 'La plus ancienne vie de S. Guénolé', in his *Mélanges d'histoire de Cornouaille* (Paris 1911), pp. 97–112.

Vita Sancti Euflami, in A. de la Borderie, 'Saint Efflam', pp. 282–96.

Vita Sancti Hervei, in A. de la Borderie, 'Saint Hervé', pp. 256–74.

Vita Sancti Machutis, ed. G. Le Duc, *La Vie de Saint Malo, évêque d'Alet, version écrite par le diacre Bili (fin du IXe siècle), textes latins et anglo-saxons, avec traductions françaises* (Dossiers du Centre Régional Archéologique d'Alet, Hors-série B-1979; Rennes 1979).

Vita Sancti Pauli Aureliani, ed. C. Cuissard, 'Vie de S. Paul de Léon en Bretagne', *Revue Celtique* 5 (1881–3), pp. 413–59.

W. Worcestre, *Itineraries*, ed. J.H. Harvey (Oxford 1969).

Wade-Evans, A.W., ed. and trans. (part), *Vitae sanctorum Britanniae et genealogiae* (Cardiff 1944).

Waitz, G., ed., 'Historia Walciodorensis monasterii', MGH, Srg 14 (1884, repr. Stuttgart 1963), pp. 505–41.

Walahfrid Strabo, *De beati Blathmaic uita et fine*, ed. E. Duemmler, MGH, Poetae latini aevi carolingici 2 (1884), pp. 297–301. *Walahfrid Strabo: Zwei Legenden. Blathmac, der Martyrer von Iona (Hy),Mammes der christliche Orpheus*, ed. M. Pörnbacher (Reichenauer Texte und Bilder 7; Sigmaringen 1997).

Walahfrid Strabo, *Passio S. Mammetis*, ed. H. Delehaye, *Analecta Bollandiana* 58 (1940), pp.128–41. *Walahfrid Strabo: Zwei Legenden. Blathmac, der Martyrer von Iona (Hy),Mammes der christliche Orpheus*, ed. M. Pörnbacher (Reichenauer Texte und Bilder 7; Sigmaringen 1997).

Walker, G., ed., *Sancti Columbani opera* (Dublin 1957).

Wallace-Hadrill, J.M., ed., *The Fourth Book of the Chronicle of Fredegar* (London 1960).

Walsh, M., and D. Ó Cróinín, ed. and trans., *Cummian's Letter* De controuersia Paschali (Toronto 1988).

Walsh, P., ed., *Genealogiae Regum et Sanctorum Hiberniae by the Four Masters* (Maynooth and Dublin 1918).

Walshe, M. O'C., ed. and trans., *Meister Eckhart, Sermons and Treatises*, vol. 2 (Shaftesbury 1987).

Warren, F.E., ed., *The Antiphonary of Bangor*, 2 vols (London 1893–5).

Watson, J.C., ed., *Mesca Ulad* (Dublin 1941).

Widric, *Vita Gerardi*, ed. G. Waitz, MGH, Srg 4 (1841), pp. 490–509.

Williams, I., ed., *Pedeir Keinc y Mabinogi* (Cardiff 1930).

Williams, I., ed., *Canu Llywarch Hen* (Cardiff 1935).

Zaccagnini, G., ed., *Vita Sancti Fridiani. Contributi di storia e di agiografia lucchese medioevale* (Lucca 1989).

SECONDARY SOURCES

Agius, T.A., 'On Pseudo-Jerome Epistle IX', *Journal of Theological Studies* 24 (1922), pp. 176–83.

Albert, B.-S., *Le pélerinage à l'époque carolingienne* (Louvain-la-Neuve 1999).

Alonso, F., 'Galician Legends about Miraculous Sea-Voyages in Stone Boats: Some Irish and Breton Parallels', *Études Celtiques* 29 (1992), pp. 89–95.

Anderson, M.O., 'St Andrews before Alexander I', in G.W.S. Barrow, ed., *The Scottish Tradition* (Edinburgh 1974), pp. 1–13.

Anderson, M.O., *Kings and Kingship in Early Scotland* (2nd ed. Edinburgh 1980).

Angenendt, A., *Monachi Peregrini. Studien zu Pirmin und den monastischen Vorstellungen des frühen Mittelalters* (Munich 1972).

An Irien, J., 'Le culte de saint Paul Aurélien et de ses disciples', in B. Tanguy and T. Daniel, eds, *Sur les pas de Paul Aurélien. Colloque International de Saint Pol-de-Léon* (Brest and Quimper 1997), pp. 93–102.

An Irien, J., 'Saints du Cornwall et saints bretons du Ve au Xe siècle', in *Landévennec et le monachisme breton dans le Haut Moyen Age. Actes du Colloque de 15e centenaire de l'abbaye de Landévennec* (Landévennec 1985), pp. 167–88.

An Irien, J., *Saint Ké, vie et culte* (Minihi-Lévénez n.d.).

Anonymous, *Dictionnaire des saints bretons* (Paris 1979).

Armitage Robinson, J., *St. Oswald and the Church of Worcester* (London [1919]).

Arrignon, J.P. et al., eds, *Christianisme et Chrétientés en Occident et en Orient (milieu VIIe-milieu XIe s.)* (Paris 1997).

Ashe, G., *Land to the West* (London 1963).

Atwell, R.R., 'From Augustine to Gregory the Great: An Evaluation of the Emergence of the Doctrine of Purgatory', *Journal of Ecclesiastical History* 38 (1987), pp. 173–86.

Ballon, J., 'L'acte de donation de la villa de Melin à l'abbaye de Waulsort par Robert Ier, comte de Namur, 2 juin 946', *Anciens pays et assemblées d'états* 38 (1966), pp. 5–47.

Bannerman, J., *Studies in the History of Dalriada* (Edinburgh 1974).

Barbier, P., *Le Trégor historique et monumental* (Saint-Brieuc 1960).

Barone, G., 'Jean de Gorze, moine de la réforme et saint original', in Iogna-Prat and Picard, eds, *Religion et culture*, pp. 31–8.

Barré , H., 'La lettre du Pseudo-Jérôme sur l'assomption est-elle antérieure à Paschase Radbert?', *Revue Bénédictine* 68 (1958), pp. 203–25.

Barrett, C.K., *From First Adam to Last: A Study in Pauline Theology* (London 1962).

Barrow, G.W.S., *The Kingdom of the Scots* (London 1973).

Bartchy, S.S., *First-Century Slavery and 1 Corinthians 7:21* (Missoula 1973).

Baudrillard, A., et al., eds, *Dictionnaire d'histoire et de géographie ecclésiastiques* (Paris 1912–).

Baumgarten, R., 'The Geographical Orientation of Ireland in Isidore and Orosius', *Peritia* 3 (1984), pp. 189–203.

Baumgarten, R.,'The syntax of Irish *ar marb, ar mbéo : ar mairb, ar mbí* ', *Ériu* 40 (1989), pp. 99–112.

Berland, J.-M., 'La nécropole "ad sanctum" de Saint-Benoît-sur-Loire', *Studia monastica* 21 (1979), pp. 303–12.

Bermann, W., 'Dicuil's *De Mensura Orbis Terrae*', in P.L. Butzer and D. Lohrmann, eds, *Science in Western and Eastern Civilization in Carolingian Times* (Basel 1993), pp. 525–37.

Berschin, W., *Biographie und Epochenstil im lateinischen Mittelalter*, 2 vols (Stuttgart 1988).

Bhreathnach, E.,'Killeshin: An Irish Monastery Surveyed', *Cambridge Medieval Celtic Studies* 27 (1994), pp. 33–47.

Bieler, L., 'Recent Research in Irish Hagiography', *Studies* 33 (1946), pp. 230–8.

Bieler, L., 'John Colgan as Editor', *Franciscan Studies* 8 (1948), pp. 1–24.

Bieler, L., 'The Place of Saint Patrick in Latin Language and Literature', *Vigiliae Christianae* 6 (1952), pp. 65–98, repr. in R. Sharpe, ed., *Studies on the Life and Legend of St. Patrick* (London 1986).

Bieler, L., 'The Celtic Hagiographer', *Studia Patristica* 5 (Texte und Untersuchungen 80; Berlin 1962), pp. 243–65.

Bieler, L., 'St. Patrick in the British Church', in M.W. Barley and R.P.C. Hanson, eds, *Christianity in Britain, 300–700* (Leicester 1968), pp. 123–30.

Billaut, A., 'La vieille femme incarnation du mal. Sortilèges macabres chez Horaces (*Satires*, I, 8), Héliodore (*Ethiopiques*, VI,12–15) et Ronsard (*Odes* II,22)', in J. Duchemin, ed., *Actes du Colloque du Grand Palais (7–8 mai 1977)* (Paris 1980).

Binchy, D.A., 'The Irish Benedictine Congregation in Medieval Germany', *Studies* 18 (1929), pp. 194–210.

Bischoff, B., 'Wendepunkte in der Geschichte der lateinischen Exegese im Frühmittelalter', *Sacris Erudiri* 6 (1954), pp. 189–281.

Bischoff, B., 'Turning-Points in the History of Latin Exegesis in the Early Middle Ages', trans. C. O'Grady in M. McNamara, ed., *Biblical Studies: The Medieval Irish Contribution* (Dublin 1976), pp. 73–160.

Bischoff, B., *Latin Palaeography: Antiquity and the Middle Ages*, trs. D. Ganz and D. Ó Cróinín (Cambridge 1990).

[Bollandists], *Novum supplementum* (Subsidia Hagiographica 70; Bruxelles 1986).

[Bollandists], *Catalogus codicum hagiographicorum latinorum antiquiorum saeculo XVI* (Paris 1889–93).

[Bollandists], *Bibliotheca hagiographia latina*, 2 vols (Subsidia Hagiographica 6; Brussels 1898–1901).

Borsje, J., 'Die tragedie van Fergus de koning en Dorn de slavin. Een prove van een Iers-Keltisch conflict: V.A Het Godsordeel of in een boot de zee op gestuurd worden als straf', in F. Dröes et al., eds, *Proeven van Vrouwenstudies Theologie*, Deel III (IIMO Research Publications 36; Utrecht 1993), pp. 222–6.

Borsje, J., 'The Monster in the River Ness in the *Vita Sancti Columbae*: A Study of a Miracle', *Peritia* 8 (1994), pp. 27–34.

Borsje, J., *From Chaos to Enemy. Encounters with Monsters in Early Irish Texts* (Instrumenta Patristica 29; Turnhout 1996).

Bourgès, A.-Y., 'Minihy-Briac, Bourbriac et Saint-Briac : étude sur les limites des lieux placés sous l'invocation de saint Briac dans le diocèse de Tréguier au Moyen Age', *Mémoires de la Société d'émulation des Côtes-du-Nord* 112 (1984), pp. 21–43.

Bourgès, A.Y., 'Archéologie du mythe. Hagiographie du Bas Moyen Age et origines fabuleuses de quelques lignages de la noblesse bretonne', *Kreiz* 4 (1995), pp. 5–28.

Bourgès, A.Y., *Le dossier hagiographique de Saint Melar* (Britannia Monastica 5; Landévennec and Lanmeur 1997).

Bourke, C., ed., *Studies in the Cult of Saint Columba* (Dublin 1997).

Boyle, A., 'St Cadroe in Scotland', *Innes Review* 31 (1980), pp. 3–6.

Boyle, P., *The Irish College in Paris from 1578 to 1901* (Dublin 1901).

Bray, D.A., *A List of Motifs in the Lives of the Early Irish Saints* (FF Communications 252; Helsinki 1992).

Bray, D., 'Allegory in the *Navigatio Sancti Brendani*', *Viator* 26 (1995), pp. 1–10.

Breatnach, C., 'Rawlinson B 502, Lebar Glinne Dá Locha and Saltair na Rann', *Éigse* 30 (1997), pp. 109–32.

Bredero, A.H., 'Cluny et le monachisme carolingien: continuité et discontinuité', in W. Lourdeaux and D. Verhelst, eds, *Benedictine Culture, 750–1050* (Louvain 1983), pp. 50–75.

Brereton, J.P., 'Sacred Space', in M. Eliade, ed., *Encyclopaedia of Religion*, 15 vols (New York 1987), xii.526–35.

Brindley, A., and J.N. Lanting, 'A Roman Boat Found in Ireland', *Archaeology Ireland* 4.3 (1990), pp. 10–1.

Brooks, N., *The Early History of the Church of Canterbury* (Leicester 1984).

Brooks, N., and C. Cubitt, eds, *St Oswald of Worcester: Life and Influence* (London 1996).

Brown, P., *Augustine of Hippo* (London 1967).

Brown, P., *The Body and Society. Men, Women and Sexual Renunciation in Early Christianity* (New York 1988).

Brown, P., *The Cult of the Saints. Its Rise and Function in Latin Christianity* (London 1981).

Brown, P., *Society and the Holy in Late Antiquity* (Berkeley 1982).

Brüning, G., 'Adamnans Vita Columbae und ihre Ableitungen', *Zeitschrift für celtische Philologie* 11 (1915–7), pp. 213–304.

Bullough, D.A., 'The Career of Columbanus', in Lapidge, *Columbanus*, pp. 1–28.

Bullough, D.A., 'St Oswald: Monk, Bishop and Archbishop', in Brooks and Cubitt, *St Oswald of Worcester*, pp. 1–22.

Bulst, N., 'Irisches Mönchtum und cluniazensische Klosterreform', in Löwe, *Die Iren und Europa*, ii.958–69.

Burkitt, F.C., 'Saint Samson of Dol', *Journal of Theological Studies* 27 (1926), pp. 42–57.

Buron, G., 'De l'origine des marais salands guérandais', *Bulletin de la Sociéte archéologique et historique de Nantes et de Loire-Atlantique* 126, pp. 9–62.

Byrne, F.J., *Irish Kings and High-Kings* (London 1973).

Byrne, F.J., and P. Francis, 'Two Lives of Saint Patrick: *Vita secunda* and *Vita quarta*', *Journal of the Royal Society of Antiquaries of Ireland* 124 (1994), pp. 5–116.

Byrne, M.E., 'On the Punishment of Sending Adrift', *Ériu* 11 (1932), pp. 97–102.

Byrne, P., 'The Community of Clonard, Sixth to Twelfth Centuries', *Peritia* 4 (1983), pp. 157–73.

Cabrol, F., 'Octave', in *The Catholic Encyclopaedia*, 16 vols (London 1907–14), xi.204–5.

Carey, J., 'Angelology in *Saltair na Rann*', *Celtica* 19 (1987), pp. 1–8.

Carey, J., 'The Ancestry of Fénius Farsaid', *Celtica* 21 (1990), pp. 104–12.

Carey, J., *The Gaelic National Origin-legend: Synthetic Pseudohistory* (Cambridge 1994).

Carey, J., 'On the Interrelationships of Some *Cín Dromma Snechtai* Texts', *Ériu* 46 (1995), pp. 71–92.

Carey, J., 'A Posthumous Quatrain', *Éigse* 29 (1996), pp. 172–4.

Carney, J., *Studies in Irish Literature and History* (Dublin 1955, repr. 1979).

Carney, J., *The Problem of St. Patrick* (Dublin 1961).

Carney, J., Review of Selmer, *Navigatio*, *Medium Ævum* 32 (1963), pp. 37–44.

Carney, J., 'The Earliest Bran Material', in J.J. O'Meara and B. Naumann, eds, *Latin Script and Letters AD 400–900* (Leiden 1976), pp. 174–93.

Carozzi, C., 'La géographie de l'au-delà et sa signification pendant le haut Moyen Age', *Settimane di Studio* 29 (1981), pp. 423–81.

Carozzi, C., *Le voyage de l'âme dans l'Au-delà d'après la littérature latine (Vᵉ–XIIIᵉ)* (Rome 1994).

Casel, O., 'Das Mysteriengedächtnis der Messliturgie', *Jahrbuch für Liturgie-wissenschaft* 6 (1926), pp. 113–204.

Charles-Edwards, T., 'The Social Background to Irish *Peregrinatio*', *Celtica* 11 (1976), pp. 43–59.

Charles-Edwards, T., 'The Pastoral Role of the Church in the Early Irish Laws', in J. Blair and R. Sharpe, eds, *Pastoral Care Before the Parish* (Leicester 1992), pp. 63–80.

Charles-Edwards, T., *Early Irish and Welsh Kinship* (Oxford 1993).

Charles-Edwards, T., *Early Christian Ireland* (Cambridge 2000).

Coccia, E., 'La cultura irlandese precarolingia. Miracolo o mito?', *Studi Medievali*, 3a serie, 8 (1967), pp. 257–420.

Contreni, J.J., *Carolingian Learning, Masters and Manuscripts* (Aldershot 1992).

Conybeare, C., 'Re-Reading St. Patrick', *Journal of Medieval Latin* 4 (1994), pp. 39–50.

Corbet, P., *Les saints ottoniens* (Beihefte der Francia 15; Sigmaringen 1986).

Couffon, R., 'Echos hagiographiques d'un congrès', *Mémoires de la Société d'émulation des Côtes-du-Nord* 86 (1957), pp. 89–93.

Couffon, R., and J. Raison du Cleuziou, 'Le dragon dans l'art et l'hagiographie en Bretagne', *Bulletin et Mémoires de la Société d'émulation des Côtes-du-Nord* 44 (1966), pp. 2–47.

Cowan, I.B., *The Medieval Church in Scotland* (Edinburgh 1995).

Cross, T.P., *Motif-Index of Early Irish Literature* (Bloomington 1952).

Cunningham, B., 'The Culture and Ideology of Irish Franciscan Historians at Louvain 1607–1650', in C. Brady, ed., *Ideology and the Historians* (Historical Studies 17, Dublin 1991), pp. 11–30, 222–7.

Cunningham, B., and R. Gillespie, '"The Most Adaptable of Saints". The Cult of St Patrick in the Seventeenth Century', *Archivium Hibernicum* 49 (1995), pp. 82–104.

D'Arbois de Jubainville, H., 'Les noms hypocoristiques d'homme et de lieu en celtique', *Mémoires de la Société linguistique de Paris* 9 (1895–6), pp. 189–91.

Darlington, R.R., 'Ecclesiastical Reform in the Late Old English Period', *English Historical Review* 51 (1936), pp. 385–428.

Davies, J.G., *Pilgrimage Yesterday and Today* (London 1988).

Davies, W., *An Early Welsh Microcosm* (London 1978).

Davies, W., 'The Latin Charter-tradition in Western Britain, Brittany and Ireland in the Early Mediaeval Period', in Whitelock, et al., *Ireland in Early Mediaeval Europe*, pp. 258–80.

Davies, W. and P. Fouracre, eds, *The Settlement of Disputes in Early Medieval Europe* (Cambridge 1986).

De Barthélemy, A., and J. Geslin de Bourgogne, *Anciens évêchés de Bretagne*, 6 vols (Saint-Brieuc/Paris 1855–79).

De Barthélemy, A., 'La légende de S. Budoc', *Mémoires de la Société d'émulation des Côtes-du-Nord* 3 (1866), pp. 235–51.

De Bhaldraithe, T., *Gaeilge Chois Fhairrge. An Deilbhíocht* (Dublin 1977).

De Bhaldraithe, T., 'Notes on the diminutive suffix -*ín* in Modern Irish', in A. T.E. Matonis and D.F. Melia, eds, *Celtic Language, Celtic Culture. A Festschrift for Eric P. Hamp* (Van Nuys, California 1990), pp. 85–95.

De Brún, P., 'John Windele and Father John Casey: Windele's Visit to Inis Tuaisceart in 1838', *Journal of the Kerry Historical and Archaeological Society* 7 (1974), pp. 71–106.

De Brún, P., S. Ó Coileán and P. Ó Riain, eds, *Folia Gadelica. Essays Presented by Former Students to R.A. Breatnach* (Cork 1983).

De Courcy Ireland, J., *Ireland and the Irish in Maritime History* (Dublin 1987).

De Gaiffier, B., 'Notes sur le culte des SS. Clément de Metz et Caddroë', *Analecta Bollandiana* 85 (1967), pp. 21–43.

De Garaby, M., *Vies des bienheureux et des saints de Bretagne, pour tous les jours de l'année* (1839, repr. Nantes 1991).

De la Borderie, A., 'Les deux saints Caradec', *Mélanges publiés par les Bibliophiles bretons* 2 (1883), pp. 210–5.

De la Borderie, A., 'S. Maudez', *Mémoires de la Société d'émulation des Côtes-du-Nord* 28 (1890), pp. 198–266.

De la Borderie, A., 'Saint Hervé, vie latine ancienne et inédite', *Mémoires de la Société d'émulation des Côtes-du-Nord* 29 (1899), pp. 251–304.

De la Borderie, A., *Histoire de Bretagne* (Rennes 1905).

Delehaye, H., 'Les premiers "Libelli miraculorum"', *Analecta Bollandiana* 29 (1910), pp. 427–34.

Delehaye, H., 'Les recueils antiques des miracles des saints', *Analecta Bollandiana* 43 (1925), pp. 74–85.

Delehaye, H., *Cinq leçons sur la méthode hagiographique* (Subsidia Hagiographica 21, Brussels 1934).

Delehaye, H., *Les légendes hagiographiques* (4th ed., Brussels 1955).

Delehaye, H., *L'œuvre des Bollandistes à travers trois siècles. 1615–1915* (Brussels 1959).

de Moreau, H., 'L'Irlande et le monachisme de saint Benoît', *Revue liturgique et monastique* 14 (1928), pp. 30–7.

Denzinger, H., and A. Schönmetzer, eds, *Enchiridion symbolorum, definitionum, et declarationum* (Freiburg 1976).

Deuffic, J.-L., *Questions d'hagiographie bretonne. Sources, bibliographie générale* (Britannia Christiana 1, 1981).

de Varebeke, H.J., 'The Benedictines in Medieval Ireland', *Journal of the Royal Society of Antiquaries of Ireland* 80 (1950), pp. 92–6.

De Vogüé, A., 'Grégoire le Grand et ses Dialogues d'après deux ouvrages récents', *Revue d'Histoire Ecclésiastique* 83 (1988), pp. 281–348.

De Vriendt, F. and M. Trigalet, 'L'indexation informatique de la *Bibliotheca hagiographica latina* et des *Catalogues de manuscrits hagiographiques*. Deux projets en cours aux Facultés universitaires de Namur', *Litterae hagiologicae, Bulletin d'Hagiologia, Atelier belge d'études sur la sainteté* 1 (1995), pp. 7–11.

Dictionnaire de théologie catholique, ed. A. Vacant, E. Mangenot and É. Amann, 15 vols (1903–50).

Dierkens, A., *Abbayes et chapitres entre Sambre et Meuse (VIIe–XIe siècles)* (Sigmaringen 1985).

Doble, G.H., 'The Mass at Vannes in the Sixteenth Century', *Pax* (1944), pp. 130–6.

Doble, G.H., *The Saints of Cornwall*, 5 vols (Chatham and Oxford 1960–70).

Doherty, C., 'The Monastic Town in Early Medieval Ireland', in H.B. Clarke and A. Simms, eds, *The Comparative History of Urban Origins in Non-Roman Europe*, 2 vols (London 1985), i.45–75.

Doherty, C., 'Some Aspects of Hagiography as a Source for Irish Economic History', *Peritia* 1 (1982), pp. 300–28.

Dronke, P., 'St. Patrick's Reading', *Cambridge Medieval Celtic Studies* 1 (1981), pp. 21–38.

Dubois, J., and J.-L. Lemaître, *Sources et méthodes de l'hagiographie médiévale* (Paris 1993).

Duby, G., *L'An Mil* (new edition in the collection entitled *Féodalité*, Paris 1996).

Du Cange, C.D., *Glossarium mediae et infimae Latinitatis*, 10 vols (Niort 1883–7, repr. Paris 1937–8).

Duft, J., and P. Meyer, *The Irish Miniatures in the Abbey Library of St. Gall* (Olten 1954).

Duine, F., *Notes sur les saints bretons. Les saints de Dol* (Rennes 1902).

Duine, F., *Bréviaires et missels des églises et abbayes bretonnes de France antérieurs au XVIIe siècle* (Rennes 1906).

Duine, F., *Origines bretonnes, étude des sources, questions d'hagiographie et Vie de saint Samson* (Paris 1914).

Duine, F., *Mémento des sources hagiographiques de l'histoire de Bretagne* (Rennes 1918).

Duine, F., *Catalogue des sources hagiographiques pour l'histoire de Bretagne jusqu'à la fin du XIIe siècle* (Paris 1922).

Duine, F., *Inventaire liturgique de l'hagiographie bretonne* (extract from *Mémoires de la Société archéologique d'Ille-et-Vilaine*, Paris 1922).

Duine, F., *Saints de Domnonée. Notes critiques, les saints de Bretagne* (Rennes n.d.).

Dumville, D.N., '*Echtrae* and *Immram*: Some Problems of Definition', *Ériu* 27 (1976), pp. 73–94.

Dumville, D.N., 'Celtic Latin Texts in Northern England, *c*.1150–*c*.1250', *Celtica* 12 (1977), pp. 19–49.

Dumville, D.N., '"Primarius Cohortis" in Adomnán's Life of Columba', *Scottish Gaelic Studies* 13 (1979–81), pp. 130–1.

Dumville, D.N., 'Some Aspects of the Earliest Irish Christianity', in P. Ní Chatháin and M. Richter, eds, *Ireland and Europe* (Stuttgart 1984), pp. 16–24.

Dumville, D.N., 'Gildas and Uinniau', in Lapidge and Dumville, *Gildas: New Approaches*, pp. 207–14.

Dumville, D.N., 'Two Approaches to the Dating of *Nauigatio Sancti Brendani*', *Studi Medievali* 3a serie, 29 (1988), pp. 87–102.

Dumville, D.N., 'A Seventeenth-Century Hiberno-Breton Hagiological Exchange', in G. Jondorf and D.N. Dumville, eds, *France and the British Isles in the Middle Ages and Renaissance* (Woodbridge 1991), pp. 249–54.

Dumville, D.N., *Wessex and England from Alfred to Edgar* (Woodbridge 1992).

Dumville, D.N., *English Caroline Script and Monastic History: Studies in Benedictinism, AD 950–1030* (Woodbridge 1993).

Dumville, D.N., 'The Eastern Terminus of the Antonine Wall: 12th- or 13th-century Evidence', *Proceedings of the Society of Antiquaries of Scotland* 124 (1994), pp. 293–8.

Dumville, D.N., 'Britain and Ireland in *Táin Bó Fraích*', *Études Celtiques* 32 (1996), pp. 175–87.

Dumville, D.N., Review of A. Smyth, *Alfred the Great*, *Cambrian Medieval Celtic Studies* 31 (1996), pp. 90–3.

Dumville, D.N., *The Churches of North Britain in the First Viking-Age* (Whithorn 1997).

Dumville, D.N., *Three Men in a Boat. Scribe, Language, and Culture in the Church of Viking-Age Europe* (Cambridge 1997).

Dumville, D.N., *A Palaeographer's Review: the Insular System of Scripts in the Early Middle Ages*, I (Osaka 1999).

Dumville, D.N., 'Cusantín mac Ferccusa, Rí Alban: a Misidentified Monastic Ditch-digger', *Scottish Gaelic Studies* 19 (1999), pp. 234–40.

Dumville, D.N., 'The Chronicle of the Kings of Alba', in S. Taylor, ed., *Kings, Clerics and Chronicles in Scotland, 500–1297* (Dublin 2000), pp. 73–86.

Dumville, D.N., et al., *Saint Patrick, AD 493–1193* (Woodbridge 1993).

Dunning, P.J., 'Pope Innocent III and the Waterford-Lismore Controversy 1108–1216', *Irish Theological Quarterly* 28 (1961), pp. 215–32.

Duval, Y.M., *Auprès des saints corps et âme. L'inhumation ad sanctos dans la chrétienté d'Orient et d'Occident du IIIe au VIIIe siècle* (Paris 1988).

Ebrard, J.H.A., *Die iroschottische Missionskirche des sechsten, siebenten und achten Jahrhunderts* (Gütersloh 1873).

Edel, D., ed., *Cultural Identity and Cultural Integration. Ireland and Europe in the Early Middle Ages* (Dublin 1995).

Emanuel, H., 'A Double-Name Formula in Welsh "Saints' Lives"', *Bulletin of the Board of Celtic Studies* 21 (1964–6), pp. 133–5.

Engelbert, P., 'Zur Frühgeschichte des Bobbieser Skriptoriums', *Revue bénédictine* 78 (1968), pp. 220–60.

Esposito, M., 'The Sources of Conchubranus' Life of St. Monenna', *English Historical Review* 35 (1920), pp. 71–8.

Esposito, M., 'Notes on a Latin Life of Saint Patrick', *Classica et Mediaevalia* 13 (1952), pp. 59–72.

Esposito, M., 'An Apocryphal Book of Enoch and Elias as a Possible Source of the *Navigatio Brendani*', *Celtica* 5 (1960), pp. 192–206.

Etchingham, C., 'The Idea of Monastic Austerity in Early Ireland', *Historical Studies* 21 (1997), pp. 14–29.

Evans, A.C., 'Saints and Skinboats', in P. Throckmorton, ed., *History from the Sea* (London 1987), pp. 108–11.

Evans, D.E., 'A Comparison of the Formation of some Continental Celtic and Early Insular Celtic personal names', *Bulletin of the Board of Celtic Studies* 24 (1970–72), pp. 415–34.

Faller, P.O., *De priorum saeculorum silentio circa assumptionem b. Mariae virginis* (Rome 1946).

Fanning, T., 'Some Field Monuments in the Townlands of Clonmelsh and Garryhundon, Co. Carlow', *Peritia* 3 (1984), pp. 43–9.

Farrell, A.W., and S. Penny, 'The Broighter Hoard: A Reassessment', *Irish Archaeological Research Forum* 2 (1975), pp. 15–28.

Fennessy, I., 'Printed Books in St Anthony's College, Louvain, 1673 (F.L.K., MS A 34)', *Collectanea Hibernica* 38 (1996), pp. 82–117.

Fick, A., *Die griechischen Personennamen nach ihrer Bildung erklärt* (Göttingen 1874).

Fingerhut, E.R., *Who First Discovered America? A Critique of Pre-Columbian Voyages* (Claremont, California 1984).

Flachenecker, H., *Schottenklöster. Irische Benediktinerkonvente im hochmittelalterlichen Deutschland* (Paderborn 1995).

Flanagan, L., 'Ships and Shipping in Pre-Viking Ireland', *Cultura Maritima* 1 (1975), pp. 3–8.

Fleming, P., ed., *Collectanea sacra seu S. Columbani Hiberni abbatis ... acta et opuscula* (Louvain 1667).

Fleuriot, L., 'Le saint breton Winniau et le pénitentiel dit de Finnian', *Études Celtiques* 15 (1976–8), pp. 607–14.

Fleuriot, L., *Les origines de la Bretagne* (Paris 1980, 2nd ed. Paris 1982).

Fleuriot, L., *A Dictionary of Old Breton – Dictionnaire du vieux Breton* (Toronto 1985).

Ford, P.K., ed., *Celtic Folklore and Christianity. Studies in Memory of William W. Heist* (Berkeley 1983).

Fouracre, P., and R.A. Gerberding, *Late Merovingian France: History and Hagiography 640–720* (Manchester and New York 1996).

Fros, H., 'L'eschatologie médiévale dans quelques écrits hagiographiques (IVe–IXe siècles)', in W. Verbeke et al., eds, *The Use and Abuse of Eschatology in the Middle Ages* (Louvain 1988), pp. 212–20.

Fuhrmann, J.P., *Irish Medieval Monasteries on the Continent* (Washington, DC 1927).

Galliou, P., *L'Armorique romaine* (Braspartz 1983).

Galliou, P., and M. Jones, *The Bretons* (Oxford 1991).

Garnsey, P., *Ideas of Slavery from Aristotle to Augustine* (Cambridge 1996).

Gilbert, J.T., 'The Manuscripts of the Former College of Irish Franciscans, Louvain', Historical Manuscripts Commission, *Fourth Report* (1874), Appendix, pp. 599–613.

Goethe, J.W. von, *Winckelmann und sein Jahrhundert* (1805, repr. Munich 1962).

Gorman, M., 'A Critique of Bischoff's Theory of Irish Exegesis: The Commentary on Genesis in Munich Clm 6302 (Wendepunkte 2)', *Journal of Medieval Latin* 7 (1997), pp. 178–233.

Gougaud, L.,'Un point obscur de l'itinéraire de S. Colomban venant en Gaule', *Annales de Bretagne* 22 (1907), pp. 327–43.

Gougaud, L., 'Inventaire des règles monastiques irlandaises' *Revue Bénédictine* 25 (1908), pp. 167–84 and 321–33.

Gougaud, L., *Les chrétientés celtiques* (1st ed. Paris 1911, 2nd ed. Crozon 1995).

Gougaud, L., *Christianity in Celtic Lands*, trans. M. Joynt (London 1932).

Gougaud, L., 'Anciennes traditions ascétiques. I. L'usage de voyager à pied', *Revue d'Ascétique et de Mystique* 3 (1922), pp. 5–59.

Gousset, M.-T., 'La représentation de la Jérusalem céleste', *Cahiers Archéologiques* 23 (1974), pp. 47–60.

Gray, P.T.R., and M.W. Herren, 'Columbanus and the Three Chapters Controversy – A New Approach', *Journal of Theological Studies*, n.s. 45 (1994), pp. 160–70.

Grogan, B., 'Eschatological Teaching in the Early Irish Church', in M. McNamara, ed., *Biblical Studies: The Medieval Irish Contribution* (Dublin 1976), pp. 46–58.

Grosjean, P., 'Catalogus codicum hagiographicorum latinorum Dubliniensium', *Analecta Bollandiana* 46 (1928), pp. 81–148.

Grosjean, P., 'Hagiographica celtica: IV. Sancti hiberni septem nunquam morituri', *Analecta Bollandiana* 55 (1937), pp. 287–95.

Grosjean, P., 'Notes d'hagiographie celtique. 20. Les Vies latines de S. Cáemgen et de S. Patrice du manuscrit 121 des Bollandistes', in *Analecta Bollandiana* 70 (1952), pp. 313–5.

Grosjean, P., 'Vie et miracles de S. Petroc', *Analecta Bollandiana* 74 (1956), pp. 470–96.

Grosjean, P., 'Notes sur quelques sources des Antiquitates de Jacques Ussher. Édition de la Vita Commani', in *Analecta Bollandiana* 77 (1959), pp. 154–87.

Grosjean, P. 'Un soldat de fortune irlandais au service des «Acta Sanctorum». Philippe O'Sullivan Beare et Jean Bolland (1634)', in *Analecta Bollandiana* 81 (1963), pp. 418–46.

Guenée, B., *Histoire et culture historique dans l'Occident médiéval* (Paris 1980).

Guerout, J., 'Fare (Sainte)', in Baudrillard et al., *Dictionnaire*, xvi.505–31.

Guerout, J., and Y. Chaussy, 'Faremoutiers', in Baudrillard et al., *Dictionnaire*, xvi.534–45.

Guigon, P., 'Les sites religieux et fortifiés du Haut Moyen-Age en Bretagne. Les églises des saints et les palais des rois', Thèse de doctorat, Rennes 1990.

Guigon, P., 'Les influences irlandaises sur l'architecture religieuse bretonne du Haut Moyen-Age à l'époque romane. Mythe ou réalité?', in Laurent and Davis, eds, *Irlande et Bretagne*, pp. 193–215.

Guillotel, H., 'Les origines du ressort de l'évêché de Dol', *Mémoires de la Société historique et archéologique de Bretagne* 54 (1977), pp. 31–68.

Guillotel, H., 'Les origines de Landévennec', in *Landévennec et le monachisme breton dans le Haut Moyen Age. Actes du Colloque de 15ème centenaire de l'abbaye de Landévennec* (Landévennec 1985), pp. 97–114.

Guillotel, H., 'Sainte-Croix de Quimperlé et Locronan', in Laurent, *Saint Ronan et la Troménie*, pp. 175–90.

Guillotin de Corson, A., 'Pluvigner et son Pardon', in *La semaine religieuse du diocèse de Vannes* (1890), pp. 104–7.

Gurevich, A., 'Au Moyen Age. Conscience individuelle et image de l'au-delà', *Annales* 37 (1982), pp. 255–75.

Guyonvarc'h, J.–C., 'Celtique commun *Letavia, gaulois Letavis*, irlandais *Letha*; la porte de l'Autre monde', *Ogam* 19 (1967), pp. 490–4; 20 (1968), p. 195.

Gwynn, A., 'Irish Monks and the Cluniac Reform', *Studies* 39 (1940), pp. 409–30.

Gwynn, A., 'Some Notes on the History of the Irish and Scottish Benedictine Monasteries in Germany', *Innes Review* 5 (1954), pp. 5–27.

Gwynn, A., *The Irish Church in the Eleventh and Twelfth Centuries* (Dublin 1992).

Hallinger, K., *Gorze-Kluny. Studien zu den monastischen Lebensformen und Gegensätzen im Hochmittelalter*, 2 vols (Rome 1950–1).

Hamlin, A., 'Crosses in Early Ireland: The Evidence from Written Sources', in M. Ryan, ed., *Ireland and Insular Art AD 500–1200* (Dublin 1987), pp. 138–40.

Hampe, K., *Germany under the Salian and Hohenstaufen Emperors* (London 1973).

Harbison, P., *The High Crosses of Ireland*, 3 vols (Bonn and Dublin 1992).

Harvey, A., 'Retrieving the Pronunciation of Early Insular Celtic Scribes: The Case of Dorbbéne', *Celtica* 22 (1991), pp. 48–65.

Harvey, A., K. Devine and F.J. Smith, eds, *Archive of Celtic Latin Literature* (Turnhout 1994).

Hauréau, B., *Notices et extraits de quelques manuscrits latins de la Bibliothèque nationale* (Paris 1892).

Hawkes, C.F.C., *Pytheas: Europe and the Greek Explorers* (Oxford 1973).

Hayes, R., 'Some Notable Limerick Doctors', *North Munster Antiquarian Journal* 1.3 (1938), 113–23.

Haywood, J., *Dark Age Naval Power* (London 1991).

Henken, E., *The Welsh Saints: A Study in Patterned Lives* (Cambridge 1991).

Hennig, J., 'A Note on the Traditions of St. Frediano and St. Silao of Lucca', *Mediaeval Studies* 13 (1951), pp. 234–42.

Herbert, M., 'Review of *The Book of Leinster* vi', *Éigse* 22 (1987), pp. 166–8.

Herbert, M., *Iona, Kells, and Derry. The History and Hagiography of the Monastic* Familia *of Columba* (Oxford 1988).

Herbert, M., 'Hagiography', in K. McCone and K. Simms, eds, *Progress in Medieval Irish Studies* (Maynooth 1996), pp. 79–90.

Herren, M., 'Mission and Monasticism in the "Confession" of Patrick', in Ó Corráin et al., *Sages, Saints and Storytellers*, pp. 76–85.

Heuclin, J., *Aux origines monastiques de la Gaule du Nord. Ermites et reclus du Ve au XIe siècle* (Lille 1988).

Hillers, B., 'Voyages between Heaven and Hell: Navigating the Early Irish *Immram* Tales', *Proceedings of the Harvard Celtic Colloquium* 13 (1993), pp. 66–81.

Hillgarth, J.N., 'St Julian of Toledo in the Middle Ages', *Journal of the Warburg and Courtauld Institutes* 21 (1958), pp. 7–26.

Historical Manuscripts Commission, *Fourth Report of the Royal Commission on Historical Manuscripts*, Part I, Report and Appendix (London 1874).

Hogan, E., 'Irish Historical Studies in the Seventeenth Century', *Irish Ecclesiastical Record* 7 (1871), pp. 31–43, 56–77, 193–216, 268–89.

Hornell, J., 'The Curraghs of Ireland', *Mariner's Mirror* 23 (1937), pp. 74–83, 148–75; 24 (1938), pp. 5–23.

Hornell, J., *British Coracles and Irish Curraghs* (London 1938).

Hourihane, C.P., and J.J. Hourihane, 'The Kilnaruane Pillar Stone, Bantry, Co. Cork', *Journal of the Cork Historical and Archaeological Society* 84 (1979), pp. 65–73.

Howlett, D., 'Seven Studies in Seventh-Century Texts', *Peritia* 10 (1996), pp. 1–70.

Hughes, K., 'The Changing Theory and Practice of Irish Pilgrimage', *Journal of Ecclesiastical History* 11 (1960), pp. 143–51, reprinted in her *Church and Society in Ireland, AD 400–1200* (London 1987), chapter XIV.

Iogna-Prat, D., and J.-C. Picard, eds, *Religion et culture autour de l'an mil. Royaume capétien et Lotharingie* (Paris 1990).

Ireland, C., 'Some Analogues of the O.E. *Seafarer* from Hiberno-Latin Sources', *Neuphilologische Mitteilungen* 92 (1991), pp. 1–14.

Jackson, K.H., *Language and History in Early Britain* (Edinburgh 1953).

James, E., 'Bede and the Tonsure Question', *Peritia* 3 (1984), pp. 85–98.

James, E., 'Ireland and Western Gaul in the Merovingian Period', in Whitelock et al., *Ireland in Early Mediaeval Europe*, pp. 362–86.

Jankulak, K., 'Some Sources of Nicholas Roscarrock's Account of the Life of St Petrock', *Devon & Cornwall Notes & Queries* 37 pt. vi (1994), pp. 185–9.

Jenner, H., 'The Irish Immigrations into Cornwall in the Late Fifth and Early Sixth Centuries', *The 84th Annual Report of the Royal Cornwall Polytechnic Society* (1917), pp. 38–85.

Jennings, B., *Michael O Cleirigh, Chief of the Four Masters and his Associates* (Dublin and Cork 1936).

John, E., 'The Sources of the English Monastic Reformation: a Comment', *Revue Bénédictine* 70 (1960), pp. 197–203.

John, E., *Orbis Britanniae and Other Studies* (Leicester 1966).

Johnstone, P., 'The Bantry Boat', *Antiquity* 38 (1964), pp. 278–9.

Johnstone, P., *The Seacraft of Prehistory* (London 1980).

Jones, G.H., 'Celtic Britain and the Pilgrim Movement', *Y Cymmrodor* 23 (1912).

Jones, M.E., *The End of Roman Britain* (Ithaca and London 1996).

Jones, M.E., 'The Literary Evidence for Mast and Sail during the Anglo–Saxon Invasions', *Studies in Medieval and Renaissance History*, n. s. 13 (1993), pp. 31–67.

Judic, B., 'Pénitence publique, pénitence privée et aveu chez Grégoire le Grand (590–604)', in Groupe de la Bussière, ed., *Pratiques de la confession. Des pères du désert à Vatican II. Quinze études d'histoire* (Paris 1983), pp. 41–51.

Jugie, M., *La mort et l'assomption de la Sainte Vierge* (Rome 1944).

Kehr, P., *Die Urkunden Otto III.* (Innsbruck 1890).

Kelly, F., *A Guide to Early Irish Law* (Dublin 1988).

Kennedy, C.A., 'Dead, Cult of the', in D.N. Freedman, ed., *Anchor Bible Dictionary*, 6 vols (New York 1992), ii.107–8.

Kenney, J., *The Sources for the Early History of Ireland (Ecclesiastical)* (Cornell 1929, repr. Dublin 1979).

Kerlouégan, F., 'Les citations d'auteurs latins profanes dans les vies de saints bretons carolingiennes', *Études Celtiques* 18 (1981), pp. 181–95.

Keynes, S., 'King Athelstan's Books', in M. Lapidge and H. Gneuss, eds, *Learning and Literature in Anglo–Saxon England* (Cambridge 1985), pp. 143–201.

Klingshirn, W.E., *Caesarius of Arles* (Cambridge 1994).

Knowles, D., *Great Historical Enterprises* (London 1962).

Koch, J.T., with J. Carey, ed., *The Celtic Heroic Age. Literary Sources for Ancient Celtic Europe and Early Ireland and Wales* (Malden, Massachusetts 1995).

Kottje, R., and H. Maurer, eds, *Monastische Reformen im 9. und 10. Jahrhundert* (Sigmaringen 1989).

Kurzawa, F., *Petite vie de saint Patrick* (Paris 1995).

Lahellec, P., 'Approche de la vie et de l'oeuvre du fondateur de l'hagiographie bretonne. Albert le Grand et "La Vies des Saincts de la Bretaigne Armorique" (1627)', Mémoire de maîtrise d'histoire, Brest 1996.

Lambot, D.C., 'L'homélie du Pseudo-Jérôme sur l'assomption et l'évangile de la nativité de Marie d'après une lettre inédite d'Hincmar', *Revue Bénédictine* 46 (1934), pp. 265–82.

Langdon, M., 'Sound symbolism in Yuman languages', in Sawyer, *Studies in American Indian languages*, pp. 149–73.

Lanzoni, F., 'Il sepolcro do S. Girolamo', *La scuola cattolica* 20 (1921), pp. 383–90; 21 (1921), pp. 458–69.

Lapidge, M., 'Beowulf, Aldhelm, the *Liber Monstrorum* and Wessex', *Studi Medievali*, 3a series, 23 (1982), pp. 151–92.

Lapidge, M., 'Schools, Learning and Literature in Tenth-century England', *Settimane di studio del Centro italiano di studi sull'alto medioevo* 38 (1991), pp. 951–1005.

Lapidge, M., 'Israel the Grammarian in Anglo-Saxon England', in H.J. Westra, ed., *From Athens to Chartres: Neoplatonism and Medieval Thought. Studies in Honour of Edouard Jeauneau* (Leiden 1992), pp. 97–114.

Lapidge, M., ed., *Columbanus: Studies on the Latin Writings* (Woodbridge 1997).

Lapidge, M. and D.N. Dumville, eds, *Gildas: New Approaches* (Woodbridge 1984).

Lapidge, M., and R. Sharpe, *A Bibliography of Celtic-Latin Literature 400–1200* (Dictionary of Medieval Latin from Celtic Sources, Ancillary Publications 1; Dublin 1985).

Largillière, R., *Les saints et l'organisation chrétienne primitive dans l'Armorique bretonne* (Rennes 1925, new ed. Crozon 1995).

Largillière, R., 'Les Minihys', *Mémoires de la Société d'histoire et d'archéologie de Bretagne*, 8 (1927), pp. 183–216.

Latham, R.E., and D. Howlett, eds, *Dictionary of Medieval Latin from British Sources* (London 1965–).

Latham, R.E., *Revised Medieval Latin Word-List from British and Irish Sources* (London 1965).

Laurent, C., and H. Davis, eds, *Irlande et Bretagne. Vingt siècles d'histoire. Actes du Colloque de Rennes, 29–31 mars 1993* (Rennes 1994).

Laurent, D., ed., *Saint Ronan et la Troménie. Actes du Colloque International, 28–30 avril 1989* (Bannalec 1995).

Lawlor, H.J., 'The Manuscripts of the Vita S. Columbani', *Transactions of the Royal Irish Academy* 32 C (1902–4), pp. 1–132.

Leclercq, J., 'Un recueil d'hagiographie colombanienne', *Analecta Bollandiana* 73 (1955), pp. 193–6.

Leclercq, J., 'Jean de Gorze et la vie religieuse au Xe siècle', in *Saint Chrodegang: Communications présentées au colloque tenue à Metz à l'occasion du douzième centenaire de sa mort* (Metz 1967), pp. 133–52.

Leclercq, J., 'La réforme bénédictine anglaise du Xe siècle vue du Continent', *Studia monastica* 24 (1982), pp. 105–25.

Le Duc, Gw., 'Bretons et Irlandais, Irlandais et Bretons', *Britannia Monastica* 1 (1990), pp. 7–12.

Le Duc, Gw., 'L'évêché mythique de Brest', in *Les débuts de l'organisation religieuse de la Bretagne armoricaine* (Britannia Monastica 3, 1994), pp. 169–99.

Le Duc, Gw., 'La Bretagne, intermédiaire entre l'Aquitaine et l'Irlande', in J.-M. Picard, ed., *Aquitaine and Ireland in the Middle Ages* (Dublin 1995), pp. 173–87.

Leerssen, J., *Mere Irish and Fíor-Ghael. Studies in the Idea of Irish Nationality, its Development and Literary Expression prior to the Nineteenth Century* (Amsterdam 1986).

Le Goff, J., *Pour un autre Moyen Age* (Paris 1977).

Le Goff, J., *Le naissance du purgatoire* (Paris 1981).

Le Mené, J.-M., *Histoire du diocèse de Vannes* (Vannes 1888).

Le Menn, Gw., *Grand choix de prénoms bretons* (Saint-Brieuc/La Baule 1975).

Le Menn, Gw., *La femme au sein d'or* (Skol-Dastum 1985).

Le Moigne, F.-Y., *Histoire de Metz* (Toulouse 1986).

Lethbridge, T.C., *Herdsmen and Hermits* (London 1950).

Levison, W., 'Conspectus codicum hagiographicorum', MGH, Srm 7 (1920), pp. 529–706.

Levison, W., *Die Politik in den Jenseitvisionen des frühen Mittelalters* (Bonn 1921).

Levison, W., *England and the Continent in the Eighth Century* (Oxford 1946).

Little, G., *Brendan the Navigator: An Interpretation* (London 1945).

Lobineau, Gw., *Les vies des saints de Bretagne et des personnages d'une éminente piété qui ont vécu dans cette province* (1725), ed. A. Tresvaux, 6 vols (Paris 1836–9).

Loth, J., *L'émigration bretonne en Armorique du Ve au VIIe siècle de notre ère* (Rennes 1883).

Loth, J., *Chrestomathie bretonne* (Paris 1890).

Loth, J., *Les noms des saints bretons* (Paris 1910); originally appeared in *Revue Celtique* 29 (1908), pp. 222–48 and 271–311, and 30 (1909), pp. 121–55, 283–320 and 395–403.

Löwe, H., 'Ein literarischer Widersacher des Bonifatius: Virgil von Salzburg und die Kosmographie des Aethicus Ister', *Abhandlungen der Akademie der Wissenschaften und der Literatur in Mainz* (1951), pp. 899–988 (Nr 11).

Löwe, H., 'Dialogus de statu sanctae ecclesiae. Das Werk eines Iren im Laon des 10. Jahrhunderts', *Deutsches Archiv für Erforschung des Mittelalters* 17 (1961), pp. 12–90.

Löwe, H., ed., *Die Iren und Europa im früheren Mittelalter*, 2 vols (Stuttgart 1982)

Lucas, L.W., *Grammar of Ros Goill Irish, Co. Donegal* (Belfast 1979).

Maarleveld, T.J., 'Type or Technique? Some Thoughts on Boat and Ship Finds as Indicative of Cultural Traditions', *International Journal of Nautical Archaeology* 24.1 (1995), pp. 3–7.

MacCaffrey, J., 'Lives of the Irish Saints', *Irish Theological Quarterly* 5 (1910), pp. 335–47.

Mac Cana, P., 'On the "Prehistory" of *Immram Brain*', *Ériu* 26 (1975), pp. 33–52.

Mac Cana, P., 'Placenames and Mythology in Irish Tradition: Places, Pilgrimages, and Things', in G.W. MacLennan, ed., *Proceedings of the First North American Congress of Celtic Studies* (Ottawa 1988), pp. 319–41.

MacCullagh, R., *Irish Currach Folk* (Dublin 1992).

MacCulloch, J.A., *The Harrowing of Hell: A Comparative Study of an Early Christian Doctrine* (Edinburgh 1930).

MacDonald, A., 'Aspects of the Monastery and Monastic Life in Adomnán's Life of Columba', *Peritia* 3 (1984), pp. 271–302.

MacDonald, A., 'Adomnán's Monastery of Iona', in Bourke, *Cult of Saint Columba*, pp. 24–44.

MacDonnell, C., 'Notice of Some of the Lives which Seem to have been Ready, or in Preparation, for the Continuation of the "Acta Sanctorum Hiberniae", at the Death of Colgan', *Proceedings of the Royal Irish Academy* 7 (1857–61), pp. 371–5.

Mac Eoin, G., 'On the Irish Legend of the Origin of the Picts', *Studia Hibernica* 4 (1964), pp. 138–54.

MacLysaght, E.A., and J. Ainsworth, 'The Arthur Manuscript', *North Munster Antiquarian Journal* 8.2 (1959), pp. 79–87.

Mac Mathúna, S., 'The Structure and Transmission of Early Irish Voyage Literature', in H.L.C. Tristram , ed., *Text und Zeittiefe* (Scriptoralia 58; Tübingen 1994), pp. 313–57.

Mac Neill, E., *Phases of Irish History* (Dublin 1919).

Mac Neill, E., *Celtic Ireland* (Dublin 1921).

Mac Neill, M., *The Festival of Lughnasa* (Oxford 1962).

Mac Niocaill, G., and P.F. Wallace, eds, *Keimelia. Studies in Medieval Archaeology and History in Memory of Tom Delaney* (Galway 1988).

Mac Shamhráin, A.S., *Church and Polity in Pre-Norman Ireland: The Case of Glendalough* (Maynooth 1996).

Marcus, G.J., *The Conquest of the North Atlantic* (Woodbridge 1980).

Marcus, G.J., 'Factors in Early Celtic Navigation', *Études Celtiques* 6 (1953–4), pp. 312–27.

Martin, D.B., *Slavery as Salvation* (New Haven 1990).

Martin, H., *Mentalités médiévales. XIe–XVe siècle* (Paris 1996).

Mayr-Harting, H., *The Coming of Christianity to Anglo-Saxon England* (London 1972).

McCarthy, D., 'The Origin of the *Latercus* Paschal Cycle of the Insular Celtic Churches', *Cambrian Medieval Celtic Studies* 28 (1994), pp. 25–49.

McCone, K., 'Brigit in the Seventh Century: a Saint with Three Lives ?', *Peritia* 1 (1982), pp. 107–45.

McCone, K., 'An Introduction to Early Irish Saints' Lives', *Maynooth Review* 11 (1984), pp. 6–59.

McCone, K., 'Werewolves, Cyclopes, *Díberga*, and *Fíanna*: Juvenile Delinquency in Early Ireland', *Cambridge Medieval Celtic Studies* 12 (1986), pp. 1–22.

McDonnell, K., 'The Descent of Jesus in the Jordan and the Descent into Hell', *Worship* 69 (1995), pp. 98–109.

McGrail, S., *Ancient Boats in Northwest Europe* (2nd ed. London 1998).

McKenzie, J.L., *Dictionary of the Bible* (London 1965).

McManus, D., *A Guide to Ogam* (Maynooth 1991).

McNamara, J.A., and J.E. Halborg, *Sainted Women of the Dark Ages* (Durham USA and London 1992).

McNamara, M., *The Apocrypha in the Irish Church* (Dublin 1975).

McNamara, M., 'Some Aspects of Early Medieval Irish Eschatology', in P. Ní Chatháin and M. Richter, eds, *Ireland and Europe in the Early Middle Ages. Learning and Literature* (Stuttgart 1996), pp. 42–75.

Melia, D., 'Law and the Shaman Saint', in Ford, *Celtic Folklore and Christianity*, pp. 113–28.

Mellinkoff, R., 'Cain's Monstrous Progeny in Beowulf. Part 1: Noachic Tradition', *Anglo-Saxon England* 8 (1979), pp. 143–62.

Mellinkoff, R., 'Cain's Monstrous Progeny in Beowulf. Part 2: Post Diluvian Survival', *Anglo-Saxon England* 9 (1980), pp. 183–97.

Merdrignac, B., *Recherches sur l'hagiographie armoricaine du VIIe au XVe siècle* (Dossiers du Centre Régional Archéologique d'Alet 1, [Saint Malo] 1986).

Merdrignac, B., 'Saints et géants dans l'hagiographie armoricaine du Haut Moyen Age', in X. Barral i Altet, ed., *Actes des VIe journées nationales de l'Association française d'archéologie mérovingienne (Rennes, juin 1984)* (Paris 1988), pp. 21–32.

Merdrignac, B., 'La première Vie de saint Samson. Étude chronologique', *Studia Monastica* 30 (1988), pp. 243–88.

Merdrignac, B., 'Bretons et Irlandais en France du nord: VIe–VIIIe siècles' in J.-M. Picard, ed., *Ireland and Northern France, AD 600–850 – Irlande et France du Nord, VIIe–IXe siècles* (Dublin 1991), pp. 119–42.

Merdrignac, B., 'Henoc, les *philosophi* et Pental', in Gw. Le Menn and J.–Y. Le Moing, eds, *Bretagne et pays celtiques. Langues, histoire, civilisation. Mélanges offerts à la mémoire de Léon Fleuriot* (Saint Brieuc and Rennes 1992), pp. 167–81.

Merdrignac, B., 'Les origines bretonnes dans les leçons des bréviaires des XVe-XVIe siècles', in *1491. La Bretagne, terre d'Europe* (Brest and Quimper, 1992), pp. 295–309.

Merdrignac, B., *Les Vies de saints bretons durant le Haut Moyen-Age* (Rennes 1993).

Merdrignac, B., 'La désacralisation du mythe celtique de la navigation vers l'Autre Monde. L'apport du dossier hagiographique de saint Malo', *Ollodagos* 5 (1993), pp. 13–43.

Merdrignac, B., 'La perception de l'Irlande dans les *Vitae* des saints bretons du haut Moyen Age (VIIe–XIIe siècles)', in Laurent and Davis, *Irlande et Bretagne*, pp. 64–75.

Merdrignac, B., 'Des "fous volants" au XIIe siècle en Grande Bretagne', *Kreiz* 3 (1994), pp. 141–6.

Merdrignac, B.,'Saint Ronan et sa *Vie* latine', in Laurent, *Saint Ronan et la Troménie*, pp. 125–56.

Meyer, K., *Hibernica minora* (Oxford 1894).

Meyer, K., 'Zur keltischen Wortkunde I–IX', *Sitzungsberichte der königlich preussischen Akademie der Wissenschaften* 1912 (38, pp. 790–803), (51, pp. 1144–57), 1913 (25, pp. 445–55), (49, pp. 950–9), 1914 (21, pp. 630–42), (35, pp. 939–58), 1917 (47, pp. 624–53), 1918 (31, pp. 618–33), 1919 (21, pp. 374–401).

Meyer, K., 'Aus dem Nachlass Heinrich Zimmers', *Zeitschrift für celtische Philologie* 9 (1913), pp. 87–120.

Miller, M., 'Matriliny by Treaty: the Pictish Foundation-legend', in Whitelock et al., *Ireland in Early Mediaeval Europe*, pp. 133-61.

Misonne, D., 'Les sources littéraires de la Vie de Saint Éloque et les amplifications walciodoriennes de la translation', *Revue bénédictine* 71 (1961), pp. 338–65.

Misonne, D., 'La charte de Raoul de Laon relative à l'établissement des moines scots à Saint-Michel-en-Thiérache (3 février 945)', *Revue bénédictine* 74 (1964), pp. 298–307.

Misonne, D., 'L'éloge de Forannan, abbé de Waulsort, dans la charte de Robert de Namur', *Anciens pays et assemblées d'états* 38 (1966), pp. 49–60.

Misonne, D., *Eilbert de Florennes. Histoire et légende* (Louvain 1967).

Mooney, C., 'Father John Colgan, O.F.M., his Work and Times and Literary Milieu', in T. O Donnell, ed., *Father John Colgan, O.F.M., 1592–1658. Essays in Commemoration of the Third Centenary of his Death* (Dublin 1959), pp. 7–40.

Morgenstern, J., 'The Gates of Righteousness', *Hebrew Union College Annual* 6 (1929), pp. 1–37.

Morice, H., *Mémoires pour servir de preuves à l'histoire ... de Bretagne*, 3 vols, (Paris 1742–46).

Moyse, G., 'Monachisme et réglementation monastique en Gaul avant Benoît d'Aniane', in *Sous la Règle de Saint Benoît: Structures monastiques et sociétés en France du moyen âge à l'époque moderne* (Geneva 1982), pp. 3–19.

Murdoch, B., 'The Holy Hostage. De filio mulieris in the Middle Cornish Play *Beunans Meriasek*', *Medium Ævum* 58 (1989), pp. 258–73.

Murdoch, B., *Cornish Literature* (Woodbridge 1993).

Murphy, F.X., 'Martyrium', in *New Catholic Encyclopaedia*, 15 vols (New York 1967), ix.526–35.

Nagy, J.F., *Conversing with Angels and Ancients. Literary Myths of Medieval Ireland* (Ithaca and Dublin 1997).

Neill, K., 'How Carson Caught the Boat', *Archaeology Ireland* 7.2 (1993), pp. 24–6.

Nelson, J., 'Queens as Jezebels: The Careers of Brunhild and Balthild in Merovingian History', in D. Baker, ed., *Medieval Women* (Oxford 1978), pp. 31–77.

Nerney, D.S., 'A Study of St. Patrick's Sources', *Irish Ecclesiastical Record* 71 (1949), pp. 497–507.

Ní Chatháin, P., 'Swineherds, Seers, and Druids', *Studia Celtica* 14/15 (1979–80), pp. 200–11.

Nicholls, K.W., 'Some Place-names from *Pontificia Hibernica*', *Dinnsheanchas* 3 (1969), pp. 85–98.

Nicholls, K.W., 'The Land of the Leinstermen', *Peritia* 3 (1984), pp. 535–58.

Nicholls, K.W., 'The Charter of John, Lord of Ireland, in Favour of the Cistercian Abbey of Baltinglass', *Peritia* 4 (1985), pp. 187–206.

Niermeyer, J.F., *Mediae Latinitatis lexicon minus* (Leiden 1976).

Nightingale, J., 'Oswald, Fleury and Continental Reform', in N. Brooks and C. Cubitt, eds, *St Oswald of Worcester*, pp. 23–45.

O'Brien, E., 'Churches of South-East County Dublin, Seventh to Twelfth Century' in Mac Niocaill and Wallace, eds, *Keimelia*, pp. 504–24.

O'Brien, E., 'Archaeological Study of Church Cemeteries: Past Present Future', in J. Blair and C. Pyrah, eds, *Church Archaeology: Research Directions for the Future* (London 1996), pp. 159–66.

O'Brien, M.A., (ed. R. Baumgarten), 'Old Irish Personal Names', *Celtica* 10 (1973), pp. 211–36.

O'Carroll, M., *Theotokos* (Dublin 1982).

Ó Corráin, D., 'The Early Irish Churches: Some Aspects of Organisation' in D. Ó Corráin, ed., *Irish Antiquity. Essays and Studies presented to Professor M.J. O'Kelly* (Cork 1981), pp. 327–41.

Ó Corráin, D., L. Breatnach and K. McCone, eds, *Sages, Saints and Storytellers. Celtic Studies in Honour of Professor James Carney* (Maynooth 1989).

Ó Criomhthain, T., *An tOileánach* (Dublin 1929).

Ó Cróinín, D., *Early Medieval Ireland 400–1200* (London 1995).

O Donnell, T., ed., *Father John Colgan O.F.M. 1592–1658* (Dublin 1959).

O'Donovan, J., 'The Ordnance Survey Letters', in P. Walsh, ed., *The Placenames of Westmeath* (Dublin 1957), pp. 1–103.

O Dwyer, P., *Célí Dé. Spiritual Reform in Ireland 750–900* (Dublin 1981).

Ó Fiaich, T., *Má Nuad* (Maynooth 1972).

Ó Fiaich, T., 'Vergil's Irish Background and Departure for France', *Seanchas Ardmhacha* 11 (1983–5), pp. 301–18.

O'Hanlon, J., *The Lives of the Irish Saints*, 10 vols (Dublin 1875–1903).

Ó hEailidhe, P., 'The Monk's Boat: A Roman Period Relic from Lough Lene, Co. Westmeath, Eire', *International Journal of Nautical Archaeology* 21 (1992), pp. 185–90.

O'Loughlin, T., 'The Exegetical Purpose of Adomnán's *De locis sanctis*', *Cambridge Medieval Celtic Studies* 24 (1992), pp. 37–53.

O'Loughlin, T., 'Adam's Burial at Hebron: Some Aspects of its Significance in the Latin Tradition', *Proceedings of the Irish Biblical Association* 15 (1992), pp. 66–88.

O'Loughlin, T., 'The Latin Version of the Scriptures in Iona in the Late Seventh Century: The Evidence from *De locis sanctis*', *Peritia* 8 (1994), pp. 18–26.

O'Loughlin, T., 'The Library of Iona in the Late Seventh Century. The Evidence from Adomnán's *De locis sanctis*', *Ériu* 45 (1994), pp. 33–52.

O'Loughlin, T., 'The Gates of Hell. From Metaphor to Fact', *Milltown Studies* 38 (1996), pp. 98–114.

O'Loughlin, T., 'The View from Iona: Adomnán's Mental Maps', *Peritia* 10 (1996), pp. 98–122.

O'Loughlin, T., '*Res, Tempus, Locus, Persona*: Adomnán's Exegetical Method', *Innes Review* 48 (1997), pp. 95–112.

O'Loughlin, T., 'Living in the Ocean', in Bourke, *Cult of Saint Columba*, pp. 11–23.

Olson, B.L. and O.J. Padel, 'A Tenth-Century List of Cornish Parochial Saints', *Cambridge Medieval Celtic Studies* 12 (1986), pp. 33–71.

Ó Luing, S., 'Celtic Scholars of Germany', *Zeitschrift für celtische Philologie* 46 (1994), pp. 249–71.

Ó Máille, T., *The Language of the Annals of Ulster* (Manchester 1910).

O'Meara, J.J., Review of Severin, *Brendan Voyage*, *Times Literary Supplement*, 14 July 1978.

O'Neill Hencken, H., *The Archaeology of Cornwall and Sicily* (London 1962).

O'Rahilly, T.F., *Early Irish History and Mythology* (Dublin 1946).

O'Reilly, J., 'Reading the Scriptures in the Life of Columba', in Bourke, *Cult of Saint Columba*, pp. 80–106.

Ó Riain, P., 'St. Finbarr: a Study in a Cult', *Journal of the Cork Historical and Archaeological Society* 82 (1977), pp. 63–82.

Ó Riain, P., 'The Book of Glendalough or Rawlinson B 502', *Éigse* 18 (1980–1), pp. 161–76.

Ó Riain, P., 'Towards a Methodology in Early Irish Hagiography', *Peritia* 1 (1982), pp. 146–59.

Ó Riain, P., 'NLI G2, f.3 and the Book of Glendalough', *Zeitschrift für celtische Philologie* 39 (1982), pp. 29–32.

Ó Riain, P., 'Cainnech *alias* Colum Cille, Patron of Ossory', in de Brún, Ó Coileáin and Ó Riain, *Folia Gadelica*, pp. 20–35.

Ó Riain, P., 'Irish Saints' Genealogies', *Nomina* 7 (1983), pp. 23–30.

Ó Riain, P., 'Finnian or Winniau', in P. Ní Chatháin and M. Richter, ed., *Irland und Europa. Ireland and Europe* (Stuttgart 1984), pp. 52–7.

Ó Riain, P., 'Les Vies de saint Fursy: les sources irlandaises', *Revue du Nord* 68 (1986), pp. 405–13.

Ó Riain, P., 'St. Abbán: The Genesis of an Irish Saint's Life', in D.E. Evans et al., eds, *Proceedings of the Seventh International Congress of Celtic Studies, Oxford, 1983* (Oxford 1986), pp. 159–70.

Ó Riain, P., 'Conservation in the Vocabulary of the Early Irish Church', in Ó Corráin et al., *Sages, Saints and Storytellers*, pp. 358–66.

Ó Riain, P., 'Finnio and Winniau: a Question of Priority', in R. Bielmeier and R. Stempel, eds, *Indogermanica et Caucasica. Festschrift für Karl Horst Schmidt zum 65. Geburtstag* (Berlin and New York 1994), pp. 407–14.

Ó Riain, P., 'Pagan Example and Christian Practice. A Reconsideration', in Edel, *Cultural Identity and Cultural Integration*, pp. 144–56.

Ó Riain, P., 'Saint Ronan de Locronan: le dossier irlandais', in Laurent, *Saint Ronan et la Troménie*, pp. 157–63.

Ó Riain, P., '*Codex Salmanticensis*: A Provenance *inter Anglos* or *inter Hibernos*?', in T. Barnard, D. Ó Cróinín and K. Simms, eds, *A Miracle of Learning. Essays in Honour of William O'Sullivan* (Aldershot 1997), pp. 91–100.

Ó Riain, P., 'Rawlinson B 502 alias Lebar Glinne Dá Locha: a Restatement of the Case', *Zeitschrift für celtische Philologie* 51 (1999), pp. 130–47.

Ó Riain, P., 'Finnio and Winniau: a Return to the Subject', in J. Carey, J.T. Koch and P-Y. Lambert, eds, *Ildánach Ildírech. A Festschrift for Proinsias Mac Cana* (Andover and Aberystwyth 1999), pp. 187–202.

Orme, N., 'Saint Breage. A Medieval Virgin Saint of Cornwall', *Analecta Bollandiana* 110 (1992), pp. 341–52.

Orme, N., *English Church Dedications* (Exeter 1996).

Ortenberg, V., 'Archbishop Sigeric's Journey to Rome in 990', *Anglo-Saxon England* 19 (1990), pp. 197–246.

O'Sullivan, W., 'Notes on the Script and Make-up of the Book of Leinster', *Celtica* 7 (1966), pp. 1–31.

O'Sullivan, W., 'A Waterford Origin for the Codex Salmanticensis', *Decies* 54 (1998), pp.17–24.

Padel, O.J., *A Popular Dictionary of Cornish Place Names* (Penzance 1988).

Pain, G., 'Actualisation des sources hagiographiques de l'histoire de Bretagne de l'Abbé Duine, notices 72 à 86', Mémoire de maîtrise d'histoire, Rennes 1996.

Parisse, M., *Histoire de la Lorraine* (Toulouse 1978).

Parisse, M., *La Lorraine monastique au moyen âge* (Nancy 1981).

Parisse, M., and O.G. Oexle, eds, *L'abbaye de Gorze au Xe siècle* (Nancy 1993).

Pérennès, H., *Dictionnaire topographique du Finistère* (Rennes 1950).

Peyresaubes, D., 'Plouagat et ses chapelles', *Les cahiers du Trégor* 16 (septembre 1986), p. 24.

Philippart, G., *Les légendiers et autres manuscrits hagiographiques* (Typologie des sources du Moyen Age occidental 24–5; Turnhout 1977, repr. 1985).

Philippart, G., 'Patrons de la bonne mort', in *Les vivants et leurs morts. Art, croyances et rites funéraires dans l'Ardenne d'autrefois* (Bastogne 1989), pp. 87–96.

Philippart, G., 'Hagiographies locale, régionale, diocésaine, universelle. Les hagiographies du saint patron dans l'aire belge du Xe siècle', in

W. Berschin, ed., *Lateinische Kultur im X. Jahrhundert. Akten des I. Internationalen Mittellateinerkongresses. Heidelberg, 12.–15.IX.1988* (Stuttgart 1991), pp. 355–67.

Philippart, G., 'Pour une histoire générale, problématique et sérielle de la littérature et de l'édition hagiographiques latines de l'antiquité et du moyen âge', *Cassiodorus* 2 (1996), pp. 197–213.

Picard, J.-M., 'Structural Patterns in Early Hiberno-Latin Hagiography', *Peritia* 4 (1985), pp. 67–82.

Picard, J.-M., 'Les celticismes des hagiographes irlandais du VIIe siècle', *Études Celtiques* 29 (1992), pp. 355–73.

Picard, J.-M., 'Adomnán's *Vita Columbae* and the Cult of Colum Cille in Continental Europe', *Proceedings of the Royal Irish Academy* 98 (1998), pp. 1–23.

Pietri, L., 'Les sépultures privilégiées en Gaule d'après les sources littéraires', in Y.M. Duval and J.C. Picard, eds, *L'inhumation privilégiée du IVe au VIIIe siècle en Occident. Actes du colloque tenu à Creteil les 16–18 mars 1984* (Paris 1986), pp. 133–42.

Pietri, L., 'L'évolution du culte des saints aux premiers siècles chrétiens: du témoin à l'intercesseur', *Les fonctions des saints dans le monde occidental (IIIe–XIIIe siècles)* (Rome 1991), pp. 15–36.

Poulin, J.-C., 'À propos du diocèse de Dol. Saint Samson et la question des enclaves', *Francia* 6 (1979), pp. 610–5.

Poulin, J.-C., 'Le dossier de saint Samson de Dol', *Francia* 15 (1987), pp. 701–14.

Poulin, J.-C., 'Méthodes de recherche en hagiographie du Haut Moyen Age', unpublished paper presented at ACFAS, McGill University, Montreal, May 1996.

Poupardin, R., 'Cartulaire de Saint-Vincent de Laon (Arch. Vatican., Misc. Arm. X. 145). Analyse et pièces inédites', *Mémoires de la Société de l'Histoire de Paris et de l'Île de France* 29 (1902), pp. 173–267.

Preston-Jones, A., and P. Rose, 'Medieval Cornwall', *Cornish Archaeology* 25 (1986), pp. 135–85.

Prete, S., 'La "Vita S. Columbani" di Ionas e il suo *prologus*', *Rivista di storia della chiesa in Italia* 22 (1968), pp. 94–111.

Price, L., 'The Antiquities and Place Names of South County Dublin', *Dublin Historical Record* 2 no. 4 (1940), pp. 121–33.

Price, L., *The Place-names of County Wicklow*, 6 vols (Dublin, 1967).

Prinz, F., *Frühes Mönchtum im Frankenreich* (Munich and Vienna 1965).

Quin, E.G., ed., *Dictionary of the Irish Language, Based Mainly on Old and Middle Irish Materials* (Dublin 1913–76, compact ed. 1983).

Raftery, B., *Pagan Celtic Ireland: The Enigma of the Irish Iron Age* (London 1994).

Raude, A.J., *L'origine géographique des Bretons armoricains* (Lorient 1996).

Reeves, W., *The Culdees of the British Islands* (Dublin 1864).

Reeves, W., 'On a Manuscript Volume of Lives of Saints (chiefly Irish), now in Primate Marsh's Library, Dublin', *Proceedings of the Royal Irish Academy*, Second Series, 1 (1869–79), pp. 339–50.

Riché, P., *Écoles et enseignement dans le haut moyen-âge* (Paris 1989).

Riché, P., 'Saint Maudez, irlandais, breton et parisien', in *Mélanges François Kerlouégan* (Besançon-Paris 1994), pp. 539–44.

Rivet, A.L.F., and C. Smith, *The Place-names of Roman Britain* (London 1979).

Riviére, J., 'Role du démon au jugement particulier chez les Pères', *Revue des Sciences Religieuses* 4 (1924), pp. 43–64.

Rohr, C., 'Hagiographie als historische Quelle: Ereignisgeschichte und Wunderberichte in der Vita Columbani des Ionas von Bobbio', *Mitteilungen des Instituts für Österreichische Geschichtsforschung* 103 (1995), pp. 229–64.

Ross, A., *Pagan Celtic Britain. Studies in Iconography and Tradition* (London and New York 1967).

Russell, K.C., 'Slavery as Reality and Metaphor in the Pauline Letters', dissertation, Pontifical University, Rome.

Russell, P., *Celtic Word-Formation: The Velar Suffixes* (Dublin 1990).

Ryan, J., *Irish Monasticism* (Dublin and Cork 1931).

Ryan, J., ed., *Féilsgríbhinn Eóin Mhic Néill* (Dublin 1940).

Ryan, M., 'Native Pottery in Early Historic Ireland', *Proceedings of the Royal Irish Academy* 73 C (1973), pp. 619–45.

Sackur, E., 'Handschriftliches aus Frankreich', *Neues Archiv der Gesellschaft für ältere deutsche Geschichtskunde* 15 (1889–90), pp. 103–39.

Sackur, E., *Die Cluniacenser in ihrer kirchlichen und allgemeingeschichtlichen Wirksamkeit bis zur Mitte des elften Jahrhunderts*, 2 vols (Halle a.S. 1892–4).

Sawyer, J., ed., *Studies in American Indian Languages* (University of California Publications in Linguistics 65; Berkeley 1991).

Sawyer, P.H., 'The Last Scandinavian Kings of York', *Northern History* 31 (1995), pp. 39–44.

Sayers, W., 'Three Charioteering Gifts in *Mesca Ulad* and *Táin Bó Cúailnge*', *Ériu* 32 (1981), pp. 163–7.

Sayers, W., 'Textual Notes on Descriptions of the Old Irish Chariot and Team', *Studia Celtica Japonica* 4 (1991), pp. 15–35.

Selmer, C., 'Israel, ein unbekannter Schotte des 10. Jahrhunderts', *Studien und Mitteilungen zur Geschichte des Benediktiner-Ordens und seiner Zweige* 62 (1949–50), pp. 62–86.

Semmler, J., 'Iren in der lothringischen Klosterreform', in Löwe, *Iren und Europa*, ii.941–57.

Severin, T., *The Brendan Voyage* (London and New York 1978).

Seymour, St J.D., 'The Eschatology of the Early Irish Church', *Zeitschrift für celtische Philologie* 14 (1928), pp. 179–211.

Shanzer, D., '"Iuvenes vestri visiones videbunt": Visions and the Literary Sources of Patrick's *Confessio*', *Journal of Medieval Latin* 3 (1993), pp. 169–201.

Sharpe, R., 'Hiberno-Latin *Laicus*, Irish *Láech* and the Devil's Men', *Ériu* 30 (1979), pp. 75–92.

Sharpe, R., 'St Patrick and the See of Armagh', *Cambridge Medieval Celtic Studies* 4 (1982), pp. 33–59.

Sharpe, R., '*Vitae S Brigidae*: the Oldest Texts', *Peritia* 1 (1982), pp. 81–106.

Sharpe, R., 'Armagh and Rome in the Seventh Century', in P. Ní Chatháin and M. Richter, eds, *Ireland and Europe. The Early Church* (Stuttgart 1984), pp. 58–72.

Sharpe, R., 'Dispute Settlement in Medieval Ireland: A Preliminary Inquiry', in Davies and Fouracre, *Settlement of Disputes*, pp. 169–89.

Sharpe, R., 'The Origin and Elaboration of the Catalogus Praecipuorum Sanctorum Hiberniae Attributed to Fr Henry Fitzsimon, S.J.', *Bodleian Library Record* 13.3 (1989), pp. 202–30.

Sharpe, R., 'Maghnus Ó Domhnaill's Source for Adomnán's *Vita S. Columbae* and Other *Vitae*', *Celtica* 21 (1990), pp. 604–7.

Sharpe, R., *Medieval Irish Saints' Lives. An Introduction to Vitae Sanctorum Hiberniae* (Oxford 1991).

Simon, M., *L'abbaye de Landévennec de S. Guénolé à nos jours* (Rennes 1985).

Simonetti, M., 'Sulla tradizione agiografica di S. Magno di Trani', in *Atti del convegno "Il paleocristiano in Ciociaria", Fiuggi 1977*, a cura dell' Accademia Bessarione (1978), pp. 97–121.

Simonetti, M., 'Un testo inedito di San Magno di Trani', in R. Cantalamessa and L.F. Pizzolato, ed., *Paradoxos Politeia. Studi patristici in onore di Giuseppe Lazzati* (Studia Patristica Mediolanensia; Milan 1979), pp. 42–54.

Skene, W.F., *Celtic Scotland*, 3 vols (Edinburgh 1876–80).

Smyth, A.P., 'The Húi Néill and the Leinstermen in the Annals of Ulster 431 to 516 A.D.', *Études Celtiques* 14 (1974), pp. 121–43.

Smyth, A.P., *Scandinavian York and Dublin*, 2 vols (Dublin 1975–9).

Smyth, A.P., *Celtic Leinster* (Dublin 1982).

Snieders, I., 'L'influence de l'hagiographie irlandaise sur les Vitae des saints irlandais de Belgique', *Revue d'histoire ecclésiastique* 24 (1928), pp. 596–627, 828–67.

Stalmans, N., 'La fonction du travail hagiographique et le rôle du saint en Irlande au VIIème et VIIIème siècles', thèse de doctorat inédite, Brussels 2000.

Stalmans, N., L'inhumation laïque en cimetière ecclésiastique en Irlande au VIIème et VIIIème siècles', in A.M. Helvétius, ed., *Sanctity and Politics* (Turnhout, forthcoming).

Stancliffe, C., *St Martin and his Hagiographer* (Oxford 1983).

Stancliffe, C., 'The Miracle Stories in Seventh-Century Irish Saints' Lives', in J. Fontaine and J.N. Hillgarth, eds, *The Seventh Century: Change and Continuity* (London 1992), pp. 87–115.

Stevenson, J., 'The Monastic Rules of Columbanus', in Lapidge, *Columbanus*, pp. 203–16.

Stevenson, J., 'Literacy and Orality in Early Medieval Ireland', in Edel, *Cultural Identity and Cultural Integration*, pp. 11–22.

Strecker, K., ed., *Die Ottonenzeit*, MGH, Poetae latini medii aevi 5 (Leipzig and Berlin 1937–9).

Synge, J.M., *In Wicklow, West Kerry and Connemara* (Dublin and London 1919).

Tanguy, B., 'Les paroisses primitives en plou- et leurs saints éponymes', *Bulletin de la Société archéologique du Finistère* 109 (1981), pp. 121–55.

Tanguy, B., *Dictionnaire des noms de communes trèves et paroisses du Finistère* (Douarnenez 1990).

Tanguy, B., 'Cornou, une ancienne paroisse disparue', in *Charpiana. Mélanges offerts par ses amis à Jacques Charpy* ([Rennes] 1991), pp. 573–8.

Tanguy, B., *Dictionnaire des noms des communes, trèves et paroisses des Côtes d'Armor*, 1 (Douarnenez, 1992).

Tanguy, B., and T. Daniel, eds, *Sur les pas de Paul Aurélien. Colloque international de Saint-Pol-de-Léon, 7–8 juin 1991* (Brest/Quimper 1997).

Theissen, G., *The Miracle Stories of the Early Christian Tradition* (Edinburgh 1983).

Thomas, C., 'Grass-Marked Pottery in Cornwall', in J.M. Coles and D.D.A. Simpson, eds, *Studies in Ancient Europe* (Leicester 1968), pp. 311–31.

Thomas, C., 'The Irish Settlements in Post-Roman Britain. A Survey of the Evidence', *Journal of the Royal Society of Cornwall* N.S. 6, pt iv (1972), pp. 251–74.

Thomas, C.,'Irish Colonists in South-West Britain', *World Archaeology* 5 (1973), pp. 5–13.

Thomas, C., *And Shall These Mute Stones Speak? Post-Roman Inscriptions in Western Britain* (Cardiff 1994).

Thompson, E.A., *Who was Saint Patrick?* (Woodbridge 1985).

Thompson, S., 'Narrative Motif-Analysis as a Folklore Method', *FF Communications* 161 (1955), pp. 1–9.

Thompson, S., *Motif-Index of Folk Literature*, 6 vols (Copenhagen 1955–8).

Thurneysen, R., *A Grammar of Old Irish*, trans. D.A. Binchy and O. Bergin (Dublin 1946).

Todd, M., *The South-West to AD 1000* (London 1987).

Toucas, A., 'Regula Waldeberti', in G. Pelliccia and G. Rocca, ed., *Dizionario degli istituti di perfezione* (Rome 1974–), vii.1602–3.

Treffort, C., *L'Eglise carolingienne et la mort. Christianisme, rites funéraires et pratiques commémoratives* (Lyon 1996).

Uhlich, J., *Die Morphologie der komponierten Personennamen des Altirischen* (Beiträge zu Sprachwissenschaften 1; Bonn 1993).

Ultan, R., 'A Case of Sound Symbolism in Konkow', in Sawyer, *Studies in American Indian Languages*, pp. 295–301.

Vallerie, E., 'Les références bretonnes et celtiques dans le Martyrologe de l'abbé Chastelain', *Bulletin de la Société archéologique du Finistère* 110 (1982), pp. 146–70 and 112 (1983), pp. 177–224.

Vallerie, E., *Diazezoù studi istorel an anvioù-Parrez – Traité de toponymie historique de la Bretagne* (Le Relecq-Kerhuon 1994).

Van den Gheyn, J., *Catalogue des manuscrits de la Bibliothèque Royale de Belgique*, V (*Histoire- Hagiographie*), (Brussels 1905).

Van der Essen, L., *Étude critique et littéraire sur les Vitae des saints mérovingiens de l'ancienne Belgique* (Louvain 1907).

Van Hamel, A.G., 'On Lebor Gabála', *Zeitschrift für celtische Philologie* 10 (1914–5), pp. 97–197.

Van Uytfanghe, M., *Stylisation biblique et condition humaine* (Bruxelles 1987).

Van Uytfanghe, M., 'L'essor du culte des saints et la question de l'eschatologie', in *Les fonctions des saints dans le monde occidental (IIIᵉ–XIIIᵉ siècle)* (Rome 1991), pp. 91–107.

Vendryes, J., 'Sur les hypocoristiques celtiques précédés de *Mo-* ou de *To-* (*Do-*)', in *Choix des études linguistiques et celtiques* (Paris 1952), pp. 182–95.

Vendryes, J., E. Bachellery, and P.-Y. Lambert, *Lexique étymologique de l'irlandais ancien* (Paris and Dublin 1959–).

Vogeler, R., 'Exkurs: Jonas und die Dialogi Gregors des Grossen', in Berschin, *Biographie*, ii.43–8.

Wallace-Hadrill, J.M., *The Frankish Church* (Oxford 1983).

Warner, R., 'The Broighter Hoard', in B.G. Scott, ed., *Studies in Early Ireland* (Belfast 1981), pp. 29–38.

Warren, C., 'Jehoshaphat, Valley of', in J. Hastings, ed., *Dictionary of the Bible*, 5 vols (Edinburgh 1898–1904), ii.561–2.

Warren, F.E., *The Liturgy and Ritual of the Celtic Church* (Oxford 1881, new ed. Woodbridge 1987).

Wattenbach, W., and R. Holtzmann, *Deutschlands Geschichtsquellen im Mittelalter*, 3 vols (Darmstadt 1967–71).

Westermann, W.L., *The Slave Systems of Greek and Roman Antiquity* (Philadelphia 1955).

Whitelock, D.,R. McKitterick and D. Dumville, eds, *Ireland in Early Mediaeval Europe: Studies in Memory of Kathleen Hughes* (Cambridge 1982).

Wood, I., 'The *Vita Columbae* and Merovingian Hagiography', *Peritia* 1 (1982), pp. 63–80.

Wood, I., *The Merovingian Kingdoms 450–71* (London and New York 1994 [*recte* 1993]).

Wooding, J.M., *Communication and Commerce along the Western Sealanes AD 400–800* (BAR International Series 654; Oxford 1996).

Wooding, J.M., 'Monastic Voyaging and the *Navigatio*', in Wooding, *Otherworld Voyage*.

Wooding, J.M., ed., *The Otherworld Voyage in Early Irish Literature. An Anthology of Criticism* (Dublin 2000).

Wooding, J.M., 'Biblical Narrative and Local Imagery on the Kilnaruane Cross-Shaft, Co. Cork', in N. Edwards and M. Redknap, eds, *Proceedings of the Fourth Insular Art Congress* (Oxford, forthcoming).

Woolf, A., 'Erik Bloodaxe Revisited', *Northern History* 34 (1998), pp. 189–93.

Wormald, P., 'Æthelwold and his Continental Counterparts: Contact, Comparison, Contrast', in B. Yorke, ed., *Bishop Æthelwold, his Career and Influence* (Woodbridge 1988), pp. 13–42.

Wright, N., 'Columbanus's Epistulae', in Lapidge, *Columbanus*, pp. 29–92.

Zimmer, H., 'Keltische Studien. 10. Zur Personnennamenbildung im Irischen' *Zeitschrift für Vergleichende Sprachforschung* 32 (1893), pp. 158–97.

Zimmer, H., 'Über direkte Handelsverbindugen Westgalliens mit Irland im Altertum und frühen Mittelalter', *Sitzungsberichte der Königlichen Preussischen Akademie der Wissenschaften* (1909–10).

Index